Managing Editor
Robert Mewis

Publisher
RSMeans

Cost Consultant
Hanscomb

Coordinators
Brian McBurney
Susan Neil

St. John's
Raymond Murray

Halifax
Raymond Murray

Montreal
Philippe Coutou

Ottawa
Brian McBurney

Toronto
Nathan Thinagarippillai

Winnipeg
Isaac Gwendo

Calgary
Mike Swick

Vancouver
Ken King

Mechanical
Murugan Thambiayah

Electrical
Mariola Ilia

Hanscomb's *Yardsticks for Costing* is published by RSMeans, part of Gordian, which serves the construction industry in the U.S., Canada, and other countries worldwide with information products and services that provide cost, product, and project activity information for design, construction, and facility management professionals.

U.S. Office: RSMeans
1099 Hingham Street, Suite 201
Rockland, MA 02370
Phone: (800) 334-3509
www.rsmeans.com
Fax: (781) 422-5180

Contents 2018

Please read before using *YARDSTICKS FOR COSTING!*

To make it easier for you to pinpoint items, the manual is divided into six sections, each coded **A, B, C, D, E**, and **F**.

Note that Sections C and D are divided into two parts: one listing metric prices and the other listing imperial prices. Both listings use a Division number at the top of the page. This number corresponds to the **MASTERFORMAT 2016** specification. The Divisions are listed below.
To further help you use this manual, you'll find a visual guide on pages 3 and 4.
This contains examples which clearly pinpoint the essential components of each section and is preceded by notes on how to use the tables. We strongly recommend that before using the data you take time to look at Section A!

Current Market Prices Divisions—Metric and Imperial

How to use the data

One of the biggest advantages of *Yardsticks for Costing* is that it lists costs for 8 major Canadian cities. Many other manuals list only 1 set of unit prices.

Note that **unit prices are for average non-residential construction involving union labor.**

Generally speaking, in most areas, unit prices for residential construction are as much as 20–30% lower.

No allowances have been included for alteration work, difficult access, crash schedules, or any other extremes.

Material and workmanship quality is assumed to be of good standard and produced under normal conditions. Special large-scale purchasing discounts have not been applied.

Overhead & Profit

For **overhead and profit**, note that all prices include site overhead and profit for all items normally subcontracted by general contractors. General trade work is priced at a net cost excluding site overhead and profit.

When preparing estimates, refer to Section D, CIQS Z1. A sum should be added to estimates to cover the general contractor's site overhead and profit on a percentage basis.

Preparation of estimates

Section C contains unit prices set out in a trade format and is ideally suited to the preparation of sub-trade preliminary estimates using approximate quantities.

Section D provides composite unit rates which are more suited to an elemental cost estimate, a faster method used to prepare preliminary estimates. Ideally, cost summaries should follow the Elemental Building Cost Breakdown shown on Page 3.

Local market conditions can have a profound effect on final building costs. Generally, the greater the volume of work in a given locality, the steeper the rises in prices for that area. In smaller cities, these conditions can be created temporarily by the inadvertent tendering of one or two large projects during the same period. These influences cannot be measured definitively, and each estimator must allow for them according to his or her own judgment.

Contingencies/ Allowances

When preparing estimates, the wise estimator allows a contingency sum for unforeseen conditions. Even where definitive prebid estimates have been prepared, a small margin should be provided for potential field changes during construction.

Escalation

Unit prices and rates are based on tendering levels experienced during January 2018. They allow for the cost of wage increases up to the end of December 2017. Tendered rates normally include provisions for escalation based on the work schedule of a particular project and depend on the contract conditions. It is impossible to ascertain the precise escalation in a rate. However, estimators should allow for escalation likely between January 2018 and the date of the estimate. Here is an example of how you can do this:

Estimate based on unit rates = $1,215,000

Proposed bid date = July 2018

6 months x 2% per annum, estimated = 1%

Total estimate July 2018 bid date = $1,227,150

Goods & Services Tax

All rates exclude the Goods and Services Tax (G.S.T.), Harmonized Sales Tax (H.S.T.) and Quebec Sales Tax (Q.S.T.). The applicable Retail Sales Tax (R.S.T.) is included in Winnipeg's rates. This approach conforms to industry bidding practices which include the submission of all tenders exclusive of G.S.T./H.S.T., the tax being added to the certified amount of each progress billing.

If you have any questions

If you have any questions regarding the content of *Yardsticks for Costing*, call the Hanscomb Hot Line in the city nearest you:

· St. John's: (902) 422-3620
· Halifax: (902) 422-3620
· Ottawa: (613) 234-8089
· Toronto: (416) 487-3811
· Winnipeg: (204) 775-3389
· Edmonton: (780) 426-7980
· Vancouver: (604) 685-1241

Questions concerning mechanical or electrical costs should be directed to the Toronto office.

To order extra copies

To order additional copies of *Yardsticks for Costing*, call (800) 334-3509 or visit http://www.hanscomb.com to download an order form.

Preparing an "Elemental Building Cost Breakdown"

When possible, estimates should carry an elemental notation using the CIQS measurement and pricing method. An example of a format prepared by Hanscomb using actual figures is shown here.

This format provides for a reduction of most sub-elemental estimates to a single rate based on a parametric unit suitable to that particular sub-element. Accumulation of these elemental unit rates over a period of time will provide an excellent source of parametric cost data, which will be useful for rapid preliminary estimating at the earliest stages of projects. This method should be used at every opportunity, rather than the square foot or cubic foot (square metre or cubic metre) single rate methods of estimating.

Project	: RETIREMENT HOME				Report date	: 1 Jan 2018

(Elemental Cost Summary table as shown)

```
Project      : RETIREMENT HOME                                  Report date : 1 Jan 2018
             : NEW DEVELOPMENT                                  Page No.    : 1
Location     : TORONTO, ONTARIO          ELEMENTAL COST SUMMARY  Bldg Type   : 447
Owner        : RETIREMENT HOMES LTD                             C.T. Index  : 0.0
Consultant   : CONSOLIDATED ARCHITECTS                          GFA         : 15,000 m2
```

Element	Ratio to GFA	Elemental Cost Quantity	Unit rate	Sub-Total	Total	Sub-Total	Total	%
A SHELL		15,000 m2			4,014,900		267.66	25.6
A1 SUBSTRUCTURE					399,900		26.60	2.5
A11 Foundations	0.235	3,525 m2	113.19	399,000		26.60	
A12 Basement Excavation				0		0.00	
A13 Special Conditions				0		0.00	
A2 STRUCTURE					1,913,100		127.54	12.2
A21 Lowest Floor Construction	0.235	3,525 m2	48.51	171,000		11.40	
A22 Upper Floor Construction	0.765	11,475 m2	115.00	1,319,600		87.97	
A23 Roof Construction	0.235	3,525 m2	119.86	422,500		28.17	
A3 EXTERIOR ENCLOSURE					1,702,800		113.52	10.9
A31 Walls Below Grade				0		0.00	
A32 Walls Above Grade	0.329	4,935 m2	234.99	1,159,700		77.31	
A33 Windows & Entrances	0.044	660 m2	400.00	264,000		17.60	
A34 Roof Coverings	0.235	3,525 m2	64.99	229,100		15.27	
A35 Projections	0.000	1 Sum	50,000.00	50,000		3.33	
B INTERIORS		15,000 m2			3,568,600		237.91	22.8
B1 PARTITIONS & DOORS					1,069,400		71.29	6.8
B11 Partitions	1.251	18,765 m2	56.99	1,069,400		71.29	
B12 Doors	0.095	1,425 No	0.00			0.00	
B2 FINISHES					1,526,200		101.75	9.7
B21 Floor Finishes	1.000	15,000 m2	45.13	677,000		45.13	
B22 Ceiling Finishes	1.000	15,000 m2	14.13	212,000		14.13	
B23 Wall Finishes	2.832	42,480 m2	15.00	637,200		42.48	
B3 FITTINGS & EQUIPMENT					973,000		64.87	6.2
B31 Fittings & Fixtures	1.000	15,000 m2	48.20	723,000		48.20	
B32 Equipment	1.000	15,000 m2	0.00			0.00	
B33 Elevators	0.000	1 No	250,000.00	250,000		16.67	
B34 Escalators						0.00	
C SERVICES		15,000 m2			6,467,500		431.17	41.2
C1 MECHANICAL					4,817,200		321.15	30.7
C11 Plumbing & Drainage	1.000	15,000 m2	75.00	1,125,000		75.00	
C12 Fire Protection	1.000	15,000 m2	25.44	381,600		25.44	
C13 HVAC	1.000	15,000 m2	200.03	3,000,500		200.03	
C14 Controls	1.000	15,000 m2	20.67	310,100		20.67	
C2 ELECTRICAL					1,650,300		110.02	10.5
C21 Service & Distribution	1.000	15,000 m2	40.27	604,100		40.27	
C22 Lighting, Devices & Heating	1.000	15,000 m2	35.81	537,200		35.81	
C23 Systems & Ancillaries	1.000	15,000 m2	33.93	509,000		33.93	
NET BUILDING COST - EXCLUDING SITE				$	14,051,000		936.73	89.6
D SITE & ANCILLARY WORK		15,000 m2			185,000		12.33	1.2
D1 SITE WORK					185,000		12.33	1.2
D11 Site Development	0.500	7,500 m2	13.33	100,000		6.67	
D12 Mechanical Site Services	0.500	7,500 m2	6.67	50,000		3.33	
D13 Electrical Site Services	0.500	7,500 m2	4.67	35,000		2.33	
D2 ANCILLARY WORK					0		0.00	0.0
D21 Demolitions				0		0.00	
D22 Alterations				0		0.00	
NET BUILDING COST - INCLUDING SITE				$	14,236,000		949.07	90.8
Z1 GENERAL REQUIREMENTS & FEE					1,446,400		96.43	9.2
Z11 General Requirements	8.0 %			1,138,900		75.93	
Z12 Fee	2.0 %			307,500		20.50	
TOTAL CONSTRUCTION ESTIMATE - EXCLUDING ALLOWANCES				$	15,682,400		1,045.49	100.0
Z2 ALLOWANCES					1,617,300		107.82	
Z21 Design & Pricing Allowance	5.0 %			784,100		52.27	
Z22 Escalation Allowance	2.0 %			329,300		21.95	
Z23 Construction Allowance	3.0 %			503,900		33.59	
TOTAL CONSTRUCTION ESTIMATE - INCLUDING ALLOWANCES				$	17,299,700		1,153.31	
HARMONIZED SALES TAX					2,249,000		149.93	
Harmonized Sales Tax	13.0 %			2,249,000		149.93	
TOTAL CONSTRUCTION ESTIMATE				$	19,548,700		1,303.25	

```
T9999 -11                        COST ESTIMATE                        Hanscomb
```

1: HOW TO READ "CURRENT MARKET PRICES" METRIC ON P. 10, IMPERIAL ON P. 76

This is the Division number and category title. The line tells you whether the page is in metric or imperial.

This line contains names of 8 major Canadian cities.

Capitalized bold-face heading shows main Division category.

This heading in bold-face shows "broadscope" listing.

Lower-case bold-face listing of sub-category.

Regular type listings showing "narrowscope" listings.

Dotted line shows supply only; solid line shows installation only.

Column shows metric or imperial unit of measurement.

Prices are shown in dollars and cents if under $1,000; dollars only if over $1,000.

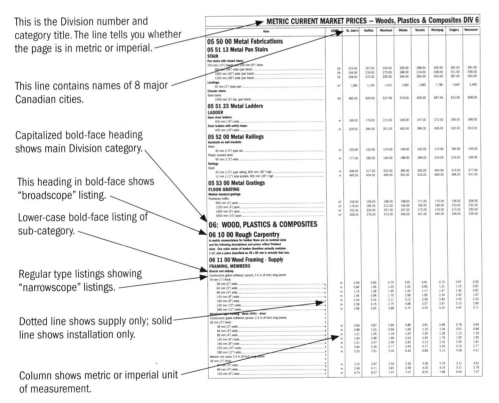

Unit prices are listed separately in **both metric and imperial** using the Division format.

Prices are based on market prices current January 2018 and include all materials, labour to install, transportation, equipment costs, and site overhead and profit for work normally done by subcontractors. Provincial taxes included where applicable, **GST/HST excluded.**

Unit prices are for use in **approximate** construction cost estimating. Prices represent **average** rates for **average** conditions. Many variables influence construction costs at a given location and a given time—the reader must gauge these conditions. The reader must note that prices shown represent normal, rather than optimum, conditions where lower or higher prices prevail.

Hanscomb recommends obtaining budget quotes from subcontractors and suppliers for specific installations.

Use caution when using unit rates for negotiating change orders.

2: HOW TO READ "COMPOSITE UNIT RATES" METRIC ON P. 140, IMPERIAL ON P. 150

Main heading shows metric or imperial listings for composite rates by material/system classification. Note that the number refers to the Canadian Institute of Quantity Surveyors (CIQS) breakdown.

Listings of composite units and rates are for use in preparing preliminary estimates or for comparative purposes. Rates in this section are basically built up from the prices appearing in Section C, Current Market Prices.

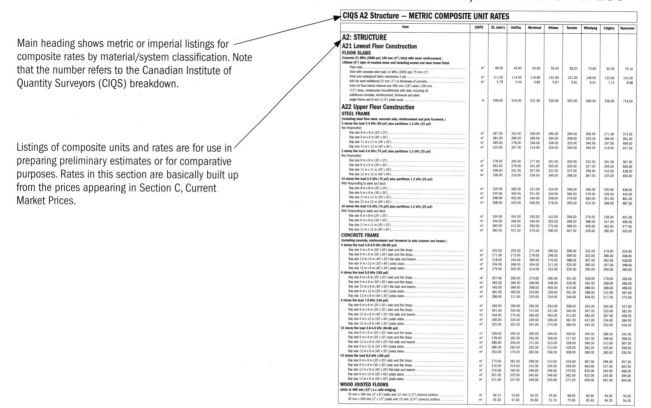

3: HOW TO READ "GROSS BLDG. COSTS—REPRESENTATIVE EXAMPLES" ON P. 159

Description of building type.

Breakdown of building elements.

First 3 columns show low and high costs per square metre, plus **average** costs for building elements.

These 3 columns show low and high costs per square foot, plus average costs for building elements.

Final column shows building element cost as a percentage of total cost.

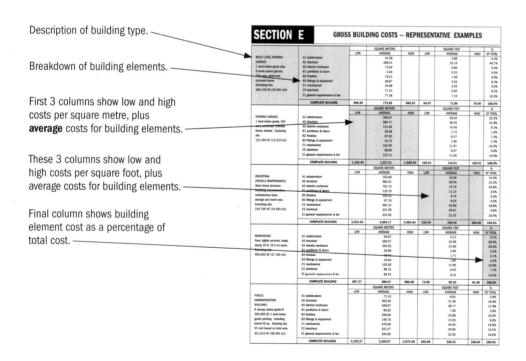

This section offers a general guide to **overall** costs of 45 building types.

Costs are shown in both metric and imperial and based on gross floor area. Costs are shown for each building element with its proportion to the total cost. Prices are based on representative projects estimated in the Toronto market and must be adjusted to local conditions.

High and low prices are shown per square foot or square metre, and these indicate the +/- 10% from the averages, respectively. In the majority of cases, prices will fall between the high and low figures.

Note that costs for site work are not included because of a wide variation regardless of gross floor area.

4

IMPORTANT! Metric Item page numbers are in bold. All other numbers denote Imperial Items.

5

IMPORTANT! Metric Item page numbers are in bold. All other numbers denote Imperial Items.

IMPORTANT! Metric Item page numbers are in bold. All other numbers denote Imperial Items.

IMPORTANT! Metric item page numbers are in bold. All other numbers denote Imperial Items.

01: GENERAL REQUIREMENTS

01 41 00 Regulatory Requirements

01 41 26 Permit Requirements

BUILDING PERMITS

These building permit fees and rates are intended as a guide only. For more information on building permits, contact your local municipal offices.

Based on value, New Construction and Renovations

Item	UNITS	St. John's	Halifax	Montreal	Ottawa	Toronto	Winnipeg	Calgary	Vancouver
Minimum Permit Fee	$	25.00	25.00	820.00	200.00	198.60	203.00	*112.00	126.00
Rates (minimum permit fee applies)									
Portion from $1 to $1000	$/1000	9.00	5.50	8.90	7.92	N/A	N/A	N/A	N/A
Portion from $1,001 to $2,000	$/1000	9.00	5.50	8.90	7.92	N/A	10.00	*11.11	N/A
Portion from $2,001 to $5,000	$/1000	9.00	5.50	8.90	7.92	N/A	10.00	*11.11	N/A
Portion from $5,001 to $50,000	$/1000	9.00	5.50	8.90	7.92	N/A	10.00	*11.11	8.10
Portion from $50,001 to $100,000	$/1000	9.00	5.50	8.90	7.92	N/A	10.00	*11.11	4.05
Portion from $100,001 to $500,000	$/1000	7.20	5.50	8.90	7.92	N/A	10.00	*11.11	4.05
Portion from $500,001 to $1,000,000	$/1000	7.20	5.50	8.90	7.92	N/A	10.00	*11.11	4.05
Portion over $1,000,001	$/1000	7.20	5.50	8.90	7.92	N/A	10.00	*11.11	4.05

Based on occupancy: New Construction Building permit rates based on occupancy are to be added to any required fees and minimum rates based on value (as listed above). For Winnipeg, building permit rates based on value are to be used only when occupancy type cannot be determined. For Ottawa this applies to only newly created GFA.

Item	UNITS	St. John's	Halifax	Montreal	Ottawa	Toronto	Winnipeg	Calgary	Vancouver
Group A - Assembly Occupancies									
(rates vary based on building use, check with local municipality)	m²	N/A	N/A	N/A	12.27	28.61	18.25	N/A	N/A
Group B - Institutional Occupancies									
(rates vary based on building use, check with local municipality)	m²	N/A	N/A	N/A	12.27	30.44	24.00	N/A	N/A
Group C - Residential Occupancies									
(rates vary based on building use, check with local municipality)	m²	N/A	N/A	N/A	8.29	17.16	13.00	N/A	N/A
Group D - Business and Personal Services Occupancies									
(rates vary based on building use, check with local municipality)									
Building shell alone	m²	N/A	N/A	N/A	5.06	17.99	15.75	N/A	N/A
Finished buildings	m²	N/A	N/A	N/A	7.53	22.62	15.75	N/A	N/A
Group E - Mercantile Occupancies									
(rates vary based on building use, check with local municipality)									
Building shell alone	m²	N/A	N/A	N/A	6.35	14.57	13.20	N/A	N/A
Finished buildings	m²	N/A	N/A	N/A	8.82	19.20	13.20	N/A	N/A
Group F - Industrial Occupancies									
(rates vary based on building use, check with local municipality)									
Building shell alone (<7,500 m²)	m²	N/A	N/A	N/A	2.91	11.43	15.25	N/A	N/A
Finished buildings (<7,500 m²)	m²	N/A	N/A	N/A	5.38	15.73	15.25	N/A	N/A

Based on occupancy, Renovations

Building permit rates based on occupancy are to be added to any required fees and rates based on value (as listed above)

Item	UNITS	St. John's	Halifax	Montreal	Ottawa	Toronto	Winnipeg	Calgary	Vancouver
Group A - Assembly Occupancies	m²	N/A	N/A	N/A	12.27	5.32	7.70	N/A	N/A
Group B - Institutional Occupancies	m²	N/A	N/A	N/A	12.27	5.32	9.70	N/A	N/A
Group C - Residential Occupancies	m²	N/A	N/A	N/A	8.29	4.93	5.30	N/A	N/A
Group D - Business and Personal Services Occupancies	m²	N/A	N/A	N/A	7.53	5.32	6.00	N/A	N/A
Group E - Mercantile Occupancies	m²	N/A	N/A	N/A	8.82	4.93	5.30	N/A	N/A
Group F - Industrial Occupancies	m²	N/A	N/A	N/A	5.38	4.93	6.10	N/A	N/A

TAXES

Sales tax on building materials:

Item	UNITS	St. John's	Halifax	Montreal	Ottawa	Toronto	Winnipeg	Calgary	Vancouver
Provincial Sales Tax (P.S.T.)	%	N/A	N/A	N/A	N/A	N/A	**8.00	N/A	7.00
Goods & Services Tax (G.S.T.)	%	N/A	N/A	5.00	N/A	N/A	5.00	5.00	5.00
Quebec Sales Tax (Q.S.T.)	%	N/A	N/A	9.975	N/A	N/A	N/A	N/A	N/A
Harmonized Sales Tax (H.S.T.)	%	15.00	15.00	N/A	13.00	13.00	N/A	N/A	N/A

* All building and demolition permits are subject to a surcharge for the Alberta Safety Codes Council. Greater of $4.50 or 4% of the total permit to a max of $560.

Item	UNITS	St. John's	Halifax	Montreal	Ottawa	Toronto	Winnipeg	Calgary	Vancouver

The unit rates given include material, labour, overhead & profit.

**R.S.T. (Retail Sales Tax) on material and labour has been included in Winnipeg mechanical and electrical unit rates.

All unit rates exclude G.S.T., Q.S.T. & H.S.T.

For calculation purposes using the unit rates provided in this book:

St. Johns: H.S.T. should be added to the unit rate.

Halifax: H.S.T. should be added to the unit rate.

Montreal: H.S.T. should be added to the unit rate.

Ottawa: H.S.T. should be added to the unit rate.

Toronto: H.S.T. should be added to the unit rate.

Winnipeg: G.S.T. should be added to the unit rate. (R.S.T. on material is included in the unit rate.)

Calgary: G.S.T. should be added to the unit rate. (there is no P.S.T.)

Vancouver: G.S.T. should be added to the unit rate.

Method for calculating a unit rate from scratch:

Assumptions:

Material (M) = $40.00

Labour (L) = $40.00

Overhead & Profit (O) = $20.00

	St. John's		Halifax		Montreal		Ottawa		Toronto		Winnipeg		Calgary		Vancouver
Material		40.00		40.00		40.00		40.00		40.00		40.00		40.00	40.00
Labour		40.00		40.00		40.00		40.00		40.00		40.00		40.00	40.00
OH&P		20.00		20.00		20.00		20.00		20.00		20.00		20.00	20.00
PST on (M)	N/A	—	N/A	—	N/A	—	N/A	—	N/A	—	N/A	—	N/A	—	5.0%	2.00
RST on (M)	N/A	—	N/A	—	N/A	—	N/A	—	N/A	—	7.0%	2.80	N/A	—	7.0%	7.14
GST on (M+L+O)	N/A	—	N/A	—	5.0%	5.00	N/A	—	N/A	—	5.0%	5.00	5.0%	5.00	7.0%	7.14
QST on sum of (M+L+O+GST)	N/A	—	N/A	—	9.98%	9.98	N/A	—	N/A	—	N/A	—	N/A	—	N/A	—
HST on (M+L+O)	13.0%	13.00	15.0%	15.00	N/A	—	13%	13.00	13%	13.00	N/A	—	N/A	—	N/A	—
TOTAL		113.00		115.00		114.98		113.00		113.00		107.80		105.00		109.14

Item	UNITS	St. John's	Halifax	Montreal	Ottawa	Toronto	Winnipeg	Calgary	Vancouver
02: EXISTING CONDITIONS									
02 41 00 Demolition									
02 41 16 Structure Demolition									
BUILDING DEMOLITION									
No salvage or haulage included, based on building volume									
Low rise building, 3 m (10') floor to floor height,									
GFA of 3700 m² (40 ksf), average cost	m³	16.20	14.80	16.00	21.60	18.20	19.20	18.70	31.90
02 41 19 Selective Demolition									
CUTOUT DEMOLITION									
Concrete									
Foundation Walls, 200 mm (8") thick									
Unreinforced	m³	175.00	176.00	194.00	213.00	208.00	215.00	185.00	285.00
Reinforced	m³	297.00	296.00	338.00	373.00	363.00	378.00	323.00	488.00
Slab-on grade:									
Unreinforced	m²	12.30	12.20	13.20	14.40	14.50	15.10	12.80	19.50
Reinforced	m²	18.70	18.10	19.40	21.30	22.30	23.10	19.70	29.80
MASONRY DEMOLITION									
Masonry									
Partitions:									
Average cost	m²	82.50	81.30	87.00	91.30	98.80	105.00	86.30	134.00
Exterior walls:									
Average cost	m²	115.00	115.00	124.00	138.00	140.00	151.00	122.00	186.00

Item	UNITS	St. John's	Halifax	Montreal	Ottawa	Toronto	Winnipeg	Calgary	Vancouver
03: CONCRETE									
03 01 00 Maintenance of Concrete									
PATCHING CONCRETE									
Epoxy									
100% solids injected to cracks:									
Slab on grade	m	72.60	72.80	77.30	72.00	85.70	102.00	89.60	108.00
Soffits or walls	m	108.00	105.00	112.00	103.00	126.00	144.00	133.00	128.00
Epoxy/sand 1:4 mortar:									
Patching to slab or deck									
12 mm (1/4") thick	m²	346.00	338.00	359.00	354.00	399.00	498.00	442.00	528.00
25 mm (1") thick	m²	576.00	581.00	602.00	587.00	663.00	868.00	758.00	879.00
Bulk grouting									
Filling to voids	m³	18,200	18,800	22,500	18,600	22,700	30,900	28,600	28,500
03 10 00 Concrete Forming and Accessories									
03 11 00 Concrete Forming									
SUBSTRUCTURE									
Footings									
Strip (wall) footings:									
Level footings	m²	100.00	124.00	104.00	120.00	108.00	181.00	114.00	132.00
Stepped footings	m²	101.00	129.00	107.00	123.00	110.00	185.00	115.00	134.00
Spread (column) footings:									
Column footings	m²	98.10	127.00	107.00	119.00	105.00	177.00	111.00	129.00
Piles caps	m²	110.00	133.00	114.00	126.00	114.00	190.00	118.00	139.00
Raft foundations	m²	105.00	136.00	116.00	126.00	114.00	190.00	118.00	139.00
Foundations walls and grade beams									
Not exceeding 3600 mm (12') high:									
Concealed finish	m²	110.00	119.00	118.00	118.00	118.00	172.00	126.00	148.00
Exposed finish	m²	120.00	127.00	125.00	124.00	124.00	182.00	134.00	158.00
STRUCTURE									
Multiple uses (minimum 4) 8 floors or more									
Flat plate slab concealed finish	m²	108.00	114.00	118.00	129.00	142.00	170.00	116.00	137.00
Exposed finish	m²	117.00	119.00	126.00	136.00	152.00	184.00	122.00	144.00
Flat slab, with drops:									
Concealed finish	m²	117.00	119.00	120.00	131.00	149.00	156.00	122.00	144.00
Exposed finish	m²	126.00	130.00	128.00	141.00	160.00	166.00	133.00	156.00
Concrete beam slab									
Concealed finish	m²	108.00	132.00	126.00	136.00	152.00	184.00	122.00	144.00
Exposed finish	m²	117.00	143.00	134.00	146.00	163.00	197.00	133.00	156.00
Walls									
Not exceeding 1200 mm (4') high									
Concealed finish	m²	103.00	114.00	108.00	113.00	113.00	163.00	118.00	140.00
Exposed finish	m²	114.00	119.00	113.00	119.00	119.00	172.00	125.00	148.00
Between 1200 mm (4') and 2400 mm (8')									
Concealed finish	m²	103.00	115.00	121.00	124.00	127.00	162.00	118.00	140.00
Exposed finish	m²	114.00	121.00	127.00	131.00	134.00	170.00	125.00	148.00
Between 2400 mm (8') and 3600 mm (12')									
Concealed finish	m²	114.00	127.00	140.00	145.00	144.00	263.00	133.00	158.00
Exposed finish	m²	131.00	137.00	148.00	155.00	155.00	277.00	141.00	166.00
Column (square or rectangular):									
Concealed finish	m²	120.00	131.00	175.00	144.00	150.00	181.00	149.00	165.00
Exposed finish	m²	129.00	135.00	182.00	152.00	155.00	190.00	158.00	173.00
Beams:									
Concealed finish	m²	120.00	121.00	182.00	162.00	163.00	216.00	163.00	179.00
Exposed finish	m²	129.00	125.00	190.00	170.00	172.00	224.00	170.00	186.00
Stairs (measure soffits only):									
Exposed finish	m²	345.00	426.00	415.00	403.00	406.00	536.00	404.00	442.00
Single use									
Flat plate slab:									
Concealed finish	m²	123.00	147.00	137.00	175.00	174.00	202.00	157.00	163.00
Exposed finish	m²	143.00	166.00	153.00	199.00	200.00	230.00	175.00	186.00
Flat slab, with drops:									
Concealed finish	m²	143.00	153.00	145.00	187.00	190.00	217.00	168.00	175.00
Exposed finish	m²	165.00	171.00	162.00	212.00	214.00	242.00	187.00	195.00
Concrete beam slab:									
Concealed finish	m²	131.00	157.00	145.00	187.00	190.00	217.00	168.00	175.00
Exposed finish	m²	152.00	174.00	162.00	210.00	214.00	242.00	187.00	195.00
Walls									
Not exceeding 1200 mm (4') high									
Concealed finish	m²	129.00	120.00	148.00	142.00	148.00	245.00	126.00	182.00
Exposed finish	m²		130.00	156.00	154.00	159.00	264.00	135.00	197.00
Between 1200 mm (4') and 2400 mm (8')									
Concealed finish	m²	129.00	130.00	148.00	142.00	148.00	245.00	126.00	182.00
Exposed finish	m²	140.00	139.00	156.00	154.00	159.00	264.00	135.00	197.00
Between 2400 mm (8') and 3600 mm (12')									
Concealed finish	m²	140.00	134.00	152.00	144.00	152.00	250.00	128.00	186.00
Exposed finish	m²	152.00	149.00	171.00	161.00	166.00	281.00	141.00	207.00

Item	UNITS	St. John's	Halifax	Montreal	Ottawa	Toronto	Winnipeg	Calgary	Vancouver
Columns (square or rectangular):									
Concealed finish	m²	147.00	148.00	190.00	170.00	168.00	234.00	167.00	211.00
Exposed finish	m²	158.00	159.00	200.00	181.00	177.00	245.00	175.00	220.00
Beams:									
Concealed finish	m²	147.00	156.00	211.00	187.00	186.00	254.00	182.00	229.00
Exposed finish	m²	158.00	162.00	221.00	201.00	191.00	265.00	192.00	240.00
Stairs (measure soffit only):									
Exposed finish	m²	436.00	449.00	508.00	463.00	458.00	630.00	453.00	565.00

03 15 00 Concrete Accessories
EXPANSION JOINT
Asphalt and fiber plain filler types to exterior

Item	UNITS	St. John's	Halifax	Montreal	Ottawa	Toronto	Winnipeg	Calgary	Vancouver
6 mm (1/4") thick contraction joint, i.e. to sidewalks									
100 mm (4") wide	m	10.70	10.10	11.40	11.50	12.80	17.80	11.90	14.70
150 mm (6") wide	m	10.40	9.83	11.00	11.20	12.60	17.40	11.60	14.30
24 mm (1") thick expansion joint, i.e. between new & existing bldgs.									
150 mm (6") wide	m	19.50	19.30	22.10	21.90	23.80	33.60	23.80	26.30
200 mm (8") wide	m	24.00	22.00	24.90	23.70	26.70	37.70	27.30	30.20
300 mm (12") wide	m	26.50	24.40	27.50	27.80	30.40	42.80	30.50	33.50

03 20 00 Concrete Reinforcement
03 21 00 Reinforcing Steel
REINFORCING IN PLACE
Deformed bars, 350 MPa (50,000 psi)

Item	UNITS	St. John's	Halifax	Montreal	Ottawa	Toronto	Winnipeg	Calgary	Vancouver
Light bars:									
To footings and slabs	kg	2.63	2.78	2.39	2.58	2.45	2.38	2.14	2.99
To walls, columns and beams	kg	2.67	2.85	2.41	2.60	2.51	2.44	2.18	3.05
Heavy bars:									
To footings and slabs	kg	2.50	2.68	2.22	2.58	2.36	2.24	2.04	2.62
To walls, columns and beams	kg	2.57	2.74	2.25	2.61	2.42	2.28	2.09	2.69
Deformed bars, 400 MPa (60,000 psi)									
Light bars:									
To footings and slabs	kg	2.53	2.85	2.39	2.40	2.52	2.45	2.18	3.12
To walls, columns and beams	kg	2.69	3.05	2.51	2.58	2.68	2.65	2.29	3.33
Heavy bars:									
To footings and slabs	kg	2.60	2.73	2.30	2.39	2.33	2.20	2.09	2.69
To walls, columns and beams	kg	2.63	2.74	2.32	2.40	2.35	2.21	2.10	2.70

COATED REINFORCING
Add for epoxy coating

Item	UNITS	St. John's	Halifax	Montreal	Ottawa	Toronto	Winnipeg	Calgary	Vancouver
Total load not exceeding 1 tonne (1.2 tons):									
Light bars	kg	1.32	1.47	1.25	0.98	1.10	1.81	1.38	1.89
Heavy bars	kg	0.96	1.06	0.89	0.72	0.79	1.31	1.00	1.37
Total load over 1 not exceeding 5 tonnes (6 tons):									
Light bars	kg	1.04	1.17	0.95	0.73	0.83	1.42	1.11	1.55
Heavy bars	kg	0.72	0.79	0.61	0.50	0.57	0.94	0.75	1.03
Total load over 5 tonnes (6 tons):									
Light bars	kg	0.82	0.93	0.81	0.64	0.70	1.14	0.89	1.22
Heavy bars	kg	0.60	0.69	0.59	0.48	0.50	0.85	0.63	0.88

03 22 00 Welded Wire Fabric
WELDED WIRE FABRIC
In slabs:

Item	UNITS	St. John's	Halifax	Montreal	Ottawa	Toronto	Winnipeg	Calgary	Vancouver
150 mm x 150 mm (6" x 6") mesh:									
6/6 gauge	m²	6.24	6.03	6.07	6.55	6.48	7.96	5.31	7.03
8/8 gauge	m²	5.30	5.05	5.11	5.55	5.48	6.76	4.50	5.93
10/10 gauge	m²	4.43	4.25	4.29	4.64	4.59	5.67	3.76	4.94
100 mm x 100 mm (4" x 4") mesh:									
8/8 gauge	m²	7.52	7.19	7.25	7.28	7.54	9.30	6.50	8.19
10/10 gauge	m²	5.22	5.05	5.02	5.44	5.39	6.59	4.52	5.69

03 23 00 Stressing Tendons
PRESTRESSING STEEL
Wire or strands

Item	UNITS	St. John's	Halifax	Montreal	Ottawa	Toronto	Winnipeg	Calgary	Vancouver
Ungrouted:									
1760 MPa (255 ksi)									
Not exceeding 30 m (100') long	kg	11.60	11.20	11.80	14.50	12.00	16.90	13.80	20.00
Over 30 m (100') not exceeding 60 m (200') long	kg	10.60	10.10	10.60	13.30	10.70	14.70	12.40	17.80
Bars									
Ungrouted									
1030 MPa (150 ksi)									
Not exceeding 30 m (100') long	kg	12.80	12.20	12.20	14.50	12.60	15.30	12.30	17.10
Grouted									
1030 MPa (150 ksi)									
Not exceeding 30 m (100') long	kg	25.50	23.50	25.40	28.20	25.90	28.10	23.60	25.00

Item	UNITS	St. John's	Halifax	Montreal	Ottawa	Toronto	Winnipeg	Calgary	Vancouver
03 30 00 Cast-In-Place Concrete									
03 31 00 Structural Concrete									
PLACING CONCRETE (placed only)									
By crane or hoist (major hoisting equipment not included)									
To foundation:									
Wall footings	m³	31.60	31.20	35.30	39.80	44.70	43.40	36.40	33.60
Column footings	m³	31.60	31.20	35.30	39.80	44.70	43.40	36.40	33.60
Raft foundations	m³	28.10	27.70	30.90	35.10	39.40	38.40	32.30	29.90
Pile caps	m³	34.40	34.00	37.90	43.20	48.50	47.20	39.70	36.70
Grade beams and foundation walls	m³	35.20	34.40	38.90	44.10	49.30	47.90	40.30	37.30
To column, walls etc.									
Columns	m³	42.90	42.10	47.60	54.10	60.30	58.90	49.60	45.70
Walls	m³	39.90	39.20	43.90	47.60	54.90	54.80	46.00	42.40
To slabs, beams etc.									
Slab-on-grade	m³	28.80	28.10	33.20	37.60	35.60	41.60	33.10	33.50
Suspended slabs (flat slabs)	m³	28.80	28.10	33.00	35.70	35.00	41.60	33.10	33.50
Suspended slabs (pans or waffles)	m³	33.30	32.40	38.30	43.20	41.00	47.90	38.30	38.60
Suspended slabs (metal deck)	m³	36.10	35.10	41.50	46.70	44.80	52.10	41.20	42.00
Beams (integrated with slabs)	m³	28.80	28.10	33.20	37.60	35.60	41.60	33.10	33.50
Beams (isolated)	m³	36.10	35.10	41.50	46.70	44.80	52.10	41.20	42.00
To miscellaneous									
Stairs	m³	67.90	66.20	78.40	88.30	83.90	97.90	77.90	79.00
Floor toppings	m³	59.10	57.50	67.90	76.50	72.70	85.30	67.50	68.50
HEAVYWEIGHT CONCRETE (supplied only)									
Portland cement									
Standard local aggregates:									
10 MPa (1,500 psi)	m³	189.00	164.00	175.00	160.00	179.00	204.00	220.00	180.00
15 MPa (2,000 psi)	m³	189.00	164.00	179.00	165.00	183.00	213.00	224.00	182.00
20 MPa (3,000 psi)	m³	190.00	174.00	187.00	186.00	183.00	212.00	238.00	309.00
25 MPa (3,500 psi)	m³	196.00	180.00	199.00	177.00	195.00	225.00	245.00	245.00
30 MPa (4,000 psi)	m³	211.00	189.00	215.00	186.00	203.00	241.00	265.00	260.00
High-early cement, type 30									
Standard aggregates:									
10 MPa (1,500 psi)	m³	205.00	173.00	183.00	158.00	194.00	228.00	231.00	197.00
15 MPa (2,000 psi)	m³	212.00	179.00	190.00	160.00	201.00	234.00	233.00	200.00
20 MPa (3,000 psi)	m³	211.00	187.00	213.00	163.00	203.00	232.00	245.00	270.00
25 MPa (3,500 psi)	m³	216.00	197.00	227.00	170.00	211.00	250.00	255.00	277.00
30 MPa (4,000 psi)	m³	196.00	180.00	237.00	180.00	220.00	261.00	272.00	294.00
03 35 00 Concrete Finishing									
FINISHING FLOORS									
Standard Finishes									
Concealed rough finishes:									
Screeding	m²	4.73	4.69	5.39	6.05	6.07	7.42	6.30	6.75
Wood float	m²	6.51	6.46	7.35	7.89	8.20	8.47	7.17	8.16
Concealed smooth finishes:									
Machine trowel	m²	10.20	11.60	14.20	13.60	16.50	19.60	16.00	16.20
Machine grinding	m²	36.40	41.30	51.60	48.20	57.90	70.30	57.40	57.80
Exposed finishes:									
Machine trowel	m²	9.79	10.30	13.80	13.40	13.40	16.40	12.70	13.20
Broom finish	m²	6.09	6.42	8.74	8.30	8.36	10.20	7.80	8.15
Acid etching	m²	4.12	4.33	5.95	5.65	5.70	6.95	5.28	5.49
Stair treads	m²	53.10	56.00	76.30	72.60	72.80	89.80	68.10	71.20
Heavy duty finishes									
Standard hardener - non-metallic									
(steel trowel finish and sealer not included):									
20 kg/10 m² (40 lbs/100 sf)	m²	4.84	4.84	5.25	5.84	6.15	8.47	5.19	8.57
30 kg/10 m² (60 lbs/100 sf)	m²	6.81	6.77	7.43	8.21	8.79	18.80	7.88	14.50
Coloured hardener - standard colours									
(steel trowel finish and sealer not included):									
20 kg/10 m² (40 lbs/100 sf)	m²	14.10	15.80	18.20	18.80	19.80	44.10	20.10	33.00
30 kg/10 m² (60 lbs/100 sf)	m²	15.30	16.80	19.10	20.30	21.10	46.20	21.30	35.00
FINISHING WALLS									
Bushhammered concrete									
Exterior walls/columns in open area, minimum 100 m² (1000 sf):									
Heavy finish	m²	138.00	137.00	124.00	138.00	135.00	137.00	145.00	137.00
Sandblasted concrete									
Exterior walls/columns in open area, minimum 500 m² (5400 sf):									
Light finish	m²	24.50	23.80	22.80	27.10	25.50	28.10	29.70	27.00
Medium finish	m²	31.80	31.50	29.70	35.70	33.70	36.90	39.10	35.20
Heavy finish	m²	42.70	41.90	39.60	47.70	44.90	49.00	51.90	47.20

Item	UNITS	St. John's	Halifax	Montreal	Ottawa	Toronto	Winnipeg	Calgary	Vancouver
03 40 00 Precast Concrete									
03 41 00 Precast Structural Concrete									
BEAMS									
Standard I section:									
1000 mm (36") deep	m	698.00	713.00	750.00	666.00	720.00	676.00	799.00	1160.00
COLUMNS									
Rectangular section:									
600 mm x 600 mm (24" x 24") single storey	m	702.00	716.00	745.00	604.00	710.00	676.00	795.00	1190.00
600 mm x 600 mm (24" x 24") multi storey	m	877.00	893.00	930.00	752.00	884.00	845.00	991.00	1480.00
PRESTRESSED CONCRETE									
Floor and roof slabs, 490 kg/m² (100 psf) live load									
Hollow core slabs, 7.3 m (24') spans, min. 500 m² (5400 sf)									
204 mm (8") hollow core	m²	N/A	122.00	124.00	138.00	127.00	147.00	151.00	177.00
305 mm (12") hollow core	m²	N/A	144.00	145.00	168.00	158.00	179.00	182.00	229.00
Double tees, 9.2 m (30') spans, min. 600 m² (6500 sf)									
610 mm (24") deep	m²	N/A	178.00	173.00	204.00	187.00	193.00	200.00	259.00
03 45 00 Precast Architectural Concrete									
WALL PANELS									
Solid, non load bearing:									
Plain grey, smooth finish	m²	404.00	381.00	323.00	307.00	328.00	491.00	367.00	478.00
Plain grey, textured finish	m²	431.00	407.00	352.00	345.00	362.00	535.00	393.00	510.00
Plain grey, exposed aggregate	m²	475.00	446.00	379.00	361.00	382.00	571.00	430.00	562.00
White, textured finish	m²	492.00	454.00	374.00	367.00	389.00	629.00	461.00	557.00
White, exposed aggregate	m²	517.00	477.00	385.00	367.00	396.00	644.00	483.00	585.00
Sandwich panels, non load panels:									
Plain grey, smooth finish	m²	461.00	435.00	370.00	352.00	376.00	563.00	422.00	588.00
Plain grey, textured finish	m²	484.00	457.00	386.00	366.00	395.00	593.00	439.00	614.00
Plain grey, exposed aggregate	m²	530.00	503.00	429.00	405.00	432.00	654.00	484.00	675.00
White, textured finish	m²	542.00	496.00	402.00	383.00	411.00	668.00	502.00	649.00
White, exposed aggregate	m²	693.00	637.00	516.00	491.00	532.00	865.00	649.00	839.00
Solid, load bearing:									
Plain grey, smooth finish	m²	468.00	446.00	383.00	357.00	382.00	532.00	430.00	562.00
White, textured finish	m²	542.00	496.00	402.00	383.00	411.00	668.00	502.00	610.00
Sandwich panels, load bearing:									
Plain grey, smooth finish	m²	511.00	484.00	414.00	387.00	417.00	575.00	468.00	650.00
White, textured finish	m²	579.00	534.00	433.00	411.00	445.00	721.00	543.00	702.00
03 60 00 Grouting									
GROUT									
Cement and sand									
Pressure grout curtain:									
Connection Charge, 1 per 3 m (10') depth	EA	467.00	460.00	516.00	491.00	495.00	694.00	485.00	634.00
Grouting material, average absorption rate 43 m³/m									
(0.25 cf/lf) of depth	m³	2,890	2,870	3,170	2,930	3,080	4,340	3,030	3,940
Filling voids:									
Average cost	m³	6,200	6,160	6,790	6,370	6,610	9,270	6,460	7,050
04: MASONRY									
04 05 00 Common Work Results for Masonry									
04 05 23 Masonry Accessories									
CONTROL JOINT									
12 mm (1/2") thick control joint, i.e. to facades									
100 mm (4") wide	m	14.80	16.60	15.70	16.80	16.50	18.50	19.60	16.70
150 mm (6") wide	m	15.90	17.60	16.30	17.80	17.40	19.60	20.40	17.60

04 20 00 Unit Masonry

The following items cover simple walls and components. Prices for composite walls can be found in Section D. No allowance has been made in the prices for decorative or special bonding. As a rule of thumb for budgeting purposes, a wall with a decorative bond would cost approximately 10% more than a comparable wall in stretcher bond, but this differential can vary depending on the volume of work, the size and type of unit, and the specific bond. No allowance has been made in the masonry prices for scaffolding or temporary work platforms.

Item	UNITS	St. John's	Halifax	Montreal	Ottawa	Toronto	Winnipeg	Calgary	Vancouver
04 21 00 Clay Unit Masonry									
FACE BRICK - UNREINFORCED									
Modular clay brick 190 x 90 x 57 mm (7-5/8 x 3-5/8 x 2-5/16")									
Veneer	m²	292.00	258.00	239.00	236.00	242.00	352.00	340.00	333.00
Tied to solid backing	m²	305.00	272.00	251.00	249.00	252.00	368.00	357.00	351.00
Utility clay brick 240 x 90 x 57 mm (9-5/8 x 3-5/8 x 2-5/16")									
Veneer	m²	289.00	256.00	237.00	233.00	240.00	348.00	333.00	330.00
Tied to solid backing	m²	300.00	268.00	246.00	244.00	250.00	364.00	354.00	346.00

Item	UNITS	St. John's	Halifax	Montreal	Ottawa	Toronto	Winnipeg	Calgary	Vancouver
Norman clay brick 290 x 90 x 57 mm (11-5/8 x 3-5/8 x 2-5/16")									
Veneer	m²	309.00	275.00	251.00	253.00	255.00	376.00	359.00	357.00
Tied to solid backing	m²	319.00	284.00	259.00	261.00	268.00	385.00	371.00	368.00
Jumbo clay brick 290 x 90 x 90 mm (11-5/8 x 3-5/8 x 3-5/8")									
Veneer	m²	276.00	244.00	223.00	225.00	232.00	331.00	322.00	318.00
Tied to solid backing	m²	293.00	259.00	238.00	237.00	243.00	353.00	341.00	336.00
Giant clay brick 390 x 90 x 190 mm (15-5/8 x 3-5/8 x 7-5/8")									
Veneer	m²	186.00	165.00	153.00	152.00	157.00	224.00	217.00	211.00
Tied to solid backing	m²	193.00	173.00	156.00	157.00	161.00	235.00	225.00	223.00

FACE BRICK - REINFORCED

Item	UNITS	St. John's	Halifax	Montreal	Ottawa	Toronto	Winnipeg	Calgary	Vancouver
Modular clay brick 190 x 90 x 57 mm (7-5/8 x 3-5/8 x 2-5/16")									
Veneer	m²	292.00	269.00	239.00	253.00	255.00	390.00	380.00	381.00
Tied to solid backing	m²	299.00	276.00	243.00	261.00	268.00	400.00	392.00	391.00
Utility clay brick 240 x 90 x 57 mm (9-5/8 x 3-5/8 x 2-5/16")									
Veneer	m²	292.00	269.00	239.00	253.00	255.00	390.00	380.00	381.00
Tied to solid backing	m²	299.00	276.00	243.00	261.00	268.00	400.00	392.00	391.00
Norman clay brick 290 x 90 x 57 mm (11-5/8 x 3-5/8 x 2-5/16")									
Veneer	m²	292.00	269.00	239.00	253.00	255.00	390.00	380.00	381.00
Tied to solid backing	m²	308.00	285.00	251.00	268.00	274.00	409.00	400.00	401.00
Jumbo clay brick 290 x 90 x 90 mm (11-5/8 x 3-5/8 x 3-5/8")									
Veneer	m²	270.00	248.00	222.00	233.00	240.00	359.00	350.00	351.00
Tied to solid backing	m²	279.00	257.00	227.00	239.00	244.00	368.00	359.00	364.00
Giant clay brick 390 x 90 x 190 mm (15-5/8 x 3-5/8 x 7-5/8")									
Veneer	m²	187.00	174.00	154.00	160.00	166.00	250.00	244.00	244.00
Tied to solid backing	m²	202.00	188.00	164.00	173.00	177.00	269.00	262.00	264.00

04 22 00 Concrete Unit Masonry

CONCRETE BLOCK - UNREINFORCED

Plain (lightweight) concrete blocks

Item	UNITS	St. John's	Halifax	Montreal	Ottawa	Toronto	Winnipeg	Calgary	Vancouver
Backup:									
100 mm (4")	m²	109.00	87.40	123.00	122.00	123.00	191.00	168.00	150.00
150 mm (6")	m²	122.00	96.90	141.00	137.00	141.00	211.00	190.00	168.00
200 mm (8")	m²	129.00	108.00	156.00	152.00	155.00	239.00	215.00	182.00
250 mm (10")	m²	157.00	126.00	177.00	178.00	180.00	275.00	245.00	218.00
300 mm (12")	m²	170.00	134.00	193.00	188.00	190.00	294.00	262.00	231.00
Freestanding jointed and pointed:									
100 mm (4")	m²	109.00	91.70	135.00	130.00	131.00	202.00	184.00	154.00
150 mm (6")	m²	117.00	96.90	143.00	138.00	142.00	218.00	195.00	166.00
200 mm (8")	m²	129.00	108.00	156.00	152.00	155.00	239.00	215.00	182.00
250 mm (10")	m²	155.00	129.00	188.00	182.00	188.00	289.00	260.00	219.00
300 mm (12")	m²	173.00	145.00	208.00	203.00	207.00	319.00	286.00	243.00
Cavity wall, cost per side									
100 mm (4")	m²	114.00	95.10	143.00	132.00	138.00	211.00	190.00	160.00
150 mm (6")	m²	121.00	102.00	151.00	141.00	147.00	227.00	199.00	171.00
200 mm (8")	m²	131.00	110.00	162.00	153.00	158.00	246.00	218.00	185.00
250 mm (10")	m²	154.00	128.00	193.00	180.00	187.00	285.00	258.00	218.00
300 mm (12")	m²	170.00	141.00	208.00	196.00	203.00	314.00	279.00	235.00

CONCRETE BLOCK - UNREINFORCED, DECORATIVE

Architectural split faced concrete blocks

Item	UNITS	St. John's	Halifax	Montreal	Ottawa	Toronto	Winnipeg	Calgary	Vancouver
Freestanding jointed and pointed:									
100 mm (4")	m²	141.00	172.00	151.00	160.00	169.00	239.00	213.00	197.00
150 mm (6")	m²	157.00	191.00	172.00	176.00	187.00	261.00	238.00	216.00
200 mm (8")	m²	176.00	215.00	189.00	198.00	212.00	297.00	266.00	244.00
250 mm (10")	m²	194.00	239.00	205.00	217.00	235.00	326.00	293.00	269.00
300 mm (12")	m²	204.00	248.00	217.00	228.00	243.00	341.00	308.00	282.00
Cavity wall, cost per side									
100 mm (4")	m²	141.00	172.00	151.00	160.00	169.00	239.00	213.00	197.00
150 mm (6")	m²	158.00	195.00	173.00	177.00	188.00	264.00	239.00	218.00
200 mm (8")	m²	177.00	216.00	190.00	199.00	213.00	298.00	267.00	245.00
250 mm (10")	m²	196.00	240.00	207.00	220.00	237.00	332.00	294.00	270.00
300 mm (12")	m²	228.00	280.00	246.00	257.00	273.00	385.00	345.00	317.00

Integrally coloured architectural split faced concrete blocks

Item	UNITS	St. John's	Halifax	Montreal	Ottawa	Toronto	Winnipeg	Calgary	Vancouver
Freestanding jointed and pointed:									
100 mm (4")	m²	158.00	195.00	173.00	177.00	188.00	264.00	239.00	218.00
150 mm (6")	m²	169.00	207.00	183.00	192.00	206.00	287.00	257.00	235.00
200 mm (8")	m²	196.00	240.00	207.00	220.00	237.00	332.00	294.00	270.00
250 mm (10")	m²	219.00	269.00	238.00	244.00	262.00	367.00	332.00	302.00
300 mm (12")	m²	255.00	312.00	276.00	286.00	308.00	431.00	386.00	353.00
Cavity wall, cost per side									
100 mm (4")	m²	158.00	195.00	173.00	177.00	188.00	264.00	239.00	218.00
150 mm (6")	m²	169.00	207.00	183.00	192.00	206.00	287.00	257.00	235.00
200 mm (8")	m²	197.00	241.00	209.00	221.00	238.00	333.00	295.00	272.00
250 mm (10")	m²	219.00	269.00	238.00	244.00	262.00	367.00	332.00	302.00
300 mm (12")	m²	259.00	316.00	279.00	292.00	313.00	437.00	392.00	360.00

CONCRETE BLOCK - REINFORCED

Plain (lightweight) concrete blocks

Item	UNITS	St. John's	Halifax	Montreal	Ottawa	Toronto	Winnipeg	Calgary	Vancouver
Backup:									
100 mm (4")	m²	142.00	103.00	137.00	149.00	160.00	236.00	196.00	196.00
150 mm (6")	m²	156.00	115.00	155.00	166.00	181.00	264.00	218.00	217.00
200 mm (8")	m²	167.00	125.00	165.00	179.00	191.00	284.00	235.00	232.00

Item	UNITS	St. John's	Halifax	Montreal	Ottawa	Toronto	Winnipeg	Calgary	Vancouver
250 mm (10")...............	m²	199.00	147.00	193.00	210.00	225.00	335.00	276.00	277.00
300 mm (12")...............	m²	207.00	156.00	204.00	218.00	236.00	349.00	289.00	287.00
Freestanding jointed and pointed:									
100 mm (4")..............	m²	148.00	114.00	153.00	160.00	167.00	256.00	217.00	204.00
150 mm (6")..............	m²	157.00	124.00	164.00	172.00	181.00	276.00	230.00	218.00
200 mm (8")..............	m²	167.00	129.00	172.00	182.00	191.00	292.00	245.00	232.00
250 mm (10").............	m²	207.00	158.00	212.00	221.00	234.00	360.00	299.00	281.00
300 mm (12").............	m²	221.00	171.00	227.00	239.00	250.00	381.00	321.00	305.00
Cavity wall, cost per side									
100 mm (4")..............	m²	149.00	114.00	156.00	162.00	170.00	261.00	220.00	206.00
150 mm (6")..............	m²	164.00	127.00	168.00	179.00	188.00	289.00	243.00	227.00
200 mm (8")..............	m²	177.00	134.00	180.00	192.00	199.00	306.00	260.00	243.00
250 mm (10").............	m²	209.00	163.00	219.00	229.00	238.00	367.00	310.00	288.00
300 mm (12").............	m²	221.00	171.00	228.00	241.00	251.00	389.00	324.00	306.00

CONCRETE BLOCK - REINFORCED, DECORATIVE
Architectural split faced concrete blocks

Item	UNITS	St. John's	Halifax	Montreal	Ottawa	Toronto	Winnipeg	Calgary	Vancouver
Freestanding jointed and pointed:									
100 mm (4")..............	m²	179.00	148.00	173.00	205.00	187.00	266.00	239.00	222.00
150 mm (6")..............	m²	194.00	160.00	187.00	223.00	203.00	290.00	259.00	241.00
200 mm (8")..............	m²	207.00	172.00	200.00	239.00	218.00	309.00	279.00	259.00
250 mm (10").............	m²	238.00	197.00	227.00	273.00	249.00	353.00	319.00	296.00
300 mm (12").............	m²	247.00	204.00	239.00	284.00	258.00	367.00	330.00	306.00
Cavity wall, cost per side									
100 mm (4")..............	m²	185.00	154.00	180.00	214.00	192.00	276.00	251.00	231.00
150 mm (6")..............	m²	200.00	168.00	194.00	232.00	212.00	298.00	270.00	253.00
200 mm (8")..............	m²	214.00	176.00	203.00	244.00	221.00	316.00	286.00	265.00
250 mm (10").............	m²	238.00	198.00	228.00	274.00	250.00	356.00	320.00	299.00
300 mm (12").............	m²	252.00	209.00	241.00	288.00	262.00	372.00	339.00	312.00

Integrally coloured architectural split faced concrete blocks

Item	UNITS	St. John's	Halifax	Montreal	Ottawa	Toronto	Winnipeg	Calgary	Vancouver
Freestanding jointed and pointed:									
100 mm (4")..............	m²	200.00	168.00	194.00	232.00	212.00	298.00	275.00	253.00
150 mm (6")..............	m²	215.00	177.00	205.00	246.00	222.00	320.00	292.00	268.00
200 mm (8")..............	m²	230.00	191.00	220.00	264.00	243.00	345.00	316.00	289.00
250 mm (10").............	m²	266.00	221.00	257.00	307.00	277.00	399.00	365.00	330.00
300 mm (12").............	m²	294.00	244.00	281.00	337.00	305.00	436.00	399.00	367.00
Cavity wall, cost per side									
100 mm (4")..............	m²	200.00	168.00	194.00	232.00	212.00	298.00	275.00	253.00
150 mm (6")..............	m²	216.00	178.00	207.00	251.00	225.00	323.00	296.00	271.00
200 mm (8")..............	m²	252.00	209.00	241.00	288.00	262.00	372.00	344.00	312.00
250 mm (10").............	m²	274.00	227.00	262.00	314.00	286.00	405.00	371.00	341.00
300 mm (12").............	m²	295.00	245.00	282.00	340.00	307.00	440.00	403.00	368.00

04 23 00 Glass Unit Masonry
GLASS BLOCK
Glass block units in straight assembly, normal view,

Item	UNITS	St. John's	Halifax	Montreal	Ottawa	Toronto	Winnipeg	Calgary	Vancouver
152 mm x 152 mm (6" x 6")..............	m²	924.00	646.00	878.00	1,010	862.00	1,260	1,100	958.00
203 mm x 203 mm (8" x 8")..............	m²	673.00	471.00	638.00	734.00	629.00	920.00	800.00	697.00
305 mm x 305 mm (12" x 12")..............	m²	619.00	435.00	590.00	679.00	581.00	846.00	740.00	645.00

04 40 00 Stone Assemblies
Including Necessary Anchor And Fixing Slots And Checks

04 43 00 Stone Masonry
GRANITE (EDGEWORK EXTRA)
Grey, 40 mm (1 1/2") thick:

Item	UNITS	St. John's	Halifax	Montreal	Ottawa	Toronto	Winnipeg	Calgary	Vancouver
Flamed finish	m²	1,150	866.00	1,120	1,160	1,250	1,290	1,220	1,290
Honed finish	m²	1,210	911.00	1,190	1,230	1,290	1,350	1,280	1,340
Polished finish	m²	1,250	950.00	1,240	1,290	1,330	1,430	1,320	1,410
Grey, 100 mm (4") thick									
Flamed finish	m²	1,400	1,050	1,370	1,430	1,530	1,600	1,480	1,560
Honed finish	m²	1,430	1,080	1,400	1,460	1,560	1,630	1,520	1,600
Polished finish	m²	1,560	1,190	1,510	1,590	1,680	1,770	1,660	1,730

LIMESTONE (EDGEWORK EXTRA)
Plain ashlar coursing:
Dimensioned stone 90 mm (3 5/8") on bed:

Item	UNITS	St. John's	Halifax	Montreal	Ottawa	Toronto	Winnipeg	Calgary	Vancouver
Sawn finish	m²	616.00	1,080	650.00	697.00	714.00	754.00	720.00	786.00
Rubbed finish	m²	672.00	1,180	710.00	760.00	780.00	823.00	786.00	858.00

MARBLE (EDGEWORK EXTRA)
White, 20 mm (3/4") thick

Item	UNITS	St. John's	Halifax	Montreal	Ottawa	Toronto	Winnipeg	Calgary	Vancouver
Honed finish	m²	994.00	1,610	1,050	1,140	1,060	1,190	1,180	1,170
White, 40 mm (1 1/2") thick									
Honed finish	m²	1,210	1,960	1,290	1,400	1,310	1,480	1,420	1,430

SANDSTONE (EDGEWORK EXTRA)
Ashlar coursing:

Item	UNITS	St. John's	Halifax	Montreal	Ottawa	Toronto	Winnipeg	Calgary	Vancouver
Standard grade..............	m²	517.00	697.00	500.00	552.00	583.00	563.00	548.00	621.00
Select grade	m²	615.00	825.00	590.00	651.00	688.00	673.00	650.00	735.00

Item	UNITS	St. John's	Halifax	Montreal	Ottawa	Toronto	Winnipeg	Calgary	Vancouver
ROUGH STONE WALL									
Fieldstone									
Split Field Stone									
Random pattern..	m²	524.00	803.00	508.00	589.00	560.00	619.00	605.00	660.00
Limestone									
Split bed split face:									
Coursed Rubble..	m²	311.00	474.00	302.00	346.00	330.00	365.00	359.00	389.00
90 mm (3 5/8") sawn bed, split face:									
Single coursing......................................	m²	259.00	397.00	255.00	289.00	277.00	303.00	298.00	325.00
Triple coursing.......................................	m²	279.00	428.00	271.00	312.00	299.00	330.00	322.00	350.00

05: METALS

05 10 00 Structural Metal Framing

05 12 00 Structural Steel Framing

STRUCTURAL STEEL

(Based on simple construction types) 350 MPa (50 ksi)

yield strength, including shop prime coat

Item	UNITS	St. John's	Halifax	Montreal	Ottawa	Toronto	Winnipeg	Calgary	Vancouver
Beams:									
Light beams not exceeding 50 kg/m (35 lbs/lf).........................	TONNE	4,510	4,100	4,410	4,550	4,700	5,050	4,110	6,040
Wide flange beams between 50 and 240 kg/m (35 and 160 lbs/lf)...........	TONNE	4,110	3,780	4,030	4,160	4,250	4,650	3,780	5,550
Welded wide flange	TONNE	4,310	3,940	4,220	4,360	4,480	4,850	3,950	5,790
Plate girders:									
Average cost	TONNE	5,040	4,620	4,960	5,120	5,250	5,690	4,630	6,800
Columns:									
Light beam, not exceeding 50 kg/m (35 lbs/lf)........................	TONNE	4,390	4,010	4,310	4,430	4,550	4,940	4,030	5,890
Wide flange, over 50 kg/m (35 lbs/lf) not exceeding 285 kg/m (190 lbs/lf)	TONNE	4,110	3,780	4,030	4,160	4,250	4,650	3,780	5,550
Welded Wide Flange..	TONNE	4,310	3,940	4,220	4,360	4,480	4,850	3,950	5,790
Hollow Structural Sections (HSS):									
All sizes	TONNE	4,770	4,380	4,690	4,830	4,960	5,390	4,380	6,430
Spandrels:									
Light beams not exceeding 50 kg/m (35 lbs/lf)........................	TONNE	4,770	4,380	4,690	4,830	4,960	5,390	4,380	6,430
Wide flange beams between 50 and 240 kg/m (35 and 160 lbs/lf)...........	TONNE	4,590	4,200	4,520	4,630	4,780	5,190	4,200	6,190
Welded wide flange beams...	TONNE	4,710	4,310	4,650	4,760	4,890	5,320	4,330	6,340
Trusses:									
Double angle or tee	TONNE	4,470	4,010	4,700	4,790	5,540	5,260	4,390	5,800
Wide flange...	TONNE	4,180	3,760	4,380	4,450	5,160	4,910	4,060	5,390
Welded wide flange	TONNE	4,400	3,950	4,620	4,700	5,460	5,180	4,300	5,710
Tubular sections	TONNE	4,750	4,280	4,990	5,100	5,890	5,600	4,650	6,170
Bracing:									
Angles	TONNE	4,470	4,010	4,700	4,790	5,540	5,260	4,390	5,800
Wide flange..	TONNE	5,210	4,670	5,450	5,550	6,450	6,120	5,070	6,750
Purlins:									
Light beam	TONNE	3,740	3,380	3,950	4,020	4,650	4,430	3,660	4,890
Wide flange..	TONNE	3,360	3,020	3,510	3,600	4,180	3,960	3,280	4,360
Girts:									
Hot rolled	TONNE	3,740	3,380	3,950	4,020	4,650	4,430	3,660	4,890
Cold formed	TONNE	6,030	5,420	6,340	6,470	7,480	7,100	5,910	7,850
Sag rods:									
Average cost	EA	39.20	35.20	41.20	41.90	48.50	45.90	38.30	51.00
Loose lintels (supply only):									
Average cost	TONNE	2,600	2,330	2,760	2,790	3,220	3,060	2,570	3,380
Base plates:									
Up to 203 mm (8") thickness Canadian..............	TONNE	4,080	3,640	4,260	4,330	5,030	4,770	3,970	5,270
Over 203 mm (8") thickness U.S.	TONNE	4,870	4,360	5,110	5,210	6,060	5,730	4,750	6,300
Stud shear connectors:									
Shop applied...	EA	3.30	2.95	3.46	3.54	4.08	3.87	3.20	4.26
Field applied...	EA	6.29	5.64	6.60	6.72	7.77	7.38	6.12	8.15
Ancillary steel:									
Average cost	TONNE	6,980	6,260	7,330	7,470	8,640	8,210	6,820	9,060

DIV 5 Metals — METRIC CURRENT MARKET PRICES

Item	UNITS	St. John's	Halifax	Montreal	Ottawa	Toronto	Winnipeg	Calgary	Vancouver
05 20 00 Metal Joists									
05 21 00 Steel Joist Framing									
OPEN WEB JOISTS									
(Based on simple construction types.)									
For bracing etc. see item 05120.									
380 MPa (55 ksi) yield strength									
Prime coated	TONNE	4,490	3,950	3,840	3,830	4,070	4,430	3,570	5,650
05 30 00 Metal Decking									
05 31 00 Steel Decking									
FLOOR DECKS - GALVANIZED									
(Based on composite decks)									
Flat (v-rib pans)									
0.38 mm (28 ga) thick	m²	19.20	19.10	21.30	20.30	20.70	19.30	20.50	31.00
38 mm (1 1/2") deep non cellular									
0.76 mm (22 ga) thick:									
With Z75 (g25) wipe coat	m²	35.90	36.50	36.00	36.90	38.90	36.00	38.50	57.40
With Z275 (g90) wipe coat	m²	37.60	38.50	37.50	38.80	40.80	37.90	40.20	60.00
0.91 mm (20 ga) thick:									
With Z75 (g25) wipe coat	m²	40.20	40.80	40.10	41.10	43.80	40.20	42.80	63.80
1.22 mm (18 ga) thick:									
With Z75 (g25) wipe coat	m²	44.40	45.10	44.20	45.70	48.00	44.50	47.40	70.60
1.63 mm (16 ga) thick:									
With Z75 (g25) wipe coat	m²	52.60	53.70	52.60	54.30	57.20	52.70	56.10	83.80
38 mm (1 1/2") deep, cellular (100% cellular)									
0.91 mm (20 ga) thick:									
With Z75 (g25) wipe coat	m²	81.40	82.80	81.10	83.70	88.40	81.70	86.90	130.00
With Z275 (g90) wipe coat	m²	92.80	94.70	92.90	95.40	101.00	93.30	99.30	148.00
76 mm (3") deep, non cellular									
0.76 mm (22 ga) thick:									
With Z75 (g25) wipe coat	m²	50.40	49.60	46.60	51.70	54.80	51.00	54.00	74.80
With Z275 (g90) wipe coat	m²	51.30	50.20	47.40	52.60	55.60	51.90	55.00	76.40
0.91 mm (20 ga) thick:									
With Z75 (g25) wipe coat	m²	55.60	54.60	51.40	57.00	60.40	56.10	59.40	82.20
1.22 mm (18 ga) thick:									
With Z75 (g25) wipe coat	m²	60.20	59.10	55.90	61.70	65.50	60.90	64.30	89.50
1.63 mm (16 ga) thick:									
With Z75 (g25) wipe coat	m²	67.00	66.10	62.10	68.90	73.20	68.00	72.00	99.70
76 mm (3") deep, cellular (100% cellular)									
0.91 mm (20 ga) thick:									
With Z75 (g25) wipe coat	m²	115.00	112.00	106.00	117.00	125.00	116.00	121.00	168.00
With Z275 (g90) wipe coat	m²	117.00	114.00	108.00	119.00	127.00	118.00	125.00	172.00
ROOF DECKS - GALVANIZED									
38 mm (1 1/2") deep, non cellular									
0.76 mm (22 ga) thick:									
Standard, Z75 (g25) wipe coat	m²	33.70	34.60	30.90	38.20	35.00	34.10	31.50	66.40
Standard, Z275 (g90) wipe coat	m²	35.60	36.50	32.50	40.40	37.10	36.00	33.30	70.40
Acoustical, Z75 (g25) wipe coat	m²	41.50	42.40	37.80	46.90	42.80	41.70	38.50	81.50
Acoustical, Z275 (g90) wipe coat	m²	42.70	44.20	39.60	48.90	44.90	43.50	40.10	85.00
0.91 mm (20 ga) thick:									
Standard, Z75 (g25) wipe coat	m²	37.50	38.70	34.40	42.40	39.00	38.20	35.30	74.10
Acoustical, Z75 (g25) wipe coat	m²	45.10	46.40	41.40	51.20	46.90	45.90	42.20	89.00
1.22 mm (18 ga) thick:									
Standard, Z75 (g25) wipe coat	m²	44.70	45.70	40.90	50.40	46.50	45.10	41.80	88.00
1.63 mm (16 ga) thick:									
Standard, Z75 (g25) wipe coat	m²	50.30	51.70	46.10	57.00	52.00	50.90	47.00	99.20
76 mm (3") deep, non cellular									
0.76 mm (22 ga) thick:									
Standard, Z75 (g25) wipe coat	m²	48.70	49.90	46.60	57.40	52.00	49.50	47.50	95.30
Standard, Z275 (g90) wipe coat	m²	50.40	51.70	48.20	59.30	54.10	50.90	48.80	98.80
Acoustical, Z75 (g25) wipe coat	m²	56.70	58.00	54.30	66.50	60.60	57.30	55.00	111.00
Acoustical, Z275 (g90) wipe coat	m²	59.40	61.00	56.80	69.90	63.30	60.40	57.60	116.00
0.91 mm (20 ga) thick:									
Standard, Z75 (g25) wipe coat	m²	55.50	56.90	52.80	65.20	59.30	56.30	53.70	108.00
Acoustical, Z75 (g25) wipe coat	m²	61.70	63.20	58.70	72.50	66.00	62.70	59.90	121.00
1.22 mm (18 ga) thick:									
Standard, Z75 (g25) wipe coat	m²	61.70	63.20	58.70	72.50	66.00	62.70	59.90	121.00
1.63 mm (16 ga) thick:									
Standard, Z75 (g25) wipe coat	m²	67.90	69.70	65.00	79.90	72.80	68.70	66.10	133.00
05 40 00 Cold-Formed Metal Framing									
FRAMING, STUD WALLS									
Solid type, 0.531 mm (25 ga)									
400 mm (16") o.c.									
41 mm (1-5/8") studs	m²	22.30	22.20	20.50	24.50	27.10	20.20	18.50	27.20
64 mm (2-1/2") studs	m²	26.00	25.70	23.90	28.00	31.20	23.30	21.60	31.60
92 mm (3-5/8") studs	m²	28.90	28.40	26.30	31.20	34.70	26.00	24.00	35.00
152 mm (6") studs	m²	46.20	45.70	41.90	50.00	55.30	41.60	38.20	56.10

Item	UNITS	St. John's	Halifax	Montreal	Ottawa	Toronto	Winnipeg	Calgary	Vancouver
05 50 00 Metal Fabrications									
05 51 13 Metal Pan Stairs									
STAIR									
Pan stairs with closed risers:									
250 mm (10") treads and 200 mm (8") risers									
900 mm (36") wide (per tread)	EA	224.00	197.00	243.00	263.00	288.00	305.00	281.00	391.00
1050 mm (42") wide (per tread)	EA	249.00	219.00	270.00	289.00	316.00	338.00	311.00	436.00
1200 mm (48") wide (per tread)	EA	308.00	270.00	335.00	360.00	394.00	420.00	387.00	540.00
Landings:									
50 mm (2") deep pan	m²	1,290	1,140	1,410	1,500	1,660	1,780	1,640	2,400
Circular stairs:									
Steel stairs:									
1500 mm (5') dia. (per tread)	EA	485.00	426.00	537.00	573.00	626.00	667.00	613.00	908.00
05 51 33 Metal Ladders									
LADDER									
Open steel ladders:									
400 mm (16") wide	m	199.00	176.00	215.00	246.00	247.00	272.00	265.00	366.00
Steel ladders with safety loops:									
400 mm (16") wide	m	326.00	284.00	351.00	400.00	398.00	436.00	432.00	610.00
05 52 00 Metal Railings									
Handrails on wall brackets									
Steel:									
40 mm (1.5") pipe rail	m	133.00	122.00	124.00	148.00	140.00	174.00	160.00	145.00
Plastic covered steel:									
40 mm (1.5") wide	m	177.00	163.00	164.00	198.00	186.00	234.00	214.00	194.00
Railings									
Steel:									
40 mm (1.5") pipe railing, 900 mm (36") high	m	348.00	317.00	323.00	385.00	363.00	454.00	415.00	377.00
12 mm (0.5") tube pickets, 900 mm (36") high	m	495.00	454.00	465.00	552.00	520.00	648.00	598.00	541.00
05 53 00 Metal Gratings									
FLOOR GRATING									
Welded standard gratings									
Pedestrian traffic:									
900 mm (3') span	m²	158.00	146.00	186.00	168.00	171.00	175.00	136.00	208.00
1200 mm (4') span	m²	179.00	165.00	212.00	190.00	195.00	199.00	153.00	232.00
1800 mm (6') span	m²	252.00	233.00	297.00	267.00	272.00	279.00	215.00	330.00
3000 mm (10') span	m²	408.00	376.00	473.00	430.00	441.00	445.00	346.00	529.00
06: WOOD, PLASTICS & COMPOSITES									
06 10 00 Rough Carpentry									
In metric nomenclature for lumber there are no nominal sizes and the following descriptions and prices reflect finished sizes. One cubic meter of lumber therefore actually contains 1 m³, and a piece described as 38 x 89 mm is actually that size.									
06 11 00 Wood Framing - Supply									
FRAMING, MEMBERS									
Boards and shiplap									
Construction grade softwood, spruce, 2.4 m (8') long pieces									
19 mm (1") thick:									
38 mm (2") wide	m	0.56	0.63	0.70	0.61	0.61	0.72	0.67	0.50
64 mm (3") wide	m	0.94	1.06	1.20	1.03	0.95	1.21	1.15	0.81
89 mm (4") wide	m	1.15	1.28	1.45	1.24	1.17	1.47	1.40	0.97
140 mm (6") wide	m	1.64	2.66	1.75	2.58	1.95	2.34	2.00	1.67
184 mm (8") wide	m	2.00	3.24	2.11	3.13	2.39	2.83	2.43	2.03
235 mm (10") wide	m	2.58	4.15	2.75	4.08	3.07	3.67	3.15	2.60
286 mm (12") wide	m	3.65	5.92	3.86	5.74	4.35	5.20	4.44	3.71
Structural light framing - studs (S4S) - dried									
Construction grade softwood, spruce, 2.4 m (8') long pieces									
38 mm (2") thick:									
38 mm (2") wide	m	0.84	0.87	0.80	0.85	0.91	0.88	0.78	0.84
64 mm (3") wide	m	0.98	1.01	0.94	1.00	1.10	1.04	0.91	0.96
89 mm (4") wide	m	1.21	1.25	1.16	1.24	1.35	1.28	1.12	1.19
140 mm (6") wide	m	1.94	2.66	1.90	2.24	2.40	1.79	1.60	1.40
184 mm (8") wide	m	2.51	3.47	2.46	2.92	3.13	2.32	2.05	1.81
235 mm (10") wide	m	3.84	5.28	3.77	4.44	4.77	3.54	3.18	2.77
286 mm (12") wide	m	5.55	7.61	5.45	6.43	6.89	5.13	4.58	4.01
Western red cedar, 2.4 m (8') long pieces									
38 mm (2") thick:									
64 mm (3") wide	m	3.23	3.87	3.55	3.39	4.09	3.79	3.12	3.52
89 mm (4") wide	m	3.46	4.11	3.81	3.59	4.35	4.03	3.31	3.76
140 mm (6") wide	m	6.75	8.07	7.47	7.07	8.55	7.89	6.50	7.37

Item	UNITS	St. John's	Halifax	Montreal	Ottawa	Toronto	Winnipeg	Calgary	Vancouver
184 mm (8") wide............	m	9.33	11.20	10.30	9.78	11.80	10.90	8.99	10.20
235 mm (10") wide...........	m	15.20	18.20	17.00	16.10	19.40	17.90	14.80	16.80
286 mm (12") wide...........	m	20.10	24.00	22.20	21.00	25.40	23.30	19.40	21.90
Pressure treated lumber, rated for ground contact									
38 mm (2") thick:									
89 mm (4") wide............	m	2.14	2.20	2.05	2.20	2.40	2.26	1.98	2.11
140 mm (6") wide...........	m	2.94	4.02	2.87	3.40	3.64	2.71	2.43	2.11
184 mm (8") wide...........	m	4.25	5.84	4.15	4.93	5.26	3.94	3.50	3.07
235 mm (10") wide..........	m	6.18	8.53	6.09	7.17	7.68	5.73	5.12	4.47
286 mm (12") wide..........	m	13.80	18.90	13.40	15.80	16.70	12.70	11.40	9.90
89 mm (4") thick:									
89 mm (4") wide............	m	4.25	5.82	4.15	4.91	5.26	3.93	3.50	3.07

06 11 00 Wood Framing - Installation
(rough hardware included)
Light framing

FRAMING, WALLS
Wall framing cost:

Item	UNITS	St. John's	Halifax	Montreal	Ottawa	Toronto	Winnipeg	Calgary	Vancouver
38 x 89 mm (2" x 4")........	m²	14.10	16.90	13.90	13.10	20.80	18.90	13.20	14.70
38 x 140 mm (2" x 6").......	m²	21.00	25.00	20.70	19.40	31.10	28.40	19.70	21.70

FRAMING, JOISTS & BEAMS
Joist or beams:

Item	UNITS	St. John's	Halifax	Montreal	Ottawa	Toronto	Winnipeg	Calgary	Vancouver
38 x 240 mm (2" x 10")......	m²	19.40	23.00	18.90	17.90	28.60	26.00	18.30	20.10
38 x 290 mm (2" x 12")......	m²	23.80	28.40	23.10	22.10	35.00	32.30	22.00	24.50

FRAMING, ROOFS
Rafters or purlins:

Item	UNITS	St. John's	Halifax	Montreal	Ottawa	Toronto	Winnipeg	Calgary	Vancouver
38 x 140 mm (2" x 6").......	m²	14.50	18.10	14.60	15.00	21.80	20.00	14.30	17.60

FRAMING, CEILINGS
Suspended ceiling framing timber :

Item	UNITS	St. John's	Halifax	Montreal	Ottawa	Toronto	Winnipeg	Calgary	Vancouver
32 x 38 mm (1 1/2" x 2").....	m²	21.10	26.60	21.20	21.90	32.00	29.20	20.80	25.70

FRAMING, BLOCKING & NAILERS
Nailers, blocking etc.:

Item	UNITS	St. John's	Halifax	Montreal	Ottawa	Toronto	Winnipeg	Calgary	Vancouver
38 x 38 mm (2" x 2")..........	m	6.11	7.28	6.01	5.67	9.08	8.28	5.73	6.35

FRAMING, FURRING & STRAPPINGS
Furring or strapping:
19 mm (1") thick

Item	UNITS	St. John's	Halifax	Montreal	Ottawa	Toronto	Winnipeg	Calgary	Vancouver
38 mm (2") wide............	m	2.34	2.77	2.28	2.17	3.44	3.16	2.16	2.41
64 mm (3") wide............	m		3.24	2.66	2.51	4.00	3.65	2.56	2.81
89 mm (4") wide............	m	2.75	3.27	2.69	2.55	4.06	3.74	2.58	2.86
38 mm (2") thick									
38 mm (2") wide............	m	3.18	3.82	3.14	2.97	4.72	4.35	2.98	3.30
64 mm (3") wide............	m	3.03	3.63	2.99	2.81	4.54	4.11	2.85	3.13
89 mm (4") wide............	m	3.57	4.28	3.52	3.32	5.33	4.87	3.33	3.71
140 mm (6") wide...........	m	3.66	4.37	3.59	3.39	5.41	4.96	3.41	3.77

06 15 00 Wood Decking - Supply
DECKING
Decking tongue and groove - dried
Select spruce:
38 mm (2") thick

Item	UNITS	St. John's	Halifax	Montreal	Ottawa	Toronto	Winnipeg	Calgary	Vancouver
140 mm (6") wide...........	m	4.48	4.64	4.72	5.72	5.42	6.11	5.23	5.57
184 mm (8") wide...........	m	5.05	5.23	5.32	6.45	6.15	6.87	5.91	6.30
64 mm (3") thick									
140 mm (6") wide...........	m	6.68	6.92	7.06	8.56	8.12	9.13	7.83	8.31
89 mm (4") thick									
140 mm (6") wide...........	m	9.95	10.30	10.50	12.80	12.20	13.60	11.80	12.30
Select fir or hemlock:									
38 mm (2") thick									
140 mm (6") wide...........	m	4.70	4.88	4.98	6.04	5.71	6.43	5.52	5.88
184 mm (8") wide...........	m	7.20	7.46	7.62	9.20	8.75	9.86	8.44	8.97
64 mm (3") thick									
140 mm (6") wide...........	m	7.48	7.75	7.90	9.60	9.11	10.20	8.77	9.32
89 mm (4") thick									
140 mm (6") wide...........	m	12.50	13.00	13.20	15.90	15.20	17.10	14.70	15.60
Select cedar:									
38 mm (2") thick									
140 mm (6") wide...........	m	10.40	10.80	10.30	13.80	11.60	13.50	10.50	10.50
184 mm (8") wide...........	m	13.50	13.90	13.40	18.10	15.10	17.50	13.70	13.50
64 mm (3") thick									
140 mm (6") wide...........	m	15.90	16.40	15.70	21.20	17.90	20.50	16.10	16.20
89 mm (4") thick									
140 mm (6") wide...........	m	24.10	24.90	24.00	32.10	27.20	31.50	24.60	24.30

Item	UNITS	St. John's	Halifax	Montreal	Ottawa	Toronto	Winnipeg	Calgary	Vancouver
06 15 00 Wood Decking - Installation									
DECKING									
Decking tongue and groove - dried									
38 mm (2") thick									
140 mm (6") wide	m²	25.70	22.70	26.60	25.80	39.40	37.10	25.90	29.10
184 mm (8") wide	m²	29.10	25.60	30.20	29.00	44.40	41.60	29.20	32.80
64 mm (3") thick									
140 mm (6") wide	m²	35.50	31.00	36.60	35.30	54.20	50.90	35.60	39.90
89 mm (4") thick									
140 mm (6") wide	m²	45.10	39.70	46.50	44.90	68.90	65.00	45.40	50.80
06 16 00 Sheathing - Supply									
SHEATHING									
Prices are based upon the standard imperial panel size which is 1220 x 2440 (4' x 8'), although 1440 x 3050 (4' x 10') and 1440 x 3660 (4' x 12') are available from most mills, at a premium.									
Unsanded fir plywood:									
12.5 mm (1/2")	m²	11.10	11.40	12.50	9.73	12.70	9.58	8.37	10.00
15.5 mm (5/8")	m²	12.50	12.80	14.10	11.00	14.30	10.80	9.45	11.30
18.5 mm (3/4")	m²	14.40	14.90	16.30	12.70	16.60	12.40	10.90	13.00
Sanded fir plywood, G1S:									
8 mm (3/8")	m²	12.20	22.30	12.10	10.90	12.30	12.20	10.60	12.10
11 mm (1/2")	m²	14.60	26.50	14.50	13.10	15.00	14.60	12.50	14.40
14 mm (5/8")	m²	18.50	33.70	18.30	16.70	18.70	18.60	16.00	18.30
17 mm (3/4")	m²	21.90	39.50	21.40	19.30	21.70	21.50	18.70	21.50
06 16 00 Sheathing - Installation									
SHEATHING									
Floors or flat roofs:									
12.5 mm (1/2")	m²	8.08	7.10	8.32	8.02	12.40	11.60	8.07	9.10
15.5 mm (5/8")	m²	9.69	8.50	10.00	9.63	14.80	13.90	9.69	10.90
18.5 mm (3/4")	m²	9.69	8.50	10.00	9.63	14.80	13.90	9.69	10.90
Walls:									
9.5 mm (3/8")	m²	9.69	8.75	9.44	9.35	14.70	13.80	10.00	11.10
12.5 mm (1/2")	m²	11.30	10.20	11.00	10.90	17.20	16.10	11.70	12.90
15.5 mm (5/8")	m²	11.30	10.20	11.00	10.90	17.20	16.10	11.70	12.90
18.5 mm (3/4")	m²	12.90	11.60	12.40	12.40	19.60	18.40	13.10	14.50
06 17 00 Shop-Fabricated Structural Wood									
STRUCTURAL JOISTS									
Composite wood joist with parallel 38 mm x 64 mm (2" x 3") top and bottom Micro-Lam flanges and 10 mm (3/8") plywood web - SUPPLY ONLY (excluding hardware)									
300 mm (11 1/8") deep	m	15.30	5.02	16.40	16.90	17.10	19.90	17.20	16.40
355 mm (14") deep	m	16.50	5.49	17.50	18.30	18.50	21.40	18.60	17.60
406 mm (16") deep	m	17.00	5.62	18.40	18.90	19.30	22.30	19.60	18.10
457 mm (18") deep	m	19.00	6.25	20.10	21.00	21.40	24.70	21.50	20.30
508 mm (20") deep	m	20.80	6.88	21.70	23.00	23.40	26.80	23.30	21.90
06 18 00 Glued-Laminated Construction									
LAMINATED FRAMING									
Structural units - SUPPLY ONLY (excluding hardware) based on actual net volumes, spruce									
Straight members 38 mm (2") material: Interior work									
Industrial grade	m³	1,570	1,540	1,560	1,470	1,750	1,910	1,660	2,520
Commercial grade	m³	1,610	1,580	1,600	1,520	1,790	1,970	1,720	2,580
Quality grade	m³	1,800	1,770	1,770	1,680	2,000	2,180	1,910	2,850
Structural units (installation only)									
Less than 23.6 m³ (10,000 fbm):									
Members not exceeding 9 m (30') long	EA	271.00	258.00	259.00	255.00	286.00	343.00	285.00	340.00
Over 9 m (30'), not exceeding 12 m (40')	EA	373.00	358.00	357.00	350.00	396.00	473.00	393.00	472.00
Over 12 m (40')	EA	745.00	715.00	715.00	700.00	793.00	945.00	786.00	945.00
23.6 m³ and over (10,000 fbm):									
Members not exceeding 9 m (30') long	EA	150.00	145.00	145.00	141.00	160.00	191.00	160.00	189.00
Over 9 m (30'), not exceeding 12 m (40')	EA	254.00	243.00	244.00	238.00	269.00	322.00	268.00	322.00
Over 12 m (40')	EA	474.00	455.00	458.00	445.00	509.00	602.00	501.00	604.00

Item	UNITS	St. John's	Halifax	Montreal	Ottawa	Toronto	Winnipeg	Calgary	Vancouver
06 20 00 Finish Carpentry									
06 26 00 Board Panelling									
PANELLING, BOARDS									
Veneered plywood panelling standard panels excluding finishing.									
For select grades for special selection or "bookmatching" application,									
multiply pricing by two.									
Fir: 6 mm (1/4") G1S	m²	63.90	64.90	66.10	69.80	80.00	87.90	74.60	92.20
Birch: 6 mm (1/4") G1S	m²	70.90	72.10	73.40	77.60	88.80	97.70	82.50	103.00
Oak: 6 mm (1/4")	m²	83.00	84.20	85.70	90.70	104.00	114.00	96.70	120.00
Mahogany: 6 mm (1/4")	m²	94.60	96.00	97.70	103.00	119.00	129.00	110.00	136.00
Walnut: 6 mm (1/4")	m²	124.00	126.00	127.00	136.00	156.00	171.00	146.00	181.00
Teak: 6 mm (1/4")	m²	131.00	133.00	135.00	142.00	163.00	178.00	153.00	189.00
Wood panelling T&G simple finish									
Knotty Pine: 19 mm x 140 mm (1" x 6") D4S	m²	70.70	72.00	79.30	80.50	98.00	102.00	86.40	121.00
Cedar: 19 mm x 140 mm (1" x 6") D4S	m²	117.00	118.00	130.00	132.00	162.00	167.00	142.00	196.00
Redwood: 19 mm x 140 mm (1" x 6") D4S	m²	159.00	161.00	178.00	181.00	220.00	229.00	194.00	272.00
Douglas Fir: 19 mm x 140 mm (1" x 6") D4S	m²	121.00	123.00	136.00	139.00	169.00	175.00	150.00	210.00
Birch: 19 mm x 140 mm (1" x 6") D4S	m²	121.00	123.00	136.00	139.00	169.00	175.00	150.00	210.00
Oak: 19 mm x 140 mm (1" x 6") D4S	m²	160.00	162.00	179.00	182.00	221.00	230.00	195.00	273.00
Mahogany: 19 mm x 140 mm (1" x 6") D4S	m²	187.00	189.00	210.00	215.00	261.00	272.00	230.00	322.00
07: THERMAL & MOISTURE PROTECTION									
07 10 00 Dampproofing and Waterproofing									
07 11 00 Dampproofing									
BITUMINOUS ASPHALT COATING									
Cutback asphalt									
Sprayed:									
1 coat	m²	7.70	7.98	8.66	9.55	8.96	8.97	7.43	10.60
2 coats	m²	11.40	12.00	13.00	14.20	13.40	13.20	11.20	16.10
07 13 00 Sheet Waterproofing									
ELASTOMERIC WATERPROOFING									
Flexible membrane									
3 mm (1/8"), polyethylene based sheet:									
On horizontal surfaces	m²	32.20	32.90	31.10	53.70	34.20	32.50	26.40	35.00
On vertical surfaces	m²	32.00	32.50	33.80	61.60	40.40	34.60	32.00	37.20
1.5 mm (1/16") rubber based sheet:									
On horizontal surfaces	m²	51.00	51.10	55.00	97.00	59.20	57.30	46.20	59.80
On vertical surfaces	m²	73.70	72.10	87.50	161.00	102.00	89.20	80.80	92.70
Rubberized asphalt hot applied									
Sheet reinforced:									
On horizontal surfaces	m²	29.80	28.10	30.20	32.90	30.70	31.00	23.90	36.00
On vertical surfaces	m²	52.90	49.50	53.60	58.10	53.90	54.30	42.60	63.90
Acrylic, epoxy or silanes, fluid applied									
On vertical surfaces:									
Low solid	m²	30.90	30.60	35.20	38.20	37.00	36.40	29.50	44.00
High solid	m²	45.00	44.40	51.10	55.40	53.90	53.00	42.80	63.90
Asphalt impregnated protection board									
3 mm (1/8") thick:									
Laid horizontally	m²	13.80	13.10	14.10	38.40	15.70	17.70	12.30	24.00
Fixed vertically	m²	17.20	16.30	17.50	48.00	19.80	22.20	15.60	30.00
MEMBRANE WATERPROOFING									
Fabric membrane									
Glass fibre mesh (embedded):									
2-ply on horizontal surfaces	m²	30.00	29.80	30.10	50.90	32.20	29.80	25.90	31.90
2-ply on vertical surfaces	m²	33.50	32.90	33.70	56.50	36.00	33.40	29.00	35.60
3-ply on horizontal surfaces	m²	33.70	33.40	33.80	57.50	36.40	33.60	29.40	35.80
3-ply on vertical surfaces	m²	42.00	41.40	41.70	71.00	45.00	41.70	36.30	44.40
PROTECTION BOARD									
Plastic protection board									
3 mm (1/8") thick:									
Laid horizontally	m²	8.08	9.30	9.44	8.65	9.35	8.49	6.03	8.16
Fixed vertically	m²	8.89	10.20	10.40	9.52	10.30	9.37	6.63	8.96
Hardboard									
6 mm (1/4") thick:									
Laid horizontally	m²	5.23	6.19	6.26	6.07	6.90	5.91	4.69	5.78
Fixed vertically	m²	6.96	8.26	8.34	8.08	9.20	7.89	6.24	7.71
Plywood									
6 mm (1/4") thick:									
Laid horizontally	m²	7.16	8.69	8.70	8.93	9.69	8.13	6.49	8.09
Fixed vertically	m²	8.89	10.90	10.80	11.40	12.10	10.20	8.09	10.20

Item	UNITS	St. John's	Halifax	Montreal	Ottawa	Toronto	Winnipeg	Calgary	Vancouver
07 16 00 Cementitious & Reactive Waterproofing									
CEMENTITIOUS WATERPROOFING									
Parging									
Exposed:									
12 mm (1/2") thick (2 coats)	m²	50.10	48.20	45.00	50.00	54.50	43.80	41.00	51.10
Concealed:									
12 mm (1/2") thick (2 coats)	m²	40.40	38.70	36.00	40.40	43.70	35.10	32.90	41.20
07 19 00 Water Repellents									
SILICONE WATER REPELLENTS									
Silicone base									
Roller applied to concrete and masonry walls:									
1 coat	m²	11.10	10.40	10.00	11.00	10.80	11.80	12.60	10.50
2 coats	m²	20.10	18.90	18.00	19.60	19.20	21.10	22.70	19.00
07 20 00 Thermal Protection									
07 21 00 Thermal Insulation									
BUILDING INSULATION									
Loose fill insulation									
Fibrous:									
Glass fibre	m³	101.00	95.80	107.00	131.00	115.00	110.00	97.40	76.30
Pelletized:									
Vermicular or perlite	m³		143.00	161.00	198.00	175.00	168.00	149.00	114.00
Board or quilt insulation									
Glass fibre af-530:									
25 mm (1")	m²	29.20	27.70	31.30	38.40	33.70	32.00	28.40	22.10
38 mm (1 1/2")	m²	29.20	27.80	31.30	38.40	33.70	32.00	28.40	22.10
51 mm (2")	m²	34.30	32.70	36.50	44.80	39.30	37.40	33.10	25.90
Expanded polystyrene:									
25 mm (1")	m²	27.30	26.20	29.40	36.10	31.50	30.10	26.80	20.80
38 mm (1 1/2")	m²	28.80	27.80	31.30	38.40	33.70	32.00	28.40	22.10
51 mm (2")	m²	32.70	31.40	35.00	43.00	38.00	36.10	32.00	25.00
Urethane panels:									
25 mm (1")	m²	43.10	40.90	46.10	56.10	49.60	47.40	41.90	32.80
38 mm (1 1/2")	m²	48.80	46.70	51.90	64.00	56.50	53.60	47.30	37.00
51 mm (2")	m²	53.70	50.90	57.10	70.20	61.90	59.00	52.20	40.60
Foamed-in-place (insulated in warm conditions)									
Polyurethane:									
Sprayed, 1 coat, average 25 mm (1") thick	m²	22.90	21.90	24.10	30.00	26.50	25.20	22.10	17.30
Poured into cavity average 25 mm (1") wide including									
jigging walls	m²	43.70	41.80	46.60	57.40	50.70	48.10	42.40	33.20
Perimeter and Under-Slab Insulation									
Polystyrene									
Moulded panels:									
25 mm (1")	m²	23.20	22.00	24.20	30.10	26.80	25.30	22.10	17.40
38 mm (1 1/2")	m²	34.10	32.30	36.00	44.50	38.90	37.20	32.90	25.70
51 mm (2")	m²	36.80	35.10	39.20	48.20	42.50	40.50	35.70	28.10
Polyurethane									
Rigid board:									
25 mm (1")	m²	25.10	23.20	28.70	14.50	30.70	32.20	22.60	20.40
38 mm (1 1/2")	m²	29.70	27.50	34.20	17.20	36.60	37.80	27.30	24.00
51 mm (2")	m²	34.60	32.10	40.00	20.00	42.60	44.30	31.70	28.10
07 22 00 Roof and Deck Insulation									
ROOF DECK INSULATION									
Wood fibreboard									
Asphalt impregnated:									
12 mm (1/2") board	m²	8.19	6.92	9.10	10.80	10.00	9.81	8.80	8.57
Glass fibreboard									
Rigid kraft faced insulation:									
19 mm (3/4")	m²	11.80	10.00	13.00	15.60	14.50	13.90	12.50	12.30
25 mm (1")	m²	15.20	12.90	17.10	20.30	18.80	18.20	16.40	16.00
50 mm (2")	m²	24.00	20.30	26.80	31.90	29.60	29.10	25.90	25.20
75 mm (3")	m²	33.70	28.40	37.60	44.60	41.30	40.40	36.30	35.30
100 mm (4") two layer	m²	48.50	40.80	53.80	64.20	59.10	57.80	51.80	50.60
Expanded polystyrene panels									
25 mm (1")	m²	14.70	12.60	16.60	19.90	18.30	17.90	15.90	15.70
38 mm (1 1/2")	m²	19.80	16.70	22.00	26.30	24.20	23.90	21.20	20.50
51 mm (2")	m²	25.40	21.50	28.20	33.80	31.10	30.40	27.30	26.50
Phenolic foam panels									
25 mm (1")	m²	16.50	13.80	18.20	21.60	19.80	19.50	17.30	17.10
38 mm (1 1/2")	m²	20.80	17.50	23.10	27.50	25.40	24.80	22.30	21.90
51 mm (2")	m²	27.30	22.90	30.40	36.10	33.30	32.40	29.30	28.50

Item	UNITS	St. John's	Halifax	Montreal	Ottawa	Toronto	Winnipeg	Calgary	Vancouver
07 26 00 Vapour Retarders									
VAPOUR RETARDERS									
Polyethylene vapour barrier, 0.15 mm (.006") thick...........	m²	1.75	1.86	1.80	2.01	1.83	2.00	2.03	1.69
07 30 00 Steep Slope Roofing									
07 31 00 Shingles and Shakes									
ASPHALT SHINGLES									
Asphalt shingles, standard pitch									
Standard butt edge:									
10.25 kg/m² (2.10 lbs/sf)	m²	32.90	30.70	24.20	28.30	26.10	24.50	24.00	38.40
Sealed butt edge:									
10.25 kg/m² (2.10 lbs/sf) self sealing	m²	32.90	30.70	24.20	28.30	26.10	24.50	24.00	38.40
SLATE									
Vermont, semi-weathering green...........	m²	169.00	177.00	180.00	189.00	205.00	190.00	182.00	189.00
WOOD									
Cedar shingles									
First grade, high pitch (4/12 min):									
450 mm (18") shingle, 140 mm (5 1/2") exposed...........	m²	78.10	76.10	73.00	69.10	77.40	89.60	74.00	96.90
600 mm (24") shingle, 190 mm (7 1/2") exposed...........	m²	83.40	81.30	77.80	73.70	82.50	95.70	78.80	103.00
07 40 00 Roofing and Siding Panels									
07 41 00 Roof Panels									
ALUMINUM/STEEL ROOFING									
38 mm (1 1/2") profile									
Exposed fasteners:									
Single skin siding									
0.711 mm (22 ga) steel, baked enamel finish	m²	94.10	93.10	93.50	105.00	107.00	113.00	97.10	113.00
0.813 mm (24 ga) aluminum, baked enamel finish	m²	121.00	120.00	120.00	135.00	139.00	147.00	125.00	145.00
Single skin fascia panels									
0.711 mm (22 ga) steel, baked enamel finish	m²	172.00	172.00	172.00	191.00	196.00	211.00	179.00	207.00
0.813 mm (24 ga) aluminum, baked enamel finish	m²	376.00	374.00	374.00	421.00	431.00	456.00	390.00	451.00
Hidden fasteners:									
Single skin siding									
0.711 mm (22 ga) steel, baked enamel finish	m²	161.00	160.00	160.00	180.00	185.00	195.00	168.00	196.00
0.813 mm (24 ga) aluminum, baked enamel finish	m²	187.00	185.00	188.00	208.00	215.00	227.00	193.00	225.00
Single skin fascia panels									
0.711 mm (22 ga) steel, baked enamel finish	m²	191.00	189.00	192.00	215.00	221.00	232.00	200.00	233.00
0.813 mm (24 ga) aluminum, baked enamel finish	m²	206.00	203.00	206.00	231.00	237.00	250.00	210.00	249.00
Factory sandwich panel 25 mm insulation									
0.711 mm (22 ga) steel, baked enamel finish	m²	186.00	185.00	188.00	206.00	205.00	240.00	200.00	242.00
0.813 mm (24 ga) aluminum, baked enamel finish	m²	205.00	205.00	210.00	228.00	229.00	269.00	220.00	271.00
07 46 00 Siding									
WOOD SIDING, BOARDS									
Wood siding									
Bevelled select cedar (unfinished):									
19 mm x 184 mm (1" x 8")	m²	120.00	124.00	120.00	129.00	121.00	143.00	125.00	138.00
19 mm x 235 mm (1" x 10")	m²	104.00	108.00	105.00	112.00	105.00	125.00	109.00	120.00
FIBRE CEMENT SIDING									
Fibre-reinforced cement siding									
Flat panels:									
6 mm (1/4") with textured finish	m²	168.00	170.00	162.00	182.00	164.00	175.00	173.00	215.00
Corrugated panels:									
6 mm (1/4") with coloured finish	m²	150.00	154.00	144.00	165.00	147.00	154.00	154.00	193.00
Sandwich panels:									
38 mm (1 1/2") with coloured finish	m²	219.00	224.00	214.00	240.00	217.00	228.00	227.00	286.00
07 50 00 Membrane Roofing									
07 51 00 Built-Up Bituminous Roofing									
BUILT-UP ROOFING									
Base treatment									
Base sheets (vapour barrier):									
Paper laminate	m²	4.26	3.60	4.47	4.88	4.46	5.01	4.39	4.67
1.95 kg/m² (0.4 lbs/sf) asphalt impregnated felt	m²	5.27	4.30	5.47	6.48	5.80	6.98	6.02	6.59
Membrane									
Asphalt impregnated felts:									
0.73 kg/m² (0.15 lbs/sf) felt (per ply)	m²	5.39	5.23	5.61	6.35	5.79	5.65	4.96	6.75
Bitumen:									
Roofing asphalt, standard	kg	1.55	1.49	1.62	1.81	1.65	1.61	1.42	1.93
Protective surface									
Granular materials:									
10 mm (3/8") roofing gravel...........	TONNE	103.00	103.00	112.00	111.00	123.00	137.00	120.00	112.00
White granite chips	TONNE	205.00	205.00	225.00	222.00	245.00	274.00	240.00	224.00

Item	UNITS	St. John's	Halifax	Montreal	Ottawa	Toronto	Winnipeg	Calgary	Vancouver
07 52 00 Modified Bituminous Membrane Roofing									
MODIFIED BITUMEN ROOFING									
Base sheet:									
#15 glass fiber felt:									
Nailed	m²	5.92	63.70	6.07	6.31	6.41	6.55	6.11	7.01
Mopped	m²	7.19	77.50	7.40	7.67	7.79	7.95	7.43	8.50
#15 organic felt:									
Nailed	m²	3.94	42.60	4.07	4.21	4.27	4.39	4.08	4.65
Mopped	m²	6.00	64.60	6.15	6.39	6.50	6.64	6.19	7.09
Cap sheet, SBS (Styrene butadiene styrene - rubber)									
modified, 4 mm (160 mils):									
Granular surface cap sheet:									
Polyester reinforced:									
Mopped	m²	13.00	146.00	13.20	14.20	14.30	14.70	13.40	15.30
Torched	m²	13.20	148.00	13.60	14.40	14.50	14.90	13.60	15.70
Glass fiber reinforced:									
Mopped	m²	9.73	109.00	10.10	10.80	10.60	10.90	9.99	11.50
Torched	m²	9.73	109.00	10.10	10.80	10.60	10.90	9.99	11.50
Smooth surface cap sheet, 3.7 mm (145 mils):									
Mopped	m²	23.60	265.00	24.60	26.00	25.80	26.60	24.20	27.90
Torched	m²	21.80	244.00	22.60	24.20	23.70	24.40	22.50	25.60
Flashing									
Granular surface flashing, torched, 3.8 mm (150 mils)	m²	13.20	145.00	13.90	13.70	13.90	15.00	13.90	16.50
07 53 00 Elastomeric Membrane Roofing									
ELASTOMERIC ROOFING									
Elastomeric (cold applied)									
On horizontal surfaces	m²	51.80	58.30	63.10	70.10	65.60	58.50	54.80	71.40
Rubberized asphalt (hot applied)									
Sheet reinforced:									
On horizontal surfaces	m²	48.00	53.80	58.50	65.10	60.60	54.10	50.70	66.40
SINGLE-PLY MEMBRANE									
Ethylene propylene diene monomer (EPDM),									
1.1 mm (45 mils), 1.37 kg/m² (0.28 P.S.F.)									
Loose-laid & ballasted with stone/gravel, 49 kg/m²									
(10 P.S.F.)	m²	26.80	37.80	27.20	28.30	26.30	28.80	25.90	35.70
Mechanically attached	m²	30.50	43.10	30.90	32.40	30.10	32.90	29.70	40.70
Fully adhered with adhesive	m²	34.20	48.40	35.00	36.60	33.80	37.00	33.30	45.70
Polyvinyl chloride (PVC), heat welded seams									
Reinforced, 1.5 mm (60 mils), 1.95 kg/m² (40 P.S.F.)									
Loose-laid & ballasted with stone/gravel, 59 kg/m²									
(12 P.S.F.)	m²	30.50	43.10	30.90	32.40	30.10	32.90	29.70	40.70
Mechanically attached	m²	34.20	48.40	35.00	36.60	33.80	37.00	33.30	45.70
Fully adhered with adhesive	m²	38.00	54.10	38.70	40.30	37.20	41.30	37.00	50.60
07 60 00 Flashing and Sheet Metal									
07 61 00 Sheet Metal Roofing									
COPPER ROOFING									
Copper									
Standing seams:									
4.88 kg/m² (1 lb/sf), 454 g (16 oz)	m²	474.00	484.00	485.00	513.00	581.00	587.00	570.00	622.00
07 65 00 Flexible Flashing									
FLASHING									
Flashings									
Galvanized steel:									
0.466 mm (26 ga)	m²	86.50	112.00	87.70	90.10	98.80	112.00	87.60	106.00
Aluminum:									
0.711 mm (24 ga)	m²	99.80	129.00	101.00	104.00	114.00	130.00	101.00	124.00
Stainless steel (eze-form)									
0.406 mm (27 ga)	m²	131.00	171.00	132.00	138.00	151.00	172.00	133.00	163.00
Copper:									
4.88 kg/m² (1 lb/sf), 454 g (16 oz)	m²	180.00	184.00	183.00	198.00	222.00	221.00	216.00	236.00
Rubber butyl:									
1.6 mm (1/16")	m²	69.10	776.00	71.60	76.70	75.60	77.70	71.00	81.80
1.6 mm (1/16") with galvanized fascia clip	m²	78.10	877.00	81.00	86.60	85.40	87.50	80.20	92.30

Item	UNITS	St. John's	Halifax	Montreal	Ottawa	Toronto	Winnipeg	Calgary	Vancouver
07 80 00 Fire and Smoke Protection									
07 81 00 Applied Fireproofing									
SPRAYED									
Sprayed fireproofing 2 hour fire rating									
Structural steel members:									
Columns, small (measure girth)	m²	32.80	67.60	30.90	32.10	33.20	33.60	32.80	32.30
Columns, large (measure girth)	m²	20.50	41.90	19.30	20.20	20.70	21.00	20.50	20.40
OWSJ (twice depth plus width)	m²	38.60	75.30	35.20	35.00	36.10	37.20	36.50	36.00
Beams (measure girth)	m²	36.80	75.50	34.80	35.80	37.10	37.70	36.80	36.20
Floor decks (measure flat area):									
76 mm (3") cellular	m²	31.70	64.60	31.20	30.00	30.90	32.00	32.20	36.00
76 mm (3") fluted	m²	31.70	64.60	31.20	30.00	30.90	32.00	32.20	36.00
38 mm (1 1/2") cellular	m²	29.80	61.20	29.50	28.30	29.10	30.40	30.30	33.70
38 mm (1 1/2") fluted	m²	30.10	61.60	29.80	28.70	29.70	30.60	30.80	33.80
NON-SPRAYED									
Intumescent paint 1 hour fire rating									
Structural steel members:									
Columns	m²	265.00	171.00	233.00	231.00	235.00	338.00	314.00	253.00
Beams	m²	200.00	129.00	176.00	175.00	177.00	255.00	237.00	191.00
07 84 00 Firestopping									
FIRESTOPPING									
2 hour floor separation									
To edges or openings in slabs	m	14.10	14.00	12.60	13.80	13.70	14.10	15.70	14.00
08: OPENINGS									
08 10 00 Doors and Frames									
08 11 00 Metal Doors and Frames									
STEEL FRAMES, KNOCK DOWN									
Fully Finished									
Door frames based on 0.9 m x 2.1 m (3' x 7') doors in									
walls 140 mm (6") thick									
2.642 mm (12 ga) thick steel	EA	515.00	480.00	505.00	573.00	521.00	638.00	615.00	653.00
2.032 mm (14 ga) thick steel	EA	300.00	281.00	295.00	336.00	305.00	374.00	361.00	381.00
1.626 mm (16 ga) thick steel	EA	242.00	227.00	237.00	268.00	245.00	302.00	291.00	307.00
1.219 mm (18 ga) thick steel	EA	230.00	211.00	222.00	255.00	230.00	284.00	274.00	290.00
0.915 mm (20 ga) thick steel	EA	197.00	183.00	192.00	220.00	199.00	244.00	235.00	250.00
COMMERCIAL STEEL DOORS									
Hollow-cored Fully Finished									
Doors 45 mm (1 3/4") thick without openings, based on									
900 mm x 2100 mm (3' x 7') doors, prepared to receive but									
excluding hardware									
Honeycombed:									
1.626 mm (16 ga) thick steel	Leaf	559.00	521.00	571.00	664.00	652.00	794.00	653.00	619.00
1.219 mm (18 ga) thick steel	Leaf	468.00	437.00	476.00	557.00	548.00	667.00	550.00	520.00
0.914 mm (20 ga) thick steel	Leaf	387.00	361.00	394.00	460.00	452.00	550.00	453.00	428.00
Stiffened									
1.626 mm (16 ga) thick steel	Leaf	744.00	693.00	761.00	884.00	870.00	1060.00	872.00	824.00
Sundries:									
Openings in door (excluding glazing)	EA	98.20	91.60	100.00	117.00	114.00	139.00	115.00	109.00
08 14 00 Wood Doors									
WOOD DOORS									
Interior Wood Flush Type									
Based on 45 mm (1-3/4") door sizes 900 mm x 2100 mm (3' x 7').									
Prices include hanging the door and fixing the hardware, but exclude									
the supply of hardware, see 08700. Prices do not allow for painting,									
staining or any other decorations, nor for any glass or glazing.									
Solid core									
Paint grade:									
Birch	Leaf	400.00	370.00	403.00	378.00	442.00	485.00	442.00	390.00
Stain grade:									
Birch, select white	Leaf	447.00	415.00	447.00	422.00	494.00	543.00	492.00	435.00
Mahogany, tiama	Leaf	479.00	445.00	481.00	453.00	529.00	579.00	527.00	466.00
Ash	Leaf	479.00	445.00	481.00	453.00	529.00	579.00	527.00	466.00
Red Oak, flat cut	Leaf	510.00	472.00	508.00	480.00	563.00	619.00	561.00	496.00
Walnut	Leaf	615.00	572.00	619.00	583.00	683.00	747.00	680.00	600.00
Teak	Leaf	694.00	644.00	694.00	659.00	768.00	840.00	763.00	676.00
Plastic Laminate 1.5 mm (1/16") thick:									
Wood grain	Leaf	524.00	486.00	528.00	495.00	580.00	636.00	577.00	511.00
Textured	Leaf	541.00	499.00	541.00	510.00	597.00	653.00	597.00	526.00
Solid colours	Leaf	556.00	515.00	556.00	525.00	613.00	672.00	612.00	540.00

Item	UNITS	St. John's	Halifax	Montreal	Ottawa	Toronto	Winnipeg	Calgary	Vancouver
Hollow core, honeycomb fill									
Paint grade:									
Birch	Leaf	337.00	289.00	310.00	278.00	328.00	355.00	293.00	329.00
Stain grade:									
Birch, select white	Leaf	445.00	380.00	410.00	368.00	433.00	468.00	386.00	436.00
Mahogany, tiama	Leaf	460.00	397.00	428.00	384.00	450.00	486.00	400.00	453.00
Ash	Leaf	532.00	458.00	493.00	443.00	520.00	561.00	464.00	522.00
Red Oak, flat cut	Leaf	528.00	455.00	487.00	438.00	513.00	558.00	461.00	518.00
Walnut	Leaf	660.00	569.00	609.00	549.00	644.00	696.00	577.00	645.00
Teak	Leaf	695.00	599.00	641.00	577.00	677.00	735.00	608.00	682.00

08 30 00 Specialty Doors and Frames
08 33 00 Coiling Doors and Grilles
COILING GRILLE

Item	UNITS	St. John's	Halifax	Montreal	Ottawa	Toronto	Winnipeg	Calgary	Vancouver
Non-Industrial									
Rolling overhead grilles									
Aluminum storefront types:									
Clear anodized finish	m²	746.00	861.00	780.00	815.00	914.00	894.00	768.00	798.00
Colour anodized finish	m²	835.00	964.00	875.00	913.00	1,020	1,000	862.00	895.00

08 36 00 Panel Doors
OVERHEAD, COMMERCIAL

Item	UNITS	St. John's	Halifax	Montreal	Ottawa	Toronto	Winnipeg	Calgary	Vancouver
Manual, sectional overhead type, hardware and glazing included									
Wood doors:									
Panel type	m²	182.00	205.00	217.00	194.00	238.00	241.00	203.00	250.00
Flush type, non insulated	m²	232.00	263.00	273.00	252.00	305.00	309.00	261.00	319.00
Flush type, insulated	m²	280.00	316.00	330.00	299.00	367.00	372.00	313.00	386.00
Steel doors:									
Single skin 0.914 mm (20 ga) thick									
Standard	m²	321.00	314.00	360.00	364.00	426.00	430.00	347.00	399.00
Reinforced	m²	358.00	348.00	403.00	405.00	474.00	477.00	386.00	443.00
Double skin 0.914 mm (20 ga) thick									
Insulated	m²	438.00	427.00	490.00	496.00	578.00	585.00	470.00	543.00
Insulated and reinforced	m²	481.00	468.00	538.00	542.00	637.00	643.00	518.00	600.00
Flush type, heavy duty	m²	664.00	648.00	743.00	753.00	879.00	887.00	712.00	825.00

OVERHEAD, INDUSTRIAL

Item	UNITS	St. John's	Halifax	Montreal	Ottawa	Toronto	Winnipeg	Calgary	Vancouver
Industrial steel doors:									
Non-labelled service door									
0.914 mm (20 ga) thick steel	m²	371.00	364.00	416.00	423.00	493.00	497.00	402.00	464.00
1.219 mm (18 ga) thick steel	m²	402.00	392.00	448.00	455.00	531.00	536.00	431.00	499.00
Class A, 3 hour labelled									
0.914 mm (20 ga) thick steel door	m²	655.00	637.00	733.00	740.00	870.00	879.00	706.00	817.00

08 40 00 Entrances, Storefronts & Curtain Walls
08 41 13 Aluminum-Framed Entrances & Storefronts
ALUMINUM FRAMES

Item	UNITS	St. John's	Halifax	Montreal	Ottawa	Toronto	Winnipeg	Calgary	Vancouver
For single glazing (glazing not included)									
50 mm x 100 mm (2" x 4") approx. Members:									
Clear anodized finish	m	151.00	141.00	144.00	173.00	152.00	188.00	142.00	162.00
Colour anodized finish	m	180.00	169.00	171.00	205.00	180.00	223.00	168.00	192.00
65 mm x 150 mm (2 1/2" x 6") approx. Members:									
Clear anodized finish	m	241.00	225.00	228.00	273.00	241.00	297.00	226.00	258.00
Colour anodized finish	m	284.00	266.00	270.00	322.00	283.00	354.00	266.00	304.00
For double glazing, thermally broken									
50 mm x 100 mm (2" x 4") approx. Members:									
Clear anodized finish	m	180.00	169.00	171.00	205.00	180.00	223.00	168.00	192.00
Colour anodized finish	m	284.00	266.00	270.00	322.00	283.00	354.00	266.00	304.00
65 mm x 150 mm (2 1/2" x 6") approx. Members:									
Clear anodized finish	m	267.00	250.00	252.00	305.00	267.00	330.00	250.00	286.00
Colour anodized finish	m	284.00	266.00	270.00	322.00	283.00	354.00	266.00	304.00
Reinforcement for aluminum framing									
Average cost	m	64.60	60.60	61.30	73.80	64.70	80.10	60.40	69.00

ALUMINUM DOORS & FRAMES

Item	UNITS	St. John's	Halifax	Montreal	Ottawa	Toronto	Winnipeg	Calgary	Vancouver
Frames based on 900 mm x 2100 mm (3' x 7') doors									
For single doors:									
Clear anodized finish	EA	587.00	567.00	617.00	770.00	697.00	723.00	585.00	721.00
Colour anodized finish	EA	640.00	621.00	673.00	841.00	760.00	788.00	639.00	784.00
Single door with 900 mm (3') transom (excluding transom panel):									
Clear anodized finish	EA	825.00	800.00	870.00	1,080	981.00	1,020	825.00	1,010
Colour anodized finish	EA	898.00	868.00	942.00	1,180	1,060	1,100	897.00	1,100
Single door with sidelight and transom (excluding glazing):									
Clear anodized finish	EA	1,450	1,390	1,500	1,890	1,720	1,780	1,450	1,750
Colour anodized finish	EA	1,730	1,650	1,800	2,250	2,060	2,110	1,700	2,120

Item	UNITS	St. John's	Halifax	Montreal	Ottawa	Toronto	Winnipeg	Calgary	Vancouver
For pair of doors:									
Clear anodized finish	EA	701.00	679.00	738.00	923.00	832.00	863.00	701.00	862.00
Colour anodized finish	EA	825.00	800.00	870.00	1,080	981.00	1,020	825.00	1,010
Pair of doors with transom (excluding transom panel):									
Clear anodized finish	EA	1,090	1,050	1,150	1,430	1,300	1,350	1,080	1,350
Colour anodized finish	EA	1,370	1,320	1,430	1,780	1,600	1,700	1,370	1,670
Pair of doors with sidelights (excluding glazing):									
Clear anodized finish	EA	1,090	1,050	1,150	1,430	1,300	1,350	1,080	1,350
Colour anodized finish	EA	1,280	1,240	1,330	1,670	1,520	1,570	1,260	1,570
Pair of doors, sidelight and transom (excluding glazing):									
Clear anodized finish	EA	1,730	1,670	1,800	2,280	2,060	2,120	1,720	2,120
Colour anodized finish	EA	2,020	1,940	2,110	2,660	2,390	2,470	2,010	2,470
Doors based on 0.9 m x 2.1 m (3' x 7') doors,									
excluding hardware and glazing									
45 mm (1-3/4") doors									
25 mm (1") stiles:									
Clear anodized finish	Leaf	1,610	1,590	1,620	2,180	1,720	2,110	1,540	1,820
Colour anodized finish	Leaf	1,620	1,600	1,670	2,190	1,730	2,140	1,570	1,840
50 mm (2") stiles:									
Clear anodized finish	Leaf	1,020	1,000	1,030	1,380	1,080	1,320	975.00	1,140
Colour anodized finish	Leaf	1,180	1,160	1,190	1,600	1,250	1,520	1,120	1,310
76 mm to 101 mm (3" to 4") stiles:									
Clear anodized finish	Leaf	1,400	1,380	1,420	1,910	1,470	1,800	1,340	1,550
Colour anodized finish	Leaf	1,710	1,680	1,720	2,310	1,830	2,210	1,630	1,890
127 mm (5") stiles:									
Clear anodized finish	Leaf	1,610	1,590	1,620	2,180	1,720	2,110	1,540	1,820
Colour anodized finish	Leaf	1,710	1,680	1,720	2,310	1,830	2,210	1,630	1,890
50 mm (2") doors									
50 mm (2") stiles:									
Clear anodized finish	Leaf	1,310	1,280	1,320	1,770	1,380	1,720	1,250	1,480
Colour anodized finish	Leaf	1,400	1,380	1,420	1,910	1,470	1,800	1,340	1,550

08 42 29 Automatic Entrances

Power operated doors

SWING ENTRANCE

Swing doors

Overhead mounted, single door	Leaf	5420.00	5380.00	5360.00	588.00	5810.00	7180.00	5410.00	5260.00
Overhead mounted, pair of doors	Pair	10,200	10,100	10,100	1,110	10,900	13,600	10,200	9,910
Mounted in floor, single door	Leaf	6570.00	6520.00	6490.00	713.00	7000.00	8680.00	6540.00	6370.00
Mounted in floor, pair of doors	Pair	10,900	10,900	10,800	1,190	11,600	14,400	11,000	10,700

SLIDING ENTRANCE

Sliding doors, doors included, glazing not included:

3650 mm (12') opening, biparting	EA	16,100	16,000	16,000	1,760	17,300	21,400	16,200	15,700

08 42 33 Revolving Door Entrances

REVOLVING DOORS

**Based on standard dimensions: diameter 2000 mm (6'6") approx.,
height 2100 mm (7'), fascia panel 76 mm (3").**

6 mm (1/4") glass

Manual type:

Anodized aluminum	EA	55,300	54,000	53,300	55,500	53,900	70,400	52,800	52,100
Bronze	EA	137,000	132,000	132,000	137,000	134,000	175,000	130,000	127,000
Stainless steel, satin finish	EA	113,000	110,000	109,000	113,000	110,000	144,000	108,000	106,000
Stainless steel, mirror finish	EA	137,000	132,000	132,000	137,000	134,000	175,000	130,000	127,000

12 mm (1/2") glass

Manual type:

Anodized aluminum	EA	58,300	56,800	56,400	58,500	56,700	74,300	55,900	55,000
Bronze	EA	144,000	140,000	136,000	145,000	141,000	183,000	137,000	136,000
Stainless steel, satin finish	EA	118,000	116,000	114,000	118,000	115,000	149,000	113,000	111,000
Stainless steel, mirror finish	EA	144,000	140,000	136,000	145,000	141,000	183,000	137,000	136,000

Accessories

Operating:

Power assistance	EA	22,400	20,100	18,600	18,400	22,700	24,100	19,600	18,800

Finishes:

Tinted glass	EA	1,970	2,460	2,030	2,120	2,280	2,520	2,160	2,600
Glass ceiling	EA	5,990	7,450	6,200	6,440	6,980	7,680	6,590	7,900
Up to 400 mm (16") fascia panels	EA	3,610	3,610	3,350	3,750	3,820	3,710	4,440	3,720

Floor grille, aluminum floor grille with galvanized

sheet metal drain pan, quadrant sized	Quarter	5,120	5,120	4,740	5,310	5,180	5,490	6,290	5,190

08 44 00 Curtain Wall & Glazed Assemblies

08 44 13 Glazed Aluminum Curtain Wall

CURTAIN WALLS (Single Glazing)

(Glazing not included)

3000-3600 mm (10-12') spans (floor to floor)

750 mm (2'6") modules (mullion spacing)

Clear anodized finish	m²	487.00	582.00	495.00	490.00	603.00	615.00	476.00	641.00
Baked enamel finish	m²	502.00	602.00	513.00	506.00	625.00	635.00	491.00	660.00

Item	UNITS	St. John's	Halifax	Montreal	Ottawa	Toronto	Winnipeg	Calgary	Vancouver
Colour anodized finish	m²	510.00	613.00	523.00	513.00	635.00	645.00	503.00	674.00
1200 mm (4') modules (mullion spacing)									
Clear anodized finish	m²	459.00	494.00	476.00	472.00	561.00	584.00	444.00	570.00
Baked enamel finish	m²	477.00	513.00	495.00	488.00	579.00	607.00	462.00	587.00
Colour anodized finish	m²	507.00	549.00	524.00	523.00	620.00	648.00	495.00	631.00
1500 mm (5') modules (mullion spacing)									
Clear anodized finish	m²	448.00	507.00	474.00	459.00	561.00	560.00	465.00	583.00
Baked enamel finish	m²	414.00	471.00	440.00	425.00	521.00	521.00	430.00	541.00
Colour anodized finish	m²	463.00	527.00	490.00	477.00	580.00	580.00	482.00	603.00

CURTAIN WALLS (Double Glazing)
(Thermally broken. Glazing not included)
3000-3600 mm (10-12') spans (floor to floor)

Item	UNITS	St. John's	Halifax	Montreal	Ottawa	Toronto	Winnipeg	Calgary	Vancouver
750 mm (2'6") modules (mullion spacing)									
Clear anodized finish	m²	582.00	700.00	596.00	589.00	725.00	736.00	572.00	768.00
Baked enamel finish	m²	630.00	756.00	645.00	637.00	786.00	797.00	619.00	832.00
Colour anodized finish	m²	647.00	776.00	663.00	654.00	805.00	818.00	635.00	853.00
1200 mm (4') modules (mullion spacing)									
Clear anodized finish	m²	548.00	592.00	568.00	565.00	669.00	700.00	533.00	680.00
Baked enamel finish	m²	572.00	618.00	592.00	588.00	699.00	730.00	556.00	711.00
Colour anodized finish	m²	612.00	660.00	635.00	631.00	748.00	781.00	595.00	757.00
1500 mm (5') modules (mullion spacing)									
Clear anodized finish	m²	520.00	592.00	551.00	533.00	652.00	653.00	541.00	680.00
Baked enamel finish	m²	546.00	619.00	574.00	557.00	683.00	686.00	565.00	712.00
Colour anodized finish	m²	577.00	656.00	611.00	589.00	724.00	724.00	599.00	752.00

08 44 33 Slope Glazing Assemblies
Sealed glazing units, tempered outer pane, laminated inner pane:

Item	UNITS	St. John's	Halifax	Montreal	Ottawa	Toronto	Winnipeg	Calgary	Vancouver
Not exceeding 45 m² (500 sf)									
Clear anodized finish	m²	1,470	1,530	1,420	1,480	1,600	1,910	1,350	1,550
Baked enamel finish	m²	1,610	1,660	1,510	1,590	1,740	2,060	1,450	1,700
Colour anodized finish	m²	1,920	2,010	1,890	1,900	2,090	2,450	1,770	2,030
Over 45 m² (500 sf)									
Clear anodized finish	m²	1,300	1,350	1,250	1,290	1,410	1,660	1,190	1,370
Baked enamel finish	m²	1,400	1,450	1,340	1,390	1,520	1,780	1,290	1,480
Colour anodized finish	m²	1,460	1,530	1,410	1,480	1,600	1,900	1,350	1,550

08 50 00 Windows

08 51 00 Metal Windows

08 51 13 Aluminum Windows
Tubular type, thermally broken (glazing not included)

Item	UNITS	St. John's	Halifax	Montreal	Ottawa	Toronto	Winnipeg	Calgary	Vancouver
Punched openings (fixed):									
Baked enamel finish	m²	225.00	233.00	217.00	271.00	236.00	283.00	208.00	213.00
Colour anodized finish	m²	258.00	265.00	247.00	308.00	271.00	320.00	236.00	244.00
Ribbon type (fixed)									
Baked enamel finish	m²	223.00	229.00	214.00	266.00	234.00	278.00	205.00	208.00
Colour anodized finish	m²	254.00	263.00	243.00	302.00	267.00	317.00	233.00	239.00
Ventilating sash:									
Average cost	EA	681.00	612.00	694.00	896.00	753.00	754.00	585.00	611.00
Units for single glazing									
Framing member for fixed units:									
Clear anodized finish	m	72.10	74.20	69.00	86.10	75.50	90.40	66.30	67.80
Baked enamel finish	m	74.70	76.80	71.70	89.10	78.20	93.80	68.70	70.10
Colour anodized finish	m	82.00	84.50	78.80	98.00	86.10	103.00	75.50	77.20
Ventilating units (add to cost of fixed units):									
Clear anodized finish	EA	392.00	354.00	397.00	515.00	432.00	433.00	336.00	352.00
Baked enamel finish	EA	455.00	408.00	464.00	600.00	504.00	503.00	391.00	408.00
Colour anodized finish	EA	515.00	464.00	525.00	680.00	570.00	571.00	442.00	464.00
Units for double glazing thermally broken									
Framing member for fixed units:									
Clear anodized finish	m	82.00	84.50	78.80	98.00	86.10	103.00	75.50	77.20
Baked enamel finish	m	86.20	88.90	82.90	103.00	90.80	109.00	79.60	81.40
Colour anodized finish	m	101.00	104.00	96.80	120.00	106.00	127.00	92.80	94.70
Ventilating units (add to cost of fixed units):									
Clear anodized finish	EA	515.00	464.00	525.00	680.00	570.00	571.00	442.00	464.00
Baked enamel finish	EA	568.00	509.00	576.00	748.00	627.00	629.00	486.00	510.00
Colour anodized finish	EA	579.00	520.00	589.00	761.00	637.00	637.00	496.00	520.00

08 51 23 Steel Windows
Industrial type (glazing not included)

Item	UNITS	St. John's	Halifax	Montreal	Ottawa	Toronto	Winnipeg	Calgary	Vancouver
Light size 500 mm x 400 mm (20" x 16"):									
Prime coat	m²	139.00	178.00	133.00	179.00	149.00	208.00	142.00	135.00
Baked enamel finish	m²	173.00	219.00	167.00	226.00	192.00	255.00	174.00	168.00
Ventilating sash (additional):									
Average cost	EA	188.00	204.00	192.00	263.00	217.00	245.00	170.00	176.00

Item	UNITS	St. John's	Halifax	Montreal	Ottawa	Toronto	Winnipeg	Calgary	Vancouver
08 52 00 Wood Windows									
WOOD WINDOWS (glazing not included)									
Fixed units									
Prime coat only:									
Pine	m²	337.00	335.00	324.00	324.00	325.00	397.00	326.00	452.00
Cedar	m²	369.00	368.00	357.00	355.00	359.00	437.00	360.00	494.00
Redwood	m²	421.00	421.00	406.00	403.00	407.00	498.00	408.00	561.00
Aluminum covered wood	m²	393.00	393.00	379.00	379.00	386.00	466.00	384.00	529.00
Plastic covered wood	m²	339.00	336.00	352.00	350.00	348.00	405.00	335.00	385.00
Ventilating units:									
Average cost	EA	196.00	196.00	208.00	205.00	191.00	232.00	193.00	235.00
08 60 00 Roof Windows & Skylights									
(measured flat on plane)									
08 62 00 Unit Skylights									
Plastic skylights									
Single skin:									
Less than 1 m² (10 sf) plan area (ea)	m²	923.00	873.00	790.00	1040.00	883.00	987.00	765.00	819.00
Double skin:									
Less than 1 m² (10 sf) plan area (ea)	m²	1,240	1,170	1,070	1,390	1,190	1,320	1,040	1,110
08 63 00 Metal-Framed Skylights									
Aluminum, standard members									
Heat strengthened laminated glass:									
Not exceeding 45 m² (500 sf)									
Clear anodized finish	m²	1,470	1,390	1,260	1,650	1,410	1,570	1,220	1,300
Baked enamel finish	m²	1,480	1,410	1,270	1,670	1,420	1,590	1,230	1,310
Colour anodized finish	m²	1,820	1,720	1,550	2,040	1,750	1,930	1,500	1,640
Over 45 m² (500 sf)									
Clear anodized finish	m²	1,420	1,340	1,210	1,600	1,370	1,530	1,180	1,260
Baked enamel finish	m²	1,450	1,370	1,240	1,630	1,390	1,550	1,200	1,280
Colour anodized finish	m²	1,630	1,570	1,410	1,850	1,570	1,750	1,370	1,450
08 70 00 Hardware									
08 71 00 Door Hardware									
Door hardware (allowance factor only)									
LOCKSET									
Locksets:									
Hotels	EA	378.00	345.00	372.00	388.00	453.00	474.00	401.00	349.00
Retail stores	EA	247.00	224.00	240.00	251.00	295.00	304.00	261.00	227.00
Apartment buildings	EA	194.00	177.00	193.00	199.00	236.00	245.00	210.00	181.00
Office buildings	EA	348.00	317.00	341.00	355.00	415.00	433.00	371.00	320.00
Hospitals	EA	311.00	280.00	301.00	313.00	367.00	386.00	325.00	302.00
Schools	EA	281.00	255.00	274.00	288.00	336.00	351.00	299.00	259.00
BUTT HINGE									
Butts:									
Hotels	EA	64.20	58.40	61.30	62.80	74.00	63.80	65.60	61.60
Retail stores	EA	64.20	58.40	61.30	62.80	74.00	63.80	65.60	61.60
Apartment buildings	EA	34.50	31.40	33.20	33.80	40.10	34.40	35.60	33.40
Office buildings	EA	64.20	58.40	61.30	62.80	74.00	63.80	65.60	61.60
Hospitals	EA	64.20	58.40	61.30	62.80	74.00	63.80	65.60	61.60
Schools	EA	64.20	58.40	61.30	62.80	74.00	63.80	65.60	61.60
PULL PLATE									
Pulls:									
Hotels	EA	70.00	63.60	67.50	71.60	81.40	91.80	71.00	92.30
Retail stores	EA	70.00	63.60	67.50	71.60	81.40	91.80	71.00	92.30
Apartment buildings	EA	38.10	34.50	36.70	38.90	44.30	49.90	38.60	50.10
Office buildings	EA	70.00	63.60	67.50	71.60	81.40	91.80	71.00	92.30
Hospitals	EA	70.00	63.60	67.50	71.60	81.40	91.80	71.00	92.30
Schools	EA	70.00	63.60	67.50	71.60	81.40	91.80	71.00	92.30
PUSH PLATE									
Push plates:									
Hotels	EA	41.70	34.60	39.00	39.40	44.40	50.00	38.20	52.80
Retail stores	EA	41.70	34.60	39.00	39.40	44.40	50.00	38.20	52.80
Apartment buildings	EA	41.70	34.60	39.00	39.40	44.40	50.00	38.20	52.80
Office buildings	EA	41.70	34.60	39.00	39.40	44.40	50.00	38.20	52.80
Hospitals	EA	41.70	34.60	39.00	39.40	44.40	50.00	38.20	52.80
Schools	EA	41.70	34.60	39.00	39.40	44.40	50.00	38.20	52.80
DOOR CLOSER									
Closers:									
Office buildings	EA	351.00	319.00	379.00	373.00	386.00	357.00	300.00	282.00
Hospitals	EA	351.00	319.00	379.00	373.00	386.00	357.00	300.00	282.00
Schools	EA	351.00	319.00	379.00	373.00	386.00	357.00	300.00	282.00

Item	UNITS	St. John's	Halifax	Montreal	Ottawa	Toronto	Winnipeg	Calgary	Vancouver
AUTOMATIC OPENERS COMMERCIAL									
Handicap actuator push buttons, 2, including 12V DC									
wiring for automatic barrier free access	Leaf	3,370	3,030	2,950	3,100	3,680	3,820	3,060	2,900

08 80 00 Glazing

08 81 00 Glass Glazing
(installed in prepared frames)

08 81 10 Float Glass
PLAIN GLASS

Item	UNITS	St. John's	Halifax	Montreal	Ottawa	Toronto	Winnipeg	Calgary	Vancouver
Clear glass									
4 mm (5/32") thick	m²	141.00	151.00	138.00	149.00	158.00	177.00	147.00	158.00
5 mm (3/16") thick	m²	168.00	180.00	168.00	176.00	188.00	208.00	178.00	188.00
6 mm (1/4") thick	m²	194.00	209.00	194.00	205.00	218.00	243.00	205.00	219.00
8 mm (5/16") thick	m²	273.00	290.00	270.00	286.00	305.00	341.00	285.00	306.00
10 mm (3/8") thick	m²	314.00	338.00	314.00	331.00	350.00	392.00	333.00	355.00
12 mm (1/2") thick	m²	395.00	425.00	395.00	418.00	443.00	498.00	418.00	445.00
Tinted glass:									
6 mm (1/4") thick	m²	220.00	237.00	218.00	233.00	247.00	278.00	231.00	249.00
8 mm (5/16") thick	m²	314.00	338.00	314.00	331.00	350.00	392.00	333.00	355.00
10 mm (3/8") thick	m²	372.00	400.00	373.00	397.00	418.00	470.00	394.00	420.00
12 mm (1/2") thick	m²	447.00	479.00	445.00	473.00	501.00	560.00	471.00	501.00
HEAT STRENGTHENED GLASS									
Clear:									
Add to cost of float glass	m²	186.00	228.00	199.00	206.00	208.00	223.00	197.00	244.00
Tinted									
Add to cost of float glass	m²	203.00	248.00	215.00	221.00	226.00	239.00	215.00	263.00

08 81 30 Insulating Glass
(based on 2.5 m², 25 sf per unit)

Item	UNITS	St. John's	Halifax	Montreal	Ottawa	Toronto	Winnipeg	Calgary	Vancouver
Clear glass:									
Two panes of 3 mm (1/8") glass	m²	304.00	338.00	302.00	313.00	310.00	336.00	268.00	357.00
Two panes of 4 mm (5/32") glass	m²	313.00	347.00	313.00	319.00	320.00	348.00	277.00	366.00
Two panes of 5 mm (3/16") glass	m²	342.00	378.00	340.00	346.00	349.00	377.00	304.00	401.00
Two panes of 6 mm (1/4") glass	m²	374.00	414.00	373.00	382.00	381.00	413.00	330.00	438.00
Per 0.5 m² (5 sf) reduction of unit size, add	%	15.00	15.00	15.00	15.00	15.00	15.00	15.00	15.00
Tinted glass (one pane only):									
Two panes of 3 mm (1/8") glass	m²	342.00	378.00	340.00	346.00	349.00	377.00	304.00	401.00
Two panes of 5 mm (3/16") glass	m²	356.00	395.00	358.00	368.00	364.00	397.00	315.00	420.00
Two panes of 6 mm (1/4") glass	m²	392.00	433.00	388.00	396.00	399.00	430.00	345.00	456.00
Per 0.5 m² (5 sf) reduction of unit size, add	%	15.00	15.00	15.00	15.00	15.00	15.00	15.00	15.00
Reflective glass (one pane only):									
Standard specification	m²	554.00	614.00	551.00	563.00	564.00	610.00	489.00	650.00
High quality specification	m²	851.00	945.00	852.00	872.00	869.00	946.00	755.00	1000.00
Custom specification	m²	989.00	1100.00	991.00	1010.00	1010.00	1100.00	875.00	1160.00

08 81 30 Insulating Glass (for sloped glazing)

Item	UNITS	St. John's	Halifax	Montreal	Ottawa	Toronto	Winnipeg	Calgary	Vancouver
Tempered exterior laminated interior:									
Clear glass	m²	674.00	786.00	683.00	684.00	725.00	751.00	585.00	645.00
Tinted glass (one pane only)	m²	674.00	786.00	683.00	684.00	725.00	751.00	585.00	645.00

08 81 45 Sheet Glass

Item	UNITS	St. John's	Halifax	Montreal	Ottawa	Toronto	Winnipeg	Calgary	Vancouver
A quality:									
2 mm (5/64") thick	m²	121.00	130.00	121.00	128.00	136.00	150.00	129.00	136.00
3 mm (1/8") thick	m²	131.00	141.00	129.00	138.00	147.00	164.00	139.00	148.00

08 81 65 Wire Glass

Item	UNITS	St. John's	Halifax	Montreal	Ottawa	Toronto	Winnipeg	Calgary	Vancouver
Transparent glass (polished):									
6 mm (1/4") thick	m²	344.00	377.00	332.00	342.00	350.00	378.00	286.00	332.00
Translucent glass (cast):									
6 mm (1/4") thick	m²	205.00	225.00	197.00	204.00	208.00	219.00	169.00	197.00
Double glass installation:									
Silver	m²	570.00	621.00	544.00	564.00	579.00	622.00	471.00	547.00
Gold	m²	585.00	638.00	561.00	581.00	595.00	643.00	487.00	563.00
Spandrel glass:									
6 mm (1/4") black	m²	360.00	393.00	347.00	360.00	369.00	397.00	300.00	348.00
6 mm (1/4") silver	m²	542.00	592.00	520.00	538.00	552.00	594.00	450.00	522.00
6 mm (1/4") gold	m²	697.00	759.00	669.00	692.00	709.00	764.00	576.00	670.00

08 83 00 Mirrors
MIRRORS
Opaque mirrors

Item	UNITS	St. John's	Halifax	Montreal	Ottawa	Toronto	Winnipeg	Calgary	Vancouver
Unframed mirrors:									
6 mm (1/4") thick (smooth edges)	m²	255.00	272.00	255.00	269.00	285.00	321.00	267.00	288.00
Framed (tamperproof) mirrors:									
6 mm (1/4") thick (stainless steel frame)	m²	447.00	479.00	445.00	473.00	501.00	560.00	471.00	501.00

Item	UNITS	St. John's	Halifax	Montreal	Ottawa	Toronto	Winnipeg	Calgary	Vancouver
08 84 00 Plastic Glazing									
Flat sheets (Installed in prepared frames)									
08 84 10 Plexiglass Acrylic									
Clear cast acrylic:									
1.6 mm (1/16") thick	m²	160.00	181.00	156.00	168.00	168.00	206.00	180.00	149.00
3.0 mm (1/8") thick	m²	150.00	169.00	145.00	153.00	155.00	191.00	166.00	140.00
5.0 mm (3/16") thick	m²	179.00	202.00	178.00	188.00	186.00	229.00	199.00	166.00
6.0 mm (1/4") thick	m²	207.00	233.00	205.00	217.00	216.00	268.00	231.00	192.00
10.0 mm (3/8") thick	m²	328.00	371.00	324.00	343.00	341.00	420.00	368.00	306.00
12.0 mm (1/2") thick	m²	438.00	495.00	431.00	455.00	456.00	561.00	488.00	408.00
White cast acrylic:									
3.0 mm (1/8") thick	m²	157.00	179.00	154.00	166.00	162.00	203.00	176.00	147.00
5.0 mm (3/16") thick	m²	187.00	211.00	185.00	195.00	194.00	241.00	208.00	173.00
6.0 mm (1/4") thick	m²	206.00	232.00	204.00	216.00	214.00	263.00	230.00	191.00
Colour cast acrylic:									
3.0 mm (1/8") thick	m²	179.00	202.00	178.00	188.00	186.00	229.00	199.00	166.00
5.0 mm (3/16") thick	m²	197.00	227.00	194.00	206.00	206.00	253.00	221.00	183.00
6.0 mm (1/4") thick	m²	223.00	254.00	221.00	233.00	232.00	288.00	247.00	207.00
08 84 20 Polycarbonate									
Clear polycarbonate:									
0.8 mm (1/32") thick	m²	143.00	165.00	139.00	148.00	148.00	181.00	159.00	134.00
1.2 mm (3/64") thick	m²	158.00	180.00	155.00	167.00	164.00	205.00	179.00	148.00
1.6 mm (1/16") thick	m²	163.00	187.00	158.00	170.00	170.00	208.00	182.00	153.00
2.0 mm (5/64") thick	m²	197.00	227.00	194.00	206.00	206.00	253.00	221.00	183.00
2.4 mm (3/32") thick	m²	208.00	234.00	206.00	218.00	218.00	269.00	232.00	194.00
3.0 mm (1/8") thick	m²	230.00	260.00	225.00	238.00	238.00	292.00	255.00	213.00
5.0 mm (3/16") thick	m²	289.00	333.00	283.00	300.00	302.00	371.00	325.00	270.00
6.0 mm (1/4") thick	m²	350.00	398.00	343.00	365.00	364.00	449.00	390.00	326.00
10.0 mm (3/8") thick	m²	606.00	689.00	594.00	631.00	629.00	777.00	673.00	563.00
12.0 mm (1/2") thick	m²	744.00	846.00	730.00	775.00	774.00	953.00	829.00	691.00
Tinted polycarbonate (bronze or green):									
3.0 mm (1/8") thick	m²	259.00	293.00	253.00	269.00	267.00	331.00	288.00	240.00
5.0 mm (3/16") thick	m²	336.00	381.00	330.00	350.00	350.00	430.00	375.00	314.00
6.0 mm (1/4") thick	m²	423.00	480.00	415.00	441.00	439.00	542.00	470.00	394.00
08 88 00 Special Function Glazing									
(installed in prepared frames)									
08 88 56 Laminated Glass									
High security laminated glass									
Single lamination									
2 mm x 3 mm (5/64" x 1/8") plus vinyl	m²	516.00	562.00	497.00	512.00	525.00	566.00	428.00	495.00
09: FINISHES									
09 20 00 Plaster and Gypsum Board									
09 22 00 Supports for Plaster & Gypsum Board									
(for steel studs see Item 05 40 00; for wood furring see Item 06 11 00; for suspension systems see 09 22 26)									
FURRING									
Steel channel furring									
Tied to steel:									
19 mm (3/4")	m	5.31	5.43	6.42	8.20	9.16	6.96	4.85	6.75
38 mm (1 1/2")	m	7.59	7.77	9.19	11.70	13.10	9.95	6.97	9.58
GYPSUM LATH									
Lath (supply only)									
Gypsum lath:									
10 mm (3/8") plain	m²	4.06	4.16	4.90	6.27	7.02	5.31	3.73	5.14
10 mm (3/8") perforated	m²	5.72	5.84	6.92	8.79	9.85	7.48	5.25	7.19
10 mm (3/8") foilback	m²	5.98	6.12	7.27	9.19	10.30	7.86	5.46	7.57
Lath (installation only)									
On wood framing to:									
Walls	m²	11.90	11.80	12.00	14.00	12.90	16.50	10.90	15.60
Ceilings and exterior soffits	m²	15.10	15.10	15.10	18.00	16.30	21.00	14.10	19.90
Beams, columns and bulkheads	m²	15.20	15.20	15.30	18.10	16.40	21.00	14.20	20.00
On steel framing to:									
Walls	m²	20.60	20.80	21.10	24.80	22.30	28.90	19.20	27.20
Ceilings and exterior soffits	m²	26.30	26.30	26.20	31.30	28.30	36.10	24.50	34.40
Beams, columns and bulkheads	m²	32.50	32.40	32.60	38.70	35.10	45.10	30.20	42.70
METAL LATH									
Metal lath; diamond mesh:									
Painted									
1.36 kg/m² (2.5 lbs/sy)	m²	4.12	4.22	4.99	6.35	7.11	5.40	3.79	5.21
1.85 kg/m² (3.4 lbs/sy)	m²	8.30	8.48	10.00	12.80	14.30	10.80	7.59	10.50
Galvanized									
1.36 kg/m² (2.5 lbs/sy)	m²	4.86	4.98	5.92	7.52	8.41	6.41	4.47	6.14
1.85 kg/m² (3.4 lbs/sy)	m²	7.82	8.00	9.46	12.00	13.40	10.20	7.17	9.89

Item	UNITS	St. John's	Halifax	Montreal	Ottawa	Toronto	Winnipeg	Calgary	Vancouver
Metal lath, 3 mm (1/8") flat rib:									
Painted									
1.90 kg/m² (3.5 lbs/sy)	m²	8.65	8.86	10.50	13.30	15.00	11.30	7.95	10.90
Galvanized									
1.90 kg/m² (3.5 lbs/sy)	m²	9.87	10.10	11.90	15.10	16.90	13.00	9.06	12.40
Metal lath, 10 mm (3/8") high rib:									
Painted									
1.90 kg/m² (3.5 lbs/sy)	m²	10.60	10.90	12.80	16.30	18.30	13.80	9.75	13.40
Galvanized									
1.90 kg/m² (3.5 lbs/sy)	m²	12.60	12.90	15.10	19.60	21.70	16.70	11.50	16.00
Stucco mesh, 1.626 mm thick (16 gauge) welded wire mesh:									
Galvanized									
50 mm x 50 mm (2" x 2"), ribbed	m²	6.59	6.73	7.99	10.10	11.40	8.64	6.04	8.32
25 mm x 25 mm (1" x 1") flat	m²	4.90	5.04	5.94	7.59	8.47	6.45	4.49	6.21

09 22 26 Suspension Systems
SUSPENDED METAL JOIST FRAMING

Item	UNITS	St. John's	Halifax	Montreal	Ottawa	Toronto	Winnipeg	Calgary	Vancouver
Suspended metal joist framing system									
to accept gypsum wall board ceiling finish:									
60 mm (24") deep, complete	m²	89.00	87.80	81.00	96.40	107.00	80.30	74.10	105.00

09 23 00 Gypsum Plastering
GYPSUM PLASTER (lath or other base not included)

Item	UNITS	St. John's	Halifax	Montreal	Ottawa	Toronto	Winnipeg	Calgary	Vancouver
Gypsum plaster, trowelled finish to									
Walls:									
2 coats on gypsum lath	m²	91.00	96.40	90.90	122.00	103.00	99.30	122.00	99.90
3 coats on metal lath	m²	136.00	142.00	137.00	183.00	157.00	145.00	179.00	149.00
3 coats on rigid insulation	m²	123.00	131.00	122.00	167.00	135.00	133.00	163.00	136.00
3 coats on masonry	m²	120.00	128.00	117.00	164.00	133.00	131.00	157.00	133.00
3 coats on concrete	m²	123.00	131.00	122.00	167.00	135.00	133.00	163.00	136.00
Ceilings:									
2 coats on gypsum lath	m²	106.00	113.00	106.00	143.00	120.00	119.00	141.00	117.00
3 coats on metal lath	m²	139.00	146.00	141.00	188.00	160.00	152.00	184.00	154.00
3 coats on rigid insulation	m²	129.00	136.00	130.00	173.00	142.00	139.00	171.00	141.00
3 coats on concrete	m²	129.00	136.00	130.00	173.00	142.00	139.00	171.00	141.00
Columns, beams and bulkheads:									
2 coats on gypsum lath	m²	135.00	141.00	136.00	182.00	154.00	144.00	178.00	147.00
3 coats on metal lath	m²	185.00	195.00	182.00	249.00	208.00	202.00	244.00	204.00
3 coats on rigid insulation	m²	155.00	166.00	157.00	207.00	176.00	171.00	207.00	172.00
3 coats on masonry	m²	155.00	166.00	157.00	207.00	176.00	171.00	207.00	172.00
3 coats on concrete	m²	148.00	159.00	151.00	200.00	170.00	166.00	200.00	166.00
Acoustical plaster, sprayed finish to									
Walls:									
2 coats to gypsum lath	m²	42.80	45.10	42.50	57.40	48.00	46.80	56.60	46.80
2 coats to metal lath	m²	53.10	56.40	53.20	71.60	60.00	58.40	70.80	58.40
2 coats to masonry	m²	49.50	52.40	49.40	66.50	56.00	54.10	65.70	54.20
2 coats to concrete	m²	50.90	53.70	50.70	68.20	57.30	55.60	67.50	55.80
3 coats to metal lath	m²	65.40	69.20	65.20	87.90	73.80	71.50	86.90	71.80
Ceilings:									
2 coats to gypsum lath	m²	44.40	46.90	44.40	59.70	50.20	48.80	59.00	48.80
2 coats to metal lath	m²	53.10	56.40	53.20	71.60	60.00	58.40	70.80	58.40
2 coats to concrete	m²	51.20	54.20	51.10	68.80	57.70	56.10	68.00	56.20
3 coats to metal lath	m²	66.00	70.00	66.10	88.90	74.70	72.40	88.00	72.70
Columns, beams and bulkheads:									
2 coats to gypsum lath	m²	53.10	56.40	53.20	71.60	60.00	58.40	70.80	58.40
2 coats to metal lath	m²	66.00	70.00	66.10	88.90	74.70	72.40	88.00	72.70
2 coats to concrete	m²	64.30	68.40	64.50	86.40	72.90	70.40	85.60	70.60
3 coats to metal lath	m²	83.90	88.90	83.80	114.00	94.60	91.80	113.00	92.20

09 26 00 Veneer Plastering
VENEER PLASTER

Item	UNITS	St. John's	Halifax	Montreal	Ottawa	Toronto	Winnipeg	Calgary	Vancouver
1 coat on gypsum board (board not included) to:									
Walls	m²	29.40	31.40	29.70	39.60	33.40	32.20	39.20	32.30
Ceilings	m²	32.50	34.30	32.60	43.60	36.70	35.60	43.10	35.40
Columns, beams and bulkheads	m²	42.80	45.10	42.50	57.40	48.00	46.80	56.60	46.80
Sprayed plaster									
1 coat, textured, to:									
Concrete	m²	21.80	22.90	21.80	29.10	24.30	23.50	28.60	23.60
Gypsum board	m²	36.20	38.40	36.10	48.70	40.90	39.50	48.10	40.10

09 29 00 Gypsum Board - Supply Only
Standard sheets 1200 mm (48") wide
GYPSUM WALLBOARD

Item	UNITS	St. John's	Halifax	Montreal	Ottawa	Toronto	Winnipeg	Calgary	Vancouver
Regular gypsum wallboard:									
10 mm (3/8") thick	m²	6.23	6.19	6.31	4.92	7.88	10.30	5.78	12.60
12 mm (1/2") thick	m²	6.23	6.19	6.31	4.92	7.88	10.30	5.78	12.60
16 mm (5/8") thick	m²	7.50	7.44	7.60	5.92	9.49	12.40	6.93	15.60
Fire-rated gypsum wallboard:									
12 mm (1/2") thick	m²	7.48	7.41	7.57	5.90	9.47	12.40	6.90	15.10
16 mm (5/8") thick	m²	7.62	7.55	7.72	6.02	9.68	12.60	7.07	15.30
Foilback gypsum wallboard:									
10 mm (3/8") thick	m²	9.95	9.83	10.10	7.81	12.50	16.50	9.18	20.00

Item	UNITS	St. John's	Halifax	Montreal	Ottawa	Toronto	Winnipeg	Calgary	Vancouver
12 mm (1/2") thick............	m²	10.20	10.20	10.40	8.00	13.00	16.90	9.46	20.70
16 mm (5/8") thick............	m²	11.10	10.90	11.20	8.72	14.10	18.10	10.20	22.40
Water resistant gypsum wallboard:									
12 mm (1/2") thick	m²	11.00	10.80	11.10	8.65	14.00	18.00	10.10	22.10
16 mm (5/8") thick	m²	13.60	13.50	13.70	10.90	17.20	22.50	12.50	27.30
Predecorated gypsum panels									
Standard panels, vinyl face on:									
12 mm (1/2") plain core	m²	21.40	21.20	21.60	17.00	27.40	35.40	19.90	43.20
Custom gypsum panels, vinyl face on:									
12 mm (1/2") plain core	m²	27.20	27.00	27.80	21.30	34.50	44.80	25.20	54.90
16 mm (5/8") plain core	m²	27.20	27.00	27.80	21.30	34.50	44.80	25.20	54.90
16 mm (5/8") fire-rated core	m²	27.50	27.50	28.00	21.80	34.90	45.70	25.40	55.60
Core boards and sheathing boards									
Gypsum (Shaftliner) coreboard 600 mm (24") wide:									
25 mm (1") thick	m²	16.40	15.70	16.60	13.70	20.90	28.70	15.20	33.00
Gypsum sheathing boards:									
12 mm (1/2") thick	m²	6.41	6.21	6.49	5.40	8.18	11.30	5.92	13.00
Fire-rated gypsum sheathing boards:									
16 mm (5/8") thick	m²	11.60	11.30	11.70	9.82	14.80	20.40	10.80	23.80
Exterior soffit boards:									
12 mm (1/2") thick	m²	10.80	10.40	10.90	9.11	13.70	18.80	9.98	22.00

09 29 00 Gypsum Board - Installation Only
GYPSUM WALLBOARD

Related waste factors included. Standard backing and soffit boards
10 mm (3/8") or 12 mm (1/2") thick:

Item	UNITS	St. John's	Halifax	Montreal	Ottawa	Toronto	Winnipeg	Calgary	Vancouver
To walls, ceilings or soffits	m²	14.10	14.00	14.20	16.80	15.10	19.40	13.20	18.50
To walls (laminated to solid backing)............	m²	12.60	12.50	12.50	15.10	13.60	17.30	11.90	16.40
To beams, columns or bulkheads	m²	17.60	17.30	17.20	20.70	18.80	23.80	16.10	22.90
16 mm (5/8") thick:									
To walls, ceilings or soffits	m²	15.10	15.10	15.10	17.90	16.30	20.90	14.10	19.90
To walls (laminated to solid backing)............	m²	14.10	14.10	14.30	16.90	15.30	19.40	13.20	18.60
To beams, columns or bulkheads	m²	18.80	18.90	18.80	22.40	20.50	25.90	17.80	24.90
Coreboards									
25 mm (1") thick									
Per 25 mm (1") laminate............	m²	16.80	17.00	17.00	20.40	18.20	23.40	15.50	22.10
Taping joints and finishing									
To walls and soffits	m²	8.72	8.74	8.80	10.40	9.42	12.00	8.14	11.50

09 30 00 Tiling
09 30 13 Ceramic Tiling
CERAMIC TILE

Glazed wall tile 6 mm (1/4") thick
Mortar bed:

Item	UNITS	St. John's	Halifax	Montreal	Ottawa	Toronto	Winnipeg	Calgary	Vancouver
100 mm x 100 mm (4" x 4")............	m²	149.00	152.00	154.00	159.00	154.00	190.00	145.00	145.00
150 mm x 150 mm (6" x 6")............	m²	149.00	152.00	154.00	159.00	154.00	190.00	145.00	145.00
Thinset:									
100 mm x 100 mm (4" x 4")............	m²	128.00	129.00	133.00	135.00	131.00	161.00	125.00	125.00
150 mm x 150 mm (6" x 6")............	m²	128.00	129.00	133.00	135.00	131.00	161.00	125.00	125.00
Unglazed floor tile 6 mm (1/4") thick									
Mortar bed:									
25 mm x 25 mm (1" x 1"), one colour............	m²	134.00	135.00	138.00	140.00	136.00	169.00	130.00	131.00
Thinset:									
25 mm x 25 mm (1" x 1"), one colour............	m²	140.00	142.00	146.00	147.00	145.00	176.00	138.00	137.00
Base Trim									
Ceramic mosaic base:									
100 mm (4") high, one colour	m	40.90	41.40	44.60	46.30	44.30	54.50	41.70	39.70

09 30 16 Quarry Tiling
QUARRY TILE

12.5 mm (1/2") thick terracotta
To walls
Mortar bed:

Item	UNITS	St. John's	Halifax	Montreal	Ottawa	Toronto	Winnipeg	Calgary	Vancouver
150 mm x 150 mm (6" x 6"), one colour............	m²	189.00	178.00	200.00	217.00	205.00	237.00	200.00	235.00
Thinset:									
150 mm x 150 mm (6" x 6"), one colour............	m²	145.00	145.00	148.00	160.00	152.00	172.00	148.00	164.00
To floors									
Mortar bed:									
150 mm x 150 mm (6" x 6"), one colour............	m²	184.00	174.00	197.00	212.00	202.00	235.00	196.00	231.00
Thinset:									
150 mm x 150 mm (6" x 6"), one colour............	m²	137.00	138.00	142.00	153.00	145.00	165.00	138.00	156.00
To stairs									
Nosing only:									
Non slip	m	82.00	81.90	83.90	90.60	86.00	96.80	83.80	93.30
Base Trim									
Quarry tile base:									
150 mm (6") high, terracotta............	m	43.20	44.10	44.20	47.90	45.20	51.20	44.00	49.10

Item	UNITS	St. John's	Halifax	Montreal	Ottawa	Toronto	Winnipeg	Calgary	Vancouver
09 50 00 Ceilings									
09 51 00 Acoustical Ceilings									
SUSPENDED CEILINGS, COMPLETE									
COMPLETE, FIXED TO SOFFIT OF HOLLOW METAL OR WOOD, WOOD DECK OR TO FIXINGS PROVIDED IN SOFFIT.									
Exposed suspension system									
Mineral fibre panel 600 mm x 1200 mm (24' x 48'):									
16 mm (5/8") thick standard	m²	44.60	48.40	43.00	48.00	48.00	47.50	37.00	64.90
16 mm (5/8") thick fire-rated	m²	48.70	52.70	46.70	52.50	52.30	51.70	40.30	70.50
Glass fibre 600 mm x 1200 mm (24" x 48"):									
Vinyl faced									
16 mm (5/8") thick	m²	46.50	46.10	46.10	49.30	57.10	49.20	41.50	48.70
20 mm (3/4") thick	m²	54.80	54.30	54.30	58.00	67.20	58.00	48.70	57.20
Glass faced									
20 mm (3/4") thick	m²	58.80	63.50	56.20	63.10	63.00	62.20	48.60	85.00
Glass fibre panel 1200 mm x 1200 mm (48" x 48"):									
Vinyl faced									
25 mm (1") thick	m²	70.70	70.00	70.00	75.00	86.40	74.80	63.00	76.30
Glass faced									
25 mm (1") thick	m²	78.30	77.80	77.80	83.00	96.00	82.80	69.80	82.10
Mineral fibre damage resistive panel 600 mm x 1200 mm (24" x 48"):									
5 mm (3/16") thick standard	m²	87.20	94.30	83.70	93.50	93.50	92.60	72.20	126.00
Semi-concealed suspension system									
Mineral fibre panel 600 mm x 1200 mm (24" x 48"):									
16 mm (5/8") thick standard	m²	49.80	53.80	50.00	54.00	58.20	53.10	49.20	53.70
16 mm (5/8") thick fire-rated	m²	52.40	56.60	52.80	56.70	61.10	56.10	51.70	55.00
Glass fibre 600 mm x 1200 mm (24" x 48"):									
Vinyl faced									
16 mm (5/8") thick	m²	42.60	46.30	43.00	46.30	49.90	45.80	42.20	44.80
20 mm (3/4") thick	m²	43.70	47.00	43.90	47.10	50.80	46.70	42.90	45.60
Glass faced									
20 mm (3/4") thick	m²	55.40	59.90	55.60	59.90	64.50	58.90	54.60	58.00
Glass fibre panel 1200 mm x 1200 mm (48" x 48"):									
Vinyl faced									
25 mm (1") thick	m²	66.20	70.00	65.00	73.40	84.30	85.00	66.30	82.50
Concealed suspension system									
Mineral fibre panel 300 mm x 600 mm (12" x 24"):									
20 mm (3/4") thick standard	m²	121.00	130.00	121.00	132.00	141.00	128.00	120.00	127.00
20 mm (3/4") thick fire-rated	m²	124.00	132.00	122.00	133.00	142.00	130.00	121.00	128.00
Mineral fibre panel 300 mm x 300 mm (12" x 12"):									
20 mm (3/4") thick standard	m²	111.00	119.00	111.00	121.00	129.00	118.00	111.00	116.00
20 mm (3/4") thick fire-rated	m²	120.00	129.00	120.00	131.00	140.00	127.00	118.00	125.00
Suspended ceiling sundries									
Extra over cost of suspended ceiling for drilling and bolting to soffit	m²	15.60	16.30	15.60	18.40	17.80	16.00	20.70	16.70
Mineral wool sound absorption blanket	m²	15.60	16.30	15.60	18.40	17.80	16.00	20.70	16.70
09 60 00 Flooring									
09 63 40 Stone Flooring									
MARBLE									
To floors									
Panels:									
19 mm (3/4") travertine	m²	616.00	646.00	340.00	646.00	704.00	712.00	658.00	738.00
To walls									
Panels:									
19 mm (3/4") travertine	m²	647.00	680.00	357.00	680.00	737.00	748.00	691.00	760.00
09 64 00 Wood Flooring									
WOOD STRIP FLOORING									
Hardwood (finished)									
57 mm (2 1/4") wide x 21 mm (3/4") thick strips:									
Birch or maple									
Second grade or better	m²	135.00	129.00	139.00	129.00	145.00	158.00	160.00	147.00
Oak, plain white									
Stain grade	m²	141.00	136.00	144.00	136.00	153.00	162.00	173.00	147.00
Finish grade	m²	151.00	145.00	154.00	148.00	166.00	174.00	190.00	157.00
WOOD PARQUET FLOORING									
Prefinished									
8 mm (5/16") thick:									
Maple, select	m²	81.10	78.60	83.00	87.40	90.90	118.00	117.00	119.00
Oak, select	m²	83.40	80.70	85.00	89.60	90.90	121.00	120.00	121.00

Item	UNITS	St. John's	Halifax	Montreal	Ottawa	Toronto	Winnipeg	Calgary	Vancouver
RESILIENT WOOD FLOORING ASSEMBLIES									
On sleepers and subfloor									
Wood subfloor and sleepers:									
Industrial grade	m²	151.00	146.00	153.00	162.00	165.00	218.00	216.00	219.00
First grade	m²	148.00	142.00	149.00	157.00	159.00	209.00	208.00	210.00
Second grade	m²	143.00	139.00	146.00	154.00	154.00	206.00	203.00	207.00
Subfloor on steel springs and sleepers									
Industrial grade	m²	168.00	163.00	172.00	180.00	184.00	243.00	242.00	244.00
First grade	m²	196.00	191.00	199.00	209.00	213.00	284.00	282.00	285.00
Second grade	m²	183.00	178.00	187.00	196.00	199.00	266.00	265.00	266.00
09 65 00 Resilient Flooring									
RESILIENT TILE FLOORING									
Rubber tile									
3 mm (1/8") thick:									
Average cost	m²	89.50	116.00	114.00	119.00	119.00	137.00	112.00	116.00
Vinyl tile									
3 mm (1/8") thick									
Marbleized	m²	46.00	53.80	53.00	56.20	62.30	71.40	57.30	57.00
Solid colours	m²	47.50	55.50	54.60	58.10	64.40	73.70	59.10	58.70
Vinyl-composite tile									
1.5 mm (1/16") thick:									
Average cost	m²	27.30	22.70	27.80	27.30	33.90	26.50	28.50	38.10
2 mm (5/64") thick:									
Average cost	m²	30.30	25.10	31.00	30.40	37.70	29.60	31.70	42.20
3 mm (1/8") thick:									
Average cost	m²	32.30	26.90	33.10	32.60	40.40	31.60	33.80	45.90
RESILIENT SHEET FLOORING									
Linoleum									
2.3 mm (5/64") thick:									
Embossed patterns	m²	76.30	71.80	76.20	81.80	85.00	71.30	74.50	71.70
3 mm (1/8") thick:									
Solid colours	m²	80.00	75.30	80.00	85.60	89.10	74.70	78.00	76.60
Polyvinyl chloride (vinyl)									
Inlaid pattern:									
1.7 mm (1/16") thick:									
Mini chips	m²	30.80	36.90	35.90	37.70	38.90	45.50	35.30	36.40
Mini chips with embossed pattern	m²	32.20	38.50	37.50	39.60	40.60	47.80	36.90	38.50
Irregular chips	m²	35.60	42.60	41.60	43.80	44.80	52.60	40.70	42.30
Square chips	m²	37.50	44.90	43.60	45.90	47.20	55.60	42.50	44.60
Surface treated	m²	37.50	44.90	43.60	45.90	47.20	55.60	42.50	44.60
1.9 mm (5/64") thick:									
With embossed pattern	m²	54.20	65.00	63.10	66.80	68.50	80.20	61.90	64.60
2.3 mm (3/32") thick									
Square chips	m²	38.40	45.90	44.50	47.20	48.30	56.90	44.00	45.80
Irregular chips	m²	54.20	65.00	63.10	66.80	68.50	80.20	61.90	64.60
With embossed pattern	m²	58.50	70.10	68.20	72.00	73.80	86.60	67.10	69.80
Inlaid pattern with cushion backing									
2.7 mm (7/64") thick:	m²	54.20	65.00	63.10	66.80	68.50	80.20	61.90	64.60
Printed pattern with cushion backing:									
1.9 mm (5/64") thick	m²	41.70	50.00	48.50	51.30	52.70	61.90	47.60	49.90
2.5 mm (3/32") thick	m²	46.00	54.90	53.40	56.50	58.00	68.10	52.70	55.00
09 66 00 Terrazzo Flooring									
PORTLAND CEMENT TERRAZZO									
To floors with 3 mm (1/8") zinc strip									
Sand cushion type:									
762 mm x 762 mm (30" x 30") grid	m²	333.00	329.00	377.00	354.00	376.00	439.00	387.00	352.00
Bonded to concrete:									
762 mm x 762 mm (30" x 30") grid	m²	299.00	296.00	339.00	320.00	339.00	395.00	347.00	323.00
Thinset:									
762 mm x 762 mm (30" x 30") grid	m²	265.00	262.00	301.00	286.00	302.00	352.00	308.00	282.00
TERRAZZO, PRECAST									
To stairs									
Treads:									
To steel stairs	m	362.00	356.00	407.00	389.00	410.00	479.00	419.00	384.00
PLASTIC MATRIX TERRAZZO									
Epoxy type									
6 mm (1/4") thick	m²	299.00	296.00	328.00	332.00	350.00	423.00	387.00	388.00
10 mm (3/8") thick	m²	314.00	310.00	341.00	347.00	366.00	445.00	406.00	400.00
Latex Type									
6 mm (1/4") thick	m²	239.00	236.00	264.00	264.00	281.00	338.00	310.00	305.00
10 mm (3/8") thick	m²	267.00	265.00	292.00	300.00	313.00	379.00	349.00	343.00
CONDUCTIVE TERRAZZO									
Epoxy type									
6 mm (1/4") thick	m²	309.00	307.00	343.00	341.00	382.00	463.00	408.00	388.00
10 mm (3/8") thick	m²	376.00	374.00	419.00	416.00	464.00	564.00	497.00	464.00

Item	UNITS	St. John's	Halifax	Montreal	Ottawa	Toronto	Winnipeg	Calgary	Vancouver
TRIM & ACCESSORIES									
Base trim									
Cove base, standard:									
100 mm (4") high	m	78.70	80.40	88.30	91.40	107.00	131.00	95.90	96.20
150 mm (6") high	m	93.30	95.50	105.00	109.00	126.00	155.00	113.00	114.00

09 67 00 Fluid-Applied Flooring

FLUID APPLIED FLOORING
Urethane liquid pour laid on prepared concrete or asphalt
including game or lane lines

Item	UNITS	St. John's	Halifax	Montreal	Ottawa	Toronto	Winnipeg	Calgary	Vancouver
Indoor:									
6 mm (1/4") thick	m^2	154.00	159.00	150.00	176.00	173.00	192.00	219.00	180.00
9 mm (3/8") thick	m^2	172.00	177.00	165.00	193.00	190.00	211.00	241.00	199.00
Outdoor with textured surface									
12 mm (1/2") thick	m^2	219.00	227.00	215.00	247.00	244.00	268.00	309.00	254.00

09 68 00 Carpeting

CARPET
Nylon:

Item	UNITS	St. John's	Halifax	Montreal	Ottawa	Toronto	Winnipeg	Calgary	Vancouver
Anti-static									
Light duty 680 g/m^2 (20 oz/sy)	m^2	38.30	38.40	39.60	40.10	47.20	51.20	40.30	52.90
Medium duty 950 g/m^2 (28 oz/sy)	m^2	48.40	48.40	50.00	50.50	59.40	64.60	51.00	68.00
Cut pile									
Heavy duty 1530 g/m^2 (45 oz/sy)	m^2	66.20	69.00	67.00	69.50	81.40	87.90	69.70	88.10
Acrylic:									
Tufted									
Light duty 1080 g/m^2 (32 oz/sy)	m^2	41.60	43.40	41.90	43.60	51.20	55.20	44.00	55.30
Woven									
Medium duty 1360 g/m^2 (40 oz/sy)	m^2	56.80	59.20	57.40	59.60	69.90	75.30	60.10	75.60
Heavy duty 1700 g/m^2 (50 oz/sy)	m^2	72.40	75.80	73.20	76.00	89.30	96.40	76.70	96.60
Polypropylene:									
Light duty 680 g/m^2 (20 oz/sy)	m^2	28.50	29.80	28.80	29.90	35.10	37.70	30.20	37.90
Medium duty 850 g/m^2 (25 oz/sy)	m^2	38.10	39.70	38.40	40.00	47.10	50.40	40.20	50.60
Heavy duty 1020 g/m^2 (30 oz/sy)	m^2	49.80	52.00	50.20	52.10	61.60	66.20	52.50	66.50
Wool (including underpadding):									
Light duty 920 g/m^2 (27 oz/sy)	m^2	65.00	67.90	65.70	68.40	80.30	86.30	68.70	86.90
Medium duty 1190 g/m^2 (35 oz/sy)	m^2	77.60	80.70	78.20	81.20	95.30	103.00	81.60	103.00
Heavy duty 1420 g/m^2 (42 oz/sy)	m^2	94.90	98.90	95.60	99.50	116.00	125.00	100.00	126.00

09 69 00 Access Flooring

RIGID GRID ACCESS FLOORING
600 mm x 600 mm (24" x 24") panels (based on 300 mm (12") height)

Item	UNITS	St. John's	Halifax	Montreal	Ottawa	Toronto	Winnipeg	Calgary	Vancouver
Steel-clad wood floor panel:									
With plastic laminated finish	m^2	275.00	270.00	272.00	302.00	291.00	264.00	256.00	16.60
With vinyl floor finish	m^2	281.00	275.00	277.00	309.00	297.00	269.00	263.00	17.00
Steel floor panels:									
With plastic laminated finish	m^2	330.00	323.00	326.00	361.00	347.00	314.00	306.00	19.90
With vinyl floor finish	m^2	338.00	330.00	332.00	368.00	357.00	324.00	316.00	20.30

SNAP ON STRINGER ACCESS FLOORING
600 mm x 600 mm (24" x 24") panels (based on 300 mm (12") height)

Item	UNITS	St. John's	Halifax	Montreal	Ottawa	Toronto	Winnipeg	Calgary	Vancouver
Steel clad wood floor panels:									
With plastic laminated floor finish	m^2	269.00	264.00	266.00	294.00	285.00	258.00	250.00	16.00
With vinyl floor finish	m^2	274.00	269.00	271.00	301.00	290.00	263.00	255.00	17.00
Steel floor panels:									
With plastic laminated floor finish	m^2	320.00	314.00	318.00	352.00	339.00	307.00	299.00	19.40
With vinyl floor finish	m^2	328.00	320.00	324.00	359.00	344.00	313.00	303.00	19.60

STRINGERLESS ACCESS FLOORING
600 mm x 600 mm (24" x 24") panels (based on 300 mm (12") height)

Item	UNITS	St. John's	Halifax	Montreal	Ottawa	Toronto	Winnipeg	Calgary	Vancouver
Steel-clad wood floor finish:									
With plastic laminated finish	m^2	237.00	232.00	235.00	258.00	248.00	226.00	219.00	14.30
With vinyl floor finish	m^2	244.00	239.00	240.00	269.00	259.00	235.00	227.00	14.70
Steel - clad concrete panel									
With plastic laminated finish	m^2	320.00	314.00	318.00	352.00	339.00	307.00	299.00	19.40
Steel floor panels:									
With plastic laminated finish	m^2	289.00	284.00	285.00	318.00	307.00	278.00	269.00	17.40
With vinyl floor finish	m^2	297.00	291.00	292.00	324.00	313.00	285.00	276.00	17.80
Aluminum floor panels:									
With plastic laminated finish	m^2	577.00	566.00	571.00	632.00	609.00	554.00	537.00	34.80
With vinyl floor finish	m^2	611.00	598.00	602.00	668.00	643.00	585.00	570.00	36.70

Item	UNITS	St. John's	Halifax	Montreal	Ottawa	Toronto	Winnipeg	Calgary	Vancouver
09 70 00 Wall Finishes									
09 72 00 Wall Coverings									
VINYL-COATED FABRIC WALL COVERING									
(Based on supply price of $10.50/m² ($1.00/SF))									
Plain patterns (double rolls)									
Untrimmed:									
To drywall	m²	37.60	33.70	34.10	34.80	37.60	40.30	32.00	48.90
To plaster	m²	35.40	31.60	32.20	32.70	35.60	38.00	30.10	46.00
Pretrimmed:									
To drywall	m²	37.60	33.70	34.10	34.80	37.60	40.30	32.00	48.90
To plaster	m²	31.80	28.60	28.90	29.70	31.90	34.30	26.90	41.40
Decorative patterns (double rolls)									
Untrimmed:									
To drywall	m²	39.40	35.30	35.90	36.80	39.80	42.50	33.40	51.10
To plaster	m²	35.40	31.60	32.20	32.70	35.60	38.00	30.10	46.00
Pretrimmed:									
To drywall	m²	38.30	34.60	35.00	35.70	38.50	41.30	32.50	50.10
To plaster	m²	34.50	31.20	31.30	32.20	34.50	37.10	29.60	45.20
VINYL WALL COVERINGS									
(15% material waste included)									
1370 mm (54") wide, plain or decorated									
To walls:									
340 g/m (15 oz per lin. yd)	m²	50.50	45.40	46.20	47.00	50.70	54.50	42.80	65.80
430 g/m (19 oz per lin. yd)	m²	53.80	48.40	49.00	50.00	53.90	57.90	45.50	70.00
770 g/m (34 oz per lin. yd)	m²	68.00	61.10	61.90	63.00	67.90	73.00	57.50	88.70
WALLPAPER									
(Based on supply price of $8.60/m² ($0.80/sf))									
Plain patterns (double rolls)									
Untrimmed:									
To drywall	m²	34.50	31.20	31.30	32.20	34.50	37.10	29.60	45.20
To plaster	m²	33.80	30.40	30.90	31.50	33.80	36.30	28.50	44.00
Pretrimmed:									
To drywall	m²	34.20	30.90	31.10	32.00	34.20	36.80	29.30	44.70
To plaster	m²	33.30	30.00	30.40	30.80	33.50	35.90	28.00	43.40
Decorative patterns (double rolls)									
Untrimmed:									
To drywall	m²	36.10	32.40	32.90	33.40	36.10	38.70	30.50	46.90
To plaster	m²	35.40	31.60	32.20	32.70	35.60	38.00	30.10	46.00
Pretrimmed:									
To drywall	m²	34.20	30.90	31.10	32.00	34.20	36.80	29.30	44.70
To plaster	m²	33.30	30.00	30.40	30.80	33.50	35.90	28.00	43.40
09 90 00 Painting and Coating									
09 91 00 Painting									
DOORS & WINDOWS, EXTERIOR									
3 coats, brush applied:									
Wood or metal windows	m²	18.60	10.50	18.70	23.10	19.70	23.40	17.90	139.00
Wooden doors	EA	85.10	48.50	86.20	107.00	91.10	107.00	82.10	641.00
Metal doors	EA	77.00	43.70	77.70	96.00	81.90	96.70	73.90	577.00
Wooden frames	EA	45.60	25.90	46.10	57.00	48.70	57.30	43.70	342.00
Metal door frames	EA	39.20	22.30	39.80	49.00	41.90	49.50	37.90	295.00
TRIM, EXTERIOR									
3 coats, brush applied:									
Metal flashing	m²	18.60	10.50	18.70	23.10	19.70	23.40	17.90	139.00
Soffits, fascias	m²	22.40	12.60	22.30	27.90	23.80	27.90	21.40	166.00
Handrails, railing etc.	m	3.44	1.95	3.46	4.25	3.64	4.31	3.30	25.70
MISCELLANEOUS, EXTERIOR									
3 coats, brush applied:									
Pipes not exceeding 150 mm (6") dia.	m	3.44	1.95	3.46	4.25	3.64	4.31	3.30	25.70
Flagpoles (before erection)	m²	12.80	7.39	12.90	16.00	13.70	16.10	12.40	96.80
Lamp standard (before erection)	m²	11.90	6.71	11.90	14.90	12.60	14.80	11.50	88.80
WALLS & CEILINGS, INTERIOR									
Ceilings									
2 coats, rolled									
Concrete, wood, plaster or drywall	m²	9.51	5.69	9.90	12.70	10.30	12.20	9.64	75.10
Acoustic tile (concealed grid)	m²	6.99	4.19	7.29	9.35	7.59	8.91	7.05	55.00
Acoustic tile (exposed grid)	m²	11.10	6.65	11.60	14.90	12.10	14.00	11.40	88.10
Steel deck (measure surface area)	m²	7.46	4.47	7.77	9.95	8.10	9.48	7.54	58.70
Surfaces associated with ceilings									
2 coats at same time as ceiling:									
OWSJ (measure twice height)	m²	7.56	4.51	7.86	10.10	8.19	9.62	7.65	59.50
Duct work	m²	7.56	4.51	7.86	10.10	8.19	9.62	7.65	59.50
2 coats separate from ceiling:									
OWSJ (measure twice height)	m²	12.60	7.52	13.00	16.70	13.60	15.90	12.60	98.90
Structural steelwork (exposed area)	m²	9.51	5.69	9.90	12.70	10.30	12.20	9.64	75.10
Duct work	m²	12.80	7.70	13.40	17.30	13.80	16.10	12.80	101.00
Pipes over 50 mm (2") dia. surface area	m²	12.80	7.70	13.40	17.30	13.80	16.10	12.80	101.00

Item	UNITS	St. John's	Halifax	Montreal	Ottawa	Toronto	Winnipeg	Calgary	Vancouver
Pipes not exceeding 50 mm (2") dia..............	m²	11.60	6.84	11.90	15.50	12.50	14.60	11.70	91.00
3 coats, rolled:									
Concrete, wood, plaster, or drywall	m²	10.40	5.92	10.50	13.00	11.10	13.10	10.00	10.80
Walls									
2 coats, rolled:									
Concrete, plywood, plaster, or drywall............	m²	9.76	5.82	10.10	13.00	10.60	12.50	9.81	76.60
Concrete block, acoustic board or panel	m²	11.30	6.78	11.70	15.30	12.30	14.40	11.50	88.80
Plywood and paneling.............................	m²	9.82	5.88	10.20	13.10	10.70	12.60	9.90	77.30
Steel and wood sashes...........................	m²	11.60	6.84	11.90	15.40	12.50	14.50	11.60	90.30
Structural steel, exposed surfaces...............	m²	10.60	6.35	11.00	14.10	11.50	13.40	10.70	83.80
3 coats, rolled:									
Concrete, plywood, plaster, or drywall............	m²	10.40	5.92	10.50	13.00	11.10	13.10	10.00	10.80
Concrete block, tile, acoustic board or panel ...	m²	13.20	7.58	13.40	16.40	14.10	16.80	12.70	98.90
Steel and wood sashes...........................	m²	15.00	8.56	15.00	18.60	15.90	18.80	14.20	111.00
Structural steel, exposed surfaces...............	m²	16.90	9.79	17.20	21.30	18.40	21.40	16.40	127.00
Baseboards not exceeding 100 mm (4") high......	m	5.38	3.05	5.43	6.73	5.77	6.80	5.20	40.50
DOORS & WINDOWS, INTERIOR									
2 coats (brush applied) on:									
Metal doors	EA	58.20	34.80	60.60	77.70	63.20	74.00	58.60	458.00
Metal door frames	EA	35.10	20.80	36.50	47.00	37.80	44.50	35.40	276.00
3 coats (brush applied) on:									
Wooden doors....................................	EA	75.20	42.70	76.00	93.90	80.30	94.60	72.30	565.00
Wooden door frames	EA	44.00	25.00	44.30	54.80	46.70	55.10	42.20	329.00
Edges of plastic faced doors	EA	26.50	15.10	27.00	33.30	28.60	33.50	25.60	199.00
MISCELLANEOUS, INTERIOR									
2 coats (brush applied) on:									
Stair treads......................................	m²	14.60	8.62	15.00	19.10	15.60	18.20	14.70	114.00
Hollow metal screens............................	m²	13.70	8.25	14.20	18.20	14.70	17.50	13.70	108.00
Handrails, balustrades etc.......................	m	4.80	2.86	4.97	6.41	5.19	6.09	4.83	37.80
3 coats (brush applied) on:									
Shelving	m²	21.00	12.00	21.00	26.30	22.30	26.40	20.20	157.00
Millwork (surface area)	m²	23.80	13.60	24.30	30.20	25.40	30.00	23.10	179.00

09 96 00 High-Performance Coatings

WALL COATINGS

Plastic paint to interior walls

Item	UNITS	St. John's	Halifax	Montreal	Ottawa	Toronto	Winnipeg	Calgary	Vancouver
3 coats:									
Concrete blockwork...............................	m²	22.80	35.50	24.30	23.70	22.70	28.20	21.20	23.00
Concrete	m²	22.40	35.00	23.80	23.20	22.40	27.80	20.70	22.50
Drywall	m²	20.80	32.30	22.10	21.50	21.00	26.00	19.20	20.90

10: SPECIALTIES

10 11 00 Visual Display Units

10 11 13 Chalkboards

CHALKBOARDS

Wall Mounted

Fixed (includes installation cost of trim)

Impregnated fibreboard 12 mm (1/2") thick:

Item	UNITS	St. John's	Halifax	Montreal	Ottawa	Toronto	Winnipeg	Calgary	Vancouver
Steel sheet, baked on acrylic finish...............	m²	124.00	121.00	129.00	336.00	119.00	150.00	140.00	237.00
Steel sheet, porcelain enamel finish..............	m²	120.00	117.00	124.00	326.00	116.00	144.00	135.00	231.00
Tempered hardboard 6 mm (1/4"):									
Baked on acrylic finish...........................	m²	60.20	58.30	62.00	161.00	57.80	71.60	67.50	115.00

ALUMINUM TRIM

(Standard products)

Edge trim and divider bars (Supply only)

6 mm (1/4") exposed face:

Item	UNITS	St. John's	Halifax	Montreal	Ottawa	Toronto	Winnipeg	Calgary	Vancouver
Clear anodized finish	m	5.01	4.91	5.15	24.40	5.03	6.22	4.98	4.90
Baked enamel finish	m	5.51	5.41	5.67	26.90	5.53	6.87	5.50	5.38
Colour anodized finish	m	5.78	5.66	5.95	28.10	5.79	7.19	5.76	5.64
18 mm (3/4") exposed face:									
Clear anodized finish	m	5.01	4.91	5.15	24.40	5.03	6.22	4.98	4.90
Baked enamel finish	m	5.60	5.48	5.75	27.20	5.61	6.96	5.57	5.44
Colour anodized finish	m	5.78	5.66	5.95	28.10	5.79	7.19	5.76	5.64
44 mm (1-3/4") exposed face:									
Clear anodized finish	m	10.50	10.30	10.80	51.20	10.50	13.10	10.40	10.20
Baked enamel finish	m	15.10	14.70	15.40	73.40	15.20	18.90	15.10	14.50
Colour anodized finish	m	15.10	14.70	15.40	73.40	15.20	18.90	15.10	14.50
Chalk rails									
Single web:									
Clear anodized finish	m	12.70	12.40	13.00	61.50	12.70	16.10	12.90	13.40
Baked enamel finish	m	13.70	13.40	14.00	65.10	13.50	17.30	13.80	14.30
Colour anodized finish	m	15.10	14.70	15.40	73.40	15.10	19.20	15.40	16.10
Boxed type:									
Clear anodized finish	m	21.90	21.40	22.30	106.00	21.90	27.80	22.30	23.10
Baked enamel finish	m	22.80	22.30	23.50	111.00	22.80	29.00	23.20	24.00
Colour anodized finish	m	22.60	22.00	23.30	109.00	22.60	28.70	23.00	23.70

DIV 10 Specialties — METRIC CURRENT MARKET PRICES

Item	UNITS	St. John's	Halifax	Montreal	Ottawa	Toronto	Winnipeg	Calgary	Vancouver
Map rails									
Mounted on wall, cork inset:									
25 mm (1") wide	m	8.62	8.45	8.86	42.10	8.63	11.00	8.81	8.24
50 mm (2") wide	m	10.20	10.00	10.60	49.60	10.30	13.10	10.50	9.79
Mounted on board or wall, 50 mm (2") h-type:									
Clear anodized finish	m	10.20	10.00	10.60	49.60	10.30	13.10	10.50	9.79
Baked enamel finish	m	11.40	11.00	11.70	55.20	11.30	14.40	11.60	10.70
Colour anodized finish	m	12.40	12.10	12.80	60.70	12.50	15.90	12.70	12.00

10 11 23 Tackboards

TACKBOARDS
Wall Mounted
Fixed (includes installation cost of trim)

Item	UNITS	St. John's	Halifax	Montreal	Ottawa	Toronto	Winnipeg	Calgary	Vancouver
Cork, natural:									
6 mm (1/4") thick............	m²	82.90	80.70	73.90	97.00	65.20	81.00	75.00	95.90
12 mm (1/2") thick............	m²	104.00	101.00	92.20	121.00	81.60	101.00	93.90	120.00
Cork, vinyl coated:									
6 mm (1/4") thick............	m²	117.00	114.00	105.00	137.00	92.60	114.00	106.00	136.00
12 mm (1/2") thick............	m²	140.00	137.00	124.00	163.00	110.00	137.00	128.00	161.00
Cork, covered with 50 g vinyl fabric:									
6 mm (1/4") thick............	m²	105.00	103.00	94.00	124.00	82.80	103.00	95.40	122.00
12 mm (1/2") thick............	m²	125.00	122.00	111.00	146.00	98.20	122.00	112.00	145.00
Cork, covered with nylon fabric:									
12 mm (1/2") thick............	m²	147.00	143.00	131.00	173.00	115.00	144.00	133.00	168.00

10 21 00 Compartments and Cubicles

10 21 13 Toilet Compartments

PARTITIONS, TOILET
Metal toilet partitions

Item	UNITS	St. John's	Halifax	Montreal	Ottawa	Toronto	Winnipeg	Calgary	Vancouver
Floor mounted, overhead braced:									
Standard cubicle	EA	807.00	795.00	809.00	854.00	773.00	881.00	822.00	772.00
Alcove type	EA	783.00	773.00	786.00	830.00	749.00	854.00	797.00	749.00
Floor mounted, pilaster type:									
Standard cubicle	EA	921.00	907.00	922.00	976.00	880.00	1000.00	938.00	881.00
Alcove type	EA	867.00	854.00	870.00	920.00	830.00	946.00	883.00	828.00
Ceiling hung:									
Standard cubicle	EA	990.00	975.00	992.00	1050.00	947.00	1080.00	1010.00	945.00
Alcove type	EA	950.00	937.00	955.00	1010.00	909.00	1040.00	971.00	908.00

10 22 00 Partitions

10 22 19 Demountable Partitions
2.74 m (9') height

PARTITIONS, MOVABLE OFFICE
Gypsum partitions

Item	UNITS	St. John's	Halifax	Montreal	Ottawa	Toronto	Winnipeg	Calgary	Vancouver
Plain drywall:									
Painted	m	328.00	313.00	331.00	271.00	364.00	363.00	311.00	495.00
Vinyl covered.........	m	379.00	365.00	386.00	316.00	422.00	424.00	363.00	576.00
Drywall with sound absorption:									
Painted	m	356.00	340.00	356.00	294.00	394.00	394.00	336.00	536.00
Vinyl covered.........	m	396.00	379.00	400.00	329.00	440.00	441.00	377.00	600.00
Steel partitions									
Baked enamel finish	m	582.00	557.00	588.00	483.00	647.00	646.00	553.00	879.00

10 22 33 Accordion Folding Partitions

ACCORDION FOLDING PARTITIONS
2.44 m (8') height
Wood:

Item	UNITS	St. John's	Halifax	Montreal	Ottawa	Toronto	Winnipeg	Calgary	Vancouver
Room divider type.........	m	597.00	574.00	579.00	624.00	652.00	623.00	590.00	619.00
Classroom type.........	m	1,070	1,030	1,040	1,120	1,170	1,120	1,060	1,110

10 22 39 Folding Panel Partitions
2.74 m (9') height

FOLDING PARTITIONS

Item	UNITS	St. John's	Halifax	Montreal	Ottawa	Toronto	Winnipeg	Calgary	Vancouver
Manually operated partitions									
Vinyl faced gypsum panes.........	m	1,310	1,310	1,370	1,390	1,660	1,530	1,460	1,370
Sound absorbing.........	m	1,650	1,640	1,710	1,740	2,070	1,910	1,830	1,700
Electrically operated panels									
Steel gymnasium pattern.........	m	1,200	1,190	1,230	1,260	1,490	1,390	1,320	1,230

BIFOLD PARTITIONS
Wood:

Item	UNITS	St. John's	Halifax	Montreal	Ottawa	Toronto	Winnipeg	Calgary	Vancouver
Gymnasium type.........	m	1,140	1,110	1,160	1,180	1,410	1,290	1,250	1,170

Item	UNITS	St. John's	Halifax	Montreal	Ottawa	Toronto	Winnipeg	Calgary	Vancouver

10 26 00 Wall and Door Protection
10 26 13 Corner Guards
CORNER GUARDS
Vinyl acrylic with aluminum retainers, 75 mm (3") legs

Item	UNITS	St. John's	Halifax	Montreal	Ottawa	Toronto	Winnipeg	Calgary	Vancouver
Flush mounted:									
L-type 6 mm (1/4") radius	m	98.10	93.50	96.10	104.00	110.00	112.00	106.00	125.00
L-type 30 mm (1 1/4") radius	m	98.10	93.50	96.10	104.00	110.00	112.00	106.00	125.00
U-type 100 mm (4") wall	m	120.00	114.00	118.00	128.00	135.00	138.00	130.00	152.00
U-type 150 mm (6") wall	m	187.00	178.00	183.00	201.00	209.00	216.00	205.00	238.00
U-type 200 mm (8") wall	m	189.00	179.00	184.00	202.00	211.00	217.00	206.00	240.00
Surface mounted:									
L-type 6 mm (1/4") radius	m	71.40	68.00	69.80	75.60	79.90	81.60	77.20	90.60
L-type 30 mm (1 1/4") radius	m	71.40	68.00	69.80	75.60	79.90	81.60	77.20	90.60
U-type 100 mm (4") wall	m	134.00	129.00	131.00	144.00	153.00	155.00	146.00	173.00
U-type 150 mm (6") wall	m	143.00	135.00	136.00	152.00	159.00	163.00	153.00	180.00
U-type 200 mm (8") wall	m	162.00	155.00	159.00	172.00	181.00	186.00	175.00	208.00
Stainless steel									
Standard sections:									
Built-in	m	102.00	104.00	95.70	130.00	167.00	110.00	108.00	117.00
Fixed to wall surface with adhesive	m	70.40	71.50	66.00	92.70	115.00	75.70	75.00	82.00

10 28 00 Toilet, Bath & Laundry Accessories
10 28 13 Toilet Accessories
BATH ACCESSORIES, DISPENSING UNITS
(Based on chrome unless noted)

Item	UNITS	St. John's	Halifax	Montreal	Ottawa	Toronto	Winnipeg	Calgary	Vancouver
Toilet tissue, roll type									
Flush mounted, single	EA	34.40	35.10	36.30	38.90	39.30	48.20	43.10	49.70
Flush mounted, double	EA	45.00	45.90	47.40	51.00	51.40	63.10	56.60	65.00
Toilet tissue, leaf type:									
Single (900 sheets)	EA	38.00	38.90	40.00	43.00	43.60	53.50	47.90	54.60
Double (1800 sheets)	EA	48.50	49.50	51.00	55.10	55.40	68.20	61.00	69.50
Toilet seat covers:									
For unfolded covers	EA	70.60	64.40	70.20	74.80	85.50	78.90	79.00	70.90
For folded covers	EA	89.80	81.40	88.70	94.90	108.00	99.90	100.00	89.90
Sanitary napkins:									
Surface mounted, single	EA	402.00	366.00	399.00	428.00	486.00	450.00	449.00	405.00
Surface mounted, double	EA	561.00	510.00	556.00	594.00	679.00	625.00	627.00	563.00
Recessed, single	EA	561.00	510.00	556.00	594.00	679.00	625.00	627.00	563.00
Recessed, double	EA	758.00	689.00	750.00	801.00	917.00	843.00	847.00	759.00
Paper towels, roll type									
Surface mounted, standard roll	EA	108.00	105.00	112.00	121.00	137.00	123.00	121.00	121.00
Surface mounted, jumbo roll	EA	128.00	125.00	132.00	146.00	164.00	148.00	146.00	145.00
Paper towel leaf type									
Surface mounted horizontal	EA	95.40	92.30	98.70	106.00	122.00	107.00	107.00	106.00
Surface mounted vertical	EA	101.00	97.90	105.00	113.00	129.00	116.00	114.00	112.00
Recessed horizontal	EA	91.00	87.90	93.90	101.00	115.00	103.00	101.00	101.00
Paper towel, universal:									
Surface mounted, 375 mm (15") high	EA	108.00	101.00	107.00	117.00	133.00	119.00	117.00	116.00
Recessed, 650 mm (26") high, stainless	EA	463.00	434.00	462.00	497.00	562.00	505.00	497.00	494.00
Facial tissue:									
Surface mounted	EA	48.90	47.40	50.60	54.80	61.80	55.60	54.90	54.60
Recessed	EA	49.90	48.30	51.60	55.90	63.00	56.70	55.90	55.30
Soap products									
Soap bars:									
Soap dish	EA	26.60	26.90	28.20	29.50	31.40	32.00	30.60	24.80
Powdered soap:									
450 ml (16 oz) capacity	EA	58.00	58.60	61.80	64.20	68.20	69.60	66.80	54.20
Liquid soap, individual tank:									
Wall type, surface mounted, 450 ml (16 oz)	EA	116.00	117.00	122.00	127.00	137.00	139.00	134.00	107.00
Wall type, surface mounted, 500 ml (18 oz)	EA	134.00	135.00	148.00	150.00	161.00	161.00	157.00	127.00
Wall type, surface mounted, 1100 ml (40 oz)	EA	163.00	165.00	173.00	180.00	192.00	196.00	187.00	152.00
Wall type, surface mounted, 1700 ml (60 oz)	EA	176.00	178.00	188.00	195.00	207.00	213.00	201.00	165.00
Wall type, recessed, 450 ml (16 oz)	EA	257.00	258.00	273.00	283.00	302.00	307.00	295.00	239.00
Lavatory mounted, 450 ml (16 oz)	EA	165.00	167.00	175.00	182.00	194.00	198.00	189.00	154.00
Liquid soap, central tank:									
(piping not included) wall type valve	EA	91.20	92.10	96.90	101.00	107.00	109.00	105.00	85.10
Wall type valve, vandal-proof	EA	222.00	223.00	237.00	245.00	262.00	266.00	256.00	208.00
Lavatory type valve	EA	205.00	207.00	219.00	227.00	241.00	244.00	235.00	191.00
Exposed tanks, 4.5 l (1 gal.)	EA	121.00	122.00	126.00	133.00	142.00	146.00	139.00	112.00
Exposed tanks, 9.1 l (2 gal.)	EA	205.00	207.00	219.00	227.00	241.00	244.00	235.00	191.00
Exposed tanks, 23 l (5 gal.)	EA	427.00	432.00	454.00	474.00	503.00	515.00	492.00	399.00
Pressure reducing tank, 23 l (5 gal.)	EA	740.00	748.00	788.00	818.00	872.00	889.00	853.00	692.00
Storage tank, 230 l (50 gal.)	EA	2,250	2,270	2,390	2,500	2,670	2,680	2,590	2,100

BATH ACCESSORIES, DISPOSAL UNITS
Sanitary napkin units

Item	UNITS	St. John's	Halifax	Montreal	Ottawa	Toronto	Winnipeg	Calgary	Vancouver
Wall mounted:									
Surface mounted	EA	187.00	197.00	200.00	208.00	221.00	239.00	233.00	221.00
Recessed	EA	214.00	226.00	230.00	241.00	255.00	273.00	265.00	254.00

Item	UNITS	St. John's	Halifax	Montreal	Ottawa	Toronto	Winnipeg	Calgary	Vancouver
Waste receptacles									
Free standing baked enamel:									
400 mm x 400 mm x 900 mm (16" x 16" x 36")...........	EA	213.00	216.00	222.00	229.00	244.00	262.00	256.00	240.00
300 mm x 300 mm x 1050 mm (12" x 12" x 42")	EA	205.00	210.00	213.00	221.00	236.00	253.00	249.00	234.00
Wall mounted:									
Surface mounted, 300 mm x 1050 mm (12" x 42")...........	EA	473.00	480.00	490.00	509.00	541.00	580.00	566.00	535.00
Semi-recessed, 300 mm x 1050 mm (12" x 42")...........	EA	486.00	494.00	504.00	524.00	556.00	598.00	581.00	550.00
Recessed, 300 mm x 1050 mm (12" x 42")	EA	407.00	414.00	422.00	437.00	467.00	501.00	486.00	461.00
Recessed, exposed door only...........	EA	77.40	78.60	80.30	83.30	88.50	94.80	92.30	87.50
Ash trays									
Surface mounted:									
Circular, 200 mm (8") dia...........	EA	186.00	190.00	193.00	201.00	214.00	229.00	221.00	212.00
Semi-circular, 330 mm (13") dia...........	EA	149.00	151.00	153.00	160.00	170.00	180.00	178.00	168.00
Rectangular, 200 mm (8") long	EA	164.00	167.00	169.00	176.00	188.00	202.00	197.00	184.00
Rectangular, 300 mm (12") long	EA	203.00	207.00	211.00	219.00	233.00	250.00	246.00	231.00
Recessed:									
200 mm (8") long	EA	225.00	226.00	232.00	241.00	256.00	275.00	265.00	253.00
300 mm (12") long	EA	330.00	334.00	343.00	354.00	376.00	405.00	395.00	372.00
BATH ACCESSORIES, COMBINATION UNITS									
Towel/waste receptacles (all units based on stainless steel)									
Surface mounted:									
350 mm x 1500 mm (14" x 60")...........	EA	741.00	748.00	763.00	794.00	846.00	902.00	883.00	850.00
Semi-recessed:									
350 mm x 1500 mm (14" x 60")...........	EA	711.00	718.00	736.00	764.00	813.00	867.00	847.00	817.00
Recessed:									
350 mm x 1500 mm (14" x 60")...........	EA	602.00	610.00	622.00	647.00	688.00	736.00	720.00	693.00

10 51 00 Lockers

10 51 13 Metal Lockers
STANDARD LOCKERS, BAKED ENAMEL
1.8 m (72") high
Single tier

Item	UNITS	St. John's	Halifax	Montreal	Ottawa	Toronto	Winnipeg	Calgary	Vancouver
300 mm (12") wide:									
375 mm (15") deep...........	EA	245.00	241.00	266.00	237.00	273.00	278.00	256.00	335.00
450 mm (18") deep...........	EA	266.00	262.00	291.00	257.00	297.00	303.00	278.00	364.00
375 mm (15") wide:									
375 mm (15") deep...........	EA	288.00	284.00	315.00	277.00	321.00	328.00	300.00	394.00
450 mm (18") deep...........	EA	304.00	299.00	332.00	293.00	339.00	345.00	318.00	416.00
Two tier									
300 mm (12") wide:									
375 mm (15") deep...........	EA	289.00	285.00	316.00	279.00	323.00	329.00	301.00	395.00
450 mm (18") deep...........	EA	330.00	325.00	360.00	318.00	368.00	374.00	345.00	451.00
Six tier									
300 mm (12") wide:									
375 mm (15") deep...........	EA	387.00	381.00	424.00	375.00	434.00	441.00	406.00	532.00
450 mm (18") deep...........	EA	406.00	400.00	444.00	391.00	453.00	461.00	422.00	554.00
Accessories									
Bases, baked enamel:									
Per locker	EA	35.50	34.90	38.70	34.00	39.50	40.20	36.90	48.20

COIN OPERATED LOCKERS, BAKED ENAMEL
1.8 m (72") high
Single tier

Item	UNITS	St. John's	Halifax	Montreal	Ottawa	Toronto	Winnipeg	Calgary	Vancouver
300 mm (12") wide:									
300 mm (12") deep...........	EA	1,110	1,080	1,220	1,070	1,240	1,260	1,170	1,520
375 mm (15") deep...........	EA	1,120	1,090	1,220	1,070	1,240	1,260	1,170	1,520
450 mm (18") deep (standard)...........	EA	1,040	1,020	1,130	999	1,150	1,170	1,080	1,420
525 mm (21") deep...........	EA	1,120	1,110	1,220	1,080	1,250	1,270	1,190	1,530
Two tier									
300 mm (12") wide:									
300 mm (12") deep...........	EA	1,220	1,190	1,320	1,180	1,360	1,380	1,270	1,640
375 mm (15") deep...........	EA	1,240	1,220	1,350	1,200	1,400	1,410	1,310	1,700
450 mm (18") deep (standard)...........	EA	1,170	1,140	1,260	1,120	1,300	1,320	1,210	1,570
525 mm (21") deep...........	EA	1,270	1,240	1,360	1,230	1,410	1,420	1,320	1,750
Accessories									
Bases, baked enamel									
Per locker	EA	60.80	59.90	66.40	58.40	67.90	69.00	63.70	83.10
Sloping tops, baked enamel:									
To suit 450 mm (18") wide tiers...........	m	259.00	255.00	284.00	250.00	289.00	294.00	270.00	355.00

10 55 00 Postal Specialties
MAIL BOXES

Item	UNITS	St. John's	Halifax	Montreal	Ottawa	Toronto	Winnipeg	Calgary	Vancouver
Apartment type:									
Back loading...........	EA	118.00	115.00	125.00	103.00	121.00	145.00	132.00	157.00
Front loading	EA	140.00	136.00	149.00	122.00	144.00	173.00	157.00	187.00
Post office type:									
Type c	EA	229.00	222.00	244.00	200.00	236.00	285.00	256.00	304.00

COLLECTION BOXES

Item	UNITS	St. John's	Halifax	Montreal	Ottawa	Toronto	Winnipeg	Calgary	Vancouver
Aluminum	EA	4,060	3,980	4,320	3,530	4,170	5,020	4,540	5,440
Bronze or stainless steel	EA	4,480	4,370	4,750	3,910	4,600	5,510	5,020	5,960

Item	UNITS	St. John's	Halifax	Montreal	Ottawa	Toronto	Winnipeg	Calgary	Vancouver
10 75 00 Flagpoles									
Erected complete									
FLAGPOLE, GROUND SET									
Stationary (including metal base and base cover and supply									
and installation of anchor bolts in prepared base)									
Tapered cone, external rope:									
11 m (35'), painted steel............	EA	3,920	3,910	4,220	3,910	4,190	4,950	4,080	4,620
11 m (35'), satin aluminum	EA	3,690	3,700	4,010	3,720	3,970	4,700	3,870	4,350
11 m (35'), clear anodized aluminum	EA	4,000	4,000	4,300	4,000	4,270	5,080	4,180	4,690
11 m (35'), colour anodized aluminum	EA	4,320	4,310	4,640	4,320	4,600	5,480	4,510	5,070
Sectional, standard external rope:									
11 m (35'), clear anodized aluminum	EA	2,480	2,480	2,660	2,480	2,650	3,150	2,590	2,910
11 m (35'), baked enamel aluminum	EA	3,440	3,430	3,690	3,430	3,660	4,350	3,590	4,040
Tilting (concrete not included)									
Tapered cone, external rope:									
11 m (35'), painted steel............	EA	4,580	4,580	4,960	4,620	4,930	5,860	4,820	5,410
11 m (35'), satin aluminum	EA	4,000	4,000	4,300	4,000	4,270	5,080	4,180	4,690
11 m (35'), clear anodized aluminum	EA	4,580	4,580	4,960	4,620	4,930	5,860	4,820	5,410
11 m (35'), colour anodized aluminum	EA	5,040	5,030	5,420	5,050	5,380	6,420	5,260	5,930
Sectional, standard, external rope:									
11 m (35'), clear anodized aluminum	EA	3,120	3,130	3,400	3,140	3,330	3,970	3,260	3,680
11 m (35'), baked enamel aluminum	EA	4,150	4,150	4,480	4,160	4,440	5,270	4,330	4,900
FLAGPOLE, STRUCTURE MOUNTED									
Wall bracket included									
Vertical Type									
Tapered cone:									
6 m (20'), satin aluminum............	EA	3,100	3,100	3,320	3,090	3,300	3,930	3,230	3,650
6 m (20'), clear anodized aluminum	EA	3,470	3,460	3,730	3,480	3,710	4,410	3,620	4,090
6 m (20'), colour anodized aluminum	EA	3,670	3,680	3,960	3,680	3,940	4,680	3,850	4,310
Sectional, standard:									
6 m (20'), clear anodized aluminum	EA	2,500	2,530	2,700	2,510	2,690	3,200	2,630	2,950
6 m (20'), colour anodized aluminum	EA	3,470	3,460	3,730	3,480	3,710	4,410	3,620	4,090
11: EQUIPMENT									
11 13 00 Loading Dock Equipment									
11 13 16 Loading Dock Seals & Shelters									
DOCK BUMPERS									
INCLUDING FIXED BOLTS									
100 mm (4") projection, horizontal 250 mm (10") high:									
355 mm (14") wide............	EA	150.00	150.00	141.00	144.00	140.00	150.00	161.00	188.00
610 mm (24") wide............	EA	177.00	175.00	160.00	169.00	163.00	176.00	190.00	223.00
910 mm (36") wide............	EA	214.00	212.00	196.00	202.00	197.00	213.00	232.00	265.00
100 mm (4") projection, vertical 510 mm (20") high:									
280 mm (11") wide............	EA	178.00	176.00	163.00	170.00	166.00	179.00	192.00	225.00
140 mm (5 1/2") projection for use with door seals									
Vertical 510 mm (20") high:									
280 mm (11") wide............	EA	198.00	197.00	189.00	189.00	186.00	198.00	215.00	247.00
TRUCK DOOR SEALS, NORMAL DUTY									
For docks 2400 mm (8'-0") wide									
With fixed head and double neoprene seal:									
2400 mm (8'-0") high............	EA	1,400	1,550	1,540	1,440	1,490	1,630	1,570	1,680
3000 mm (10'-0") high............	EA	1,480	1,630	1,620	1,500	1,550	1,710	1,660	1,770
Additional costs:									
Extra for heavy duty door seals............	EA	595.00	659.00	657.00	610.00	636.00	694.00	668.00	714.00
RAIL DOCK SHELTERS, NORMAL DUTY									
Not exceeding 1500 mm (60") projection									
3 sides:									
Not exceeding 10 m² (100 sf)............	EA	2,940	2,390	2,270	2,740	2,520	2,860	3,140	2,360
Over 10 m² (100 sf) not exceeding 14 m² (150 sf)............	EA	3,320	2,690	2,510	3,110	2,880	3,210	3,500	2,670
4 sides:									
Not exceeding 10 m² (100 sf)............	EA	3,040	2,600	2,410	3,000	2,810	3,070	3,380	2,580
Over 10 m² (100 sf) not exceeding 14 m² (150 sf)............	EA	3,630	3,140	2,890	3,620	3,370	3,700	4,040	3,070
11 13 19 Stationary Loading Dock Equipment									
DOCK LEVELLERS									
Platform levellers									
Mechanical:									
Size 1800 mm x 1800 mm (6' x 6')............	EA	4,420	4,630	4,900	4,670	5,160	5,620	5,210	4,970
Size 1800 mm x 2400 mm (6' x 8')............	EA	4,830	5,050	5,350	5,120	5,630	6,130	5,700	5,430
Hydraulic:									
Size 1800 mm x 1800 mm (6' x 6')............	EA	6,800	6,600	7,180	7,070	7,350	8,200	7,680	7,280
Size 1800 mm x 2400 mm (6' x 8')............	EA	7,560	7,340	8,000	7,880	8,160	9,140	8,560	8,110

Item	UNITS	St. John's	Halifax	Montreal	Ottawa	Toronto	Winnipeg	Calgary	Vancouver
11 24 00 Maintenance Equipment									
11 24 23 Façade Access Equipment									
POWERED WINDOW WASHING EQUIPMENT									
Equipment									
Stage 6 m (20') long:									
2 point suspension, drop not exceeding 90 m (300')......	EA	78,100	75,700	75,000	78,500	76,900	80,800	83,700	82,400
4 point suspension, drop over 90 m (300')......	EA	99,500	96,400	95,700	100,000	97,900	103,000	106,000	105,000
Tracks									
Steel	m	531.00	510.00	495.00	609.00	618.00	572.00	626.00	556.00
11 53 00 Laboratory Equipment									
LABORATORY EQUIPMENT									
Fume hoods including 1500 mm (5') hood, base cabinet,									
counter top and basic fittings (motor and blower not included)									
Steel cabinet	m	10,400	10,400	10,400	10,400	11,000	10,300	10,500	12,600
LABORATORY FURNITURE									
Tables or counters 600 mm (24") wide									
Plastic	m	1,600	1,570	1,590	1,620	1,810	1,880	1,800	1,870
Resin impregnated stone	m	1,900	1,870	1,890	1,930	2,160	2,230	2,140	2,230
Stainless steel	m	2,150	2,130	2,280	2,220	2,460	2,280	2,320	2,170
Solid front storage units 2.1 m (7') high									
Plastic or wood	m	1,450	1,430	1,440	1,480	1,630	1,710	1,630	1,690
Stainless steel	m	2,380	2,350	2,510	2,440	2,720	2,500	2,540	2,390
Solid front wall storage units									
Plastic or wood	m	728.00	717.00	724.00	741.00	824.00	856.00	823.00	851.00
Stainless steel	m	1,470	1,460	1,590	1,520	1,700	1,560	1,600	1,480
Laboratory stools 760 mm (30") high									
Any type	EA	385.00	381.00	381.00	391.00	436.00	452.00	435.00	449.00
14: CONVEYING EQUIPMENT									
14 20 00 Elevators									
14 21 00 Electric Traction Elevators									
GEARED ELEVATOR EQUIPMENT									
(Cars and entrances included, new building, front opening only)									
Passenger elevator, maximum speed 100 m/min (350 fpm),									
capacity 1140 kg (2,500 lbs), stainless steel doors, machine									
overhead mounted, basic cost for average commercial building									
Single door from one side									
8 floors	EA	260,000	273,000	268,000	290,000	299,000	278,000	251,000	250,000
Centre biparting									
8 floors	EA	276,000	286,000	282,000	309,000	314,000	292,000	265,000	265,000
14 24 00 Hydraulic Elevators									
HYDRAULIC ELEVATOR EQUIPMENT									
(Cars and entrances included, new building, front opening only)									
Passenger elevator, Class A, maximum speed 50 m/min (150 fpm) 5 floors,									
capacity 900 kg (2,000 lbs), basic cost for average commercial building									
Single door from one side	EA	135,000	128,000	149,000	143,000	152,000	137,000	131,000	160,000
Centre biparting									
Basic prime coat finish	EA	141,000	138,000	159,000	152,000	161,000	150,000	143,000	172,000
Stainless steel	EA	142,000	136,000	156,000	150,000	159,000	146,000	138,000	172,000
Freight elevator, Class C, maximum speed 15 m/min (50 fpm),									
3 floors, capacity 4,500 kg (10,000 lbs), average cost	EA	270,000	265,000	278,000	289,000	299,000	307,000	268,000	271,000
14 30 00 Escalators and Moving Stairs									
14 31 00 Escalators									
ESCALATORS									
1200 mm (48") wide (tread width)									
4.6 m (15') rise:									
Inclined stainless steel balustrade	EA	271,000	249,000	284,000	302,000	304,000	325,000	269,000	389,000
Inclined glass balustrade	EA	264,000	245,000	278,000	294,000	299,000	318,000	265,000	380,000
14 32 00 Moving Walks									
MOVING RAMPS & WALKS									
Horizontal type (based on minimum length of 30 m (100'))									
900 mm (36") wide:									
Stainless steel balustrade	m	14,100	13,900	15,800	16,200	16,300	17,200	14,800	17,000
Standard glass balustrade	m	14,400	14,200	16,000	16,400	16,500	17,400	15,100	17,200
Inclined type, 4.9 (16') rise									
Glass or stainless steel panels:									
900 mm (36") wide	EA	683,000	667,000	751,000	777,000	781,000	829,000	715,000	822,000

Item	UNITS	St. John's	Halifax	Montreal	Ottawa	Toronto	Winnipeg	Calgary	Vancouver
14 90 00 Other Conveying Equipment									
14 91 00 Facility Chutes									
CHUTES									
Garbage and Linen chutes, including doors, sprinklers, sanitizing system and sound insulation, 3658 mm (12') floor height									
Aluminized steel:									
600 mm (24") dia., 1.219 mm (18 ga) thick, complete system	FLOOR	2,300	2,300	2,180	2,190	2,150	2,180	2,050	2,540
Stainless steel:									
600 mm (24") dia., 1.219 mm (18 ga) thick, complete system	FLOOR	4,180	4,190	3,930	4,240	4,160	4,190	3,890	4,740
Chute accessories									
Sanitizer	EA	321.00	322.00	298.00	325.00	318.00	318.00	298.00	364.00
14 92 00 Pneumatic Tube Systems									
PNEUMATIC TUBE SYSTEM									
Price per station, average 91 m (300') apart, 2 zones and up									
fully automatic system controlled:									
100 mm (4") dia.	EA	35,000	35,000	35,000	35,700	29,800	41,200	37,500	34,800
150 mm (6") dia.	EA	44,700	44,700	44,000	45,600	37,900	51,700	48,000	43,900
21: FIRE SUPPRESSION									
21 11 00 Facility Fire-Suppression Water-Service Piping									
SPECIALTIES									
Siamese pumper connection:									
100 mm x 65 mm (4" x 2 1/2")	EA	1,390	1,280	1,300	1,320	1,310	1,410	1,350	1,410
Check valve, 100 mm (4") dia.	EA	951.00	875.00	888.00	906.00	897.00	964.00	924.00	969.00
Double gate and check valves, assembly with bronze trimmings:									
100 mm (4") dia.	EA	11,900	10,900	11,100	11,300	11,200	12,000	11,500	12,100
21 12 00 Fire-Suppression Standpipes									
STANDPIPE & FIRE HOSE EQUIPMENT									
Cabinets, c/w glass panel, valve, hose, rack and ABC fire extinguisher									
Surface mounted	EA	1,630	1,500	1,520	1,560	1,540	1,660	1,590	1,660
Recessed	EA	1,660	1,530	1,550	1,590	1,570	1,690	1,620	1,700
Recessed, stainless steel	EA	2,340	2,150	2,190	2,230	2,210	2,380	2,280	2,390
21 13 00 Fire-Suppression Sprinkler Systems									
SPRINKLERS									
Systems priced per head including all required piping,									
accessories and equipment for a complete system									
Sprinkler heads 1 per 9.3 m² (100 sf)	EA	261.00	240.00	244.00	248.00	246.00	264.00	253.00	266.00
Sprinkler heads 1 per 13.9 m² (150 sf)	EA	285.00	262.00	266.00	272.00	269.00	289.00	277.00	291.00
21 20 00 Fire-Extinguishing Systems									
CARBON DIOXIDE EQUIPMENT									
Extinguishing systems									
Kitchen hood extinguishing system including carbon dioxide cylinder, distribution piping and 2 heads	EA	7,230	6,650	6,750	6,890	6,820	7,330	7,020	7,370
Extinguishers									
5 kg (10 lbs) capacity with wall bracket	EA	541.00	497.00	505.00	515.00	510.00	548.00	525.00	551.00
PRESSURIZED EXTINGUISHERS & FIRE BLANKETS									
Pressurized extinguishers									
Water extinguisher, 11 l (2.5 gal) capacity with wall bracket	EA	252.00	232.00	236.00	240.00	238.00	256.00	245.00	257.00
Fire blankets									
Size 1830 mm x 1830 mm (72" x 72")	EA	245.00	225.00	229.00	233.00	231.00	248.00	238.00	249.00
21 30 00 Fire Pumps									
Fire pump, electric driven, c/w jockey pump and controller									
16 l/s (250 GPM)	EA	77,400	71,200	72,300	73,700	73,000	78,500	75,200	78,800
32 l/s (500 GPM)	EA	90,300	83,100	84,300	86,100	85,200	91,600	87,800	92,000
63 l/s (1000 GPM)	EA	102,000	93,600	95,000	97,000	96,000	103,000	98,900	104,000
95 l/s (1500 GPM)	EA	123,000	113,000	115,000	117,000	116,000	125,000	119,000	125,000
Fire pump, diesel driven, c/w jockey pump and controller									
16 l/s (250 GPM)	EA	87,100	80,100	81,400	83,000	82,200	88,400	84,700	88,800
32 l/s (500 GPM)	EA	98,200	90,300	91,700	93,500	92,600	99,500	95,400	100,000
63 l/s (1000 GPM)	EA	104,000	95,500	96,900	98,900	97,900	105,000	101,000	106,000
95 l/s (1500 GPM)	EA	120,000	110,000	112,000	114,000	113,000	121,000	116,000	122,000

Item	UNITS	St. John's	Halifax	Montreal	Ottawa	Toronto	Winnipeg	Calgary	Vancouver
22: PLUMBING									
22 05 00 Common Work Results for Plumbing									
VALVES, BRONZE									
VALVES AND COCKS (manual)									
Gate valves									
Bronze 1380 kPa (200 psi) water or 860 kPa (125 psi) steam									
pressure, screwed or soldered:									
12 mm (1/2")	EA	124.00	114.00	116.00	118.00	117.00	126.00	121.00	126.00
20 mm (3/4")	EA	154.00	141.00	144.00	146.00	145.00	156.00	149.00	157.00
25 mm (1")	EA	186.00	171.00	173.00	177.00	175.00	188.00	180.00	189.00
32 mm (1 1/4")	EA	239.00	219.00	223.00	227.00	225.00	242.00	232.00	243.00
38 mm (1 1/2")	EA	286.00	263.00	267.00	273.00	270.00	290.00	278.00	292.00
50 mm (2")	EA	324.00	298.00	303.00	309.00	306.00	329.00	315.00	330.00
I.b.b.m. Outside screw and yoke:									
1380 kPa (200 psi) water or 860 kPa (125 psi) steam pressure,									
flanged:									
65 mm (2 1/2")	EA	822.00	756.00	767.00	783.00	775.00	833.00	798.00	837.00
75 mm (3")	EA	914.00	840.00	853.00	871.00	862.00	927.00	888.00	931.00
100 mm (4")	EA	1,340	1,230	1,250	1,270	1,260	1,350	1,300	1,360
150 mm (6")	EA	2,150	1,980	2,010	2,050	2,030	2,180	2,090	2,190
200 mm (8")	EA	3,510	3,230	3,280	3,340	3,310	3,560	3,410	3,570
Globe valves									
Bronze 2070 kPa (300 psi) water or 1035 kPa (150 psi) steam									
pressure, screwed or soldered:									
12 mm (1/2")	EA	157.00	144.00	147.00	149.00	148.00	159.00	152.00	160.00
20 mm (3/4")	EA	180.00	166.00	168.00	172.00	170.00	183.00	175.00	184.00
25 mm (1")	EA	264.00	243.00	247.00	251.00	249.00	268.00	256.00	269.00
32 mm (1 1/4")	EA	395.00	364.00	369.00	377.00	373.00	401.00	384.00	403.00
38 mm (1 1/2")	EA	424.00	390.00	396.00	404.00	400.00	430.00	412.00	432.00
50 mm (2")	EA	594.00	546.00	554.00	566.00	560.00	602.00	577.00	605.00
I.b.b.m. Outside screw and yoke:									
1380 kPa (200 psi) water or 860 kPa (125 psi) steam pressure,									
flanged:									
65 mm (2 1/2")	EA	961.00	884.00	898.00	916.00	907.00	975.00	934.00	980.00
75 mm (3")	EA	1,080	995.00	1,010	1,030	1,020	1,100	1,050	1,100
100 mm (4")	EA	1,690	1,550	1,570	1,610	1,590	1,710	1,640	1,720
150 mm (6")	EA	2,780	2,550	2,590	2,650	2,620	2,820	2,700	2,830
200 mm (8")	EA	4,660	4,290	4,360	4,440	4,400	4,730	4,530	4,750
Swing check valves									
Bronze 2070 kPa (300 psi) water or 1035 kPa (150 psi) steam									
pressure, screwed or soldered:									
12 mm (1/2")	EA	110.00	101.00	103.00	105.00	104.00	112.00	107.00	112.00
20 mm (3/4")	EA	136.00	125.00	127.00	129.00	128.00	138.00	132.00	138.00
25 mm (1")	EA	180.00	166.00	168.00	172.00	170.00	183.00	175.00	184.00
32 mm (1 1/4")	EA	224.00	206.00	209.00	213.00	211.00	227.00	217.00	228.00
38 mm (1 1/2")	EA	286.00	263.00	267.00	273.00	270.00	290.00	278.00	292.00
50 mm (2")	EA	401.00	369.00	374.00	382.00	378.00	406.00	389.00	408.00
I.b.b.m. 1380 kPa (200 psi) water or 860 kPa (125 psi) steam									
pressure, flanged:									
65 mm (2 1/2")	EA	670.00	616.00	626.00	638.00	632.00	679.00	651.00	683.00
75 mm (3")	EA	747.00	687.00	698.00	712.00	705.00	758.00	726.00	761.00
100 mm (4")	EA	1,160	1,060	1,080	1,100	1,090	1,170	1,120	1,180
150 mm (6")	EA	2,070	1,900	1,930	1,970	1,950	2,100	2,010	2,110
200 mm (8")	EA	3,490	3,210	3,260	3,320	3,290	3,540	3,390	3,550
Ball valves									
Bronze 4140 kPa (600 psi) water pressure, screwed or soldered:									
12 mm (1/2")	EA	50.00	46.00	46.70	47.70	47.20	50.70	48.60	51.00
20 mm (3/4")	EA	68.40	62.90	63.90	65.10	64.50	69.30	66.40	69.70
25 mm (1")	EA	90.70	83.50	84.70	86.50	85.60	92.00	88.20	92.40
32 mm (1 1/4")	EA	125.00	115.00	117.00	119.00	118.00	127.00	122.00	127.00
38 mm (1 1/2")	EA	149.00	137.00	140.00	142.00	141.00	152.00	145.00	152.00
50 mm (2")	EA	210.00	193.00	196.00	200.00	198.00	213.00	204.00	214.00
Butterfly valves									
Bronze disc, wafer type, buna seat:									
65 mm (2 1/2")	EA	582.00	535.00	544.00	554.00	549.00	590.00	565.00	593.00
75 mm (3")	EA	603.00	555.00	563.00	575.00	569.00	612.00	586.00	615.00
100 mm (4")	EA	670.00	616.00	626.00	638.00	632.00	679.00	651.00	683.00
150 mm (6")	EA	822.00	756.00	767.00	783.00	775.00	833.00	798.00	837.00
200 mm (8")	EA	1,140	1,050	1,070	1,090	1,080	1,160	1,110	1,170
WATER METER ASSEMBLY									
Including communication register c/w by-pass									
Sealed register meter, positive displacement type									
25 mm (1") pipe size	EA	1,690	1,550	1,570	1,610	1,590	1,710	1,640	1,720
50 mm (2") pipe size	EA	3,750	3,450	3,500	3,580	3,540	3,810	3,650	3,820
Compound water meter									
75 mm (3") pipe size	EA	11,100	10,200	10,400	10,600	10,500	11,300	10,800	11,300
Turbine type water meter, c/w integral strainer and test outlet									
100 mm (4") pipe size	EA	12,900	11,900	12,100	12,300	12,200	13,100	12,600	13,200
150 mm (6") pipe size	EA	25,400	23,400	23,800	24,200	24,000	25,800	24,700	25,900
200 mm (8") pipe size	EA	34,700	31,900	32,400	33,000	32,700	35,200	33,700	35,300

Item	UNITS	St. John's	Halifax	Montreal	Ottawa	Toronto	Winnipeg	Calgary	Vancouver
22 07 00 Plumbing Insulation									
PIPE INSULATION									
Glass fibre, factory jacket									
12 mm (1/2") thick:									
12 mm (1/2")	m	20.10	18.50	18.80	19.20	19.00	20.40	19.60	20.50
20 mm (3/4")	m	21.70	20.00	20.30	20.70	20.50	22.00	21.10	22.10
25 mm (1")	m	22.20	20.40	20.70	21.10	20.90	22.50	21.50	22.60
32 mm (1 1/4")	m	23.00	21.20	21.50	21.90	21.70	23.30	22.40	23.40
38 mm (1 1/2")	m	25.20	23.20	23.60	24.00	23.80	25.60	24.50	25.70
50 mm (2")	m	26.50	24.40	24.80	25.30	25.00	26.90	25.80	27.00
65 mm (2 1/2")	m	27.50	25.30	25.60	26.20	25.90	27.80	26.70	28.00
75 mm (3")	m	29.70	27.30	27.70	28.30	28.00	30.10	28.80	30.20
100 mm (4")	m	0.02	0.02	0.02	0.02	0.02	0.02	0.02	0.02
125 mm (5")	m	0.02	0.02	0.02	0.02	0.02	0.02	0.02	0.02
150 mm (6")	m	0.02	0.02	0.02	0.02	0.02	0.02	0.02	0.02
25 mm (1") thick:									
12 mm (1/2")	m	23.00	21.20	21.50	21.90	21.70	23.30	22.40	23.40
20 mm (3/4")	m	24.40	22.40	22.80	23.20	23.00	24.70	23.70	24.80
25 mm (1")	m	25.40	23.40	23.80	24.20	24.00	25.80	24.70	25.90
32 mm (1 1/4")	m	26.80	24.70	25.00	25.60	25.30	27.20	26.10	27.30
38 mm (1 1/2")	m	28.30	26.00	26.40	27.00	26.70	28.70	27.50	28.80
50 mm (2")	m	30.00	27.60	28.00	28.60	28.30	30.40	29.10	30.60
65 mm (2 1/2")	m	33.00	30.30	30.80	31.40	31.10	33.40	32.00	33.60
75 mm (3")	m	34.80	32.00	32.50	33.10	32.80	35.30	33.80	35.40
100 mm (4")	m	43.50	40.00	40.60	41.40	41.00	44.10	42.20	44.30
125 mm (5")	m	54.40	50.00	50.80	51.80	51.30	55.10	52.80	55.40
150 mm (6")	m	54.70	50.30	51.10	52.10	51.60	55.50	53.10	55.70
200 mm (8")	m	66.50	61.10	62.10	63.30	62.70	67.40	64.60	67.70
250 mm (10")	m	75.40	69.30	70.40	71.80	71.10	76.40	73.20	76.80
300 mm (12")	m	95.00	87.40	88.70	90.50	89.60	96.30	92.30	96.80
COVER FOR PIPE INSULATION									
200 g/m² (6 oz.) canvas									
12 mm (1/2")	m	19.10	17.60	17.80	18.20	18.00	19.40	18.50	19.40
20 mm (3/4")	m	19.50	17.90	18.20	18.60	18.40	19.80	19.00	19.90
25 mm (1")	m	19.70	18.10	18.40	18.80	18.60	20.00	19.20	20.10
32 mm (1 1/4")	m	19.90	18.30	18.60	19.00	18.80	20.20	19.40	20.30
38 mm (1 1/2")	m	20.20	18.60	18.90	19.30	19.10	20.50	19.70	20.60
50 mm (2")	m	21.00	19.30	19.60	20.00	19.80	21.30	20.40	21.40
65 mm (2 1/2")	m	22.40	20.60	20.90	21.30	21.10	22.70	21.70	22.80
75 mm (3")	m	23.60	21.70	22.10	22.50	22.30	24.00	23.00	24.10
100 mm (4")	m	24.60	22.60	23.00	23.40	23.20	24.90	23.90	25.10
125 mm (5")	m	26.20	24.10	24.50	24.90	24.70	26.60	25.40	26.70
150 mm (6")	m	29.80	27.40	27.80	28.40	28.10	30.20	28.90	30.30
200 mm (8")	m	32.60	30.00	30.50	31.10	30.80	33.10	31.70	33.30
250 mm (10")	m	36.90	33.90	34.50	35.10	34.80	37.40	35.80	37.60
300 mm (12")	m	38.60	35.50	36.00	36.80	36.40	39.10	37.50	39.30
22 10 00 Plumbing Piping									
PIPE, COPPER									
Copper pressure piping, based on 3 m (10') of pipe, including									
one pipe support, and solder									
Type m:									
12 mm (1/2")	m	44.80	41.20	41.90	42.70	42.30	45.50	43.60	45.70
20 mm (3/4")	m	52.90	48.70	49.40	50.40	49.90	53.60	51.40	53.90
25 mm (1")	m	63.80	58.70	59.60	60.80	60.20	64.70	62.00	65.00
32 mm (1 1/4")	m	81.80	75.30	76.40	78.00	77.20	83.00	79.50	83.40
38 mm (1 1/2")	m	101.00	93.30	94.70	96.70	95.70	103.00	98.60	103.00
50 mm (2")	m	151.00	138.00	141.00	143.00	142.00	153.00	146.00	153.00
65 mm (2 1/2")	m	209.00	192.00	195.00	199.00	197.00	212.00	203.00	213.00
75 mm (3")	m	263.00	242.00	246.00	250.00	248.00	267.00	255.00	268.00
Type l:									
12 mm (1/2")	m	49.90	45.90	46.60	47.60	47.10	50.60	48.50	50.90
20 mm (3/4")	m	60.60	55.80	56.60	57.80	57.20	61.50	58.90	61.80
25 mm (1")	m	76.40	70.30	71.40	72.80	72.10	77.50	74.30	77.90
32 mm (1 1/4")	m	93.40	85.90	87.20	89.00	88.10	94.70	90.70	95.10
38 mm (1 1/2")	m	112.00	103.00	105.00	107.00	106.00	114.00	109.00	114.00
50 mm (2")	m	166.00	153.00	155.00	159.00	157.00	169.00	162.00	170.00
65 mm (2 1/2")	m	233.00	215.00	218.00	222.00	220.00	237.00	227.00	238.00
75 mm (3")	m	298.00	274.00	278.00	284.00	281.00	302.00	289.00	303.00
Type k:									
12 mm (1/2")	m	56.70	52.20	53.00	54.00	53.50	57.50	55.10	57.80
20 mm (3/4")	m	78.00	71.80	72.90	74.30	73.60	79.10	75.80	79.50
25 mm (1")	m	94.60	87.00	88.30	90.10	89.20	95.90	91.90	96.30
32 mm (1 1/4")	m	112.00	103.00	105.00	107.00	106.00	114.00	109.00	114.00
38 mm (1 1/2")	m	137.00	126.00	128.00	130.00	129.00	139.00	133.00	139.00
50 mm (2")	m	196.00	180.00	183.00	187.00	185.00	199.00	191.00	200.00
65 mm (2 1/2")	m	272.00	251.00	254.00	260.00	257.00	276.00	265.00	278.00
75 mm (3")	m	358.00	330.00	335.00	341.00	338.00	363.00	348.00	365.00

Item	UNITS	St. John's	Halifax	Montreal	Ottawa	Toronto	Winnipeg	Calgary	Vancouver
22 13 00 Facility Sanitary Sewerage									
Copper drainage piping, based on 3 m (10') of pipe, including									
one support, and solder									
Drainage waste and vent:									
32 mm (1 1/4")	m	69.20	63.70	64.60	66.00	65.30	70.20	67.30	70.50
38 mm (1 1/2")	m	77.70	71.50	72.60	74.00	73.30	78.80	75.50	79.20
50 mm (2")	m	100.00	92.40	93.90	95.70	94.80	102.00	97.60	102.00
75 mm (3")	m	142.00	131.00	133.00	135.00	134.00	144.00	138.00	145.00
PIPE, CAST IRON									
Cast iron drainage piping, based on 3 m (10') of pipe, including,									
one support and jointing material									
Hub and spigot:									
75 mm (3")	m	107.00	98.50	100.00	102.00	101.00	109.00	104.00	109.00
100 mm (4")	m	131.00	121.00	123.00	125.00	124.00	133.00	128.00	134.00
150 mm (6")	m	207.00	190.00	193.00	197.00	195.00	210.00	201.00	211.00
200 mm (8")	m	304.00	280.00	284.00	290.00	287.00	309.00	296.00	310.00
250 mm (10")	m	448.00	412.00	419.00	427.00	423.00	455.00	436.00	457.00
300 mm (12")	m	541.00	497.00	505.00	515.00	510.00	548.00	525.00	551.00
Mechanical joint:									
75 mm (3")	m	89.10	82.00	83.30	84.90	84.10	90.40	86.60	90.80
100 mm (4")	m	107.00	98.50	100.00	102.00	101.00	109.00	104.00	109.00
150 mm (6")	m	161.00	148.00	150.00	154.00	152.00	163.00	157.00	164.00
200 mm (8")	m	241.00	221.00	225.00	229.00	227.00	244.00	234.00	245.00
250 mm (10")	m	354.00	326.00	331.00	337.00	334.00	359.00	344.00	361.00
PIPE, PLASTIC									
Plastic drainage piping, based on 3 m (10') of pipe, including									
one support and jointing material									
ABS drainage waste and vent:									
32 mm (1 1/4")	m	50.50	46.40	47.10	48.10	47.60	51.20	49.00	51.40
38 mm (1 1/2")	m	50.20	46.20	46.90	47.90	47.40	51.00	48.80	51.20
50 mm (2")	m	56.70	52.20	53.00	54.00	53.50	57.50	55.10	57.80
75 mm (3")	m	87.70	80.60	81.90	83.50	82.70	88.90	85.20	89.30
22 13 19 Sanitary Waste Piping Specialties									
TRAPS									
Trap primer including 7.5 m (25') type I, 12 mm (1/2") copper									
pressure pipe									
Bronze, 12 mm (1/2") dia.	EA	642.00	591.00	600.00	612.00	606.00	651.00	624.00	654.00
DRAINS									
Floor drain including 3 m of connecting drainage pipe									
Cast iron body, nickel bronze top:									
50 mm (2")	EA	531.00	488.00	496.00	506.00	501.00	539.00	516.00	541.00
75 mm (3")	EA	585.00	538.00	546.00	558.00	552.00	593.00	569.00	596.00
100 mm (4")	EA	669.00	615.00	625.00	637.00	631.00	678.00	650.00	681.00
Funnel type, cast iron body, polished brass top:									
50 mm (2")	EA	673.00	619.00	629.00	641.00	635.00	683.00	654.00	686.00
75 mm (3")	EA	728.00	670.00	680.00	694.00	687.00	739.00	708.00	742.00
100 mm (4")	EA	812.00	747.00	758.00	774.00	766.00	823.00	789.00	827.00
GRATE & FRAME									
Trench grating									
Medium duty golden duct alloy grate and frame:									
150 mm (6")	m	516.00	475.00	482.00	492.00	487.00	524.00	502.00	526.00
300 mm (12")	m	817.00	752.00	763.00	779.00	771.00	829.00	794.00	833.00
375 mm (15")	m	849.00	781.00	793.00	809.00	801.00	861.00	825.00	865.00
Heavy duty golden duct alloy grate and frame:									
300 mm (12")	m	795.00	731.00	743.00	758.00	750.00	806.00	773.00	810.00
Extra heavy duty golden duct alloy grate and frame:									
225 mm (9")	m	858.00	789.00	801.00	817.00	809.00	870.00	833.00	874.00
450 mm (18")	m	1,540	1,410	1,440	1,460	1,450	1,560	1,490	1,570
Roof drains including 3 m (10') of connecting drainage pipe									
Cast iron body with underdeck clamp:									
50 mm (2")	EA	642.00	591.00	600.00	612.00	606.00	651.00	624.00	654.00
75 mm (3")	EA	697.00	642.00	651.00	665.00	658.00	707.00	678.00	711.00
100 mm (4")	EA	782.00	720.00	731.00	745.00	738.00	793.00	760.00	797.00
150 mm (6")	EA	867.00	798.00	810.00	826.00	818.00	879.00	843.00	883.00
Cast iron body meter flow with underdeck clamp:									
50 mm (2")	EA	734.00	675.00	685.00	699.00	692.00	744.00	713.00	747.00
75 mm (3")	EA	823.00	757.00	768.00	784.00	776.00	834.00	799.00	838.00
100 mm (4")	EA	851.00	783.00	795.00	811.00	803.00	863.00	827.00	867.00
150 mm (6")	EA	1,110	1,020	1,040	1,060	1,050	1,130	1,080	1,130
CLEANOUTS									
Cleanouts									
Galvanized with cut-off caulking, ferrule and nickel bronze cover:									
50 mm (2")	EA	318.00	293.00	297.00	303.00	300.00	323.00	309.00	324.00
75 mm (3")	EA	348.00	320.00	325.00	331.00	328.00	353.00	338.00	354.00
100 mm (4")	EA	400.00	368.00	373.00	381.00	377.00	405.00	388.00	407.00
150 mm (6")	EA	734.00	675.00	685.00	699.00	692.00	744.00	713.00	747.00

Item	UNITS	St. John's	Halifax	Montreal	Ottawa	Toronto	Winnipeg	Calgary	Vancouver
22 31 00 Domestic Water Softeners									
WATER SOFTENER									
Water softeners (according to grain capacity)									
Semi-automatic									
20,000	EA	1,380	1,270	1,290	1,310	1,300	1,400	1,340	1,400
Fully automatic									
20,000	EA	1,740	1,600	1,620	1,660	1,640	1,760	1,690	1,770
30,000	EA	1,790	1,650	1,670	1,710	1,690	1,820	1,740	1,830
40,000	EA	1,970	1,810	1,840	1,880	1,860	2,000	1,920	2,010
60,000	EA	2,120	1,950	1,980	2,020	2,000	2,150	2,060	2,160
105,000	EA	3,360	3,090	3,140	3,200	3,170	3,410	3,270	3,420
22 33 00 Electric Domestic Water Heaters									
WATER HEATERS									
Hot water storage heaters, no wiring or plumbing included.									
Electric:									
55 l (12 imp. gals.)	EA	1,060	975	990	1,010	1,000	1,080	1,030	1,080
100 l (22.1 imp. gals.)	EA	1,070	985	1,000	1,020	1,010	1,090	1,040	1,090
136 l (30 imp. gals.)	EA	1,070	985	1,000	1,020	1,010	1,090	1,040	1,090
182 l (40 imp. gals.)	EA	1,130	1,040	1,060	1,080	1,070	1,150	1,100	1,160
273 l (60 imp. gals.)	EA	1,310	1,210	1,230	1,250	1,240	1,330	1,280	1,340
22 34 00 Fuel-Fired Domestic Water Heaters									
WATER HEATERS									
Hot water storage heaters, no wiring or plumbing included.									
Fuel fired:									
114 l (25.0 imp. gals.)	EA	1,330	1,220	1,240	1,260	1,250	1,340	1,290	1,350
151 l (33.3 imp. gals.)	EA	1,460	1,350	1,370	1,390	1,380	1,480	1,420	1,490
189 l (41.6 imp. gals.)	EA	1,830	1,690	1,710	1,750	1,730	1,860	1,780	1,870
22 40 00 Plumbing Fixtures									
Including plumbing brass and 4500 mm (15') of connecting pipe for each service, carrier not included.									
WATER CLOSETS									
Vitreous china water closets									
Floor mounted:									
One-piece closet, combination	EA	2,300	2,120	2,150	2,190	2,170	2,330	2,240	2,340
With tank, regular rim	EA	1,620	1,490	1,510	1,550	1,530	1,640	1,580	1,650
With tank, elongated rim	EA	1,690	1,550	1,570	1,610	1,590	1,710	1,640	1,720
With flush valve, elongated rim	EA	2,100	1,930	1,960	2,000	1,980	2,130	2,040	2,140
Wall mounted:									
With tank, regular rim	EA	1,870	1,720	1,740	1,780	1,760	1,890	1,810	1,900
With flush valve, elongated rim	EA	2,190	2,020	2,050	2,090	2,070	2,230	2,130	2,240
Shower mixing valves									
Thermostatic control	EA	616.00	566.00	575.00	587.00	581.00	625.00	598.00	627.00
URINALS									
Vitreous china urinals									
Floor mounted:									
With tank	EA	2,760	2,540	2,570	2,630	2,600	2,800	2,680	2,810
With flush valve	EA	2,410	2,210	2,250	2,290	2,270	2,440	2,340	2,450
Wall mounted:									
With tank	EA	2,600	2,390	2,430	2,470	2,450	2,630	2,520	2,650
With flush valve	EA	2,330	2,150	2,180	2,220	2,200	2,370	2,270	2,380
LAVATORIES									
Lavatories									
Vitreous china:									
Wall hung, 510 mm x 460 mm (20" x 18")	EA	1,710	1,570	1,590	1,630	1,610	1,730	1,660	1,740
Countertop, 530 mm x 480 mm (21" x 19")	EA	1,710	1,570	1,590	1,630	1,610	1,730	1,660	1,740
Countertop, 480 mm x 410 mm (19" x 16"), oval	EA	1,690	1,550	1,570	1,610	1,590	1,710	1,640	1,720
Cast iron enamelled:									
Wall hung, 480 mm x 430 mm (19" x 17")	EA	2,020	1,860	1,890	1,930	1,910	2,050	1,970	2,060
Countertop, 530 mm x 430 mm (21" x 17")	EA	1,890	1,740	1,760	1,800	1,780	1,910	1,830	1,920
Steel enamelled:									
Countertop, 530 mm x 430 mm (21" x 17")	EA	1,730	1,590	1,610	1,650	1,630	1,750	1,680	1,760
Countertop, 460 mm (18") dia.	EA	1,730	1,590	1,610	1,650	1,630	1,750	1,680	1,760
SINKS									
Kitchen sinks									
Stainless steel:									
Single bowl, 510 mm x 520 mm x 180 mm (20" x 20 1/2" x 7")	EA	1,630	1,500	1,520	1,560	1,540	1,660	1,590	1,660
Double bowl, 520 mm x 790 mm x 180 mm (20 1/2" x 31" x 7")	EA	1,820	1,680	1,700	1,740	1,720	1,850	1,770	1,860
Service sinks									
Cast iron enamelled:									
Wall hung, 560 mm x 460 mm (22" x 18")	EA	3,980	3,660	3,710	3,790	3,750	4,030	3,860	4,050
Mop receptor, floor type:									
560 mm x 460 mm (22" x 18")	EA	3,590	3,310	3,360	3,420	3,390	3,640	3,490	3,660

Item	UNITS	St. John's	Halifax	Montreal	Ottawa	Toronto	Winnipeg	Calgary	Vancouver
LAUNDRY SINKS									
Laundry sinks and trays									
Steel enamelled sinks:									
Single bowl, 610 mm x 530 mm (24" x 21")	EA	1,730	1,590	1,610	1,650	1,630	1,750	1,680	1,760
Double bowl, 810 mm x 530 mm (32" x 21")	EA	2,020	1,860	1,890	1,930	1,910	2,050	1,970	2,060
Single compartment, 560 mm x 560 mm (22" x 22")	EA	1,860	1,710	1,730	1,770	1,750	1,880	1,800	1,890
Double compartment, 1130 mm x 560 mm (44 1/2" x 22")	EA	2,240	2,060	2,090	2,130	2,110	2,270	2,170	2,280
BATHS									
Bathtubs									
Cast iron enamelled, recessed:									
1500 mm (5') long	EA	4,650	4,280	4,350	4,430	4,390	4,720	4,520	4,740
Steel enamelled, recessed:									
1500 mm (5') long	EA	3,080	2,840	2,880	2,940	2,910	3,130	3,000	3,140
Fibreglass, one piece with sidewalls:									
1500 mm (5') long	EA	4,240	3,900	3,960	4,040	4,000	4,300	4,120	4,320
SHOWERS									
Showers									
Shower head and pressure balancing valve	EA	1,140	1,050	1,070	1,090	1,080	1,160	1,110	1,170
Prefabricated shower, medium duty valve, rod and curtain	EA	2,590	2,380	2,420	2,460	2,440	2,620	2,510	2,640
Prefabricated shower, medium duty valve and door	EA	2,980	2,740	2,780	2,840	2,810	3,020	2,890	3,030
CARRIERS/SUPPORTS									
Fixture chair carriers									
Lavatory	EA	324.00	298.00	303.00	309.00	306.00	329.00	315.00	330.00
Water closet	EA	530.00	488.00	495.00	505.00	500.00	538.00	515.00	540.00
Urinal	EA	276.00	254.00	257.00	263.00	260.00	280.00	268.00	281.00
HYDRANTS									
Wall hydrants non-freeze type 20 mm (3/4") dia., 300 mm (12")									
wall including 4500 mm (15') of connecting pipe									
Exposed	EA	778.00	716.00	727.00	741.00	734.00	789.00	756.00	793.00
Concealed	EA	969.00	891.00	905.00	923.00	914.00	983.00	941.00	987.00

22 47 00 Drinking Fountains and Water Coolers

Based on stainless steel fixture including plumbing brass and 4500 mm (15') of connecting pipe for each service, carrier not incl.

Item	UNITS	St. John's	Halifax	Montreal	Ottawa	Toronto	Winnipeg	Calgary	Vancouver
DRINKING FOUNTAIN									
Non-refrigerated drinking fountains:									
Wall hung, basic unit	EA	1,880	1,730	1,750	1,790	1,770	1,900	1,820	1,910
Wall hung, hi-lo dual unit	EA	3,950	3,640	3,690	3,770	3,730	4,010	3,840	4,030
Refrigerated drinking fountains:									
Wall hung, basic unit	EA	3,980	3,660	3,710	3,790	3,750	4,030	3,860	4,050
Wall hung, hi-lo dual unit	EA	5,460	5,020	5,100	5,200	5,150	5,540	5,300	5,560

22 66 00 Chemical-Waste Systems for Laboratory and Healthcare Facilities

PIPE, GLASS

Glass drainage piping, based on 3 m (10') of pipe, including pipe supports and jointing material

Item	UNITS	St. John's	Halifax	Montreal	Ottawa	Toronto	Winnipeg	Calgary	Vancouver
Glass pipe:									
38 mm (1 1/2")	m	124.00	114.00	116.00	118.00	117.00	126.00	121.00	126.00
50 mm (2")	m	155.00	142.00	145.00	147.00	146.00	157.00	150.00	158.00
75 mm (3")	m	208.00	191.00	194.00	198.00	196.00	211.00	202.00	212.00
100 mm (4")	m	339.00	312.00	317.00	323.00	320.00	344.00	330.00	346.00
150 mm (6")	m	573.00	527.00	536.00	546.00	541.00	582.00	557.00	584.00

23: HEATING, VENTILATING, & AIR CONDITIONING

23 07 00 HVAC Insulation

DUCTWORK INSULATION

Internal

Item	UNITS	St. John's	Halifax	Montreal	Ottawa	Toronto	Winnipeg	Calgary	Vancouver
Glass fibre acoustic lining:									
12 mm (1/2")	m²	50.90	46.80	47.50	48.50	48.00	51.60	49.40	51.80
25 mm (1")	m²	57.20	52.70	53.50	54.50	54.00	58.10	55.60	58.30
External									
Glass fibre thermal flexible:									
25 mm (1")	m²	49.80	45.80	46.50	47.50	47.00	50.50	48.40	50.80
50 mm (2")	m²	60.00	55.20	56.00	57.20	56.60	60.80	58.30	61.10
Glass fibre thermal rigid, c/w canvas jacket:									
25 mm (1")	m²	82.00	75.50	76.60	78.20	77.40	83.20	79.70	83.60
50 mm (2")	m²	95.70	88.00	89.40	91.20	90.30	97.10	93.00	97.50

Item	UNITS	St. John's	Halifax	Montreal	Ottawa	Toronto	Winnipeg	Calgary	Vancouver
23 10 00 Facility Fuel Systems									
UNDERGROUND STORAGE TANKS									
Oil storage tanks									
Underground steel tank including hold-down straps, anchors, saddles									
excavation, bedding and backfilling									
Small/domestic									
1,100 l (250 gals.)	EA	4,260	3,920	3,980	4,060	4,020	4,320	4,140	4,340
2,200 l (500 gals.)	EA	6,430	5,920	6,010	6,130	6,070	6,530	6,250	6,560
Large/commercial									
4,400 l (1,000 gals.)	EA	9,650	8,870	9,010	9,190	9,100	9,780	9,370	9,830
10,000 l (2,200 gals.)	EA	15,100	13,800	14,100	14,300	14,200	15,300	14,600	15,300
25,000 l (5,500 gals.)	EA	42,600	39,200	39,800	40,600	40,200	43,200	41,400	43,400
50,000 l (11,000 gals.)	EA	67,800	62,400	63,400	64,600	64,000	68,800	65,900	69,100
910 mm (36") access sleeve to grade with 610 mm (24") manhole	EA	7,590	6,980	7,090	7,230	7,160	7,700	7,370	7,730
23 21 13 Hydronic Piping									
PIPE, STEEL									
Galvanized steel pressure piping, based on 3 m (10') of pipe									
for screwed piping and 6 m (20') of pipe for flanged piping,									
including pipe support, and jointing material									
Schedule 40, screwed:									
12 mm (1/2")	m	72.20	66.40	67.40	68.80	68.10	73.20	70.10	73.50
20 mm (3/4")	m	81.00	74.50	75.60	77.20	76.40	82.10	78.70	82.50
25 mm (1")	m	101.00	92.60	94.10	96.00	95.00	102.00	97.90	103.00
32 mm (1 1/4")	m	118.00	108.00	110.00	112.00	111.00	119.00	114.00	120.00
38 mm (1 1/2")	m	136.00	125.00	127.00	129.00	128.00	138.00	132.00	138.00
50 mm (2")	m	177.00	163.00	165.00	169.00	167.00	180.00	172.00	180.00
Black steel pressure piping, based on 3 m (10') for screwed									
piping and 6m (20') of pipe for welded piping including									
pipe support, and jointing material									
Schedule 40, screwed:									
12 mm (1/2")	m	60.30	55.50	56.30	57.50	56.90	61.20	58.60	61.50
20 mm (3/4")	m	67.00	61.60	62.60	63.80	63.20	67.90	65.10	68.30
25 mm (1")	m	81.50	75.00	76.10	77.70	76.90	82.70	79.20	83.10
32 mm (1 1/4")	m	94.10	86.60	87.90	89.70	88.80	95.50	91.50	95.90
38 mm (1 1/2")	m	107.00	98.50	100.00	102.00	101.00	109.00	104.00	109.00
50 mm (2")	m	138.00	127.00	129.00	131.00	130.00	140.00	134.00	140.00
Schedule 40, welded:									
65 mm (2 1/2")	m	171.00	157.00	159.00	163.00	161.00	173.00	166.00	174.00
75 mm (3")	m	195.00	179.00	182.00	186.00	184.00	198.00	190.00	199.00
100 mm (4")	m	253.00	233.00	237.00	241.00	239.00	257.00	246.00	258.00
150 mm (6")	m	411.00	378.00	384.00	392.00	388.00	417.00	400.00	419.00
200 mm (8")	m	583.00	536.00	545.00	556.00	550.00	591.00	567.00	594.00
Schedule 40, grooved:									
65 mm (2 1/2")	m	177.00	163.00	165.00	169.00	167.00	180.00	172.00	180.00
75 mm (3")	m	220.00	203.00	206.00	210.00	208.00	224.00	214.00	225.00
100 mm (4")	m	250.00	230.00	234.00	238.00	236.00	254.00	243.00	255.00
150 mm (6")	m	454.00	417.00	424.00	432.00	428.00	460.00	441.00	462.00
200 mm (8")	m	659.00	606.00	616.00	628.00	622.00	669.00	641.00	672.00
23 21 23 Pumps									
PUMPS									
In-line circulators									
Bronze body:									
20 mm to 38 mm (3/4" to 1 1/2")	EA	1,070	985.00	1,000	1,020	1,010	1,090	1,040	1,090
Iron body:									
20 mm to 38 mm (3/4" to 1 1/2")	EA	739.00	680.00	690.00	704.00	697.00	749.00	718.00	753.00
50 mm (2")	EA	1,200	1,100	1,120	1,140	1,130	1,210	1,160	1,220
65 mm (2 1/2")	EA	1,370	1,260	1,280	1,300	1,290	1,390	1,330	1,390
75 mm (3")	EA	1,820	1,680	1,700	1,740	1,720	1,850	1,770	1,860
Base mounted, ball bearing type									
Iron body:									
0.75 kW (1 hp)	EA	2,860	2,630	2,670	2,730	2,700	2,900	2,780	2,920
2.24 kW (3 hp)	EA	3,490	3,210	3,260	3,320	3,290	3,540	3,390	3,550
3.73 kW (5 hp)	EA	3,990	3,670	3,720	3,800	3,760	4,040	3,870	4,060
5.59 kW (7.5hp)	EA	6,410	5,900	5,990	6,110	6,050	6,500	6,230	6,530
7.46 kW (10 hp)	EA	7,450	6,850	6,960	7,100	7,030	7,560	7,240	7,590
23 30 00 HVAC Air Distribution									
DUCTWORK									
Rigid ducts, sheet metal including cleats and normal suspension									
Galvanized steel	kg	20.60	18.90	19.20	19.60	19.40	20.90	20.00	21.00
Aluminum	kg	36.90	33.90	34.50	35.10	34.80	37.40	35.80	37.60
Stainless steel	kg	29.20	26.80	27.20	27.80	27.50	29.60	28.30	29.70
Flexible ducts, aluminum, insulated									
100 mm (4") dia.	m	14.10	13.00	13.20	13.40	13.30	14.30	13.70	14.40
125 mm (5") dia.	m	16.40	15.10	15.30	15.70	15.50	16.70	16.00	16.70
150 mm (6") dia.	m	19.40	17.80	18.10	18.50	18.30	19.70	18.80	19.80
175 mm (7") dia.	m	22.80	21.00	21.30	21.70	21.50	23.10	22.10	23.20
200 mm (8") dia.	m	27.10	25.00	25.30	25.90	25.60	27.50	26.40	27.60

Item	UNITS	St. John's	Halifax	Montreal	Ottawa	Toronto	Winnipeg	Calgary	Vancouver
225 mm (9") dia.	m	30.50	28.10	28.50	29.10	28.80	31.00	29.70	31.10
250 mm (10") dia.	m	34.50	31.70	32.20	32.80	32.50	34.90	33.50	35.10
300 mm (12") dia.	m	46.00	42.30	43.00	43.80	43.40	46.70	44.70	46.90
350 mm (14") dia.	m	56.40	51.90	52.70	53.70	53.20	57.20	54.80	57.50
400 mm (16") dia.	m	72.20	66.40	67.40	68.80	68.10	73.20	70.10	73.50
Galvanized spiral ducts, uninsulated									
75 mm (3") dia.	m	15.30	14.00	14.30	14.50	14.40	15.50	14.80	15.60
100 mm (4") dia.	m	19.00	17.50	17.70	18.10	17.90	19.20	18.40	19.30
125 mm (5") dia.	m	22.70	20.90	21.20	21.60	21.40	23.00	22.00	23.10
150 mm (6") dia.	m	26.50	24.40	24.80	25.30	25.00	26.90	25.80	27.00
175 mm (7") dia.	m	28.20	25.90	26.30	26.90	26.60	28.60	27.40	28.70
200 mm (8") dia.	m	31.90	29.30	29.80	30.40	30.10	32.40	31.00	32.50
225 mm (9") dia.	m	35.60	32.80	33.30	33.90	33.60	36.10	34.60	36.30
250 mm (10") dia.	m	39.50	36.20	36.70	37.50	37.10	39.90	38.20	40.10
300 mm (12") dia.	m	46.70	43.00	43.70	44.50	44.10	47.40	45.40	47.60
350 mm (14") dia.	m	56.50	52.00	52.80	53.80	53.30	57.30	54.90	57.60
400 mm (16") dia.	m	62.50	57.50	58.40	59.60	59.00	63.40	60.80	63.70
450 mm (18") dia.	m	78.40	72.20	73.30	74.70	74.00	79.60	76.20	79.90
500 mm (20") dia.	m	85.30	78.50	79.70	81.30	80.50	86.50	82.90	86.90
550 mm (22") dia.	m	94.30	86.80	88.10	89.90	89.00	95.70	91.70	96.10
600 mm (24") dia.	m	103.00	95.00	96.40	98.40	97.40	105.00	100.00	105.00
700 mm (28") dia.	m	134.00	123.00	125.00	127.00	126.00	135.00	130.00	136.00
800 mm (32") dia.	m	155.00	142.00	145.00	147.00	146.00	157.00	150.00	158.00

CENTRAL AIR HANDLING UNITS

**Central station modular units, with insulated casing, fans motors
and drives, heating and cooling coils, with filters, humidifier
and mixing box. Automatic controls not included.**

Low pressure type:

Item	UNITS	St. John's	Halifax	Montreal	Ottawa	Toronto	Winnipeg	Calgary	Vancouver
0.7 m³/s (1,500 cfm)	EA	24,000	22,000	22,400	22,800	22,600	24,300	23,300	24,400
1.4 m³/s (3,000 cfm)	EA	33,300	30,600	31,100	31,700	31,400	33,800	32,300	33,900
2.8 m³/s (6,000 cfm)	EA	44,800	41,200	41,900	42,700	42,300	45,500	43,600	45,700
4.7 m³/s (10,000 cfm)	EA	57,000	52,500	53,300	54,300	53,800	57,800	55,400	58,100
Medium pressure type:									
7.1 m³/s (15,000 cfm)	EA	90,900	83,700	84,900	86,700	85,800	92,200	88,400	92,700
9.4 m³/s (20,000 cfm)	EA	118,000	108,000	110,000	112,000	111,000	119,000	114,000	120,000
14.2 m³/s (30,000 cfm)	EA	165,000	152,000	154,000	158,000	156,000	168,000	161,000	168,000

23 34 00 HVAC Fans

FANS

Vane axial fans, for suspended mounting
Direct connected tubular belt driven fan class 1

Item	UNITS	St. John's	Halifax	Montreal	Ottawa	Toronto	Winnipeg	Calgary	Vancouver
1.4 m³/s (3,000 cfm)	EA	3,060	2,820	2,860	2,920	2,890	3,110	2,980	3,120
2.4 m³/s (5,000 cfm)	EA	4,970	4,570	4,640	4,740	4,690	5,040	4,830	5,070
3.3 m³/s (7,000 cfm)	EA	5,180	4,770	4,840	4,940	4,890	5,260	5,040	5,280
4.7 m³/s (10,000 cfm)	EA	5,480	5,040	5,120	5,220	5,170	5,560	5,330	5,580
7.1 m³/s (15,000 cfm)	EA	7,430	6,830	6,940	7,080	7,010	7,540	7,220	7,570
9.4 m³/s (20,000 cfm)	EA	14,400	13,300	13,500	13,700	13,600	14,600	14,000	14,700
Propeller fans									
Direct driven through the wall plate type, unit not including									
exhaust wall shutter:									
305 mm (12") dia., 0.5 m³/s (1,000 cfm)	EA	1,210	1,110	1,130	1,150	1,140	1,230	1,170	1,230
406 mm (16") dia., 0.9 m³/s (2,000 cfm)	EA	1,460	1,350	1,370	1,390	1,380	1,480	1,420	1,490
610 mm (24") dia., 2.4 m³/s (5,000 cfm)	EA	1,960	1,800	1,830	1,870	1,850	1,990	1,910	2,000
762 mm (30") dia., 3.8 m³/s (8,000 cfm)	EA	2,370	2,180	2,220	2,260	2,240	2,410	2,310	2,420
914 mm (36") dia., 7.1 m³/s (15,000 cfm)	EA	2,870	2,640	2,680	2,740	2,710	2,910	2,790	2,930
1067 mm (42") dia., 9.4 m³/s (20,000 cfm)	EA	3,160	2,910	2,950	3,010	2,980	3,200	3,070	3,220
1219 mm (48") dia., 14.2 m³/s (30,000 cfm)	EA	3,740	3,440	3,490	3,570	3,530	3,790	3,640	3,810
1372 mm (54") dia., 18.9 m³/s (40,000 cfm)	EA	4,340	3,990	4,050	4,130	4,090	4,400	4,210	4,420
1524 mm (60") dia., 23.6 m³/s (50,000 cfm)	EA	5,770	5,300	5,390	5,490	5,440	5,850	5,600	5,880
1829 mm (72") dia., 28.3 m³/s (60,000 cfm)	EA	8,640	7,950	8,070	8,230	8,150	8,760	8,390	8,800
Roof exhaust fans, back draft damper, prefabricated curb									
and speed controller not included									
Centrifugal, aluminum, direct drive:									
0.1 m³/s (200 cfm)	EA	897.00	825.00	838.00	854.00	846.00	909.00	871.00	914.00
0.2 m³/s (420 cfm)	EA	942.00	867.00	880.00	898.00	889.00	956.00	916.00	960.00
0.3 m³/s (630 cfm)	EA	957.00	880.00	894.00	912.00	903.00	971.00	930.00	975.00
0.4 m³/s (850 cfm)	EA	1,140	1,050	1,070	1,090	1,080	1,160	1,110	1,170
0.7 m³/s (1,480 cfm)	EA	1,460	1,350	1,370	1,390	1,380	1,480	1,420	1,490
1.1 m³/s (2,330 cfm)	EA	1,800	1,660	1,680	1,720	1,700	1,830	1,750	1,840
Centrifugal, aluminum, belt driven:									
0.3 m³/s (630 cfm)	EA	1,100	1,010	1,030	1,050	1,040	1,120	1,070	1,120
0.6 m³/s (1,270 cfm)	EA	1,460	1,350	1,370	1,390	1,380	1,480	1,420	1,490
0.9 m³/s (1,910 cfm)	EA	1,660	1,530	1,550	1,590	1,570	1,690	1,620	1,700
2.0 m³/s (4,240 cfm)	EA	1,900	1,750	1,770	1,810	1,790	1,920	1,840	1,930
2.8 m³/s (6,000 cfm)	EA	2,200	2,030	2,060	2,100	2,080	2,240	2,140	2,250
4.5 m³/s (9,500 cfm)	EA	4,400	4,050	4,110	4,190	4,150	4,460	4,270	4,480
6.8 m³/s (14,400 cfm)	EA	4,710	4,330	4,400	4,480	4,440	4,770	4,570	4,800

Item	UNITS	St. John's	Halifax	Montreal	Ottawa	Toronto	Winnipeg	Calgary	Vancouver
23 37 00 Air Outlets and Inlets									
LOUVERS									
Louvers									
Fresh and exhaust air:									
Galvanized steel	m²	508.00	467.00	474.00	484.00	479.00	515.00	493.00	517.00
Aluminum	m²	580.00	533.00	542.00	552.00	547.00	588.00	563.00	591.00
23 40 00 HVAC Air Cleaning Devices									
AIR FILTERS									
Permanent washable type, metal frame:									
50 mm (2") thick	m²	981.00	902.00	916.00	934.00	925.00	994.00	953.00	999.00
Electronic air cleaner									
Standard, residential type	EA	2,260	2,080	2,110	2,150	2,130	2,290	2,190	2,300
Glass fibre, throwaway type									
25 mm-508 mm x 508 mm (1"-20" x 20")	EA	8.86	8.15	8.28	8.44	8.36	8.99	8.61	9.03
50 mm-508 mm x 508 mm (2"-20" x 20")	EA	11.90	10.90	11.10	11.30	11.20	12.00	11.50	12.10
23 50 00 Central Heating Equipment									
23 51 00 Breechings, Chimneys, and Stacks									
CHIMNEY									
Chimney									
B vent c/w rain cap, 6 m (20 lf)									
150 mm (6") duct size	EA	818.00	753.00	764.00	780.00	772.00	830.00	795.00	834.00
200 mm (8") duct size	EA	1,120	1,030	1,050	1,070	1,060	1,140	1,090	1,140
250 mm (10") duct size	EA	1,960	1,800	1,830	1,870	1,850	1,990	1,910	2,000
300 mm (12") duct size	EA	2,290	2,110	2,140	2,180	2,160	2,320	2,220	2,330
400 mm (16") duct size	EA	3,210	2,950	3,000	3,060	3,030	3,260	3,120	3,270
23 52 00 Heating Boilers									
BOILERS									
Copper water tube boilers									
Atmospheric gas fired, commercial on/off type, hot water:									
60 kW (204 mbh)	EA	5,000	4,600	4,670	4,770	4,720	5,070	4,860	5,100
116 kW (396 mbh)	EA	6,320	5,810	5,900	6,020	5,960	6,410	6,140	6,440
184 kW (627 mbh)	EA	9,210	8,470	8,600	8,780	8,690	9,340	8,950	9,390
282 kW (962 mbh)	EA	11,600	10,600	10,800	11,000	10,900	11,700	11,200	11,800
615 kW (2100 mbh)	EA	19,600	18,000	18,300	18,700	18,500	19,900	19,100	20,000
Atmospheric gas fired, commercial modulating type, hot water:									
116 kW (396 mbh)	EA	7,930	7,290	7,410	7,550	7,480	8,040	7,700	8,080
184 kW (627 mbh)	EA	9,850	9,060	9,200	9,380	9,290	9,990	9,570	10,000
282 kW (962 mbh)	EA	15,900	14,600	14,900	15,200	15,000	16,100	15,500	16,200
615 kW (2100 mbh)	EA	25,500	23,500	23,900	24,300	24,100	25,900	24,800	26,000
Packaged steel boilers									
Oil fired, hot water:									
48 kW (5 bhp)	EA	6,720	6,180	6,280	6,400	6,340	6,820	6,530	6,850
73 kW (7.5 bhp)	EA	8,560	7,880	8,000	8,160	8,080	8,690	8,320	8,730
97 kW (10 bhp)	EA	23,000	21,200	21,500	21,900	21,700	23,300	22,400	23,400
193 kW (20 bhp)	EA	25,700	23,600	24,000	24,400	24,200	26,000	24,900	26,100
387 kW (40 bhp)	EA	38,800	35,700	36,200	37,000	36,600	39,300	37,700	39,500
580 kW (60 bhp)	EA	45,100	41,400	42,100	42,900	42,500	45,700	43,800	45,900
774 kW (80 bhp)	EA	57,100	52,600	53,400	54,400	53,900	57,900	55,500	58,200
967 kW (100 bhp)	EA	65,200	60,000	60,900	62,100	61,500	66,100	63,300	66,400
1210 kW (125 bhp)	EA	71,400	65,700	66,700	68,100	67,400	72,500	69,400	72,800
Gas fired, hot water:									
48 kW (5 bhp)	EA	6,350	5,840	5,930	6,050	5,990	6,440	6,170	6,470
73 kW (7.5 bhp)	EA	8,110	7,460	7,570	7,730	7,650	8,220	7,880	8,260
97 kW (10 bhp)	EA	26,100	24,000	24,400	24,800	24,600	26,400	25,300	26,600
193 kW (20 bhp)	EA	29,000	26,700	27,100	27,700	27,400	29,500	28,200	29,600
387 kW (40 bhp)	EA	41,200	37,900	38,500	39,300	38,900	41,800	40,100	42,000
580 kW (60 bhp)	EA	49,600	45,600	46,300	47,300	46,800	50,300	48,200	50,500
774 kW (80 bhp)	EA	60,600	55,800	56,600	57,800	57,200	61,500	58,900	61,800
967 kW (100 bhp)	EA	71,800	66,000	67,000	68,400	67,700	72,800	69,700	73,100
1210 kW (125 bhp)	EA	73,400	67,500	68,500	69,900	69,200	74,400	71,300	74,700
Sectional cast iron boilers									
Gas fired, steam, capacity net ibr:									
132 kW (450 mbh)	EA	23,700	21,800	22,200	22,600	22,400	24,100	23,100	24,200
264 kW (900 mbh)	EA	35,100	32,300	32,800	33,400	33,100	35,600	34,100	35,700

Item	UNITS	St. John's	Halifax	Montreal	Ottawa	Toronto	Winnipeg	Calgary	Vancouver
455 kW (1550 mbh)	EA	54,100	49,700	50,500	51,500	51,000	54,800	52,500	55,100
637 kW (2175 mbh)	EA	71,900	66,100	67,100	68,500	67,800	72,900	69,800	73,200
Gas fired, hot water, capacity net ibr:									
153 kW (520 mbh)	EA	23,100	21,300	21,600	22,000	21,800	23,400	22,500	23,500
305 kW (1045 mbh)	EA	37,700	34,700	35,200	36,000	35,600	38,300	36,700	38,400
510 kW (1740 mbh)	EA	52,400	48,200	48,900	49,900	49,400	53,100	50,900	53,400
714 kW (2435 mbh)	EA	70,000	64,400	65,300	66,700	66,000	71,000	68,000	71,300

23 60 00 Central Cooling Equipment
23 62 00 Packaged Compressor & Condenser Units
CHILLERS
Self contained air cooled liquid chiller w/50% propylene glycol

Item	UNITS	St. John's	Halifax	Montreal	Ottawa	Toronto	Winnipeg	Calgary	Vancouver
70 kW (20 Ton)	EA	43,100	39,700	40,300	41,100	40,700	43,800	41,900	44,000
176 kW (50 Ton)	EA	85,600	78,800	80,000	81,600	80,800	86,900	83,200	87,300
351 kW (100 Ton)	EA	195,000	179,000	182,000	186,000	184,000	198,000	190,000	199,000
702 kW (200 Ton)	EA	280,000	257,000	261,000	267,000	264,000	284,000	272,000	285,000

23 64 00 Packaged Water Chillers
CHILLERS
Chillers complete with starter and accessories
Centrifugal water chiller, average 0.65 kW/Ton energy consumption:

Item	UNITS	St. John's	Halifax	Montreal	Ottawa	Toronto	Winnipeg	Calgary	Vancouver
351 kW (100 Ton)	EA	176,000	162,000	164,000	168,000	166,000	178,000	171,000	179,000
702 kW (200 Ton)	EA	229,000	211,000	214,000	218,000	216,000	232,000	222,000	233,000
1404 kW (400 Ton)	EA	302,000	278,000	282,000	288,000	285,000	306,000	294,000	308,000
2106 kW (600 Ton)	EA	363,000	333,000	339,000	345,000	342,000	368,000	352,000	369,000
2808 kW (800 Ton)	EA	514,000	473,000	480,000	490,000	485,000	521,000	500,000	524,000
3510 kW (1000 Ton)	EA	563,000	518,000	526,000	536,000	531,000	571,000	547,000	573,000

23 65 00 Cooling Towers
COOLING TOWERS
Two speed fan motors (capacity controls) c/w sump heater package
galvanized steel construction
Centrifugal/induced draft fan based on 35/30.5/24.4 deg C (95/87/76 deg F) temp condition:

Item	UNITS	St. John's	Halifax	Montreal	Ottawa	Toronto	Winnipeg	Calgary	Vancouver
351 kW (100 Ton)	EA	39,300	36,200	36,700	37,500	37,100	39,900	38,200	40,100
702 kW (200 Ton)	EA	58,900	54,200	55,000	56,200	55,600	59,800	57,300	60,000
1404 kW (400 Ton)	EA	88,800	81,700	83,000	84,600	83,800	90,100	86,300	90,500
2106 kW (600 Ton)	EA	139,000	128,000	130,000	132,000	131,000	141,000	135,000	141,000
3510 kW (1000 Ton)	EA	216,000	199,000	202,000	206,000	204,000	219,000	210,000	220,000

Propeller/forced draft fan based on 35/30.5/24.4 deg C (95/87/76 deg F) temp condition:

Item	UNITS	St. John's	Halifax	Montreal	Ottawa	Toronto	Winnipeg	Calgary	Vancouver
702 kW (200 Ton)	EA	54,500	50,100	50,900	51,900	51,400	55,300	52,900	55,500
1404 kW (400 Ton)	EA	68,800	63,300	64,300	65,500	64,900	69,800	66,800	70,100
2106 kW (600 Ton)	EA	96,400	88,600	90,000	91,800	90,900	97,700	93,600	98,200
3510 kW (1000 Ton)	EA	146,000	135,000	137,000	139,000	138,000	148,000	142,000	149,000

Closed circuit cooler based on 37.8/32.2/24.4 deg C (100/90/76 deg F) temp condition:

Item	UNITS	St. John's	Halifax	Montreal	Ottawa	Toronto	Winnipeg	Calgary	Vancouver
351 kW (100 Ton)	EA	92,400	85,000	86,300	88,100	87,200	93,700	89,800	94,200
1055 (300 Ton)	EA	232,000	214,000	217,000	221,000	219,000	235,000	226,000	237,000
2106 kW (600 Ton)	EA	477,000	439,000	446,000	455,000	450,000	484,000	464,000	486,000

23 72 00 Air-to-Air Energy Recovery Equipment
HEAT RECOVERY VENTILATORS
2 operational modes, c/w main controls, basic de-humidistat
Light commercial series:

Item	UNITS	St. John's	Halifax	Montreal	Ottawa	Toronto	Winnipeg	Calgary	Vancouver
238 - 333 l/s (500 - 700 CFM)	EA	9,560	8,790	8,930	9,110	9,020	9,700	9,290	9,740
476 - 619 l/s (1000 - 1300 CFM)	EA	11,000	10,100	10,300	10,500	10,400	11,200	10,700	11,200

23 82 00 Convection Heating and Cooling Units
HYDRONIC HEATING
Terminal Heat Transfer Units
(Not including piping or accessories)
Unit heaters with diffusers
Steam at 14 kPa (2 lbs) pressure:

Item	UNITS	St. John's	Halifax	Montreal	Ottawa	Toronto	Winnipeg	Calgary	Vancouver
10.6 kW (35 mbh)	EA	1,580	1,450	1,480	1,500	1,490	1,600	1,530	1,610
18.5 kW (63 mbh)	EA	1,860	1,710	1,730	1,770	1,750	1,880	1,800	1,890
36.6 kW (125 mbh)	EA	2,410	2,210	2,250	2,290	2,270	2,440	2,340	2,450
52.8 kW (180 mbh)	EA	3,190	2,930	2,980	3,040	3,010	3,240	3,100	3,250
70.3 kW (240 mbh)	EA	4,070	3,740	3,800	3,880	3,840	4,130	3,960	4,150
103.2 kW (352 mbh)	EA	6,230	5,730	5,820	5,940	5,880	6,320	6,060	6,350
Hot water entering at 93 deg C (200 deg F)									
6.7 kW (23 mbh)	EA	1,620	1,490	1,510	1,550	1,530	1,640	1,580	1,650
11.7 kW (40 mbh)	EA	1,910	1,760	1,780	1,820	1,800	1,940	1,850	1,940
23.4 kW (80 mbh)	EA	2,550	2,350	2,390	2,430	2,410	2,590	2,480	2,600
33.7 kW (115 mbh)	EA	3,520	3,240	3,290	3,350	3,320	3,570	3,420	3,590
47.2 kW (161 mbh)	EA	4,360	4,010	4,070	4,150	4,110	4,420	4,230	4,440
73.3 kW (250 mbh)	EA	6,230	5,730	5,820	5,940	5,880	6,320	6,060	6,350

Item	UNITS	St. John's	Halifax	Montreal	Ottawa	Toronto	Winnipeg	Calgary	Vancouver
Force flow units									
Steam at 14 kPa (2 lbs) pressure or hot water entering at 93 deg C (200 deg F)									
surface or recess mounted including thermostat:									
4.9 kW (16.7 mbh) steam or 2.8 kW (9.4 mbh) hot water capacity	EA	3,320	3,050	3,100	3,160	3,130	3,360	3,220	3,380
10.1 kW (34.6 mbh) steam or 7.6 kW (25.9 mbh) hot water capacity	EA	3,770	3,470	3,520	3,600	3,560	3,830	3,670	3,840
14.7 kW (50.0) steam or 10.4 kW (33.5 mbh) hot water capacity	EA	4,710	4,330	4,400	4,480	4,440	4,770	4,570	4,800
26.0 kW (89.0 mbh) steam or 19.0 kW (65.0 mbh) hot water capacity	EA	6,230	5,730	5,820	5,940	5,880	6,320	6,060	6,350
Semi-recessed mounted, all sizes:									
Add	EA	649.00	597.00	606.00	618.00	612.00	658.00	630.00	661.00
Convectors and radiators									
Baseboard:									
Cast iron	m	385.00	354.00	359.00	367.00	363.00	390.00	374.00	392.00
Wall finned	m	116.00	106.00	108.00	110.00	109.00	117.00	112.00	118.00
Convectors-radiators, floor type:									
1.5 kW (5.0 mbh)	EA	530.00	488.00	495.00	505.00	500.00	538.00	515.00	540.00
3.0 kW (10.2 mbh)	EA	660.00	607.00	617.00	629.00	623.00	670.00	642.00	673.00
4.2 kW (14.4 mbh)	EA	789.00	725.00	737.00	751.00	744.00	800.00	766.00	804.00

23 83 00 Radiant Heating Units

23 83 26 Gas-Fired Radiant Heaters

Item	UNITS	St. John's	Halifax	Montreal	Ottawa	Toronto	Winnipeg	Calgary	Vancouver
Natural gas fired, output capacity									
11.7 kW (40 mbh)	EA	2,590	2,380	2,420	2,460	2,440	2,620	2,510	2,640
23.4 kW (80 mbh)	EA	3,070	2,830	2,870	2,930	2,900	3,120	2,990	3,130
35.2 kW (120 mbh)	EA	3,580	3,300	3,350	3,410	3,380	3,630	3,480	3,650
46.9 kW (160 mbh)	EA	4,050	3,720	3,780	3,860	3,820	4,110	3,930	4,130
58.6 kW (200 mbh)	EA	4,630	4,260	4,330	4,410	4,370	4,700	4,500	4,720
93.8 kW (320 mbh)	EA	6,890	6,340	6,440	6,570	6,500	6,990	6,700	7,020

23 83 33 Electric Radiant Heaters
ELECTRIC HEATERS PROPELLERS FAN TYPE

Item	UNITS	St. John's	Halifax	Montreal	Ottawa	Toronto	Winnipeg	Calgary	Vancouver
Wall type force flow									
208 V, integrated thermostat:									
1500 W	EA	944.00	869.00	882.00	900.00	891.00	958.00	918.00	962.00
2000 W	EA	975.00	897.00	911.00	929.00	920.00	989.00	948.00	994.00
3000 W	EA	1,020	938.00	952.00	972.00	962.00	1,030	991.00	1,040
4000 W	EA	1,170	1,070	1,090	1,110	1,100	1,180	1,130	1,190

ELECTRICAL BASEBOARD
208 V, integrated thermostat

Item	UNITS	St. John's	Halifax	Montreal	Ottawa	Toronto	Winnipeg	Calgary	Vancouver
Baked enamel finish (white):									
500 W	EA	217.00	200.00	203.00	207.00	205.00	220.00	211.00	221.00
750 W	EA	225.00	207.00	210.00	214.00	212.00	228.00	218.00	229.00
1000 W	EA	266.00	245.00	248.00	254.00	251.00	270.00	259.00	271.00
1250 W	EA	319.00	293.00	298.00	304.00	301.00	324.00	310.00	325.00
1500 W	EA	384.00	353.00	358.00	366.00	362.00	389.00	373.00	391.00
2000 W	EA	452.00	415.00	422.00	430.00	426.00	458.00	439.00	460.00

23 84 00 Humidity Control Equipment
HUMIDIFIERS

Item	UNITS	St. John's	Halifax	Montreal	Ottawa	Toronto	Winnipeg	Calgary	Vancouver
Installed in air handling units									
Gas fired									
90 kg / hr (200 lb / hr)	EA	35,700	32,900	33,400	34,000	33,700	36,200	34,700	36,400
180 kg / hr (400 lb / hr)	EA	58,800	54,100	54,900	56,100	55,500	59,700	57,200	59,900
270 kg / hr (600 lb / hr)	EA	65,500	60,300	61,200	62,400	61,800	66,400	63,700	66,700
360 kg / hr (800 lb / hr)	EA	114,000	105,000	107,000	109,000	108,000	116,000	111,000	117,000
455 kg / hr (1000 lb / hr)	EA	131,000	121,000	123,000	125,000	124,000	133,000	128,000	134,000

26: ELECTRICAL

26 05 00 Common Work Results
for Electrical

26 05 13 Medium-Voltage Electrical Power
Conductors and Cables
CONDUCTORS

Item	UNITS	St. John's	Halifax	Montreal	Ottawa	Toronto	Winnipeg	Calgary	Vancouver
Building wire installed in conduit									
High tension, 5 kV single copper conductor, x-link shielded PVC:									
No. 8	m	27.80	25.50	25.90	26.50	26.20	28.20	27.00	28.30
No. 6	m	28.80	26.50	26.90	27.50	27.20	29.20	28.00	29.40
No. 4	m	33.10	30.40	30.90	31.50	31.20	33.50	32.10	33.70
No. 2	m	41.70	38.30	38.90	39.70	39.30	42.20	40.50	42.40
No. 1	m	43.80	40.30	40.90	41.70	41.30	44.40	42.50	44.60
No. 1/0	m	53.40	49.10	49.90	50.90	50.40	54.20	51.90	54.40
No. 2/0	m	64.10	59.00	59.90	61.10	60.50	65.00	62.30	65.30
No. 3/0	m	73.80	67.90	68.90	70.30	69.60	74.80	71.70	75.20
No. 4/0	m	86.50	79.60	80.80	82.40	81.60	87.70	84.00	88.10
250 mcm	m	94.00	86.50	87.80	89.60	88.70	95.40	91.40	95.80

Item	UNITS	St. John's	Halifax	Montreal	Ottawa	Toronto	Winnipeg	Calgary	Vancouver
300 mcm	m	103.00	94.40	95.80	97.80	96.80	104.00	99.70	105.00
350 mcm	m	109.00	100.00	102.00	104.00	103.00	111.00	106.00	111.00
400 mcm	m	125.00	115.00	117.00	119.00	118.00	127.00	122.00	127.00
500 mcm	m	147.00	136.00	138.00	140.00	139.00	149.00	143.00	150.00
750 mcm	m	169.00	155.00	157.00	161.00	159.00	171.00	164.00	172.00
High tension, 15 kV single copper conductor, x-link shielded PVC:									
No. 1	m	62.00	57.00	57.90	59.10	58.50	62.90	60.30	63.20
No. 1/0	m	72.60	66.80	67.80	69.20	68.50	73.60	70.60	74.00
No. 2/0	m	79.10	72.70	73.90	75.30	74.60	80.20	76.80	80.60
No. 3/0	m	90.80	83.60	84.80	86.60	85.70	92.10	88.30	92.60
No. 4/0	m	108.00	99.50	101.00	103.00	102.00	110.00	105.00	110.00
250 mcm	m	117.00	107.00	109.00	111.00	110.00	118.00	113.00	119.00
300 mcm	m	125.00	115.00	117.00	119.00	118.00	127.00	122.00	127.00
350 mcm	m	142.00	131.00	133.00	135.00	134.00	144.00	138.00	145.00
400 mcm	m	159.00	146.00	149.00	152.00	150.00	161.00	155.00	162.00
500 mcm	m	169.00	155.00	157.00	161.00	159.00	171.00	164.00	172.00
750 mcm	m	201.00	185.00	188.00	192.00	190.00	204.00	196.00	205.00
High tension, 25 kV single copper conductor, x-link shielded PVC:									
No. 1	m	69.40	63.90	64.80	66.20	65.50	70.40	67.50	70.70
No. 1/0	m	79.10	72.70	73.90	75.30	74.60	80.20	76.80	80.60
No. 2/0	m	90.80	83.60	84.80	86.60	85.70	92.10	88.30	92.60
No. 4/0	m	112.00	103.00	105.00	107.00	106.00	114.00	109.00	114.00
250 mcm	m	128.00	118.00	120.00	122.00	121.00	130.00	125.00	131.00
300 mcm	m	142.00	131.00	133.00	135.00	134.00	144.00	138.00	145.00
350 mcm	m	157.00	144.00	147.00	149.00	148.00	159.00	152.00	160.00
400 mcm	m	161.00	148.00	150.00	154.00	152.00	163.00	157.00	164.00
500 mcm	m	189.00	174.00	176.00	180.00	178.00	191.00	183.00	192.00
750 mcm	m	234.00	215.00	219.00	223.00	221.00	238.00	228.00	239.00

FEEDER CIRCUIT

60-400 A (support and fittings included, exposed installation, copper conductors)

Rigid galvanized conduit:

Item	UNITS	St. John's	Halifax	Montreal	Ottawa	Toronto	Winnipeg	Calgary	Vancouver
60 A, 3 wire	m	68.70	63.20	64.20	65.40	64.80	69.70	66.70	70.00
60 A, 4 wire	m	75.00	69.00	70.10	71.50	70.80	76.10	72.90	76.50
100 A, 3 wire	m	79.40	73.00	74.20	75.60	74.90	80.50	77.10	80.90
100 A, 4 wire	m	101.00	92.70	94.10	96.10	95.10	102.00	98.00	103.00
150 A, 3 wire	m	124.00	114.00	116.00	118.00	117.00	126.00	121.00	126.00
150 A, 4 wire	m	164.00	151.00	153.00	157.00	155.00	167.00	160.00	167.00
200 A, 3 wire	m	175.00	161.00	163.00	167.00	165.00	177.00	170.00	178.00
200 A, 4 wire	m	201.00	185.00	188.00	192.00	190.00	204.00	196.00	205.00
300 A, 3 wire	m	275.00	253.00	256.00	262.00	259.00	278.00	267.00	280.00
300 A, 4 wire	m	358.00	330.00	335.00	341.00	338.00	363.00	348.00	365.00
400 A, 3 wire	m	427.00	393.00	399.00	407.00	403.00	433.00	415.00	435.00
400 A, 4 wire	m	598.00	550.00	558.00	570.00	564.00	606.00	581.00	609.00

Electric metallic (E.M.T.) conduit:

Item	UNITS	St. John's	Halifax	Montreal	Ottawa	Toronto	Winnipeg	Calgary	Vancouver
60 A, 3 wire	m	47.90	44.10	44.70	45.70	45.20	48.60	46.60	48.80
60 A, 4 wire	m	54.00	49.60	50.40	51.40	50.90	54.70	52.40	55.00
100 A, 3 wire	m	59.50	54.70	55.50	56.70	56.10	60.30	57.80	60.60
100 A, 4 wire	m	80.00	73.60	74.70	76.30	75.50	81.20	77.80	81.50
150 A, 3 wire	m	99.40	91.50	92.90	94.70	93.80	101.00	96.60	101.00
150 A, 4 wire	m	123.00	113.00	115.00	117.00	116.00	125.00	119.00	125.00
200 A, 3 wire	m	135.00	124.00	126.00	128.00	127.00	137.00	131.00	137.00
200 A, 4 wire	m	159.00	146.00	149.00	152.00	150.00	161.00	155.00	162.00
300 A, 3 wire	m		194.00	197.00	201.00	199.00	214.00	205.00	215.00
300 A, 4 wire	m	268.00	247.00	250.00	256.00	253.00	272.00	261.00	273.00
400 A, 3 wire	m	356.00	328.00	333.00	339.00	336.00	361.00	346.00	363.00
400 A, 4 wire	m	443.00	408.00	414.00	422.00	418.00	449.00	431.00	451.00

26 05 19 Low-Voltage Electrical Power Conductors and Cables

CONDUCTORS

Building wire installed in conduit

Rw-90 copper:

Item	UNITS	St. John's	Halifax	Montreal	Ottawa	Toronto	Winnipeg	Calgary	Vancouver
No. 14	hm	177.00	163.00	165.00	169.00	167.00	180.00	172.00	180.00
No. 12	hm	227.00	209.00	212.00	216.00	214.00	230.00	220.00	231.00
No. 10	hm	313.00	288.00	292.00	298.00	295.00	317.00	304.00	319.00
No. 8	hm	441.00	406.00	412.00	420.00	416.00	447.00	428.00	449.00
No. 6	hm	584.00	537.00	545.00	557.00	551.00	592.00	568.00	595.00
No. 4	hm	822.00	756.00	767.00	783.00	775.00	833.00	798.00	837.00
No. 3	hm	962.00	885.00	899.00	917.00	908.00	976.00	935.00	981.00
No. 2	hm	1,170	1,070	1,090	1,110	1,100	1,180	1,130	1,190
No. 1	hm	1,400	1,290	1,310	1,330	1,320	1,420	1,360	1,430
No. 1/0	hm	1,640	1,510	1,530	1,570	1,550	1,670	1,600	1,670
No. 2/0	hm	2,000	1,840	1,870	1,910	1,890	2,030	1,950	2,040
No. 3/0	hm	2,440	2,240	2,280	2,320	2,300	2,470	2,370	2,480
No. 4/0	hm	2,960	2,720	2,760	2,820	2,790	3,000	2,870	3,010
250 mcm	hm	3,410	3,140	3,190	3,250	3,220	3,460	3,320	3,480
300 mcm	hm	3,990	3,670	3,720	3,800	3,760	4,040	3,870	4,060
350 mcm	hm	4,600	4,230	4,300	4,380	4,340	4,670	4,470	4,690
400 mcm	hm	5,170	4,760	4,830	4,930	4,880	5,250	5,030	5,270
500 mcm	hm	6,160	5,660	5,750	5,870	5,810	6,250	5,980	6,270
600 mcm	hm	7,340	6,750	6,850	6,990	6,920	7,440	7,130	7,470

Item	UNITS	St. John's	Halifax	Montreal	Ottawa	Toronto	Winnipeg	Calgary	Vancouver
750 mcm	hm	10,000	9,220	9,370	9,550	9,460	10,200	9,740	10,200
1000 mcm	hm	13,400	12,300	12,500	12,700	12,600	13,500	13,000	13,600
Rw-90 aluminum									
No. 1	hm	1,040	959.00	974.00	994.00	984.00	1,060	1,010	1,060
No. 1/0	hm	1,220	1,120	1,140	1,160	1,150	1,240	1,180	1,240
No. 2/0	hm	1,350	1,240	1,260	1,280	1,270	1,370	1,310	1,370
No. 3/0	hm	1,710	1,570	1,590	1,630	1,610	1,730	1,660	1,740
No. 4/0	hm	1,950	1,790	1,820	1,860	1,840	1,980	1,900	1,990
250 mcm	hm	2,320	2,140	2,170	2,210	2,190	2,350	2,260	2,370
300 mcm	hm	2,750	2,530	2,560	2,620	2,590	2,780	2,670	2,800
350 mcm	hm	3,240	2,980	3,030	3,090	3,060	3,290	3,150	3,300
400 mcm	hm	3,590	3,310	3,360	3,420	3,390	3,640	3,490	3,660
500 mcm	hm	4,120	3,790	3,850	3,930	3,890	4,180	4,010	4,200
600 mcm	hm	4,390	4,040	4,100	4,180	4,140	4,450	4,260	4,470
750 mcm	hm	5,350	4,920	5,000	5,100	5,050	5,430	5,200	5,450
1000 mcm	hm	7,470	6,870	6,980	7,120	7,050	7,580	7,260	7,610
AC 90 copper (BX)									
2C / 14	hm	657.00	605.00	614.00	626.00	620.00	667.00	639.00	670.00
2C / 12	hm	748.00	688.00	699.00	713.00	706.00	759.00	727.00	762.00
2C / 10	hm	860.00	791.00	803.00	819.00	811.00	872.00	835.00	876.00
3C / 14	hm	760.00	699.00	710.00	724.00	717.00	771.00	739.00	774.00
3C / 12	hm	823.00	757.00	768.00	784.00	776.00	834.00	799.00	838.00
3C / 10	hm	966.00	888.00	902.00	920.00	911.00	979.00	938.00	984.00
3C / 8	hm	1,550	1,420	1,450	1,470	1,460	1,570	1,500	1,580
3C / 6	hm	1,840	1,700	1,720	1,760	1,740	1,870	1,790	1,880
3C / 4	hm	2,400	2,200	2,240	2,280	2,260	2,430	2,330	2,440
3C / 3	hm	2,660	2,450	2,480	2,540	2,510	2,700	2,590	2,710
3C / 2	hm	2,880	2,650	2,690	2,750	2,720	2,920	2,800	2,940
4C / 14	hm	823.00	757.00	768.00	784.00	776.00	834.00	799.00	838.00
4C / 12	hm	909.00	837.00	849.00	867.00	858.00	922.00	884.00	927.00
4C / 10	hm	1,350	1,240	1,260	1,280	1,270	1,370	1,310	1,370
Corflex, single copper conductor, low tension, 600 V PVC jacket:									
No. 1/0	m	29.30	26.90	27.30	27.90	27.60	29.70	28.40	29.80
No. 2/0	m	31.40	28.90	29.30	29.90	29.60	31.80	30.50	32.00
No. 3/0	m	37.90	34.90	35.40	36.20	35.80	38.50	36.90	38.70
No. 4/0	m	41.20	37.90	38.50	39.30	38.90	41.80	40.10	42.00
250 mcm	m	49.90	45.90	46.60	47.60	47.10	50.60	48.50	50.90
300 mcm	m	54.30	49.90	50.70	51.70	51.20	55.00	52.70	55.30
350 mcm	m	61.90	56.90	57.80	59.00	58.40	62.80	60.20	63.10
400 mcm	m	67.20	61.80	62.80	64.00	63.40	68.20	65.30	68.50
500 mcm	m	73.80	67.90	68.90	70.30	69.60	74.80	71.70	75.20
750 mcm	m	127.00	117.00	119.00	121.00	120.00	129.00	124.00	130.00
1000 mcm	m	154.00	141.00	144.00	146.00	145.00	156.00	149.00	157.00
Mineral insulated cable, 600V, 2 hours fire rated feeder									
60A / 4w - 4/C #6 MI	m	130.00	120.00	122.00	124.00	123.00	132.00	127.00	133.00
100A / 4w - 4 x 1/C #6 MI	m	194.00	178.00	181.00	185.00	183.00	197.00	188.00	198.00
120A / 4w - 4 x 1/C #4 MI	m	251.00	231.00	235.00	239.00	237.00	255.00	244.00	256.00
150A / 4w - 4 x 1/C #3 MI	m	289.00	266.00	270.00	276.00	273.00	293.00	281.00	295.00
200A / 4w - 4 x 1/C #1 MI	m	328.00	301.00	306.00	312.00	309.00	332.00	318.00	334.00
250A / 4w - 4 x 1/C #2/0 MI	m	324.00	298.00	303.00	309.00	306.00	329.00	315.00	330.00
300A / 4w - 4 x 1/C #3/0 MI	m	506.00	465.00	472.00	482.00	477.00	513.00	491.00	515.00
400A / 4w - 4 x 1/C #250 mcm MI	m	682.00	627.00	637.00	649.00	643.00	691.00	662.00	694.00
500A / 4w - 4 x 1/C #350 mcm MI	m	805.00	740.00	751.00	767.00	759.00	816.00	782.00	820.00
600A / 4w - 4 x 1/C #500 mcm MI	m	1,060	975.00	990.00	1,010	1,000	1,080	1,030	1,080
600V Mineral insulated cable termination									
16 mm (1/2")	m	118.00	108.00	110.00	112.00	111.00	119.00	114.00	120.00
21 mm (3/4")	m	209.00	192.00	195.00	199.00	197.00	212.00	203.00	213.00
27 mm (1")	m	457.00	420.00	427.00	435.00	431.00	463.00	444.00	465.00
35 mm (1 1/4")	m	649.00	597.00	606.00	618.00	612.00	658.00	630.00	661.00

26 05 33 Raceway and Boxes for Electrical Systems

CONDUIT

Material Price Carried At Trade

RACEWAYS INSTALLED COMPLETE

Embedded in slab excluding elbows and pull boxes:

Item	UNITS	St. John's	Halifax	Montreal	Ottawa	Toronto	Winnipeg	Calgary	Vancouver
Rigid galvanized steel									
16 mm (1/2")	m	25.20	23.20	23.60	24.00	23.80	25.60	24.50	25.70
21 mm (3/4")	m	27.60	25.40	25.70	26.30	26.00	28.00	26.80	28.10
27 mm (1")	m	37.30	34.30	34.80	35.60	35.20	37.80	36.30	38.00
35 mm (1 1/4")	m	47.30	43.50	44.20	45.00	44.60	47.90	45.90	48.20
41 mm (1 1/2")	m	53.80	49.50	50.30	51.30	50.80	54.60	52.30	54.90
53 mm (2")	m	65.90	60.60	61.60	62.80	62.20	66.90	64.10	67.20
Electric metallic (E.M.T.)									
16 mm (1/2")	m	13.30	12.20	12.40	12.60	12.50	13.40	12.90	13.50
21 mm (3/4")	m	16.00	14.70	14.90	15.30	15.10	16.20	15.60	16.30
27 mm (1")	m	19.40	17.80	18.10	18.50	18.30	19.70	18.80	19.80
35 mm (1 1/4")	m	24.70	22.70	23.10	23.50	23.30	25.00	24.00	25.20
41 mm (1 1/2")	m	28.70	26.40	26.80	27.40	27.10	29.10	27.90	29.30
53 mm (2")	m	33.20	30.50	31.00	31.60	31.30	33.60	32.20	33.80
Rigid PVC									
16 mm (1/2")	m	13.80	12.70	12.90	13.10	13.00	14.00	13.40	14.00
21 mm (3/4")	m	14.80	13.70	13.90	14.10	14.00	15.10	14.40	15.10
27 mm (1")	m	18.00	16.60	16.80	17.20	17.00	18.30	17.50	18.40

Item	UNITS	St. John's	Halifax	Montreal	Ottawa	Toronto	Winnipeg	Calgary	Vancouver
35 mm (1 1/4")................................	m	21.20	19.50	19.80	20.20	20.00	21.50	20.60	21.60
41 mm (1 1/2")................................	m	25.40	23.40	23.80	24.20	24.00	25.80	24.70	25.90
53 mm (2")................................	m	29.70	27.30	27.70	28.30	28.00	30.10	28.80	30.20
Surface mounted 2400 mm (8') average high one pull box, one elbow per 30 m (100 LF), and supports:									
Rigid galvanized steel									
16 mm (1/2")................................	m	33.80	31.10	31.60	32.20	31.90	34.30	32.90	34.50
21 mm (3/4")................................	m	36.80	33.80	34.40	35.00	34.70	37.30	35.70	37.50
27 mm (1")................................	m	47.00	43.20	43.90	44.70	44.30	47.60	45.60	47.80
35 mm (1 1/4")................................	m	62.50	57.50	58.40	59.60	59.00	63.40	60.80	63.70
41 mm (1 1/2")................................	m	70.40	64.70	65.70	67.10	66.40	71.40	68.40	71.70
53 mm (2")................................	m	88.40	81.30	82.60	84.20	83.40	89.70	85.90	90.10
63 mm (2 1/2")................................	m	141.00	130.00	132.00	134.00	133.00	143.00	137.00	144.00
78 mm (3")................................	m	177.00	163.00	165.00	169.00	167.00	180.00	172.00	180.00
91 mm (3 1/2")................................	m	232.00	214.00	217.00	221.00	219.00	235.00	226.00	237.00
103 mm (4")................................	m	285.00	262.00	266.00	272.00	269.00	289.00	277.00	291.00
129 mm (5")................................	m	501.00	461.00	468.00	478.00	473.00	508.00	487.00	511.00
155 mm (6")................................	m	693.00	638.00	647.00	661.00	654.00	703.00	674.00	706.00
Electric metallic (E.M.T.)									
16 mm (1/2")................................	m	17.40	16.00	16.20	16.60	16.40	17.60	16.90	17.70
21 mm (3/4")................................	m	20.40	18.70	19.00	19.40	19.20	20.60	19.80	20.70
27 mm (1")................................	m	25.50	23.50	23.90	24.30	24.10	25.90	24.80	26.00
35 mm (1 1/4")................................	m	36.30	33.30	33.90	34.50	34.20	36.80	35.20	36.90
41 mm (1 1/2")................................	m	40.80	37.50	38.10	38.90	38.50	41.40	39.70	41.60
53 mm (2")................................	m	47.90	44.10	44.70	45.70	45.20	48.60	46.60	48.80
63 mm (2 1/2")................................	m	72.30	66.50	67.50	68.90	68.20	73.30	70.20	73.70
78 mm (3")................................	m	87.70	80.60	81.90	83.50	82.70	88.90	85.20	89.30
103 mm (4")................................	m	125.00	115.00	117.00	119.00	118.00	127.00	122.00	127.00
Rigid PVC									
16 mm (1/2")................................	m	20.10	18.50	18.80	19.20	19.00	20.40	19.60	20.50
21 mm (3/4")................................	m	21.20	19.50	19.80	20.20	20.00	21.50	20.60	21.60
27 mm (1")................................	m	25.40	23.40	23.80	24.20	24.00	25.80	24.70	25.90
35 mm (1 1/4")................................	m	28.60	26.30	26.70	27.30	27.00	29.00	27.80	29.20
41 mm (1 1/2")................................	m	33.90	31.20	31.70	32.30	32.00	34.40	33.00	34.60
53 mm (2")................................	m	40.30	37.10	37.60	38.40	38.00	40.90	39.10	41.00
63 mm (2 1/2")................................	m	56.20	51.70	52.50	53.50	53.00	57.00	54.60	57.20
78 mm (3")................................	m	67.80	62.40	63.40	64.60	64.00	68.80	65.90	69.10
91 mm (3 1/2")................................	m	81.60	75.10	76.20	77.80	77.00	82.80	79.30	83.20
103 mm (4")................................	m	95.40	87.80	89.10	90.90	90.00	96.80	92.70	97.20
Rigid aluminum									
16 mm (1/2")................................	m	23.70	21.80	22.20	22.60	22.40	24.10	23.10	24.20
21 mm (3/4")................................	m	28.40	26.10	26.50	27.10	26.80	28.80	27.60	28.90
27 mm (1")................................	m	34.80	32.00	32.50	33.10	32.80	35.30	33.80	35.40
35 mm (1 1/4")................................	m	46.30	42.60	43.30	44.10	43.70	47.00	45.00	47.20
41 mm (1 1/2")................................	m	53.20	48.90	49.70	50.70	50.20	54.00	51.70	54.20
53 mm (2")................................	m	69.60	64.10	65.00	66.40	65.70	70.60	67.70	71.00
63 mm (2 1/2")................................	m	117.00	107.00	109.00	111.00	110.00	118.00	113.00	119.00
78 mm (3")................................	m	139.00	128.00	130.00	132.00	131.00	141.00	135.00	141.00
91 mm (3 1/2")................................	m	187.00	172.00	174.00	178.00	176.00	189.00	181.00	190.00
103 mm (4")................................	m	243.00	223.00	227.00	231.00	229.00	246.00	236.00	247.00

WIRING CHANNELS

Wiring channels

Square section, steel:

Item	UNITS	St. John's	Halifax	Montreal	Ottawa	Toronto	Winnipeg	Calgary	Vancouver
65 mm (2 1/2") x 65 mm (2 1/2")................	m	142.00	131.00	133.00	135.00	134.00	144.00	138.00	145.00
100 mm (4") x 100 mm (4")................	m	197.00	181.00	184.00	188.00	186.00	200.00	192.00	201.00
150 mm (6") x 150 mm (6")................	m	258.00	237.00	241.00	245.00	243.00	261.00	250.00	262.00

OUTLET BOXES

Wiring outlet boxes

Ceiling type 100 mm x 100 mm (4" x 4"):

Item	UNITS	St. John's	Halifax	Montreal	Ottawa	Toronto	Winnipeg	Calgary	Vancouver
Surface	EA	35.00	32.20	32.70	33.30	33.00	35.50	34.00	35.60
Recessed	EA	25.40	23.40	23.80	24.20	24.00	25.80	24.70	25.90
Cast iron	EA	143.00	132.00	134.00	136.00	135.00	145.00	139.00	146.00
Wall type device box:									
Surface, 1 gang	EA	30.70	28.30	28.70	29.30	29.00	31.20	29.90	31.30
Surface, 2 gang	EA	31.80	29.30	29.70	30.30	30.00	32.30	30.90	32.40
Recessed, 1 gang	EA	41.30	38.00	38.60	39.40	39.00	41.90	40.20	42.10
Recessed, 2 gang	EA	46.60	42.90	43.60	44.40	44.00	47.30	45.30	47.50

PULL BOXES & CABINETS

Pull box or metering cabinets:

Item	UNITS	St. John's	Halifax	Montreal	Ottawa	Toronto	Winnipeg	Calgary	Vancouver
500 mm x 500 mm x 250 mm (20" x 20" x 10")	EA	305.00	281.00	285.00	291.00	288.00	310.00	297.00	311.00
500 mm x 750 mm x 250 mm (20" x 30" x 10")	EA	357.00	329.00	334.00	340.00	337.00	362.00	347.00	364.00
750 mm x 750 mm x 250 mm (30" x 30" x 10")	EA	446.00	410.00	417.00	425.00	421.00	453.00	434.00	455.00
910 mm x 910 mm x 250 mm (36" x 36" x 10")	EA	641.00	590.00	599.00	611.00	605.00	650.00	623.00	653.00
910 mm x 910 mm x 300 mm (36" x 36" x 12")	EA	650.00	598.00	607.00	619.00	613.00	659.00	631.00	662.00
1220 mm x 1220 mm x 300 mm (48" x 48" x 12")	EA	1,030	946.00	960.00	980.00	970.00	1,040	999.00	1,050

26 05 36 Cable Trays for Electrical Systems

CABLE TRAY

Cable tray including fittings and supports

Ventilated type:

Galvanized steel

Item	UNITS	St. John's	Halifax	Montreal	Ottawa	Toronto	Winnipeg	Calgary	Vancouver
150 mm (6") wide................	m	154.00	141.00	144.00	146.00	145.00	156.00	149.00	157.00

Item	UNITS	St. John's	Halifax	Montreal	Ottawa	Toronto	Winnipeg	Calgary	Vancouver
300 mm (12") wide	m	167.00	154.00	156.00	160.00	158.00	170.00	163.00	171.00
450 mm (18") wide	m	211.00	194.00	197.00	201.00	199.00	214.00	205.00	215.00
600 mm (24") wide	m	237.00	218.00	222.00	226.00	224.00	241.00	231.00	242.00
Aluminum									
150 mm (6") wide	m	180.00	166.00	168.00	172.00	170.00	183.00	175.00	184.00
300 mm (12") wide	m	200.00	184.00	187.00	191.00	189.00	203.00	195.00	204.00
450 mm (18") wide	m	240.00	220.00	224.00	228.00	226.00	243.00	233.00	244.00
600 mm (24") wide	m	283.00	260.00	264.00	270.00	267.00	287.00	275.00	288.00
Ladder type:									
Galvanized steel									
150 mm (6") wide	m	144.00	133.00	135.00	137.00	136.00	146.00	140.00	147.00
300 mm (12") wide	m	163.00	150.00	152.00	156.00	154.00	166.00	159.00	166.00
450 mm (18") wide	m	193.00	177.00	180.00	184.00	182.00	196.00	187.00	197.00
600 mm (24") wide	m	222.00	204.00	207.00	211.00	209.00	225.00	215.00	226.00
Aluminum									
150 mm (6") wide	m	175.00	161.00	163.00	167.00	165.00	177.00	170.00	178.00
300 mm (12") wide	m	183.00	169.00	171.00	175.00	173.00	186.00	178.00	187.00
450 mm (18") wide	m	219.00	202.00	205.00	209.00	207.00	223.00	213.00	224.00
600 mm (24") wide	m	251.00	231.00	235.00	239.00	237.00	255.00	244.00	256.00

26 05 83 Wiring Connections
WIRING DEVICES
(Stainless steel switch cover included, wired to junction box)
Switches, 120-347 V

Item	UNITS	St. John's	Halifax	Montreal	Ottawa	Toronto	Winnipeg	Calgary	Vancouver
Toggle switches, premium grade, connected:									
Single pole, 120 V	EA	135.00	124.00	126.00	128.00	127.00	137.00	131.00	137.00
3-way, 120 V	EA	159.00	146.00	149.00	152.00	150.00	161.00	155.00	162.00
4-way, 120 V	EA	228.00	210.00	213.00	217.00	215.00	231.00	221.00	232.00
Single pole, 347 V	EA	140.00	129.00	131.00	133.00	132.00	142.00	136.00	143.00
3-way, 347 V	EA	165.00	152.00	154.00	158.00	156.00	168.00	161.00	168.00
4-way, 347 V	EA	243.00	223.00	227.00	231.00	229.00	246.00	236.00	247.00
(Stainless steel receptacle cover included, wired to junction box)									
15 A receptacles									
Standard:									
Duplex u ground	EA	137.00	126.00	128.00	130.00	129.00	139.00	133.00	139.00
Duplex u ground, specification grade	EA	148.00	137.00	139.00	141.00	140.00	151.00	144.00	151.00
Duplex isolated ground	EA	175.00	161.00	163.00	167.00	165.00	177.00	170.00	178.00
Duplex GFI	EA	158.00	145.00	148.00	150.00	149.00	160.00	153.00	161.00
Duplex TVSS	EA	200.00	184.00	187.00	191.00	189.00	203.00	195.00	204.00
Weatherproof:									
Duplex u ground	EA	177.00	163.00	165.00	169.00	167.00	180.00	172.00	180.00
20 A receptacles									
Standard:									
Duplex u ground	EA	152.00	139.00	142.00	144.00	143.00	154.00	147.00	154.00
Duplex GFI	EA	158.00	145.00	148.00	150.00	149.00	160.00	153.00	161.00
30 A receptacles									
Dryer type:									
4 wire, 120/240 V	EA	360.00	332.00	337.00	343.00	340.00	366.00	350.00	367.00
50 A receptacles									
Range type:									
4 wire, 120/240 V	EA	533.00	490.00	498.00	508.00	503.00	541.00	518.00	543.00

MOTOR CONNECTION AND DISCONNECT ONLY

Item	UNITS	St. John's	Halifax	Montreal	Ottawa	Toronto	Winnipeg	Calgary	Vancouver
7.5 kW (10 hp) motors	EA	572.00	527.00	535.00	545.00	540.00	581.00	556.00	583.00
11.2 kW (15 hp) motors	EA	588.00	541.00	549.00	561.00	555.00	597.00	572.00	599.00
18.6 kW (25 hp) motors	EA	791.00	727.00	739.00	753.00	746.00	802.00	768.00	806.00
37.5 kW (50 hp) motors	EA	1,070	985.00	1,000	1,020	1,010	1,090	1,040	1,090
56 kW (75 hp) motors	EA	1,240	1,140	1,160	1,180	1,170	1,260	1,210	1,260
75 kW (100 hp) motors	EA	1,830	1,690	1,710	1,750	1,730	1,860	1,780	1,870

26 22 00 Low-Voltage Transformers
TRANSFORMERS
Dry type
Three phase 600 V / 120-208 V:

Item	UNITS	St. John's	Halifax	Montreal	Ottawa	Toronto	Winnipeg	Calgary	Vancouver
3 kVA	EA	1,140	1,050	1,070	1,090	1,080	1,160	1,110	1,170
6 kVA	EA	1,480	1,370	1,390	1,410	1,400	1,510	1,440	1,510
9 kVA	EA	1,840	1,700	1,720	1,760	1,740	1,870	1,790	1,880
15 kVA	EA	2,140	1,970	2,000	2,040	2,020	2,170	2,080	2,180
30 kVA	EA	2,810	2,580	2,620	2,680	2,650	2,850	2,730	2,860
45 kVA	EA	3,640	3,340	3,400	3,460	3,430	3,690	3,530	3,700
75 kVA	EA	5,620	5,170	5,250	5,350	5,300	5,700	5,460	5,720
112.5 kVA	EA	7,500	6,900	7,010	7,150	7,080	7,610	7,290	7,650
150 kVA	EA	9,120	8,390	8,510	8,690	8,600	9,250	8,860	9,290
225 kVA	EA	13,900	12,800	13,000	13,200	13,100	14,100	13,500	14,100
300 kVA	EA	16,300	15,000	15,200	15,600	15,400	16,600	15,900	16,600
450 kVA	EA	24,400	22,400	22,800	23,200	23,000	24,700	23,700	24,800
500 kVA	EA	27,000	24,900	25,200	25,800	25,500	27,400	26,300	27,500
600 kVA	EA	32,300	29,700	30,200	30,800	30,500	32,800	31,400	32,900
750 kVA	EA	37,200	34,200	34,700	35,500	35,100	37,700	36,200	37,900

Item	UNITS	St. John's	Halifax	Montreal	Ottawa	Toronto	Winnipeg	Calgary	Vancouver
26 24 00 Switchboards and Panelboards									
PANELBOARDS									
Lighting / power panels complete with bolt on breakers									
120/240 V, 1 phase, NBLP main lugs:									
100 A									
12 circuits, 15 A	EA	1,070	985.00	1,000	1,020	1,010	1,090	1,040	1,090
18 circuits, 15 A	EA	1,350	1,240	1,260	1,280	1,270	1,370	1,310	1,370
24 circuits, 15 A	EA	1,690	1,550	1,570	1,610	1,590	1,710	1,640	1,720
225 A									
24 circuits, 15 A	EA	1,740	1,600	1,620	1,660	1,640	1,760	1,690	1,770
30 circuits, 15 A	EA	2,080	1,910	1,940	1,980	1,960	2,110	2,020	2,120
36 circuits, 15 A	EA	2,400	2,200	2,240	2,280	2,260	2,430	2,330	2,440
42 circuits, 15 A	EA	2,620	2,410	2,450	2,490	2,470	2,660	2,540	2,670
60 circuits, 15 A	EA	3,380	3,110	3,160	3,220	3,190	3,430	3,290	3,450
84 circuits, 15 A	EA	4,130	3,800	3,860	3,940	3,900	4,190	4,020	4,210
Tub only with main lug:									
400 A									
42 spaces	EA	3,300	3,030	3,080	3,140	3,110	3,340	3,200	3,360
60 spaces	EA	4,290	3,950	4,010	4,090	4,050	4,350	4,170	4,370
84 spaces	EA	6,480	5,960	6,050	6,170	6,110	6,570	6,290	6,600
120/240 V, 1 phase, NBLP main breaker c/w bolt on breakers:									
100 A									
12 circuits, 15 A	EA	1,260	1,160	1,180	1,200	1,190	1,280	1,230	1,290
18 circuits, 15 A	EA	1,570	1,440	1,470	1,490	1,480	1,590	1,520	1,600
24 circuits, 15 A	EA	1,910	1,760	1,780	1,820	1,800	1,940	1,850	1,940
225 A									
24 circuits, 15 A	EA	2,400	2,200	2,240	2,280	2,260	2,430	2,330	2,440
30 circuits, 15 A	EA	2,720	2,510	2,540	2,600	2,570	2,760	2,650	2,780
36 circuits, 15 A	EA	3,040	2,800	2,840	2,900	2,870	3,090	2,960	3,100
42 circuits, 15 A	EA	3,410	3,140	3,190	3,250	3,220	3,460	3,320	3,480
60 circuits, 15 A	EA	4,030	3,710	3,760	3,840	3,800	4,090	3,910	4,100
84 circuits, 15 A	EA	4,800	4,420	4,480	4,580	4,530	4,870	4,670	4,890
120/208 V, 3 phase, NBLP with lugs:									
100 A									
18 circuits, 15 A	EA	1,390	1,280	1,300	1,320	1,310	1,410	1,350	1,410
24 circuits, 15 A	EA	1,720	1,580	1,600	1,640	1,620	1,740	1,670	1,750
30 circuits, 15 A	EA	2,200	2,030	2,060	2,100	2,080	2,240	2,140	2,250
42 circuits, 15 A	EA	2,630	2,420	2,460	2,500	2,480	2,670	2,550	2,680
225 A									
18 circuits, 15 A	EA	1,420	1,310	1,330	1,350	1,340	1,440	1,380	1,450
24 circuits, 15 A	EA	1,760	1,620	1,640	1,680	1,660	1,780	1,710	1,790
30 circuits, 15 A	EA	2,250	2,070	2,100	2,140	2,120	2,280	2,180	2,290
42 circuits, 15 A	EA	2,680	2,470	2,500	2,560	2,530	2,720	2,610	2,730
60 circuits, 15 A	EA	3,500	3,220	3,270	3,330	3,300	3,550	3,400	3,560
72 circuits, 15 A	EA	3,920	3,610	3,660	3,740	3,700	3,980	3,810	4,000
84 circuits, 15 A	EA	4,460	4,100	4,170	4,250	4,210	4,530	4,340	4,550
120/208 V, 3 phase, NBLP main breaker:									
100 A									
15 circuits, 15 A	EA	1,700	1,560	1,580	1,620	1,600	1,720	1,650	1,730
24 circuits, 15 A	EA	2,370	2,180	2,220	2,260	2,240	2,410	2,310	2,420
30 circuits, 15 A	EA	2,850	2,620	2,660	2,720	2,690	2,890	2,770	2,910
42 circuits, 15 A	EA	3,290	3,020	3,070	3,130	3,100	3,330	3,190	3,350
225 A									
18 circuits, 15 A	EA	2,080	1,910	1,940	1,980	1,960	2,110	2,020	2,120
24 circuits, 15 A	EA	2,440	2,240	2,280	2,320	2,300	2,470	2,370	2,480
30 circuits, 15 A	EA	2,890	2,660	2,700	2,760	2,730	2,930	2,810	2,950
42 circuits, 15 A	EA	3,380	3,110	3,160	3,220	3,190	3,430	3,290	3,450
347/600 V CDP Style									
100 A									
24 circuits, 15 A single pole 347 V	EA	4,460	4,100	4,170	4,250	4,210	4,530	4,340	4,550
42 circuits, 15 A single pole 347 V	EA	6,190	5,690	5,780	5,900	5,840	6,280	6,020	6,310
225 A									
24 circuits, 15 A single pole 347 V	EA	4,650	4,280	4,350	4,430	4,390	4,720	4,520	4,740
30 circuits, 15 A single pole 347 V	EA	5,620	5,170	5,250	5,350	5,300	5,700	5,460	5,720
42 circuits, 15 A single pole 347 V	EA	6,410	5,900	5,990	6,110	6,050	6,500	6,230	6,530
347/600 V CDP style main lugs:									
225 A, 42 spaces	EA	2,020	1,860	1,890	1,930	1,910	2,050	1,970	2,060
26 24 16 Panelboards									
OVERCURRENT PROTECTION DEVICES									
Distribution panel fusible type									
Base and main lugs 250 or 600 V, copper:									
3 poles, 3 wires									
250 A	EA	2,400	2,200	2,240	2,280	2,260	2,430	2,330	2,440
400 A	EA	2,620	2,410	2,450	2,490	2,470	2,660	2,540	2,670
600 A	EA	2,920	2,680	2,720	2,780	2,750	2,960	2,830	2,970
800 A	EA	3,230	2,970	3,020	3,080	3,050	3,280	3,140	3,290
1200 A	EA	4,240	3,900	3,960	4,040	4,000	4,300	4,120	4,320
3 poles, 4 wires									
250 A	EA	2,510	2,310	2,350	2,390	2,370	2,550	2,440	2,560
400 A	EA	2,810	2,580	2,620	2,680	2,650	2,850	2,730	2,860
600 A	EA	3,170	2,920	2,960	3,020	2,990	3,210	3,080	3,230

Item	UNITS	St. John's	Halifax	Montreal	Ottawa	Toronto	Winnipeg	Calgary	Vancouver
800 A	EA	3,630	3,330	3,390	3,450	3,420	3,680	3,520	3,690
1200 A	EA	4,620	4,250	4,320	4,400	4,360	4,690	4,490	4,710
Door in trim	EA	943.00	868.00	881.00	899.00	890.00	957.00	917.00	961.00
Fusible units for distribution panel, fuses not included									
600 V:									
2 poles									
30 A	EA	350.00	322.00	327.00	333.00	330.00	355.00	340.00	356.00
60 A	EA	392.00	361.00	366.00	374.00	370.00	398.00	381.00	400.00
100 A	EA	647.00	595.00	604.00	616.00	610.00	656.00	628.00	659.00
200 A	EA	1,090	1,000	1,020	1,040	1,030	1,110	1,060	1,110
400 A	EA	2,510	2,310	2,350	2,390	2,370	2,550	2,440	2,560
600 A	EA	3,020	2,780	2,820	2,880	2,850	3,060	2,940	3,080
800 A	EA	4,520	4,150	4,220	4,300	4,260	4,580	4,390	4,600
1200 A	EA	7,720	7,100	7,210	7,350	7,280	7,830	7,500	7,860
3 poles									
30 A, twin mounted	EA	1,040	956.00	970.00	990.00	980.00	1,050	1,010	1,060
60 A, twin mounted	EA	1,090	1,000	1,020	1,040	1,030	1,110	1,060	1,110
100 A, twin mounted	EA	1,180	1,080	1,100	1,120	1,110	1,190	1,140	1,200
200 A	EA	1,290	1,190	1,210	1,230	1,220	1,310	1,260	1,320
400 A	EA	2,480	2,280	2,320	2,360	2,340	2,520	2,410	2,530
600 A	EA	3,200	2,940	2,990	3,050	3,020	3,250	3,110	3,260
800 A	EA	4,870	4,480	4,540	4,640	4,590	4,930	4,730	4,960
1200 A	EA	6,540	6,020	6,110	6,230	6,170	6,630	6,360	6,660
Distribution panel, breaker type base, main breaker, no circuit breakers									
250 or 600 V:									
3 poles, 3 wires									
250 A	EA	3,980	3,660	3,710	3,790	3,750	4,030	3,860	4,050
400 A	EA	5,270	4,850	4,920	5,020	4,970	5,340	5,120	5,370
600 A	EA	6,870	6,320	6,420	6,540	6,480	6,970	6,670	7,000
800 A	EA	8,650	7,960	8,080	8,240	8,160	8,770	8,400	8,810
1200 A	EA	14,600	13,500	13,700	13,900	13,800	14,800	14,200	14,900
3 poles, 4 wires									
250 A	EA	4,000	3,680	3,730	3,810	3,770	4,050	3,880	4,070
400 A	EA	5,290	4,870	4,940	5,040	4,990	5,360	5,140	5,390
600 A	EA	6,890	6,340	6,440	6,570	6,500	6,990	6,700	7,020
800 A	EA	8,690	8,000	8,120	8,280	8,200	8,820	8,450	8,860
1200 A	EA	14,600	13,500	13,700	13,900	13,800	14,800	14,200	14,900
TVSS filter	EA	2,770	2,540	2,580	2,640	2,610	2,810	2,690	2,820

26 24 19 Motor-Control Centers
MOTOR STARTERS & CONTROLS

Magnetic starter (full voltage non-reversible general purpose enclosure with overload relays)
600 V 3 phase:

Item	UNITS	St. John's	Halifax	Montreal	Ottawa	Toronto	Winnipeg	Calgary	Vancouver
Motors up to 1.5 kW (2 hp)	EA	583.00	536.00	545.00	556.00	550.00	591.00	567.00	594.00
Motors up to 3.7 kW (5 hp)	EA	657.00	605.00	614.00	626.00	620.00	667.00	639.00	670.00
Motors up to 7.5 kW (10 hp)	EA	1,160	1,060	1,080	1,100	1,090	1,170	1,120	1,180
Motors up to 18.6 kW (25 hp)	EA	1,810	1,670	1,690	1,730	1,710	1,840	1,760	1,850
Motors up to 37.5 kW (50 hp)	EA	3,950	3,640	3,690	3,770	3,730	4,010	3,840	4,030

Combination magnetic/fusible type (full voltage non-reversible general purpose enclosure with fuses and overload relays)
600 V 3 phase:

Item	UNITS	St. John's	Halifax	Montreal	Ottawa	Toronto	Winnipeg	Calgary	Vancouver
Motors up to 3.7 kW (5 hp)	EA	1,580	1,450	1,480	1,500	1,490	1,600	1,530	1,610
Motors up to 7.5 kW (10 hp)	EA	1,640	1,510	1,530	1,570	1,550	1,670	1,600	1,670
Motors up to 18.6 kW (25 hp)	EA	2,290	2,110	2,140	2,180	2,160	2,320	2,220	2,330
Motors up to 37.5 kW (50 hp)	EA	3,340	3,070	3,120	3,180	3,150	3,390	3,240	3,400

26 25 00 Enclosed Bus Assemblies
BUS DUCT

Copper low impedance ventilated including supports and fitting, excluding elbows
Feeder type:
600 V

Item	UNITS	St. John's	Halifax	Montreal	Ottawa	Toronto	Winnipeg	Calgary	Vancouver
1000 A	m	1,180	1,080	1,100	1,120	1,110	1,190	1,140	1,200
1350 A	m	1,740	1,600	1,620	1,660	1,640	1,760	1,690	1,770
1600 A	m	2,080	1,910	1,940	1,980	1,960	2,110	2,020	2,120
2000 A	m	2,610	2,400	2,440	2,480	2,460	2,640	2,530	2,660
2500 A	m	3,260	3,000	3,050	3,110	3,080	3,310	3,170	3,330
3000 A	m	3,890	3,580	3,630	3,710	3,670	3,950	3,780	3,960
3500 A	m	4,430	4,080	4,140	4,220	4,180	4,490	4,310	4,510
4000 A	m	5,060	4,650	4,720	4,820	4,770	5,130	4,910	5,150
4500 A	m	5,420	4,980	5,060	5,160	5,110	5,490	5,260	5,520
5000 A	m	5,890	5,420	5,500	5,620	5,560	5,980	5,730	6,000
347/600 V									
1000 A	m	1,620	1,490	1,510	1,550	1,530	1,640	1,580	1,650
1350 A	m	2,220	2,040	2,070	2,110	2,090	2,250	2,150	2,260
1600 A	m	2,670	2,460	2,490	2,550	2,520	2,710	2,600	2,720
2000 A	m	3,260	3,000	3,050	3,110	3,080	3,310	3,170	3,330
2500 A	m	4,000	3,680	3,730	3,810	3,770	4,050	3,880	4,070
3000 A	m	5,080	4,670	4,740	4,840	4,790	5,150	4,930	5,170
3500 A	m	5,720	5,270	5,350	5,450	5,400	5,810	5,560	5,830
4000 A	m	6,240	5,740	5,830	5,950	5,890	6,330	6,070	6,360
4500 A	m	6,890	6,340	6,440	6,570	6,500	6,990	6,700	7,020

Item	UNITS	St. John's	Halifax	Montreal	Ottawa	Toronto	Winnipeg	Calgary	Vancouver
5000 A	m	7,570	6,960	7,070	7,210	7,140	7,680	7,350	7,710
Plug in type:									
600 V									
1000 A	m	1,190	1,090	1,110	1,130	1,120	1,200	1,150	1,210
1350 A	m	1,750	1,610	1,630	1,670	1,650	1,770	1,700	1,780
1600 A	m	2,090	1,920	1,950	1,990	1,970	2,120	2,030	2,130
2000 A	m	2,620	2,410	2,450	2,490	2,470	2,660	2,540	2,670
2500 A	m	3,280	3,010	3,060	3,120	3,090	3,320	3,180	3,340
3000 A	m	3,900	3,590	3,640	3,720	3,680	3,960	3,790	3,970
3500 A	m	4,470	4,110	4,180	4,260	4,220	4,540	4,350	4,560
4000 A	m	5,070	4,660	4,730	4,830	4,780	5,140	4,920	5,160
4500 A	m	5,430	4,990	5,070	5,170	5,120	5,500	5,270	5,530
347/600 V									
600 A	m	1,180	1,080	1,100	1,120	1,110	1,190	1,140	1,200
1000 A	m	1,630	1,500	1,520	1,560	1,540	1,660	1,590	1,660
1350 A	m	2,230	2,050	2,080	2,120	2,100	2,260	2,160	2,270
1600 A	m	2,680	2,470	2,500	2,560	2,530	2,720	2,610	2,730
2000 A	m	3,280	3,010	3,060	3,120	3,090	3,320	3,180	3,340
2500 A	m	4,010	3,690	3,740	3,820	3,780	4,060	3,890	4,080
3000 A	m	5,090	4,680	4,750	4,850	4,800	5,160	4,940	5,180
3500 A	m	5,730	5,270	5,360	5,460	5,410	5,820	5,570	5,840
4000 A	m	6,250	5,750	5,840	5,960	5,900	6,340	6,080	6,370
4500 A	m	6,820	6,270	6,370	6,490	6,430	6,910	6,620	6,940
Aluminum low impedance ventilated including supports and fitting, excluding elbows									
Feeder type:									
600 V									
600 A	m	678.00	624.00	634.00	646.00	640.00	688.00	659.00	691.00
1000 A	m	784.00	722.00	733.00	747.00	740.00	796.00	762.00	799.00
1350 A	m	1,110	1,020	1,040	1,060	1,050	1,130	1,080	1,130
1600 A	m	1,260	1,160	1,180	1,200	1,190	1,280	1,230	1,290
2000 A	m	1,490	1,370	1,400	1,420	1,410	1,520	1,450	1,520
2500 A	m	1,870	1,720	1,740	1,780	1,760	1,890	1,810	1,900
3000 A	m	2,130	1,960	1,990	2,030	2,010	2,160	2,070	2,170
3500 A	m	2,390	2,190	2,230	2,270	2,250	2,420	2,320	2,430
4000 A	m	2,960	2,720	2,760	2,820	2,790	3,000	2,870	3,010
4500 A	m	3,320	3,050	3,100	3,160	3,130	3,360	3,220	3,380
347/600 V									
600 A	m	784.00	722.00	733.00	747.00	740.00	796.00	762.00	799.00
1000 A	m	954.00	878.00	891.00	909.00	900.00	968.00	927.00	972.00
1350 A	m	1,330	1,220	1,240	1,260	1,250	1,340	1,290	1,350
1600 A	m	1,460	1,350	1,370	1,390	1,380	1,480	1,420	1,490
2000 A	m	1,800	1,660	1,680	1,720	1,700	1,830	1,750	1,840
2500 A	m	2,050	1,880	1,910	1,950	1,930	2,070	1,990	2,080
3000 A	m	2,370	2,180	2,220	2,260	2,240	2,410	2,310	2,420
3500 A	m	2,980	2,740	2,780	2,840	2,810	3,020	2,890	3,030
4000 A	m	3,670	3,370	3,430	3,490	3,460	3,720	3,560	3,740
4500 A	m	4,090	3,760	3,820	3,900	3,860	4,150	3,980	4,170
Plug in type:									
600 V									
600 A	m	700.00	644.00	653.00	667.00	660.00	710.00	680.00	713.00
1000 A	m	763.00	702.00	713.00	727.00	720.00	774.00	742.00	778.00
1350 A	m	1,140	1,050	1,070	1,090	1,080	1,160	1,110	1,170
1600 A	m	1,380	1,270	1,290	1,310	1,300	1,400	1,340	1,400
2000 A	m	1,640	1,510	1,530	1,570	1,550	1,670	1,600	1,670
2500 A	m	2,080	1,910	1,940	1,980	1,960	2,110	2,020	2,120
3000 A	m	2,330	2,150	2,180	2,220	2,200	2,370	2,270	2,380
3500 A	m	2,630	2,420	2,460	2,500	2,480	2,670	2,550	2,680
4000 A	m	3,290	3,020	3,070	3,130	3,100	3,330	3,190	3,350
347/600 V									
600 A	m	795.00	731.00	743.00	758.00	750.00	806.00	773.00	810.00
1000 A	m	965.00	887.00	901.00	919.00	910.00	978.00	937.00	983.00
1350 A	m	1,340	1,230	1,250	1,270	1,260	1,350	1,300	1,360
1600 A	m	1,470	1,360	1,380	1,400	1,390	1,490	1,430	1,500
2000 A	m	1,810	1,670	1,690	1,730	1,710	1,840	1,760	1,850
2500 A	m	2,070	1,900	1,930	1,970	1,950	2,100	2,010	2,110
3000 A	m	2,390	2,190	2,230	2,270	2,250	2,420	2,320	2,430
3500 A	m	2,990	2,750	2,790	2,850	2,820	3,030	2,900	3,050
4000 A	m	3,690	3,390	3,450	3,510	3,480	3,740	3,580	3,760
Bus duct plug in units									
Fusible units (including fuses):									
600 V									
30 A	EA	625.00	575.00	584.00	596.00	590.00	634.00	608.00	637.00
60 A	EA	689.00	634.00	644.00	657.00	650.00	699.00	670.00	702.00
100 A	EA	965.00	887.00	901.00	919.00	910.00	978.00	937.00	983.00
200 A	EA	1,700	1,560	1,580	1,620	1,600	1,720	1,650	1,730
400 A	EA	3,560	3,280	3,330	3,390	3,360	3,610	3,460	3,630
600 A	EA	5,230	4,810	4,880	4,980	4,930	5,300	5,080	5,320
800 A	EA	8,720	8,020	8,150	8,310	8,230	8,850	8,480	8,890
1000 A	EA	10,900	10,000	10,200	10,400	10,300	11,100	10,600	11,100
1200 A	EA	16,700	15,400	15,600	16,000	15,800	17,000	16,300	17,100
347/600V									
30 A	EA	678.00	624.00	634.00	646.00	640.00	688.00	659.00	691.00

Item	UNITS	St. John's	Halifax	Montreal	Ottawa	Toronto	Winnipeg	Calgary	Vancouver
60 A	EA	731.00	673.00	683.00	697.00	690.00	742.00	711.00	745.00
100 A	EA	1,050	965.00	980.00	1,000	990.00	1,060	1,020	1,070
200 A	EA	1,780	1,640	1,660	1,700	1,680	1,810	1,730	1,810
400 A	EA	3,710	3,410	3,470	3,540	3,500	3,760	3,610	3,780
600 A	EA	5,450	5,010	5,090	5,190	5,140	5,530	5,290	5,550
800 A	EA	9,900	9,110	9,250	9,430	9,340	10,000	9,620	10,100
1000 A	EA	11,000	10,100	10,300	10,500	10,400	11,200	10,700	11,200
1200 A	EA	16,400	15,100	15,300	15,700	15,500	16,700	16,000	16,700

26 28 00 Low-Voltage Circuit Protective Devices
SWITCHES
Switches, fusible type, without fuses (individual mounting)
600 V

Item	UNITS	St. John's	Halifax	Montreal	Ottawa	Toronto	Winnipeg	Calgary	Vancouver
30 A 3 poles 3 W	EA	360.00	332.00	337.00	343.00	340.00	366.00	350.00	367.00
30 A 3 poles 4 W	EA	382.00	351.00	356.00	364.00	360.00	387.00	371.00	389.00
60 A 3 poles 3 W	EA	424.00	390.00	396.00	404.00	400.00	430.00	412.00	432.00
60 A 3 poles 4 W	EA	488.00	449.00	455.00	465.00	460.00	495.00	474.00	497.00
100 A 3 poles 3 W	EA	753.00	692.00	703.00	717.00	710.00	763.00	731.00	767.00
100 A 3 poles 4 W	EA	816.00	751.00	762.00	778.00	770.00	828.00	793.00	832.00
200 A 3 poles 3 W	EA	1,290	1,190	1,210	1,230	1,220	1,310	1,260	1,320
200 A 3 poles 4 W	EA	1,410	1,300	1,320	1,340	1,330	1,430	1,370	1,440
400 A 3 poles 3 W	EA	2,900	2,670	2,710	2,770	2,740	2,950	2,820	2,960
400 A 3 poles 4 W	EA	3,080	2,840	2,880	2,940	2,910	3,130	3,000	3,140
600 A 3 poles 3 W	EA	3,770	3,470	3,520	3,600	3,560	3,830	3,670	3,840
600 A 3 poles 4 W	EA	4,030	3,710	3,760	3,840	3,800	4,090	3,910	4,100
800 A 3 poles 3 W	EA	6,610	6,080	6,180	6,300	6,240	6,710	6,430	6,740
800 A 3 poles 4 W	EA	7,090	6,520	6,620	6,760	6,690	7,190	6,890	7,230
1200 A 3 poles 3 W	EA	8,490	7,810	7,930	8,090	8,010	8,610	8,250	8,650
1200 A 3 poles 4 W	EA	9,440	8,690	8,820	9,000	8,910	9,580	9,180	9,620

Switches, non fusible
250 or 600 V:

Item	UNITS	St. John's	Halifax	Montreal	Ottawa	Toronto	Winnipeg	Calgary	Vancouver
30 A 2 poles 2 W	EA	307.00	283.00	287.00	293.00	290.00	312.00	299.00	313.00
30 A 3 poles 3 W	EA	339.00	312.00	317.00	323.00	320.00	344.00	330.00	346.00
30 A 3 poles 4 W	EA	339.00	312.00	317.00	323.00	320.00	344.00	330.00	346.00
60 A 2 poles 2 W	EA	350.00	322.00	327.00	333.00	330.00	355.00	340.00	356.00
60 A 3 poles 3 W	EA	424.00	390.00	396.00	404.00	400.00	430.00	412.00	432.00
60 A 3 poles 4 W	EA	445.00	410.00	416.00	424.00	420.00	452.00	433.00	454.00
100 A 2 poles 2 W	EA	594.00	546.00	554.00	566.00	560.00	602.00	577.00	605.00
100 A 3 poles 3 W	EA	700.00	644.00	653.00	667.00	660.00	710.00	680.00	713.00
100 A 3 poles 4 W	EA	742.00	683.00	693.00	707.00	700.00	753.00	721.00	756.00
200 A 2 poles 2 W	EA	1,020	936.00	950.00	970.00	960.00	1,030	989.00	1,040
200 A 3 poles 3 W	EA	1,280	1,180	1,200	1,220	1,210	1,300	1,250	1,310
200 A 3 poles 4 W	EA	1,290	1,190	1,210	1,230	1,220	1,310	1,260	1,320
400 A 2 poles 2 W	EA	2,530	2,330	2,370	2,410	2,390	2,570	2,460	2,580
400 A 3 poles 3 W	EA	2,860	2,630	2,670	2,730	2,700	2,900	2,780	2,920
400 A 3 poles 4 W	EA	2,970	2,730	2,770	2,830	2,800	3,010	2,880	3,020
600 A 2 poles 2 W	EA	3,490	3,210	3,260	3,320	3,290	3,540	3,390	3,550
600 A 3 poles 3 W	EA	3,750	3,450	3,500	3,580	3,540	3,810	3,650	3,820
600 A 3 poles 4 W	EA	3,760	3,460	3,510	3,590	3,550	3,820	3,660	3,830
800 A 2 poles 2 W	EA	5,950	5,470	5,550	5,670	5,610	6,030	5,780	6,060
800 A 3 poles 3 W	EA	6,020	5,540	5,620	5,740	5,680	6,110	5,850	6,130
800 A 3 poles 4 W	EA	6,600	6,070	6,170	6,290	6,230	6,700	6,420	6,730
1200 A 2 poles 2 W	EA	7,160	6,580	6,680	6,820	6,750	7,260	6,950	7,290
1200 A 3 poles 3 W	EA	7,170	6,590	6,690	6,830	6,760	7,270	6,960	7,300
1200 A 3 poles 4 W	EA	7,880	7,240	7,360	7,500	7,430	7,990	7,650	8,020

Splitters troughs
125 A:

Item	UNITS	St. John's	Halifax	Montreal	Ottawa	Toronto	Winnipeg	Calgary	Vancouver
1000 mm (3') 3 poles	EA	232.00	214.00	217.00	221.00	219.00	235.00	226.00	237.00
1000 mm (3') 4 poles	EA	301.00	277.00	281.00	287.00	284.00	305.00	293.00	307.00
225 A:									
1000 mm (3') 3 poles	EA	392.00	361.00	366.00	374.00	370.00	398.00	381.00	400.00
1000 mm (3') 4 poles	EA	498.00	458.00	465.00	475.00	470.00	505.00	484.00	508.00
400 A:									
1200 mm (4') 3 poles	EA	625.00	575.00	584.00	596.00	590.00	634.00	608.00	637.00
1200 mm (4') 4 poles	EA	700.00	644.00	653.00	667.00	660.00	710.00	680.00	713.00
600 A:									
1200 mm (4') 3 poles	EA	1,060	975	990	1,010	1,000	1,080	1,030	1,080
1200 mm (4') 4 poles	EA	1,170	1,070	1,090	1,110	1,100	1,180	1,130	1,190

26 28 16 Enclosed Switches and Circuit Breakers
CIRCUIT BREAKERS
Circuit Breakers:
347/600 V, single pole

Item	UNITS	St. John's	Halifax	Montreal	Ottawa	Toronto	Winnipeg	Calgary	Vancouver
15-30A	EA	146.00	135.00	137.00	139.00	138.00	148.00	142.00	149.00
40-60A	EA	173.00	159.00	161.00	165.00	163.00	175.00	168.00	176.00
70-100A	EA	220.00	203.00	206.00	210.00	208.00	224.00	214.00	225.00
600 V, 2 poles									
15-30A	EA	353.00	325.00	330.00	336.00	333.00	358.00	343.00	360.00
40-60A	EA	418.00	384.00	390.00	398.00	394.00	424.00	406.00	426.00
70-100A	EA	455.00	418.00	425.00	433.00	429.00	461.00	442.00	463.00
125-225A	EA	1,060	971.00	986.00	1,010	996.00	1,070	1,030	1,080
250A	EA	1,740	1,600	1,620	1,660	1,640	1,760	1,690	1,770
300-400A	EA	2,190	2,020	2,050	2,090	2,070	2,230	2,130	2,240

Item	UNITS	St. John's	Halifax	Montreal	Ottawa	Toronto	Winnipeg	Calgary	Vancouver
600A	EA	3,220	2,960	3,010	3,070	3,040	3,270	3,130	3,280
800A	EA	5,830	5,360	5,450	5,560	5,500	5,910	5,670	5,940
1000-1200A	EA	10,600	9,750	9,900	10,100	10,000	10,800	10,300	10,800
600 V, 3 poles									
15-30A	EA	444.00	409.00	415.00	423.00	419.00	450.00	432.00	453.00
40-60A	EA	517.00	476.00	483.00	493.00	488.00	525.00	503.00	527.00
70-100A	EA	572.00	527.00	535.00	545.00	540.00	581.00	556.00	583.00
125-225A	EA	1,270	1,170	1,190	1,210	1,200	1,290	1,240	1,300
250A	EA	1,830	1,690	1,710	1,750	1,730	1,860	1,780	1,870
300-400A	EA	2,730	2,520	2,550	2,610	2,580	2,770	2,660	2,790
600A	EA	4,230	3,890	3,950	4,030	3,990	4,290	4,110	4,310
800A	EA	6,070	5,590	5,670	5,790	5,730	6,160	5,900	6,190
1000-1200A	EA	11,300	10,400	10,600	10,800	10,700	11,500	11,000	11,600
120/208 V, single pole									
15-25A	EA	41.30	38.00	38.60	39.40	39.00	41.90	40.20	42.10
30-60A	EA	49.80	45.80	46.50	47.50	47.00	50.50	48.40	50.80
70A	EA	64.70	59.50	60.40	61.60	61.00	65.60	62.80	65.90
90-100A	EA	212.00	195.00	198.00	202.00	200.00	215.00	206.00	216.00
120/208 V, 2 poles									
15-25A	EA	75.30	69.20	70.30	71.70	71.00	76.30	73.10	76.70
30-60A	EA	90.10	82.90	84.20	85.90	85.00	91.40	87.60	91.80
70A	EA	121.00	111.00	113.00	115.00	114.00	123.00	117.00	123.00
90A	EA	173.00	159.00	161.00	165.00	163.00	175.00	168.00	176.00
100A	EA	517.00	476.00	483.00	493.00	488.00	525.00	503.00	527.00
125-225A	EA	1,010	933.00	947.00	967.00	957.00	1,030	986.00	1,030
250A	EA	1,530	1,400	1,430	1,450	1,440	1,550	1,480	1,560
300-400A	EA	2,090	1,920	1,950	1,990	1,970	2,120	2,030	2,130
600A	EA	3,100	2,850	2,890	2,950	2,920	3,140	3,010	3,150
800A	EA	5,600	5,150	5,230	5,330	5,280	5,680	5,440	5,700
1000-1200A	EA	10,200	9,410	9,550	9,750	9,650	10,400	9,940	10,400
120/208 V, 3 poles									
15-25A	EA	186.00	171.00	173.00	177.00	175.00	188.00	180.00	189.00
30-60A	EA	201.00	185.00	188.00	192.00	190.00	204.00	196.00	205.00
70A	EA	257.00	236.00	240.00	244.00	242.00	260.00	249.00	261.00
90A	EA	297.00	273.00	277.00	283.00	280.00	301.00	288.00	302.00
100A	EA	626.00	576.00	585.00	597.00	591.00	635.00	609.00	638.00
125-150A	EA	1,210	1,110	1,130	1,150	1,140	1,230	1,170	1,230
175-225A	EA	1,230	1,130	1,150	1,170	1,160	1,250	1,190	1,250
250A	EA	1,610	1,480	1,500	1,540	1,520	1,630	1,570	1,640
300-400A	EA	2,670	2,460	2,490	2,550	2,520	2,710	2,600	2,720
600A	EA	4,140	3,810	3,870	3,950	3,910	4,200	4,030	4,220
800A	EA	5,940	5,460	5,540	5,660	5,600	6,020	5,770	6,050
1000-1200A	EA	11,100	10,200	10,400	10,600	10,500	11,300	10,800	11,300
Ground Fault Circuit Breakers:									
120/208 V, single pole									
15-30A	EA	211.00	194.00	197.00	201.00	199.00	214.00	205.00	215.00
40A	EA	237.00	218.00	222.00	226.00	224.00	241.00	231.00	242.00
120/208 V, 2 poles									
15-30A	EA	393.00	362.00	367.00	375.00	371.00	399.00	382.00	401.00
40-50A	EA	443.00	408.00	414.00	422.00	418.00	449.00	431.00	451.00

26 32 00 Packaged Generator Assemblies
POWER GENERATION
Complete operating system, including 2 ATS for emergency and essential power

347-600 V	UNITS	St. John's	Halifax	Montreal	Ottawa	Toronto	Winnipeg	Calgary	Vancouver
50 kW	EA	46,600	42,900	43,600	44,400	44,000	47,300	45,300	47,500
60 kW	EA	60,300	55,500	56,300	57,500	56,900	61,200	58,600	61,500
100 kW	EA	77,200	71,000	72,100	73,500	72,800	78,300	75,000	78,600
150 kW	EA	98,100	90,200	91,600	93,400	92,500	99,400	95,300	99,900
200 kW	EA	114,000	105,000	107,000	109,000	108,000	116,000	111,000	117,000
300 kW	EA	157,000	144,000	147,000	149,000	148,000	159,000	152,000	160,000
500 kW	EA	232,000	214,000	217,000	221,000	219,000	235,000	226,000	237,000
800 kW	EA	370,000	340,000	346,000	352,000	349,000	375,000	359,000	377,000

26 50 00 Lighting
26 51 00 Interior Lighting
INTERIOR LIGHTING FIXTURES
Fluorescent, medium quality (T-8 lamps included)
Surface mounted, strip fixture (no louvre or guard):

Item	UNITS	St. John's	Halifax	Montreal	Ottawa	Toronto	Winnipeg	Calgary	Vancouver
1220 mm (48"), 1 tube	EA	147.00	136.00	138.00	140.00	139.00	149.00	143.00	150.00
1220 mm (48"), 2 tube	EA	159.00	146.00	149.00	152.00	150.00	161.00	155.00	162.00
1220 mm (48"), 4 tube, tandem	EA	240.00	220.00	224.00	228.00	226.00	243.00	233.00	244.00
Surface mounted, wrap-around lens:									
1220 mm (48"), 2 tube	EA	193.00	177.00	180.00	184.00	182.00	196.00	187.00	197.00
1220 mm (48"), 4 tube	EA	275.00	253.00	256.00	262.00	259.00	278.00	267.00	280.00
Surface mounted, lay-in lens:									
1220 mm (48"), 2 tube	EA	237.00	218.00	222.00	226.00	224.00	241.00	231.00	242.00
1220 mm (48"), 4 tube	EA	268.00	247.00	250.00	256.00	253.00	272.00	261.00	273.00
Surface mounted, damp locations:									
1220 mm (48"), 2 tube	EA	444.00	409.00	415.00	423.00	419.00	450.00	432.00	453.00

Item	UNITS	St. John's	Halifax	Montreal	Ottawa	Toronto	Winnipeg	Calgary	Vancouver
Suspended fixtures:									
1220 mm (48"), 2 tube	EA	240.00	220.00	224.00	228.00	226.00	243.00	233.00	244.00
1220 mm (48"), 4 tube	EA	268.00	247.00	250.00	256.00	253.00	272.00	261.00	273.00
2240 mm (96"), 2 tube high bay, high output	EA	482.00	444.00	450.00	460.00	455.00	489.00	469.00	491.00
Recessed, acrylic lens:									
1220 mm (48"), 2 tube	EA	235.00	216.00	220.00	224.00	222.00	239.00	229.00	240.00
1220 mm (48"), 4 tube	EA	269.00	248.00	251.00	257.00	254.00	273.00	262.00	274.00
Recessed, direct / indirect									
1220 mm (48"), 2 tube	EA	258.00	237.00	241.00	245.00	243.00	261.00	250.00	262.00
1220 mm (48"), 4 tube	EA	299.00	275.00	279.00	285.00	282.00	303.00	290.00	305.00
Incandescent (lamps and stems included)									
Industrial type:									
RLM dome, 200 W	EA	288.00	265.00	269.00	275.00	272.00	292.00	280.00	294.00
Vapourtight, 150 W	EA	578.00	531.00	540.00	550.00	545.00	586.00	561.00	589.00
Explosion proof, 150 W	EA	972.00	894.00	908.00	926.00	917.00	986.00	945.00	990.00
Commercial type:									
Compact fluorescent	EA	278.00	255.00	259.00	265.00	262.00	282.00	270.00	283.00
Wall-washer, compact fluorescent	EA	288.00	265.00	269.00	275.00	272.00	292.00	280.00	294.00
HID (ballast, lamps etc. included)									
High bay type:									
400 W, single MH	EA	676.00	622.00	632.00	644.00	638.00	686.00	657.00	689.00
400 W, twin MH	EA	959.00	882.00	896.00	914.00	905.00	973.00	932.00	977.00
Low bay type:									
400 W, single MH	EA	349.00	321.00	326.00	332.00	329.00	354.00	339.00	355.00
400 W, twin MH	EA	959.00	882.00	896.00	914.00	905.00	973.00	932.00	977.00
LED luminaire (housing, trim and lamp included)									
Commercial type:									
LED downlight, 100 mm (4") diameter	EA	373.00	343.00	348.00	356.00	352.00	378.00	363.00	380.00
LED downlight, 150 mm (6") diameter	EA	545.00	501.00	509.00	519.00	514.00	553.00	529.00	555.00
Linear LED, including driver	m	332.00	305.00	310.00	316.00	313.00	336.00	322.00	338.00
LED recessed, including dimmable driver	EA	615.00	566.00	574.00	586.00	580.00	624.00	597.00	626.00
LED decorative wall wash	EA	579.00	532.00	541.00	551.00	546.00	587.00	562.00	590.00

26 52 00 Emergency Lighting
EXIT & EMERGENCY LIGHTING

Item	UNITS	St. John's	Halifax	Montreal	Ottawa	Toronto	Winnipeg	Calgary	Vancouver
Exit lights:									
1 face (ceiling or wall), LED, universal mount	EA	308.00	284.00	288.00	294.00	291.00	313.00	300.00	314.00
Emergency battery unit includes twin head, receptacle and mounting brackets									
24 V:									
200 W	EA	958.00	881.00	895.00	913.00	904.00	972.00	931.00	976.00
300 W	EA	1,070	985.00	1,000	1,020	1,010	1,090	1,040	1,090
12 V:									
200 W	EA	851.00	783.00	795.00	811.00	803.00	863.00	827.00	867.00
300 W	EA	1,010	933.00	947.00	967.00	957.00	1,030	986.00	1,030
360 W	EA	1,110	1,020	1,040	1,060	1,050	1,130	1,080	1,130
Heads operative average distance 6000 mm (20')									
12 V or 24 V, single	EA	130.00	120.00	122.00	124.00	123.00	132.00	127.00	133.00
12 V or 24 V, twin	EA	158.00	145.00	148.00	150.00	149.00	160.00	153.00	161.00

26 56 00 Exterior Lighting
WALL AND POLE MOUNTED

Item	UNITS	St. John's	Halifax	Montreal	Ottawa	Toronto	Winnipeg	Calgary	Vancouver
Exterior wall pack:									
70 W, MH	EA	578.00	531.00	540.00	550.00	545.00	586.00	561.00	589.00
250 W, MH	EA	684.00	629.00	639.00	651.00	645.00	693.00	664.00	697.00
400 W, MH	EA	702.00	645.00	655.00	669.00	662.00	712.00	682.00	715.00
LED, including cut-off shield	EA	1,280	1,180	1,200	1,220	1,210	1,300	1,250	1,310
Exterior pole mounted, includes 9140 mm (30') pole:									
1 x 400 W, MH	EA	3,130	2,880	2,920	2,980	2,950	3,170	3,040	3,190
2 x 400 W, MH	EA	3,760	3,460	3,510	3,590	3,550	3,820	3,660	3,830
LED, including cut-off shield	EA	4,940	4,540	4,610	4,710	4,660	5,010	4,800	5,030

27: COMMUNICATIONS
27 15 00 Communications Horizontal Cabling

Item	UNITS	St. John's	Halifax	Montreal	Ottawa	Toronto	Winnipeg	Calgary	Vancouver
Components									
Cat 6 cable drop	EA	230.00	212.00	215.00	219.00	217.00	233.00	224.00	234.00
Cat 6 communication horizontal cable	m	2.86	2.63	2.67	2.73	2.70	2.90	2.78	2.92
Communication data rack and patch panel	EA	3,660	3,360	3,420	3,480	3,450	3,710	3,550	3,730
Voice data outlet (jack and empty conduit)	EA	172.00	158.00	160.00	164.00	162.00	174.00	167.00	175.00

Item	UNITS	St. John's	Halifax	Montreal	Ottawa	Toronto	Winnipeg	Calgary	Vancouver
28: ELECTRONIC SAFETY & SECURITY									
28 16 00 Intrusion Detection									
CARD ACCESS & ALARM SYSTEM									
Card Access & Alarm System									
Basic computer / processor unit, keyboard, printer, control terminal, cabinet and multiplexer panels, wiring and conduit with 15 card reading stations, 30 devices and 1000 photo access cards.									
Price per system	EA	64,700	59,500	60,400	61,600	61,000	65,600	62,800	65,900
Components									
Card readers	EA	862.00	793.00	805.00	821.00	813.00	874.00	837.00	878.00
Door switch	EA	428.00	394.00	400.00	408.00	404.00	434.00	416.00	436.00
Door contact	EA	257.00	236.00	240.00	244.00	242.00	260.00	249.00	261.00
Electrical strike	EA	578.00	531.00	540.00	550.00	545.00	586.00	561.00	589.00
Mag lock	EA	1,050	965.00	980.00	1,000	990.00	1,060	1,020	1,070
Request to exit	EA	428.00	394.00	400.00	408.00	404.00	434.00	416.00	436.00
28 23 00 Video Surveillance									
Card Access & Alarm System									
Components									
CCTV camera	EA	2,000	1,840	1,870	1,910	1,890	2,030	1,950	2,040
CCTV camera PTZ	EA	2,930	2,690	2,730	2,790	2,760	2,970	2,840	2,980
CCTV camera PTZ, weatherproof	EA	3,520	3,240	3,290	3,350	3,320	3,570	3,420	3,590
28 30 00 Electronic Detection and Alarm									
28 31 00 Fire Detection and Alarm									
FIRE ALARM SYSTEMS - ADDRESSABLE									
Fire alarm systems, not wired, price of components only									
1 stage, with smoke protection (batteries included):									
Control panel 4 zones	EA	4,490	4,130	4,200	4,280	4,240	4,560	4,370	4,580
Control panel 8 zones	EA	5,460	5,020	5,100	5,200	5,150	5,540	5,300	5,560
Control panel 12 zones	EA	6,930	6,380	6,470	6,610	6,540	7,030	6,740	7,060
Control panel 24 zones	EA	11,100	10,200	10,400	10,600	10,500	11,300	10,800	11,300
Annunciator 4 zones	EA	1,350	1,240	1,260	1,280	1,270	1,370	1,310	1,370
Annunciator 8 zones	EA	1,860	1,710	1,730	1,770	1,750	1,880	1,800	1,890
Annunciator 12 zones	EA	2,340	2,150	2,190	2,230	2,210	2,380	2,280	2,390
Annunciator 24 zones	EA	3,480	3,200	3,250	3,310	3,280	3,530	3,380	3,540
2 stage, with smoke detection (batteries included):									
Control panel 4 zones	EA	6,030	5,550	5,630	5,750	5,690	6,120	5,860	6,150
Control panel 8 zones	EA	7,730	7,110	7,220	7,360	7,290	7,840	7,510	7,870
Control panel 12 zones	EA	9,720	8,940	9,080	9,260	9,170	9,860	9,450	9,900
Control panel 24 zones	EA	13,500	12,400	12,600	12,800	12,700	13,700	13,100	13,700
Components:									
Bells	EA	278.00	255.00	259.00	265.00	262.00	282.00	270.00	283.00
Manual station, 1 stage	EA	257.00	236.00	240.00	244.00	242.00	260.00	249.00	261.00
Manual station, 2 stage	EA	267.00	246.00	249.00	255.00	252.00	271.00	260.00	272.00
Fire detection	EA	364.00	334.00	340.00	346.00	343.00	369.00	353.00	370.00
Smoke detector, surface type	EA	331.00	304.00	309.00	315.00	312.00	335.00	321.00	337.00
Smoke detector, duct type	EA	738.00	679.00	689.00	703.00	696.00	748.00	717.00	752.00
Horns	EA	283.00	260.00	264.00	270.00	267.00	287.00	275.00	288.00
Strobes	EA	283.00	260.00	264.00	270.00	267.00	287.00	275.00	288.00
Horn / strobe	EA	324.00	298.00	303.00	309.00	306.00	329.00	315.00	330.00
31: EARTHWORK									
31 13 13 Selective Tree and Shrub Removal									
SELECTIVE TREE REMOVAL & TRIMMING									
Tree removal in restricted areas									
Complete removal:									
600 mm (24") diameter	EA	957.00	963.00	862.00	990.00	1,040	994.00	926.00	1,250
31 22 00 Grading									
LOAM OR TOPSOIL									
Rough Grading									
Strip and stockpile topsoil:									
Pull scraper not exceeding 150 m (500') haul	m³	4.71	4.48	4.63	4.66	4.29	5.24	3.83	4.73
Cut, fill and compact:									
Pull scraper not exceeding 200 m (700') haul	m³	5.07	4.81	5.00	4.95	4.65	5.68	4.12	5.15
Self propelled scraper not exceeding 500 m (1600') haul	m³	6.16	5.86	6.10	6.04	5.69	6.86	5.13	6.26
Cut and stockpile:									
Front end loader operation	m³	5.11	4.65	4.82	4.73	4.46	5.49	3.98	4.99
Scraper operation	m³	4.88	4.46	4.61	4.57	4.29	5.07	3.83	4.62
Fill and compact from stockpile:									
Pull scraper not exceeding 200 m (700') haul	m³	5.42	4.90	4.98	5.19	4.81	5.56	4.32	5.16
Self propelled scraper not exceeding 500 m (1600') haul	m³	6.51	6.04	6.15	6.20	5.79	6.66	5.21	6.22
Fill with imported granular material (not exceeding 15 km (10 mile) haul):									
Machine operation	m³	42.60	42.20	42.90	43.90	39.90	48.80	34.70	44.10
Hand operation	m³	111.00	103.00	109.00	111.00	101.00	122.00	88.20	111.00

Item	UNITS	St. John's	Halifax	Montreal	Ottawa	Toronto	Winnipeg	Calgary	Vancouver
FINE GRADE									
Finish grading									
By machine:									
Grader	m²	2.04	1.82	2.00	1.92	1.78	2.18	1.60	1.97
Roller	m²	1.10	0.96	1.05	1.04	0.99	1.16	0.87	1.08
By hand:									
To rough grades	m²	4.85	4.22	4.77	4.56	4.16	5.05	3.62	4.62
To finish grades	m²	7.05	6.18	6.93	6.68	6.07	7.41	5.21	6.71

31 23 00 Excavation and Fill

31 23 16 Excavation

EXCAVATING

Item	UNITS	St. John's	Halifax	Montreal	Ottawa	Toronto	Winnipeg	Calgary	Vancouver
Machine excavation - building (excluding hauling cost)									
Bulk excavation medium soil (including checker/labourer):									
Backhoe operation, 60 m³/hour (80 cy/hour)	m³	5.95	6.10	5.49	5.87	5.95	6.81	5.50	9.26
Front end loader operation, 60 m³/hour (80 cy/hour)	m³	4.60	4.70	4.50	4.60	4.75	5.41	4.45	7.25
Bulk excavation, rock:									
Ripping	m³	17.70	17.10	13.50	13.10	15.20	18.90	15.20	16.30
Trench and footing excavation medium soil									
For foundation walls									
Not exceeding 1800 mm (6') deep	m³	18.00	17.90	17.80	17.00	18.60	27.70	20.30	32.20
Over 1800 mm (6') not exceeding 3600 mm (12') deep	m³	12.10	12.10	11.80	11.30	12.40	18.10	13.30	20.30
For column footings									
Not exceeding 1800 mm (6') deep	m³	21.60	21.00	22.20	19.90	21.30	31.80	23.00	37.30
Over 1800 mm (6') not exceeding 3600 mm (12') deep	m³	17.40	16.60	17.40	15.50	17.20	24.70	18.30	27.60
Excavation below level of basement:									
For wall footings not exceeding 600 mm (2') deep	m³	9.51	9.31	8.90	7.24	10.20	15.00	11.50	17.70
Trench and footing excavation, rock:									
For foundation walls not exceeding 3600 mm (12') deep	m³	205.00	198.00	214.00	237.00	231.00	299.00	214.00	232.00
For footings	m³	218.00	217.00	232.00	249.00	245.00	313.00	228.00	245.00
Hand excavation									
Not exceeding 1800 mm (6') deep:									
Normal soil	m³	93.60	101.00	126.00	111.00	119.00	177.00	123.00	205.00
Rock (hand-held compressor tool)	m³	497.00	492.00	535.00	525.00	553.00	712.00	530.00	556.00
Clean off rock face	m²	43.50	40.50	41.30	38.90	41.20	53.50	39.30	41.20
Bulk excavation, overburden (external), minimum volume 2000 m³ (2600 CY)									
Wide open areas	m³	29.00	37.20	37.60	38.90	38.40	49.40	33.80	53.00
Adjacent building 30 m (100') distant	m³	80.20	104.00	104.00	108.00	108.00	140.00	95.40	151.00
Trench excavation, overburden (external) for retaining wall									
Wide open areas	m³	65.40	79.30	94.50	80.70	83.90	112.00	73.50	121.00
Adjacent buildings 30 m (100') distant	m³	186.00	229.00	276.00	236.00	245.00	326.00	212.00	353.00

31 23 19 Dewatering

DEWATERING

Item	UNITS	St. John's	Halifax	Montreal	Ottawa	Toronto	Winnipeg	Calgary	Vancouver
Pumping prices include attendance consumables and 10 m (33') of discharge pipe									
Electrically powered:									
1.5 l/s (20 gpm), 1.5 kW (2 hp) submersible	DAY	64.80	60.00	60.00	73.60	77.00	77.40	58.10	61.60
45 l/s (600 gpm), 22 kW (30 hp)	DAY	216.00	200.00	207.00	252.00	257.00	264.00	194.00	205.00
Gas or diesel powered:									
45 l/s (600 gpm), 22 kW (30 hp)	DAY	352.00	335.00	355.00	416.00	427.00	436.00	335.00	331.00
Drainage trenches and pits									
Trenches 1800 mm (6') wide including backfill:									
600 mm (2') deep by machine	m	14.70	14.60	14.10	14.00	15.20	22.80	16.30	26.20
900 mm (3') deep by machine	m	18.80	19.00	18.40	18.80	19.90	29.80	21.40	34.10
1200 mm (4') deep by machine	m	24.10	23.60	24.00	23.80	25.40	37.50	26.40	43.10
Wellpoint system, single stage. 150 metre (500') system consisting of 38 mm (1 1/2") diameter wellpoints at 1500 mm (5') o.c. spacing and 200 mm (8") diameter header pipe, to maximum depth of 7300 mm (24')									
Installation of 150 m (500') header system									
including all labour & materials	EA	N/A	35,600	40,000	N/A	46,800	43,000	37,500	50,700
Rental of 150 m (500') installed system - first month	MONTH	N/A	23,400	23,900	N/A	27,600	28,900	25,300	23,200
Add for rental of system for each subsequent month	MONTH	N/A	17,900	17,800	N/A	20,900	21,800	19,200	18,400
Daily maintenance of system including site checks,									
oil, filters, fuel	DAY	N/A	593.00	725.00	N/A	823.00	725.00	641.00	748.00
24 hour supervision of system (OPTIONAL)	DAY	N/A	2,140	2,380	N/A	2,610	2,700	2,350	2,140

31 23 23 Fill

BACKFILL

Item	UNITS	St. John's	Halifax	Montreal	Ottawa	Toronto	Winnipeg	Calgary	Vancouver
Backfill and compaction									
Excavated materials, place & compact for grading	m³	13.20	15.00	14.20	14.00	15.60	21.00	18.60	24.80
Pit run gravel not exceeding 15 km (10 mile) haul	m³	34.50	38.30	35.90	35.30	39.70	53.40	47.00	61.10
Crushed stone to weeping tiles	m³	66.10	73.30	68.30	67.00	75.80	101.00	88.90	119.00
20 mm (3/4") crushed stone to under side of									
slab-on-grade, not exceeding 15 km (10 mile) haul	m³	59.90	66.70	62.40	61.50	68.80	93.50	80.30	109.00

Item	UNITS	St. John's	Halifax	Montreal	Ottawa	Toronto	Winnipeg	Calgary	Vancouver
HAULING									
Waste material disposal									
Hauling:									
1 hour return trip	m³	15.50	15.20	20.80	15.90	18.60	20.00	19.10	34.70
Dump charges for typical urban city, tipping fees only									
(rates vary based on material types, check with local municipality)									
Building construction materials............................	TONNE	N/A	N/A	N/A	N/A	N/A	N/A	N/A	N/A
Excavated clean soil, non-hazardous material............	TONNE	N/A	N/A	N/A	N/A	N/A	N/A	N/A	N/A
31 40 00 Shoring and Underpinning									
SHEET PILING									
Steel									
Left in place:									
8000 mm (25') deep, 150 kg/m² (30 lbs/sf)..................	m²	623.00	620.00	690.00	785.00	678.00	1,180	1,090	1,130
UNDERPINNING									
Average Cost	m³	1,390	1,480	1,600	1,870	151	2,720	2,490	2,850
31 50 00 Excavation Support and Protection									
SOLDIER PILES & LAGGING									
6000 mm (20') deep	m²	492.00	469.00	508.00	665.00	714.00	999.00	738.00	900.00
10000 mm (35') deep	m²	542.00	531.00	564.00	729.00	792.00	1,100.00	808.00	995.00
31 60 00 Special Foundations & Load-Bearing Elements									
31 62 00 Driven Piles									
PILES, CONCRETE									
Concrete piles									
Precast piles:									
300 mm x 300 mm (12" x 12") hexagonal	m	335.00	335.00	N/A	N/A	N/A	283.00	N/A	275.00
400 mm x 400 mm (16" x 16") hexagonal	m	392.00	392.00	N/A	N/A	N/A	313.00	N/A	304.00
PILES, STEEL									
Steel piles									
Steel H-piles:									
300 mm (12"), 79 kg/m (53 lb/ft).............................	m	326.00	259.00	273.00	279.00	275.00	442.00	314.00	565.00
Steel pipe piles:									
250 mm (10") dia., concrete filled...........................	m	267.00	215.00	220.00	220.00	222.00	357.00	260.00	456.00
31 63 00 Bored Piles									
CAISSONS									
Drilled Caissons									
In normal soil									
No lining:									
600 mm (24") dia.	m	178.00	160.00	167.00	182.00	197.00	282.00	157.00	357.00
750 mm (30") dia.	m	288.00	261.00	272.00	291.00	319.00	456.00	249.00	586.00
900 mm (36") dia.	m	396.00	362.00	369.00	404.00	440.00	637.00	347.00	798.00
Lining removed:									
600 mm (24") dia.	m	225.00	199.00	211.00	231.00	250.00	357.00	196.00	454.00
750 mm (30") dia.	m	337.00	306.00	316.00	348.00	374.00	547.00	297.00	683.00
900 mm (36") dia.	m	463.00	403.00	426.00	479.00	511.00	730.00	406.00	943.00
In wet soil, pumping included									
Lining removed:									
750 mm (30") dia.	m	390.00	346.00	352.00	394.00	430.00	614.00	339.00	767.00
Lining left in place:									
750 mm (30") dia.	m	778.00	714.00	724.00	809.00	888.00	1,280	702.00	1,640
In shale or soft rock									
No lining:									
750 mm (30") dia.	m	800.00	760.00	750.00	845.00	910.00	1,320	710.00	1,640

Item	UNITS	St. John's	Halifax	Montreal	Ottawa	Toronto	Winnipeg	Calgary	Vancouver
32: EXTERIOR IMPROVEMENTS									
32 11 00 Base Courses									
BASE COURSES									
Base courses									
Grading:									
Prepare sub-base	m²	1.67	1.66	1.71	1.64	1.62	1.98	1.43	1.90
Granular bases:									
Pit run gravel, 300 mm (12") thick	m³	39.00	38.50	40.00	37.70	38.20	45.80	33.20	44.10
20 mm crushed stone	m³	72.60	71.10	75.20	72.00	71.30	85.90	62.10	82.30
32 12 00 Flexible Paving									
PAVING									
Bituminous paving									
One layer:									
50 mm	m²	17.40	17.90	16.20	16.80	15.60	21.40	20.00	70.70
Two layers:									
100 mm	m²	32.20	36.00	30.00	32.40	29.00	40.30	36.50	133.00
32 14 00 Unit Paving									
PRECAST CONCRETE PAVING SLABS									
Precast concrete pavers									
50 mm (2") thick precast pavers complete, basic									
100mm x 200mm (4" x 8")	m²	110.00	104.00	92.60	95.50	105.00	99.10	100.00	225.00
32 16 00 Curbs, Gutters, Sidewalks, and Driveways									
CURBS									
Precast concrete curb									
200 mm x 150 mm (8"x6"x8')	m	56.90	26.20	40.00	42.00	46.40	57.10	49.00	194.00
32 31 00 Fences and Gates									
FENCE, CHAIN LINK									
Chain link fence - galvanized steel									
4.935 mm (6 gauge) wire - 50 mm (2") mesh:									
Penitentiary type:									
1800 mm (6') high	m	101.00	109.00	101.00	110.00	106.00	97.20	104.00	117.00
2400 mm (8') high	m	137.00	145.00	138.00	155.00	145.00	129.00	142.00	158.00
3600 mm (12') high	m	174.00	187.00	177.00	191.00	185.00	169.00	183.00	205.00
3.797 mm (9 gauge) wire - 50 mm (2") mesh:									
Standard type:									
1800 mm (6') high	m	81.90	84.30	80.50	87.80	84.70	78.30	76.10	94.60
2400 mm (8') high	m	98.40	100.00	96.50	105.00	102.00	94.20	92.00	113.00
3600 mm (12') high	m	123.00	127.00	120.00	133.00	126.00	116.00	115.00	142.00
3.038 mm (11 gauge) wire - 50 mm (2") mesh:									
Light commercial type:									
1800 mm (6') high	m	61.50	52.40	54.20	58.20	57.40	51.30	55.60	65.30
2400 mm (8') high	m	89.10	70.80	78.70	84.60	82.90	73.50	80.40	94.50
3600 mm (12') high	m	120.00	98.00	108.00	115.00	113.00	101.00	109.00	124.00
Barbed wire top protection:									
3 strands	m	11.00	9.80	10.40	11.50	11.20	9.98	10.60	13.00
Galvanized steel gates:									
50 mm (2") mesh, 1800 mm (6') high	m	272.00	257.00	261.00	283.00	276.00	245.00	269.00	321.00
32 90 00 Planting									
32 91 00 Planting Preparation									
SOIL PREPARATION									
Spread and grade topsoil by machine									
From site stockpile	m³	15.00	14.30	16.30	15.60	15.20	16.80	10.90	15.50
Import (including cost of soil)	m³	55.60	52.50	47.80	57.40	56.90	53.80	40.60	53.10
Fine grade topsoil by hand									
To slopes, banks and the like	m²	5.75	5.79	6.07	6.25	6.28	6.11	4.77	6.32
32 92 00 Turf and Grasses									
SEEDING									
Seeding, mechanical application assumes soil prepared and									
and work carried out in best sowing periods									
Lawns (area not exceeding 10000 m² (12,000 SY)									
$4.50/kg ($2.00/lb), 25 kg/1000 m² (45 lbs/1000 SY)	m²	1.24	0.85	1.54	1.29	1.38	1.81	1.72	1.48
Hydro seeding, over 10000 m² (12,000 SY)									
Level areas (wood fibre mulch)	m²	1.40	0.87	1.30	1.07	1.36	1.58	1.71	1.52
Sloping areas (liquid plastic)	m²	1.64	1.00	1.51	1.21	1.53	1.81	1.92	1.74
SODDING									
Sodding									
6 mm (1/4") to 20 mm (3/4") thick cut nursery sod:									
No. 1 grade to level ground	m²	6.34	5.00	5.55	5.50	6.00	8.40	7.65	7.22
No. 1 grade to slopes	m²	8.15	6.43	7.11	7.09	7.72	10.70	9.79	9.21

Item	UNITS	St. John's	Halifax	Montreal	Ottawa	Toronto	Winnipeg	Calgary	Vancouver
32 93 00 Plants									
SHRUBS & TREES									
All trees earth balled and burlapped. All plantings to be staked and guyed as necessary. Prices cover excavation and reinstatement and include maintenance and full guarantee. Planting assumed in normal season. All trees nursery grown.									
Trees, deciduous									
Sugar maple and linden and ash:									
3000-4000 mm (10-12') high (40 mm (1 1/2") calliper)	EA	436.00	329.00	392.00	410.00	418.00	484.00	417.00	477.00
50-60 mm (2-2 1/2") calliper	EA	794.00	615.00	718.00	758.00	774.00	893.00	774.00	882.00
75-90 mm (3-3 1/2") calliper	EA	1,170	883.00	1,040	1,090	1,110	1,280	1,110	1,290
Silver maple:									
3000-4000 mm (10-12') high (40 mm (1 1/2") calliper)	EA	387.00	300.00	350.00	360.00	388.00	473.00	397.00	500.00
50-60 mm calliper (2-2 1/2")	EA	601.00	471.00	547.00	555.00	600.00	731.00	609.00	767.00
75-90 mm calliper (3-3 1/2")	EA	1,070	867.00	990.00	1,010	1,090	1,320	1,110	1,390
Red maple and honey locust:									
3000-4000 mm (10-12') high (40 mm (1 1/2") calliper)	EA	493.00	414.00	469.00	433.00	464.00	636.00	521.00	490.00
50-60 mm (2-2 1/2") calliper	EA	783.00	663.00	742.00	697.00	740.00	1010.00	831.00	783.00
75-90 mm (3-3 1/2") calliper	EA	1,470	1,250	1,390	1,300	1,380	1,900	1,560	1,470
Trees, evergreen									
Cedar:									
1200-1500 mm (4-5') high	EA	150.00	154.00	179.00	163.00	174.00	173.00	201.00	197.00
1500-1800 mm (5-6') high	EA	330.00	338.00	390.00	351.00	379.00	368.00	444.00	412.00
1800-2400 mm (6-8') high	EA	534.00	549.00	644.00	580.00	619.00	608.00	722.00	675.00
Spruce:									
1200-1500 mm (4-5') high	EA	274.00	273.00	298.00	323.00	294.00	277.00	356.00	325.00
1500-1800 mm (5-6') high	EA	427.00	429.00	475.00	506.00	464.00	439.00	498.00	519.00
1800-2400 mm (6-8') high	EA	607.00	612.00	673.00	716.00	658.00	622.00	810.00	736.00
Pine:									
1200-1500 mm (4-5') high	EA	300.00	282.00	313.00	336.00	309.00	301.00	333.00	325.00
1500-1800 mm (5-6') high	EA	497.00	472.00	512.00	548.00	504.00	488.00	543.00	539.00
1800-2400 mm (6-8') high	EA	751.00	745.00	780.00	837.00	767.00	750.00	834.00	802.00
Shrubs									
Forsythia and honey suckle:									
1000-1200 mm (3-4') high	EA	61.70	62.50	57.20	55.70	62.70	62.20	57.40	56.60
1200-1500 mm (4-5') high	EA	79.50	80.30	73.70	72.10	80.60	79.70	73.50	72.20
Oleaster (Russian Olive):									
1000-1200 mm (3-4') high	EA	68.20	62.50	57.20	55.70	62.70	62.20	57.40	56.60
1200-1500 mm (4-5') high	EA	77.60	71.60	65.50	63.40	71.50	71.20	66.10	63.60
Flowering crab-tree:									
1000-1200 mm (3-4') high	EA	109.00	93.80	90.00	89.70	102.00	100.00	91.00	94.40
1200-1500 mm (4-5') high	EA	130.00	113.00	106.00	108.00	121.00	120.00	109.00	111.00
Beautybush:									
1000-1200 mm (3-4') high	EA	75.30	73.20	72.20	66.90	80.60	76.70	67.40	75.40
1200-1500 mm (4-5') high	EA	97.90	94.60	92.40	86.30	104.00	99.20	86.60	94.40
Spirea:									
600-1200 mm (2-4') high	EA	51.90	48.30	50.80	46.50	53.80	54.60	45.60	51.60
1200-1500 mm (4-5') high	EA	69.00	64.30	67.00	60.90	71.50	72.80	60.30	66.90
Dogwood:									
1000-1200 mm (3-4') high	EA	60.00	56.30	47.50	46.50	55.40	54.60	51.30	51.60
1200-1500 mm (4-5') high	EA	99.30	93.00	81.70	77.00	92.30	91.20	86.60	85.80
Hedges									
Yews:									
800-900 mm (30-36") high	m	218.00	206.00	198.00	169.00	226.00	252.00	168.00	207.00
900-1000 mm (36-42") high	m	344.00	321.00	304.00	266.00	357.00	402.00	266.00	331.00
Privet:									
1000-1200 mm (3-4') high	m	56.60	56.30	59.80	54.30	62.70	67.60	54.40	56.60
1200-1500 mm (4-5') high	m	72.20	71.90	76.90	69.30	80.60	86.70	70.40	75.40
Boxwood:									
250-300 mm (10-12") high	m	184.00	189.00	271.00	217.00	243.00	292.00	217.00	218.00
300-400 mm (12-15") high	m	209.00	219.00	308.00	248.00	279.00	335.00	249.00	265.00
Flowering currant (Alpine):									
450-600 mm (18-24") high	m	70.60	61.70	59.50	58.00	63.20	71.20	47.80	56.60
600-900 mm (2-3') high	m	90.60	78.50	76.90	74.40	80.60	91.20	60.40	75.40

Item	UNITS	St. John's	Halifax	Montreal	Ottawa	Toronto	Winnipeg	Calgary	Vancouver

33: UTILITIES
33 11 00 Water Utility Distribution Piping
PIPING, WATER DISTRIBUTION SYSTEMS

Cast iron pressure pipe based on 30 m (100') of pipe, one
tee, two 90 degree elbows, buried 1500 mm (5') deep,
including excavation, bedding, anchoring and backfill.

Item	UNITS	St. John's	Halifax	Montreal	Ottawa	Toronto	Winnipeg	Calgary	Vancouver
Class 2 titon cast iron pipe:									
100 mm (4")	m	269.00	248.00	251.00	257.00	254.00	273.00	262.00	274.00
150 mm (6")	m	314.00	289.00	293.00	299.00	296.00	318.00	305.00	320.00
200 mm (8")	m	372.00	342.00	347.00	355.00	351.00	377.00	362.00	379.00
250 mm (10")	m	477.00	439.00	446.00	455.00	450.00	484.00	464.00	486.00
300 mm (12")	m	561.00	516.00	524.00	534.00	529.00	569.00	545.00	571.00
350 mm (14")	m	679.00	625.00	635.00	647.00	641.00	689.00	660.00	692.00
400 mm (16")	m	801.00	737.00	748.00	764.00	756.00	813.00	779.00	816.00
450 mm (18")	m	917.00	843.00	856.00	874.00	865.00	930.00	891.00	934.00
500 mm (20")	m	1,050	962.00	977.00	997.00	987.00	1,060	1,020	1,070
600 mm (24")	m	1,380	1,270	1,290	1,310	1,300	1,400	1,340	1,400

Schedule 40 pvc pressure pipe with cast iron fittings based on
30 m of pipe, one tee, two 90-degree elbows, buried 1500 mm (5')
deep, including excavation, bedding, anchoring and backfill.

Item	UNITS	St. John's	Halifax	Montreal	Ottawa	Toronto	Winnipeg	Calgary	Vancouver
C900 PVC pipe:									
100 mm (4")	m	242.00	222.00	226.00	230.00	228.00	245.00	235.00	246.00
150 mm (6")	m	260.00	239.00	243.00	247.00	245.00	263.00	252.00	265.00
200 mm (8")	m	355.00	327.00	332.00	338.00	335.00	360.00	345.00	362.00
250 mm (10")	m	421.00	387.00	393.00	401.00	397.00	427.00	409.00	429.00
300 mm (12")	m	522.00	480.00	487.00	497.00	492.00	529.00	507.00	531.00

Soft copper pressure pipe (in coil) based on 40 m (132') of pipe,
one coupling, one adapter, buried 1500 mm (5') deep, including
excavation, bedding and backfill.

Item	UNITS	St. John's	Halifax	Montreal	Ottawa	Toronto	Winnipeg	Calgary	Vancouver
Soft copper pipe type k:									
12 mm (1/2")	m	293.00	269.00	273.00	279.00	276.00	297.00	284.00	298.00
20 mm (3/4")	m	318.00	293.00	297.00	303.00	300.00	323.00	309.00	324.00
25 mm (1")	m	360.00	332.00	337.00	343.00	340.00	366.00	350.00	367.00
32 mm (1 1/4")	m	398.00	366.00	371.00	379.00	375.00	403.00	386.00	405.00
38 mm (1 1/2")	m	430.00	396.00	402.00	410.00	406.00	436.00	418.00	438.00

33 12 00 Water Utility Distribution Equipment
Curb stop including box buried 1500 mm (5') deep

Item	UNITS	St. John's	Halifax	Montreal	Ottawa	Toronto	Winnipeg	Calgary	Vancouver
Copper service pipe:									
12 mm (1/2")	EA	558.00	513.00	521.00	531.00	526.00	565.00	542.00	568.00
20 mm (3/4")	EA	605.00	557.00	565.00	577.00	571.00	614.00	588.00	617.00
25 mm (1")	EA	727.00	669.00	679.00	693.00	686.00	737.00	707.00	741.00
32 mm (1 1/4")	EA	1,180	1,080	1,100	1,120	1,110	1,190	1,140	1,200
38 mm (1 1/2")	EA	1,430	1,320	1,340	1,360	1,350	1,450	1,390	1,460
Cast iron service pipe:									
100 mm (4")	EA	2,370	2,180	2,220	2,260	2,240	2,410	2,310	2,420
150 mm (6")	EA	3,230	2,970	3,020	3,080	3,050	3,280	3,140	3,290
200 mm (8")	EA	4,780	4,400	4,460	4,560	4,510	4,850	4,650	4,870

33 31 00 Sanitary Utility Sewerage Piping
PIPING, DRAINAGE & SEWAGE, POLYVINYL CHLORIDE
PVC

Item	UNITS	St. John's	Halifax	Montreal	Ottawa	Toronto	Winnipeg	Calgary	Vancouver
Perforated:									
100 mm (4") dia.	m	49.70	45.70	46.40	47.40	46.90	50.40	48.30	50.70
150 mm (6") dia.	m	72.00	66.20	67.20	68.60	67.90	73.00	69.90	73.30

PIPING, DRAINAGE & SEWAGE, VITRIFIED CLAY
Vitrified clay
Farm tile, 300 mm (1'-0") length

Item	UNITS	St. John's	Halifax	Montreal	Ottawa	Toronto	Winnipeg	Calgary	Vancouver
100 mm (4") dia.	m	54.70	50.30	51.10	52.10	51.60	55.50	53.10	55.70
150 mm (6") dia.	m	64.20	59.10	60.00	61.20	60.60	65.10	62.40	65.40

PIPING, DRAINAGE & SEWAGE, CONCRETE
Concrete drainage piping based on 30 m (100') of pipe including jointing,
buried 1.5 m (5') deep, including excavation, bedding and backfilling.

Item	UNITS	St. John's	Halifax	Montreal	Ottawa	Toronto	Winnipeg	Calgary	Vancouver
Type C-76 class 3 concrete sewer pipe									
150 mm (6")	m	227.00	209.00	212.00	216.00	214.00	230.00	220.00	231.00
200 mm (8")	m	271.00	250.00	253.00	259.00	256.00	275.00	264.00	276.00
250 mm (10")	m	341.00	314.00	319.00	325.00	322.00	346.00	332.00	348.00
300 mm (12")	m	367.00	337.00	343.00	349.00	346.00	372.00	356.00	374.00
375 mm (15")	m	413.00	380.00	386.00	394.00	390.00	419.00	402.00	421.00
450 mm (18")	m	462.00	425.00	432.00	440.00	436.00	469.00	449.00	471.00
525 mm (21")	m	523.00	481.00	488.00	498.00	493.00	530.00	508.00	532.00
600 mm (24")	m		583.00	592.00	604.00	598.00	643.00	616.00	646.00
675 mm (27")	m	744.00	684.00	695.00	709.00	702.00	755.00	723.00	758.00
750 mm (30")	m	895.00	823.00	836.00	852.00	844.00	907.00	869.00	912.00
900 mm (36")	m	1,160	1,060	1,080	1,100	1,090	1,170	1,120	1,180
1050 mm (42")	m	1,420	1,310	1,330	1,350	1,340	1,440	1,380	1,450

Item	UNITS	St. John's	Halifax	Montreal	Ottawa	Toronto	Winnipeg	Calgary	Vancouver
33 36 00 Utility Septic Tanks									
SEPTIC TANKS									
Including excavation, stone bedding and backfilling									
Septic tank									
Steel horizontal:									
3,270 l (791.0 imp.gals.)	EA	4,630	4,260	4,330	4,410	4,370	4,700	4,500	4,720
9,090 l (2,375.0 imp.gals.)	EA	14,600	13,500	13,700	13,900	13,800	14,800	14,200	14,900
22,730 l (5,000.0 imp.gals.)	EA	28,700	26,400	26,800	27,400	27,100	29,100	27,900	29,300
Disposal bed header pipes									
Cast iron, mechanical joint:									
100 mm (4")	m	232.00	214.00	217.00	221.00	219.00	235.00	226.00	237.00
Plastic:									
100 mm (4")	m	189.00	174.00	176.00	180.00	178.00	191.00	183.00	192.00
Plastic perforated:									
100 mm (4")	m	122.00	112.00	114.00	116.00	115.00	124.00	118.00	124.00
33 49 00 Storm Drainage Structures									
CATCH BASINS OR MANHOLES									
Catch basins, excavation and backfill included with pipe									
Poured concrete:									
610 mm x 610 mm x 1220 mm deep (2'0" x 2'0" x 4'0" deep)	EA	2,600	2,390	2,430	2,470	2,450	2,630	2,520	2,650
Add for each additional 300 mm (1') in depth	EA	314.00	289.00	293.00	299.00	296.00	318.00	305.00	320.00
Precast concrete:									
610 mm (2'0") dia. x 1220 mm (4'0") deep	EA	2,190	2,020	2,050	2,090	2,070	2,230	2,130	2,240
Add for each additional 300 mm (1') depth	EA	320.00	294.00	299.00	305.00	302.00	325.00	311.00	326.00
Manholes, excavation and backfill included with pipe									
Poured concrete:									
760 mm x 760 mm x 2130 mm deep (2'6" x 2'6" x 7'0" deep)	EA	4,020	3,700	3,750	3,830	3,790	4,070	3,900	4,090
Add for each additional 300 mm (1') depth	EA	373.00	343.00	348.00	356.00	352.00	378.00	363.00	380.00
Precast concrete:									
760 mm (2'6") dia. x 2130 mm (7'0") deep	EA	3,400	3,130	3,180	3,240	3,210	3,450	3,310	3,470
Add for each additional 300 mm (1') depth	EA	403.00	371.00	376.00	384.00	380.00	409.00	391.00	410.00
33 61 00 Hydronic Energy Distribution									
CHILLED WATER, DISTRIBUTION									
Including fittings, supports, guides and anchors,									
expansion joints and loops.									
Schedule 40 A-53 pipe									
In tunnel with 50 mm (2") glass fibre insulation:									
75 mm (3") dia.	m	846.00	778.00	790.00	806.00	798.00	858.00	822.00	862.00
100 mm (4") dia.	m	938.00	863.00	876.00	894.00	885.00	951.00	912.00	956.00
125 mm (5") dia.	m	1,110	1,020	1,040	1,060	1,050	1,130	1,080	1,130
150 mm (6") dia.	m	1,240	1,140	1,160	1,180	1,170	1,260	1,210	1,260
200 mm (8") dia.	m	1,520	1,390	1,420	1,440	1,430	1,540	1,470	1,540
250 mm (10") dia.	m	1,950	1,790	1,820	1,860	1,840	1,980	1,900	1,990
300 mm (12") dia.	m	2,480	2,280	2,320	2,360	2,340	2,520	2,410	2,530
350 mm (14") dia.	m	2,690	2,480	2,510	2,570	2,540	2,730	2,620	2,740
In steel conduit including excavation & backfilling, av. 1800 mm (6') deep:									
75 mm (3") dia.	m	1,260	1,160	1,180	1,200	1,190	1,280	1,230	1,290
100 mm (4") dia.	m	1,440	1,330	1,350	1,370	1,360	1,460	1,400	1,470
125 mm (5") dia.	m	1,900	1,750	1,770	1,810	1,790	1,920	1,840	1,930
150 mm (6") dia.	m	2,160	1,990	2,020	2,060	2,040	2,190	2,100	2,200
200 mm (8") dia.	m	2,630	2,420	2,460	2,500	2,480	2,670	2,550	2,680
250 mm (10") dia.	m	3,150	2,900	2,940	3,000	2,970	3,190	3,060	3,210
300 mm (12") dia.	m	4,610	4,240	4,310	4,390	4,350	4,680	4,480	4,700
350 mm (14") dia.	m	5,530	5,090	5,170	5,270	5,220	5,610	5,380	5,640
33 63 00 Steam Energy Distribution									
STEAM DISTRIBUTION									
Including fittings, supports, guides and anchors, expansion joints and loops.									
Schedule 40 A-53 steam, schedule 80 seamless condensate.									
In tunnel with 50 mm (2") calcium silicate insulation on steam and 25 mm (1") glass fibre on condensate:									
75 mm (3"), 38 mm (1 1/2")	m	840.00	772.00	784.00	800.00	792.00	851.00	816.00	855.00
100 mm (4"), 50 mm (2")	m	888.00	817.00	830.00	846.00	838.00	901.00	863.00	905.00
125 mm (5"), 75 mm (3")	m	1,060	975.00	990.00	1,010	1,000	1,080	1,030	1,080
150 mm (6"), 75 mm (3")	m	1,210	1,110	1,130	1,150	1,140	1,230	1,170	1,230
200 mm (8"), 100 mm (4")	m	1,360	1,250	1,270	1,290	1,280	1,380	1,320	1,380
250 mm (10"), 125 mm (5")	m	1,910	1,760	1,780	1,820	1,800	1,940	1,850	1,940
300 mm (12"), 150 mm (6")	m	2,060	1,890	1,920	1,960	1,940	2,090	2,000	2,100
350 mm (14"), 150 mm (6")	m	2,610	2,400	2,440	2,480	2,460	2,640	2,530	2,660
In steel conduit including manhole, excavation and backfilling, average 1800 mm (6') deep:									
75 mm (3"), 38 mm (1 1/2")	m	1,480	1,370	1,390	1,410	1,400	1,510	1,440	1,510
100 mm (4"), 50 mm (2")	m	1,740	1,600	1,620	1,660	1,640	1,760	1,690	1,770
125 mm (5"), 75 mm (3")	m	1,990	1,830	1,860	1,900	1,880	2,020	1,940	2,030
150 mm (6"), 75 mm (3")	m	2,230	2,050	2,080	2,120	2,100	2,260	2,160	2,270
200 mm (8"), 100 mm (4")	m	2,680	2,470	2,500	2,560	2,530	2,720	2,610	2,730

Item	UNITS	St. John's	Halifax	Montreal	Ottawa	Toronto	Winnipeg	Calgary	Vancouver
250 mm (10"), 125 mm (5")	m	3,370	3,100	3,150	3,210	3,180	3,420	3,280	3,430
300 mm (12"), 150 mm (6")	m	4,540	4,170	4,240	4,320	4,280	4,600	4,410	4,620
350 mm (14"), 150 mm (6")	m	4,880	4,490	4,550	4,650	4,600	4,950	4,740	4,970

33 71 19 Electrical Underground Ducts & Manholes

MANHOLES

Concrete manholes

Item	UNITS	St. John's	Halifax	Montreal	Ottawa	Toronto	Winnipeg	Calgary	Vancouver
1500 mm x 1500 mm (5' x 5') single	EA	6,460	5,940	6,030	6,150	6,090	6,550	6,270	6,580
1500 mm x 3000 mm (5' x 10') double	EA	11,300	10,400	10,600	10,800	10,700	11,500	11,000	11,600

UNDERGROUND DUCT BANKS

**Underground duct banks, 100 mm (4") PVC pipe ducts & fittings
including all excavation, concrete and backfilling**

In soft earth with backfill:

Item	UNITS	St. John's	Halifax	Montreal	Ottawa	Toronto	Winnipeg	Calgary	Vancouver
1 duct	m	182.00	168.00	170.00	174.00	172.00	185.00	177.00	186.00
2 ducts	m	212.00	195.00	198.00	202.00	200.00	215.00	206.00	216.00
3 ducts	m	275.00	253.00	256.00	262.00	259.00	278.00	267.00	280.00
4 ducts	m	334.00	307.00	312.00	318.00	315.00	339.00	324.00	340.00
5 ducts	m	402.00	370.00	375.00	383.00	379.00	407.00	390.00	409.00
6 ducts	m	469.00	431.00	438.00	446.00	442.00	475.00	455.00	477.00
7 ducts	m	531.00	488.00	496.00	506.00	501.00	539.00	516.00	541.00
8 ducts	m	613.00	564.00	572.00	584.00	578.00	621.00	595.00	624.00
9 ducts	m	653.00	601.00	610.00	622.00	616.00	662.00	634.00	665.00
10 ducts	m	697.00	642.00	651.00	665.00	658.00	707.00	678.00	711.00
11 ducts	m	779.00	717.00	728.00	742.00	735.00	790.00	757.00	794.00
12 ducts	m	835.00	768.00	780.00	796.00	788.00	847.00	812.00	851.00
13 ducts	m	882.00	811.00	824.00	840.00	832.00	894.00	857.00	899.00
14 ducts	m	990.00	911.00	925.00	943.00	934.00	1,000	962.00	1,010
15 ducts	m	1,050	967.00	982.00	1,000	992.00	1,070	1,020	1,070

In soft earth with granular backfill:

Item	UNITS	St. John's	Halifax	Montreal	Ottawa	Toronto	Winnipeg	Calgary	Vancouver
1 duct	m	205.00	188.00	191.00	195.00	193.00	207.00	199.00	208.00
2 ducts	m	273.00	252.00	255.00	261.00	258.00	277.00	266.00	279.00
3 ducts	m	303.00	279.00	283.00	289.00	286.00	307.00	295.00	309.00
4 ducts	m	455.00	418.00	425.00	433.00	429.00	461.00	442.00	463.00
5 ducts	m	514.00	473.00	480.00	490.00	485.00	521.00	500.00	524.00
6 ducts	m	541.00	497.00	505.00	515.00	510.00	548.00	525.00	551.00
7 ducts	m	656.00	604.00	613.00	625.00	619.00	665.00	638.00	669.00
8 ducts	m	703.00	646.00	656.00	670.00	663.00	713.00	683.00	716.00
9 ducts	m	755.00	694.00	705.00	719.00	712.00	765.00	733.00	769.00
10 ducts	m	870.00	800.00	813.00	829.00	821.00	883.00	846.00	887.00
11 ducts	m	905.00	833.00	845.00	863.00	854.00	918.00	880.00	922.00
12 ducts	m	962.00	885.00	899.00	917.00	908.00	976.00	935.00	981.00
13 ducts	m	1,080	995.00	1,010	1,030	1,020	1,100	1,050	1,100
14 ducts	m	1,120	1,030	1,050	1,070	1,060	1,140	1,090	1,140
15 ducts	m	1,220	1,120	1,140	1,160	1,150	1,240	1,180	1,240

In soft rock with granular backfill:

Item	UNITS	St. John's	Halifax	Montreal	Ottawa	Toronto	Winnipeg	Calgary	Vancouver
1 duct	m	255.00	235.00	239.00	243.00	241.00	259.00	248.00	260.00
2 ducts	m	322.00	296.00	301.00	307.00	304.00	327.00	313.00	328.00
3 ducts	m	349.00	321.00	326.00	332.00	329.00	354.00	339.00	355.00
4 ducts	m	560.00	515.00	523.00	533.00	528.00	568.00	544.00	570.00
5 ducts	m	633.00	582.00	591.00	603.00	597.00	642.00	615.00	645.00
6 ducts	m	658.00	605.00	615.00	627.00	621.00	668.00	640.00	671.00
7 ducts	m	757.00	696.00	707.00	721.00	714.00	768.00	735.00	771.00
8 ducts	m	825.00	759.00	770.00	786.00	778.00	836.00	801.00	840.00
9 ducts	m	906.00	834.00	846.00	864.00	855.00	919.00	881.00	923.00
10 ducts	m	1,030	950.00	964.00	984.00	974.00	1,050	1,000	1,050
11 ducts	m	1,060	975.00	990.00	1,010	1,000	1,080	1,030	1,080
12 ducts	m	1,110	1,020	1,040	1,060	1,050	1,130	1,080	1,130
13 ducts	m	1,220	1,120	1,140	1,160	1,150	1,240	1,180	1,240
14 ducts	m	1,250	1,150	1,170	1,190	1,180	1,270	1,220	1,270
15 ducts	m	1,310	1,210	1,230	1,250	1,240	1,330	1,280	1,340

01: GENERAL REQUIREMENTS

01 41 00 Regulatory Requirements

01 41 26 Permit Requirements

BUILDING PERMITS

These building permit fees and rates are intended as a guide only. For more information on building permits, contact your local municipal offices.

Item	UNITS	St. John's	Halifax	Montreal	Ottawa	Toronto	Winnipeg	Calgary	Vancouver
Based on value, New Construction and Renovations									
Minimum Permit Fee	$	25.00	25.00	820.00	200.00	198.60	203.00	*112.00	126.00
Rates (minimum permit fee applies)									
Portion from $1 to $1000	$/1000	9.00	5.50	8.90	7.92	N/A	N/A	N/A	N/A
Portion from $1,001 to $2,000	$/1000	9.00	5.50	8.90	7.92	N/A	10.00	*11.11	N/A
Portion from $2,001 to $5,000	$/1000	9.00	5.50	8.90	7.92	N/A	10.00	*11.11	N/A
Portion from $5,001 to $50,000	$/1000	9.00	5.50	8.90	7.92	N/A	10.00	*11.11	8.10
Portion from $50,001 to $100,000	$/1000	9.00	5.50	8.90	7.92	N/A	10.00	*11.11	4.05
Portion from $100,001 to $500,000	$/1000	7.20	5.50	8.90	7.92	N/A	10.00	*11.11	4.05
Portion from $500,001 to $1,000,000	$/1000	7.20	5.50	8.90	7.92	N/A	10.00	*11.11	4.05
Portion over $1,000,001	$/1000	7.20	5.50	8.90	7.92	N/A	10.00	*11.11	4.05
Based on occupancy, New Construction									
Building permit rates based on occupancy are to be added to any required fees and minimum rates based on value (as listed above). For Winnipeg, building permit rates based on value are to be used only when occupancy type cannot be determined.									
Group A - Assembly Occupancies									
(rates vary based on building use, check with local municipality)	SF	N/A	N/A	N/A	1.14	2.66	1.70	N/A	N/A
Group B - Institutional Occupancies									
(rates vary based on building use, check with local municipality)	SF	N/A	N/A	N/A	1.14	2.83	2.23	N/A	N/A
Group C - Residential Occupancies									
(rates vary based on building use, check with local municipality)	SF	N/A	N/A	N/A	0.77	1.59	1.21	N/A	N/A
Group D - Business and Personal Services Occupancies									
(rates vary based on building use, check with local municipality)									
Building shell alone	SF	N/A	N/A	N/A	0.47	1.67	1.46	N/A	N/A
Finished buildings	SF	N/A	N/A	N/A	0.70	2.10	1.46	N/A	N/A
Group E - Mercantile Occupancies									
(rates vary based on building use, check with local municipality)									
Building shell alone	SF	N/A	N/A	N/A	0.59	1.35	1.23	N/A	N/A
Finished buildings	SF	N/A	N/A	N/A	0.82	1.78	1.23	N/A	N/A
Group F - Industrial Occupancies									
(rates vary based on building use, check with local municipality)									
Building shell alone (< 80,700 SF)	SF	N/A	N/A	N/A	0.27	1.06	1.42	N/A	N/A
Finished buildings (< 80,700 SF)	SF	N/A	N/A	N/A	0.50	1.46	1.42	N/A	N/A
Based on occupancy, Renovations									
Building permit rates based on occupancy are to be added to any required fees and rates based on value (as listed above)									
Group A - Assembly Occupancies	SF	N/A	N/A	N/A	1.14	0.49	0.72	N/A	N/A
Group B - Institutional Occupancies	SF	N/A	N/A	N/A	1.14	0.49	0.90	N/A	N/A
Group C - Residential Occupancies	SF	N/A	N/A	N/A	0.77	0.46	0.49	N/A	N/A
Group D - Business and Personal Services Occupancies	SF	N/A	N/A	N/A	0.70	0.49	0.56	N/A	N/A
Group E - Mercantile Occupancies	SF	N/A	N/A	N/A	0.82	0.46	0.49	N/A	N/A
Group F - Industrial Occupancies	SF	N/A	N/A	N/A	0.50	0.46	0.57	N/A	N/A
TAXES									
Sales tax on building materials:									
Provincial Sales Tax (P.S.T.)	%	N/A	N/A	N/A	N/A	N/A	**8.00	N/A	7.00
Goods & Services Tax (G.S.T.)	%	N/A	N/A	5.00	N/A	N/A	5.00	5.00	5.00
Quebec Sales Tax (Q.S.T.)	%	N/A	N/A	9.975	N/A	N/A	N/A	N/A	N/A
Harmonized Sales Tax (H.S.T.)	%	15.00	15.00	N/A	13.00	13.00	N/A	N/A	N/A

* All building and demolition permits are subject to a surcharge for the Alberta Safety Codes Council. Greater of $4.50 or 4% of the total permit to a max of $560.

Item	UNITS	St. John's	Halifax	Montreal	Ottawa	Toronto	Winnipeg	Calgary	Vancouver

The unit rates given include material, labour, overhead & profit.

**R.S.T. (Retail Sales Tax) on material and labour has been included in Winnipeg mechanical and electrical unit rates.

All unit rates exclude G.S.T., Q.S.T. & H.S.T.

For calculation purposes using the unit rates provided in this book:

St. Johns: H.S.T. should be added to the unit rate.

Halifax: H.S.T. should be added to the unit rate.

Montreal: H.S.T. should be added to the unit rate.

Ottawa: H.S.T. should be added to the unit rate.

Toronto: H.S.T. should be added to the unit rate.

Winnipeg: G.S.T. should be added to the unit rate. (R.S.T. on material is included in the unit rate.)

Calgary: G.S.T. should be added to the unit rate. (there is no P.S.T.)

Vancouver: H.S.T. should be added to the unit rate.

Method for calculating a unit rate from scratch:

Assumptions:

Material (M) = $40.00

Labour (L) = $40.00

Overhead & Profit (O) = $20.00

	St. John's		Halifax		Montreal		Ottawa		Toronto		Winnipeg		Calgary		Vancouver	
Material		40.00		40.00		40.00		40.00		40.00		40.00		40.00		40.00
Labour		40.00		40.00		40.00		40.00		40.00		40.00		40.00		40.00
OH&P		20.00		20.00		20.00		20.00		20.00		20.00		20.00		20.00
PST on (M)	N/A	–	N/A	–	N/A	–	N/A	–	N/A	–	N/A	–	N/A	–	5.0%	2.00
RST on (M)	N/A	–	N/A	–	N/A	–	N/A	–	N/A	–	7.0%	2.80	N/A	–	N/A	–
GST on (M+L+O)	N/A	–	N/A	–	5.0%	5.00	N/A	–	N/A	–	5.0%	5.00	5.0%	5.00	7.0%	7.14
QST on sum of (M+L+O+GST)	N/A	–	N/A	–	10.0%	9.98	N/A	–	N/A	–	N/A	–	N/A	–	N/A	–
HST on (M+L+O)	13.0%	13.00	15.0%	15.00	N/A	–	13%	13.00	13%	13.00	N/A	–	N/A	–	N/A	–
TOTAL		113.00		115.00		114.98		113.00		113.00		107.80		105.00		109.14

Item	UNITS	St. John's	Halifax	Montreal	Ottawa	Toronto	Winnipeg	Calgary	Vancouver
02: EXISTING CONDITIONS									
02 41 00 Demolition									
02 41 16 Structure Demolition									
BUILDING DEMOLITION									
No salvage or haulage included, based on building volume									
Low rise building, 10' floor to floor height,									
GFA of 40 ksf, average cost	CF	0.46	0.42	0.45	0.61	0.52	0.54	0.53	0.90
02 41 19 Selective Demolition									
CUTOUT DEMOLITION									
Concrete									
Foundation Walls:									
Unreinforced	CF	4.96	4.98	5.49	6.03	5.89	6.09	5.24	8.07
Reinforced	CF	8.41	8.38	9.57	10.60	10.30	10.70	9.15	13.80
Slab-on grade:									
Unreinforced	SF	1.14	1.13	1.23	1.34	1.35	1.40	1.19	1.81
Reinforced	SF	1.74	1.68	1.80	1.98	2.07	2.15	1.83	2.77
MASONRY DEMOLITION									
Masonry									
Partitions:									
Average cost	SF	7.66	7.55	8.08	8.48	9.18	9.75	8.02	12.40
Exterior walls:									
Average cost	SF	10.70	10.70	11.50	12.80	13.00	14.00	11.30	17.30

Item	UNITS	St. John's	Halifax	Montreal	Ottawa	Toronto	Winnipeg	Calgary	Vancouver
03: CONCRETE									
03 01 00 Maintenance of Concrete									
PATCHING CONCRETE									
Epoxy									
100% solids injected to cracks:									
Slab on grade	LF	22.10	22.20	23.60	21.90	26.10	31.10	27.30	32.90
Soffits or walls	LF	32.90	32.00	34.10	31.40	38.40	43.90	40.50	39.00
Epoxy/sand 1:4 mortar:									
Patching to slab or deck									
1/4" thick	SF	32.10	31.40	33.40	32.90	37.10	46.30	41.10	49.10
1" thick	SF	53.50	54.00	55.90	54.50	61.60	80.60	70.40	81.70
Bulk grouting									
Filling to voids	CF	515.00	532.00	637.00	527.00	643.00	875.00	810.00	807.00
03 10 00 Concrete Forming and Accessories									
03 11 00 Concrete Forming									
SUBSTRUCTURE									
Footings									
Strip (wall) footings:									
Level footings	SF	9.29	11.50	9.66	11.10	10.00	16.80	10.60	12.30
Stepped footings	SF	9.38	12.00	9.94	11.40	10.20	17.20	10.70	12.40
Spread (column) footings:									
Column footings	SF	9.11	11.80	9.94	11.10	9.75	16.40	10.30	12.00
Piles caps	SF	10.20	12.40	10.60	11.70	10.60	17.70	11.00	12.90
Raft foundations	SF	9.75	12.60	10.80	11.70	10.60	17.70	11.00	12.90
Foundations walls and grade beams									
Not exceeding 12' high:									
Concealed finish	SF	10.20	11.10	11.00	11.00	11.00	16.00	11.70	13.70
Exposed finish	SF	11.10	11.80	11.60	11.50	11.50	16.90	12.40	14.70
STRUCTURE									
Multiple uses (minimum 4) 8 floors or more									
Flat plate slab concealed finish	SF	10.00	10.60	11.00	12.00	13.20	15.80	10.80	12.70
Exposed finish	SF	10.90	11.10	11.70	12.60	14.10	17.10	11.30	13.40
Flat slab, with drops:									
Concealed finish	SF	10.90	11.10	11.10	12.20	13.80	14.50	11.30	13.40
Exposed finish	SF	11.70	12.10	11.90	13.10	14.90	15.40	12.40	14.50
Concrete beam slab									
Concealed finish	SF	10.00	12.30	11.70	12.60	14.10	17.10	11.30	13.40
Exposed finish	SF	10.90	13.30	12.40	13.60	15.10	18.30	12.40	14.50
Walls									
Not exceeding 4' high									
Concealed finish	SF	9.57	10.60	10.00	10.50	10.50	15.10	11.00	13.00
Exposed finish	SF	10.60	11.10	10.50	11.10	11.10	16.00	11.60	13.70
Between 4' and 8'									
Concealed finish	SF	9.57	10.70	11.20	11.50	11.80	15.10	11.00	13.00
Exposed finish	SF	10.60	11.20	11.80	12.20	12.40	15.80	11.60	13.70
Between 8' and 12'									
Concealed finish	SF	10.60	11.80	13.00	13.50	13.40	24.40	12.40	14.70
Exposed finish	SF	12.20	12.70	13.70	14.40	14.40	25.70	13.10	15.40
Column (square or rectangular):									
Concealed finish	SF	11.10	12.20	16.30	13.40	13.90	16.80	13.80	15.30
Exposed finish	SF	12.00	12.50	16.90	14.10	14.40	17.70	14.70	16.10
Beams:									
Concealed finish	SF	11.10	11.20	16.90	15.10	15.10	20.10	15.10	16.60
Exposed finish	SF	12.00	11.60	17.70	15.80	16.00	20.80	15.80	17.30
Stairs (measure soffits only):									
Exposed finish	SF	32.10	39.60	38.60	37.40	37.70	49.80	37.50	41.10
Single use									
Flat plate slab:									
Concealed finish	SF	11.40	13.70	12.70	16.30	16.20	18.80	14.60	15.10
Exposed finish	SF	13.30	15.40	14.20	18.50	18.60	21.40	16.30	17.30
Flat slab, with drops:									
Concealed finish	SF	13.30	14.20	13.50	17.40	17.70	20.20	15.60	16.30
Exposed finish	SF	15.30	15.90	15.10	19.70	19.90	22.50	17.40	18.10
Concrete beam slab:									
Concealed finish	SF	12.20	14.60	13.50	17.40	17.70	20.20	15.60	16.30
Exposed finish	SF	14.10	16.20	15.10	19.50	19.90	22.50	17.40	18.10
Walls									
Not exceeding 4' high									
Concealed finish	SF	12.00	11.10	13.70	13.20	13.70	22.80	11.70	16.90
Exposed finish	SF	13.00	12.10	14.50	14.30	14.80	24.50	12.50	18.30
Between 4' and 8'									
Concealed finish	SF	12.00	12.10	13.70	13.20	13.70	22.80	11.70	16.90
Exposed finish	SF	13.00	12.90	14.50	14.30	14.80	24.50	12.50	18.30
Between 8' and 12'									
Concealed finish	SF	13.00	12.40	14.10	13.40	14.10	23.20	11.90	17.30
Exposed finish	SF	14.10	13.80	15.90	15.00	15.40	26.10	13.10	19.20

Item	UNITS	St. John's	Halifax	Montreal	Ottawa	Toronto	Winnipeg	Calgary	Vancouver
Columns (square or rectangular):									
Concealed finish	SF	13.70	13.70	17.70	15.80	15.60	21.70	15.50	19.60
Exposed finish	SF	14.70	14.80	18.60	16.80	16.40	22.80	16.30	20.40
Beams:									
Concealed finish	SF	13.70	14.50	19.60	17.40	17.30	23.60	16.90	21.30
Exposed finish	SF	14.70	15.10	20.50	18.70	17.70	24.60	17.80	22.30
Stairs (measure soffit only):									
Exposed finish	SF	40.50	41.70	47.20	43.00	42.50	58.50	42.10	52.50

03 15 00 Concrete Accessories
EXPANSION JOINT
Asphalt and fiber plain filler types to exterior
1/4" thick contraction joint, i.e. to sidewalks

Item	UNITS	St. John's	Halifax	Montreal	Ottawa	Toronto	Winnipeg	Calgary	Vancouver
4" wide	LF	3.26	3.08	3.47	3.51	3.90	5.43	3.63	4.48
6" wide	LF	3.17	3.00	3.35	3.41	3.84	5.30	3.54	4.36
1" thick expansion joint, i.e. between new & existing bldgs.									
6" wide	LF	5.94	5.88	6.74	6.68	7.25	10.20	7.25	8.02
8" wide	LF	7.32	6.71	7.59	7.22	8.14	11.50	8.32	9.20
12" wide	LF	8.08	7.44	8.38	8.47	9.27	13.00	9.30	10.20

03 20 00 Concrete Reinforcement
03 21 00 Reinforcing Steel
REINFORCING IN PLACE
Deformed bars, 50,000 psi
Light bars:

Item	UNITS	St. John's	Halifax	Montreal	Ottawa	Toronto	Winnipeg	Calgary	Vancouver
To footings and slabs	LBS	1.19	1.26	1.08	1.17	1.11	1.08	0.97	1.36
To walls columns and beams	LBS	1.21	1.29	1.09	1.18	1.14	1.11	0.99	1.38
Heavy bars:									
To footings and slabs	LBS	1.13	1.22	1.01	1.17	1.07	1.02	0.93	1.19
To walls columns and beams	LBS	1.17	1.24	1.02	1.18	1.10	1.03	0.95	1.22
Deformed bars, 60,000 psi									
Light bars:									
To footings and slabs	LBS	1.15	1.29	1.08	1.09	1.14	1.11	0.99	1.42
To walls columns and beams	LBS	1.22	1.38	1.14	1.17	1.22	1.20	1.04	1.51
Heavy bars:									
To footings and slabs	LBS	1.18	1.24	1.04	1.08	1.06	1.00	0.95	1.22
To walls columns and beams	LBS	1.19	1.24	1.05	1.09	1.07	1.00	0.95	1.22

COATED REINFORCING
Add for epoxy coating
Total load not exceeding 1 ton:

Item	UNITS	St. John's	Halifax	Montreal	Ottawa	Toronto	Winnipeg	Calgary	Vancouver
Light bars	LBS	0.60	0.67	0.57	0.44	0.50	0.82	0.63	0.86
Heavy bars	LBS	0.44	0.48	0.40	0.33	0.36	0.59	0.45	0.62
Total load over 1 not exceeding 6 tons:									
Light bars	LBS	0.47	0.53	0.43	0.33	0.38	0.64	0.50	0.70
Heavy bars	LBS	0.33	0.36	0.28	0.23	0.26	0.43	0.34	0.47
Total load over 6 tons:									
Light bars	LBS	0.37	0.42	0.37	0.29	0.32	0.52	0.40	0.55
Heavy bars	LBS	0.27	0.31	0.27	0.22	0.23	0.39	0.29	0.40

03 22 00 Welded Wire Fabric
WELDED WIRE FABRIC
In slabs:
6"x6" mesh:

Item	UNITS	St. John's	Halifax	Montreal	Ottawa	Toronto	Winnipeg	Calgary	Vancouver
6/6 gauge	SF	0.58	0.56	0.56	0.61	0.60	0.74	0.49	0.65
8/8 gauge	SF	0.49	0.47	0.47	0.52	0.51	0.63	0.42	0.55
10/10 gauge	SF	0.41	0.39	0.40	0.43	0.43	0.53	0.35	0.46
4"x4" mesh:									
8/8 gauge	SF	0.70	0.67	0.67	0.68	0.70	0.86	0.60	0.76
10/10 gauge	SF	0.48	0.47	0.47	0.51	0.50	0.61	0.42	0.53

03 23 00 Stressing Tendons
PRESTRESSING STEEL
Wire or strands
Ungrouted:
255 ksi

Item	UNITS	St. John's	Halifax	Montreal	Ottawa	Toronto	Winnipeg	Calgary	Vancouver
Not exceeding 100' long	LBS	5.26	5.08	5.35	6.58	5.44	7.67	6.26	9.07
Over 100' not exceeding 200' long	LBS	4.81	4.58	4.81	6.03	4.85	6.67	5.62	8.07
Bars									
Ungrouted									
150 ksi									
Not exceeding 100' long	LBS	5.81	5.53	5.53	6.58	5.72	6.94	5.58	7.76
Grouted									
150 ksi									
Not exceeding 100' long	LBS	11.60	10.70	11.50	12.80	11.70	12.70	10.70	11.30

Item	UNITS	St. John's	Halifax	Montreal	Ottawa	Toronto	Winnipeg	Calgary	Vancouver
03 30 00 Cast-In-Place Concrete									
03 31 00 Structural Concrete									
PLACING CONCRETE (placed only)									
By crane or hoist (major hoisting equipment not included)									
To foundation:									
Wall footings	CY	24.20	23.90	27.00	30.40	34.20	33.20	27.80	25.70
Column footings	CY	24.20	23.90	27.00	30.40	34.20	33.20	27.80	25.70
Raft foundations	CY	21.50	21.20	23.60	26.80	30.10	29.40	24.70	22.90
Pile caps	CY	26.30	26.00	29.00	33.00	37.10	36.10	30.40	28.10
Grade beams and foundation walls	CY	26.90	26.30	29.70	33.70	37.70	36.60	30.80	28.50
To column, walls etc.									
Columns	CY	32.80	32.20	36.40	41.40	46.10	45.00	37.90	34.90
Walls	CY	30.50	30.00	33.60	36.40	42.00	41.90	35.20	32.40
To slabs, beams etc.									
Slab-on-grade	CY	22.00	21.50	25.40	28.70	27.20	31.80	25.30	25.60
Suspended slabs (flat slabs)	CY	22.00	21.50	25.20	27.30	26.80	31.80	25.30	25.60
Suspended slabs (pans or waffles)	CY	25.50	24.80	29.30	33.00	31.30	36.60	29.30	29.50
Suspended slabs (metal deck)	CY	27.60	26.80	31.70	35.70	34.30	39.80	31.50	32.10
Beams (integrated with slabs)	CY	22.00	21.50	25.40	28.70	27.20	31.80	25.30	25.60
Beams (isolated)	CY	27.60	26.80	31.70	35.70	34.30	39.80	31.50	32.10
To miscellaneous									
Stairs	CY	51.90	50.60	59.90	67.50	64.10	74.80	59.60	60.40
Floor toppings	CY	45.20	44.00	51.90	58.50	55.60	65.20	51.60	52.40
HEAVYWEIGHT CONCRETE (supplied only)									
Portland cement									
Standard local aggregates:									
1,500 psi	CY	145.00	125.00	134.00	122.00	137.00	156.00	168.00	138.00
2,000 psi	CY	145.00	125.00	137.00	126.00	140.00	163.00	171.00	139.00
3,000 psi	CY	145.00	133.00	143.00	142.00	140.00	162.00	182.00	236.00
3,500 psi	CY	150.00	138.00	152.00	135.00	149.00	172.00	187.00	187.00
4,000 psi	CY	161.00	145.00	164.00	142.00	155.00	184.00	203.00	199.00
High-early cement, type 30									
Standard aggregates:									
1,500 psi	CY	157.00	132.00	140.00	121.00	148.00	174.00	177.00	151.00
2,000 psi	CY	162.00	137.00	145.00	122.00	154.00	179.00	178.00	153.00
3,000 psi	CY	161.00	143.00	163.00	125.00	155.00	177.00	187.00	206.00
3,500 psi	CY	165.00	151.00	174.00	130.00	161.00	191.00	195.00	212.00
4,000 psi	CY	150.00	138.00	181.00	138.00	168.00	200.00	208.00	225.00
03 35 00 Concrete Finishing									
FINISHING FLOORS									
Standard finishes									
Concealed rough finishes:									
Screeding	SF	0.44	0.44	0.50	0.56	0.56	0.69	0.59	0.63
Wood float	SF	0.60	0.60	0.68	0.73	0.76	0.79	0.67	0.76
Concealed smooth finishes:									
Machine trowel	SF	0.95	1.08	1.32	1.26	1.53	1.82	1.49	1.51
Machine grinding	SF	3.38	3.84	4.79	4.48	5.38	6.53	5.33	5.37
Exposed finishes:									
Machine trowel	SF	0.91	0.96	1.28	1.24	1.24	1.52	1.18	1.23
Broom finish	SF	0.57	0.60	0.81	0.77	0.78	0.95	0.72	0.76
Acid etching	SF	0.38	0.40	0.55	0.52	0.53	0.65	0.49	0.51
Stair treads	SF	4.93	5.20	7.09	6.74	6.76	8.34	6.33	6.61
Heavy duty finishes									
Standard hardener - non-metallic									
(steel trowel finish and sealer not included):									
40 lbs/100 sf	SF	0.45	0.45	0.49	0.54	0.57	0.79	0.48	0.80
60 lbs/100 sf	SF	0.63	0.63	0.69	0.76	0.82	1.75	0.73	1.35
Coloured hardener - standard colours									
(steel trowel finish and sealer not included):									
40 lbs/100 sf	SF	1.31	1.47	1.69	1.75	1.84	4.10	1.87	3.07
60 lbs/100 sf	SF	1.42	1.56	1.77	1.89	1.96	4.29	1.98	3.25
FINISHING WALLS									
Bushhammered concrete									
Exterior walls/columns in open area, minimum 1000 sf:									
Heavy finish	SF	12.80	12.70	11.50	12.80	12.50	12.70	13.50	12.70
Sandblasted concrete									
Exterior walls/columns in open area, minimum 5400 sf:									
Light finish	SF	2.28	2.21	2.12	2.52	2.37	2.61	2.76	2.51
Medium finish	SF	2.95	2.93	2.76	3.32	3.13	3.43	3.63	3.27
Heavy finish	SF	3.97	3.89	3.68	4.43	4.17	4.55	4.82	4.39
03 40 00 Precast Concrete									
03 41 00 Precast Structural Concrete									
BEAMS									
Standard I section:									
36" deep	LF	213.00	217.00	229.00	203.00	219.00	206.00	244.00	354.00

Item	UNITS	St. John's	Halifax	Montreal	Ottawa	Toronto	Winnipeg	Calgary	Vancouver
COLUMNS									
Rectangular section:									
24" x 24" single storey........................	LF	214.00	218.00	227.00	184.00	216.00	206.00	242.00	363.00
24" x 24" multi storey.........................	LF	267.00	272.00	283.00	229.00	269.00	258.00	302.00	451.00
PRESTRESSED CONCRETE									
Floor and roof slabs, 100 psf live load									
Hollow core slabs, 24' spans, min. 5400 sf									
8" hollow core........................	SF	N/A	11.30	11.50	12.80	11.80	13.70	14.00	16.40
12" hollow core.......................	SF	N/A	13.40	13.50	15.60	14.70	16.60	16.90	21.30
Double tees, 30' spans, min. 6500 sf									
24" deep	SF	N/A	16.50	16.10	19.00	17.40	17.90	18.60	24.10

03 45 00 Precast Architectural Concrete

Item	UNITS	St. John's	Halifax	Montreal	Ottawa	Toronto	Winnipeg	Calgary	Vancouver
WALL PANELS									
Solid, non load bearing:									
Plain grey, smooth finish................	SF	37.50	35.40	30.00	28.50	30.50	45.60	34.10	44.40
Plain grey, textured finish..............	SF	40.00	37.80	32.70	32.10	33.60	49.70	36.50	47.40
Plain grey, exposed aggregate..........	SF	44.10	41.40	35.20	33.50	35.50	53.00	39.90	52.20
White, textured finish...................	SF	45.70	42.20	34.70	34.10	36.10	58.40	42.80	51.70
White, exposed aggregate...............	SF	48.00	44.30	35.80	34.10	36.80	59.80	44.90	54.30
Sandwich panels, non load panels:									
Plain grey, smooth finish................	SF	42.80	40.40	34.40	32.70	34.90	52.30	39.20	54.60
Plain grey, textured finish..............	SF	45.00	42.50	35.90	34.00	36.70	55.10	40.80	57.00
Plain grey, exposed aggregate..........	SF	49.20	46.70	39.90	37.60	40.10	60.80	45.00	62.70
White, textured finish...................	SF	50.40	46.10	37.30	35.60	38.20	62.10	46.60	60.30
White, exposed aggregate...............	SF	64.40	59.20	47.90	45.60	49.40	80.40	60.30	77.90
Solid, load bearing:									
Plain grey, smooth finish................	SF	43.50	41.40	35.60	33.20	35.50	49.40	39.90	52.20
White, textured finish...................	SF	50.40	46.10	37.30	35.60	38.20	62.10	46.60	56.70
Sandwich panels, load bearing:									
Plain grey, smooth finish................	SF	47.50	45.00	38.50	36.00	38.70	53.40	43.50	60.40
White, textured finish...................	SF	53.80	49.60	40.20	38.20	41.30	67.00	50.40	65.20

03 60 00 Grouting

Item	UNITS	St. John's	Halifax	Montreal	Ottawa	Toronto	Winnipeg	Calgary	Vancouver
GROUT									
Cement and sand									
Pressure grout curtain:									
Connection charge, 1 per 10' depth	EA	467.00	460.00	516.00	491.00	495.00	694.00	485.00	634.00
Grouting material, average absorption rate 0.25 cf/lf									
of depth	CF	81.80	81.30	89.80	83.00	87.20	123.00	85.80	112.00
Filling voids:									
Average cost............................	CF	176.00	174.00	192.00	180.00	187.00	262.00	183.00	200.00

04: MASONRY

04 05 00 Common Work Results for Masonry

04 05 23 Masonry Accessories

Item	UNITS	St. John's	Halifax	Montreal	Ottawa	Toronto	Winnipeg	Calgary	Vancouver
CONTROL JOINT									
1/2" thick control joint, i.e. to facades									
4" wide	LF	4.51	5.06	4.79	5.12	5.03	5.64	5.97	5.09
6" wide	LF	4.85	5.36	4.97	5.43	5.30	5.97	6.22	5.36

04 20 00 Unit Masonry

The following items cover simple walls and components. Prices for composite walls can be found in Section D. No allowance has been made in the prices for decorative or special bonding. As a rule of thumb for budgeting purposes, a wall with a decorative bond would cost approximately 10% more than a comparable wall in stretcher bond, but this differential can vary depending on the volume of work, the size and type of unit, and the specific bond. No allowance has been made in the masonry prices for scaffolding or temporary work platforms.

04 21 00 Clay Unit Masonry

Item	UNITS	St. John's	Halifax	Montreal	Ottawa	Toronto	Winnipeg	Calgary	Vancouver
FACE BRICK - UNREINFORCED									
4" modular clay brick 7-5/8" x 3-5/8" x 2-5/16"									
Veneer	SF	27.10	24.00	22.20	21.90	22.50	32.70	31.60	30.90
Tied to solid backing.....................	SF	28.30	25.30	23.30	23.10	23.40	34.20	33.20	32.60
4" utility clay brick 9-5/8" x 3-5/8" x 2-5/8"									
Veneer	SF	26.80	23.80	22.00	21.60	22.30	32.30	30.90	30.70
Tied to solid backing.....................	SF	27.90	24.90	22.90	22.70	23.20	33.80	32.90	32.10
4" norman clay brick 11-5/8" x 3-5/8" x 2-5/16"									
Veneer	SF	28.70	25.50	23.30	23.50	23.70	34.90	33.40	33.20
Tied to solid backing.....................	SF	29.60	26.40	24.10	24.20	24.90	35.80	34.50	34.20
4" jumbo clay brick 11-5/8 x 3-5/8" x 3-5/8"									
Veneer	SF	25.60	22.70	20.70	20.90	21.60	30.80	29.90	29.50
Tied to solid backing.....................	SF	27.20	24.10	22.10	22.00	22.60	32.80	31.70	31.20
4" giant clay brick 15-5/8" x 3-5/8" x 7-5/8"									

Item	UNITS	St. John's	Halifax	Montreal	Ottawa	Toronto	Winnipeg	Calgary	Vancouver
Veneer	SF	17.30	15.30	14.20	14.10	14.60	20.80	20.20	19.60
Tied to solid backing	SF	17.90	16.10	14.50	14.60	15.00	21.80	20.90	20.70

FACE BRICK - REINFORCED
Modular clay brick 7-5/8" x 3-5/8" x 2-5/16"

Item	UNITS	St. John's	Halifax	Montreal	Ottawa	Toronto	Winnipeg	Calgary	Vancouver
Veneer	SF	27.10	25.00	22.20	23.50	23.70	36.20	35.30	35.40
Tied to solid backing	SF	27.80	25.60	22.60	24.20	24.90	37.20	36.40	36.30
Utility clay brick 9-5/8" x 3-5/8" x 2-5/16"									
Veneer	SF	27.10	25.00	22.20	23.50	23.70	36.20	35.30	35.40
Tied to solid backing	SF	27.80	25.60	22.60	24.20	24.90	37.20	36.40	36.30
Norman clay brick 11-5/8" x 3-5/8" x 2-5/16"									
Veneer	SF	27.10	25.00	22.20	23.50	23.70	36.20	35.30	35.40
Tied to solid backing	SF	28.60	26.50	23.30	24.90	25.50	38.00	37.20	37.30
Jumbo clay brick 11-5/8" x 3-5/8" x 3-5/8"									
Veneer	SF	25.10	23.00	20.60	21.60	22.30	33.40	32.50	32.60
Tied to solid backing	SF	25.90	23.90	21.10	22.20	22.70	34.20	33.40	33.80
Giant clay brick 15-5/8" x 3-5/8" x 7-5/8"									
Veneer	SF	17.40	16.20	14.30	14.90	15.40	23.20	22.70	22.70
Tied to solid backing	SF	18.80	17.50	15.20	16.10	16.40	25.00	24.30	24.50

04 22 00 Concrete Unit Masonry
CONCRETE BLOCK - UNREINFORCED
Plain (lightweight) concrete blocks
Backup:

Item	UNITS	St. John's	Halifax	Montreal	Ottawa	Toronto	Winnipeg	Calgary	Vancouver
4"	SF	10.10	8.12	11.40	11.30	11.40	17.70	15.60	13.90
6"	SF	11.30	9.00	13.10	12.70	13.10	19.60	17.70	15.60
8"	SF	12.00	10.00	14.50	14.10	14.40	22.20	20.00	16.90
10"	SF	14.60	11.70	16.40	16.50	16.70	25.50	22.80	20.30
12"	SF	15.80	12.40	17.90	17.50	17.70	27.30	24.30	21.50

Freestanding jointed and pointed:

Item	UNITS	St. John's	Halifax	Montreal	Ottawa	Toronto	Winnipeg	Calgary	Vancouver
4"	SF	10.10	8.52	12.50	12.10	12.20	18.80	17.10	14.30
6"	SF	10.90	9.00	13.30	12.80	13.20	20.30	18.10	15.40
8"	SF	12.00	10.00	14.50	14.10	14.40	22.20	20.00	16.90
10"	SF	14.40	12.00	17.50	16.90	17.50	26.80	24.20	20.30
12"	SF	16.10	13.50	19.30	18.90	19.20	29.60	26.60	22.60

Cavity wall, cost per side

Item	UNITS	St. John's	Halifax	Montreal	Ottawa	Toronto	Winnipeg	Calgary	Vancouver
4"	SF	10.60	8.84	13.30	12.30	12.80	19.60	17.70	14.90
6"	SF	11.20	9.48	14.00	13.10	13.70	21.10	18.50	15.90
8"	SF	12.20	10.20	15.10	14.20	14.70	22.90	20.30	17.20
10"	SF	14.30	11.90	17.90	16.70	17.40	26.50	24.00	20.30
12"	SF	15.80	13.10	19.30	18.20	18.90	29.20	25.90	21.80

CONCRETE BLOCK - UNREINFORCED, DECORATIVE
Architectural split faced concrete blocks
Freestanding jointed and pointed:

Item	UNITS	St. John's	Halifax	Montreal	Ottawa	Toronto	Winnipeg	Calgary	Vancouver
4"	SF	13.10	16.00	14.00	14.90	15.70	22.20	19.80	18.30
6"	SF	14.60	17.70	16.00	16.40	17.40	24.20	22.10	20.10
8"	SF	16.40	20.00	17.60	18.40	19.70	27.60	24.70	22.70
10"	SF	18.00	22.20	19.00	20.20	21.80	30.30	27.20	25.00
12"	SF	19.00	23.00	20.20	21.20	22.60	31.70	28.60	26.20

Cavity wall, cost per side

Item	UNITS	St. John's	Halifax	Montreal	Ottawa	Toronto	Winnipeg	Calgary	Vancouver
4"	SF	13.10	16.00	14.00	14.90	15.70	22.20	19.80	18.30
6"	SF	14.70	18.10	16.10	16.40	17.50	24.50	22.20	20.30
8"	SF	16.40	20.10	17.70	18.50	19.80	27.70	24.80	22.80
10"	SF	18.20	22.30	19.20	20.40	22.00	30.80	27.30	25.10
12"	SF	21.20	26.00	22.90	23.90	25.40	35.80	32.10	29.50

Integrally coloured architectural split faced concrete blocks
Freestanding jointed and pointed:

Item	UNITS	St. John's	Halifax	Montreal	Ottawa	Toronto	Winnipeg	Calgary	Vancouver
4"	SF	14.70	18.10	16.10	16.40	17.50	24.50	22.20	20.30
6"	SF	15.70	19.20	17.00	17.80	19.10	26.70	23.90	21.80
8"	SF	18.20	22.30	19.20	20.40	22.00	30.80	27.30	25.10
10"	SF	20.30	25.00	22.10	22.70	24.30	34.10	30.80	28.10
12"	SF	23.70	29.00	25.60	26.60	28.60	40.00	35.90	32.80

Cavity wall, cost per side

Item	UNITS	St. John's	Halifax	Montreal	Ottawa	Toronto	Winnipeg	Calgary	Vancouver
4"	SF	14.70	18.10	16.10	16.40	17.50	24.50	22.20	20.30
6"	SF	15.70	19.20	17.00	17.80	19.10	26.70	23.90	21.80
8"	SF	18.30	22.40	19.40	20.50	22.10	30.90	27.40	25.30
10"	SF	20.30	25.00	22.10	22.70	24.30	34.10	30.80	28.10
12"	SF	24.10	29.40	25.90	27.10	29.10	40.60	36.40	33.40

CONCRETE BLOCK - REINFORCED
Plain (lightweight) concrete blocks
Backup:

Item	UNITS	St. John's	Halifax	Montreal	Ottawa	Toronto	Winnipeg	Calgary	Vancouver
4"	SF	13.20	9.57	12.70	13.80	14.90	21.90	18.20	18.20
6"	SF	14.50	10.70	14.40	15.40	16.80	24.50	20.30	20.20
8"	SF	15.50	11.60	15.30	16.60	17.70	26.40	21.80	21.60
10"	SF	18.50	13.70	17.90	19.50	20.90	31.10	25.60	25.70
12"	SF	19.20	14.50	19.00	20.30	21.90	32.40	26.80	26.70

Freestanding jointed and pointed:

Item	UNITS	St. John's	Halifax	Montreal	Ottawa	Toronto	Winnipeg	Calgary	Vancouver
4"	SF	13.70	10.60	14.20	14.90	15.50	23.80	20.20	19.00
6"	SF	14.60	11.50	15.20	16.00	16.80	25.60	21.40	20.30
8"	SF	15.50	12.00	16.00	16.90	17.70	27.10	22.80	21.60
10"	SF	19.20	14.70	19.70	20.50	21.70	33.40	27.80	26.10
12"	SF	20.50	15.90	21.10	22.20	23.20	35.40	29.80	28.30

Item	UNITS	St. John's	Halifax	Montreal	Ottawa	Toronto	Winnipeg	Calgary	Vancouver
Cavity wall, cost per side									
4"	SF	13.80	10.60	14.50	15.10	15.80	24.20	20.40	19.10
6"	SF	15.20	11.80	15.60	16.60	17.50	26.80	22.60	21.10
8"	SF	16.40	12.40	16.70	17.80	18.50	28.40	24.20	22.60
10"	SF	19.40	15.10	20.30	21.30	22.10	34.10	28.80	26.80
12"	SF	20.50	15.90	21.20	22.40	23.30	36.10	30.10	28.40
CONCRETE BLOCK - REINFORCED, DECORATIVE									
Architectural split faced concrete blocks									
Freestanding jointed and pointed:									
4"	SF	16.60	13.70	16.10	19.00	17.40	24.70	22.20	20.60
6"	SF	18.00	14.90	17.40	20.70	18.90	26.90	24.10	22.40
8"	SF	19.20	16.00	18.60	22.20	20.30	28.70	25.90	24.10
10"	SF	22.10	18.30	21.10	25.40	23.10	32.80	29.60	27.50
12"	SF	22.90	19.00	22.20	26.40	24.00	34.10	30.70	28.40
Cavity wall, cost per side									
4"	SF	17.20	14.30	16.70	19.90	17.80	25.60	23.30	21.50
6"	SF	18.60	15.60	18.00	21.60	19.70	27.70	25.10	23.50
8"	SF	19.90	16.40	18.90	22.70	20.50	29.40	26.60	24.60
10"	SF	22.10	18.40	21.20	25.50	23.20	33.10	29.70	27.80
12"	SF	23.40	19.40	22.40	26.80	24.30	34.60	31.50	29.00
Integrally coloured architectural split faced concrete blocks									
Freestanding jointed and pointed:									
4"	SF	18.60	15.60	18.00	21.60	19.70	27.70	25.50	23.50
6"	SF	20.00	16.40	19.00	22.90	20.60	29.70	27.10	24.90
8"	SF	21.40	17.70	20.40	24.50	22.60	32.10	29.40	26.80
10"	SF	24.70	20.50	23.90	28.50	25.70	37.10	33.90	30.70
12"	SF	27.30	22.70	26.10	31.30	28.30	40.50	37.10	34.10
Cavity wall, cost per side									
4"	SF	18.60	15.60	18.00	21.60	19.70	27.70	25.50	23.50
6"	SF	20.10	16.50	19.20	23.30	20.90	30.00	27.50	25.20
8"	SF	23.40	19.40	22.40	26.80	24.30	34.60	32.00	29.00
10"	SF	25.50	21.10	24.30	29.20	26.60	37.60	34.50	31.70
12"	SF	27.40	22.80	26.20	31.60	28.50	40.90	37.40	34.20
04 23 00 Glass Unit Masonry									
GLASS BLOCK									
Glass block units in straight assembly, normal view,									
6" x 6"	SF	85.80	60.00	81.60	93.80	80.10	117.00	102.00	89.00
8" x 8"	SF	62.50	43.80	59.30	68.20	58.40	85.50	74.30	64.80
12" x 12"	SF	57.50	40.40	54.80	63.10	54.00	78.60	68.70	59.90
04 40 00 Stone Assemblies									
Including Necessary Anchor And Fixing Slots And Checks									
04 43 00 Stone Masonry									
GRANITE (EDGEWORK EXTRA)									
Grey, 1 1/2" thick:									
Flamed finish	SF	107.00	80.50	104.00	108.00	116.00	120.00	113.00	120.00
Honed finish	SF	112.00	84.60	111.00	114.00	120.00	125.00	119.00	124.00
Polished finish	SF	116.00	88.30	115.00	120.00	124.00	133.00	123.00	131.00
Grey, 4" thick:									
Flamed finish	SF	130.00	97.50	127.00	133.00	142.00	149.00	137.00	145.00
Honed finish	SF	133.00	100.00	130.00	136.00	145.00	151.00	141.00	149.00
Polished finish	SF	145.00	111.00	140.00	148.00	156.00	164.00	154.00	161.00
LIMESTONE (EDGEWORK EXTRA)									
Plain ashlar coursing:									
Dimensioned stone 3 5/8" on bed:									
Sawn finish	SF	57.20	100.00	60.40	64.80	66.30	70.00	66.90	73.00
Rubbed finish	SF	62.40	110.00	66.00	70.60	72.50	76.50	73.00	79.70
MARBLE (EDGEWORK EXTRA)									
White, 3/4" thick									
Honed finish	SF	92.30	150.00	97.50	106.00	98.50	111.00	110.00	109.00
White, 1 1/2" thick									
Honed finish	SF	112.00	182.00	120.00	130.00	122.00	137.00	132.00	133.00
SANDSTONE (EDGEWORK EXTRA)									
Ashlar coursing:									
Standard grade	SF	48.00	64.80	46.50	51.30	54.20	52.30	50.90	57.70
Select grade	SF	57.10	76.60	54.80	60.50	63.90	62.50	60.40	68.30
ROUGH STONE WALL									
Fieldstone									
Split Field Stone									
Random pattern	SF	48.70	74.60	47.20	54.70	52.00	57.50	56.20	61.30
Limestone									
Split bed split face:									
Coursed Rubble	SF	28.90	44.00	28.10	32.10	30.70	33.90	33.40	36.10
3 5/8" sawn bed, split face:									
Single coursing	SF	24.10	36.90	23.70	26.80	25.70	28.10	27.70	30.20
Triple coursing	SF	25.90	39.80	25.20	29.00	27.80	30.70	29.90	32.50

Item	UNITS	St. John's	Halifax	Montreal	Ottawa	Toronto	Winnipeg	Calgary	Vancouver
05: METALS									
05 10 00 Structural Metal Framing									
05 12 00 Structural Steel Framing									
STRUCTURAL STEEL									
(Based on simple construction types) 50 ksi yield									
strength, including shop prime coat									
Beams:									
Light beams not exceeding 35 lbs/lf	TON	4,090	3,720	4,000	4,130	4,260	4,580	3,730	5,480
Wide flange beams between 35 lbs/lf and 160 lbs/lf	TON	3,730	3,430	3,660	3,770	3,860	4,220	3,430	5,030
Welded wide flange	TON	3,910	3,570	3,830	3,960	4,060	4,400	3,580	5,250
Plate girders:									
Average cost	TON	4,570	4,190	4,500	4,640	4,760	5,160	4,200	6,170
Columns:									
Light beam, not exceeding 35 lbs/lf	TON	3,980	3,640	3,910	4,020	4,130	4,480	3,660	5,340
Wide flange, over 35 lbs/lf not exceeding 190 lbs/lf	TON	3,730	3,430	3,660	3,770	3,860	4,220	3,430	5,030
Welded wide flange	TON	3,910	3,570	3,830	3,960	4,060	4,400	3,580	5,250
Hollow Structural Sections (HSS):									
All sizes	TON	4,330	3,970	4,250	4,380	4,500	4,890	3,970	5,830
Spandrels:									
Light beams not exceeding 35 lbs/lf	TON	4,330	3,970	4,250	4,380	4,500	4,890	3,970	5,830
Wide flange beams between 35 lbs/lf and 160 lbs/lf	TON	4,160	3,810	4,100	4,200	4,340	4,710	3,810	5,620
Welded wide flange beams	TON	4,270	3,910	4,220	4,320	4,440	4,830	3,930	5,750
Trusses:									
Double angle or tee	TON	4,060	3,640	4,260	4,350	5,030	4,770	3,980	5,260
Wide flange	TON	3,790	3,410	3,970	4,040	4,680	4,450	3,680	4,890
Welded wide flange	TON	3,990	3,580	4,190	4,260	4,950	4,700	3,900	5,180
Tubular sections	TON	4,310	3,880	4,530	4,630	5,340	5,080	4,220	5,600
Bracing:									
Angles	TON	4,060	3,640	4,260	4,350	5,030	4,770	3,980	5,260
Wide flange	TON	4,730	4,240	4,940	5,030	5,850	5,550	4,600	6,120
Purlins:									
Light beam	TON	3,390	3,070	3,580	3,650	4,220	4,020	3,320	4,440
Wide flange	TON	3,050	2,740	3,180	3,270	3,790	3,590	2,980	3,960
Girts:									
Hot rolled	TON	3,390	3,070	3,580	3,650	4,220	4,020	3,320	4,440
Cold formed	TON	5,470	4,920	5,750	5,870	6,790	6,440	5,360	7,120
Sag rods:									
Average cost	EA	39.20	35.20	41.20	41.90	48.50	45.90	38.30	51.00
Loose lintels (supply only):									
Average cost	TON	2,360	2,110	2,500	2,530	2,920	2,780	2,330	3,070
Base plates:									
Up to 8" thickness Canadian	TON	3,700	3,300	3,860	3,930	4,560	4,330	3,600	4,780
Over 8" thickness U.S.	TON	4,420	3,960	4,640	4,730	5,500	5,200	4,310	5,720
Stud shear connectors:									
Shop applied	EA	3.30	2.95	3.46	3.54	4.08	3.87	3.20	4.26
Field applied	EA	6.29	5.64	6.60	6.72	7.77	7.38	6.12	8.15
Ancillary steel:									
Average cost	TON	6,330	5,680	6,650	6,780	7,840	7,450	6,190	8,220
05 20 00 Metal Joists									
05 21 00 Steel Joist Framing									
OPEN WEB JOISTS									
(Based on simple construction types.)									
For bracing etc. see item 05120.									
55 ksi yield strength									
Prime coated	TON	4,070	3,580	3,480	3,470	3,690	4,020	3,240	5,130
05 30 00 Metal Decking									
05 31 00 Steel Decking									
FLOOR DECKS - GALVANIZED									
(Based on composite decks)									
Flat (v-rib pans)									
28 gauge	SF	1.78	1.77	1.98	1.89	1.92	1.79	1.90	2.88
1 1/2" deep, non cellular									
22 gauge:									
With g25 wipe coat	SF	3.34	3.39	3.34	3.43	3.61	3.34	3.58	5.33
With g90 wipe coat	SF	3.49	3.58	3.48	3.60	3.79	3.52	3.73	5.57
20 gauge:									
With g25 wipe coat	SF	3.73	3.79	3.73	3.82	4.07	3.73	3.98	5.93
18 gauge:									
With g25 wipe coat	SF	4.12	4.19	4.11	4.25	4.46	4.13	4.40	6.56
16 gauge:									
With g25 wipe coat	SF	4.89	4.99	4.89	5.04	5.31	4.90	5.21	7.79

Item	UNITS	St. John's	Halifax	Montreal	Ottawa	Toronto	Winnipeg	Calgary	Vancouver
1 1/2" deep, cellular (100% cellular)									
20 gauge:									
With g25 wipe coat	SF	7.56	7.69	7.53	7.78	8.21	7.59	8.07	12.10
With g90 wipe coat	SF	8.62	8.80	8.63	8.86	9.38	8.67	9.23	13.70
3" deep, non cellular									
22 gauge:									
With g25 wipe coat	SF	4.68	4.61	4.33	4.80	5.09	4.74	5.02	6.95
With g90 wipe coat	SF	4.77	4.66	4.40	4.89	5.17	4.82	5.11	7.10
20 gauge:									
With g25 wipe coat	SF	5.17	5.07	4.78	5.30	5.61	5.21	5.52	7.64
18 gauge:									
With g25 wipe coat	SF	5.59	5.49	5.19	5.73	6.09	5.66	5.97	8.31
16 gauge:									
With g25 wipe coat	SF	6.22	6.14	5.77	6.40	6.80	6.32	6.69	9.26
3" deep, cellular (100% cellular)									
20 gauge:									
With g25 wipe coat	SF	10.70	10.40	9.85	10.90	11.60	10.80	11.20	15.60
With g90 wipe coat	SF	10.90	10.60	10.00	11.10	11.80	11.00	11.60	16.00
ROOF DECKS - GALVANIZED									
1 1/2" deep, non cellular									
22 gauge:									
Standard, g25 wipe coat	SF	3.13	3.21	2.87	3.55	3.25	3.17	2.93	6.17
Standard, g90 wipe coat	SF	3.31	3.39	3.02	3.75	3.45	3.34	3.09	6.54
Acoustical, g25 wipe coat	SF	3.86	3.94	3.51	4.36	3.98	3.87	3.58	7.57
Acoustical, g90 wipe coat	SF	3.97	4.11	3.68	4.54	4.17	4.04	3.73	7.90
20 gauge:									
Standard, g25 wipe coat	SF	3.48	3.60	3.20	3.94	3.62	3.55	3.28	6.88
Acoustical, g25 wipe coat	SF	4.19	4.31	3.85	4.76	4.36	4.26	3.92	8.27
18 gauge:									
Standard, g25 wipe coat	SF	4.15	4.25	3.80	4.68	4.32	4.19	3.88	8.18
16 gauge:									
Standard, g25 wipe coat	SF	4.67	4.80	4.28	5.30	4.83	4.73	4.37	9.22
3" deep, non cellular									
22 gauge:									
Standard, g25 wipe coat	SF	4.52	4.64	4.33	5.33	4.83	4.60	4.41	8.85
Standard, g90 wipe coat	SF	4.68	4.80	4.48	5.51	5.03	4.73	4.53	9.18
Acoustical, g25 wipe coat	SF	5.27	5.39	5.04	6.18	5.63	5.32	5.11	10.30
Acoustical, g90 wipe coat	SF	5.52	5.67	5.28	6.49	5.88	5.61	5.35	10.80
20 gauge:									
Standard, g25 wipe coat	SF	5.16	5.29	4.91	6.06	5.51	5.23	4.99	10.00
Acoustical, g25 wipe coat	SF	5.73	5.87	5.45	6.74	6.13	5.83	5.56	11.20
18 gauge:									
Standard, g25 wipe coat	SF	5.73	5.87	5.45	6.74	6.13	5.83	5.56	11.20
16 gauge:									
Standard, g25 wipe coat	SF	6.31	6.48	6.04	7.42	6.76	6.38	6.14	12.40

05 40 00 Cold-Formed Metal Framing

FRAMING, STUD WALLS

Solid type, 25 gauge

16" o.c.

Item	UNITS	St. John's	Halifax	Montreal	Ottawa	Toronto	Winnipeg	Calgary	Vancouver
1 5/8" studs	SF	2.07	2.06	1.90	2.28	2.52	1.88	1.72	2.53
2 1/2" studs	SF	2.42	2.39	2.22	2.60	2.90	2.16	2.01	2.94
3 5/8" studs	SF	2.68	2.64	2.44	2.90	3.22	2.42	2.23	3.25
6" studs	SF	4.29	4.25	3.89	4.65	5.14	3.86	3.55	5.21

05 50 00 Metal Fabrications

05 51 13 Metal Pan Stairs

STAIR

Pan stairs with closed risers:

10" treads and 8" risers

Item	UNITS	St. John's	Halifax	Montreal	Ottawa	Toronto	Winnipeg	Calgary	Vancouver
36" wide (per tread)	EA	224.00	197.00	243.00	263.00	288.00	305.00	281.00	391.00
42" wide (per tread)	EA	249.00	219.00	270.00	289.00	316.00	338.00	311.00	436.00
48" wide (per tread)	EA	308.00	270.00	335.00	360.00	394.00	420.00	387.00	540.00
Landings:									
2" deep pan	SF	120.00	106.00	131.00	139.00	154.00	165.00	152.00	223.00
Circular stairs:									
Steel stairs:									
5' dia. (per tread)	EA	485.00	426.00	537.00	573.00	626.00	667.00	613.00	908.00

05 51 33 Metal Ladders

LADDER

Open steel ladders:

Item	UNITS	St. John's	Halifax	Montreal	Ottawa	Toronto	Winnipeg	Calgary	Vancouver
16" wide	LF	60.70	53.60	65.50	75.00	75.30	82.90	80.80	112.00
Steel ladders with safety loops:									
16" wide	LF	99.40	86.60	107.00	122.00	121.00	133.00	132.00	186.00

05 52 00 Metal Railings

HANDRAILS ON WALL BRACKETS

Steel:

Item	UNITS	St. John's	Halifax	Montreal	Ottawa	Toronto	Winnipeg	Calgary	Vancouver
1.5" pipe rail	LF	40.50	37.20	37.80	45.10	42.70	53.00	48.80	44.20

Item	UNITS	St. John's	Halifax	Montreal	Ottawa	Toronto	Winnipeg	Calgary	Vancouver
Plastic covered steel:									
1.5" wide	LF	53.90	49.70	50.00	60.40	56.70	71.30	65.20	59.10
Railings									
Steel:									
1.5" pipe railing, 36" high	LF	106.00	96.60	98.50	117.00	111.00	138.00	126.00	115.00
1/2" tube pickets, 36" high	LF	151.00	138.00	142.00	168.00	158.00	198.00	182.00	165.00

05 53 00 Metal Gratings
FLOOR GRATING
Welded standard gratings

Item	UNITS	St. John's	Halifax	Montreal	Ottawa	Toronto	Winnipeg	Calgary	Vancouver
Pedestrian traffic:									
3' span	SF	14.70	13.60	17.30	15.60	15.90	16.30	12.60	19.30
4' span	SF	16.60	15.30	19.70	17.70	18.10	18.50	14.20	21.60
6' span	SF	23.40	21.60	27.60	24.80	25.30	25.90	20.00	30.70
10' span	SF	37.90	34.90	43.90	39.90	41.00	41.30	32.10	49.10

06: WOOD, PLASTICS & COMPOSITES

06 10 00 Rough Carpentry

06 11 00 Wood Framing - Supply
FRAMING, MEMBERS
Boards and shiplap
Construction grade softwood, spruce, 8 foot long pieces
1" thick:

Item	UNITS	St. John's	Halifax	Montreal	Ottawa	Toronto	Winnipeg	Calgary	Vancouver
2" wide	LF	0.17	0.19	0.21	0.19	0.19	0.22	0.20	0.15
3" wide	LF	0.29	0.32	0.37	0.31	0.29	0.37	0.35	0.25
4" wide	LF	0.35	0.39	0.44	0.38	0.36	0.45	0.43	0.30
6" wide	LF	0.50	0.81	0.53	0.79	0.59	0.71	0.61	0.51
8" wide	LF	0.61	0.99	0.64	0.95	0.73	0.86	0.74	0.62
10" wide	LF	0.79	1.26	0.84	1.24	0.94	1.12	0.96	0.79
12" wide	LF	1.11	1.80	1.18	1.75	1.33	1.58	1.35	1.13
Structural light framing - studs (S4S) - dried									
Construction grade softwood, spruce, 8 foot long pieces									
2" thick:									
2" wide	LF	0.26	0.27	0.24	0.26	0.28	0.27	0.24	0.26
3" wide	LF	0.30	0.31	0.29	0.30	0.34	0.32	0.28	0.29
4" wide	LF	0.37	0.38	0.35	0.38	0.41	0.39	0.34	0.36
6" wide	LF	0.59	0.81	0.58	0.68	0.73	0.55	0.49	0.43
8" wide	LF	0.77	1.06	0.75	0.89	0.95	0.71	0.62	0.55
10" wide	LF	1.17	1.61	1.15	1.35	1.45	1.08	0.97	0.84
12" wide	LF	1.69	2.32	1.66	1.96	2.10	1.56	1.40	1.22
Western red cedar, 8 foot long pieces									
2" thick:									
3" wide	LF	0.98	1.18	1.08	1.03	1.25	1.16	0.95	1.07
4" wide	LF	1.05	1.25	1.16	1.09	1.33	1.23	1.01	1.15
6" wide	LF	2.06	2.46	2.28	2.15	2.61	2.40	1.98	2.25
8" wide	LF	2.84	3.41	3.14	2.98	3.60	3.32	2.74	3.11
10" wide	LF	4.63	5.55	5.18	4.91	5.91	5.46	4.51	5.12
12" wide	LF	6.13	7.32	6.77	6.40	7.74	7.10	5.91	6.68
Pressure treated lumber, rated for ground contact									
2" thick:									
4" wide	LF	0.65	0.67	0.62	0.67	0.73	0.69	0.60	0.64
6" wide	LF	0.90	1.23	0.87	1.04	1.11	0.83	0.74	0.64
8" wide	LF	1.30	1.78	1.26	1.50	1.60	1.20	1.07	0.94
10" wide	LF	1.88	2.60	1.86	2.19	2.34	1.75	1.56	1.36
12" wide	LF	4.21	5.76	4.08	4.82	5.09	3.87	3.47	3.02
4" thick:									
4" wide	LF	1.30	1.77	1.26	1.50	1.60	1.20	1.07	0.94

06 11 00 Wood Framing - Installation
(Rough hardware included)
Light framing
FRAMING, WALLS
Wall framing cost:

Item	UNITS	St. John's	Halifax	Montreal	Ottawa	Toronto	Winnipeg	Calgary	Vancouver
2" x 4"	SF	1.31	1.57	1.29	1.22	1.93	1.76	1.23	1.37
2" x 6"	SF	1.95	2.32	1.92	1.80	2.89	2.64	1.83	2.02

FRAMING, JOISTS & BEAMS
Joist or beams:

Item	UNITS	St. John's	Halifax	Montreal	Ottawa	Toronto	Winnipeg	Calgary	Vancouver
2" x 10"	SF	1.80	2.14	1.76	1.66	2.66	2.42	1.70	1.87
2" x 12"	SF	2.21	2.64	2.15	2.05	3.25	3.00	2.04	2.28

FRAMING, ROOFS
Rafters or purlins:

Item	UNITS	St. John's	Halifax	Montreal	Ottawa	Toronto	Winnipeg	Calgary	Vancouver
2" x 6"	SF	1.35	1.68	1.36	1.39	2.03	1.86	1.33	1.64

FRAMING, CEILINGS
Suspended ceiling framing:

Item	UNITS	St. John's	Halifax	Montreal	Ottawa	Toronto	Winnipeg	Calgary	Vancouver
1 1/2" x 2"	SF	1.96	2.47	1.97	2.03	2.97	2.71	1.93	2.39

Item	UNITS	St. John's	Halifax	Montreal	Ottawa	Toronto	Winnipeg	Calgary	Vancouver
FRAMING, BLOCKING & NAILERS									
Nailers, blocking, etc.:									
2" x 2"	LF	1.86	2.22	1.83	1.73	2.77	2.52	1.75	1.94
FRAMING, FURRING & STRAPPINGS									
Furring or strapping:									
1" thick									
2" wide	LF	0.71	0.84	0.69	0.66	1.05	0.96	0.66	0.73
3" wide	LF	0.83	0.99	0.81	0.77	1.22	1.11	0.78	0.86
4" wide	LF	0.84	1.00	0.82	0.78	1.24	1.14	0.79	0.87
2" thick									
2" wide	LF	0.97	1.16	0.96	0.91	1.44	1.33	0.91	1.01
3" wide	LF	0.92	1.11	0.91	0.86	1.38	1.25	0.87	0.95
4" wide	LF	1.09	1.30	1.07	1.01	1.62	1.48	1.01	1.13
6" wide	LF	1.12	1.33	1.09	1.03	1.65	1.51	1.04	1.15

06 15 00 Wood Decking - Supply

DECKING

Item	UNITS	St. John's	Halifax	Montreal	Ottawa	Toronto	Winnipeg	Calgary	Vancouver
Decking tongue and groove - dried									
Select spruce:									
2" thick									
6" wide	LF	1.37	1.41	1.44	1.74	1.65	1.86	1.59	1.70
8" wide	LF	1.54	1.59	1.62	1.97	1.87	2.09	1.80	1.92
3" thick									
6" wide	LF	2.04	2.11	2.15	2.61	2.47	2.78	2.39	2.53
4" thick									
6" wide	LF	3.03	3.14	3.20	3.90	3.72	4.15	3.60	3.75
Select fir or hemlock:									
2" thick									
6" wide	LF	1.43	1.49	1.52	1.84	1.74	1.96	1.68	1.79
8" wide	LF	2.19	2.27	2.32	2.80	2.67	3.01	2.57	2.73
3" thick									
6" wide	LF	2.28	2.36	2.41	2.93	2.78	3.11	2.67	2.84
4" thick									
6" wide	LF	3.81	3.96	4.02	4.85	4.63	5.21	4.48	4.75
Select cedar:									
2" thick									
6" wide	LF	3.17	3.29	3.14	4.21	3.54	4.11	3.20	3.20
8" wide	LF	4.11	4.24	4.08	5.52	4.60	5.33	4.18	4.11
3" thick									
6" wide	LF	4.85	5.00	4.79	6.46	5.46	6.25	4.91	4.94
4" thick									
6" wide	LF	7.35	7.59	7.32	9.78	8.29	9.60	7.50	7.41

06 15 00 Wood Decking - Installation

DECKING

Item	UNITS	St. John's	Halifax	Montreal	Ottawa	Toronto	Winnipeg	Calgary	Vancouver
Decking tongue and groove - dried									
2" thick									
6" wide	SF	2.39	2.11	2.47	2.40	3.66	3.45	2.41	2.70
8" wide	SF	2.70	2.38	2.81	2.69	4.12	3.86	2.71	3.05
3" thick									
6" wide	SF	3.30	2.88	3.40	3.28	5.04	4.73	3.31	3.71
4" thick									
6" wide	SF	4.19	3.69	4.32	4.17	6.40	6.04	4.22	4.72

06 16 00 Sheathing - Supply

SHEATHING

Item	UNITS	St. John's	Halifax	Montreal	Ottawa	Toronto	Winnipeg	Calgary	Vancouver
Prices are based upon the standard imperial panel size which is 4' x 8', although 4' x 10' and 4' x 12' are available from most mills at a premium.									
Unsanded fir plywood:									
1/2"	SF	1.03	1.06	1.16	0.90	1.18	0.89	0.78	0.93
5/8"	SF	1.16	1.19	1.31	1.02	1.33	1.00	0.88	1.05
3/4"	SF	1.34	1.38	1.51	1.18	1.54	1.15	1.01	1.21
Sanded fir plywood, G1S:									
3/8"	SF	1.13	2.07	1.12	1.01	1.14	1.13	0.98	1.12
1/2"	SF	1.36	2.46	1.35	1.22	1.39	1.36	1.16	1.34
5/8"	SF	1.72	3.13	1.70	1.55	1.74	1.73	1.49	1.70
3/4"	SF	2.03	3.67	1.99	1.79	2.02	2.00	1.74	2.00

06 16 00 Sheathing - Installation

SHEATHING

Item	UNITS	St. John's	Halifax	Montreal	Ottawa	Toronto	Winnipeg	Calgary	Vancouver
Floors or flat roofs:									
1/2"	SF	0.75	0.66	0.77	0.75	1.15	1.08	0.75	0.85
5/8"	SF	0.90	0.79	0.93	0.89	1.37	1.29	0.90	1.01
3/4"	SF	0.90	0.79	0.93	0.89	1.37	1.29	0.90	1.01
Walls:									
3/8"	SF	0.90	0.81	0.88	0.87	1.37	1.28	0.93	1.03
1/2"	SF	1.05	0.95	1.02	1.01	1.60	1.50	1.09	1.20
5/8"	SF	1.05	0.95	1.02	1.01	1.60	1.50	1.09	1.20
3/4"	SF	1.20	1.08	1.15	1.15	1.82	1.71	1.22	1.35

Item	UNITS	St. John's	Halifax	Montreal	Ottawa	Toronto	Winnipeg	Calgary	Vancouver
06 17 00 Shop-Fabricated Structural Wood									
STRUCTURAL JOISTS									
Composite wood joist with parallel 2" x 3"									
top and bottom Micro-Lam flanges and 3/8"									
plywood web - SUPPLY ONLY (excluding hardware)									
11 1/8" deep	LF	4.66	1.53	5.00	5.15	5.21	6.07	5.24	5.00
14" deep	LF	5.03	1.67	5.33	5.58	5.64	6.52	5.67	5.36
16" deep	LF	5.18	1.71	5.61	5.76	5.88	6.80	5.97	5.52
18" deep	LF	5.79	1.91	6.13	6.40	6.52	7.53	6.55	6.19
20" deep	LF	6.34	2.10	6.61	7.01	7.13	8.17	7.10	6.68
06 18 00 Glued-Laminated Construction									
LAMINATED FRAMING									
Structural units - SUPPLY ONLY (excluding hardware) based on									
actual net volumes, spruce									
Straight members 2" material: Interior work									
Industrial grade	MFBM	3,700	3,630	3,680	3,470	4,130	4,510	3,920	5,950
Commercial grade	MFBM	3,800	3,730	3,780	3,590	4,220	4,650	4,060	6,090
Quality grade	MFBM	4,250	4,180	4,180	3,960	4,720	5,140	4,510	6,730
Structural units - INSTALLATION ONLY									
Less than 10,000 fbm:									
Members not exceeding 30' long	EA	271.00	258.00	259.00	255.00	286.00	343.00	285.00	340.00
Over 30', not exceeding 40'	EA	373.00	358.00	357.00	350.00	396.00	473.00	393.00	472.00
Over 40'	EA	745.00	715.00	715.00	700.00	793.00	945.00	786.00	945.00
Over 10,000 fbm:									
Members not exceeding 30' long	EA	150.00	145.00	145.00	141.00	160.00	191.00	160.00	189.00
Over 30', not exceeding 40'	EA	254.00	243.00	244.00	238.00	269.00	322.00	268.00	322.00
Over 40'	EA	474.00	455.00	458.00	445.00	509.00	602.00	501.00	604.00
06 20 00 Finish Carpentry									
06 26 00 Board Panelling									
PANELLING, BOARDS									
Veneered plywood panelling standard panels excluding finishing.									
For select grades for special selection or "bookmatching" application,									
multiply pricing by two.									
Fir: 1/4" G1S	SF	5.94	6.03	6.14	6.48	7.43	8.17	6.93	8.57
Birch: 1/4" G1S	SF	6.59	6.70	6.82	7.21	8.25	9.08	7.66	9.57
Oak: 1/4"	SF	7.71	7.82	7.96	8.43	9.66	10.60	8.98	11.10
Mahogany: 1/4"	SF	8.79	8.92	9.08	9.57	11.10	12.00	10.20	12.60
Walnut: 1/4"	SF	11.50	11.70	11.80	12.60	14.50	15.90	13.60	16.80
Teak: 1/4"	SF	12.20	12.40	12.50	13.20	15.10	16.50	14.20	17.60
Wood panelling T&G simple finish									
Knotty Pine: 1" x 6" D4S	SF	6.57	6.69	7.37	7.48	9.10	9.48	8.03	11.20
Cedar: 1" x 6" D4S	SF	10.90	11.00	12.10	12.30	15.10	15.50	13.20	18.20
Redwood: 1" x 6" D4S	SF	14.80	15.00	16.50	16.80	20.40	21.30	18.00	25.30
Douglas Fir: 1" x 6" D4S	SF	11.20	11.40	12.60	12.90	15.70	16.30	13.90	19.50
Birch: 1" x 6" D4S	SF	11.20	11.40	12.60	12.90	15.70	16.30	13.90	19.50
Oak: 1" x 6" D4S	SF	14.90	15.10	16.60	16.90	20.50	21.40	18.10	25.40
Mahogany: 1" x 6" D4S	SF	17.40	17.60	19.50	20.00	24.20	25.30	21.40	29.90
07: THERMAL & MOISTURE PROTECTION									
07 10 00 Dampproofing and Waterproofing									
07 11 00 Dampproofing									
BITUMINOUS ASPHALT COATING									
Cutback asphalt									
Sprayed:									
1 coat	SF	0.72	0.74	0.80	0.89	0.83	0.83	0.69	0.98
2 coats	SF	1.06	1.11	1.21	1.32	1.24	1.23	1.04	1.50
07 13 00 Sheet Waterproofing									
ELASTOMERIC WATERPROOFING									
Flexible membrane									
1/8" polyethylene based sheet:									
On horizontal surfaces	SF	2.99	3.06	2.89	4.99	3.18	3.02	2.45	3.25
On vertical surfaces	SF	2.97	3.02	3.14	5.72	3.75	3.21	2.97	3.46
1/16" rubber based sheet:									
On horizontal surfaces	SF	4.74	4.75	5.11	9.01	5.50	5.32	4.29	5.56
On vertical surfaces	SF	6.85	6.70	8.13	15.00	9.48	8.29	7.51	8.61
Rubberized asphalt hot applied									
Sheet reinforced:									
On horizontal surfaces	SF	2.77	2.61	2.81	3.06	2.85	2.88	2.22	3.34
On vertical surfaces	SF	4.91	4.60	4.98	5.40	5.01	5.04	3.96	5.94

Item	UNITS	St. John's	Halifax	Montreal	Ottawa	Toronto	Winnipeg	Calgary	Vancouver
Acrylic, epoxy or silanes, fluid applied									
On vertical surfaces:									
Low solid	SF	2.87	2.84	3.27	3.55	3.44	3.38	2.74	4.09
High solid	SF	4.18	4.12	4.75	5.15	5.01	4.92	3.98	5.94
Asphalt impregnated protection board									
3 mm (1/8") thick:									
Laid horizontally	SF	1.28	1.22	1.31	3.57	1.46	1.64	1.14	2.23
Fixed vertically	SF	1.60	1.51	1.63	4.46	1.84	2.06	1.45	2.79
MEMBRANE WATERPROOFING									
Fabric membrane									
Glass fibre mesh (embedded):									
2-ply on horizontal surfaces	SF	2.79	2.77	2.80	4.73	2.99	2.77	2.41	2.96
2-ply on vertical surfaces	SF	3.11	3.06	3.13	5.25	3.34	3.10	2.69	3.31
3-ply on horizontal surfaces	SF	3.13	3.10	3.14	5.34	3.38	3.12	2.73	3.33
3-ply on vertical surfaces	SF	3.90	3.85	3.87	6.60	4.18	3.87	3.37	4.12
PROTECTION BOARD									
Plastic protection board									
3 mm (1/8") thick:									
Laid horizontally	SF	0.75	0.86	0.88	0.80	0.87	0.79	0.56	0.76
Fixed vertically	SF	0.83	0.95	0.97	0.88	0.96	0.87	0.62	0.83
Hardboard									
1/4" thick:									
Laid horizontally	SF	0.49	0.58	0.58	0.56	0.64	0.55	0.44	0.54
Fixed vertically	SF	0.65	0.77	0.77	0.75	0.85	0.73	0.58	0.72
Plywood									
1/4" thick:									
Laid horizontally	SF	0.67	0.81	0.81	0.83	0.90	0.76	0.60	0.75
Fixed vertically	SF	0.83	1.01	1.00	1.06	1.12	0.95	0.75	0.95

07 16 00 Cementitious & Reactive Waterproofing
CEMENTITIOUS WATERPROOFING

Item	UNITS	St. John's	Halifax	Montreal	Ottawa	Toronto	Winnipeg	Calgary	Vancouver
Parging									
Exposed:									
1/2" thick (2 coats)	SF	4.65	4.48	4.18	4.65	5.06	4.07	3.81	4.75
Concealed:									
1/2" thick (2 coats)	SF	3.75	3.60	3.34	3.75	4.06	3.26	3.06	3.83

07 19 00 Water Repellents
SILICONE WATER REPELLENTS

Item	UNITS	St. John's	Halifax	Montreal	Ottawa	Toronto	Winnipeg	Calgary	Vancouver
Silicone base									
Roller applied to concrete and masonry walls:									
1 coat	SF	1.03	0.97	0.93	1.02	1.00	1.10	1.17	0.98
2 coats	SF	1.87	1.76	1.67	1.82	1.78	1.96	2.11	1.77

07 20 00 Thermal Protection
07 21 00 Thermal Insulation
BUILDING INSULATION

Item	UNITS	St. John's	Halifax	Montreal	Ottawa	Toronto	Winnipeg	Calgary	Vancouver
Loose fill insulation									
Fibrous:									
Glass fibre	CF	2.86	2.71	3.03	3.71	3.26	3.11	2.76	2.16
Pelletized:									
Vermicular or perlite	CF	4.28	4.05	4.56	5.61	4.96	4.76	4.22	3.23
Board or quilt insulation									
Glass fibre af-530:									
1"	SF	2.71	2.57	2.91	3.57	3.13	2.97	2.64	2.05
1 1/2"	SF	2.71	2.58	2.91	3.57	3.13	2.97	2.64	2.05
2"	SF	3.19	3.04	3.39	4.16	3.65	3.47	3.08	2.41
Expanded polystyrene:									
1"	SF	2.54	2.43	2.73	3.35	2.93	2.80	2.49	1.93
1 1/2"	SF	2.68	2.58	2.91	3.57	3.13	2.97	2.64	2.05
2"	SF	3.04	2.92	3.25	3.99	3.53	3.35	2.97	2.32
Urethane panels:									
1"	SF	4.00	3.80	4.28	5.21	4.61	4.40	3.89	3.05
1 1/2"	SF	4.53	4.34	4.82	5.95	5.25	4.98	4.39	3.44
2"	SF	4.99	4.73	5.30	6.52	5.75	5.48	4.85	3.77
Foamed-in-place (insulated in warm conditions)									
Polyurethane:									
Sprayed, 1 coat, average 1" thick	SF	2.13	2.03	2.24	2.79	2.46	2.34	2.05	1.61
Poured into cavity average 1" wide including jigging walls	SF	4.06	3.88	4.33	5.33	4.71	4.47	3.94	3.08
Perimeter and Under-Slab Insulation									
Polystyrene									
Moulded panels:									
1"	SF	2.16	2.04	2.25	2.80	2.49	2.35	2.05	1.62
1 1/2"	SF	3.17	3.00	3.34	4.13	3.61	3.46	3.06	2.39
2"	SF	3.42	3.26	3.64	4.48	3.95	3.76	3.32	2.61
Polyurethane									
Rigid board:									
1"	SF	2.33	2.16	2.67	1.35	2.85	2.99	2.10	1.90

Item	UNITS	St. John's	Halifax	Montreal	Ottawa	Toronto	Winnipeg	Calgary	Vancouver
1 1/2"	SF	2.76	2.55	3.18	1.60	3.40	3.51	2.54	2.23
2"	SF	3.21	2.98	3.72	1.86	3.96	4.12	2.95	2.61

07 22 00 Roof and Deck Insulation
ROOF DECK INSULATION
Wood fibreboard
Asphalt impregnated:

Item	UNITS	St. John's	Halifax	Montreal	Ottawa	Toronto	Winnipeg	Calgary	Vancouver
1/2" board	SF	0.76	0.64	0.85	1.00	0.93	0.91	0.82	0.80

Glass fibreboard
Rigid kraft faced insulation:

Item	UNITS	St. John's	Halifax	Montreal	Ottawa	Toronto	Winnipeg	Calgary	Vancouver
3/4"	SF	1.10	0.93	1.21	1.45	1.35	1.29	1.16	1.14
1"	SF	1.41	1.20	1.59	1.89	1.75	1.69	1.52	1.49
2"	SF	2.23	1.89	2.49	2.96	2.75	2.70	2.41	2.34
3"	SF	3.13	2.64	3.49	4.14	3.84	3.75	3.37	3.28
4", two layers	SF	4.51	3.79	5.00	5.96	5.49	5.37	4.81	4.70

Expanded polystyrene panels

Item	UNITS	St. John's	Halifax	Montreal	Ottawa	Toronto	Winnipeg	Calgary	Vancouver
1"	SF	1.37	1.17	1.54	1.85	1.70	1.66	1.48	1.46
1 1/2"	SF	1.84	1.55	2.04	2.44	2.25	2.22	1.97	1.90
2"	SF	2.36	2.00	2.62	3.14	2.89	2.82	2.54	2.46

Phenolic foam panels

Item	UNITS	St. John's	Halifax	Montreal	Ottawa	Toronto	Winnipeg	Calgary	Vancouver
1"	SF	1.53	1.28	1.69	2.01	1.84	1.81	1.61	1.59
1 1/2"	SF	1.93	1.63	2.15	2.55	2.36	2.30	2.07	2.03
2"	SF	2.54	2.13	2.82	3.35	3.09	3.01	2.72	2.65

07 26 00 Vapour Retarders
VAPOUR RETARDERS

Item	UNITS	St. John's	Halifax	Montreal	Ottawa	Toronto	Winnipeg	Calgary	Vancouver
Polyethylene vapour barrier, .006" thick	SF	0.16	0.17	0.17	0.19	0.17	0.19	0.19	0.16

07 30 00 Steep Slope Roofing
07 31 00 Shingles and Shakes
ASPHALT SHINGLES
Asphalt shingles, standard pitch
Standard butt edge:

Item	UNITS	St. John's	Halifax	Montreal	Ottawa	Toronto	Winnipeg	Calgary	Vancouver
2.10 lbs/sf	SF	3.06	2.85	2.25	2.63	2.42	2.28	2.23	3.57

Sealed butt edge:

Item	UNITS	St. John's	Halifax	Montreal	Ottawa	Toronto	Winnipeg	Calgary	Vancouver
2.10 lbs/sf self sealing	SF	3.06	2.85	2.25	2.63	2.42	2.28	2.23	3.57

SLATE

Item	UNITS	St. John's	Halifax	Montreal	Ottawa	Toronto	Winnipeg	Calgary	Vancouver
Vermont, semi-weathering green	SF	15.70	16.40	16.70	17.60	19.00	17.70	16.90	17.60

WOOD
Cedar shingles
First grade, high pitch (4/12 min):

Item	UNITS	St. John's	Halifax	Montreal	Ottawa	Toronto	Winnipeg	Calgary	Vancouver
18" shingle, 5 1/2" exposed	SF	7.26	7.07	6.78	6.42	7.19	8.32	6.87	9.00
24" shingle, 7 1/2" exposed	SF	7.75	7.55	7.23	6.85	7.66	8.89	7.32	9.57

07 40 00 Roofing and Siding Panels
07 41 00 Roof Panels
ALUMINUM/STEEL ROOFING
1 1/2" profile
Exposed fasteners:
Single skin siding

Item	UNITS	St. John's	Halifax	Montreal	Ottawa	Toronto	Winnipeg	Calgary	Vancouver
22 ga steel, baked enamel finish	SF	8.74	8.65	8.69	9.75	9.94	10.50	9.02	10.50
24 ga aluminum, baked enamel finish	SF	11.20	11.10	11.10	12.50	12.90	13.70	11.60	13.50

Single skin fascia panels

Item	UNITS	St. John's	Halifax	Montreal	Ottawa	Toronto	Winnipeg	Calgary	Vancouver
22 ga steel, baked enamel finish	SF	16.00	16.00	16.00	17.70	18.20	19.60	16.60	19.20
24 ga aluminum baked enamel finish	SF	34.90	34.70	34.70	39.10	40.00	42.40	36.20	41.90

Hidden fasteners:
Single skin siding

Item	UNITS	St. John's	Halifax	Montreal	Ottawa	Toronto	Winnipeg	Calgary	Vancouver
22 ga steel, baked enamel finish	SF	15.00	14.90	14.90	16.70	17.20	18.10	15.60	18.20
24 ga aluminum, baked enamel finish	SF	17.40	17.20	17.50	19.30	20.00	21.10	17.90	20.90

Single skin fascia panels

Item	UNITS	St. John's	Halifax	Montreal	Ottawa	Toronto	Winnipeg	Calgary	Vancouver
22 ga steel, baked enamel finish	SF	17.70	17.60	17.80	20.00	20.50	21.60	18.60	21.60
24 ga aluminum, baked enamel finish	SF	19.10	18.90	19.10	21.50	22.00	23.20	19.50	23.10

Factory sandwich panel 1" insulation

Item	UNITS	St. John's	Halifax	Montreal	Ottawa	Toronto	Winnipeg	Calgary	Vancouver
22 ga steel, baked enamel finish	SF	17.30	17.20	17.50	19.10	19.00	22.30	18.60	22.50
24 ga aluminum, baked enamel finish	SF	19.00	19.00	19.50	21.20	21.30	25.00	20.40	25.20

07 46 00 Siding
WOOD SIDING, BOARDS
Wood siding
Bevelled select cedar (unfinished):

Item	UNITS	St. John's	Halifax	Montreal	Ottawa	Toronto	Winnipeg	Calgary	Vancouver
1" x 8"	SF	11.10	11.50	11.10	12.00	11.20	13.30	11.60	12.80
1" x 10"	SF	9.66	10.00	9.75	10.40	9.75	11.60	10.10	11.10

FIBRE CEMENT SIDING
Fibre-reinforced cement siding
Flat panels:

Item	UNITS	St. John's	Halifax	Montreal	Ottawa	Toronto	Winnipeg	Calgary	Vancouver
1/4" with textured finish	SF	15.60	15.80	15.10	16.90	15.20	16.30	16.10	20.00

Corrugated panels:

Item	UNITS	St. John's	Halifax	Montreal	Ottawa	Toronto	Winnipeg	Calgary	Vancouver
1/4" with coloured finish	SF	13.90	14.30	13.40	15.30	13.70	14.30	14.30	17.90

Item	UNITS	St. John's	Halifax	Montreal	Ottawa	Toronto	Winnipeg	Calgary	Vancouver
Sandwich panels:									
1 1/2" with coloured finish	SF	20.30	20.80	19.90	22.30	20.20	21.20	21.10	26.60

07 50 00 Membrane Roofing
07 51 00 Built-Up Bituminous Roofing
BUILT-UP ROOFING

Item	UNITS	St. John's	Halifax	Montreal	Ottawa	Toronto	Winnipeg	Calgary	Vancouver
Base treatment									
Base sheets (vapour barrier):									
Paper laminate	SF	0.40	0.33	0.42	0.45	0.41	0.47	0.41	0.43
0.4 lbs/sf asphalt impregnated felt	SF	0.49	0.40	0.51	0.60	0.54	0.65	0.56	0.61
Membrane									
Asphalt impregnated felts:									
0.15 lbs/sf felt (per ply)	SF	0.50	0.49	0.52	0.59	0.54	0.52	0.46	0.63
Bitumen:									
Roofing asphalt, standard	LBS	0.70	0.68	0.73	0.82	0.75	0.73	0.64	0.88
Protective surface									
Granular materials:									
3/8" roofing gravel	TON	93.40	93.40	102.00	101.00	112.00	124.00	109.00	102.00
White granite chips	TON	186.00	186.00	204.00	201.00	222.00	249.00	218.00	203.00

07 52 00 Modified Bituminous Membrane Roofing
MODIFIED BITUMEN ROOFING

Item	UNITS	St. John's	Halifax	Montreal	Ottawa	Toronto	Winnipeg	Calgary	Vancouver
Base sheet:									
#15 glass fiber felt:									
Nailed	SF	0.55	5.92	0.56	0.59	0.60	0.61	0.57	0.65
Mopped	SF	0.67	7.20	0.69	0.71	0.72	0.74	0.69	0.79
#15 organic felt:									
Nailed	SF	0.37	3.96	0.38	0.39	0.40	0.41	0.38	0.43
Mopped	SF	0.56	6.00	0.57	0.59	0.60	0.62	0.58	0.66
Cap sheet, SBS (Styrene butadiene styrene - rubber)									
modified, 160 mils:									
Granular surface cap sheet:									
Polyester reinforced:									
Mopped	SF	1.21	13.60	1.23	1.32	1.33	1.37	1.24	1.42
Torched	SF	1.23	13.70	1.26	1.34	1.35	1.38	1.26	1.46
Glass fiber reinforced:									
Mopped	SF	0.90	10.10	0.94	1.00	0.98	1.01	0.93	1.07
Torched	SF	0.90	10.10	0.94	1.00	0.98	1.01	0.93	1.07
Smooth surface cap sheet, 145 mils:									
Mopped	SF	2.19	24.60	2.29	2.42	2.40	2.47	2.25	2.59
Torched	SF	2.03	22.70	2.10	2.25	2.20	2.27	2.09	2.38
Flashing									
Granular surface flashing, torched, 150 mils	SF	1.23	13.50	1.29	1.27	1.29	1.39	1.29	1.53

07 53 00 Elastomeric Membrane Roofing
ELASTOMERIC ROOFING

Item	UNITS	St. John's	Halifax	Montreal	Ottawa	Toronto	Winnipeg	Calgary	Vancouver
Elastomeric (cold applied)									
On horizontal surfaces	SF	4.81	5.42	5.86	6.51	6.09	5.43	5.09	6.63
Rubberized asphalt (hot applied)									
Sheet reinforced:									
On horizontal surfaces	SF	4.46	5.00	5.43	6.05	5.63	5.03	4.71	6.17

SINGLE-PLY MEMBRANE

Item	UNITS	St. John's	Halifax	Montreal	Ottawa	Toronto	Winnipeg	Calgary	Vancouver
Ethylene propylene diene monomer (EPDM),									
45 mils, 0.28 P.S.F.									
Loose-laid & ballasted with stone/gravel,									
10 P.S.F.	SF	2.49	3.51	2.53	2.63	2.44	2.68	2.41	3.32
Mechanically attached	SF	2.83	4.00	2.87	3.01	2.80	3.06	2.76	3.78
Fully adhered with adhesive	SF	3.18	4.50	3.25	3.40	3.14	3.44	3.09	4.25
Polyvinyl chloride (PVC), heat welded seams									
Reinforced, 60 mils, 40 P.S.F.									
Loose-laid & ballasted with stone/gravel,									
12 P.S.F.	SF	2.83	4.00	2.87	3.01	2.80	3.06	2.76	3.78
Mechanically attached	SF	3.18	4.50	3.25	3.40	3.14	3.44	3.09	4.25
Fully adhered with adhesive	SF	3.53	5.03	3.60	3.74	3.46	3.84	3.44	4.70

07 60 00 Flashing and Sheet Metal
07 61 00 Sheet Metal Roofing
COPPER ROOFING

Item	UNITS	St. John's	Halifax	Montreal	Ottawa	Toronto	Winnipeg	Calgary	Vancouver
Copper									
Standing seams:									
1 lb/sf, 16 oz	SF	44.00	45.00	45.10	47.70	54.00	54.50	53.00	57.80

07 65 00 Flexible Flashing
FLASHING

Item	UNITS	St. John's	Halifax	Montreal	Ottawa	Toronto	Winnipeg	Calgary	Vancouver
Flashings									
Galvanized steel:									
26 gauge	SF	8.04	10.40	8.15	8.37	9.18	10.40	8.14	9.85
Aluminum:									
24 gauge	SF	9.27	12.00	9.38	9.66	10.60	12.10	9.38	11.50

Item	UNITS	St. John's	Halifax	Montreal	Ottawa	Toronto	Winnipeg	Calgary	Vancouver
Stainless steel (eze-form)									
27 gauge	SF	12.20	15.90	12.30	12.80	14.00	16.00	12.40	15.10
Copper:									
1 lb/sf, 16 oz	SF	16.70	17.10	17.00	18.40	20.60	20.50	20.10	21.90
Rubber butyl:									
1/16"	SF	6.42	72.10	6.65	7.13	7.02	7.22	6.60	7.60
1/16" with galvanized fascia clip	SF	7.26	81.50	7.53	8.05	7.93	8.13	7.45	8.57

07 80 00 Fire and Smoke Protection

07 81 00 Applied Fireproofing

SPRAYED

Sprayed fireproofing 2 hour fire rating

Structural steel members:

Item	UNITS	St. John's	Halifax	Montreal	Ottawa	Toronto	Winnipeg	Calgary	Vancouver
Columns, small (measure girth)	SF	3.05	6.28	2.87	2.98	3.08	3.12	3.05	3.00
Columns, large (measure girth)	SF	1.90	3.89	1.79	1.88	1.92	1.95	1.90	1.90
OWSJ (twice depth plus width)	SF	3.59	7.00	3.27	3.25	3.35	3.46	3.39	3.34
Beams (measure girth)	SF	3.42	7.01	3.23	3.33	3.45	3.50	3.42	3.36
Floor decks (measure flat area):									
3" cellular	SF	2.95	6.00	2.90	2.79	2.87	2.97	2.99	3.34
3" fluted	SF	2.95	6.00	2.90	2.79	2.87	2.97	2.99	3.34
1 1/2" cellular	SF	2.77	5.69	2.74	2.63	2.70	2.82	2.81	3.13
1 1/2" fluted	SF	2.80	5.72	2.77	2.67	2.76	2.84	2.86	3.14

NON-SPRAYED

Intumescent paint 1 hour fire rating

Structural steel members:

Item	UNITS	St. John's	Halifax	Montreal	Ottawa	Toronto	Winnipeg	Calgary	Vancouver
Columns	SF	24.60	15.90	21.60	21.50	21.80	31.40	29.20	23.50
Beams	SF	18.60	12.00	16.40	16.30	16.40	23.70	22.00	17.70

07 84 00 Firestopping

FIRESTOPPING

2 hour fire separation

Item	UNITS	St. John's	Halifax	Montreal	Ottawa	Toronto	Winnipeg	Calgary	Vancouver
To edges or openings in slabs	LF	4.30	4.27	3.84	4.21	4.18	4.30	4.79	4.27

08: OPENINGS

08 10 00 Doors and Frames

08 11 00 Metal Doors and Frames

STEEL FRAMES, KNOCK DOWN

Fully Finished

Door frames based on 3' x 7' doors in walls

6" thick

Item	UNITS	St. John's	Halifax	Montreal	Ottawa	Toronto	Winnipeg	Calgary	Vancouver
12 gauge	EA	515.00	480.00	505.00	573.00	521.00	638.00	615.00	653.00
14 gauge	EA	300.00	281.00	295.00	336.00	305.00	374.00	361.00	381.00
16 gauge	EA	242.00	227.00	237.00	268.00	245.00	302.00	291.00	307.00
18 gauge	EA	230.00	211.00	222.00	255.00	230.00	284.00	274.00	290.00
20 gauge	EA	197.00	183.00	192.00	220.00	199.00	244.00	235.00	250.00

COMMERCIAL STEEL DOORS

Hollow-cored fully finished

Doors 1 3/4" thick without openings,

based on 3' x 7' prepared to receive but

excluding hardware

Honeycombed:

Item	UNITS	St. John's	Halifax	Montreal	Ottawa	Toronto	Winnipeg	Calgary	Vancouver
16 gauge	Leaf	559.00	521.00	571.00	664.00	652.00	794.00	653.00	619.00
18 gauge	Leaf	468.00	437.00	476.00	557.00	548.00	667.00	550.00	520.00
20 gauge	Leaf	387.00	361.00	394.00	460.00	452.00	550.00	453.00	428.00
Stiffened									
16 gauge	Leaf	744.00	693.00	761.00	884.00	870.00	1,060	872.00	824.00
Sundries:									
Openings in door (excluding glazing)	EA	98.20	91.60	100.00	117.00	114.00	139.00	115.00	109.00

08 14 00 Wood Doors

WOOD DOORS

Interior Wood Flush Type

Based on 1-3/4" door sizes 3'x7'. Prices include hanging the
door and fixing the hardware but exclude the supply of hardware—
see 08700. Prices do not allow for painting, staining, or any other
decorations, nor for any glass or glazing.

Solid core

Paint grade:

Item	UNITS	St. John's	Halifax	Montreal	Ottawa	Toronto	Winnipeg	Calgary	Vancouver
Birch	Leaf	400.00	370.00	403.00	378.00	442.00	485.00	442.00	390.00
Stain grade:									
Birch, select white	Leaf	447.00	415.00	447.00	422.00	494.00	543.00	492.00	435.00
Mahogany, tiama	Leaf	479.00	445.00	481.00	453.00	529.00	579.00	527.00	466.00
Ash	Leaf	479.00	445.00	481.00	453.00	529.00	579.00	527.00	466.00
Red Oak, flat cut	Leaf	510.00	472.00	508.00	480.00	563.00	619.00	561.00	496.00
Walnut	Leaf	615.00	572.00	619.00	583.00	683.00	747.00	680.00	600.00
Teak	Leaf	694.00	644.00	694.00	659.00	768.00	840.00	763.00	676.00

Item	UNITS	St. John's	Halifax	Montreal	Ottawa	Toronto	Winnipeg	Calgary	Vancouver
Plastic laminate 1/16" thick:									
Wood grain	Leaf	524.00	486.00	528.00	495.00	580.00	636.00	577.00	511.00
Textured	Leaf	541.00	499.00	541.00	510.00	597.00	653.00	597.00	526.00
Solid colours	Leaf	556.00	515.00	556.00	525.00	613.00	672.00	612.00	540.00
Hollow core, honeycomb fill									
Paint grade:									
Birch	Leaf	337.00	289.00	310.00	278.00	328.00	355.00	293.00	329.00
Stain grade:									
Birch, select white	Leaf	445.00	380.00	410.00	368.00	433.00	468.00	386.00	436.00
Mahogany, tiama	Leaf	460.00	397.00	428.00	384.00	450.00	486.00	400.00	453.00
Ash	Leaf	532.00	458.00	493.00	443.00	520.00	561.00	464.00	522.00
Red Oak, flat cut	Leaf	528.00	455.00	487.00	438.00	513.00	558.00	461.00	518.00
Walnut	Leaf	660.00	569.00	609.00	549.00	644.00	696.00	577.00	645.00
Teak	Leaf	695.00	599.00	641.00	577.00	677.00	735.00	608.00	682.00

08 30 00 Specialty Doors and Frames

08 33 00 Coiling Doors and Grilles

COILING GRILLE

Non-Industrial

Rolling overhead grilles

Aluminum storefront types:

Item	UNITS	St. John's	Halifax	Montreal	Ottawa	Toronto	Winnipeg	Calgary	Vancouver
Clear anodized finish	SF	69.30	80.00	72.50	75.70	84.90	83.10	71.30	74.10
Colour anodized finish	SF	77.60	89.60	81.30	84.80	94.80	92.90	80.10	83.10

08 36 00 Panel Doors

OVERHEAD, COMMERCIAL

Manual, sectional overhead type, hardware and glazing included

Wood doors:

Item	UNITS	St. John's	Halifax	Montreal	Ottawa	Toronto	Winnipeg	Calgary	Vancouver
Panel type	SF	16.90	19.00	20.20	18.00	22.10	22.40	18.90	23.20
Flush type, non insulated	SF	21.60	24.40	25.40	23.40	28.30	28.70	24.20	29.60
Flush type, insulated	SF	26.00	29.40	30.70	27.80	34.10	34.60	29.10	35.90
Steel doors:									
Single skin, 20 ga									
Standard	SF	29.80	29.20	33.40	33.80	39.60	39.90	32.20	37.10
Reinforced	SF	33.30	32.30	37.40	37.60	44.00	44.30	35.90	41.20
Double skin, 20 ga									
Insulated	SF	40.70	39.70	45.50	46.10	53.70	54.30	43.70	50.40
Insulated and reinforced	SF	44.70	43.50	50.00	50.40	59.20	59.70	48.10	55.70
Flush type, heavy duty	SF	61.70	60.20	69.00	70.00	81.70	82.40	66.10	76.60

OVERHEAD, INDUSTRIAL

Industrial steel doors:

Non-labelled service door

Item	UNITS	St. John's	Halifax	Montreal	Ottawa	Toronto	Winnipeg	Calgary	Vancouver
20 ga steel	SF	34.50	33.80	38.60	39.30	45.80	46.20	37.30	43.10
18 ga steel	SF	37.30	36.40	41.60	42.30	49.30	49.80	40.00	46.40
Class A, 3 hour labelled									
20 ga, thick steel door	SF	60.90	59.20	68.10	68.70	80.80	81.70	65.60	75.90

08 40 00 Entrances, Storefronts & Curtain Walls

08 41 13 Aluminum-Framed Entrances & Storefronts

ALUMINUM FRAMES

For single glazing (glazing not included)

2" x 4" approx. Members:

Item	UNITS	St. John's	Halifax	Montreal	Ottawa	Toronto	Winnipeg	Calgary	Vancouver
Clear anodized finish	LF	46.00	43.00	43.90	52.70	46.30	57.30	43.30	49.40
Colour anodized finish	LF	54.90	51.50	52.10	62.50	54.90	68.00	51.20	58.50
2 1/2" x 6" approx. Members:									
Clear anodized finish	LF	73.50	68.60	69.50	83.20	73.50	90.50	68.90	78.60
Colour anodized finish	LF	86.60	81.10	82.30	98.10	86.30	108.00	81.10	92.70
For double glazing, thermally broken									
2" x 4" approx. Members:									
Clear anodized finish	LF	54.90	51.50	52.10	62.50	54.90	68.00	51.20	58.50
Colour anodized finish	LF	86.60	81.10	82.30	98.10	86.30	108.00	81.10	92.70
2 1/2" x 6" approx. Members:									
Clear anodized finish	LF	81.40	76.20	76.80	93.00	81.40	101.00	76.20	87.20
Colour anodized finish	LF	86.60	81.10	82.30	98.10	86.30	108.00	81.10	92.70
Reinforcement for aluminum framing									
Average cost	LF	19.70	18.50	18.70	22.50	19.70	24.40	18.40	21.00

ALUMINUM DOORS & FRAMES

Frames based on 3'x7' doors

For single doors:

Item	UNITS	St. John's	Halifax	Montreal	Ottawa	Toronto	Winnipeg	Calgary	Vancouver
Clear anodized finish	EA	587.00	567.00	617.00	770.00	697.00	723.00	585.00	721.00
Colour anodized finish	EA	640.00	621.00	673.00	841.00	760.00	788.00	639.00	784.00
Single door with 3' transom (excluding transom panel):									
Clear anodized finish	EA	825.00	800.00	870.00	1,080	981.00	1,020	825.00	1,010
Colour anodized finish	EA	898.00	868.00	942.00	1,180	1,060	1,100	897.00	1,100

Item	UNITS	St. John's	Halifax	Montreal	Ottawa	Toronto	Winnipeg	Calgary	Vancouver
Single door with sidelight and transom (excluding glazing):									
Clear anodized finish	EA	1,450	1,390	1,500	1,890	1,720	1,780	1,450	1,750
Colour anodized finish	EA	1,730	1,650	1,800	2,250	2,060	2,110	1,700	2,120
For pair of doors:									
Clear anodized finish	EA	701.00	679.00	738.00	923.00	832.00	863.00	701.00	862.00
Colour anodized finish	EA	825.00	800.00	870.00	1,080	981.00	1,020	825.00	1,010
Pair of doors with transom (excluding transom panel):									
Clear anodized finish	EA	1,090	1,050	1,150	1,430	1,300	1,350	1,080	1,350
Colour anodized finish	EA	1,370	1,320	1,430	1,780	1,600	1,700	1,370	1,670
Pair of doors with sidelights (excluding glazing):									
Clear anodized finish	EA	1,090	1,050	1,150	1,430	1,300	1,350	1,080	1,350
Colour anodized finish	EA	1,280	1,240	1,330	1,670	1,520	1,570	1,260	1,570
Pair of doors, sidelight and transom (excluding glazing):									
Clear anodized finish	EA	1,730	1,670	1,800	2,280	2,060	2,120	1,720	2,120
Colour anodized finish	EA	2,020	1,940	2,110	2,660	2,390	2,470	2,010	2,470
Doors based on 3' x 7' doors,									
excluding hardware and glazing									
1 3/4" doors									
1" stiles:									
Clear anodized finish	Leaf	1,610	1,590	1,620	2,180	1,720	2,110	1,540	1,820
Colour anodized finish	Leaf	1,620	1,600	1,670	2,190	1,730	2,140	1,570	1,840
2" stiles:									
Clear anodized finish	Leaf	1,020	1,000	1,030	1,380	1,080	1,320	975	1,140
Colour anodized finish	Leaf	1,180	1,160	1,190	1,600	1,250	1,520	1,120	1,310
3" to 4" stiles:									
Clear anodized finish	Leaf	1,400	1,380	1,420	1,910	1,470	1,800	1,340	1,550
Colour anodized finish	Leaf	1,710	1,680	1,720	2,310	1,830	2,210	1,630	1,890
5" stiles:									
Clear anodized finish	Leaf	1,610	1,590	1,620	2,180	1,720	2,110	1,540	1,820
Colour anodized finish	Leaf	1,710	1,680	1,720	2,310	1,830	2,210	1,630	1,890
2" doors									
2" stiles:									
Clear anodized finish	Leaf	1,310	1,280	1,320	1,770	1,380	1,720	1,250	1,480
Colour anodized finish	Leaf	1,400	1,380	1,420	1,910	1,470	1,800	1,340	1,550

08 42 29 Automatic Entrances

Power operated doors

SWING ENTRANCE

Swing doors:

Item	UNITS	St. John's	Halifax	Montreal	Ottawa	Toronto	Winnipeg	Calgary	Vancouver
Overhead mounted, single door	Leaf	5,420	5,380	5,360	588	5,810	7,180	5,410	5,260
Overhead mounted, pair of doors	Pair	10,200	10,100	10,100	1,110	10,900	13,600	10,200	9,910
Mounted in floor, single door	Leaf	6,570	6,520	6,490	713	7,000	8,680	6,540	6,370
Mounted in floor, pair of doors	Pair	10,900	10,900	10,800	1,190	11,600	14,400	11,000	10,700

SLIDING ENTRANCE

Sliding doors, doors included, glazing not included:

Item	UNITS	St. John's	Halifax	Montreal	Ottawa	Toronto	Winnipeg	Calgary	Vancouver
12' opening, biparting	EA	16,100	16,000	16,000	1,760	17,300	21,400	16,200	15,700

08 42 33 Revolving Door Entrances

REVOLVING DOORS

Based on standard dimensions: diameter 6'6" approx.,
height 7', fascia panel 3".
1/4" glass

Manual type:

Item	UNITS	St. John's	Halifax	Montreal	Ottawa	Toronto	Winnipeg	Calgary	Vancouver
Anodized aluminum	EA	55,300	54,000	53,300	55,500	53,900	70,400	52,800	52,100
Bronze	EA	137,000	132,000	132,000	137,000	134,000	175,000	130,000	127,000
Stainless steel, satin finish	EA	113,000	110,000	109,000	113,000	110,000	144,000	108,000	106,000
Stainless steel, mirror finish	EA	137,000	132,000	132,000	137,000	134,000	175,000	130,000	127,000
1/2" glass									
Manual type:									
Anodized aluminum	EA	58,300	56,800	56,400	58,500	56,700	74,300	55,900	55,000
Bronze	EA	144,000	140,000	136,000	145,000	141,000	183,000	137,000	136,000
Stainless steel, satin finish	EA	118,000	116,000	114,000	118,000	115,000	149,000	113,000	111,000
Stainless steel, mirror finish	EA	144,000	140,000	136,000	145,000	141,000	183,000	137,000	136,000
Accessories									
Operating:									
Power assistance	EA	22,400	20,100	18,600	18,400	22,700	24,100	19,600	18,800
Finishes:									
Tinted glass	EA	1,970	2,460	2,030	2,120	2,280	2,520	2,160	2,600
Glass ceiling	EA	5,990	7,450	6,200	6,440	6,980	7,680	6,590	7,900
Up to 16" fascia panels	EA	3,610	3,610	3,350	3,750	3,820	3,710	4,440	3,720
Floor grille, aluminum floor grille with galvanized									
sheet metal drain pan, quadrant sized	Quarter	5,120	5,120	4,740	5,310	5,180	5,490	6,290	5,190

Item	UNITS	St. John's	Halifax	Montreal	Ottawa	Toronto	Winnipeg	Calgary	Vancouver
08 44 00 Curtain Wall & Glazed Assemblies									
08 44 13 Glazed Aluminum Curtain Wall									
CURTAIN WALLS (Single Glazing)									
(Glazing not included)									
10'-12' spans (floor to floor)									
2'6" modules (mullion spacing)									
Clear anodized finish	SF	45.20	54.10	46.00	45.50	56.00	57.10	44.20	59.60
Baked enamel finish	SF	46.60	55.90	47.70	47.00	58.10	59.00	45.60	61.30
Colour anodized finish	SF	47.40	56.90	48.60	47.70	59.00	59.90	46.70	62.60
4' modules (mullion spacing)									
Clear anodized finish	SF	42.60	45.90	44.20	43.90	52.10	54.30	41.20	53.00
Baked enamel finish	SF	44.30	47.70	46.00	45.30	53.80	56.40	42.90	54.50
Colour anodized finish	SF	47.10	51.00	48.70	48.60	57.60	60.20	46.00	58.60
5' modules (mullion spacing)									
Clear anodized finish	SF	41.60	47.10	44.00	42.60	52.10	52.00	43.20	54.20
Baked enamel finish	SF	38.50	43.80	40.90	39.50	48.40	48.40	39.90	50.30
Colour anodized finish	SF	43.00	49.00	45.50	44.30	53.90	53.90	44.80	56.00
CURTAIN WALLS (Double Glazing)									
(Thermally broken. Glazing not included)									
10'-12' spans (floor to floor)									
2'6" modules (mullion spacing)									
Clear anodized finish	SF	54.10	65.00	55.40	54.70	67.40	68.40	53.10	71.30
Baked enamel finish	SF	58.50	70.20	59.90	59.20	73.00	74.00	57.50	77.30
Colour anodized finish	SF	60.10	72.10	61.60	60.80	74.80	76.00	59.00	79.20
4' modules (mullion spacing)									
Clear anodized finish	SF	50.90	55.00	52.80	52.50	62.20	65.00	49.50	63.20
Baked enamel finish	SF	53.10	57.40	55.00	54.60	64.90	67.80	51.70	66.10
Colour anodized finish	SF	56.90	61.30	59.00	58.60	69.50	72.60	55.30	70.30
5' modules (mullion spacing)									
Clear anodized finish	SF	48.30	55.00	51.20	49.50	60.60	60.70	50.30	63.20
Baked enamel finish	SF	50.70	57.50	53.30	51.70	63.50	63.70	52.50	66.10
Colour anodized finish	SF	53.60	60.90	56.80	54.70	67.30	67.30	55.60	69.90
08 44 33 Slope Glazing Assemblies									
Sealed glazing units, tempered outer pane, laminated inner pane:									
Not exceeding 500 sf									
Clear anodized finish	SF	137.00	142.00	132.00	137.00	149.00	177.00	125.00	144.00
Baked enamel finish	SF	150.00	154.00	140.00	148.00	162.00	191.00	135.00	158.00
Colour anodized finish	SF	178.00	187.00	176.00	177.00	194.00	228.00	164.00	189.00
Over 500 sf									
Clear anodized finish	SF	121.00	125.00	116.00	120.00	131.00	154.00	111.00	127.00
Baked enamel finish	SF	130.00	135.00	124.00	129.00	141.00	165.00	120.00	137.00
Colour anodized finish	SF	136.00	142.00	131.00	137.00	149.00	177.00	125.00	144.00
08 50 00 Windows									
08 51 00 Metal Windows									
08 51 13 Aluminum Windows									
Tubular type, thermally broken (glazing not included)									
Punched openings (fixed):									
Baked enamel finish	SF	20.90	21.60	20.20	25.20	21.90	26.30	19.30	19.80
Colour anodized finish	SF	24.00	24.60	22.90	28.60	25.20	29.70	21.90	22.70
Ribbon type (fixed)									
Baked enamel finish	SF	20.70	21.30	19.90	24.70	21.70	25.80	19.00	19.30
Colour anodized finish	SF	23.60	24.40	22.60	28.10	24.80	29.50	21.60	22.20
Ventilating sash:									
Average cost	EA	681.00	612.00	694.00	896.00	753.00	754.00	585.00	611.00
Units for single glazing									
Framing member for fixed units:									
Clear anodized finish	LF	22.00	22.60	21.00	26.20	23.00	27.60	20.20	20.70
Baked enamel finish	LF	22.80	23.40	21.90	27.20	23.80	28.60	20.90	21.40
Colour anodized finish	LF	25.00	25.80	24.00	29.90	26.20	31.40	23.00	23.50
Ventilating units (add to cost of fixed units):									
Clear anodized finish	EA	392.00	354.00	397.00	515.00	432.00	433.00	336.00	352.00
Baked enamel finish	EA	455.00	408.00	464.00	600.00	504.00	503.00	391.00	408.00
Colour anodized finish	EA	515.00	464.00	525.00	680.00	570.00	571.00	442.00	464.00
Units for double glazing thermally broken									
Framing member for fixed units:									
Clear anodized finish	LF	25.00	25.80	24.00	29.90	26.20	31.40	23.00	23.50
Baked enamel finish	LF	26.30	27.10	25.30	31.40	27.70	33.20	24.30	24.80
Colour anodized finish	LF	30.80	31.70	29.50	36.60	32.30	38.70	28.30	28.90
Ventilating units (add to cost of fixed units):									
Clear anodized finish	EA	515.00	464.00	525.00	680.00	570.00	571.00	442.00	464.00
Baked enamel finish	EA	568.00	509.00	576.00	748.00	627.00	629.00	486.00	510.00
Colour anodized finish	EA	579.00	520.00	589.00	761.00	637.00	637.00	496.00	520.00

Item	UNITS	St. John's	Halifax	Montreal	Ottawa	Toronto	Winnipeg	Calgary	Vancouver
08 51 23 Steel Windows									
Industrial type (glazing not included)									
Light size 20" x 16":									
Prime coat	SF	12.90	16.50	12.40	16.60	13.80	19.30	13.20	12.50
Baked enamel finish	SF	16.10	20.30	15.50	21.00	17.80	23.70	16.20	15.60
Ventilating sash (additional):									
Average cost	EA	188.00	204.00	192.00	263.00	217.00	245.00	170.00	176.00
08 52 00 Wood Windows									
WOOD WINDOWS (glazing not included)									
Fixed units									
Prime coat only:									
Pine	SF	31.30	31.10	30.10	30.10	30.20	36.90	30.30	42.00
Cedar	SF	34.30	34.20	33.20	33.00	33.40	40.60	33.40	45.90
Redwood	SF	39.10	39.10	37.70	37.40	37.80	46.30	37.90	52.10
Aluminum covered wood	SF	36.50	36.50	35.20	35.20	35.90	43.30	35.70	49.10
Plastic covered wood	SF	31.50	31.20	32.70	32.50	32.30	37.60	31.10	35.80
Ventilating units:									
Average cost	EA	196.00	196.00	208.00	205.00	191.00	232.00	193.00	235.00
08 60 00 Roof Windows & Skylights									
(measured flat on plane)									
08 62 00 Unit Skylights									
Plastic skylights									
Single skin:									
Less than 10 sf plan area (ea)	SF	85.70	81.10	73.40	96.60	82.00	91.70	71.10	76.10
Double skin:									
Less than 10 sf plan area (ea)	SF	115.00	109.00	99.40	129.00	111.00	123.00	96.60	103.00
08 63 00 Metal-Framed Skylights									
Aluminum, standard members									
Heat strengthened laminated glass:									
Not exceeding 500 sf									
Clear anodized finish	SF	137.00	129.00	117.00	153.00	131.00	146.00	113.00	121.00
Baked enamel finish	SF	137.00	131.00	118.00	155.00	132.00	148.00	114.00	122.00
Colour anodized finish	SF	169.00	160.00	144.00	190.00	163.00	179.00	139.00	152.00
Over 500 sf									
Clear anodized finish	SF	132.00	124.00	112.00	149.00	127.00	142.00	110.00	117.00
Baked enamel finish	SF	135.00	127.00	115.00	151.00	129.00	144.00	111.00	119.00
Colour anodized finish	SF	151.00	146.00	131.00	172.00	146.00	163.00	127.00	135.00
08 70 00 Hardware									
08 71 00 Door Hardware									
Door hardware (allowance factor only)									
LOCKSET									
Locksets:									
Hotels	EA	378.00	345.00	372.00	388.00	453.00	474.00	401.00	349.00
Retail stores	EA	247.00	224.00	240.00	251.00	295.00	304.00	261.00	227.00
Apartment buildings	EA	194.00	177.00	193.00	199.00	236.00	245.00	210.00	181.00
Office buildings	EA	348.00	317.00	341.00	355.00	415.00	433.00	371.00	320.00
Hospitals	EA	311.00	280.00	301.00	313.00	367.00	386.00	325.00	302.00
Schools	EA	281.00	255.00	274.00	288.00	336.00	351.00	299.00	259.00
BUTT HINGE									
Butts:									
Hotels	EA	64.20	58.40	61.30	62.80	74.00	63.80	65.60	61.60
Retail stores	EA	64.20	58.40	61.30	62.80	74.00	63.80	65.60	61.60
Apartment buildings	EA	34.50	31.40	33.20	33.80	40.10	34.40	35.60	33.40
Office buildings	EA	64.20	58.40	61.30	62.80	74.00	63.80	65.60	61.60
Hospitals	EA	64.20	58.40	61.30	62.80	74.00	63.80	65.60	61.60
Schools	EA	64.20	58.40	61.30	62.80	74.00	63.80	65.60	61.60
PULL PLATE									
Pulls:									
Hotels	EA	70.00	63.60	67.50	71.60	81.40	91.80	71.00	92.30
Retail stores	EA	70.00	63.60	67.50	71.60	81.40	91.80	71.00	92.30
Apartment buildings	EA	38.10	34.50	36.70	38.90	44.30	49.90	38.60	50.10
Office buildings	EA	70.00	63.60	67.50	71.60	81.40	91.80	71.00	92.30
Hospitals	EA	70.00	63.60	67.50	71.60	81.40	91.80	71.00	92.30
Schools	EA	70.00	63.60	67.50	71.60	81.40	91.80	71.00	92.30
PUSH PLATE									
Push plates:									
Hotels	EA	41.70	34.60	39.00	39.40	44.40	50.00	38.20	52.80
Retail stores	EA	41.70	34.60	39.00	39.40	44.40	50.00	38.20	52.80
Apartment buildings	EA	41.70	34.60	39.00	39.40	44.40	50.00	38.20	52.80
Office buildings	EA	41.70	34.60	39.00	39.40	44.40	50.00	38.20	52.80
Hospitals	EA	41.70	34.60	39.00	39.40	44.40	50.00	38.20	52.80
Schools	EA	41.70	34.60	39.00	39.40	44.40	50.00	38.20	52.80

Item	UNITS	St. John's	Halifax	Montreal	Ottawa	Toronto	Winnipeg	Calgary	Vancouver
DOOR CLOSER									
Closers:									
Office buildings	EA	351.00	319.00	379.00	373.00	386.00	357.00	300.00	282.00
Hospitals	EA	351.00	319.00	379.00	373.00	386.00	357.00	300.00	282.00
Schools	EA	351.00	319.00	379.00	373.00	386.00	357.00	300.00	282.00
AUTOMATIC OPENERS COMMERCIAL									
Handicap actuator push buttons, 2, including 12V DC									
wiring for automatic barrier free access	Leaf	3,370	3,030	2,950	3,100	3,680	3,820	3,060	2,900

08 80 00 Glazing

08 81 00 Glass Glazing
(installed in prepared frames)

08 81 10 Float Glass

Item	UNITS	St. John's	Halifax	Montreal	Ottawa	Toronto	Winnipeg	Calgary	Vancouver
PLAIN GLASS									
Clear glass									
5/32" thick	SF	13.10	14.00	12.80	13.80	14.70	16.40	13.70	14.70
3/16" thick	SF	15.60	16.70	15.60	16.40	17.50	19.30	16.50	17.50
1/4" thick	SF	18.00	19.40	18.00	19.00	20.30	22.60	19.00	20.30
5/16" thick	SF	25.40	26.90	25.10	26.60	28.30	31.70	26.50	28.40
3/8" thick	SF	29.20	31.40	29.20	30.80	32.50	36.40	30.90	33.00
1/2" thick	SF	36.70	39.50	36.70	38.80	41.20	46.30	38.80	41.30
Tinted glass:									
1/4" thick	SF	20.40	22.00	20.30	21.60	22.90	25.80	21.50	23.10
5/16" thick	SF	29.20	31.40	29.20	30.80	32.50	36.40	30.90	33.00
3/8" thick	SF	34.60	37.20	34.70	36.90	38.80	43.70	36.60	39.00
1/2" thick	SF	41.50	44.50	41.30	43.90	46.50	52.00	43.80	46.50
HEAT STRENGTHENED GLASS									
Clear:									
Add to cost of float glass	SF	17.30	21.20	18.50	19.10	19.30	20.70	18.30	22.70
Tinted									
Add to cost of float glass	SF	18.90	23.00	20.00	20.50	21.00	22.20	20.00	24.40

08 81 30 Insulating Glass
(based on 2.5 m2, 25 sf per unit)

Item	UNITS	St. John's	Halifax	Montreal	Ottawa	Toronto	Winnipeg	Calgary	Vancouver
Clear glass:									
Two panes of 1/8" glass	SF	28.20	31.40	28.10	29.10	28.80	31.20	24.90	33.20
Two panes of 5/32" glass	SF	29.10	32.20	29.10	29.60	29.70	32.30	25.70	34.00
Two panes of 3/16" glass	SF	31.80	35.10	31.60	32.10	32.40	35.00	28.20	37.30
Two panes of 1/4" glass	SF	34.70	38.50	34.70	35.50	35.40	38.40	30.70	40.70
Per 5 sf reduction of unit size, add	%	15.00	15.00	15.00	15.00	15.00	15.00	15.00	15.00
Tinted glass (one pane only):									
Two panes of 1/8" glass	SF	31.80	35.10	31.60	32.10	32.40	35.00	28.20	37.30
Two panes of 3/16" glass	SF	33.10	36.70	33.30	34.20	33.80	36.90	29.30	39.00
Two panes of 1/4" glass	SF	36.40	40.20	36.00	36.80	37.10	39.90	32.10	42.40
Per 5 sf reduction of unit size, add	%	15.00	15.00	15.00	15.00	15.00	15.00	15.00	15.00
Reflective glass (one pane only):									
Standard specification	SF	51.50	57.00	51.20	52.30	52.40	56.70	45.40	60.40
High quality specification	SF	79.10	87.80	79.20	81.00	80.70	87.90	70.10	92.90
Custom specification	SF	91.90	102.00	92.10	93.80	93.80	102.00	81.30	108.00

08 81 30 Insulating Glass (for sloped glazing)

Item	UNITS	St. John's	Halifax	Montreal	Ottawa	Toronto	Winnipeg	Calgary	Vancouver
Tempered exterior laminated interior:									
Clear glass	SF	62.60	73.00	63.50	63.50	67.40	69.80	54.30	59.90
Tinted glass (one pane only)	SF	62.60	73.00	63.50	63.50	67.40	69.80	54.30	59.90

08 81 45 Sheet Glass

Item	UNITS	St. John's	Halifax	Montreal	Ottawa	Toronto	Winnipeg	Calgary	Vancouver
A quality:									
5/64" thick	SF	11.20	12.10	11.20	11.90	12.60	13.90	12.00	12.60
1/8" thick	SF	12.20	13.10	12.00	12.80	13.70	15.20	12.90	13.70

08 81 65 Wire Glass

Item	UNITS	St. John's	Halifax	Montreal	Ottawa	Toronto	Winnipeg	Calgary	Vancouver
Transparent glass (polished):									
1/4" thick	SF	32.00	35.00	30.80	31.80	32.50	35.10	26.60	30.80
Translucent glass (cast):									
1/4" thick	SF	19.00	20.90	18.30	19.00	19.30	20.30	15.70	18.30
Double glass installation:									
Silver	SF	53.00	57.70	50.50	52.40	53.80	57.80	43.80	50.80
Gold	SF	54.30	59.30	52.10	54.00	55.30	59.70	45.20	52.30
Spandrel glass:									
1/4" black	SF	33.40	36.50	32.20	33.40	34.30	36.90	27.90	32.30
1/4" silver	SF	50.40	55.00	48.30	50.00	51.30	55.20	41.80	48.50
1/4" gold	SF	64.80	70.50	62.20	64.30	65.90	71.00	53.50	62.20

08 83 00 Mirrors

Item	UNITS	St. John's	Halifax	Montreal	Ottawa	Toronto	Winnipeg	Calgary	Vancouver
MIRRORS									
Opaque mirrors									
Unframed mirrors:									
1/4" thick (smooth edges)	SF	23.70	25.30	23.70	25.00	26.50	29.80	24.80	26.80

Item	UNITS	St. John's	Halifax	Montreal	Ottawa	Toronto	Winnipeg	Calgary	Vancouver
Framed (tamperproof) mirrors:									
1/4" thick (stainless steel frame)	SF	41.50	44.50	41.30	43.90	46.50	52.00	43.80	46.50

08 84 00 Plastic Glazing
Flat sheets (Installed in prepared frames)

08 84 10 Plexiglass Acrylic

Item	UNITS	St. John's	Halifax	Montreal	Ottawa	Toronto	Winnipeg	Calgary	Vancouver
Clear cast acrylic:									
1/16" thick	SF	14.90	16.80	14.50	15.60	15.60	19.10	16.70	13.80
1/8" thick	SF	13.90	15.70	13.50	14.20	14.40	17.70	15.40	13.00
3/16" thick	SF	16.60	18.80	16.50	17.50	17.30	21.30	18.50	15.40
1/4" thick	SF	19.20	21.60	19.00	20.20	20.10	24.90	21.50	17.80
3/8" thick	SF	30.50	34.50	30.10	31.90	31.70	39.00	34.20	28.40
1/2" thick	SF	40.70	46.00	40.00	42.30	42.40	52.10	45.30	37.90
White cast acrylic:									
1/8" thick	SF	14.60	16.60	14.30	15.40	15.10	18.90	16.40	13.70
3/16" thick	SF	17.40	19.60	17.20	18.10	18.00	22.40	19.30	16.10
1/4" thick	SF	19.10	21.60	19.00	20.10	19.90	24.40	21.40	17.70
Colour cast acrylic:									
1/8" thick	SF	16.60	18.80	16.50	17.50	17.30	21.30	18.50	15.40
3/16" thick	SF	18.30	21.10	18.00	19.10	19.10	23.50	20.50	17.00
1/4" thick	SF	20.70	23.60	20.50	21.60	21.60	26.80	22.90	19.20

08 84 20 Polycarbonate

Item	UNITS	St. John's	Halifax	Montreal	Ottawa	Toronto	Winnipeg	Calgary	Vancouver
Clear polycarbonate:									
1/32" thick	SF	13.30	15.30	12.90	13.70	13.70	16.80	14.80	12.40
3/64" thick	SF	14.70	16.70	14.40	15.50	15.20	19.00	16.60	13.70
1/16" thick	SF	15.10	17.40	14.70	15.80	15.80	19.30	16.90	14.20
5/64" thick	SF	18.30	21.10	18.00	19.10	19.10	23.50	20.50	17.00
3/32" thick	SF	19.30	21.70	19.10	20.30	20.30	25.00	21.60	18.00
1/8" thick	SF	21.40	24.20	20.90	22.10	22.10	27.10	23.70	19.80
3/16" thick	SF	26.80	30.90	26.30	27.90	28.10	34.50	30.20	25.10
1/4" thick	SF	32.50	37.00	31.90	33.90	33.80	41.70	36.20	30.30
3/8" thick	SF	56.30	64.00	55.20	58.60	58.40	72.20	62.50	52.30
1/2" thick	SF	69.10	78.60	67.80	72.00	71.90	88.50	77.00	64.20
Tinted polycarbonate (bronze or green):									
1/8" thick	SF	24.10	27.20	23.50	25.00	24.80	30.80	26.80	22.30
3/16" thick	SF	31.20	35.40	30.70	32.50	32.50	39.90	34.80	29.20
1/4" thick	SF	39.30	44.60	38.60	41.00	40.80	50.40	43.70	36.60

08 88 00 Special Function Glazing
(installed in prepared frames)

08 88 56 Laminated Glass
High security laminated glass
Single lamination

Item	UNITS	St. John's	Halifax	Montreal	Ottawa	Toronto	Winnipeg	Calgary	Vancouver
5/64" x 1/8" plus vinyl	SF	47.90	52.20	46.20	47.60	48.80	52.60	39.80	46.00

09: FINISHES

09 20 00 Plaster and Gypsum Board

09 22 00 Supports for Plaster & Gypsum Board
(for steel studs see Item 05 40 00; for wood furring see
Item 06 11 00; for suspension systems see 09 22 26)

FURRING
Steel channel furring

Item	UNITS	St. John's	Halifax	Montreal	Ottawa	Toronto	Winnipeg	Calgary	Vancouver
Tied to steel:									
3/4"	LF	1.62	1.66	1.96	2.50	2.79	2.12	1.48	2.06
1 1/2"	LF	2.31	2.37	2.80	3.57	3.99	3.03	2.12	2.92

GYPSUM LATH
Lath (supply only)
Gypsum lath:

Item	UNITS	St. John's	Halifax	Montreal	Ottawa	Toronto	Winnipeg	Calgary	Vancouver
3/8" plain	SY	3.39	3.48	4.10	5.24	5.87	4.44	3.12	4.30
3/8" perforated	SY	4.78	4.88	5.79	7.35	8.24	6.25	4.39	6.01
3/8" foilback	SY	5.00	5.12	6.08	7.68	8.61	6.57	4.57	6.33

Lath (installation only)
On wood framing to:

Item	UNITS	St. John's	Halifax	Montreal	Ottawa	Toronto	Winnipeg	Calgary	Vancouver
Walls	SY	9.95	9.87	10.00	11.70	10.80	13.80	9.11	13.00
Ceilings and exterior soffits	SY	12.60	12.60	12.60	15.10	13.60	17.60	11.80	16.60
Beams, columns and bulkheads	SY	12.70	12.70	12.80	15.10	13.70	17.60	11.90	16.70
On steel framing to:									
Walls	SY	17.20	17.40	17.60	20.70	18.60	24.20	16.10	22.70
Ceilings and exterior soffits	SY	22.00	22.00	21.90	26.20	23.70	30.20	20.50	28.80
Beams, columns and bulkheads	SY	27.20	27.10	27.30	32.40	29.30	37.70	25.30	35.70

METAL LATH
Metal lath; diamond mesh:
Painted

Item	UNITS	St. John's	Halifax	Montreal	Ottawa	Toronto	Winnipeg	Calgary	Vancouver
2.5 lbs/sy	SY	3.44	3.53	4.17	5.31	5.94	4.52	3.17	4.36
3.4 lbs/sy	SY	6.94	7.09	8.36	10.70	12.00	9.03	6.35	8.78

DIV 9 Finishes — IMPERIAL CURRENT MARKET PRICES

Item	UNITS	St. John's	Halifax	Montreal	Ottawa	Toronto	Winnipeg	Calgary	Vancouver
Galvanized									
2.5 lbs/sy............	SY	4.06	4.16	4.95	6.29	7.03	5.36	3.74	5.13
3.4 lbs/sy............	SY	6.54	6.69	7.91	10.00	11.20	8.53	6.00	8.27
Metal lath, 1/8" flat rib:									
Painted									
3.5 lbs/sy............	SY	7.23	7.41	8.78	11.10	12.50	9.45	6.65	9.11
Galvanized									
3.5 lbs/sy............	SY	8.25	8.44	9.95	12.60	14.10	10.90	7.58	10.40
Metal lath, 3/8" high rib:									
Painted									
3.5 lbs/sy............	SY	8.86	9.11	10.70	13.60	15.30	11.50	8.15	11.20
Galvanized									
3.5 lbs/sy............	SY	10.50	10.80	12.60	16.40	18.10	14.00	9.62	13.40
Stucco mesh, 16 gauge welded wire mesh:									
Galvanized									
2" x 2", ribbed............	SY	5.51	5.63	6.68	8.44	9.53	7.22	5.05	6.96
1" x 1" flat............	SY	4.10	4.21	4.97	6.35	7.08	5.39	3.75	5.19

09 22 26 Suspension Systems
SUSPENDED METAL JOIST FRAMING
Suspended metal joist framing system
to accept gypsum wall board ceiling finish:

Item	UNITS	St. John's	Halifax	Montreal	Ottawa	Toronto	Winnipeg	Calgary	Vancouver
24" deep, complete............	SF	8.27	8.16	7.53	8.96	9.94	7.46	6.88	9.75

09 23 00 Gypsum Plastering
GYPSUM PLASTER (lath or other base not included)
Gypsum plaster, trowelled finish to
Walls:

Item	UNITS	St. John's	Halifax	Montreal	Ottawa	Toronto	Winnipeg	Calgary	Vancouver
2 coats on gypsum lath............	SY	76.10	80.60	76.00	102.00	86.10	83.00	102.00	83.50
3 coats on metal lath............	SY	114.00	119.00	115.00	153.00	131.00	121.00	150.00	125.00
3 coats on rigid insulation............	SY	103.00	110.00	102.00	140.00	113.00	111.00	136.00	114.00
3 coats on masonry............	SY	100.00	107.00	97.80	137.00	111.00	110.00	131.00	111.00
3 coats on concrete............	SY	103.00	110.00	102.00	140.00	113.00	111.00	136.00	114.00
Ceilings:									
2 coats on gypsum lath............	SY	88.60	94.50	88.60	120.00	100.00	99.50	118.00	97.80
3 coats on metal lath............	SY	116.00	122.00	118.00	157.00	134.00	127.00	154.00	129.00
3 coats on rigid insulation............	SY	108.00	114.00	109.00	145.00	119.00	116.00	143.00	118.00
3 coats on concrete............	SY	108.00	114.00	109.00	145.00	119.00	116.00	143.00	118.00
Columns, beams and bulkheads:									
2 coats on gypsum lath............	SY	113.00	118.00	114.00	152.00	129.00	120.00	149.00	123.00
3 coats on metal lath............	SY	155.00	163.00	152.00	208.00	174.00	169.00	204.00	171.00
3 coats on rigid insulation............	SY	130.00	139.00	131.00	173.00	147.00	143.00	173.00	144.00
3 coats on masonry............	SY	130.00	139.00	131.00	173.00	147.00	143.00	173.00	144.00
3 coats on concrete............	SY	124.00	133.00	126.00	167.00	142.00	139.00	167.00	139.00
Acoustical plaster, sprayed finish to									
Walls:									
2 coats to gypsum lath............	SY	35.80	37.70	35.50	48.00	40.10	39.10	47.30	39.10
2 coats to metal lath............	SY	44.40	47.20	44.50	59.90	50.20	48.80	59.20	48.80
2 coats to masonry............	SY	41.40	43.80	41.30	55.60	46.80	45.20	54.90	45.30
2 coats to concrete............	SY	42.60	44.90	42.40	57.00	47.90	46.50	56.40	46.70
3 coats to metal lath............	SY	54.70	57.90	54.50	73.50	61.70	59.80	72.70	60.00
Ceilings:									
2 coats to gypsum lath............	SY	37.10	39.20	37.10	49.90	42.00	40.80	49.30	40.80
2 coats to metal lath............	SY	44.40	47.20	44.50	59.90	50.20	48.80	59.20	48.80
2 coats to concrete............	SY	42.80	45.30	42.70	57.50	48.20	46.90	56.90	47.00
3 coats to metal lath............	SY	55.20	58.50	55.30	74.30	62.50	60.50	73.60	60.80
Columns, beams and bulkheads:									
2 coats to gypsum lath............	SY	44.40	47.20	44.50	59.90	50.20	48.80	59.20	48.80
2 coats to metal lath............	SY	55.20	58.50	55.30	74.30	62.50	60.50	73.60	60.80
2 coats to concrete............	SY	53.80	57.20	53.90	72.20	61.00	58.90	71.60	59.00
3 coats to metal lath............	SY	70.20	74.30	70.10	95.30	79.10	76.80	94.50	77.10

09 26 00 Veneer Plastering
VENEER PLASTER
1 coat on gypsum board (board not included) to:

Item	UNITS	St. John's	Halifax	Montreal	Ottawa	Toronto	Winnipeg	Calgary	Vancouver
Walls............	SY	24.60	26.30	24.80	33.10	27.90	26.90	32.80	27.00
Ceilings............	SY	27.20	28.70	27.30	36.50	30.70	29.80	36.00	29.60
Columns, beams and bulkheads............	SY	35.80	37.70	35.50	48.00	40.10	39.10	47.30	39.10
Sprayed plaster									
1 coat, textured, to:									
Concrete............	SY	18.20	19.10	18.20	24.30	20.30	19.60	23.90	19.70
Gypsum board (2 coats)............	SY	30.30	32.10	30.20	40.70	34.20	33.00	40.20	33.50

09 29 00 Gypsum Board - Supply Only
Standard sheets 48" wide
GYPSUM WALLBOARD
Regular gypsum wallboard:

Item	UNITS	St. John's	Halifax	Montreal	Ottawa	Toronto	Winnipeg	Calgary	Vancouver
3/8" thick............	SF	0.58	0.58	0.59	0.46	0.73	0.96	0.54	1.17
1/2" thick............	SF	0.58	0.58	0.59	0.46	0.73	0.96	0.54	1.17
5/8" thick............	SF	0.70	0.69	0.71	0.55	0.88	1.15	0.64	1.45
Fire-rated gypsum wallboard:									
1/2" thick............	SF	0.69	0.69	0.70	0.55	0.88	1.15	0.64	1.40

Item	UNITS	St. John's	Halifax	Montreal	Ottawa	Toronto	Winnipeg	Calgary	Vancouver
5/8" thick..................	SF	0.71	0.70	0.72	0.56	0.90	1.17	0.66	1.42
Foil-back gypsum wallboard:									
3/8" thick..................	SF	0.92	0.91	0.94	0.73	1.16	1.53	0.85	1.86
1/2" thick..................	SF	0.95	0.95	0.97	0.74	1.21	1.57	0.88	1.92
5/8" thick..................	SF	1.03	1.01	1.04	0.81	1.31	1.68	0.95	2.08
Water resistant gypsum wallboard:									
1/2" thick..................	SF	1.02	1.00	1.03	0.80	1.30	1.67	0.94	2.05
5/8" thick..................	SF	1.26	1.25	1.27	1.01	1.60	2.09	1.16	2.54
Predecorated gypsum panels									
Standard panels, vinyl face on:									
1/2" plain core..................	SF	1.99	1.97	2.01	1.58	2.55	3.29	1.85	4.01
Custom gypsum panels, vinyl face on:									
1/2" plain core..................	SF	2.53	2.51	2.58	1.98	3.21	4.16	2.34	5.10
5/8" plain core..................	SF	2.53	2.51	2.58	1.98	3.21	4.16	2.34	5.10
5/8" fire-rated core..................	SF	2.55	2.55	2.60	2.03	3.24	4.25	2.36	5.17
Core boards and sheathing boards									
Gypsum (Shaftliner) coreboard 24" wide:									
1" thick	SF	1.52	1.46	1.54	1.27	1.94	2.67	1.41	3.07
Gypsum sheathing boards:									
1/2" thick..................	SF	0.60	0.58	0.60	0.50	0.76	1.05	0.55	1.21
Fire-rated gypsum sheathing boards:									
5/8" thick..................	SF	1.08	1.05	1.09	0.91	1.37	1.90	1.00	2.21
Exterior soffit boards:									
1/2" thick..................	SF	1.00	0.97	1.01	0.85	1.27	1.75	0.93	2.04

09 29 00 Gypsum Board - Installation Only
GYPSUM WALLBOARD
Related waste factors included. Standard backing and soffit boards

Item	UNITS	St. John's	Halifax	Montreal	Ottawa	Toronto	Winnipeg	Calgary	Vancouver
3/8" or 1/2" thick:									
To walls, ceilings or soffits	SF	1.31	1.30	1.32	1.56	1.40	1.80	1.23	1.72
To walls (laminated to solid backing)..................	SF	1.17	1.16	1.16	1.40	1.26	1.61	1.11	1.52
To beams, columns or bulkheads	SF	1.64	1.61	1.60	1.92	1.75	2.21	1.50	2.13
5/8" thick:									
To walls, ceilings or soffits	SF	1.40	1.40	1.40	1.66	1.51	1.94	1.31	1.85
To walls (laminated to solid backing)..................	SF	1.31	1.31	1.33	1.57	1.42	1.80	1.23	1.73
To beams, columns or bulkheads	SF	1.75	1.76	1.75	2.08	1.90	2.41	1.65	2.31
Coreboards									
1" thick									
Per 1" laminate..................	SF	1.56	1.58	1.58	1.90	1.69	2.17	1.44	2.05
Taping joints and finishing									
To walls and soffits..................	SF	0.81	0.81	0.82	0.97	0.88	1.11	0.76	1.07

09 30 00 Tiling
09 30 13 Ceramic Tiling
CERAMIC TILE
Glazed wall tile 1/4" thick

Item	UNITS	St. John's	Halifax	Montreal	Ottawa	Toronto	Winnipeg	Calgary	Vancouver
Mortar bed:									
4" x 4"	SF	13.80	14.10	14.30	14.80	14.30	17.70	13.50	13.50
6" x 6"	SF	13.80	14.10	14.30	14.80	14.30	17.70	13.50	13.50
Thinset:									
4" x 4"	SF	11.90	12.00	12.40	12.50	12.20	15.00	11.60	11.60
6" x 6"	SF	11.90	12.00	12.40	12.50	12.20	15.00	11.60	11.60
Unglazed floor tile 1/4" thick									
Mortar bed:									
1" x 1", one colour	SF	12.40	12.50	12.80	13.00	12.60	15.70	12.10	12.20
Thinset:									
1" x 1", one colour	SF	13.00	13.20	13.60	13.70	13.50	16.40	12.80	12.70
Base Trim									
Ceramic mosaic base:									
4" high, one colour..................	LF	12.50	12.60	13.60	14.10	13.50	16.60	12.70	12.10

09 30 16 Quarry Tiling
QUARRY TILE
1/2" thick terra-cotta
To walls

Item	UNITS	St. John's	Halifax	Montreal	Ottawa	Toronto	Winnipeg	Calgary	Vancouver
Mortar bed:									
6" x 6", one colour..................	SF	17.60	16.50	18.60	20.20	19.00	22.00	18.60	21.80
Thinset:									
6" x 6", one colour..................	SF	13.50	13.50	13.70	14.90	14.10	16.00	13.70	15.20
To floors									
Mortar bed:									
6" x 6", one colour..................	SF	17.10	16.20	18.30	19.70	18.80	21.80	18.20	21.50
Thinset:									
6" x 6", one colour..................	SF	12.70	12.80	13.20	14.20	13.50	15.30	12.80	14.50
To stairs									
Nosing only:									
Non slip	LF	25.00	25.00	25.60	27.60	26.20	29.50	25.50	28.40
Base Trim									
Quarry tile base:									
4" high, terra-cotta..................	LF	13.20	13.40	13.50	14.60	13.80	15.60	13.40	15.00

Item	UNITS	St. John's	Halifax	Montreal	Ottawa	Toronto	Winnipeg	Calgary	Vancouver
09 50 00 Ceilings									
09 51 00 Acoustical Ceilings									
SUSPENDED CEILINGS, COMPLETE									
COMPLETE, FIXED TO SOFFIT OF HOLLOW METAL OR WOOD, WOOD DECK OR TO FIXINGS PROVIDED IN SOFFIT.									
Exposed suspension system									
Mineral fibre panel 24" x 48":									
5/8" thick standard	SF	4.14	4.50	3.99	4.46	4.46	4.41	3.44	6.03
5/8" thick fire-rated	SF	4.52	4.90	4.34	4.88	4.86	4.80	3.74	6.55
Glass fibre 24" x 48":									
Vinyl faced									
5/8" thick	SF	4.32	4.28	4.28	4.58	5.30	4.57	3.86	4.52
3/4" thick	SF	5.09	5.04	5.04	5.39	6.24	5.39	4.52	5.31
Glass faced									
3/4" thick	SF	5.46	5.90	5.22	5.86	5.85	5.78	4.52	7.90
Glass fibre panel 48" x 48":									
Vinyl faced									
1" thick	SF	6.57	6.50	6.50	6.97	8.03	6.95	5.85	7.09
Glass faced									
1" thick	SF	7.27	7.23	7.23	7.71	8.92	7.69	6.48	7.63
Mineral fibre damage resistive panel 24" x 48":									
3/16" thick standard	SF	8.10	8.76	7.78	8.69	8.69	8.60	6.71	11.70
Semi-concealed suspension system									
Mineral fibre panel 24" x 48":									
5/8" thick standard	SF	4.63	5.00	4.65	5.02	5.41	4.93	4.57	4.99
5/8" thick fire-rated	SF	4.87	5.26	4.91	5.27	5.68	5.21	4.80	5.11
Glass fibre 24" x 48":									
Vinyl faced									
5/8" thick	SF	3.96	4.30	3.99	4.30	4.64	4.25	3.92	4.16
3/4" thick	SF	4.06	4.37	4.08	4.38	4.72	4.34	3.99	4.24
Glass faced									
3/4" thick	SF	5.15	5.56	5.17	5.56	5.99	5.47	5.07	5.39
Glass fibre panel 48" x 48":									
Vinyl faced									
1" thick	SF	6.15	6.50	6.04	6.82	7.83	7.90	6.16	7.66
Concealed suspension system									
Mineral fibre panel 12" x 24":									
3/4" thick standard	SF	11.20	12.10	11.20	12.30	13.10	11.90	11.10	11.80
3/4" thick fire-rated	SF	11.50	12.30	11.30	12.40	13.20	12.10	11.20	11.90
Mineral fibre panel 12" x 12":									
3/4" thick standard	SF	10.30	11.10	10.30	11.20	12.00	11.00	10.30	10.80
3/4" thick fire-rated	SF	11.10	12.00	11.10	12.20	13.00	11.80	11.00	11.60
Suspended ceiling sundries									
Extra over cost of suspended ceiling									
for drilling and bolting to soffit	SF	1.45	1.51	1.45	1.71	1.65	1.49	1.92	1.55
Mineral wool sound absorption blanket	SF	1.45	1.51	1.45	1.71	1.65	1.49	1.92	1.55
09 60 00 Flooring									
09 63 40 Stone Flooring									
MARBLE									
To floors									
Panels:									
3/4" travertine	SF	57.20	60.00	31.60	60.00	65.40	66.10	61.10	68.60
To walls									
Panels:									
3/4" travertine	SF	60.10	63.20	33.20	63.20	68.50	69.50	64.20	70.60
09 64 00 Wood Flooring									
WOOD STRIP FLOORING									
Hardwood (finished)									
2 1/4" wide x 25/32" thick strips:									
Birch or maple									
Second grade or better	SF	12.50	12.00	12.90	12.00	13.50	14.70	14.90	13.70
Oak, plain white									
Stain grade	SF	13.10	12.60	13.40	12.60	14.20	15.10	16.10	13.70
Finish grade	SF	14.00	13.50	14.30	13.70	15.40	16.20	17.70	14.60
WOOD PARQUET FLOORING									
Prefinished									
5/16" thick:									
Maple, select	SF	7.53	7.30	7.71	8.12	8.44	11.00	10.90	11.10
Oak, select	SF	7.75	7.50	7.90	8.32	8.44	11.20	11.10	11.20
RESILIENT WOOD FLOORING ASSEMBLIES									
On sleepers and subfloor									
Wood subfloor and sleepers:									
Industrial grade	SF	14.00	13.60	14.20	15.10	15.30	20.30	20.10	20.30
First grade	SF	13.70	13.20	13.80	14.60	14.80	19.40	19.30	19.50
Second grade	SF	13.30	12.90	13.60	14.30	14.30	19.10	18.90	19.20

Item	UNITS	St. John's	Halifax	Montreal	Ottawa	Toronto	Winnipeg	Calgary	Vancouver
Subfloor on steel springs and sleepers									
Industrial grade	SF	15.60	15.10	16.00	16.70	17.10	22.60	22.50	22.70
First grade	SF	18.20	17.70	18.50	19.40	19.80	26.40	26.20	26.50
Second grade	SF	17.00	16.50	17.40	18.20	18.50	24.70	24.60	24.70

09 65 00 Resilient Flooring
RESILIENT TILE FLOORING
Rubber tile
1/8" thick:

Item	UNITS	St. John's	Halifax	Montreal	Ottawa	Toronto	Winnipeg	Calgary	Vancouver
Average cost	SF	8.31	10.80	10.60	11.10	11.10	12.70	10.40	10.80

Vinyl tile
1/8" thick

Item	UNITS	St. John's	Halifax	Montreal	Ottawa	Toronto	Winnipeg	Calgary	Vancouver
Marbleized	SF	4.27	5.00	4.92	5.22	5.79	6.63	5.32	5.30
Solid colours	SF	4.41	5.16	5.07	5.40	5.98	6.85	5.49	5.45

Vinyl composite tile
1/16" thick

Item	UNITS	St. John's	Halifax	Montreal	Ottawa	Toronto	Winnipeg	Calgary	Vancouver
Average cost	SF	2.54	2.11	2.58	2.54	3.15	2.46	2.65	3.54

5/64" thick

Item	UNITS	St. John's	Halifax	Montreal	Ottawa	Toronto	Winnipeg	Calgary	Vancouver
Average cost	SF	2.81	2.33	2.88	2.82	3.50	2.75	2.95	3.92

1/8" thick

Item	UNITS	St. John's	Halifax	Montreal	Ottawa	Toronto	Winnipeg	Calgary	Vancouver
Average cost	SF	3.00	2.50	3.08	3.03	3.75	2.94	3.14	4.26

RESILIENT SHEET FLOORING
Linoleum
5/64" thick:

Item	UNITS	St. John's	Halifax	Montreal	Ottawa	Toronto	Winnipeg	Calgary	Vancouver
Embossed patterns	SF	7.09	6.67	7.08	7.60	7.90	6.62	6.92	6.66

1/8" thick:

Item	UNITS	St. John's	Halifax	Montreal	Ottawa	Toronto	Winnipeg	Calgary	Vancouver
Solid colours	SF	7.43	7.00	7.43	7.95	8.28	6.94	7.25	7.12

Polyvinyl chloride (vinyl)
Inlaid pattern:
1/16" thick

Item	UNITS	St. John's	Halifax	Montreal	Ottawa	Toronto	Winnipeg	Calgary	Vancouver
Mini chips	SF	2.86	3.43	3.34	3.50	3.61	4.23	3.28	3.38
Mini chips with embossed pattern	SF	2.99	3.58	3.48	3.68	3.77	4.44	3.43	3.58
Irregular chips	SF	3.31	3.96	3.86	4.07	4.16	4.89	3.78	3.93
Square chips	SF	3.48	4.17	4.05	4.26	4.39	5.17	3.95	4.14
Surface treated	SF	3.48	4.17	4.05	4.26	4.39	5.17	3.95	4.14

5/64" thick

Item	UNITS	St. John's	Halifax	Montreal	Ottawa	Toronto	Winnipeg	Calgary	Vancouver
With embossed pattern	SF	5.04	6.04	5.86	6.21	6.36	7.45	5.75	6.00

3/32" thick

Item	UNITS	St. John's	Halifax	Montreal	Ottawa	Toronto	Winnipeg	Calgary	Vancouver
Square chips	SF	3.57	4.26	4.13	4.39	4.49	5.29	4.09	4.25
Irregular chips	SF	5.04	6.04	5.86	6.21	6.36	7.45	5.75	6.00
With embossed pattern	SF	5.43	6.51	6.34	6.69	6.86	8.05	6.23	6.48

Inlaid pattern with cushion backing
7/64" thick

Item	UNITS	St. John's	Halifax	Montreal	Ottawa	Toronto	Winnipeg	Calgary	Vancouver
	SF	5.04	6.04	5.86	6.21	6.36	7.45	5.75	6.00

Printed pattern with cushion backing:

Item	UNITS	St. John's	Halifax	Montreal	Ottawa	Toronto	Winnipeg	Calgary	Vancouver
5/64" thick	SF	3.87	4.65	4.51	4.77	4.90	5.75	4.42	4.64
3/32" thick	SF	4.27	5.10	4.96	5.25	5.39	6.33	4.90	5.11

09 66 00 Terrazzo Flooring
PORTLAND CEMENT TERRAZZO
To floors with 1/8" zinc strip
Sand cushion type:

Item	UNITS	St. John's	Halifax	Montreal	Ottawa	Toronto	Winnipeg	Calgary	Vancouver
30" x 30" grid	SF	30.90	30.60	35.00	32.90	34.90	40.80	36.00	32.70

Bonded to concrete:

Item	UNITS	St. John's	Halifax	Montreal	Ottawa	Toronto	Winnipeg	Calgary	Vancouver
30" x 30" grid	SF	27.80	27.50	31.50	29.70	31.50	36.70	32.20	30.00

Thinset:

Item	UNITS	St. John's	Halifax	Montreal	Ottawa	Toronto	Winnipeg	Calgary	Vancouver
30" x 30" grid	SF	24.60	24.30	28.00	26.60	28.10	32.70	28.60	26.20

TERRAZZO, PRECAST
To stairs
Treads:

Item	UNITS	St. John's	Halifax	Montreal	Ottawa	Toronto	Winnipeg	Calgary	Vancouver
To steel stairs	LF	110.00	109.00	124.00	119.00	125.00	146.00	128.00	117.00

PLASTIC MATRIX TERRAZZO
Epoxy type

Item	UNITS	St. John's	Halifax	Montreal	Ottawa	Toronto	Winnipeg	Calgary	Vancouver
1/4" thick	SF	27.80	27.50	30.50	30.80	32.50	39.30	36.00	36.00
3/8" thick	SF	29.20	28.80	31.70	32.20	34.00	41.30	37.70	37.20

Latex type

Item	UNITS	St. John's	Halifax	Montreal	Ottawa	Toronto	Winnipeg	Calgary	Vancouver
1/4" thick	SF	22.20	21.90	24.50	24.50	26.10	31.40	28.80	28.30
3/8" thick	SF	24.80	24.60	27.10	27.90	29.10	35.20	32.40	31.90

CONDUCTIVE TERRAZZO
Epoxy type

Item	UNITS	St. John's	Halifax	Montreal	Ottawa	Toronto	Winnipeg	Calgary	Vancouver
1/4" thick	SF	28.70	28.50	31.90	31.70	35.50	43.00	37.90	36.00
3/8" thick	SF	34.90	34.70	38.90	38.60	43.10	52.40	46.20	43.10

TRIM & ACCESSORIES
Base trim
Cove base, standard:

Item	UNITS	St. John's	Halifax	Montreal	Ottawa	Toronto	Winnipeg	Calgary	Vancouver
4" high	LF	24.00	24.50	26.90	27.90	32.60	39.90	29.20	29.30
6" high	LF	28.40	29.10	32.00	33.20	38.40	47.20	34.40	34.70

Item	UNITS	St. John's	Halifax	Montreal	Ottawa	Toronto	Winnipeg	Calgary	Vancouver
09 67 00 Fluid-Applied Flooring									
FLUID APPLIED FLOORING									
Urethane liquid pour laid on prepared concrete or asphalt									
including game or lane lines									
Indoor:									
1/4" thick	SF	14.30	14.80	13.90	16.40	16.10	17.80	20.30	16.70
3/8" thick	SF	16.00	16.40	15.30	17.90	17.70	19.60	22.40	18.50
Outdoor with textured surface									
1/2" thick	SF	20.30	21.10	20.00	22.90	22.70	24.90	28.70	23.60
09 68 00 Carpeting									
CARPET									
Nylon:									
Anti-static									
Light duty 20 oz/sy	SF	3.56	3.57	3.68	3.73	4.39	4.76	3.74	4.91
Medium duty 28 oz/sy	SF	4.50	4.50	4.65	4.69	5.52	6.00	4.74	6.32
Cut pile									
Heavy duty 45 oz/sy	SF	6.15	6.41	6.22	6.46	7.56	8.17	6.48	8.18
Acrylic:									
Tufted									
Light duty 32 oz/sy	SF	3.86	4.03	3.89	4.05	4.76	5.13	4.09	5.14
Woven									
Medium duty 40 oz/sy	SF	5.28	5.50	5.33	5.54	6.49	7.00	5.58	7.02
Heavy duty 50 oz/sy	SF	6.73	7.04	6.80	7.06	8.30	8.96	7.13	8.97
Polypropylene:									
Light duty 20 oz/sy	SF	2.65	2.77	2.68	2.78	3.26	3.50	2.81	3.52
Medium duty 25 oz/sy	SF	3.54	3.69	3.57	3.72	4.38	4.68	3.73	4.70
Heavy duty 30 oz/sy	SF	4.63	4.83	4.66	4.84	5.72	6.15	4.88	6.18
Wool (including underpadding):									
Light duty 27 oz/sy	SF	6.04	6.31	6.10	6.35	7.46	8.02	6.38	8.07
Medium duty 35 oz/sy	SF	7.21	7.50	7.27	7.54	8.85	9.57	7.58	9.57
Heavy duty 42 oz/sy	SF	8.82	9.19	8.88	9.24	10.80	11.60	9.29	11.70
09 69 00 Access Flooring									
RIGID GRID ACCESS FLOORING									
24" x 24" panels (based on 12" height):									
Steel-clad wood floor panel:									
With plastic laminated finish	SF	25.50	25.10	25.30	28.10	27.00	24.50	23.80	1.54
With vinyl floor finish	SF	26.10	25.50	25.70	28.70	27.60	25.00	24.40	1.58
Steel floor panels:									
With plastic laminated finish	SF	30.70	30.00	30.30	33.50	32.20	29.20	28.40	1.85
With vinyl floor finish	SF	31.40	30.70	30.80	34.20	33.20	30.10	29.40	1.89
SNAP ON STRINGER ACCESS FLOORING									
24" x 24" panels (based on 12" height)									
Steel clad wood floor panels									
With plastic laminated floor finish	SF	25.00	24.50	24.70	27.30	26.50	24.00	23.20	1.49
With vinyl floor finish	SF	25.50	25.00	25.20	28.00	26.90	24.40	23.70	1.58
Steel floor panels									
With plastic laminated floor finish	SF	29.70	29.20	29.50	32.70	31.50	28.50	27.80	1.80
With vinyl floor finish	SF	30.50	29.70	30.10	33.40	32.00	29.10	28.10	1.82
STRINGERLESS ACCESS FLOORING									
24" x 24" panels (based on 12" height)									
Steel-clad wood floor finish:									
With plastic laminated finish	SF	22.00	21.60	21.80	24.00	23.00	21.00	20.30	1.33
With vinyl floor finish	SF	22.70	22.20	22.30	25.00	24.10	21.80	21.10	1.37
Steel - clad concrete panel									
With vinyl floor finish	SF	29.70	29.20	29.50	32.70	31.50	28.50	27.80	1.80
Steel floor panels:									
With plastic laminated finish	SF	26.80	26.40	26.50	29.50	28.50	25.80	25.00	1.62
With vinyl floor finish	SF	27.60	27.00	27.10	30.10	29.10	26.50	25.60	1.65
Aluminum floor panels:									
With plastic laminated finish	SF	53.60	52.60	53.00	58.70	56.60	51.50	49.90	3.23
With vinyl floor finish	SF	56.80	55.60	55.90	62.10	59.70	54.30	53.00	3.41
09 70 00 Wall Finishes									
09 72 00 Wall Coverings									
VINYL-COATED FABRIC WALL COVERING									
(Based on supply price of $1.00/SF)									
Plain patterns (double rolls)									
Untrimmed:									
To drywall	SF	3.49	3.13	3.17	3.23	3.49	3.74	2.97	4.54
To plaster	SF	3.29	2.94	2.99	3.04	3.31	3.53	2.80	4.27
Pretrimmed:									
To drywall	SF	3.49	3.13	3.17	3.23	3.49	3.74	2.97	4.54
To plaster	SF	2.95	2.66	2.68	2.76	2.96	3.19	2.50	3.85

Item	UNITS	St. John's	Halifax	Montreal	Ottawa	Toronto	Winnipeg	Calgary	Vancouver
Decorative patterns (double rolls)									
Untrimmed:									
To drywall	SF	3.66	3.28	3.34	3.42	3.70	3.95	3.10	4.75
To plaster	SF	3.29	2.94	2.99	3.04	3.31	3.53	2.80	4.27
Pretrimmed:									
To drywall	SF	3.56	3.21	3.25	3.32	3.58	3.84	3.02	4.65
To plaster	SF	3.21	2.90	2.91	2.99	3.21	3.45	2.75	4.20
VINYL WALL COVERINGS									
(15% material waste included)									
54" wide, plain or decorated									
To walls:									
15 oz per lin. yd	SF	4.69	4.22	4.29	4.37	4.71	5.06	3.98	6.11
19 oz per lin. yd	SF	5.00	4.50	4.55	4.65	5.01	5.38	4.23	6.50
34 oz per lin. yd	SF	6.32	5.68	5.75	5.85	6.31	6.78	5.34	8.24
WALLPAPER									
(Based on supply price of $0.80/sf)									
Plain patterns (double rolls)									
Untrimmed:									
To drywall	SF	3.21	2.90	2.91	2.99	3.21	3.45	2.75	4.20
To plaster	SF	3.14	2.82	2.87	2.93	3.14	3.37	2.65	4.09
Pretrimmed:									
To drywall	SF	3.18	2.87	2.89	2.97	3.18	3.42	2.72	4.15
To plaster	SF	3.09	2.79	2.82	2.86	3.11	3.34	2.60	4.03
Decorative patterns (double rolls)									
Untrimmed:									
To drywall	SF	3.35	3.01	3.06	3.10	3.35	3.60	2.83	4.36
To plaster	SF	3.29	2.94	2.99	3.04	3.31	3.53	2.80	4.27
Pretrimmed:									
To drywall	SF	3.18	2.87	2.89	2.97	3.18	3.42	2.72	4.15
To plaster	SF	3.09	2.79	2.82	2.86	3.11	3.34	2.60	4.03

09 90 00 Painting and Coating

09 91 00 Painting

DOORS & WINDOWS, EXTERIOR

Item	UNITS	St. John's	Halifax	Montreal	Ottawa	Toronto	Winnipeg	Calgary	Vancouver
3 coats, brush applied:									
Wood or metal windows	SF	1.73	0.98	1.74	2.15	1.83	2.17	1.66	12.90
Wooden doors	EA	85.10	48.50	86.20	107.00	91.10	107.00	82.10	641.00
Metal doors	EA	77.00	43.70	77.70	96.00	81.90	96.70	73.90	577.00
Wooden frames	EA	45.60	25.90	46.10	57.00	48.70	57.30	43.70	342.00
Metal door frames	EA	39.20	22.30	39.80	49.00	41.90	49.50	37.90	295.00

TRIM, EXTERIOR

Item	UNITS	St. John's	Halifax	Montreal	Ottawa	Toronto	Winnipeg	Calgary	Vancouver
3 coats, brush applied:									
Metal flashing	SF	1.73	0.98	1.74	2.15	1.83	2.17	1.66	12.90
Soffits, fascias	SF	2.08	1.17	2.07	2.59	2.21	2.59	1.99	15.40
Handrails, railing etc.	LF	1.05	0.59	1.05	1.30	1.11	1.31	1.01	7.83

MISCELLANEOUS, EXTERIOR

Item	UNITS	St. John's	Halifax	Montreal	Ottawa	Toronto	Winnipeg	Calgary	Vancouver
3 coats, brush applied:									
Pipes not exceeding 6" dia.	LF	1.05	0.59	1.05	1.30	1.11	1.31	1.01	7.83
Flagpoles (before erection)	SF	1.19	0.69	1.20	1.49	1.27	1.50	1.15	8.99
Lamp standard (before erection)	SF	1.11	0.62	1.11	1.38	1.17	1.37	1.07	8.25

WALLS & CEILINGS, INTERIOR

Ceilings

Item	UNITS	St. John's	Halifax	Montreal	Ottawa	Toronto	Winnipeg	Calgary	Vancouver
2 coats, rolled									
Concrete, wood, plaster or drywall	SF	0.88	0.53	0.92	1.18	0.96	1.13	0.90	6.98
Acoustic tile (concealed grid)	SF	0.65	0.39	0.68	0.87	0.71	0.83	0.65	5.11
Acoustic tile (exposed grid)	SF	1.03	0.62	1.08	1.38	1.12	1.30	1.06	8.18
Steel deck (measure surface area)	SF	0.69	0.42	0.72	0.92	0.75	0.88	0.70	5.45
Surfaces associated with ceilings									
2 coats at same time as ceiling:									
OWSJ (measure twice height)	SF	0.70	0.42	0.73	0.94	0.76	0.89	0.71	5.53
Duct work	SF	0.70	0.42	0.73	0.94	0.76	0.89	0.71	5.53
2 coats separate from ceiling:									
OWSJ (measure twice height)	SF	1.17	0.70	1.21	1.55	1.26	1.48	1.17	9.19
Structural steel work (exposed area)	SF	0.88	0.53	0.92	1.18	0.96	1.13	0.90	6.98
Duct work	SF	1.19	0.72	1.24	1.61	1.28	1.50	1.19	9.38
Pipes over 2" dia. surface area	SF	1.19	0.72	1.24	1.61	1.28	1.50	1.19	9.38
Pipes not exceeding 2" dia.	SF	1.08	0.64	1.11	1.44	1.16	1.36	1.09	8.45
3 coats, rolled:									
Concrete, wood, plaster, or drywall	SF	0.97	0.55	0.98	1.21	1.03	1.22	0.93	1.00
Walls									
2 coats, rolled:									
Concrete, plywood, plaster, or drywall	SF	0.91	0.54	0.94	1.21	0.98	1.16	0.91	7.12
Concrete block, acoustic board or panel	SF	1.05	0.63	1.09	1.42	1.14	1.34	1.07	8.25
Plywood and paneling	SF	0.91	0.55	0.95	1.22	0.99	1.17	0.92	7.18
Steel and wood sashes	SF	1.08	0.64	1.11	1.43	1.16	1.35	1.08	8.39
Structural steel, exposed surfaces	SF	0.98	0.59	1.02	1.31	1.07	1.24	0.99	7.79
3 coats, rolled:									
Concrete, plywood, plaster, or drywall	SF	0.97	0.55	0.98	1.21	1.03	1.22	0.93	1.00
Concrete block, tile, acoustic board or panel	SF	1.23	0.70	1.24	1.52	1.31	1.56	1.18	9.19

Instructions for use, page 2. Main index, page 5.

Item	UNITS	St. John's	Halifax	Montreal	Ottawa	Toronto	Winnipeg	Calgary	Vancouver
Steel and wood sashes	SF	1.39	0.80	1.39	1.73	1.48	1.75	1.32	10.30
Structural steel, exposed surfaces	SF	1.57	0.91	1.60	1.98	1.71	1.99	1.52	11.80
Baseboards not exceeding (4") high	LF	1.64	0.93	1.66	2.05	1.76	2.07	1.58	12.30
DOORS & WINDOWS, INTERIOR									
2 coats (brush applied) on:									
Metal doors	EA	58.20	34.80	60.60	77.70	63.20	74.00	58.60	458.00
Metal door frames	EA	35.10	20.80	36.50	47.00	37.80	44.50	35.40	276.00
3 coats (brush applied) on:									
Wooden doors	EA	75.20	42.70	76.00	93.90	80.30	94.60	72.30	565.00
Wooden door frames	EA	44.00	25.00	44.30	54.80	46.70	55.10	42.20	329.00
Edges of plastic faced doors	EA	26.50	15.10	27.00	33.30	28.60	33.50	25.60	199.00
MISCELLANEOUS, INTERIOR									
2 coats (brush applied) on:									
Stair treads	SF	1.36	0.80	1.39	1.77	1.45	1.69	1.37	10.60
Hollow metal screens	SF	1.27	0.77	1.32	1.69	1.37	1.63	1.27	10.00
Handrails, balustrades etc.	LF	1.46	0.87	1.51	1.95	1.58	1.86	1.47	11.50
3 coats (brush applied) on:									
Shelving	SF	1.95	1.11	1.95	2.44	2.07	2.45	1.88	14.60
Millwork (surface area)	SF	2.21	1.26	2.26	2.81	2.36	2.79	2.15	16.60

09 96 00 High-Performance Coatings

WALL COATINGS

Plastic paint to interior walls

3 coats:									
Concrete blockwork	SF	2.12	3.30	2.26	2.20	2.11	2.62	1.97	2.14
Concrete	SF	2.08	3.25	2.21	2.16	2.08	2.58	1.92	2.09
Drywall	SF	1.93	3.00	2.05	2.00	1.95	2.42	1.78	1.94

10: SPECIALTIES

10 11 00 Visual Display Units

10 11 13 Chalkboards

CHALKBOARDS

Wall Mounted

Fixed (includes installation cost of trim)

Impregnated fibreboard 1/2" thick:									
Steel sheet, baked on acrylic finish	SF	11.50	11.20	12.00	31.20	11.10	13.90	13.00	22.00
Steel sheet, porcelain enamel finish	SF	11.10	10.90	11.50	30.30	10.80	13.40	12.50	21.50
Tempered hardboard 1/4":									
Baked on acrylic finish	SF	5.59	5.42	5.76	15.00	5.37	6.65	6.27	10.70

ALUMINUM TRIM

(Standard products)

Edge trim and divider bars (Supply only)

1/4" exposed face:									
Clear anodized finish	LF	1.53	1.50	1.57	7.44	1.53	1.90	1.52	1.49
Baked enamel finish	LF	1.68	1.65	1.73	8.20	1.69	2.09	1.68	1.64
Colour anodized finish	LF	1.76	1.73	1.81	8.56	1.76	2.19	1.76	1.72
3/4" exposed face:									
Clear anodized finish	LF	1.53	1.50	1.57	7.44	1.53	1.90	1.52	1.49
Baked enamel finish	LF	1.71	1.67	1.75	8.29	1.71	2.12	1.70	1.66
Colour anodized finish	LF	1.76	1.73	1.81	8.56	1.76	2.19	1.76	1.72
1-3/4" exposed face:									
Clear anodized finish	LF	3.20	3.14	3.29	15.60	3.20	3.99	3.17	3.11
Baked enamel finish	LF	4.60	4.48	4.69	22.40	4.63	5.76	4.60	4.42
Colour anodized finish	LF	4.60	4.48	4.69	22.40	4.63	5.76	4.60	4.42

Chalk rails

Single web:									
Clear anodized finish	LF	3.87	3.78	3.96	18.70	3.87	4.91	3.93	4.08
Baked enamel finish	LF	4.18	4.08	4.27	19.80	4.11	5.27	4.21	4.36
Colour anodized finish	LF	4.60	4.48	4.69	22.40	4.60	5.85	4.69	4.91
Boxed type:									
Clear anodized finish	LF	6.68	6.52	6.80	32.30	6.68	8.47	6.80	7.04
Baked enamel finish	LF	6.95	6.80	7.16	33.80	6.95	8.84	7.07	7.32
Colour anodized finish	LF	6.89	6.71	7.10	33.20	6.89	8.75	7.01	7.22

Map rails

Mounted on wall, cork inset:									
1" wide	LF	2.63	2.58	2.70	12.80	2.63	3.35	2.69	2.51
2" wide	LF	3.11	3.05	3.23	15.10	3.14	3.99	3.20	2.98
Mounted on board or wall, 2" h-type:									
Clear anodized finish	LF	3.11	3.05	3.23	15.10	3.14	3.99	3.20	2.98
Baked enamel finish	LF	3.47	3.35	3.57	16.80	3.44	4.39	3.54	3.26
Colour anodized finish	LF	3.78	3.69	3.90	18.50	3.81	4.85	3.87	3.66

10 11 23 Tackboards

TACKBOARDS

Wall Mounted

Fixed (includes installation cost of trim)

Cork, natural:									
1/4" thick	SF	7.70	7.50	6.87	9.01	6.06	7.53	6.97	8.91

Item	UNITS	St. John's	Halifax	Montreal	Ottawa	Toronto	Winnipeg	Calgary	Vancouver
1/2" thick........	SF	9.66	9.38	8.57	11.20	7.58	9.38	8.72	11.10
Cork, vinyl coated:									
1/4" thick........	SF	10.90	10.60	9.75	12.70	8.60	10.60	9.85	12.60
1/2" thick........	SF	13.00	12.70	11.50	15.10	10.20	12.70	11.90	15.00
Cork, covered with 50 g vinyl fabric:									
1/4" thick........	SF	9.75	9.57	8.73	11.50	7.69	9.57	8.86	11.30
1/2" thick........	SF	11.60	11.30	10.30	13.60	9.12	11.30	10.40	13.50
Cork, covered with nylon fabric:									
1/2" thick........	SF	13.70	13.30	12.20	16.10	10.70	13.40	12.40	15.60

10 21 00 Compartments and Cubicles

10 21 13 Toilet Compartments

PARTITIONS, TOILET

Metal toilet partitions

Item	UNITS	St. John's	Halifax	Montreal	Ottawa	Toronto	Winnipeg	Calgary	Vancouver
Floor mounted, overhead braced:									
Standard cubicle	EA	807.00	795.00	809.00	854.00	773.00	881.00	822.00	772.00
Alcove type	EA	783.00	773.00	786.00	830.00	749.00	854.00	797.00	749.00
Floor mounted, pilaster type:									
Standard cubicle	EA	921.00	907.00	922.00	976.00	880.00	1000.00	938.00	881.00
Alcove type	EA	867.00	854.00	870.00	920.00	830.00	946.00	883.00	828.00
Ceiling hung:									
Standard cubicle	EA	990.00	975.00	992.00	1,050	947.00	1,080	1,010	945.00
Alcove type	EA	950.00	937.00	955.00	1,010	909.00	1,040	971.00	908.00

10 22 00 Partitions

10 22 19 Demountable Partitions

PARTITIONS, MOVABLE OFFICE

9' height

Gypsum partitions

Item	UNITS	St. John's	Halifax	Montreal	Ottawa	Toronto	Winnipeg	Calgary	Vancouver
Plain drywall:									
Painted	LF	100.00	95.40	101.00	82.60	111.00	111.00	94.80	151.00
Vinyl covered........	LF	116.00	111.00	118.00	96.30	129.00	129.00	111.00	176.00
Drywall with sound absorption:									
Painted	LF	109.00	104.00	109.00	89.60	120.00	120.00	102.00	163.00
Vinyl covered........	LF	121.00	116.00	122.00	100.00	134.00	134.00	115.00	183.00
Steel partitions									
Baked enamel finish	LF	177.00	170.00	179.00	147.00	197.00	197.00	169.00	268.00

10 22 33 Accordion Folding Partitions

ACCORDION FOLDING PARTITIONS

8' height

Item	UNITS	St. John's	Halifax	Montreal	Ottawa	Toronto	Winnipeg	Calgary	Vancouver
Wood:									
Room divider type	LF	182.00	175.00	176.00	190.00	199.00	190.00	180.00	189.00
Classroom type........	LF	326.00	314.00	317.00	341.00	357.00	341.00	323.00	338.00

10 22 39 Folding Panel Partitions

FOLDING PARTITIONS

9' height

Item	UNITS	St. John's	Halifax	Montreal	Ottawa	Toronto	Winnipeg	Calgary	Vancouver
Manually operated partitions									
Vinyl faced gypsum panes........	LF	399.00	399.00	418.00	424.00	506.00	466.00	445.00	418.00
Sound absorbing	LF	503.00	500.00	521.00	530.00	631.00	582.00	558.00	518.00
Electrically operated panels									
Steel gymnasium pattern	LF	366.00	363.00	375.00	384.00	454.00	424.00	402.00	375.00

BIFOLD PARTITIONS

Item	UNITS	St. John's	Halifax	Montreal	Ottawa	Toronto	Winnipeg	Calgary	Vancouver
Wood:									
Gymnasium type........	LF	347.00	338.00	354.00	360.00	430.00	393.00	381.00	357.00

10 26 00 Wall and Door Protection

10 26 13 Corner Guards

CORNER GUARDS

Vinyl acrylic with aluminum retainers, 3" legs

Item	UNITS	St. John's	Halifax	Montreal	Ottawa	Toronto	Winnipeg	Calgary	Vancouver
Flush mounted:									
L-type 1/4" radius	LF	29.90	28.50	29.30	31.70	33.50	34.10	32.30	38.10
L-type 1 1/4" radius	LF	29.90	28.50	29.30	31.70	33.50	34.10	32.30	38.10
U-type 4" wall	LF	36.60	34.70	36.00	39.00	41.10	42.10	39.60	46.30
U-type 6" wall	LF	57.00	54.30	55.80	61.30	63.70	65.80	62.50	72.50
U-type 8" wall	LF	57.60	54.60	56.10	61.60	64.30	66.10	62.80	73.20
Surface mounted:									
L-type 1/4" radius	LF	21.80	20.70	21.30	23.00	24.40	24.90	23.50	27.60
L-type 1 1/4" radius	LF	21.80	20.70	21.30	23.00	24.40	24.90	23.50	27.60
U-type 4" wall	LF	40.80	39.30	39.90	43.90	46.60	47.20	44.50	52.70
U-type 6" wall	LF	43.60	41.10	41.50	46.30	48.50	49.70	46.60	54.90
U-type 8" wall	LF	49.40	47.20	48.50	52.40	55.20	56.70	53.30	63.40
Stainless steel									
Standard sections:									
Built-in	LF	31.10	31.70	29.20	39.60	50.90	33.50	32.90	35.70
Fixed to wall surface with adhesive	LF	21.50	21.80	20.10	28.30	35.10	23.10	22.90	25.00

10 28 00 Toilet, Bath & Laundry Accessories

10 28 13 Toilet Accessories

BATH ACCESSORIES, DISPENSING UNITS

(Based on chrome unless noted)

Item	UNITS	St. John's	Halifax	Montreal	Ottawa	Toronto	Winnipeg	Calgary	Vancouver
Toilet tissue, roll type									
Flush mounted, single	EA	34.40	35.10	36.30	38.90	39.30	48.20	43.10	49.70
Flush mounted, double	EA	45.00	45.90	47.40	51.00	51.40	63.10	56.60	65.00
Toilet tissue, leaf type:									
Single (900 sheets)	EA	38.00	38.90	40.00	43.00	43.60	53.50	47.90	54.60
Double (1800 sheets)	EA	48.50	49.50	51.00	55.10	55.40	68.20	61.00	69.50
Toilet seat covers:									
For unfolded covers	EA	70.60	64.40	70.20	74.80	85.50	78.90	79.00	70.90
For folded covers	EA	89.80	81.40	88.70	94.90	108.00	99.90	100.00	89.90
Sanitary napkins:									
Surface mounted, single	EA	402.00	366.00	399.00	428.00	486.00	450.00	449.00	405.00
Surface mounted, double	EA	561.00	510.00	556.00	594.00	679.00	625.00	627.00	563.00
Recessed, single	EA	561.00	510.00	556.00	594.00	679.00	625.00	627.00	563.00
Recessed, double	EA	758.00	689.00	750.00	801.00	917.00	843.00	847.00	759.00
Paper towels, roll type									
Surface mounted, standard roll	EA	108.00	105.00	112.00	121.00	137.00	123.00	121.00	121.00
Surface mounted, jumbo roll	EA	128.00	125.00	132.00	146.00	164.00	148.00	146.00	145.00
Paper towel leaf type									
Surface mounted horizontal	EA	95.40	92.30	98.70	106.00	122.00	107.00	107.00	106.00
Surface mounted vertical	EA	101.00	97.90	105.00	113.00	129.00	116.00	114.00	112.00
Recessed horizontal	EA	91.00	87.90	93.90	101.00	115.00	103.00	101.00	101.00
Paper towel, universal:									
Surface mounted, 15" high	EA	108.00	101.00	107.00	117.00	133.00	119.00	117.00	116.00
Recessed, 26" high, stainless	EA	463.00	434.00	462.00	497.00	562.00	505.00	497.00	494.00
Facial tissue:									
Surface mounted	EA	48.90	47.40	50.60	54.80	61.80	55.60	54.90	54.60
Recessed	EA	49.90	48.30	51.60	55.90	63.00	56.70	55.90	55.30
Soap products									
Soap bars:									
Soap dish	EA	26.60	26.90	28.20	29.50	31.40	32.00	30.60	24.80
Powdered soap:									
16 oz capacity	EA	58.00	58.60	61.80	64.20	68.20	69.60	66.80	54.20
Liquid soap, individual tank:									
Wall type, surface mounted, 16 oz	EA	116.00	117.00	122.00	127.00	137.00	139.00	134.00	107.00
Wall type, surface mounted, 18 oz	EA	134.00	135.00	148.00	150.00	161.00	161.00	157.00	127.00
Wall type, surface mounted, 40 oz	EA	163.00	165.00	173.00	180.00	192.00	196.00	187.00	152.00
Wall type, surface mounted, 60 oz	EA	176.00	178.00	188.00	195.00	207.00	213.00	201.00	165.00
Wall type, recessed, 16 oz	EA	257.00	258.00	273.00	283.00	302.00	307.00	295.00	239.00
Lavatory mounted, 16 oz	EA	165.00	167.00	175.00	182.00	194.00	198.00	189.00	154.00
Liquid soap, central tank:									
(piping not included) wall type valve	EA	91.20	92.10	96.90	101.00	107.00	109.00	105.00	85.10
Wall type valve, vandal-proof	EA	222.00	223.00	237.00	245.00	262.00	266.00	256.00	208.00
Lavatory type valve	EA	205.00	207.00	219.00	227.00	241.00	244.00	235.00	191.00
Exposed tanks, 1 gal	EA	121.00	122.00	126.00	133.00	142.00	146.00	139.00	112.00
Exposed tanks, 2 gal	EA	205.00	207.00	219.00	227.00	241.00	244.00	235.00	191.00
Exposed tanks, 5 gal	EA	427.00	432.00	454.00	474.00	503.00	515.00	492.00	399.00
Pressure reducing tank, 5 gal	EA	740.00	748.00	788.00	818	872.00	889.00	853.00	692.00
Storage tank, 50 gal	EA	2,250	2,270	2,390	2,500	2,670	2,680	2,590	2,100
BATH ACCESSORIES, DISPOSAL UNITS									
Sanitary napkin units									
Wall mounted:									
Surface mounted	EA	187.00	197.00	200.00	208.00	221.00	239.00	233.00	221.00
Recessed	EA	214.00	226.00	230.00	241.00	255.00	273.00	265.00	254.00
Waste receptacles									
Free standing baked enamel:									
16" x 16" x 36"	EA	213.00	216.00	222.00	229.00	244.00	262.00	256.00	240.00
12" x 12" x 42"	EA	205.00	210.00	213.00	221.00	236.00	253.00	249.00	234.00
Wall mounted:									
Surface mounted, 12" x 42"	EA	473.00	480.00	490.00	509.00	541.00	580.00	566.00	535.00
Semi-recessed, 12" x 42"	EA	486.00	494.00	504.00	524.00	556.00	598.00	581.00	550.00
Recessed, 12" x 42"	EA	407.00	414.00	422.00	437.00	467.00	501.00	486.00	461.00
Recessed, exposed door only	EA	77.40	78.60	80.30	83.30	88.50	94.80	92.30	87.50
Ash trays									
Surface mounted:									
Circular, 8" dia.	EA	186.00	190.00	193.00	201.00	214.00	229.00	221.00	212.00
Semi-circular, 13" dia.	EA	149.00	151.00	153.00	160.00	170.00	180.00	178.00	168.00
Rectangular, 8" long	EA	164.00	167.00	169.00	176.00	188.00	202.00	197.00	184.00
Rectangular, 12" long	EA	203.00	207.00	211.00	219.00	233.00	250.00	246.00	231.00
Recessed:									
8" long	EA	225.00	226.00	232.00	241.00	256.00	275.00	265.00	253.00
12" long	EA	330.00	334.00	343.00	354.00	376.00	405.00	395.00	372.00

Item	UNITS	St. John's	Halifax	Montreal	Ottawa	Toronto	Winnipeg	Calgary	Vancouver
BATH ACCESSORIES, COMBINATION UNITS									
Towel/waste receptacles (all units based on stainless steel)									
Surface mounted:									
14" x 60"	EA	741.00	748.00	763.00	794.00	846.00	902.00	883.00	850.00
Semi-recessed:									
14" x 60"	EA	711.00	718.00	736.00	764.00	813.00	867.00	847.00	817.00
Recessed:									
14" x 60"	EA	602.00	610.00	622.00	647.00	688.00	736.00	720.00	693.00

10 51 00 Lockers

10 51 13 Metal Lockers
STANDARD LOCKERS, BAKED ENAMEL

Item	UNITS	St. John's	Halifax	Montreal	Ottawa	Toronto	Winnipeg	Calgary	Vancouver
72" high									
Single tier									
12" wide:									
15" deep	EA	245.00	241.00	266.00	237.00	273.00	278.00	256.00	335.00
18" deep	EA	266.00	262.00	291.00	257.00	297.00	303.00	278.00	364.00
15" wide:									
15" deep	EA	288.00	284.00	315.00	277.00	321.00	328.00	300.00	394.00
18" deep	EA	304.00	299.00	332.00	293.00	339.00	345.00	318.00	416.00
Two tier									
12" wide:									
15" deep	EA	289.00	285.00	316.00	279.00	323.00	329.00	301.00	395.00
18" deep	EA	330.00	325.00	360.00	318.00	368.00	374.00	345.00	451.00
Six tier									
12" wide:									
15" deep	EA	387.00	381.00	424.00	375.00	434.00	441.00	406.00	532.00
18" deep	EA	406.00	400.00	444.00	391.00	453.00	461.00	422.00	554.00
Accessories									
Bases, baked enamel:									
Per locker	EA	35.50	34.90	38.70	34.00	39.50	40.20	36.90	48.20

COIN OPERATED LOCKERS, BAKED ENAMEL

Item	UNITS	St. John's	Halifax	Montreal	Ottawa	Toronto	Winnipeg	Calgary	Vancouver
72" high									
Single tier									
12" wide:									
12" deep	EA	1,110	1,080	1,220	1,070	1,240	1,260	1,170	1,520
15" deep	EA	1,120	1,090	1,220	1,070	1,240	1,260	1,170	1,520
18" deep (standard)	EA	1,040	1,020	1,130	999	1,150	1,170	1,080	1,420
21" deep	EA	1,120	1,110	1,220	1,080	1,250	1,270	1,190	1,530
Two tier									
12" wide:									
12" deep	EA	1,220	1,190	1,320	1,180	1,360	1,380	1,270	1,640
15" deep	EA	1,240	1,220	1,350	1,200	1,400	1,410	1,310	1,700
18" deep (standard)	EA	1,170	1,140	1,260	1,120	1,300	1,320	1,210	1,570
21" deep	EA	1,270	1,240	1,360	1,230	1,410	1,420	1,320	1,750
Accessories									
Bases, baked enamel									
Per locker	EA	60.80	59.90	66.40	58.40	67.90	69.00	63.70	83.10
Sloping tops, baked enamel:									
To suit 18" wide tiers	LF	78.90	77.70	86.60	76.20	88.10	89.60	82.30	108.00

10 55 00 Postal Specialties

MAIL BOXES

Item	UNITS	St. John's	Halifax	Montreal	Ottawa	Toronto	Winnipeg	Calgary	Vancouver
Apartment type:									
Back loading	EA	118.00	115.00	125.00	103.00	121.00	145.00	132.00	157.00
Front loading	EA	140.00	136.00	149.00	122.00	144.00	173.00	157.00	187.00
Post office type:									
Type c	EA	229.00	222.00	244.00	200.00	236.00	285.00	256.00	304.00

COLLECTION BOXES

Item	UNITS	St. John's	Halifax	Montreal	Ottawa	Toronto	Winnipeg	Calgary	Vancouver
Aluminum	EA	4,060	3,980	4,320	3,530	4,170	5,020	4,540	5,440
Bronze or stainless steel	EA	4,480	4,370	4,750	3,910	4,600	5,510	5,020	5,960

10 75 00 Flagpoles
Erected complete

FLAGPOLE, GROUND SET

Item	UNITS	St. John's	Halifax	Montreal	Ottawa	Toronto	Winnipeg	Calgary	Vancouver
Stationary (including metal base and base cover and supply and installation of anchor bolts in prepared base)									
Tapered cone, external rope:									
35', painted steel	EA	3,920	3,910	4,220	3,910	4,190	4,950	4,080	4,620
35', satin aluminum	EA	3,690	3,700	4,010	3,720	3,970	4,700	3,870	4,350
35', clear anodized aluminum	EA	4,000	4,000	4,300	4,000	4,270	5,080	4,180	4,690
35', colour anodized aluminum	EA	4,320	4,310	4,640	4,320	4,600	5,480	4,510	5,070
Sectional, standard external rope:									
35', clear anodized aluminum	EA	2,480	2,480	2,660	2,480	2,650	3,150	2,590	2,910
35', baked enamel aluminum	EA	3,440	3,430	3,690	3,430	3,660	4,350	3,590	4,040
Tilting (concrete not included)									
Tapered cone, external rope:									
35', painted steel	EA	4,580	4,580	4,960	4,620	4,930	5,860	4,820	5,410
35', satin aluminum	EA	4,000	4,000	4,300	4,000	4,270	5,080	4,180	4,690
35', clear anodized aluminum	EA	4,580	4,580	4,960	4,620	4,930	5,860	4,820	5,410

Item	UNITS	St. John's	Halifax	Montreal	Ottawa	Toronto	Winnipeg	Calgary	Vancouver
35', colour anodized aluminum	EA	5,040	5,030	5,420	5,050	5,380	6,420	5,260	5,930
Sectional, standard, external rope:									
35', clear anodized aluminum	EA	3,120	3,130	3,400	3,140	3,330	3,970	3,260	3,680
35', baked enamel aluminum	EA	4,150	4,150	4,480	4,160	4,440	5,270	4,330	4,900

FLAGPOLE, STRUCTURE MOUNTED
Wall bracket included
Vertical Type
Tapered cone:

	UNITS	St. John's	Halifax	Montreal	Ottawa	Toronto	Winnipeg	Calgary	Vancouver
20', stain aluminum	EA	3,100	3,100	3,320	3,090	3,300	3,930	3,230	3,650
20', clear anodized aluminum	EA	3,470	3,460	3,730	3,480	3,710	4,410	3,620	4,090
20', colour anodized aluminum	EA	3,670	3,680	3,960	3,680	3,940	4,680	3,850	4,310
Sectional, standard:									
20', clear anodized aluminum	EA	2,500	2,530	2,700	2,510	2,690	3,200	2,630	2,950
20', colour anodized aluminum	EA	3,470	3,460	3,730	3,480	3,710	4,410	3,620	4,090

11: EQUIPMENT

11 13 00 Loading Dock Equipment

11 13 16 Loading Dock Seals & Shelters
DOCK BUMPERS
INCLUDING FIXED BOLTS
4" projection, horizontal 10" high:

	UNITS	St. John's	Halifax	Montreal	Ottawa	Toronto	Winnipeg	Calgary	Vancouver
14" wide	EA	150.00	150.00	141.00	144.00	140.00	150.00	161.00	188.00
24" wide	EA	177.00	175.00	160.00	169.00	163.00	176.00	190.00	223.00
20" wide	EA	214.00	212.00	196.00	202.00	197.00	213.00	232.00	265.00
4" projection, vertical 20" high:									
11" wide	EA	178.00	176.00	163.00	170.00	166.00	179.00	192.00	225.00
5 1/2" projection for use with door seals									
Vertical 20" high:									
11" wide	EA	198.00	197.00	189.00	189.00	186.00	198.00	215.00	247.00

TRUCK DOOR SEALS, NORMAL DUTY
For docks 8' wide
With fixed head and double neoprene seal:

	UNITS	St. John's	Halifax	Montreal	Ottawa	Toronto	Winnipeg	Calgary	Vancouver
8' high	EA	1,400	1,550	1,540	1,440	1,490	1,630	1,570	1,680
10' high	EA	1,480	1,630	1,620	1,500	1,550	1,710	1,660	1,770
Additional costs:									
Extra for heavy duty door seals	EA	595.00	659.00	657.00	610.00	636.00	694.00	668.00	714.00

RAIL DOCK SHELTERS, NORMAL DUTY
Not exceeding 60" projection
3 sides:

	UNITS	St. John's	Halifax	Montreal	Ottawa	Toronto	Winnipeg	Calgary	Vancouver
Not exceeding 100 sf	EA	2,940	2,390	2,270	2,740	2,520	2,860	3,140	2,360
Over 100 sf not exceeding 150 sf	EA	3,320	2,690	2,510	3,110	2,880	3,210	3,500	2,670
4 sides:									
Not exceeding 100 sf	EA	3,040	2,600	2,410	3,000	2,810	3,070	3,380	2,580
Over 100 sf not exceeding 150 sf	EA	3,630	3,140	2,890	3,620	3,370	3,700	4,040	3,070

11 13 19 Stationary Loading Dock Equipment
DOCK LEVELLERS
Platform levellers
Mechanical:

	UNITS	St. John's	Halifax	Montreal	Ottawa	Toronto	Winnipeg	Calgary	Vancouver
Size 6' x 6'	EA	4,420	4,630	4,900	4,670	5,160	5,620	5,210	4,970
Size 6' x 8'	EA	4,830	5,050	5,350	5,120	5,630	6,130	5,700	5,430
Hydraulic:									
Size 6' x 6'	EA	6,800	6,600	7,180	7,070	7,350	8,200	7,680	7,280
Size 6' x 8'	EA	7,560	7,340	8,000	7,880	8,160	9,140	8,560	8,110

11 24 00 Maintenance Equipment

11 24 23 Façade Access Equipment
POWERED WINDOW WASHING EQUIPMENT
Equipment.
Powered stage 20' long (with support arms):

	UNITS	St. John's	Halifax	Montreal	Ottawa	Toronto	Winnipeg	Calgary	Vancouver
2 point suspension, drop not exceeding 300'	EA	78,100	75,700	75,000	78,500	76,900	80,800	83,700	82,400
4 point suspension, drop over 300'	EA	99,500	96,400	95,700	100,000	97,900	103,000	106,000	105,000
Tracks									
Steel	LF	162.00	155.00	151.00	186.00	188.00	174.00	191.00	169.00

11 53 00 Laboratory Equipment
LABORATORY EQUIPMENT
Fume hoods including 5' hood, base cabinet, counter top and basic fittings (motor and blower not included)

	UNITS	St. John's	Halifax	Montreal	Ottawa	Toronto	Winnipeg	Calgary	Vancouver
Steel cabinet	LF	3,170	3,170	3,170	3,170	3,350	3,140	3,200	3,840

LABORATORY FURNITURE
Tables or counters 24" wide

	UNITS	St. John's	Halifax	Montreal	Ottawa	Toronto	Winnipeg	Calgary	Vancouver
Plastic	LF	488.00	479.00	485.00	494.00	552.00	573.00	549.00	570.00
Resin impregnated stone	LF	579.00	570.00	576.00	588.00	658.00	680.00	652.00	680.00
Stainless steel	LF	655.00	649.00	695.00	677.00	750.00	695.00	707.00	661.00

Item	UNITS	St. John's	Halifax	Montreal	Ottawa	Toronto	Winnipeg	Calgary	Vancouver
Solid front storage units 7' high									
Plastic or wood	LF	442.00	436.00	439.00	451.00	497.00	521.00	497.00	515.00
Stainless steel	LF	725.00	716.00	765.00	744.00	829.00	762.00	774.00	728.00
Solid front wall storage units									
Plastic or wood	LF	222.00	219.00	221.00	226.00	251.00	261.00	251.00	259.00
Stainless steel	LF	448.00	445.00	485.00	463.00	518.00	475.00	488.00	451.00
Laboratory stools 30" high									
Any type	EA	385.00	381.00	381.00	391.00	436.00	452.00	435.00	449.00

14: CONVEYING EQUIPMENT

14 20 00 Elevators

14 21 00 Electric Traction Elevators

GEARED ELEVATOR EQUIPMENT

(Cars and entrances included, new building, front opening only)

Passenger elevator, maximum speed 350 fpm,
capacity 2,500 lbs, stainless steel doors, machine
overhead side mounted, basic cost for average commercial building
Single door from one side

Item	UNITS	St. John's	Halifax	Montreal	Ottawa	Toronto	Winnipeg	Calgary	Vancouver
8 floors	EA	260,000	273,000	268,000	290,000	299,000	278,000	251,000	250,000
Centre biparting									
8 floors	EA	276,000	286,000	282,000	309,000	314,000	292,000	265,000	265,000

14 24 00 Hydraulic Elevators

HYDRAULIC ELEVATOR EQUIPMENT

(Cars and entrances included, new building, front opening only)

Passenger elevator, Class A, maximum speed 150 fpm 5 floors,
capacity 2,000 lbs, basic cost for average commercial building

Item	UNITS	St. John's	Halifax	Montreal	Ottawa	Toronto	Winnipeg	Calgary	Vancouver
Single door from one side	EA	135,000	128,000	149,000	143,000	152,000	137,000	131,000	160,000
Centre biparting									
Basic prime coat finish	EA	141,000	138,000	159,000	152,000	161,000	150,000	143,000	172,000
Stainless steel	EA	142,000	136,000	156,000	150,000	159,000	146,000	138,000	172,000
Freight elevator, Class C, maximum speed 50 fpm,									
3 floors, capacity 10,000 lbs, average cost	EA	270,000	265,000	278,000	289,000	299,000	307,000	268,000	271,000

14 30 00 Escalators and Moving Stairs

14 31 00 Escalators

ESCALATORS

32" wide (tread width)

15' rise:

Item	UNITS	St. John's	Halifax	Montreal	Ottawa	Toronto	Winnipeg	Calgary	Vancouver
Stainless steel balustrade	EA	271,000	249,000	284,000	302,000	304,000	325,000	269,000	389,000
Glass balustrade	EA	264,000	245,000	278,000	294,000	299,000	318,000	265,000	380,000

14 32 00 Moving Walks

MOVING RAMPS & WALKS

Horizontal type (based on minimum length of 100')

36" wide:

Item	UNITS	St. John's	Halifax	Montreal	Ottawa	Toronto	Winnipeg	Calgary	Vancouver
Stainless steel balustrade	LF	4,300	4,240	4,820	4,940	4,970	5,240	4,510	5,180
Glass balustrade	LF	4,390	4,330	4,880	5,000	5,030	5,300	4,600	5,240
Inclined type, 16' rise									
Glass or stainless steel panels:									
36" wide	EA	683,000	667,000	751,000	777,000	781,000	829,000	715,000	822,000

14 90 00 Other Conveying Equipment

14 91 00 Facility Chutes

CHUTES

Garbage and Linen chutes, including doors, sprinklers,
sanitizing system and sound insulation, 12' floor height

Aluminized steel:

Item	UNITS	St. John's	Halifax	Montreal	Ottawa	Toronto	Winnipeg	Calgary	Vancouver
24" dia., 18 ga, complete system	FLOOR	2,300	2,300	2,180	2,190	2,150	2,180	2,050	2,540
Stainless steel:									
24" dia., 18 ga, complete system	FLOOR	4,180	4,190	3,930	4,240	4,160	4,190	3,890	4,740
Chute accessories									
Sanitizer	EA	321.00	322.00	298.00	325.00	318.00	318.00	298.00	364.00

14 92 00 Pneumatic Tube Systems

PNEUMATIC TUBE SYSTEM

Price per station, average 300' apart, 2 zones and up
fully automatic system controlled:

Item	UNITS	St. John's	Halifax	Montreal	Ottawa	Toronto	Winnipeg	Calgary	Vancouver
4" dia.	EA	35,000	35,000	35,000	35,700	29,800	41,200	37,500	34,800
6" dia.	EA	44,700	44,700	44,000	45,600	37,900	51,700	48,000	43,900

Item	UNITS	St. John's	Halifax	Montreal	Ottawa	Toronto	Winnipeg	Calgary	Vancouver
21: FIRE SUPPRESSION									
21 11 00 Facility Fire-Suppression Water-Service Piping									
SPECIALTIES									
Siamese pumper connection:									
4" x 2 1/2"	EA	1,390	1,280	1,300	1,320	1,310	1,410	1,350	1,410
Check valve, 4" dia.	EA	951.00	875.00	888.00	906.00	897.00	964.00	924.00	969.00
Double gate and check valves, assembly with bronze trimmings:									
4" dia.	EA	11,900	10,900	11,100	11,300	11,200	12,000	11,500	12,100
21 12 00 Fire-Suppression Standpipes									
STANDPIPE & FIRE HOSE EQUIPMENT									
Cabinets, c/w glass panel, valve, hose, rack and ABC fire extinguisher									
Surface mounted	EA	1,630	1,500	1,520	1,560	1,540	1,660	1,590	1,660
Recessed	EA	1,660	1,530	1,550	1,590	1,570	1,690	1,620	1,700
Recessed, stainless steel	EA	2,340	2,150	2,190	2,230	2,210	2,380	2,280	2,390
21 13 00 Fire-Suppression Sprinkler Systems									
SPRINKLERS									
Systems priced per head including all required piping,									
accessories and equipment for a complete system									
Sprinkler heads 1 per 100 sf	EA	261.00	240.00	244.00	248.00	246.00	264.00	253.00	266.00
Sprinkler heads 1 per 150 sf	EA	285.00	262.00	266.00	272.00	269.00	289.00	277.00	291.00
21 20 00 Fire-Extinguishing Systems									
CARBON DIOXIDE EQUIPMENT									
Extinguishing systems									
Kitchen hood extinguishing system including carbon dioxide									
cylinder, distribution piping and 2 heads	EA	7,230	6,650	6,750	6,890	6,820	7,330	7,020	7,370
Extinguishers									
10 lbs capacity with wall brackets	EA	541.00	497.00	505.00	515.00	510.00	548.00	525.00	551.00
PRESSURIZED EXTINGUISHERS & FIRE BLANKETS									
Pressurized extinguishers									
Water extinguisher, 2.5 gal capacity with wall bracket	EA	252.00	232.00	236.00	240.00	238.00	256.00	245.00	257.00
Fire blankets									
Size 72" x 72"	EA	245.00	225.00	229.00	233.00	231.00	248.00	238.00	249.00
21 30 00 Fire Pumps									
Fire pump, electric driven, c/w jockey pump and controller									
250 GPM	EA	77,400	71,200	72,300	73,700	73,000	78,500	75,200	78,800
500 GPM	EA	90,300	83,100	84,300	86,100	85,200	91,600	87,800	92,000
1000 GPM	EA	102,000	93,600	95,000	97,000	96,000	103,000	98,900	104,000
1500 GPM	EA	123,000	113,000	115,000	117,000	116,000	125,000	119,000	125,000
Fire pump, diesel driven, c/w jockey pump and controller									
250 GPM	EA	87,100	80,100	81,400	83,000	82,200	88,400	84,700	88,800
500 GPM	EA	98,200	90,300	91,700	93,500	92,600	99,500	95,400	100,000
1000 GPM	EA	104,000	95,500	96,900	98,900	97,900	105,000	101,000	106,000
1500 GPM	EA	120,000	110,000	112,000	114,000	113,000	121,000	116,000	122,000
22: PLUMBING									
22 05 00 Common Work Results for Plumbing									
VALVES, BRONZE									
VALVES AND COCKS (manual)									
Gate valves									
Bronze 200 psi water or 125 psi steam pressure, screwed									
or soldered:									
1/2"	EA	124.00	114.00	116.00	118.00	117.00	126.00	121.00	126.00
3/4"	EA	154.00	141.00	144.00	146.00	145.00	156.00	149.00	157.00
1"	EA	186.00	171.00	173.00	177.00	175.00	188.00	180.00	189.00
1 1/4"	EA	239.00	219.00	223.00	227.00	225.00	242.00	232.00	243.00
1 1/2"	EA	286.00	263.00	267.00	273.00	270.00	290.00	278.00	292.00
2"	EA	324.00	298.00	303.00	309.00	306.00	329.00	315.00	330.00
I.b.b.m. Outside screw and yoke:									
200 psi water or 125 psi steam pressure,									
flanged:									
2 1/2"	EA	822.00	756.00	767.00	783.00	775.00	833.00	798.00	837.00
3"	EA	914.00	840.00	853.00	871.00	862.00	927.00	888.00	931.00
4"	EA	1,340	1,230	1,250	1,270	1,260	1,350	1,300	1,360
6"	EA	2,150	1,980	2,010	2,050	2,030	2,180	2,090	2,190
8"	EA	3,510	3,230	3,280	3,340	3,310	3,560	3,410	3,570

Item	UNITS	St. John's	Halifax	Montreal	Ottawa	Toronto	Winnipeg	Calgary	Vancouver
Globe valves									
Bronze 300 psi water or 150 psi steam pressure, screwed or									
soldered:									
1/2"	EA	157.00	144.00	147.00	149.00	148.00	159.00	152.00	160.00
3/4"	EA	180.00	166.00	168.00	172.00	170.00	183.00	175.00	184.00
1"	EA	264.00	243.00	247.00	251.00	249.00	268.00	256.00	269.00
1 1/4"	EA	395.00	364.00	369.00	377.00	373.00	401.00	384.00	403.00
1 1/2"	EA	424.00	390.00	396.00	404.00	400.00	430.00	412.00	432.00
2"	EA	594.00	546.00	554.00	566.00	560.00	602.00	577.00	605.00
I.b.b.m. Outside screw and yoke:									
200 psi water or 125 psi steam pressure,									
flanged:									
2 1/2"	EA	961.00	884.00	898.00	916.00	907.00	975.00	934.00	980.00
3"	EA	1,080	995	1,010	1,030	1,020	1,100	1,050	1,100
4"	EA	1,690	1,550	1,570	1,610	1,590	1,710	1,640	1,720
6"	EA	2,780	2,550	2,590	2,650	2,620	2,820	2,700	2,830
8"	EA	4,660	4,290	4,360	4,440	4,400	4,730	4,530	4,750
Swing check valves									
Bronze 300 psi water or 150 psi steam pressure, screwed									
or soldered:									
1/2"	EA	110.00	101.00	103.00	105.00	104.00	112.00	107.00	112.00
3/4"	EA	136.00	125.00	127.00	129.00	128.00	138.00	132.00	138.00
1"	EA	180.00	166.00	168.00	172.00	170.00	183.00	175.00	184.00
1 1/4"	EA	224.00	206.00	209.00	213.00	211.00	227.00	217.00	228.00
1 1/2"	EA	286.00	263.00	267.00	273.00	270.00	290.00	278.00	292.00
2"	EA	401.00	369.00	374.00	382.00	378.00	406.00	389.00	408.00
I.b.b.m. 200 psi water or 125 psi steam pressure,									
flanged:									
2 1/2"	EA	670.00	616.00	626.00	638.00	632.00	679.00	651.00	683.00
3"	EA	747.00	687.00	698.00	712.00	705.00	758.00	726.00	761.00
4"	EA	1,160	1,060	1,080	1,100	1,090	1,170	1,120	1,180
6"	EA	2,070	1,900	1,930	1,970	1,950	2,100	2,010	2,110
8"	EA	3,490	3,210	3,260	3,320	3,290	3,540	3,390	3,550
Ball valves									
Bronze 600 psi water pressure, screwed or soldered:									
1/2"	EA	50.00	46.00	46.70	47.70	47.20	50.70	48.60	51.00
3/4"	EA	68.40	62.90	63.90	65.10	64.50	69.30	66.40	69.70
1"	EA	90.70	83.50	84.70	86.50	85.60	92.00	88.20	92.40
1 1/4"	EA	125.00	115.00	117.00	119.00	118.00	127.00	122.00	127.00
1 1/2"	EA	149.00	137.00	140.00	142.00	141.00	152.00	145.00	152.00
2"	EA	210.00	193.00	196.00	200.00	198.00	213.00	204.00	214.00
Butterfly valves									
Bronze disc, wafer type, buna seat:									
2 1/2"	EA	582.00	535.00	544.00	554.00	549.00	590.00	565.00	593.00
3"	EA	603.00	555.00	563.00	575.00	569.00	612.00	586.00	615.00
4"	EA	670.00	616.00	626.00	638.00	632.00	679.00	651.00	683.00
6"	EA	822.00	756.00	767.00	783.00	775.00	833.00	798.00	837.00
8"	EA	1,140	1,050	1,070	1,090	1,080	1,160	1,110	1,170
WATER METER ASSEMBLY									
Including communication register c/w by-pass									
Sealed register meter, positive displacement type									
1" pipe size	EA	1,690	1,550	1,570	1,610	1,590	1,710	1,640	1,720
2" pipe size	EA	3,750	3,450	3,500	3,580	3,540	3,810	3,650	3,820
Compound water meter									
3" pipe size	EA	11,100	10,200	10,400	10,600	10,500	11,300	10,800	11,300
Turbine type water meter, c/w integral strainer and test outlet									
4" pipe size	EA	12,900	11,900	12,100	12,300	12,200	13,100	12,600	13,200
6" pipe size	EA	25,400	23,400	23,800	24,200	24,000	25,800	24,700	25,900
8" pipe size	EA	34,700	31,900	32,400	33,000	32,700	35,200	33,700	35,300

22 07 00 Plumbing Insulation
PIPE INSULATION

Item	UNITS	St. John's	Halifax	Montreal	Ottawa	Toronto	Winnipeg	Calgary	Vancouver
Glass fibre, factory jacket									
1/2" thick:									
1/2"	LF	6.14	5.65	5.73	5.85	5.79	6.23	5.96	6.25
3/4"	LF	6.62	6.09	6.19	6.31	6.25	6.72	6.44	6.75
1"	LF	6.75	6.21	6.31	6.43	6.37	6.85	6.56	6.88
1 1/4"	LF	7.01	6.45	6.55	6.68	6.61	7.11	6.81	7.14
1 1/2"	LF	7.69	7.07	7.18	7.33	7.25	7.80	7.47	7.83
2"	LF	8.08	7.43	7.54	7.70	7.62	8.19	7.85	8.23
2 1/2"	LF	8.37	7.70	7.82	7.97	7.89	8.49	8.13	8.53
3"	LF	9.05	8.32	8.45	8.62	8.53	9.17	8.79	9.22
4"	LF	0.01	0.01	0.01	0.01	0.01	0.01	0.01	0.01
5"	LF	0.01	0.01	0.01	0.01	0.01	0.01	0.01	0.01
6"	LF	0.01	0.01	0.01	0.01	0.01	0.01	0.01	0.01
1" thick:									
1/2"	LF	7.01	6.45	6.55	6.68	6.61	7.11	6.81	7.14
3/4"	LF	7.43	6.84	6.94	7.08	7.01	7.54	7.22	7.57
1"	LF	7.75	7.13	7.24	7.39	7.32	7.86	7.53	7.90
1 1/4"	LF	8.17	7.52	7.63	7.79	7.71	8.29	7.94	8.33
1 1/2"	LF	8.63	7.93	8.06	8.22	8.14	8.75	8.38	8.79
2"	LF	9.14	8.41	8.54	8.71	8.63	9.27	8.88	9.32

Item	UNITS	St. John's	Halifax	Montreal	Ottawa	Toronto	Winnipeg	Calgary	Vancouver
2 1/2"	LF	10.00	9.24	9.38	9.57	9.48	10.20	9.76	10.20
3"	LF	10.60	9.75	9.90	10.10	10.00	10.70	10.30	10.80
4"	LF	13.20	12.20	12.40	12.60	12.50	13.40	12.90	13.50
5"	LF	16.60	15.20	15.50	15.80	15.60	16.80	16.10	16.90
6"	LF	16.70	15.30	15.60	15.90	15.70	16.90	16.20	17.00
8"	LF	20.30	18.60	18.90	19.30	19.10	20.50	19.70	20.60
10"	LF	23.00	21.10	21.50	21.90	21.70	23.30	22.30	23.40
12"	LF	28.90	26.60	27.00	27.60	27.30	29.40	28.10	29.50

COVER FOR PIPE INSULATION
6 oz. canvas

Item	UNITS	St. John's	Halifax	Montreal	Ottawa	Toronto	Winnipeg	Calgary	Vancouver
1/2"	LF	5.82	5.35	5.43	5.54	5.49	5.90	5.65	5.93
3/4"	LF	5.94	5.47	5.55	5.66	5.61	6.03	5.78	6.06
1"	LF	6.01	5.53	5.61	5.73	5.67	6.09	5.84	6.12
1 1/4"	LF	6.07	5.59	5.67	5.79	5.73	6.16	5.90	6.19
1 1/2"	LF	6.17	5.68	5.76	5.88	5.82	6.26	6.00	6.29
2"	LF	6.40	5.88	5.97	6.10	6.04	6.49	6.22	6.52
2 1/2"	LF	6.82	6.27	6.37	6.50	6.43	6.91	6.62	6.95
3"	LF	7.20	6.63	6.73	6.87	6.80	7.31	7.00	7.34
4"	LF	7.50	6.89	7.00	7.14	7.07	7.60	7.28	7.64
5"	LF	7.98	7.34	7.45	7.60	7.53	8.09	7.75	8.13
6"	LF	9.08	8.35	8.48	8.65	8.56	9.21	8.82	9.25
8"	LF	9.95	9.15	9.29	9.48	9.39	10.10	9.67	10.10
10"	LF	11.20	10.30	10.50	10.70	10.60	11.40	10.90	11.50
12"	LF	11.80	10.80	11.00	11.20	11.10	11.90	11.40	12.00

22 10 00 Plumbing Piping

PIPE, COPPER
Copper pressure piping, based on 3 m (10') of pipe, including one pipe support, and solder

Type m:

Item	UNITS	St. John's	Halifax	Montreal	Ottawa	Toronto	Winnipeg	Calgary	Vancouver
1/2"	LF	13.70	12.60	12.80	13.00	12.90	13.90	13.30	13.90
3/4"	LF	16.10	14.80	15.10	15.40	15.20	16.40	15.70	16.40
1"	LF	19.40	17.90	18.20	18.50	18.30	19.70	18.90	19.80
1 1/4"	LF	24.90	22.90	23.30	23.80	23.50	25.30	24.20	25.40
1 1/2"	LF	30.90	28.40	28.90	29.50	29.20	31.40	30.00	31.50
2"	LF	45.90	42.20	42.80	43.70	43.30	46.50	44.60	46.70
2 1/2"	LF	63.60	58.50	59.40	60.60	60.00	64.50	61.80	64.80
3"	LF	80.10	73.70	74.80	76.30	75.60	81.30	77.90	81.60

Type l:

Item	UNITS	St. John's	Halifax	Montreal	Ottawa	Toronto	Winnipeg	Calgary	Vancouver
1/2"	LF	15.20	14.00	14.20	14.50	14.40	15.40	14.80	15.50
3/4"	LF	18.50	17.00	17.30	17.60	17.40	18.70	18.00	18.80
1"	LF	23.30	21.40	21.80	22.20	22.00	23.60	22.60	23.70
1 1/4"	LF	28.50	26.20	26.60	27.10	26.90	28.90	27.70	29.00
1 1/2"	LF	34.20	31.50	32.00	32.60	32.30	34.70	33.30	34.90
2"	LF	50.70	46.70	47.40	48.30	47.90	51.40	49.30	51.70
2 1/2"	LF	71.10	65.40	66.40	67.70	67.10	72.10	69.10	72.40
3"	LF	90.80	83.50	84.80	86.50	85.60	92.10	88.20	92.50

Type k:

Item	UNITS	St. John's	Halifax	Montreal	Ottawa	Toronto	Winnipeg	Calgary	Vancouver
1/2"	LF	17.30	15.90	16.10	16.50	16.30	17.50	16.80	17.60
3/4"	LF	23.80	21.90	22.20	22.70	22.40	24.10	23.10	24.20
1"	LF	28.80	26.50	26.90	27.50	27.20	29.20	28.00	29.40
1 1/4"	LF	34.20	31.50	32.00	32.60	32.30	34.70	33.30	34.90
1 1/2"	LF	41.70	38.30	38.90	39.70	39.30	42.30	40.50	42.50
2"	LF	59.80	55.00	55.80	57.00	56.40	60.60	58.10	60.90
2 1/2"	LF	83.00	76.40	77.60	79.10	78.30	84.20	80.70	84.60
3"	LF	109.00	100.00	102.00	104.00	103.00	111.00	106.00	111.00

22 13 00 Facility Sanitary Sewerage
Copper drainage piping, based on 3 m (10') of pipe, including one support, and solder

Drainage waste and vent:

Item	UNITS	St. John's	Halifax	Montreal	Ottawa	Toronto	Winnipeg	Calgary	Vancouver
1 1/4"	LF	21.10	19.40	19.70	20.10	19.90	21.40	20.50	21.50
1 1/2"	LF	23.70	21.80	22.10	22.60	22.30	24.00	23.00	24.10
2"	LF	30.60	28.20	28.60	29.20	28.90	31.10	29.80	31.20
3"	LF	43.30	39.80	40.40	41.30	40.80	43.90	42.10	44.10

PIPE, CAST IRON
Cast iron drainage piping, based on 3 m (10') of pipe, including, one support and jointing material

Hub and spigot:

Item	UNITS	St. John's	Halifax	Montreal	Ottawa	Toronto	Winnipeg	Calgary	Vancouver
3"	LF	32.60	30.00	30.50	31.10	30.80	33.10	31.70	33.20
4"	LF	40.10	36.90	37.40	38.20	37.80	40.60	38.90	40.80
6"	LF	63.00	58.00	58.80	60.00	59.40	63.90	61.20	64.20
8"	LF	92.70	85.30	86.60	88.40	87.50	94.00	90.10	94.50
10"	LF	137.00	126.00	128.00	130.00	129.00	139.00	133.00	139.00
12"	LF	165.00	152.00	154.00	157.00	155.00	167.00	160.00	168.00

Mechanical joint:

Item	UNITS	St. John's	Halifax	Montreal	Ottawa	Toronto	Winnipeg	Calgary	Vancouver
3"	LF	27.20	25.00	25.40	25.90	25.60	27.60	26.40	27.70
4"	LF	32.60	30.00	30.50	31.10	30.80	33.10	31.70	33.20
6"	LF	49.10	45.20	45.90	46.80	46.30	49.80	47.70	50.00
8"	LF	73.30	67.50	68.50	69.90	69.20	74.40	71.30	74.70
10"	LF	108.00	99.30	101.00	103.00	102.00	109.00	105.00	110.00

Item	UNITS	St. John's	Halifax	Montreal	Ottawa	Toronto	Winnipeg	Calgary	Vancouver
PIPE, PLASTIC									
Plastic drainage piping, based on 3 m (10') of pipe, including									
one support and jointing material									
ABS drainage waste and vent:									
1 1/4"	LF	15.40	14.10	14.40	14.70	14.50	15.60	14.90	15.70
1 1/2"	LF	15.30	14.10	14.30	14.60	14.40	15.50	14.90	15.60
2"	LF	17.30	15.90	16.10	16.50	16.30	17.50	16.80	17.60
3"	LF	26.70	24.60	25.00	25.50	25.20	27.10	26.00	27.20

22 13 19 Sanitary Waste Piping Specialties

TRAPS

Item	UNITS	St. John's	Halifax	Montreal	Ottawa	Toronto	Winnipeg	Calgary	Vancouver
Trap primer including 25' type I, 1/2" copper									
pressure pipe									
Bronze, 1/2" dia.	EA	642.00	591.00	600.00	612.00	606.00	651.00	624.00	654.00

DRAINS

Item	UNITS	St. John's	Halifax	Montreal	Ottawa	Toronto	Winnipeg	Calgary	Vancouver
Floor drain including 10' of connecting drainage pipe									
Cast iron body, nickel bronze top:									
2"	EA	531.00	488.00	496.00	506.00	501.00	539.00	516.00	541.00
3"	EA	585.00	538.00	546.00	558.00	552.00	593.00	569.00	596.00
4"	EA	669.00	615.00	625.00	637.00	631.00	678.00	650.00	681.00
Funnel type, cast iron body, polished brass top:									
2"	EA	673.00	619.00	629.00	641.00	635.00	683.00	654.00	686.00
3"	EA	728.00	670.00	680.00	694.00	687.00	739.00	708.00	742.00
4"	EA	812.00	747.00	758.00	774.00	766.00	823.00	789.00	827.00

GRATE & FRAME

Item	UNITS	St. John's	Halifax	Montreal	Ottawa	Toronto	Winnipeg	Calgary	Vancouver
Trench grating									
Medium duty golden duct alloy grate and frame:									
6"	LF	157.00	145.00	147.00	150.00	148.00	160.00	153.00	160.00
12"	LF	249.00	229.00	233.00	237.00	235.00	253.00	242.00	254.00
15"	LF	259.00	238.00	242.00	247.00	244.00	262.00	251.00	264.00
Heavy duty golden duct alloy grate and frame:									
12"	LF	242.00	223.00	226.00	231.00	229.00	246.00	235.00	247.00
Extra heavy duty golden duct alloy grate and frame:									
9"	LF	261.00	240.00	244.00	249.00	247.00	265.00	254.00	266.00
18"	LF	468.00	431.00	438.00	446.00	442.00	475.00	455.00	477.00
Roof drains including 10' of connecting drainage pipe									
Cast iron body with underdeck clamp:									
2"	EA	642.00	591.00	600.00	612.00	606.00	651.00	624.00	654.00
3"	EA	697.00	642.00	651.00	665.00	658.00	707.00	678.00	711.00
4"	EA	782.00	720.00	731.00	745.00	738.00	793.00	760.00	797.00
6"	EA	867.00	798.00	810.00	826.00	818.00	879.00	843.00	883.00
Cast iron body meter flow with underdeck clamp:									
2"	EA	734.00	675.00	685.00	699.00	692.00	744.00	713.00	747.00
3"	EA	823.00	757.00	768.00	784.00	776.00	834.00	799.00	838.00
4"	EA	851.00	783.00	795.00	811.00	803.00	863.00	827.00	867.00
6"	EA	1,110	1,020	1,040	1,060	1,050	1,130	1,080	1,130

CLEANOUTS

Item	UNITS	St. John's	Halifax	Montreal	Ottawa	Toronto	Winnipeg	Calgary	Vancouver
Cleanouts									
Galvanized with cut-off caulking, ferrule and nickel bronze cover:									
2"	EA	318.00	293.00	297.00	303.00	300.00	323.00	309.00	324.00
3"	EA	348.00	320.00	325.00	331.00	328.00	353.00	338.00	354.00
4"	EA	400.00	368.00	373.00	381.00	377.00	405.00	388.00	407.00
6"	EA	734.00	675.00	685.00	699.00	692.00	744.00	713.00	747.00

22 31 00 Domestic Water Softeners

WATER SOFTENER

Item	UNITS	St. John's	Halifax	Montreal	Ottawa	Toronto	Winnipeg	Calgary	Vancouver
Water softeners (according to grain capacity)									
Semi-automatic									
20,000	EA	1,380	1,270	1,290	1,310	1,300	1,400	1,340	1,400
Fully automatic									
20,000	EA	1,740	1,600	1,620	1,660	1,640	1,760	1,690	1,770
30,000	EA	1,790	1,650	1,670	1,710	1,690	1,820	1,740	1,830
40,000	EA	1,970	1,810	1,840	1,880	1,860	2,000	1,920	2,010
60,000	EA	2,120	1,950	1,980	2,020	2,000	2,150	2,060	2,160
105,000	EA	3,360	3,090	3,140	3,200	3,170	3,410	3,270	3,420

22 33 00 Electric Domestic Water Heaters

WATER HEATERS

Item	UNITS	St. John's	Halifax	Montreal	Ottawa	Toronto	Winnipeg	Calgary	Vancouver
Hot water storage heaters, no wiring or plumbing included.									
Electric:									
12.0 imp. gals.	EA	1,060	975	990	1,010	1,000	1,080	1,030	1,080
22.1 imp.gals.	EA	1,070	985	1,000	1,020	1,010	1,090	1,040	1,090
30.0 imp.gals.	EA	1,070	985	1,000	1,020	1,010	1,090	1,040	1,090
40.0 imp. gals.	EA	1,130	1,040	1,060	1,080	1,070	1,150	1,100	1,160
60.0 imp. gals.	EA	1,310	1,210	1,230	1,250	1,240	1,330	1,280	1,340

Item	UNITS	St. John's	Halifax	Montreal	Ottawa	Toronto	Winnipeg	Calgary	Vancouver
22 34 00 Fuel-Fired Domestic Water Heaters									
WATER HEATERS									
Hot water storage heaters, no wiring or plumbing included.									
Fuel fired:									
25.0 imp. gals.	EA	1,330	1,220	1,240	1,260	1,250	1,340	1,290	1,350
33.3 imp. gals.	EA	1,460	1,350	1,370	1,390	1,380	1,480	1,420	1,490
41.6 imp. gals.	EA	1,830	1,690	1,710	1,750	1,730	1,860	1,780	1,870
22 40 00 Plumbing Fixtures									
Including plumbing brass and 15' of connecting pipe for									
each service, carrier not included.									
WATER CLOSETS									
Vitreous china water closets									
Floor mounted:									
One-piece closet, combination...........	EA	2,300	2,120	2,150	2,190	2,170	2,330	2,240	2,340
With tank, regular rim...........	EA	1,620	1,490	1,510	1,550	1,530	1,640	1,580	1,650
With tank, elongated rim...........	EA	1,690	1,550	1,570	1,610	1,590	1,710	1,640	1,720
With flush valve, elongated rim...........	EA	2,100	1,930	1,960	2,000	1,980	2,130	2,040	2,140
Wall mounted:									
With tank, regular rim...........	EA	1,870	1,720	1,740	1,780	1,760	1,890	1,810	1,900
With flush valve, elongated rim...........	EA	2,190	2,020	2,050	2,090	2,070	2,230	2,130	2,240
Shower mixing valves									
Thermostatic control...........	EA	616.00	566.00	575.00	587.00	581.00	625.00	598.00	627.00
URINALS									
Vitreous china urinals									
Floor mounted:									
With tank	EA	2,760	2,540	2,570	2,630	2,600	2,800	2,680	2,810
With flush valve...........	EA	2,410	2,210	2,250	2,290	2,270	2,440	2,340	2,450
Wall mounted:									
With tank	EA	2,600	2,390	2,430	2,470	2,450	2,630	2,520	2,650
With flush valve...........	EA	2,330	2,150	2,180	2,220	2,200	2,370	2,270	2,380
LAVATORIES									
Lavatories									
Vitreous china:									
Wall hung, 20" x 18"...........	EA	1,710	1,570	1,590	1,630	1,610	1,730	1,660	1,740
Countertop, 21" x 19"...........	EA	1,710	1,570	1,590	1,630	1,610	1,730	1,660	1,740
Countertop, 19" x 16", oval...........	EA	1,690	1,550	1,570	1,610	1,590	1,710	1,640	1,720
Cast iron enamelled:									
Wall hung, 19" x 17"...........	EA	2,020	1,860	1,890	1,930	1,910	2,050	1,970	2,060
Countertop, 21" x 17"...........	EA	1,890	1,740	1,760	1,800	1,780	1,910	1,830	1,920
Steel enamelled									
Countertop, 21" x 17"...........	EA	1,730	1,590	1,610	1,650	1,630	1,750	1,680	1,760
Countertop, 18" dia...........	EA	1,730	1,590	1,610	1,650	1,630	1,750	1,680	1,760
SINKS									
Kitchen sinks									
Stainless steel:									
Single bowl, 20" x 20 1/2" x 7"...........	EA	1,630	1,500	1,520	1,560	1,540	1,660	1,590	1,660
Double bowl, 20 1/2" x 31" x 7"...........	EA	1,820	1,680	1,700	1,740	1,720	1,850	1,770	1,860
Service sinks									
Cast iron enamelled:									
Wall hung, 22" x 18"...........	EA	3,980	3,660	3,710	3,790	3,750	4,030	3,860	4,050
Mop receptor, floor type:									
22" x 18"...........	EA	3,590	3,310	3,360	3,420	3,390	3,640	3,490	3,660
LAUNDRY SINKS									
Laundry sinks and trays									
Steel enamelled sinks:									
Single bowl, 24" x 21"...........	EA	1,730	1,590	1,610	1,650	1,630	1,750	1,680	1,760
Double bowl, 32" x 21"...........	EA	2,020	1,860	1,890	1,930	1,910	2,050	1,970	2,060
Single compartment, 22" x 22"...........	EA	1,860	1,710	1,730	1,770	1,750	1,880	1,800	1,890
Double compartment, 44 1/2" x 22"...........	EA	2,240	2,060	2,090	2,130	2,110	2,270	2,170	2,280
BATHS									
Bathtubs									
Cast iron enamelled, recessed:									
5' long	EA	4,650	4,280	4,350	4,430	4,390	4,720	4,520	4,740
Steel enamelled, recessed:									
5' long	EA	3,080	2,840	2,880	2,940	2,910	3,130	3,000	3,140
Fibreglass, one piece with sidewalls:									
5' long	EA	4,240	3,900	3,960	4,040	4,000	4,300	4,120	4,320
SHOWERS									
Showers									
Shower head and pressure balancing valve...........	EA	1,140	1,050	1,070	1,090	1,080	1,160	1,110	1,170
Prefabricated shower, medium duty valve, rod and curtain...........	EA	2,590	2,380	2,420	2,460	2,440	2,620	2,510	2,640
Prefabricated shower, medium duty valve and door...........	EA	2,980	2,740	2,780	2,840	2,810	3,020	2,890	3,030
CARRIERS/SUPPORTS									
Fixture chair carriers									
Lavatory	EA	324.00	298.00	303.00	309.00	306.00	329.00	315.00	330.00
Water closet...........	EA	530.00	488.00	495.00	505.00	500.00	538.00	515.00	540.00
Urinal	EA	276.00	254.00	257.00	263.00	260.00	280.00	268.00	281.00

Item	UNITS	St. John's	Halifax	Montreal	Ottawa	Toronto	Winnipeg	Calgary	Vancouver
HYDRANTS									
Wall hydrants non-freeze type 3/4" dia., 12" wall									
including 15' of connecting pipe									
Exposed	EA	778.00	716.00	727.00	741.00	734.00	789.00	756.00	793.00
Concealed	EA	969.00	891.00	905.00	923.00	914.00	983.00	941.00	987.00
22 47 00 Drinking Fountains and Water Coolers									
Based on stainless steel fixture including plumbing brass and									
15' of connecting pipe for each service, carrier not incl.									
DRINKING FOUNTAIN									
Non-refrigerated drinking fountains:									
Wall hung, basic unit	EA	1,880	1,730	1,750	1,790	1,770	1,900	1,820	1,910
Wall hung, hi-lo dual unit	EA	3,950	3,640	3,690	3,770	3,730	4,010	3,840	4,030
Refrigerated drinking fountains:									
Wall hung, basic unit	EA	3,980	3,660	3,710	3,790	3,750	4,030	3,860	4,050
Wall hung, hi-lo dual unit	EA	5,460	5,020	5,100	5,200	5,150	5,540	5,300	5,560
22 66 00 Chemical-Waste Systems for Laboratory									
and Healthcare Facilities									
PIPE, GLASS									
Glass drainage piping, based on 3 m (10') of pipe, including									
pipe supports and jointing material									
Glass pipe:									
1 1/2"	LF	37.80	34.80	35.30	36.00	35.70	38.30	36.70	38.50
2"	LF	47.20	43.40	44.10	44.90	44.50	47.80	45.80	48.10
3"	LF	63.30	58.20	59.10	60.30	59.70	64.20	61.50	64.50
4"	LF	103.00	95.10	96.60	98.50	97.50	105.00	100.00	105.00
6"	LF	175.00	161.00	163.00	167.00	165.00	177.00	170.00	178.00

23: HEATING, VENTILATING, & AIR CONDITIONING

23 07 00 HVAC Insulation

Item	UNITS	St. John's	Halifax	Montreal	Ottawa	Toronto	Winnipeg	Calgary	Vancouver
DUCTWORK INSULATION									
Internal									
Glass fibre acoustic lining:									
1/2"	SF	4.73	4.35	4.41	4.50	4.46	4.79	4.59	4.82
1"	SF	5.32	4.89	4.97	5.07	5.02	5.39	5.17	5.42
External									
Glass fibre thermal flexible:									
1"	SF	4.63	4.26	4.32	4.41	4.37	4.69	4.50	4.72
2"	SF	5.57	5.13	5.21	5.31	5.26	5.65	5.42	5.68
Glass fibre thermal rigid, c/w canvas jacket:									
1"	SF	7.62	7.01	7.12	7.26	7.19	7.73	7.41	7.77
2"	SF	8.89	8.18	8.31	8.47	8.39	9.02	8.64	9.06

23 10 00 Facility Fuel Systems

Item	UNITS	St. John's	Halifax	Montreal	Ottawa	Toronto	Winnipeg	Calgary	Vancouver
UNDERGROUND STORAGE TANKS									
Oil storage tanks									
Underground steel tank including hold-down straps,									
anchors, saddles, excavation, bedding and backfilling									
Small/domestic									
250 gals.	EA	4,260	3,920	3,980	4,060	4,020	4,320	4,140	4,340
500 gals.	EA	6,430	5,920	6,010	6,130	6,070	6,530	6,250	6,560
Large/commercial									
1,000 gals.	EA	9,650	8,870	9,010	9,190	9,100	9,780	9,370	9,830
2,200 gals.	EA	15,100	13,800	14,100	14,300	14,200	15,300	14,600	15,300
5,500 gals.	EA	42,600	39,200	39,800	40,600	40,200	43,200	41,400	43,400
11,000 gals.	EA	67,800	62,400	63,400	64,600	64,000	68,800	65,900	69,100
36" access sleeve to grade with 24" manhole	EA	7,590	6,980	7,090	7,230	7,160	7,700	7,370	7,730

23 21 13 Hydronic Piping

Item	UNITS	St. John's	Halifax	Montreal	Ottawa	Toronto	Winnipeg	Calgary	Vancouver
PIPE, STEEL									
Galvanized steel pressure piping, based on 3 m (10') of pipe									
for screwed piping and 6 m (20') of pipe for flanged piping,									
including pipe support, and jointing material									
Schedule 40, screwed:									
1/2"	LF	22.00	20.20	20.50	21.00	20.80	22.30	21.40	22.40
3/4"	LF	24.70	22.70	23.10	23.50	23.30	25.00	24.00	25.10
1"	LF	30.70	28.20	28.70	29.20	29.00	31.10	29.80	31.30
1 1/4"	LF	35.90	33.00	33.50	34.20	33.80	36.40	34.80	36.50
1 1/2"	LF	41.40	38.00	38.60	39.40	39.00	41.90	40.20	42.10
2"	LF	54.00	49.60	50.40	51.40	50.90	54.70	52.40	55.00

Item	UNITS	St. John's	Halifax	Montreal	Ottawa	Toronto	Winnipeg	Calgary	Vancouver
Black steel pressure piping, based on 3 m (10') for screwed piping and 6 m (20') of pipe for welded piping including pipe support and jointing material									
Schedule 40, screwed:									
1/2"	LF	18.40	16.90	17.20	17.50	17.30	18.60	17.90	18.70
3/4"	LF	20.40	18.80	19.10	19.50	19.30	20.70	19.80	20.80
1"	LF	24.80	22.90	23.20	23.70	23.40	25.20	24.10	25.30
1 1/4"	LF	28.70	26.40	26.80	27.30	27.10	29.10	27.90	29.20
1 1/2"	LF	32.60	30.00	30.50	31.10	30.80	33.10	31.70	33.20
2"	LF	42.00	38.60	39.20	40.00	39.60	42.60	40.80	42.80
Schedule 40, welded:									
2 1/2"	LF	52.00	47.80	48.60	49.60	49.10	52.80	50.50	53.00
3"	LF	59.40	54.70	55.50	56.60	56.10	60.30	57.80	60.60
4"	LF	77.20	71.00	72.10	73.60	72.80	78.30	75.00	78.70
6"	LF	125.00	115.00	117.00	119.00	118.00	127.00	122.00	128.00
8"	LF	178.00	163.00	166.00	169.00	168.00	180.00	173.00	181.00
Schedule 40, grooved:									
2 1/2"	LF	54.00	49.60	50.40	51.40	50.90	54.70	52.40	55.00
3"	LF	67.20	61.80	62.80	64.00	63.40	68.20	65.30	68.50
4"	LF	76.20	70.10	71.20	72.70	71.90	77.30	74.10	77.70
6"	LF	138.00	127.00	129.00	132.00	130.00	140.00	134.00	141.00
8"	LF	201.00	185.00	188.00	191.00	190.00	204.00	195.00	205.00

23 21 23 Pumps
PUMPS

Item	UNITS	St. John's	Halifax	Montreal	Ottawa	Toronto	Winnipeg	Calgary	Vancouver
In-line circulators									
Bronze body:									
3/4" to 1 1/2"	EA	1,070	985.00	1,000	1,020	1,010	1,090	1,040	1,090
Iron body:									
3/4" to 1 1/2"	EA	739.00	680.00	690.00	704.00	697.00	749.00	718.00	753.00
2"	EA	1,200	1,100	1,120	1,140	1,130	1,210	1,160	1,220
2 1/2"	EA	1,370	1,260	1,280	1,300	1,290	1,390	1,330	1,390
3"	EA	1,820	1,680	1,700	1,740	1,720	1,850	1,770	1,860
Base mounted, ball bearing type									
Iron body:									
1 hp	EA	2,860	2,630	2,670	2,730	2,700	2,900	2,780	2,920
3 hp	EA	3,490	3,210	3,260	3,320	3,290	3,540	3,390	3,550
5 hp	EA	3,990	3,670	3,720	3,800	3,760	4,040	3,870	4,060
7.5 hp	EA	6,410	5,900	5,990	6,110	6,050	6,500	6,230	6,530
10 hp	EA	7,450	6,850	6,960	7,100	7,030	7,560	7,240	7,590

23 30 00 HVAC Air Distribution
DUCTWORK

Item	UNITS	St. John's	Halifax	Montreal	Ottawa	Toronto	Winnipeg	Calgary	Vancouver
Rigid ducts, sheet metal including cleats and normal suspension									
Galvanized steel	LB	9.33	8.58	8.71	8.89	8.80	9.46	9.06	9.50
Aluminum	LB	16.70	15.40	15.60	15.90	15.80	17.00	16.30	17.00
Stainless steel	LB	13.20	12.20	12.30	12.60	12.50	13.40	12.80	13.50
Flexible ducts, aluminum, insulated									
4" dia.	LF	4.30	3.95	4.01	4.09	4.05	4.36	4.18	4.38
5" dia.	LF	5.01	4.61	4.68	4.77	4.72	5.08	4.87	5.10
6" dia.	LF	5.91	5.44	5.52	5.63	5.58	6.00	5.75	6.02
7" dia.	LF	6.95	6.39	6.49	6.62	6.55	7.04	6.75	7.08
8" dia.	LF	8.27	7.61	7.72	7.88	7.80	8.39	8.04	8.43
9" dia.	LF	9.30	8.56	8.69	8.87	8.78	9.44	9.04	9.48
10" dia.	LF	10.50	9.66	9.81	10.00	9.91	10.60	10.20	10.70
12" dia.	LF	14.00	12.90	13.10	13.40	13.20	14.20	13.60	14.30
14" dia.	LF	17.20	15.80	16.10	16.40	16.20	17.40	16.70	17.50
16" dia.	LF	22.00	20.20	20.50	21.00	20.80	22.30	21.40	22.40
Galvanized spiral ducts, uninsulated									
3" dia.	LF	4.65	4.28	4.35	4.43	4.39	4.72	4.52	4.74
4" dia.	LF	5.78	5.32	5.40	5.51	5.46	5.87	5.62	5.89
5" dia.	LF	6.91	6.36	6.46	6.59	6.52	7.01	6.72	7.04
6" dia.	LF	8.08	7.43	7.54	7.70	7.62	8.19	7.85	8.23
7" dia.	LF	8.59	7.90	8.03	8.19	8.11	8.72	8.35	8.76
8" dia.	LF	9.72	8.95	9.08	9.27	9.17	9.86	9.45	9.91
9" dia.	LF	10.90	9.99	10.10	10.30	10.20	11.00	10.50	11.10
10" dia.	LF	12.00	11.00	11.20	11.40	11.30	12.20	11.60	12.20
12" dia.	LF	14.20	13.10	13.30	13.60	13.40	14.40	13.80	14.50
14" dia.	LF	17.20	15.80	16.10	16.40	16.20	17.50	16.70	17.50
16" dia.	LF	19.10	17.50	17.80	18.20	18.00	19.30	18.50	19.40
18" dia.	LF	23.90	22.00	22.30	22.80	22.60	24.20	23.20	24.40
20" dia.	LF	26.00	23.90	24.30	24.80	24.50	26.40	25.30	26.50
22" dia.	LF	28.80	26.40	26.90	27.40	27.10	29.20	27.90	29.30
24" dia.	LF	31.50	28.90	29.40	30.00	29.70	31.90	30.60	32.10
28" dia.	LF	40.70	37.40	38.00	38.80	38.40	41.30	39.60	41.50
32" dia.	LF	47.20	43.40	44.10	44.90	44.50	47.80	45.80	48.10

CENTRAL AIR HANDLING UNITS

Central station modular units, with insulated casing, fans motors and drives, heating and cooling coils, with filters, humidifier and mixing box. Automatic controls not included.

Item	UNITS	St. John's	Halifax	Montreal	Ottawa	Toronto	Winnipeg	Calgary	Vancouver
Low pressure type:									
1,500 cfm	EA	24,000	22,000	22,400	22,800	22,600	24,300	23,300	24,400

Item	UNITS	St. John's	Halifax	Montreal	Ottawa	Toronto	Winnipeg	Calgary	Vancouver
3,000 cfm	EA	33,300	30,600	31,100	31,700	31,400	33,800	32,300	33,900
6,000 cfm	EA	44,800	41,200	41,900	42,700	42,300	45,500	43,600	45,700
10,000 cfm	EA	57,000	52,500	53,300	54,300	53,800	57,800	55,400	58,100
Medium pressure type:									
15,000 cfm	EA	90,900	83,700	84,900	86,700	85,800	92,200	88,400	92,700
20,000 cfm	EA	118,000	108,000	110,000	112,000	111,000	119,000	114,000	120,000
30,000 cfm	EA	165,000	152,000	154,000	158,000	156,000	168,000	161,000	168,000

23 34 00 HVAC Fans

FANS

Vane axial fans, for suspended mounting
Direct connected tubular belt driven fan class 1

Item	UNITS	St. John's	Halifax	Montreal	Ottawa	Toronto	Winnipeg	Calgary	Vancouver
3,000 cfm	EA	3,060	2,820	2,860	2,920	2,890	3,110	2,980	3,120
5,000 cfm	EA	4,970	4,570	4,640	4,740	4,690	5,040	4,830	5,070
7,000 cfm	EA	5,180	4,770	4,840	4,940	4,890	5,260	5,040	5,280
10,000 cfm	EA	5,480	5,040	5,120	5,220	5,170	5,560	5,330	5,580
15,000 cfm	EA	7,430	6,830	6,940	7,080	7,010	7,540	7,220	7,570
20,000 cfm	EA	14,400	13,300	13,500	13,700	13,600	14,600	14,000	14,700

Propeller fans
Direct driven through the wall plate type, unit not including
exhaust wall shutter:

Item	UNITS	St. John's	Halifax	Montreal	Ottawa	Toronto	Winnipeg	Calgary	Vancouver
12" dia., 1,000 cfm	EA	1,210	1,110	1,130	1,150	1,140	1,230	1,170	1,230
16" dia., 2,000 cfm	EA	1,460	1,350	1,370	1,390	1,380	1,480	1,420	1,490
24" dia., 5,000 cfm	EA	1,960	1,800	1,830	1,870	1,850	1,990	1,910	2,000
30" dia., 8,000 cfm	EA	2,370	2,180	2,220	2,260	2,240	2,410	2,310	2,420
36" dia., 15,000 cfm	EA	2,870	2,640	2,680	2,740	2,710	2,910	2,790	2,930
42" dia., 20,000 cfm	EA	3,160	2,910	2,950	3,010	2,980	3,200	3,070	3,220
48" dia., 30,000 cfm	EA	3,740	3,440	3,490	3,570	3,530	3,790	3,640	3,810
54" dia., 40,000 cfm	EA	4,340	3,990	4,050	4,130	4,090	4,400	4,210	4,420
60" dia., 50,000 cfm	EA	5,770	5,300	5,390	5,490	5,440	5,850	5,600	5,880
72" dia., 60,000 cfm	EA	8,640	7,950	8,070	8,230	8,150	8,760	8,390	8,800

Roof exhaust fans, back draft damper, prefabricated curb and
speed controller not included:
Centrifugal, aluminum, direct drive:

Item	UNITS	St. John's	Halifax	Montreal	Ottawa	Toronto	Winnipeg	Calgary	Vancouver
200 cfm	EA	897.00	825.00	838.00	854.00	846.00	909.00	871.00	914.00
420 cfm	EA	942.00	867.00	880.00	898.00	889.00	956.00	916.00	960.00
630 cfm	EA	957.00	880.00	894.00	912.00	903.00	971.00	930.00	975.00
850 cfm	EA	1,140	1,050	1,070	1,090	1,080	1,160	1,110	1,170
1,480 cfm	EA	1,460	1,350	1,370	1,390	1,380	1,480	1,420	1,490
2,330 cfm	EA	1,800	1,660	1,680	1,720	1,700	1,830	1,750	1,840
Centrifugal, aluminum, belt driven:									
630 cfm	EA	1,100	1,010	1,030	1,050	1,040	1,120	1,070	1,120
1,270 cfm	EA	1,460	1,350	1,370	1,390	1,380	1,480	1,420	1,490
1,910 cfm	EA	1,660	1,530	1,550	1,590	1,570	1,690	1,620	1,700
4,240 cfm	EA	1,900	1,750	1,770	1,810	1,790	1,920	1,840	1,930
6,000 cfm	EA	2,200	2,030	2,060	2,100	2,080	2,240	2,140	2,250
9,500 cfm	EA	4,400	4,050	4,110	4,190	4,150	4,460	4,270	4,480
14,400 cfm	EA	4,710	4,330	4,400	4,480	4,440	4,770	4,570	4,800

23 37 00 Air Outlets and Inlets

LOUVERS

Louvers
Fresh and exhaust air:

Item	UNITS	St. John's	Halifax	Montreal	Ottawa	Toronto	Winnipeg	Calgary	Vancouver
Galvanized steel	SF	47.20	43.40	44.10	44.90	44.50	47.80	45.80	48.10
Aluminum	SF	53.90	49.50	50.30	51.30	50.80	54.60	52.30	54.90

23 40 00 HVAC Air Cleaning Devices

AIR FILTERS

Permanent washable type, metal frame:

Item	UNITS	St. John's	Halifax	Montreal	Ottawa	Toronto	Winnipeg	Calgary	Vancouver
2" thick	SF	91.10	83.80	85.10	86.80	85.90	92.40	88.50	92.80
Electronic air cleaner									
Standard, residential type	EA	2,260	2,080	2,110	2,150	2,130	2,290	2,190	2,300
Glass fibre, throwaway type									
1"-20" x 20"	EA	8.86	8.15	8.28	8.44	8.36	8.99	8.61	9.03
2"-20" x 20"	EA	11.90	10.90	11.10	11.30	11.20	12.00	11.50	12.10

Item	UNITS	St. John's	Halifax	Montreal	Ottawa	Toronto	Winnipeg	Calgary	Vancouver
23 50 00 Central Heating Equipment									
23 51 00 Breechings, Chimneys, and Stacks									
CHIMNEY									
Chimney									
B vent c/w rain cap, 20 lf									
6" duct size	EA	818.00	753.00	764.00	780.00	772.00	830.00	795.00	834.00
8" duct size	EA	1,120	1,030	1,050	1,070	1,060	1,140	1,090	1,140
10" duct size	EA	1,960	1,800	1,830	1,870	1,850	1,990	1,910	2,000
12" duct size	EA	2,290	2,110	2,140	2,180	2,160	2,320	2,220	2,330
16" duct size	EA	3,210	2,950	3,000	3,060	3,030	3,260	3,120	3,270
23 52 00 Heating Boilers									
BOILERS									
Copper water tube boilers									
Atmospheric gas fired, commercial on/off type, hot water:									
204 mbh	EA	5,000	4,600	4,670	4,770	4,720	5,070	4,860	5,100
396 mbh	EA	6,320	5,810	5,900	6,020	5,960	6,410	6,140	6,440
627 mbh	EA	9,210	8,470	8,600	8,780	8,690	9,340	8,950	9,390
962 mbh	EA	11,600	10,600	10,800	11,000	10,900	11,700	11,200	11,800
2100 mbh	EA	19,600	18,000	18,300	18,700	18,500	19,900	19,100	20,000
Atmospheric gas fired, commercial modulating type, hot water:									
396 mbh	EA	7,930	7,290	7,410	7,550	7,480	8,040	7,700	8,080
627 mbh	EA	9,850	9,060	9,200	9,380	9,290	9,990	9,570	10,000
962 mbh	EA	15,900	14,600	14,900	15,200	15,000	16,100	15,500	16,200
2100 mbh	EA	25,500	23,500	23,900	24,300	24,100	25,900	24,800	26,000
Packaged steel boilers									
Oil fired, hot water:									
5 bhp	EA	6,720	6,180	6,280	6,400	6,340	6,820	6,530	6,850
7.5 bhp	EA	8,560	7,880	8,000	8,160	8,080	8,690	8,320	8,730
10 bhp	EA	23,000	21,200	21,500	21,900	21,700	23,300	22,400	23,400
20 bhp	EA	25,700	23,600	24,000	24,400	24,200	26,000	24,900	26,100
40 bhp	EA	38,800	35,700	36,200	37,000	36,600	39,300	37,700	39,500
60 bhp	EA	45,100	41,400	42,100	42,900	42,500	45,700	43,800	45,900
80 bhp	EA	57,100	52,600	53,400	54,400	53,900	57,900	55,500	58,200
100 bhp	EA	65,200	60,000	60,900	62,100	61,500	66,100	63,300	66,400
125 bhp	EA	71,400	65,700	66,700	68,100	67,400	72,500	69,400	72,800
Gas fired, hot water:									
5 bhp	EA	6,350	5,840	5,930	6,050	5,990	6,440	6,170	6,470
7.5 bhp	EA	8,110	7,460	7,570	7,730	7,650	8,220	7,880	8,260
10 bhp	EA	26,100	24,000	24,400	24,800	24,600	26,400	25,300	26,600
20 bhp	EA	29,000	26,700	27,100	27,700	27,400	29,500	28,200	29,600
40 bhp	EA	41,200	37,900	38,500	39,300	38,900	41,800	40,100	42,000
60 bhp	EA	49,600	45,600	46,300	47,300	46,800	50,300	48,200	50,500
80 bhp	EA	60,600	55,800	56,600	57,800	57,200	61,500	58,900	61,800
100 bhp	EA	71,800	66,000	67,000	68,400	67,700	72,800	69,700	73,100
125 bhp	EA	73,400	67,500	68,500	69,900	69,200	74,400	71,300	74,700
Sectional cast iron boilers									
Gas fired, steam, capacity net ibr:									
450 mbh	EA	23,700	21,800	22,200	22,600	22,400	24,100	23,100	24,200
900 mbh	EA	35,100	32,300	32,800	33,400	33,100	35,600	34,100	35,700
1550 mbh	EA	54,100	49,700	50,500	51,500	51,000	54,800	52,500	55,100
2175 mbh	EA	71,900	66,100	67,100	68,500	67,800	72,900	69,800	73,200
Gas fired, hot water, capacity net ibr:									
520 mbh	EA	23,100	21,300	21,600	22,000	21,800	23,400	22,500	23,500
1045 mbh	EA	37,700	34,700	35,200	36,000	35,600	38,300	36,700	38,400
1740 mbh	EA	52,400	48,200	48,900	49,900	49,400	53,100	50,900	53,400
2435 mbh	EA	70,000	64,400	65,300	66,700	66,000	71,000	68,000	71,300
23 60 00 Central Cooling Equipment									
23 62 00 Packaged Compressor & Condenser Units									
CHILLERS									
Self contained air cooled liquid chiller w/50% propylene glycol									
20 Ton	EA	43,100	39,700	40,300	41,100	40,700	43,800	41,900	44,000
50 Ton	EA	85,600	78,800	80,000	81,600	80,800	86,900	83,200	87,300
100 Ton	EA	195,000	179,000	182,000	186,000	184,000	198,000	190,000	199,000
200 Ton	EA	280,000	257,000	261,000	267,000	264,000	284,000	272,000	285,000
23 64 00 Packaged Water Chillers									
CHILLERS									
Chillers complete with starter and accessories									
Centrifugal water chiller, average 0.65 kW/Ton energy consumption:									
100 Ton	EA	176,000	162,000	164,000	168,000	166,000	178,000	171,000	179,000
200 Ton	EA	229,000	211,000	214,000	218,000	216,000	232,000	222,000	233,000
400 Ton	EA	302,000	278,000	282,000	288,000	285,000	306,000	294,000	308,000
600 Ton	EA	363,000	333,000	339,000	345,000	342,000	368,000	352,000	369,000
800 Ton	EA	514,000	473,000	480,000	490,000	485,000	521,000	500,000	524,000
1000 Ton	EA	563,000	518,000	526,000	536,000	531,000	571,000	547,000	573,000

Item	UNITS	St. John's	Halifax	Montreal	Ottawa	Toronto	Winnipeg	Calgary	Vancouver
23 65 00 Cooling Towers									
COOLING TOWERS									
Two speed fan motors (capacity controls) c/w sump heater package									
galvanized steel construction									
Centrifugal / induced draft fan based on 95/87/76 deg F temp condition:									
100 Ton	EA	39,300	36,200	36,700	37,500	37,100	39,900	38,200	40,100
200 Ton	EA	58,900	54,200	55,000	56,200	55,600	59,800	57,300	60,000
400 Ton	EA	88,800	81,700	83,000	84,600	83,800	90,100	86,300	90,500
600 Ton	EA	139,000	128,000	130,000	132,000	131,000	141,000	135,000	141,000
1000 Ton	EA	216,000	199,000	202,000	206,000	204,000	219,000	210,000	220,000
Propeller / forced draft fan based on 95/87/76 deg F temp condition:									
200 Ton	EA	54,500	50,100	50,900	51,900	51,400	55,300	52,900	55,500
400 Ton	EA	68,800	63,300	64,300	65,500	64,900	69,800	66,800	70,100
600 Ton	EA	96,400	88,600	90,000	91,800	90,900	97,700	93,600	98,200
1000 Ton	EA	146,000	135,000	137,000	139,000	138,000	148,000	142,000	149,000
Closed circuit cooler based on 100/90/76 deg F temp condition:									
100 Ton	EA	92,400	85,000	86,300	88,100	87,200	93,700	89,800	94,200
300 Ton	EA	232,000	214,000	217,000	221,000	219,000	235,000	226,000	237,000
600 Ton	EA	477,000	439,000	446,000	455,000	450,000	484,000	464,000	486,000
23 72 00 Air-to-Air Energy Recovery Equipment									
HEAT RECOVERY VENTILATORS									
2 operational modes, c/w main controls, basic de-humidistat									
Light commercial series:									
500 - 700 CFM	EA	9,560	8,790	8,930	9,110	9,020	9,700	9,290	9,740
1000 - 1300 CFM	EA	11,000	10,100	10,300	10,500	10,400	11,200	10,700	11,200
23 82 00 Convection Heating and Cooling Units									
HYDRONIC HEATING									
Terminal Heat Transfer Units									
(Not including piping or accessories)									
Unit heaters with diffusers									
Steam at 2 lbs pressure:									
35 mbh	EA	1,580	1,450	1,480	1,500	1,490	1,600	1,530	1,610
63 mbh	EA	1,860	1,710	1,730	1,770	1,750	1,880	1,800	1,890
125 mbh	EA	2,410	2,210	2,250	2,290	2,270	2,440	2,340	2,450
180 mbh	EA	3,190	2,930	2,980	3,040	3,010	3,240	3,100	3,250
240 mbh	EA	4,070	3,740	3,800	3,880	3,840	4,130	3,960	4,150
352 mbh	EA	6,230	5,730	5,820	5,940	5,880	6,320	6,060	6,350
Hot water entering at 200 deg F									
23 mbh	EA	1,620	1,490	1,510	1,550	1,530	1,640	1,580	1,650
40 mbh	EA	1,910	1,760	1,780	1,820	1,800	1,940	1,850	1,940
80 mbh	EA	2,550	2,350	2,390	2,430	2,410	2,590	2,480	2,600
115 mbh	EA	3,520	3,240	3,290	3,350	3,320	3,570	3,420	3,590
161 mbh	EA	4,360	4,010	4,070	4,150	4,110	4,420	4,230	4,440
250 mbh	EA	6,230	5,730	5,820	5,940	5,880	6,320	6,060	6,350
Force flow units									
Steam at 2 lbs pressure or water entering at 200 deg F (93 deg C)									
surface recess mounted including thermostat:									
16.7 mbh steam or 9.4 mbh hot water capacity	EA	3,320	3,050	3,100	3,160	3,130	3,360	3,220	3,380
34.6 mbh steam or 25.9 mbh hot water capacity	EA	3,770	3,470	3,520	3,600	3,560	3,830	3,670	3,840
50.0 mbh steam or 33.5 mbh hot water capacity	EA	4,710	4,330	4,400	4,480	4,440	4,770	4,570	4,800
89.0 mbh steam or 65.0 mbh hot water capacity	EA	6,230	5,730	5,820	5,940	5,880	6,320	6,060	6,350
Semi-recessed mounted, all sizes:									
Add	EA	649.00	597.00	606.00	618.00	612.00	658.00	630.00	661.00
Convectors and radiators									
Baseboard:									
Cast iron	LF	117.00	108.00	110.00	112.00	111.00	119.00	114.00	119.00
Wall finned	LF	35.20	32.40	32.90	33.60	33.20	35.70	34.20	35.90
Convectors-radiators, floor type:									
5.0 mbh	EA	530.00	488.00	495.00	505.00	500.00	538.00	515.00	540.00
10.2 mbh	EA	660.00	607.00	617.00	629.00	623.00	670.00	642.00	673.00
14.4 mbh	EA	789.00	725.00	737.00	751.00	744.00	800.00	766.00	804.00
23 83 00 Radiant Heating Units									
23 83 26 Gas-Fired Radiant Heaters									
Natural gas fired, output capacity									
40 mbh	EA	2,590	2,380	2,420	2,460	2,440	2,620	2,510	2,640
80 mbh	EA	3,070	2,830	2,870	2,930	2,900	3,120	2,990	3,130
120 mbh	EA	3,580	3,300	3,350	3,410	3,380	3,630	3,480	3,650
160 mbh	EA	4,050	3,720	3,780	3,860	3,820	4,110	3,930	4,130

Item	UNITS	St. John's	Halifax	Montreal	Ottawa	Toronto	Winnipeg	Calgary	Vancouver
200 mbh	EA	4,630	4,260	4,330	4,410	4,370	4,700	4,500	4,720
320 mbh	EA	6,890	6,340	6,440	6,570	6,500	6,990	6,700	7,020

23 83 33 Electric Radiant Heaters
ELECTRIC HEATERS PROPELLERS FAN TYPE
Wall type force flow
208 V, integrated thermostat:

1500 W	EA	944.00	869.00	882.00	900.00	891.00	958.00	918.00	962.00
2000 W	EA	975.00	897.00	911.00	929.00	920.00	989.00	948.00	994.00
3000 W	EA	1,020	938.00	952.00	972.00	962.00	1,030	991.00	1,040
4000 W	EA	1,170	1,070	1,090	1,110	1,100	1,180	1,130	1,190

ELECTRICAL BASEBOARD
208 V, integrated thermostat
Baked enamel finish (white):

500 W	EA	217.00	200.00	203.00	207.00	205.00	220.00	211.00	221.00
750 W	EA	225.00	207.00	210.00	214.00	212.00	228.00	218.00	229.00
1000 W	EA	266.00	245.00	248.00	254.00	251.00	270.00	259.00	271.00
1250 W	EA	319.00	293.00	298.00	304.00	301.00	324.00	310.00	325.00
1500 W	EA	384.00	353.00	358.00	366.00	362.00	389.00	373.00	391.00
2000 W	EA	452.00	415.00	422.00	430.00	426.00	458.00	439.00	460.00

23 84 00 Humidity Control Equipment
HUMIDIFIERS
Installed in air handling units
Gas fired

200 lb / hr	EA	35,700	32,900	33,400	34,000	33,700	36,200	34,700	36,400
400 lb / hr	EA	58,800	54,100	54,900	56,100	55,500	59,700	57,200	59,900
600 lb / hr	EA	65,500	60,300	61,200	62,400	61,800	66,400	63,700	66,700
800 lb / hr	EA	114,000	105,000	107,000	109,000	108,000	116,000	111,000	117,000
1000 lb / hr	EA	131,000	121,000	123,000	125,000	124,000	133,000	128,000	134,000

26: ELECTRICAL
26 05 00 Common Work Results for Electrical
26 05 13 Medium-Voltage Electrical Power Conductors and Cables
CONDUCTORS
Building wire installed in conduit
High tension, 5 kV single copper conductor, x-link shielded PVC:

No. 8	LF	8.46	7.79	7.91	8.07	7.99	8.58	8.23	8.62
No. 6	LF	8.79	8.08	8.21	8.37	8.29	8.91	8.54	8.95
No. 4	LF	10.10	9.27	9.41	9.60	9.51	10.20	9.80	10.30
No. 2	LF	12.70	11.70	11.90	12.10	12.00	12.90	12.30	12.90
No. 1	LF	13.30	12.30	12.50	12.70	12.60	13.50	13.00	13.60
No. 1/0	LF	16.30	15.00	15.20	15.50	15.40	16.50	15.80	16.60
No. 2/0	LF	19.50	18.00	18.30	18.60	18.40	19.80	19.00	19.90
No. 3/0	LF	22.50	20.70	21.00	21.40	21.20	22.80	21.90	22.90
No. 4/0	LF	26.40	24.20	24.60	25.10	24.90	26.70	25.60	26.90
250 mcm	LF	28.70	26.40	26.80	27.30	27.00	29.10	27.80	29.20
300 mcm	LF	31.30	28.80	29.20	29.80	29.50	31.70	30.40	31.90
350 mcm	LF	33.30	30.60	31.10	31.70	31.40	33.70	32.30	33.90
400 mcm	LF	38.10	35.10	35.60	36.30	36.00	38.70	37.00	38.80
500 mcm	LF	44.90	41.30	41.90	42.80	42.40	45.50	43.60	45.80
750 mcm	LF	51.40	47.30	48.00	48.90	48.50	52.10	49.90	52.30

High tension, 15 kV single copper conductor, x-link shielded PVC:

No. 1	LF	18.90	17.40	17.70	18.00	17.80	19.20	18.40	19.30
No. 1/0	LF	22.10	20.40	20.70	21.10	20.90	22.40	21.50	22.50
No. 2/0	LF	24.10	22.20	22.50	23.00	22.70	24.40	23.40	24.60
No. 3/0	LF	27.70	25.50	25.90	26.40	26.10	28.10	26.90	28.20
No. 4/0	LF	33.00	30.30	30.80	31.40	31.10	33.40	32.00	33.60
250 mcm	LF	35.50	32.70	33.20	33.90	33.50	36.00	34.50	36.20
300 mcm	LF	38.10	35.10	35.60	36.30	36.00	38.70	37.00	38.80
350 mcm	LF	43.30	39.80	40.40	41.30	40.80	43.90	42.10	44.10
400 mcm	LF	48.50	44.60	45.30	46.20	45.70	49.10	47.10	49.40
500 mcm	LF	51.40	47.30	48.00	48.90	48.50	52.10	49.90	52.30
750 mcm	LF	61.40	56.50	57.30	58.50	57.90	62.30	59.60	62.50

High tension, 25 kV single copper conductor, x-link shielded PVC:

No. 1	LF	21.20	19.50	19.80	20.20	20.00	21.50	20.60	21.60
No. 1/0	LF	24.10	22.20	22.50	23.00	22.70	24.40	23.40	24.60
No. 2/0	LF	27.70	25.50	25.90	26.40	26.10	28.10	26.90	28.20
No. 4/0	LF	34.20	31.50	32.00	32.60	32.30	34.70	33.30	34.90
250 mcm	LF	39.10	36.00	36.50	37.20	36.90	39.60	38.00	39.80
300 mcm	LF	43.30	39.80	40.40	41.30	40.80	43.90	42.10	44.10
350 mcm	LF	47.80	44.00	44.70	45.60	45.10	48.50	46.50	48.70
400 mcm	LF	49.10	45.20	45.90	46.80	46.30	49.80	47.70	50.00
500 mcm	LF	57.50	52.90	53.70	54.80	54.30	58.30	55.90	58.60
750 mcm	LF	71.40	65.70	66.70	68.00	67.40	72.40	69.40	72.70

Item	UNITS	St. John's	Halifax	Montreal	Ottawa	Toronto	Winnipeg	Calgary	Vancouver
FEEDER CIRCUIT									
60-400 A (support and fittings included, exposed installation, copper conductors)									
Rigid galvanized conduit:									
60 A, 3 wire	LF	20.90	19.30	19.60	19.90	19.80	21.20	20.30	21.30
60 A, 4 wire	LF	22.90	21.00	21.40	21.80	21.60	23.20	22.20	23.30
100 A, 3 wire	LF	24.20	22.30	22.60	23.10	22.80	24.50	23.50	24.70
100 A, 4 wire	LF	30.70	28.30	28.70	29.30	29.00	31.20	29.90	31.30
150 A, 3 wire	LF	37.80	34.80	35.30	36.00	35.70	38.30	36.70	38.50
150 A, 4 wire	LF	50.10	46.10	46.80	47.70	47.20	50.80	48.70	51.00
200 A, 3 wire	LF	53.30	49.00	49.80	50.80	50.30	54.10	51.80	54.30
200 A, 4 wire	LF	61.40	56.50	57.30	58.50	57.90	62.30	59.60	62.50
300 A, 3 wire	LF	83.70	77.00	78.20	79.70	78.90	84.90	81.30	85.30
300 A, 4 wire	LF	109.00	100.00	102.00	104.00	103.00	111.00	106.00	111.00
400 A, 3 wire	LF	130.00	120.00	122.00	124.00	123.00	132.00	127.00	133.00
400 A, 4 wire	LF	182.00	168.00	170.00	174.00	172.00	185.00	177.00	186.00
Electric metallic (E.M.T.) conduit:									
60 A, 3 wire	LF	14.60	13.40	13.60	13.90	13.80	14.80	14.20	14.90
60 A, 4 wire	LF	16.40	15.10	15.40	15.70	15.50	16.70	16.00	16.80
100 A, 3 wire	LF	18.10	16.70	16.90	17.30	17.10	18.40	17.60	18.50
100 A, 4 wire	LF	24.40	22.40	22.80	23.20	23.00	24.70	23.70	24.90
150 A, 3 wire	LF	30.30	27.90	28.30	28.90	28.60	30.70	29.40	30.90
150 A, 4 wire	LF	37.50	34.50	35.00	35.70	35.40	38.00	36.40	38.20
200 A, 3 wire	LF	41.00	37.70	38.30	39.10	38.70	41.60	39.90	41.80
200 A, 4 wire	LF	48.50	44.60	45.30	46.20	45.70	49.10	47.10	49.40
300 A, 3 wire	LF	64.30	59.10	60.00	61.30	60.70	65.20	62.50	65.50
300 A, 4 wire	LF	81.70	75.20	76.30	77.90	77.10	82.90	79.40	83.30
400 A, 3 wire	LF	109.00	99.90	101.00	103.00	102.00	110.00	105.00	111.00
400 A, 4 wire	LF	135.00	124.00	126.00	129.00	127.00	137.00	131.00	138.00

26 05 19 Low-Voltage Electrical Power Conductors and Cables

Item	UNITS	St. John's	Halifax	Montreal	Ottawa	Toronto	Winnipeg	Calgary	Vancouver
CONDUCTORS									
Building wire installed in conduit									
Rw-90 copper:									
No. 14	CLF	54.00	49.60	50.40	51.40	50.90	54.70	52.40	55.00
No. 12	CLF	69.10	63.60	64.60	65.90	65.20	70.10	67.20	70.40
No. 10	CLF	95.30	87.70	89.00	90.80	89.90	96.70	92.60	97.10
No. 8	CLF	134.00	124.00	126.00	128.00	127.00	136.00	131.00	137.00
No. 6	CLF	178.00	164.00	166.00	170.00	168.00	181.00	173.00	181.00
No. 4	CLF	250.00	230.00	234.00	239.00	236.00	254.00	243.00	255.00
No. 3	CLF	293.00	270.00	274.00	280.00	277.00	298.00	285.00	299.00
No. 2	CLF	355.00	327.00	332.00	339.00	335.00	360.00	345.00	362.00
No. 1	CLF	426.00	392.00	398.00	406.00	402.00	433.00	414.00	435.00
No. 1/0	CLF	501.00	461.00	468.00	477.00	472.00	508.00	487.00	510.00
No. 2/0	CLF	611.00	562.00	570.00	582.00	576.00	619.00	593.00	622.00
No. 3/0	CLF	743.00	684.00	694.00	708.00	701.00	754.00	722.00	757.00
No. 4/0	CLF	901.00	829.00	842.00	859.00	850.00	914.00	876.00	918.00
250 mcm	CLF	1,040	957.00	972.00	991.00	981.00	1,060	1,010	1,060
300 mcm	CLF	1,210	1,120	1,130	1,160	1,150	1,230	1,180	1,240
350 mcm	CLF	1,400	1,290	1,310	1,340	1,320	1,420	1,360	1,430
400 mcm	CLF	1,580	1,450	1,470	1,500	1,490	1,600	1,530	1,610
500 mcm	CLF	1,880	1,730	1,750	1,790	1,770	1,900	1,820	1,910
600 mcm	CLF	2,240	2,060	2,090	2,130	2,110	2,270	2,170	2,280
750 mcm	CLF	3,060	2,810	2,850	2,910	2,880	3,100	2,970	3,110
1000 mcm	CLF	4,070	3,740	3,800	3,880	3,840	4,130	3,960	4,150
Rw-90 aluminum:									
No. 1	CLF	318.00	292.00	297.00	303.00	300.00	322.00	309.00	324.00
No. 1/0	CLF	372.00	342.00	347.00	354.00	351.00	377.00	361.00	379.00
No. 2/0	CLF	410.00	377.00	383.00	391.00	387.00	416.00	399.00	418.00
No. 3/0	CLF	520.00	478.00	486.00	496.00	491.00	528.00	505.00	530.00
No. 4/0	CLF	594.00	547.00	555.00	566.00	561.00	603.00	578.00	606.00
250 mcm	CLF	708.00	651.00	661.00	674.00	668.00	718.00	688.00	721.00
300 mcm	CLF	837.00	770.00	782.00	797.00	789.00	849.00	813.00	853.00
350 mcm	CLF	989.00	909.00	923.00	942.00	933.00	1,000	961.00	1,010
400 mcm	CLF	1,100	1,010	1,020	1,040	1,030	1,110	1,060	1,120
500 mcm	CLF	1,260	1,160	1,170	1,200	1,190	1,270	1,220	1,280
600 mcm	CLF	1,340	1,230	1,250	1,270	1,260	1,360	1,300	1,360
750 mcm	CLF	1,630	1,500	1,520	1,550	1,540	1,650	1,590	1,660
1000 mcm	CLF	2,280	2,100	2,130	2,170	2,150	2,310	2,210	2,320
AC 90 copper (BX)									
2C / 14	CLF	200.00	184.00	187.00	191.00	189.00	203.00	195.00	204.00
2C / 12	CLF	228.00	210.00	213.00	217.00	215.00	231.00	222.00	232.00
2C / 10	CLF	262.00	241.00	245.00	250.00	247.00	266.00	255.00	267.00
3C / 14	CLF	232.00	213.00	216.00	221.00	219.00	235.00	225.00	236.00
3C / 12	CLF	251.00	231.00	234.00	239.00	237.00	254.00	244.00	255.00
3C / 10	CLF	294.00	271.00	275.00	280.00	278.00	298.00	286.00	300.00
3C / 8	CLF	472.00	434.00	441.00	449.00	445.00	478.00	458.00	481.00
3C / 6	CLF	562.00	517.00	525.00	536.00	530.00	570.00	546.00	573.00
3C / 4	CLF	730.00	672.00	682.00	696.00	689.00	741.00	710.00	744.00
3C / 3	CLF	811.00	746.00	757.00	773.00	765.00	822.00	788.00	826.00
3C / 2	CLF	879.00	808.00	821.00	837.00	829.00	891.00	854.00	895.00

Item	UNITS	St. John's	Halifax	Montreal	Ottawa	Toronto	Winnipeg	Calgary	Vancouver
4C / 14	CLF	251.00	231.00	234.00	239.00	237.00	254.00	244.00	255.00
4C / 12	CLF	277.00	255.00	259.00	264.00	262.00	281.00	269.00	282.00
4C / 10	CLF	410.00	377.00	383.00	391.00	387.00	416.00	399.00	418.00
Corflex, single copper conductor, low tension, 600 V PVC jacket:									
No. 1/0	LF	8.92	8.20	8.33	8.50	8.41	9.04	8.66	9.09
No. 2/0	LF	9.56	8.80	8.93	9.11	9.02	9.70	9.29	9.74
No. 3/0	LF	11.60	10.60	10.80	11.00	10.90	11.70	11.20	11.80
No. 4/0	LF	12.60	11.60	11.70	12.00	11.90	12.70	12.20	12.80
250 mcm	LF	15.20	14.00	14.20	14.50	14.40	15.40	14.80	15.50
300 mcm	LF	16.50	15.20	15.40	15.80	15.60	16.80	16.10	16.90
350 mcm	LF	18.90	17.40	17.60	18.00	17.80	19.10	18.30	19.20
400 mcm	LF	20.50	18.80	19.10	19.50	19.30	20.80	19.90	20.90
500 mcm	LF	22.50	20.70	21.00	21.40	21.20	22.80	21.90	22.90
750 mcm	LF	38.80	35.70	36.20	36.90	36.60	39.30	37.70	39.50
1000 mcm	LF	46.80	43.10	43.80	44.60	44.20	47.50	45.50	47.70
Mineral insulated cable, 600V, 2 hours fire rated feeder									
60A / 4w - 4/C #6 MI	LF	39.70	36.60	37.10	37.90	37.50	40.30	38.60	40.50
100A / 4w - 4 x 1/C #6 MI	LF	59.10	54.40	55.20	56.30	55.80	60.00	57.50	60.20
120A / 4w - 4 x 1/C #4 MI	LF	76.60	70.40	71.50	73.00	72.20	77.70	74.40	78.00
150A / 4w - 4 x 1/C #3 MI	LF	88.20	81.10	82.40	84.00	83.20	89.50	85.70	89.90
200A / 4w - 4 x 1/C #1 MI	LF	99.80	91.80	93.20	95.10	94.10	101.00	97.00	102.00
250A / 4w - 4 x 1/C #2/0 MI	LF	98.90	90.90	92.30	94.20	93.30	100.00	96.10	101.00
300A / 4w - 4 x 1/C #3/0 MI	LF	154.00	142.00	144.00	147.00	145.00	156.00	150.00	157.00
400A / 4w - 4 x 1/C #250 mcm MI	LF	208.00	191.00	194.00	198.00	196.00	211.00	202.00	212.00
500A / 4w - 4 x 1/C #350 mcm MI	LF	245.00	226.00	229.00	234.00	231.00	249.00	238.00	250.00
600A / 4w - 4 x 1/C #500 mcm MI	LF	323.00	297.00	302.00	308.00	305.00	328.00	314.00	329.00
600V mineral insulated cable termination									
16 mm (1/2")	LF	35.90	33.00	33.50	34.20	33.80	36.40	34.80	36.50
21 mm (3/4")	LF	63.60	58.50	59.40	60.60	60.00	64.50	61.80	64.80
27 mm (1")	LF	139.00	128.00	130.00	133.00	131.00	141.00	135.00	142.00
35 mm (1 1/4")	LF	198.00	182.00	185.00	188.00	187.00	201.00	192.00	201.00

26 05 33 Raceway and Boxes for Electrical Systems

CONDUIT
Material Price Carried At Trade

RACEWAYS INSTALLED COMPLETE
Embedded in slab excluding elbows and pull boxes:

Item	UNITS	St. John's	Halifax	Montreal	Ottawa	Toronto	Winnipeg	Calgary	Vancouver
Rigid galvanized steel									
1/2"	LF	7.69	7.07	7.18	7.33	7.25	7.80	7.47	7.83
3/4"	LF	8.40	7.73	7.85	8.00	7.92	8.52	8.16	8.56
1"	LF	11.40	10.50	10.60	10.80	10.70	11.50	11.10	11.60
1 1/4"	LF	14.40	13.30	13.50	13.70	13.60	14.60	14.00	14.70
1 1/2"	LF	16.40	15.10	15.30	15.60	15.50	16.60	15.90	16.70
2"	LF	20.10	18.50	18.80	19.10	19.00	20.40	19.50	20.50
Electric metallic (E.M.T.)									
1/2"	LF	4.04	3.71	3.77	3.85	3.81	4.10	3.92	4.11
3/4"	LF	4.88	4.49	4.56	4.65	4.60	4.95	4.74	4.97
1"	LF	5.91	5.44	5.52	5.63	5.58	6.00	5.75	6.02
1 1/4"	LF	7.53	6.92	7.03	7.17	7.10	7.63	7.31	7.67
1 1/2"	LF	8.76	8.05	8.18	8.34	8.26	8.88	8.51	8.92
2"	LF	10.10	9.30	9.44	9.64	9.54	10.30	9.83	10.30
Rigid PVC									
1/2"	LF	4.20	3.86	3.92	4.00	3.96	4.26	4.08	4.28
3/4"	LF	4.52	4.16	4.22	4.31	4.27	4.59	4.40	4.61
1"	LF	5.49	5.05	5.13	5.23	5.18	5.57	5.34	5.60
1 1/4"	LF	6.46	5.94	6.04	6.16	6.10	6.55	6.28	6.58
1 1/2"	LF	7.75	7.13	7.24	7.39	7.32	7.86	7.53	7.90
2"	LF	9.05	8.32	8.45	8.62	8.53	9.17	8.79	9.22

Surface mounted 8' average high one pull box, one elbow per 100 LF, and supports:

Item	UNITS	St. John's	Halifax	Montreal	Ottawa	Toronto	Winnipeg	Calgary	Vancouver
Rigid galvanized steel									
1/2"	LF	10.30	9.48	9.63	9.82	9.72	10.50	10.00	10.50
3/4"	LF	11.20	10.30	10.50	10.70	10.60	11.40	10.90	11.40
1"	LF	14.30	13.20	13.40	13.60	13.50	14.50	13.90	14.60
1 1/4"	LF	19.10	17.50	17.80	18.20	18.00	19.30	18.50	19.40
1 1/2"	LF	21.50	19.70	20.00	20.40	20.20	21.80	20.80	21.90
2"	LF	26.90	24.80	25.20	25.70	25.40	27.30	26.20	27.50
2 1/2"	LF	43.00	39.50	40.10	40.90	40.50	43.60	41.80	43.80
3"	LF	54.00	49.60	50.40	51.40	50.90	54.70	52.40	55.00
3 1/2"	LF	70.80	65.10	66.10	67.40	66.80	71.80	68.80	72.10
4"	LF	86.90	79.90	81.20	82.80	82.00	88.10	84.50	88.60
5"	LF	153.00	141.00	143.00	146.00	144.00	155.00	148.00	156.00
6"	LF	211.00	194.00	197.00	201.00	199.00	214.00	205.00	215.00
Electric metallic (E.M.T.)									
1/2"	LF	5.30	4.87	4.95	5.05	5.00	5.37	5.15	5.40
3/4"	LF	6.20	5.71	5.79	5.91	5.85	6.29	6.03	6.32
1"	LF	7.79	7.16	7.27	7.42	7.35	7.90	7.57	7.93
1 1/4"	LF	11.00	10.20	10.30	10.50	10.40	11.20	10.70	11.30
1 1/2"	LF	12.40	11.40	11.60	11.90	11.70	12.60	12.10	12.70
2"	LF	14.60	13.40	13.60	13.90	13.80	14.80	14.20	14.90
2 1/2"	LF	22.00	20.30	20.60	21.00	20.80	22.30	21.40	22.50
3"	LF	26.70	24.60	25.00	25.50	25.20	27.10	26.00	27.20
4"	LF	38.10	35.10	35.60	36.30	36.00	38.70	37.00	38.80

Item	UNITS	St. John's	Halifax	Montreal	Ottawa	Toronto	Winnipeg	Calgary	Vancouver
Rigid PVC									
1/2"	LF	6.14	5.65	5.73	5.85	5.79	6.23	5.96	6.25
3/4"	LF	6.46	5.94	6.04	6.16	6.10	6.55	6.28	6.58
1"	LF	7.75	7.13	7.24	7.39	7.32	7.86	7.53	7.90
1 1/4"	LF	8.72	8.02	8.15	8.31	8.23	8.85	8.48	8.89
1 1/2"	LF	10.30	9.51	9.66	9.85	9.75	10.50	10.00	10.50
2"	LF	12.30	11.30	11.50	11.70	11.60	12.50	11.90	12.50
2 1/2"	LF	17.10	15.80	16.00	16.30	16.20	17.40	16.60	17.40
3"	LF	20.70	19.00	19.30	19.70	19.50	21.00	20.10	21.10
3 1/2"	LF	24.90	22.90	23.20	23.70	23.50	25.20	24.20	25.30
4"	LF	29.10	26.70	27.20	27.70	27.40	29.50	28.30	29.60
Rigid aluminum									
1/2"	LF	7.24	6.66	6.76	6.90	6.83	7.34	7.03	7.37
3/4"	LF	8.66	7.96	8.09	8.25	8.17	8.78	8.41	8.82
1"	LF	10.60	9.75	9.90	10.10	10.00	10.70	10.30	10.80
1 1/4"	LF	14.10	13.00	13.20	13.50	13.30	14.30	13.70	14.40
1 1/2"	LF	16.20	14.90	15.10	15.50	15.30	16.40	15.80	16.50
2"	LF	21.20	19.50	19.80	20.20	20.00	21.50	20.60	21.60
2 1/2"	LF	35.50	32.70	33.20	33.90	33.50	36.00	34.50	36.20
3"	LF	42.30	38.90	39.50	40.30	39.90	42.90	41.10	43.10
3 1/2"	LF	56.90	52.30	53.10	54.20	53.60	57.70	55.30	57.90
4"	LF	74.00	68.10	69.10	70.50	69.80	75.00	71.90	75.40

WIRING CHANNELS

Wiring channels

Square section, steel:

Item	UNITS	St. John's	Halifax	Montreal	Ottawa	Toronto	Winnipeg	Calgary	Vancouver
2 1/2" x 2 1/2"	LF	43.30	39.80	40.40	41.30	40.80	43.90	42.10	44.10
4" x 4"	LF	60.10	55.30	56.10	57.30	56.70	60.90	58.40	61.20
6" x 6"	LF	78.50	72.20	73.30	74.80	74.10	79.60	76.30	80.00

OUTLET BOXES

Wiring outlet boxes

Ceiling type 4" x 4":

Item	UNITS	St. John's	Halifax	Montreal	Ottawa	Toronto	Winnipeg	Calgary	Vancouver
Surface	EA	35.00	32.20	32.70	33.30	33.00	35.50	34.00	35.60
Recessed	EA	25.40	23.40	23.80	24.20	24.00	25.80	24.70	25.90
Cast iron	EA	143.00	132.00	134.00	136.00	135.00	145.00	139.00	146.00
Wall type device box:									
Surface, 1 gang	EA	30.70	28.30	28.70	29.30	29.00	31.20	29.90	31.30
Surface, 2 gang	EA	31.80	29.30	29.70	30.30	30.00	32.30	30.90	32.40
Recessed, 1 gang	EA	41.30	38.00	38.60	39.40	39.00	41.90	40.20	42.10
Recessed, 2 gang	EA	46.60	42.90	43.60	44.40	44.00	47.30	45.30	47.50

PULL BOXES & CABINETS

Pull box or metering cabinets:

Item	UNITS	St. John's	Halifax	Montreal	Ottawa	Toronto	Winnipeg	Calgary	Vancouver
20" x 20" x 10"	EA	305.00	281.00	285.00	291.00	288.00	310.00	297.00	311.00
20" x 30" x 10"	EA	357.00	329.00	334.00	340.00	337.00	362.00	347.00	364.00
30" x 30" x 10"	EA	446.00	410.00	417.00	425.00	421.00	453.00	434.00	455.00
36" x 36" x 10"	EA	641.00	590.00	599.00	611.00	605.00	650.00	623.00	653.00
36" x 36" x 12"	EA	650.00	598.00	607.00	619.00	613.00	659.00	631.00	662.00
48" x 48" x 12"	EA	1,030	946.00	960.00	980.00	970.00	1,040	999.00	1,050

26 05 36 Cable Trays for Electrical Systems

CABLE TRAY

Cable tray including fittings and supports

Ventilated type:

Galvanized steel

Item	UNITS	St. John's	Halifax	Montreal	Ottawa	Toronto	Winnipeg	Calgary	Vancouver
6" wide	LF	46.80	43.10	43.80	44.60	44.20	47.50	45.50	47.70
12" wide	LF	51.00	47.00	47.70	48.60	48.20	51.80	49.60	52.00
18" wide	LF	64.30	59.10	60.00	61.30	60.70	65.20	62.50	65.50
24" wide	LF	72.40	66.60	67.60	69.00	68.30	73.40	70.30	73.70
Aluminum									
6" wide	LF	54.90	50.50	51.30	52.30	51.80	55.70	53.40	56.00
12" wide	LF	61.10	56.20	57.00	58.20	57.60	61.90	59.30	62.20
18" wide	LF	73.00	67.20	68.20	69.60	68.90	74.10	71.00	74.40
24" wide	LF	86.30	79.30	80.60	82.20	81.40	87.50	83.80	87.90
Ladder type:									
Galvanized steel									
6" wide	LF	43.90	40.40	41.00	41.90	41.50	44.60	42.70	44.80
12" wide	LF	49.80	45.80	46.50	47.40	46.90	50.50	48.30	50.70
18" wide	LF	58.80	54.10	54.90	56.00	55.50	59.60	57.10	59.90
24" wide	LF	67.50	62.10	63.10	64.30	63.70	68.50	65.60	68.80
Aluminum									
6" wide	LF	53.30	49.00	49.80	50.80	50.30	54.10	51.80	54.30
12" wide	LF	55.90	51.40	52.20	53.30	52.70	56.70	54.30	56.90
18" wide	LF	66.90	61.50	62.50	63.70	63.10	67.80	65.00	68.10
24" wide	LF	76.60	70.40	71.50	73.00	72.20	77.70	74.40	78.00

26 05 83 Wiring Connections

WIRING DEVICES

(Stainless steel switch cover included, wired to junction box)

Switches, 120-347 V

Toggle switches, premium grade, connected:

Item	UNITS	St. John's	Halifax	Montreal	Ottawa	Toronto	Winnipeg	Calgary	Vancouver
Single pole, 120 V	EA	135.00	124.00	126.00	128.00	127.00	137.00	131.00	137.00
3-way, 120 V	EA	159.00	146.00	149.00	152.00	150.00	161.00	155.00	162.00
4-way, 120 V	EA	228.00	210.00	213.00	217.00	215.00	231.00	221.00	232.00

Item	UNITS	St. John's	Halifax	Montreal	Ottawa	Toronto	Winnipeg	Calgary	Vancouver
Single pole, 347 V	EA	140.00	129.00	131.00	133.00	132.00	142.00	136.00	143.00
3-way, 347 V	EA	165.00	152.00	154.00	158.00	156.00	168.00	161.00	168.00
4-way, 347 V	EA	243.00	223.00	227.00	231.00	229.00	246.00	236.00	247.00
(Stainless steel receptacle cover included, wired to junction box)									
15 A receptacles									
Standard:									
Duplex u ground	EA	137.00	126.00	128.00	130.00	129.00	139.00	133.00	139.00
Duplex u ground, specification grade	EA	148.00	137.00	139.00	141.00	140.00	151.00	144.00	151.00
Duplex isolated ground	EA	175.00	161.00	163.00	167.00	165.00	177.00	170.00	178.00
Duplex GFI	EA	158.00	145.00	148.00	150.00	149.00	160.00	153.00	161.00
Duplex TVSS	EA	200.00	184.00	187.00	191.00	189.00	203.00	195.00	204.00
Weatherproof:									
Duplex u ground	EA	177.00	163.00	165.00	169.00	167.00	180.00	172.00	180.00
20 A receptacles									
Standard:									
Duplex u ground	EA	152.00	139.00	142.00	144.00	143.00	154.00	147.00	154.00
Duplex GFI	EA	158.00	145.00	148.00	150.00	149.00	160.00	153.00	161.00
30 A receptacles									
Range and dryer type:									
4 wire, 120/240 V	EA	360.00	332.00	337.00	343.00	340.00	366.00	350.00	367.00
50 A receptacles									
Range and dryer type:									
4 wire, 120/240 V	EA	533.00	490.00	498.00	508.00	503.00	541.00	518.00	543.00
MOTOR CONNECTION AND DISCONNECT ONLY									
10 hp motors	EA	572.00	527.00	535.00	545.00	540.00	581.00	556.00	583.00
15 hp motors	EA	588.00	541.00	549.00	561.00	555.00	597.00	572.00	599.00
25 hp motors	EA	791.00	727.00	739.00	753.00	746.00	802.00	768.00	806.00
50 hp motors	EA	1,070	985	1,000	1,020	1,010	1,090	1,040	1,090
75 hp motors	EA	1,240	1,140	1,160	1,180	1,170	1,260	1,210	1,260
100 hp motors	EA	1,830	1,690	1,710	1,750	1,730	1,860	1,780	1,870

26 22 00 Low-Voltage Transformers
TRANSFORMERS
Dry type
Three phase 600 V/120-208 V:

Item	UNITS	St. John's	Halifax	Montreal	Ottawa	Toronto	Winnipeg	Calgary	Vancouver
3 kVA	EA	1,140	1,050	1,070	1,090	1,080	1,160	1,110	1,170
6 kVA	EA	1,480	1,370	1,390	1,410	1,400	1,510	1,440	1,510
9 kVA	EA	1,840	1,700	1,720	1,760	1,740	1,870	1,790	1,880
15 kVA	EA	2,140	1,970	2,000	2,040	2,020	2,170	2,080	2,180
30 kVA	EA	2,810	2,580	2,620	2,680	2,650	2,850	2,730	2,860
45 kVA	EA	3,640	3,340	3,400	3,460	3,430	3,690	3,530	3,700
75 kVA	EA	5,620	5,170	5,250	5,350	5,300	5,700	5,460	5,720
112.5 kVA	EA	7,500	6,900	7,010	7,150	7,080	7,610	7,290	7,650
150 kVA	EA	9,120	8,390	8,510	8,690	8,600	9,250	8,860	9,290
225 kVA	EA	13,900	12,800	13,000	13,200	13,100	14,100	13,500	14,100
300 kVA	EA	16,300	15,000	15,200	15,600	15,400	16,600	15,900	16,600
450 kVA	EA	24,400	22,400	22,800	23,200	23,000	24,700	23,700	24,800
500 kVA	EA	27,000	24,900	25,200	25,800	25,500	27,400	26,300	27,500
600 kVA	EA	32,300	29,700	30,200	30,800	30,500	32,800	31,400	32,900
750 kVA	EA	37,200	34,200	34,700	35,500	35,100	37,700	36,200	37,900

26 24 00 Switchboards and Panelboards
PANELBOARDS
Lighting / power panels complete with bolt on breakers
120/240 V, 1 phase, NBLP main lugs:
100 A

Item	UNITS	St. John's	Halifax	Montreal	Ottawa	Toronto	Winnipeg	Calgary	Vancouver
12 circuits, 15 A	EA	1,070	985	1,000	1,020	1,010	1,090	1,040	1,090
18 circuits, 15 A	EA	1,350	1,240	1,260	1,280	1,270	1,370	1,310	1,370
24 circuits, 15 A	EA	1,690	1,550	1,570	1,610	1,590	1,710	1,640	1,720
225 A									
24 circuits, 15 A	EA	1,740	1,600	1,620	1,660	1,640	1,760	1,690	1,770
30 circuits, 15 A	EA	2,080	1,910	1,940	1,980	1,960	2,110	2,020	2,120
36 circuits, 15 A	EA	2,400	2,200	2,240	2,280	2,260	2,430	2,330	2,440
42 circuits, 15 A	EA	2,620	2,410	2,450	2,490	2,470	2,660	2,540	2,670
60 circuits, 15 A	EA	3,380	3,110	3,160	3,220	3,190	3,430	3,290	3,450
84 circuits, 15 A	EA	4,130	3,800	3,860	3,940	3,900	4,190	4,020	4,210
Tub only with main lug:									
400 A									
42 spaces	EA	3,300	3,030	3,080	3,140	3,110	3,340	3,200	3,360
60 spaces	EA	4,290	3,950	4,010	4,090	4,050	4,350	4,170	4,370
84 spaces	EA	6,480	5,960	6,050	6,170	6,110	6,570	6,290	6,600
120/240 V, 1 phase, NBLP main breaker c/w bolt on breakers:									
100 A									
12 circuits, 15 A	EA	1,260	1,160	1,180	1,200	1,190	1,280	1,230	1,290
18 circuits, 15 A	EA	1,570	1,440	1,470	1,490	1,480	1,590	1,520	1,600
24 circuits, 15 A	EA	1,910	1,760	1,780	1,820	1,800	1,940	1,850	1,940
225 A									
24 circuits, 15 A	EA	2,400	2,200	2,240	2,280	2,260	2,430	2,330	2,440
30 circuits, 15 A	EA	2,720	2,510	2,540	2,600	2,570	2,760	2,650	2,780
36 circuits, 15 A	EA	3,040	2,800	2,840	2,900	2,870	3,090	2,960	3,100
42 circuits, 15 A	EA	3,410	3,140	3,190	3,250	3,220	3,460	3,320	3,480
60 circuits, 15 A	EA	4,030	3,710	3,760	3,840	3,800	4,090	3,910	4,100

Item	UNITS	St. John's	Halifax	Montreal	Ottawa	Toronto	Winnipeg	Calgary	Vancouver
84 circuits, 15 A	EA	4,800	4,420	4,480	4,580	4,530	4,870	4,670	4,890
120/208 V, 3 phase, NBLP with lugs:									
100 A									
18 circuits, 15 A	EA	1,390	1,280	1,300	1,320	1,310	1,410	1,350	1,410
24 circuits, 15 A	EA	1,720	1,580	1,600	1,640	1,620	1,740	1,670	1,750
30 circuits, 15 A	EA	2,200	2,030	2,060	2,100	2,080	2,240	2,140	2,250
42 circuits, 15 A	EA	2,630	2,420	2,460	2,500	2,480	2,670	2,550	2,680
225 A									
18 circuits, 15 A	EA	1,420	1,310	1,330	1,350	1,340	1,440	1,380	1,450
24 circuits, 15 A	EA	1,760	1,620	1,640	1,680	1,660	1,780	1,710	1,790
30 circuits, 15 A	EA	2,250	2,070	2,100	2,140	2,120	2,280	2,180	2,290
42 circuits, 15 A	EA	2,680	2,470	2,500	2,560	2,530	2,720	2,610	2,730
60 circuits, 15 A	EA	3,500	3,220	3,270	3,330	3,300	3,550	3,400	3,560
72 circuits, 15 A	EA	3,920	3,610	3,660	3,740	3,700	3,980	3,810	4,000
84 circuits, 15 A	EA	4,460	4,100	4,170	4,250	4,210	4,530	4,340	4,550
120/208 V, 3 phase, NBLP main breaker:									
100 A									
15 circuits, 15 A	EA	1,700	1,560	1,580	1,620	1,600	1,720	1,650	1,730
24 circuits, 15 A	EA	2,370	2,180	2,220	2,260	2,240	2,410	2,310	2,420
30 circuits, 15 A	EA	2,850	2,620	2,660	2,720	2,690	2,890	2,770	2,910
42 circuits, 15 A	EA	3,290	3,020	3,070	3,130	3,100	3,330	3,190	3,350
225 A									
18 circuits, 15 A	EA	2,080	1,910	1,940	1,980	1,960	2,110	2,020	2,120
24 circuits, 15 A	EA	2,440	2,240	2,280	2,320	2,300	2,470	2,370	2,480
30 circuits, 15 A	EA	2,890	2,660	2,700	2,760	2,730	2,930	2,810	2,950
42 circuits, 15 A	EA	3,380	3,110	3,160	3,220	3,190	3,430	3,290	3,450
347/600 V CDP style									
100 A									
24 circuits, 15 A single pole 347 V	EA	4,460	4,100	4,170	4,250	4,210	4,530	4,340	4,550
42 circuits, 15 A single pole 347 V	EA	6,190	5,690	5,780	5,900	5,840	6,280	6,020	6,310
225 A									
24 circuits, 15 A single pole 347 V	EA	4,650	4,280	4,350	4,430	4,390	4,720	4,520	4,740
30 circuits, 15 A single pole 347 V	EA	5,620	5,170	5,250	5,350	5,300	5,700	5,460	5,720
42 circuits, 15 A single pole 347 V	EA	6,410	5,900	5,990	6,110	6,050	6,500	6,230	6,530
347/600 V CDP style main lugs:									
225 A, 42 spaces	EA	2,020	1,860	1,890	1,930	1,910	2,050	1,970	2,060

26 24 16 Panelboards
OVERCURRENT PROTECTION DEVICES
Distribution panel fusible type
Base and main lugs 250 or 600 V, copper:

Item	UNITS	St. John's	Halifax	Montreal	Ottawa	Toronto	Winnipeg	Calgary	Vancouver
3 poles, 3 wires									
250 A	EA	2,400	2,200	2,240	2,280	2,260	2,430	2,330	2,440
400 A	EA	2,620	2,410	2,450	2,490	2,470	2,660	2,540	2,670
600 A	EA	2,920	2,680	2,720	2,780	2,750	2,960	2,830	2,970
800 A	EA	3,230	2,970	3,020	3,080	3,050	3,280	3,140	3,290
1200 A	EA	4,240	3,900	3,960	4,040	4,000	4,300	4,120	4,320
3 poles, 4 wires									
250 A	EA	2,510	2,310	2,350	2,390	2,370	2,550	2,440	2,560
400 A	EA	2,810	2,580	2,620	2,680	2,650	2,850	2,730	2,860
600 A	EA	3,170	2,920	2,960	3,020	2,990	3,210	3,080	3,230
800 A	EA	3,630	3,330	3,390	3,450	3,420	3,680	3,520	3,690
1200 A	EA	4,620	4,250	4,320	4,400	4,360	4,690	4,490	4,710
Door in trim	EA	943.00	868.00	881.00	899.00	890.00	957.00	917.00	961.00

Fusible units for distribution panel, fuses not included
600 V:

Item	UNITS	St. John's	Halifax	Montreal	Ottawa	Toronto	Winnipeg	Calgary	Vancouver
2 poles									
30 A	EA	350.00	322.00	327.00	333.00	330.00	355.00	340.00	356.00
60 A	EA	392.00	361.00	366.00	374.00	370.00	398.00	381.00	400.00
100 A	EA	647.00	595.00	604.00	616.00	610.00	656.00	628.00	659.00
200 A	EA	1,090	1,000	1,020	1,040	1,030	1,110	1,060	1,110
400 A	EA	2,510	2,310	2,350	2,390	2,370	2,550	2,440	2,560
600 A	EA	3,020	2,780	2,820	2,880	2,850	3,060	2,940	3,080
800 A	EA	4,520	4,150	4,220	4,300	4,260	4,580	4,390	4,600
1200 A	EA	7,720	7,100	7,210	7,350	7,280	7,830	7,500	7,860
3 poles									
30 A, twin mounted	EA	1,040	956.00	970.00	990.00	980.00	1,050	1,010	1,060
60 A, twin mounted	EA	1,090	1,000	1,020	1,040	1,030	1,110	1,060	1,110
100 A, twin mounted	EA	1,180	1,080	1,100	1,120	1,110	1,190	1,140	1,200
200 A	EA	1,290	1,190	1,210	1,230	1,220	1,310	1,260	1,320
400 A	EA	2,480	2,280	2,320	2,360	2,340	2,520	2,410	2,530
600 A	EA	3,200	2,940	2,990	3,050	3,020	3,250	3,110	3,260
800 A	EA	4,870	4,480	4,540	4,640	4,590	4,930	4,730	4,960
1200 A	EA	6,540	6,020	6,110	6,230	6,170	6,630	6,360	6,660

Distribution panel, breaker type base, main breaker, no circuit breakers
250 or 600 V:

Item	UNITS	St. John's	Halifax	Montreal	Ottawa	Toronto	Winnipeg	Calgary	Vancouver
3 poles, 3 wires									
250 A	EA	3,980	3,660	3,710	3,790	3,750	4,030	3,860	4,050
400 A	EA	5,270	4,850	4,920	5,020	4,970	5,340	5,120	5,370
600 A	EA	6,870	6,320	6,420	6,540	6,480	6,970	6,670	7,000
800 A	EA	8,650	7,960	8,080	8,240	8,160	8,770	8,400	8,810
1200 A	EA	14,600	13,500	13,700	13,900	13,800	14,800	14,200	14,900

Item	UNITS	St. John's	Halifax	Montreal	Ottawa	Toronto	Winnipeg	Calgary	Vancouver
3 poles, 4 wires									
250 A	EA	4,000	3,680	3,730	3,810	3,770	4,050	3,880	4,070
400 A	EA	5,290	4,870	4,940	5,040	4,990	5,360	5,140	5,390
600 A	EA	6,890	6,340	6,440	6,570	6,500	6,990	6,700	7,020
800 A	EA	8,690	8,000	8,120	8,280	8,200	8,820	8,450	8,860
1200 A	EA	14,600	13,500	13,700	13,900	13,800	14,800	14,200	14,900
TVSS filter	EA	2,770	2,540	2,580	2,640	2,610	2,810	2,690	2,820

26 24 19 Motor-Control Centers
MOTOR STARTERS & CONTROLS
Magnetic starter (full voltage non-reversible general purpose enclosure with overload relays)
600 V 3 phase:

Item	UNITS	St. John's	Halifax	Montreal	Ottawa	Toronto	Winnipeg	Calgary	Vancouver
Motors up to 2 hp	EA	583.00	536.00	545.00	556.00	550.00	591.00	567.00	594.00
Motors up to 5 hp	EA	657.00	605.00	614.00	626.00	620.00	667.00	639.00	670.00
Motors up to 10 hp	EA	1,160	1,060	1,080	1,100	1,090	1,170	1,120	1,180
Motors up to 25 hp	EA	1,810	1,670	1,690	1,730	1,710	1,840	1,760	1,850
Motors up to 50 hp	EA	3,950	3,640	3,690	3,770	3,730	4,010	3,840	4,030

Combination magnetic/fusible type (full voltage non-reversible general purpose enclosure with fuses and overload relays)
600 V 3 phase:

Item	UNITS	St. John's	Halifax	Montreal	Ottawa	Toronto	Winnipeg	Calgary	Vancouver
Motors up to 5 hp	EA	1,580	1,450	1,480	1,500	1,490	1,600	1,530	1,610
Motors up to 10 hp	EA	1,640	1,510	1,530	1,570	1,550	1,670	1,600	1,670
Motors up to 25 hp	EA	2,290	2,110	2,140	2,180	2,160	2,320	2,220	2,330
Motors up to 50 hp	EA	3,340	3,070	3,120	3,180	3,150	3,390	3,240	3,400

26 25 00 Enclosed Bus Assemblies
BUS DUCT
Copper low impedance ventilated including supports and fitting, excluding elbows
Feeder type:
600 V

Item	UNITS	St. John's	Halifax	Montreal	Ottawa	Toronto	Winnipeg	Calgary	Vancouver
1000 A	LF	359.00	330.00	335.00	342.00	338.00	364.00	348.00	365.00
1350 A	LF	530.00	487.00	495.00	505.00	500.00	537.00	515.00	540.00
1600 A	LF	633.00	582.00	591.00	603.00	597.00	642.00	615.00	645.00
2000 A	LF	795.00	731.00	742.00	757.00	750.00	806.00	772.00	810.00
2500 A	LF	995.00	915.00	929.00	948.00	939.00	1,010	967.00	1,010
3000 A	LF	1,190	1,090	1,110	1,130	1,120	1,200	1,150	1,210
3500 A	LF	1,350	1,240	1,260	1,290	1,270	1,370	1,310	1,380
4000 A	LF	1,540	1,420	1,440	1,470	1,450	1,560	1,500	1,570
4500 A	LF	1,650	1,520	1,540	1,570	1,560	1,670	1,600	1,680
5000 A	LF	1,800	1,650	1,680	1,710	1,690	1,820	1,750	1,830
347/600 V									
1000 A	LF	494.00	455.00	462.00	471.00	466.00	501.00	480.00	504.00
1350 A	LF	675.00	621.00	631.00	643.00	637.00	685.00	656.00	688.00
1600 A	LF	814.00	749.00	760.00	776.00	768.00	826.00	791.00	830.00
2000 A	LF	995.00	915.00	929.00	948.00	939.00	1,010	967.00	1,010
2500 A	LF	1,220	1,120	1,140	1,160	1,150	1,240	1,180	1,240
3000 A	LF	1,550	1,420	1,450	1,470	1,460	1,570	1,500	1,580
3500 A	LF	1,740	1,600	1,630	1,660	1,650	1,770	1,700	1,780
4000 A	LF	1,900	1,750	1,780	1,810	1,800	1,930	1,850	1,940
4500 A	LF	2,100	1,930	1,960	2,000	1,980	2,130	2,040	2,140
5000 A	LF	2,310	2,120	2,150	2,200	2,180	2,340	2,240	2,350
Plug in type:									
600 V									
1000 A	LF	362.00	333.00	338.00	345.00	341.00	367.00	352.00	369.00
1350 A	LF	533.00	490.00	498.00	508.00	503.00	541.00	518.00	543.00
1600 A	LF	636.00	585.00	594.00	606.00	600.00	645.00	618.00	648.00
2000 A	LF	798.00	734.00	745.00	760.00	753.00	809.00	775.00	813.00
2500 A	LF	998.00	918.00	932.00	951.00	942.00	1,010	970.00	1,020
3000 A	LF	1,190	1,090	1,110	1,130	1,120	1,210	1,160	1,210
3500 A	LF	1,360	1,250	1,270	1,300	1,290	1,380	1,320	1,390
4000 A	LF	1,540	1,420	1,440	1,470	1,460	1,570	1,500	1,570
4500 A	LF	1,650	1,520	1,540	1,580	1,560	1,680	1,610	1,690
347/600 V									
600 A	LF	359.00	330.00	335.00	342.00	338.00	364.00	348.00	365.00
1000 A	LF	498.00	458.00	465.00	474.00	469.00	505.00	483.00	507.00
1350 A	LF	678.00	624.00	634.00	646.00	640.00	688.00	659.00	691.00
1600 A	LF	817.00	752.00	763.00	779.00	771.00	829.00	794.00	833.00
2000 A	LF	998.00	918.00	932.00	951.00	942.00	1,010	970.00	1,020
2500 A	LF	1,220	1,120	1,140	1,160	1,150	1,240	1,190	1,240
3000 A	LF	1,550	1,430	1,450	1,480	1,460	1,570	1,510	1,580
3500 A	LF	1,750	1,610	1,630	1,670	1,650	1,770	1,700	1,780
4000 A	LF	1,910	1,750	1,780	1,820	1,800	1,930	1,850	1,940
4500 A	LF	2,080	1,910	1,940	1,980	1,960	2,110	2,020	2,120

Aluminum low impedance ventilated including supports and fitting, excluding elbows
Feeder type:
600 V

Item	UNITS	St. John's	Halifax	Montreal	Ottawa	Toronto	Winnipeg	Calgary	Vancouver
600 A	LF	207.00	190.00	193.00	197.00	195.00	210.00	201.00	211.00
1000 A	LF	239.00	220.00	223.00	228.00	226.00	242.00	232.00	244.00
1350 A	LF	339.00	312.00	317.00	323.00	320.00	344.00	330.00	346.00
1600 A	LF	384.00	354.00	359.00	366.00	363.00	390.00	374.00	392.00

Item	UNITS	St. John's	Halifax	Montreal	Ottawa	Toronto	Winnipeg	Calgary	Vancouver
2000 A	LF	456.00	419.00	425.00	434.00	430.00	462.00	443.00	464.00
2500 A	LF	569.00	523.00	531.00	542.00	536.00	577.00	553.00	579.00
3000 A	LF	649.00	597.00	607.00	619.00	613.00	659.00	631.00	662.00
3500 A	LF	727.00	669.00	679.00	693.00	686.00	737.00	706.00	741.00
4000 A	LF	901.00	829.00	842.00	859.00	850.00	914.00	876.00	918.00
4500 A	LF	1,010	930.00	944.00	964.00	954.00	1,030	983.00	1,030
347/600 V									
600 A	LF	239.00	220.00	223.00	228.00	226.00	242.00	232.00	244.00
1000 A	LF	291.00	267.00	272.00	277.00	274.00	295.00	283.00	296.00
1350 A	LF	404.00	371.00	377.00	385.00	381.00	410.00	392.00	411.00
1600 A	LF	446.00	410.00	416.00	425.00	421.00	452.00	433.00	454.00
2000 A	LF	549.00	505.00	513.00	523.00	518.00	557.00	534.00	560.00
2500 A	LF	624.00	574.00	582.00	594.00	588.00	632.00	606.00	635.00
3000 A	LF	724.00	666.00	676.00	690.00	683.00	734.00	703.00	737.00
3500 A	LF	908.00	835.00	848.00	865.00	856.00	921.00	882.00	925.00
4000 A	LF	1,120	1,030	1,040	1,070	1,050	1,130	1,090	1,140
4500 A	LF	1,250	1,150	1,160	1,190	1,180	1,260	1,210	1,270
Plug in type:									
600 V									
600 A	LF	213.00	196.00	199.00	203.00	201.00	216.00	207.00	217.00
1000 A	LF	233.00	214.00	217.00	222.00	219.00	236.00	226.00	237.00
1350 A	LF	349.00	321.00	326.00	332.00	329.00	354.00	339.00	356.00
1600 A	LF	420.00	386.00	392.00	400.00	396.00	426.00	408.00	428.00
2000 A	LF	501.00	461.00	468.00	477.00	472.00	508.00	487.00	510.00
2500 A	LF	633.00	582.00	591.00	603.00	597.00	642.00	615.00	645.00
3000 A	LF	711.00	654.00	664.00	677.00	671.00	721.00	691.00	724.00
3500 A	LF	801.00	737.00	748.00	763.00	756.00	813.00	779.00	816.00
4000 A	LF	1,000	921.00	935.00	954.00	945.00	1,020	973.00	1,020
347/600 V									
600 A	LF	242.00	223.00	226.00	231.00	229.00	246.00	235.00	247.00
1000 A	LF	294.00	270.00	275.00	280.00	277.00	298.00	286.00	300.00
1350 A	LF	407.00	374.00	380.00	388.00	384.00	413.00	396.00	415.00
1600 A	LF	449.00	413.00	419.00	428.00	424.00	455.00	436.00	458.00
2000 A	LF	552.00	508.00	516.00	526.00	521.00	560.00	537.00	563.00
2500 A	LF	630.00	580.00	588.00	600.00	594.00	639.00	612.00	642.00
3000 A	LF	727.00	669.00	679.00	693.00	686.00	737.00	706.00	741.00
3500 A	LF	911.00	838.00	851.00	868.00	860.00	924.00	885.00	928.00
4000 A	LF	1,120	1,030	1,050	1,070	1,060	1,140	1,090	1,150
Bus duct plug in units									
Fusible units (including fuses):									
600 V									
30 A	EA	625.00	575.00	584.00	596.00	590.00	634.00	608.00	637.00
60 A	EA	689.00	634.00	644.00	657.00	650.00	699.00	670.00	702.00
100 A	EA	965.00	887.00	901.00	919.00	910.00	978.00	937.00	983.00
200 A	EA	1,700	1,560	1,580	1,620	1,600	1,720	1,650	1,730
400 A	EA	3,560	3,280	3,330	3,390	3,360	3,610	3,460	3,630
600 A	EA	5,230	4,810	4,880	4,980	4,930	5,300	5,080	5,320
800 A	EA	8,720	8,020	8,150	8,310	8,230	8,850	8,480	8,890
1000 A	EA	10,900	10,000	10,200	10,400	10,300	11,100	10,600	11,100
1200 A	EA	16,700	15,400	15,600	16,000	15,800	17,000	16,300	17,100
347/600 V									
30 A	EA	678.00	624.00	634.00	646.00	640.00	688.00	659.00	691.00
60 A	EA	731.00	673.00	683.00	697.00	690.00	742.00	711.00	745.00
100 A	EA	1,050	965.00	980.00	1,000	990.00	1,060	1,020	1,070
200 A	EA	1,780	1,640	1,660	1,700	1,680	1,810	1,730	1,810
400 A	EA	3,710	3,410	3,470	3,540	3,500	3,760	3,610	3,780
600 A	EA	5,450	5,010	5,090	5,190	5,140	5,530	5,290	5,550
800 A	EA	9,900	9,110	9,250	9,430	9,340	10,000	9,620	10,100
1000 A	EA	11,000	10,100	10,300	10,500	10,400	11,200	10,700	11,200
1200 A	EA	16,400	15,100	15,300	15,700	15,500	16,700	16,000	16,700

26 28 00 Low-Voltage Circuit Protective Devices
SWITCHES
Switches, fusible type, without fuses (individual mounting)

Item	UNITS	St. John's	Halifax	Montreal	Ottawa	Toronto	Winnipeg	Calgary	Vancouver
600 V									
30 A 3 poles 3 W	EA	360.00	332.00	337.00	343.00	340.00	366.00	350.00	367.00
30 A 3 poles 4 W	EA	382.00	351.00	356.00	364.00	360.00	387.00	371.00	389.00
60 A 3 poles 3 W	EA	424.00	390.00	396.00	404.00	400.00	430.00	412.00	432.00
60 A 3 poles 4 W	EA	488.00	449.00	455.00	465.00	460.00	495.00	474.00	497.00
100 A 3 poles 3 W	EA	753.00	692.00	703.00	717.00	710.00	763.00	731.00	767.00
100 A 3 poles 4 W	EA	816.00	751.00	762.00	778.00	770.00	828.00	793.00	832.00
200 A 3 poles 3 W	EA	1,290	1,190	1,210	1,230	1,220	1,310	1,260	1,320
200 A 3 poles 4 W	EA	1,410	1,300	1,320	1,340	1,330	1,430	1,370	1,440
400 A 3 poles 3 W	EA	2,900	2,670	2,710	2,770	2,740	2,950	2,820	2,960
400 A 3 poles 4 W	EA	3,080	2,840	2,880	2,940	2,910	3,130	3,000	3,140
600 A 3 poles 3 W	EA	3,770	3,470	3,520	3,600	3,560	3,830	3,670	3,840
600 A 3 poles 4 W	EA	4,030	3,710	3,760	3,840	3,800	4,090	3,910	4,100
800 A 3 poles 3 W	EA	6,610	6,080	6,180	6,300	6,240	6,710	6,430	6,740
800 A 3 poles 4 W	EA	7,090	6,520	6,620	6,760	6,690	7,190	6,890	7,230
1200 A 3 poles 3 W	EA	8,490	7,810	7,930	8,090	8,010	8,610	8,250	8,650
1200 A 3 poles 4 W	EA	9,440	8,690	8,820	9,000	8,910	9,580	9,180	9,620

Item	UNITS	St. John's	Halifax	Montreal	Ottawa	Toronto	Winnipeg	Calgary	Vancouver
Switches, non fusible									
250 or 600 V:									
30 A 2 poles 2 W	EA	307.00	283.00	287.00	293.00	290.00	312.00	299.00	313.00
30 A 3 poles 3 W	EA	339.00	312.00	317.00	323.00	320.00	344.00	330.00	346.00
30 A 3 poles 4 W	EA	339.00	312.00	317.00	323.00	320.00	344.00	330.00	346.00
60 A 2 poles 2 W	EA	350.00	322.00	327.00	333.00	330.00	355.00	340.00	356.00
60 A 3 poles 3 W	EA	424.00	390.00	396.00	404.00	400.00	430.00	412.00	432.00
60 A 3 poles 4 W	EA	445.00	410.00	416.00	424.00	420.00	452.00	433.00	454.00
100 A 2 poles 2 W	EA	594.00	546.00	554.00	566.00	560.00	602.00	577.00	605.00
100 A 3 poles 3 W	EA	700.00	644.00	653.00	667.00	660.00	710.00	680.00	713.00
100 A 3 poles 4 W	EA	742.00	683.00	693.00	707.00	700.00	753.00	721.00	756.00
200 A 2 poles 2 W	EA	1,020	936	950	970	960	1,030	989	1,040
200 A 3 poles 3 W	EA	1,280	1,180	1,200	1,220	1,210	1,300	1,250	1,310
200 A 3 poles 4 W	EA	1,290	1,190	1,210	1,230	1,220	1,310	1,260	1,320
400 A 2 poles 2 W	EA	2,530	2,330	2,370	2,410	2,390	2,570	2,460	2,580
400 A 3 poles 3 W	EA	2,860	2,630	2,670	2,730	2,700	2,900	2,780	2,920
400 A 3 poles 4 W	EA	2,970	2,730	2,770	2,830	2,800	3,010	2,880	3,020
600 A 2 poles 2 W	EA	3,490	3,210	3,260	3,320	3,290	3,540	3,390	3,550
600 A 3 poles 3 W	EA	3,750	3,450	3,500	3,580	3,540	3,810	3,650	3,820
600 A 3 poles 4 W	EA	3,760	3,460	3,510	3,590	3,550	3,820	3,660	3,830
800 A 2 poles 2 W	EA	5,950	5,470	5,550	5,670	5,610	6,030	5,780	6,060
800 A 3 poles 3 W	EA	6,020	5,540	5,620	5,740	5,680	6,110	5,850	6,130
800 A 3 poles 4 W	EA	6,600	6,070	6,170	6,290	6,230	6,700	6,420	6,730
1200 A 2 poles 2 W	EA	7,160	6,580	6,680	6,820	6,750	7,260	6,950	7,290
1200 A 3 poles 3 W	EA	7,170	6,590	6,690	6,830	6,760	7,270	6,960	7,300
1200 A 3 poles 4 W	EA	7,880	7,240	7,360	7,500	7,430	7,990	7,650	8,020
Splitters troughs									
125 A:									
3', 3 poles	EA	232.00	214.00	217.00	221.00	219.00	235.00	226.00	237.00
3', 4 poles	EA	301.00	277.00	281.00	287.00	284.00	305.00	293.00	307.00
225 A:									
3', 3 poles	EA	392.00	361.00	366.00	374.00	370.00	398.00	381.00	400.00
3', 4 poles	EA	498.00	458.00	465.00	475.00	470.00	505.00	484.00	508.00
400 A									
4', 3 poles	EA	625.00	575.00	584.00	596.00	590.00	634.00	608.00	637.00
4', 4 poles	EA	700.00	644.00	653.00	667.00	660.00	710.00	680.00	713.00
600 A:									
4', 3 poles	EA	1,060	975	990	1,010	1,000	1,080	1,030	1,080
4', 4 poles	EA	1,170	1,070	1,090	1,110	1,100	1,180	1,130	1,190

26 28 16 Enclosed Switches and Circuit Breakers
CIRCUIT BREAKERS

Item	UNITS	St. John's	Halifax	Montreal	Ottawa	Toronto	Winnipeg	Calgary	Vancouver
Circuit Breakers:									
347/600 V, single pole									
15-30A	EA	146.00	135.00	137.00	139.00	138.00	148.00	142.00	149.00
40-60A	EA	173.00	159.00	161.00	165.00	163.00	175.00	168.00	176.00
70-100A	EA	220.00	203.00	206.00	210.00	208.00	224.00	214.00	225.00
600 V, 2 poles									
15-30A	EA	353.00	325.00	330.00	336.00	333.00	358.00	343.00	360.00
40-60A	EA	418.00	384.00	390.00	398.00	394.00	424.00	406.00	426.00
70-100A	EA	455.00	418.00	425.00	433.00	429.00	461.00	442.00	463.00
125-225A	EA	1,060	971.00	986.00	1,010	996.00	1,070	1,030	1,080
250A	EA	1,740	1,600	1,620	1,660	1,640	1,760	1,690	1,770
300-400A	EA	2,190	2,020	2,050	2,090	2,070	2,230	2,130	2,240
600A	EA	3,220	2,960	3,010	3,070	3,040	3,270	3,130	3,280
800A	EA	5,830	5,360	5,450	5,560	5,500	5,910	5,670	5,940
1000-1200A	EA	10,600	9,750	9,900	10,100	10,000	10,800	10,300	10,800
600 V, 3 poles									
15-30A	EA	444.00	409.00	415.00	423.00	419.00	450.00	432.00	453.00
40-60A	EA	517.00	476.00	483.00	493.00	488.00	525.00	503.00	527.00
70-100A	EA	572.00	527.00	535.00	545.00	540.00	581.00	556.00	583.00
125-225A	EA	1,270	1,170	1,190	1,210	1,200	1,290	1,240	1,300
250A	EA	1,830	1,690	1,710	1,750	1,730	1,860	1,780	1,870
300-400A	EA	2,730	2,520	2,550	2,610	2,580	2,770	2,660	2,790
600A	EA	4,230	3,890	3,950	4,030	3,990	4,290	4,110	4,310
800A	EA	6,070	5,590	5,670	5,790	5,730	6,160	5,900	6,190
1000-1200A	EA	11,300	10,400	10,600	10,800	10,700	11,500	11,000	11,600
120/208 V, single pole									
15-25A	EA	41.30	38.00	38.60	39.40	39.00	41.90	40.20	42.10
30-60A	EA	49.80	45.80	46.50	47.50	47.00	50.50	48.40	50.80
70A	EA	64.70	59.50	60.40	61.60	61.00	65.60	62.80	65.90
90-100A	EA	212.00	195.00	198.00	202.00	200.00	215.00	206.00	216.00
120/208 V, 2 poles									
15-25A	EA	75.30	69.20	70.30	71.70	71.00	76.30	73.10	76.70
30-60A	EA	90.10	82.90	84.20	85.90	85.00	91.40	87.60	91.80
70A	EA	121.00	111.00	113.00	115.00	114.00	123.00	117.00	123.00
90A	EA	173.00	159.00	161.00	165.00	163.00	175.00	168.00	176.00
100A	EA	517.00	476.00	483.00	493.00	488.00	525.00	503.00	527.00
125-225A	EA	1,010	933.00	947.00	967.00	957.00	1,030	986.00	1,030
250A	EA	1,530	1,400	1,430	1,450	1,440	1,550	1,480	1,560
300-400A	EA	2,090	1,920	1,950	1,990	1,970	2,120	2,030	2,130
600A	EA	3,100	2,850	2,890	2,950	2,920	3,140	3,010	3,150
800A	EA	5,600	5,150	5,230	5,330	5,280	5,680	5,440	5,700

Item	UNITS	St. John's	Halifax	Montreal	Ottawa	Toronto	Winnipeg	Calgary	Vancouver
1000-1200A	EA	10,200	9,410	9,550	9,750	9,650	10,400	9,940	10,400
120/208 V, 3 poles									
15-25A	EA	186.00	171.00	173.00	177.00	175.00	188.00	180.00	189.00
30-60A	EA	201.00	185.00	188.00	192.00	190.00	204.00	196.00	205.00
70A	EA	257.00	236.00	240.00	244.00	242.00	260.00	249.00	261.00
90A	EA	297.00	273.00	277.00	283.00	280.00	301.00	288.00	302.00
100A	EA	626.00	576.00	585.00	597.00	591.00	635.00	609.00	638.00
125-150A	EA	1,210	1,110	1,130	1,150	1,140	1,230	1,170	1,230
175-225A	EA	1,230	1,130	1,150	1,170	1,160	1,250	1,190	1,250
250A	EA	1,610	1,480	1,500	1,540	1,520	1,630	1,570	1,640
300-400A	EA	2,670	2,460	2,490	2,550	2,520	2,710	2,600	2,720
600A	EA	4,140	3,810	3,870	3,950	3,910	4,200	4,030	4,220
800A	EA	5,940	5,460	5,540	5,660	5,600	6,020	5,770	6,050
1000-1200A	EA	11,100	10,200	10,400	10,600	10,500	11,300	10,800	11,300
Ground Fault Circuit Breakers:									
120/208 V, single pole									
15-30A	EA	211.00	194.00	197.00	201.00	199.00	214.00	205.00	215.00
40A	EA	237.00	218.00	222.00	226.00	224.00	241.00	231.00	242.00
120/208 V, 2 poles									
15-30A	EA	393.00	362.00	367.00	375.00	371.00	399.00	382.00	401.00
40-50A	EA	443.00	408.00	414.00	422.00	418.00	449.00	431.00	451.00

26 32 00 Packaged Generator Assemblies
POWER GENERATION

Complete operating system, including 2 ATS for
emergency and essential power

Item	UNITS	St. John's	Halifax	Montreal	Ottawa	Toronto	Winnipeg	Calgary	Vancouver
347-600 V									
50 kW	EA	46,600	42,900	43,600	44,400	44,000	47,300	45,300	47,500
60 kW	EA	60,300	55,500	56,300	57,500	56,900	61,200	58,600	61,500
100 kW	EA	77,200	71,000	72,100	73,500	72,800	78,300	75,000	78,600
150 kW	EA	98,100	90,200	91,600	93,400	92,500	99,400	95,300	99,900
200 kW	EA	114,000	105,000	107,000	109,000	108,000	116,000	111,000	117,000
300 kW	EA	157,000	144,000	147,000	149,000	148,000	159,000	152,000	160,000
500 kW	EA	232,000	214,000	217,000	221,000	219,000	235,000	226,000	237,000
800 kW	EA	370,000	340,000	346,000	352,000	349,000	375,000	359,000	377,000

26 50 00 Lighting
26 51 00 Interior Lighting
INTERIOR LIGHTING FIXTURES

Fluorescent, medium quality (T-8 lamps included)

Item	UNITS	St. John's	Halifax	Montreal	Ottawa	Toronto	Winnipeg	Calgary	Vancouver
Surface mounted, strip fixture (no louvre or guard):									
48", 1 tube	EA	147.00	136.00	138.00	140.00	139.00	149.00	143.00	150.00
48", 2 tube	EA	159.00	146.00	149.00	152.00	150.00	161.00	155.00	162.00
48", 4 tube, tandem	EA	240.00	220.00	224.00	228.00	226.00	243.00	233.00	244.00
Surface mounted, wrap-around lens:									
48", 2 tube	EA	193.00	177.00	180.00	184.00	182.00	196.00	187.00	197.00
48", 4 tube	EA	275.00	253.00	256.00	262.00	259.00	278.00	267.00	280.00
Surface mounted, lay-in lens:									
48", 2 tube	EA	237.00	218.00	222.00	226.00	224.00	241.00	231.00	242.00
48", 4 tube	EA	268.00	247.00	250.00	256.00	253.00	272.00	261.00	273.00
Surface mounted, damp locations:									
48", 2 tube	EA	444.00	409.00	415.00	423.00	419.00	450.00	432.00	453.00
Suspended fixtures:									
48", 2 tube	EA	240.00	220.00	224.00	228.00	226.00	243.00	233.00	244.00
48", 4 tube	EA	268.00	247.00	250.00	256.00	253.00	272.00	261.00	273.00
96", 2 tube high bay, high output	EA	482.00	444.00	450.00	460.00	455.00	489.00	469.00	491.00
Recessed, acrylic lens:									
48", 2 tube	EA	235.00	216.00	220.00	224.00	222.00	239.00	229.00	240.00
48", 4 tube	EA	269.00	248.00	251.00	257.00	254.00	273.00	262.00	274.00
Recessed, direct / indirect									
48", 2 tube	EA	258.00	237.00	241.00	245.00	243.00	261.00	250.00	262.00
48", 4 tube	EA	299.00	275.00	279.00	285.00	282.00	303.00	290.00	305.00
Incandescent (lamps and stems included)									
Industrial type:									
RLM dome, 200 W	EA	288.00	265.00	269.00	275.00	272.00	292.00	280.00	294.00
Vapourtight, 150 W	EA	578.00	531.00	540.00	550.00	545.00	586.00	561.00	589.00
Explosion proof, 150 W	EA	972.00	894.00	908.00	926.00	917.00	986.00	945.00	990.00
Commercial type:									
Compact fluorescent	EA	278.00	255.00	259.00	265.00	262.00	282.00	270.00	283.00
Wall-washer, compact fluorescent	EA	288.00	265.00	269.00	275.00	272.00	292.00	280.00	294.00
HID (ballast, lamps etc. included)									
High bay type:									
400 W, single MH	EA	676.00	622.00	632.00	644.00	638.00	686.00	657.00	689.00
400 W, twin MH	EA	959.00	882.00	896.00	914.00	905.00	973.00	932.00	977.00
Low bay type:									
400 W, single MH	EA	349.00	321.00	326.00	332.00	329.00	354.00	339.00	355.00
400 W, twin MH	EA	959.00	882.00	896.00	914.00	905.00	973.00	932.00	977.00
LED luminaire (housing, trim and lamp included)									
Commercial type:									
LED downlight, 4" diameter	EA	373.00	343.00	348.00	356.00	352.00	378.00	363.00	380.00
LED downlight, 6" diameter	EA	545.00	501.00	509.00	519.00	514.00	553.00	529.00	555.00
Linear LED, including driver	LF	101.00	93.00	94.40	96.40	95.40	103.00	98.30	103.00

Item	UNITS	St. John's	Halifax	Montreal	Ottawa	Toronto	Winnipeg	Calgary	Vancouver
LED recessed, including dimmable driver	EA	615.00	566.00	574.00	586.00	580.00	624.00	597.00	626.00
LED decorative wall wash	EA	579.00	532.00	541.00	551.00	546.00	587.00	562.00	590.00

26 52 00 Emergency Lighting
EXIT & EMERGENCY LIGHTING
Exit lights:

Item	UNITS	St. John's	Halifax	Montreal	Ottawa	Toronto	Winnipeg	Calgary	Vancouver
1 face (ceiling or wall), LED, universal mount	EA	308.00	284.00	288.00	294.00	291.00	313.00	300.00	314.00

Emergency battery unit includes twin head, receptacle and mounting brackets
24 V:

Item	UNITS	St. John's	Halifax	Montreal	Ottawa	Toronto	Winnipeg	Calgary	Vancouver
200 W	EA	958.00	881.00	895.00	913.00	904.00	972.00	931.00	976.00
300 W	EA	1,070	985.00	1,000	1,020	1,010	1,090	1,040	1,090

12 V:

Item	UNITS	St. John's	Halifax	Montreal	Ottawa	Toronto	Winnipeg	Calgary	Vancouver
200 W	EA	851.00	783.00	795.00	811.00	803.00	863.00	827.00	867.00
300 W	EA	1,010	933.00	947.00	967.00	957.00	1,030	986.00	1,030
360 W	EA	1,110	1,020	1,040	1,060	1,050	1,130	1,080	1,130

Heads operative average distance 20'

Item	UNITS	St. John's	Halifax	Montreal	Ottawa	Toronto	Winnipeg	Calgary	Vancouver
12 V or 24 V, single	EA	130.00	120.00	122.00	124.00	123.00	132.00	127.00	133.00
12 V or 24 V, twin	EA	158.00	145.00	148.00	150.00	149.00	160.00	153.00	161.00

26 56 00 Exterior Lighting
WALL AND POLE MOUNTED
Exterior wall pack:

Item	UNITS	St. John's	Halifax	Montreal	Ottawa	Toronto	Winnipeg	Calgary	Vancouver
70 W, MH	EA	578.00	531.00	540.00	550.00	545.00	586.00	561.00	589.00
250 W, MH	EA	684.00	629.00	639.00	651.00	645.00	693.00	664.00	697.00
400 W, MH	EA	702.00	645.00	655.00	669.00	662.00	712.00	682.00	715.00
LED, including cut-off shield	EA	1,280	1,180	1,200	1,220	1,210	1,300	1,250	1,310

Exterior pole mounted, includes 30' pole:

Item	UNITS	St. John's	Halifax	Montreal	Ottawa	Toronto	Winnipeg	Calgary	Vancouver
1 x 400 W, MH	EA	3,130	2,880	2,920	2,980	2,950	3,170	3,040	3,190
2 x 400 W, MH	EA	3,760	3,460	3,510	3,590	3,550	3,820	3,660	3,830
LED, including cut-off shield	EA	4,940	4,540	4,610	4,710	4,660	5,010	4,800	5,030

27: COMMUNICATIONS
27 15 00 Communications Horizontal Cabling
Components

Item	UNITS	St. John's	Halifax	Montreal	Ottawa	Toronto	Winnipeg	Calgary	Vancouver
Cat 6 cable drop	EA	230.00	212.00	215.00	219.00	217.00	233.00	224.00	234.00
Cat 6 communication horizontal cable	LF	0.87	0.80	0.81	0.83	0.82	0.88	0.85	0.89
Communication data rack and patch panel	EA	3,660	3,360	3,420	3,480	3,450	3,710	3,550	3,730
Voice data outlet (jack and empty conduit)	EA	172.00	158.00	160.00	164.00	162.00	174.00	167.00	175.00

28: ELECTRONIC SAFETY & SECURITY
28 16 00 Intrusion Detection
CARD ACCESS & ALARM SYSTEM
Card Access & Alarm System
Basic computer / processor unit, keyboard, printer, control terminal, cabinet and multiplexer panels, wiring and conduit with 15 card reading stations, 30 devices and 1000 photo access cards

Item	UNITS	St. John's	Halifax	Montreal	Ottawa	Toronto	Winnipeg	Calgary	Vancouver
Price per system	EA	64,700	59,500	60,400	61,600	61,000	65,600	62,800	65,900

Components

Item	UNITS	St. John's	Halifax	Montreal	Ottawa	Toronto	Winnipeg	Calgary	Vancouver
Card readers	EA	862.00	793.00	805.00	821.00	813.00	874.00	837.00	878.00
Door switch	EA	428.00	394.00	400.00	408.00	404.00	434.00	416.00	436.00
Door contact	EA	257.00	236.00	240.00	244.00	242.00	260.00	249.00	261.00
Electrical strike	EA	578.00	531.00	540.00	550.00	545.00	586.00	561.00	589.00
Mag lock	EA	1,050	965.00	980.00	1,000	990.00	1,060	1,020	1,070
Request to exit	EA	428.00	394.00	400.00	408.00	404.00	434.00	416.00	436.00

28 23 00 Video Surveillance
Card Access & Alarm System
Components

Item	UNITS	St. John's	Halifax	Montreal	Ottawa	Toronto	Winnipeg	Calgary	Vancouver
CCTV camera	EA	2,000	1,840	1,870	1,910	1,890	2,030	1,950	2,040
CCTV camera PTZ	EA	2,930	2,690	2,730	2,790	2,760	2,970	2,840	2,980
CCTV camera PTZ, weatherproof	EA	3,520	3,240	3,290	3,350	3,320	3,570	3,420	3,590

28 30 00 Electronic Detection and Alarm
28 31 00 Fire Detection and Alarm
FIRE ALARM SYSTEMS - ADDRESSABLE
Fire alarm systems, not wired, price of components only
1 stage, with smoke protection (batteries included):

Item	UNITS	St. John's	Halifax	Montreal	Ottawa	Toronto	Winnipeg	Calgary	Vancouver
Control panel 4 zones	EA	4,490	4,130	4,200	4,280	4,240	4,560	4,370	4,580
Control panel 8 zones	EA	5,460	5,020	5,100	5,200	5,150	5,540	5,300	5,560
Control panel 12 zones	EA	6,930	6,380	6,470	6,610	6,540	7,030	6,740	7,060
Control panel 24 zones	EA	11,100	10,200	10,400	10,600	10,500	11,300	10,800	11,300
Annunciator 4 zones	EA	1,350	1,240	1,260	1,280	1,270	1,370	1,310	1,370
Annunciator 8 zones	EA	1,860	1,710	1,730	1,770	1,750	1,880	1,800	1,890
Annunciator 12 zones	EA	2,340	2,150	2,190	2,230	2,210	2,380	2,280	2,390
Annunciator 24 zones	EA	3,480	3,200	3,250	3,310	3,280	3,530	3,380	3,540

Item	UNITS	St. John's	Halifax	Montreal	Ottawa	Toronto	Winnipeg	Calgary	Vancouver
2 stage, with smoke detection (batteries included):									
Control panel 4 zones	EA	6,030	5,550	5,630	5,750	5,690	6,120	5,860	6,150
Control panel 8 zones	EA	7,730	7,110	7,220	7,360	7,290	7,840	7,510	7,870
Control panel 12 zones	EA	9,720	8,940	9,080	9,260	9,170	9,860	9,450	9,900
Control panel 24 zones	EA	13,500	12,400	12,600	12,800	12,700	13,700	13,100	13,700
Components:									
Bells	EA	278.00	255.00	259.00	265.00	262.00	282.00	270.00	283.00
Manual station, 1 stage	EA	257.00	236.00	240.00	244.00	242.00	260.00	249.00	261.00
Manual station, 2 stage	EA	267.00	246.00	249.00	255.00	252.00	271.00	260.00	272.00
Fire detection	EA	364.00	334.00	340.00	346.00	343.00	369.00	353.00	370.00
Smoke detector, surface type	EA	331.00	304.00	309.00	315.00	312.00	335.00	321.00	337.00
Smoke detector, duct type	EA	738.00	679.00	689.00	703.00	696.00	748.00	717.00	752.00
Horns	EA	283.00	260.00	264.00	270.00	267.00	287.00	275.00	288.00
Strobes	EA	283.00	260.00	264.00	270.00	267.00	287.00	275.00	288.00
Horn / strobe	EA	324.00	298.00	303.00	309.00	306.00	329.00	315.00	330.00

31: EARTHWORK

31 13 13 Selective Tree and Shrub Removal
SELECTIVE TREE REMOVAL & TRIMMING
Tree removal in restricted areas

Item	UNITS	St. John's	Halifax	Montreal	Ottawa	Toronto	Winnipeg	Calgary	Vancouver
Complete removal:									
24" diameter	EA	957.00	963.00	862.00	990.00	1,040.00	994.00	926.00	1,250.00

31 22 00 Grading
LOAM OR TOPSOIL
Rough Grading

Item	UNITS	St. John's	Halifax	Montreal	Ottawa	Toronto	Winnipeg	Calgary	Vancouver
Strip and stockpile topsoil:									
Pull scraper not exceeding 500' haul	CY	3.60	3.43	3.54	3.56	3.28	4.01	2.93	3.62
Cut, fill and compact:									
Pull scraper not exceeding 700' haul	CY	3.88	3.68	3.82	3.78	3.56	4.34	3.15	3.94
Self propelled scraper not exceeding 1600' haul	CY	4.71	4.48	4.66	4.62	4.35	5.24	3.92	4.79
Cut and stockpile:									
Front end loader operation	CY	3.91	3.56	3.69	3.62	3.41	4.20	3.04	3.82
Scraper operation	CY	3.73	3.41	3.52	3.49	3.28	3.88	2.93	3.53
Fill and compact from stockpile:									
Pull scraper not exceeding 700' haul	CY	4.14	3.75	3.81	3.97	3.68	4.25	3.30	3.95
Self propelled scraper not exceeding 1600' haul	CY	4.98	4.62	4.70	4.74	4.43	5.09	3.98	4.76
Fill with imported granular material (not exceeding:									
10 mile haul):									
Machine operation	CY	32.60	32.30	32.80	33.60	30.50	37.30	26.50	33.70
Hand operation	CY	84.90	78.70	83.30	84.90	77.20	93.30	67.40	84.90

FINE GRADE
Finish grading

Item	UNITS	St. John's	Halifax	Montreal	Ottawa	Toronto	Winnipeg	Calgary	Vancouver
By machine:									
Grader	SY	1.71	1.52	1.67	1.61	1.49	1.82	1.34	1.65
Roller	SY	0.92	0.80	0.88	0.87	0.83	0.97	0.73	0.90
By hand:									
To rough grades	SY	4.06	3.53	3.99	3.81	3.48	4.22	3.03	3.86
To finish grades	SY	5.89	5.17	5.79	5.59	5.08	6.20	4.36	5.61

31 23 00 Excavation and Fill
31 23 16 Excavation
EXCAVATING
Machine excavation - building (excluding hauling cost)

Item	UNITS	St. John's	Halifax	Montreal	Ottawa	Toronto	Winnipeg	Calgary	Vancouver
Bulk excavation medium soil (including checker/labourer):									
Backhoe operation, 80 cy/hour	CY	4.55	4.66	4.20	4.49	4.55	5.21	4.21	7.08
Front end loader operation, 80 cy/hour	CY	3.52	3.59	3.44	3.52	3.63	4.14	3.40	5.54
Bulk excavation, rock:									
Ripping	CY	13.50	13.10	10.30	10.00	11.60	14.50	11.60	12.50
Trench and footing excavation medium soil									
For foundation walls									
Not exceeding 6' deep	CY	13.80	13.70	13.60	13.00	14.20	21.20	15.50	24.60
Over 6' not exceeding 12' deep	CY	9.25	9.25	9.02	8.64	9.48	13.80	10.20	15.50
For column footings									
Not exceeding 6' deep	CY	16.50	16.10	17.00	15.20	16.30	24.30	17.60	28.50
Over 6' not exceeding 12' deep	CY	13.30	12.70	13.30	11.90	13.20	18.90	14.00	21.10
Excavation below level of basement:									
For wall footings not exceeding 2' deep	CY	7.27	7.12	6.80	5.54	7.80	11.50	8.79	13.50
Trench and footing excavation, rock:									
For foundation walls not exceeding 12' deep	CY	157.00	151.00	164.00	181.00	177.00	229.00	164.00	177.00
For footings	CY	167.00	166.00	177.00	190.00	187.00	239.00	174.00	187.00
Hand excavation									
Not exceeding 6' deep:									
Normal soil	CY	71.60	77.20	96.30	84.90	91.00	135.00	94.00	157.00
Rock (hand-held compressor tool)	CY	380.00	376.00	409.00	401.00	423.00	544.00	405.00	425.00
Clean off rock face	SF	33.30	31.00	31.60	29.70	31.50	40.90	30.00	31.50
Bulk excavation, normal soil (external), minimum volume									
2600 CY									
Wide open areas	CY	22.20	28.40	28.70	29.70	29.40	37.80	25.80	40.50
Adjacent building 100' distant	CY	61.30	79.50	79.50	82.60	82.60	107.00	72.90	115.00

Item	UNITS	St. John's	Halifax	Montreal	Ottawa	Toronto	Winnipeg	Calgary	Vancouver
Trench excavation, normal soil (external)									
Wide open areas....................	CY	50.00	60.60	72.30	61.70	64.10	85.60	56.20	92.50
Adjacent buildings 100' distant....................	CY	142.00	175.00	211.00	180.00	187.00	249.00	162.00	270.00

31 23 19 Dewatering
DEWATERING
Pumping prices include attendance consumables and 33' of discharge pipe

Item	UNITS	St. John's	Halifax	Montreal	Ottawa	Toronto	Winnipeg	Calgary	Vancouver
Electrically powered:									
20 gpm, 2 hp submersible	DAY	64.80	60.00	60.00	73.60	77.00	77.40	58.10	61.60
600 gpm, 30 hp	DAY	216.00	200.00	207.00	252.00	257.00	264.00	194.00	205.00
Gas or diesel powered:									
600 gpm, 30 hp	DAY	352.00	335.00	355.00	416.00	427.00	436.00	335.00	331.00
Drainage trenches and pits									
Trenches 6' wide including backfill:									
2' deep by machine	LF	4.48	4.45	4.30	4.27	4.63	6.95	4.97	7.99
3' deep by machine	LF	5.73	5.79	5.61	5.73	6.07	9.08	6.52	10.40
4' deep by machine	LF	7.35	7.19	7.32	7.25	7.74	11.40	8.05	13.10
Wellpoint system, single stage. 500' system consisting of 1 1/2" diameter wellpoints at 5' o.c. spacing and 8" diameter header pipe, to maximum depth of 24'									
Installation of 500' header system									
including all labour & materials	EA	N/A	35,600.00	40,000.00	N/A	46,800.00	43,000.00	37,500.00	50,700.00
Rental of 500' installed system - first month	MONTH	N/A	23,400.00	23,900.00	N/A	27,600.00	28,900.00	25,300.00	23,200.00
Add for rental of system for each subsequent month............	MONTH	N/A	17,900.00	17,800.00	N/A	20,900.00	21,800.00	19,200.00	18,400.00
Daily maintenance of system including site checks, oil, filters, fuel	DAY	N/A	593.00	725.00	N/A	823.00	725.00	641.00	748.00
24 hour supervision of system (OPTIONAL)	DAY	N/A	2,140.00	2,380.00	N/A	2,610.00	2,700.00	2,350.00	2,140.00

31 23 23 Fill
BACKFILL
Backfill and compaction

Item	UNITS	St. John's	Halifax	Montreal	Ottawa	Toronto	Winnipeg	Calgary	Vancouver
Excavated materials, place & compact for grading............	CY	10.10	11.50	10.90	10.70	11.90	16.10	14.20	19.00
Pit run gravel not exceeding 10 mile haul............	CY	26.40	29.30	27.40	27.00	30.40	40.80	35.90	46.70
Crushed stone to weeping tiles............	CY	50.50	56.00	52.20	51.20	58.00	77.20	68.00	91.00
3/4" crushed stone to under side of slab-on-grade, not exceeding 10 mile haul	CY	45.80	51.00	47.70	47.00	52.60	71.50	61.40	83.30

HAULING
Waste material disposal

Item	UNITS	St. John's	Halifax	Montreal	Ottawa	Toronto	Winnipeg	Calgary	Vancouver
Hauling:									
1 hour return trip	CY	11.90	11.60	15.90	12.20	14.20	15.30	14.60	26.50
Dump charges for typical urban city, tipping fees only									
(rates vary based on material types, check with local municipality)									
Building construction materials	TON	N/A	N/A	N/A	N/A	N/A	N/A	N/A	N/A
Excavated clean soil, non-hazardous material............	TON	N/A	N/A	N/A	N/A	N/A	N/A	N/A	N/A

31 40 00 Shoring and Underpinning
SHEET PILING
Steel

Item	UNITS	St. John's	Halifax	Montreal	Ottawa	Toronto	Winnipeg	Calgary	Vancouver
Left in place:									
25' deep, 30 lbs/sf............	SF	57.90	57.60	64.10	72.90	63.00	110.00	101.00	105.00

UNDERPINNING

Item	UNITS	St. John's	Halifax	Montreal	Ottawa	Toronto	Winnipeg	Calgary	Vancouver
Average Cost............	CY	1,060.00	1,130.00	1,220.00	1,430.00	115.00	2,080.00	1,900.00	2,180.00

31 50 00 Excavation Support and Protection
SOLDIER PILES & LAGGING

Item	UNITS	St. John's	Halifax	Montreal	Ottawa	Toronto	Winnipeg	Calgary	Vancouver
20' deep	SF	45.70	43.60	47.20	61.80	66.30	92.80	68.60	83.60
35' deep	SF	50.40	49.30	52.40	67.70	73.60	102.00	75.10	92.40

31 60 00 Special Foundations
& Load-Bearing Elements
31 62 00 Driven Piles
PILES, CONCRETE
Concrete piles

Item	UNITS	St. John's	Halifax	Montreal	Ottawa	Toronto	Winnipeg	Calgary	Vancouver
Precast piles:									
12" x 12" hexagonal	LF	102.00	102.00	N/A	N/A	N/A	86.30	N/A	83.80
16" x 16" hexagonal	LF	119.00	119.00	N/A	N/A	N/A	95.40	N/A	92.70

PILES, STEEL
Steel piles

Item	UNITS	St. John's	Halifax	Montreal	Ottawa	Toronto	Winnipeg	Calgary	Vancouver
Steel H-piles:									
12", 53 lb/ft............	LF	99.40	78.90	83.20	85.00	83.80	135.00	95.70	172.00
Steel pipe piles:									
10" dia., concrete filled............	LF	81.40	65.50	67.10	67.10	67.70	109.00	79.20	139.00

31 63 00 Bored Piles
CAISSONS
Drilled Caissons
In normal soil

Item	UNITS	St. John's	Halifax	Montreal	Ottawa	Toronto	Winnipeg	Calgary	Vancouver
No lining:									
24" dia.	LF	54.30	48.80	50.90	55.50	60.00	86.00	47.90	109.00
30" dia.	LF	87.80	79.60	82.90	88.70	97.20	139.00	75.90	179.00

Item	UNITS	St. John's	Halifax	Montreal	Ottawa	Toronto	Winnipeg	Calgary	Vancouver
36" dia.	LF	121.00	110.00	112.00	123.00	134.00	194.00	106.00	243.00
Lining removed:									
24" dia.	LF	68.60	60.70	64.30	70.40	76.20	109.00	59.70	138.00
30" dia.	LF	103.00	93.30	96.30	106.00	114.00	167.00	90.50	208.00
36" dia.	LF	141.00	123.00	130.00	146.00	156.00	223.00	124.00	287.00
In wet soil, pumping included									
Lining removed:									
30" dia.	LF	119.00	105.00	107.00	120.00	131.00	187.00	103.00	234.00
Lining left in place:									
30" dia.	LF	237.00	218.00	221.00	247.00	271.00	390.00	214.00	500.00
In shale or soft rock									
No lining:									
30" dia.	LF	244.00	232.00	229.00	258.00	277.00	402.00	216.00	500.00

32: EXTERIOR IMPROVEMENTS

32 11 00 Base Courses

BASE COURSES

Base courses

Grading:

Item	UNITS	St. John's	Halifax	Montreal	Ottawa	Toronto	Winnipeg	Calgary	Vancouver
Prepare sub-base	SY	1.40	1.39	1.43	1.37	1.35	1.66	1.20	1.59
Granular bases:									
Pit run gravel, 12" thick	CY	29.80	29.40	30.60	28.80	29.20	35.00	25.40	33.70
3/4" crushed stone	CY	55.50	54.40	57.50	55.00	54.50	65.70	47.50	62.90

32 12 00 Flexible Paving

PAVING

Bituminous paving

One layer:

Item	UNITS	St. John's	Halifax	Montreal	Ottawa	Toronto	Winnipeg	Calgary	Vancouver
2"	SY	14.50	15.00	13.50	14.00	13.00	17.90	16.70	59.10
Two layers:									
4"	SY	26.90	30.10	25.10	27.10	24.20	33.70	30.50	111.00

32 14 00 Unit Paving

PRECAST CONCRETE PAVING SLABS

Precast concrete pavers

2" thick precast pavers complete, basic

Item	UNITS	St. John's	Halifax	Montreal	Ottawa	Toronto	Winnipeg	Calgary	Vancouver
4" x 8"	SF	10.20	9.66	8.60	8.87	9.75	9.21	9.29	20.90

32 16 00 Curbs, Gutters, Sidewalks, and Driveways

CURBS

Precast concrete curb

Item	UNITS	St. John's	Halifax	Montreal	Ottawa	Toronto	Winnipeg	Calgary	Vancouver
8" x 6" x 8'	LF	17.30	7.99	12.20	12.80	14.10	17.40	14.90	59.10

32 31 00 Fences and Gates

FENCE, CHAIN LINK

Chain link fence - galvanized steel

6 gauge wire - 2" mesh:

Penitentiary type:

Item	UNITS	St. John's	Halifax	Montreal	Ottawa	Toronto	Winnipeg	Calgary	Vancouver
6' high	LF	30.80	33.20	30.80	33.50	32.30	29.60	31.70	35.70
8' high	LF	41.80	44.20	42.10	47.20	44.20	39.30	43.30	48.20
12' high	LF	53.00	57.00	53.90	58.20	56.40	51.50	55.80	62.50
9 gauge wire - 2" mesh:									
Standard type:									
6' high	LF	25.00	25.70	24.50	26.80	25.80	23.90	23.20	28.80
8' high	LF	30.00	30.50	29.40	32.00	31.10	28.70	28.00	34.40
12' high	LF	37.50	38.70	36.60	40.50	38.40	35.40	35.10	43.30
11 gauge wire - 2" mesh:									
Light commercial type:									
6' high	LF	18.70	16.00	16.50	17.70	17.50	15.60	16.90	19.90
8' high	LF	27.20	21.60	24.00	25.80	25.30	22.40	24.50	28.80
12' high	LF	36.60	29.90	32.90	35.10	34.40	30.80	33.20	37.80
Barbed wire top protection:									
3 strands	LF	3.35	2.99	3.17	3.51	3.41	3.04	3.23	3.96
Galvanized steel gates:									
2" mesh, 6' high	LF	82.90	78.30	79.60	86.30	84.10	74.70	82.00	97.80

32 90 00 Planting

32 91 00 Planting Preparation

SOIL PREPARATION

Spread and grade topsoil by machine

Item	UNITS	St. John's	Halifax	Montreal	Ottawa	Toronto	Winnipeg	Calgary	Vancouver
From site stockpile	CY	11.50	10.90	12.50	11.90	11.60	12.80	8.33	11.90
Import (including cost of soil)	CY	42.50	40.10	36.50	43.90	43.50	41.10	31.00	40.60

Fine grade topsoil by hand

Item	UNITS	St. John's	Halifax	Montreal	Ottawa	Toronto	Winnipeg	Calgary	Vancouver
To slopes, banks and the like	SY	4.81	4.84	5.08	5.23	5.25	5.11	3.99	5.28

DIV 32 Exterior Improvements – IMPERIAL CURRENT MARKET PRICES

Item	UNITS	St. John's	Halifax	Montreal	Ottawa	Toronto	Winnipeg	Calgary	Vancouver
32 92 00 Turf and Grasses									
SEEDING									
Seeding, mechanical application assumes soil prepared and work carried out in best sowing periods									
Lawns (area not exceeding 12,000 sy)									
$2.00/lb, 45 lbs/1000 sy	SY	1.04	0.71	1.29	1.08	1.15	1.51	1.44	1.24
Hydro seeding, over 12,000 sy									
Level areas (wood fibre mulch)	SY	1.17	0.73	1.09	0.89	1.14	1.32	1.43	1.27
Sloping areas (liquid plastic)	SY	1.37	0.84	1.26	1.01	1.28	1.51	1.61	1.45
SODDING									
Sodding									
1/4" to 3/4" thick cut nursery sod:									
No. 1 grade to level ground	SY	5.30	4.18	4.64	4.60	5.02	7.02	6.40	6.04
No. 1 grade to slopes	SY	6.81	5.38	5.94	5.93	6.45	8.95	8.19	7.70
32 93 00 Plants									
SHRUBS & TREES									
All trees earth balled and burlapped. All plantings to be staked and guyed as necessary. Prices cover excavation and reinstatement and include maintenance and full guarantee. Planting assumed in normal season. All trees nursery grown.									
Trees, deciduous									
Sugar maple and linden and ash:									
10-12' high (1 1/2" calliper)	EA	436.00	329.00	392.00	410.00	418.00	484.00	417.00	477.00
2-2 1/2" calliper	EA	794.00	615.00	718.00	758.00	774.00	893.00	774.00	882.00
3-3 1/2" calliper	EA	1,170	883.00	1,040	1,090	1,110	1,280	1,110	1,290
Silver maple:									
10-12' high (1 1/2" calliper)	EA	387.00	300.00	350.00	360.00	388.00	473.00	397.00	500.00
2-2 1/2" calliper	EA	601.00	471.00	547.00	555.00	600.00	731.00	609.00	767.00
3-3 1/2" calliper	EA	1,070	867.00	990.00	1,010	1,090	1,320	1,110	1,390
Red maple and honey locust:									
10-12' high (1 1/2" calliper)	EA	493.00	414.00	469.00	433.00	464.00	636.00	521.00	490.00
2-2 1/2" calliper	EA	783.00	663.00	742.00	697.00	740.00	1,010	831.00	783.00
3-3 1/2" calliper	EA	1,470	1,250	1,390	1,300	1,380	1,900	1,560	1,470
Trees, evergreen									
Cedar:									
4-5' high	EA	150.00	154.00	179.00	163.00	174.00	173.00	201.00	197.00
5-6' high	EA	330.00	338.00	390.00	351.00	379.00	368.00	444.00	412.00
6-8' high	EA	534.00	549.00	644.00	580.00	619.00	608.00	722.00	675.00
Spruce:									
4-5' high	EA	274.00	273.00	298.00	323.00	294.00	277.00	356.00	325.00
5-6' high	EA	427.00	429.00	475.00	506.00	464.00	439.00	498.00	519.00
6-8' high	EA	607.00	612.00	673.00	716.00	658.00	622.00	810.00	736.00
Pine:									
4-5' high	EA	300.00	282.00	313.00	336.00	309.00	301.00	333.00	325.00
5-6' high	EA	497.00	472.00	512.00	548.00	504.00	488.00	543.00	539.00
6-8' high	EA	751.00	745.00	780.00	837.00	767.00	750.00	834.00	802.00
Shrubs									
Forsythia and honey suckle:									
3-4' high	EA	61.70	62.50	57.20	55.70	62.70	62.20	57.40	56.60
4-5' high	EA	79.50	80.30	73.70	72.10	80.60	79.70	73.50	72.20
Oleaster (Russian Olive):									
3-4' high	EA	68.20	62.50	57.20	55.70	62.70	62.20	57.40	56.60
4-5' high	EA	77.60	71.60	65.50	63.40	71.50	71.20	66.10	63.60
Flowering crab-tree:									
3-4' high	EA	109.00	93.80	90.00	89.70	102.00	100.00	91.00	94.40
4-5' high	EA	130.00	113.00	106.00	108.00	121.00	120.00	109.00	111.00
Beautybush:									
3-4' high	EA	75.30	73.20	72.20	66.90	80.60	76.70	67.40	75.40
4-5' high	EA	97.90	94.60	92.40	86.30	104.00	99.20	86.60	94.40
Spirea:									
2-4' high	EA	51.90	48.30	50.80	46.50	53.80	54.60	45.60	51.60
4-5' high	EA	69.00	64.30	67.00	60.90	71.50	72.80	60.30	66.90
Dogwood:									
3-4' high	EA	60.00	56.30	47.50	46.50	55.40	54.60	51.30	51.60
4-5' high	EA	99.30	93.00	81.70	77.00	92.30	91.20	86.60	85.80
Hedges									
Yews:									
30-36" high	LF	66.40	62.80	60.40	51.50	68.90	76.80	51.20	63.10
36-42" high	LF	105.00	97.80	92.70	81.10	109.00	123.00	81.10	101.00
Privet:									
3-4' high	LF	17.30	17.20	18.20	16.60	19.10	20.60	16.60	17.30
4-5' high	LF	22.00	21.90	23.40	21.10	24.60	26.40	21.50	23.00
Boxwood:									
10-12" high	LF	56.10	57.60	82.60	66.10	74.10	89.00	66.10	66.40
12-15" high	LF	63.70	66.80	93.90	75.60	85.00	102.00	75.90	80.80
Flowering currant (Alpine):									
18-24" high	LF	21.50	18.80	18.10	17.70	19.30	21.70	14.60	17.30
2-3' high	LF	27.60	23.90	23.40	22.70	24.60	27.80	18.40	23.00

Item	UNITS	St. John's	Halifax	Montreal	Ottawa	Toronto	Winnipeg	Calgary	Vancouver

33: UTILITIES

33 11 00 Water Utility Distribution Piping

PIPING, WATER DISTRIBUTION SYSTEMS

Cast iron pressure pipe based on 100' of pipe, one tee, two 90 degree elbows buried 5' deep, including excavation, bedding, anchoring and backfill.

Class 2 titon cast iron pipe:

Item	UNITS	St. John's	Halifax	Montreal	Ottawa	Toronto	Winnipeg	Calgary	Vancouver
4"	LF	82.10	75.50	76.60	78.20	77.40	83.20	79.70	83.60
6"	LF	95.60	88.00	89.30	91.10	90.20	97.00	92.90	97.40
8"	LF	113.00	104.00	106.00	108.00	107.00	115.00	110.00	116.00
10"	LF	145.00	134.00	136.00	139.00	137.00	147.00	141.00	148.00
12"	LF	171.00	157.00	160.00	163.00	161.00	173.00	166.00	174.00
14"	LF	207.00	190.00	193.00	197.00	195.00	210.00	201.00	211.00
16"	LF	244.00	225.00	228.00	233.00	230.00	248.00	237.00	249.00
18"	LF	279.00	257.00	261.00	266.00	264.00	283.00	272.00	285.00
20"	LF	319.00	293.00	298.00	304.00	301.00	323.00	310.00	325.00
24"	LF	420.00	386.00	392.00	400.00	396.00	426.00	408.00	428.00

Schedule 40 PVC pressure pipe with cast iron fittings based on 100' of pipe, one tee, two 90-degree elbows, buried 5' deep, including excavation, bedding, anchoring and backfill:

C900 PVC pipe:

Item	UNITS	St. John's	Halifax	Montreal	Ottawa	Toronto	Winnipeg	Calgary	Vancouver
4"	LF	73.70	67.80	68.80	70.20	69.50	74.70	71.60	75.10
6"	LF	79.20	72.80	73.90	75.40	74.70	80.30	76.90	80.70
8"	LF	108.00	99.60	101.00	103.00	102.00	110.00	105.00	110.00
10"	LF	128.00	118.00	120.00	122.00	121.00	130.00	125.00	131.00
12"	LF	159.00	146.00	148.00	151.00	150.00	161.00	154.00	162.00

Soft copper pressure pipe (in coil) based on 132' of pipe, one coupling, one adapter, buried 5' deep, including excavation, bedding and backfill.

Soft copper pipe type k:

Item	UNITS	St. John's	Halifax	Montreal	Ottawa	Toronto	Winnipeg	Calgary	Vancouver
1/2"	LF	89.20	82.00	83.30	85.00	84.10	90.40	86.60	90.90
3/4"	LF	96.90	89.20	90.50	92.40	91.40	98.30	94.20	98.80
1"	LF	110.00	101.00	103.00	105.00	104.00	111.00	107.00	112.00
1 1/4"	LF	121.00	111.00	113.00	115.00	114.00	123.00	118.00	123.00
1 1/2"	LF	131.00	121.00	123.00	125.00	124.00	133.00	127.00	134.00

33 12 00 Water Utility Distribution Equipment

Curb stop including box buried 5' deep

Copper service pipe:

Item	UNITS	St. John's	Halifax	Montreal	Ottawa	Toronto	Winnipeg	Calgary	Vancouver
1/2"	EA	558.00	513.00	521.00	531.00	526.00	565.00	542.00	568.00
3/4"	EA	605.00	557.00	565.00	577.00	571.00	614.00	588.00	617.00
1"	EA	727.00	669.00	679.00	693.00	686.00	737.00	707.00	741.00
1 1/4"	EA	1,180	1,080	1,100	1,120	1,110	1,190	1,140	1,200
1 1/2"	EA	1,430	1,320	1,340	1,360	1,350	1,450	1,390	1,460

Cast iron service pipe:

Item	UNITS	St. John's	Halifax	Montreal	Ottawa	Toronto	Winnipeg	Calgary	Vancouver
4"	EA	2,370	2,180	2,220	2,260	2,240	2,410	2,310	2,420
6"	EA	3,230	2,970	3,020	3,080	3,050	3,280	3,140	3,290
8"	EA	4,780	4,400	4,460	4,560	4,510	4,850	4,650	4,870

33 31 00 Sanitary Utility Sewerage Piping

PIPING, DRAINAGE & SEWAGE, POLYVINYL CHLORIDE

PVC

Perforated:

Item	UNITS	St. John's	Halifax	Montreal	Ottawa	Toronto	Winnipeg	Calgary	Vancouver
4" dia.	LF	15.20	13.90	14.20	14.40	14.30	15.40	14.70	15.40
6" dia.	LF	21.90	20.20	20.50	20.90	20.70	22.20	21.30	22.40

PIPING, DRAINAGE & SEWAGE, VITRIFIED CLAY

Vitrified clay

Farm tile, 1' length

Item	UNITS	St. John's	Halifax	Montreal	Ottawa	Toronto	Winnipeg	Calgary	Vancouver
4" dia.	LF	16.70	15.30	15.60	15.90	15.70	16.90	16.20	17.00
6" dia.	LF	19.60	18.00	18.30	18.70	18.50	19.90	19.00	19.90

PIPING, DRAINAGE & SEWAGE, CONCRETE

Concrete drainage piping based on 100' of pipe including jointing, buried 5' deep, including excavation, bedding and backfilling.

Type C-76 class 3 concrete sewer pipe

Item	UNITS	St. John's	Halifax	Montreal	Ottawa	Toronto	Winnipeg	Calgary	Vancouver
6"	LF	69.10	63.60	64.60	65.90	65.20	70.10	67.20	70.40
8"	LF	82.70	76.10	77.20	78.80	78.00	83.90	80.40	84.30
10"	LF	104.00	95.70	97.20	99.10	98.10	106.00	101.00	106.00
12"	LF	112.00	103.00	104.00	107.00	105.00	113.00	109.00	114.00
15"	LF	126.00	116.00	118.00	120.00	119.00	128.00	122.00	128.00
18"	LF	141.00	130.00	132.00	134.00	133.00	143.00	137.00	144.00
21"	LF	159.00	147.00	149.00	152.00	150.00	162.00	155.00	162.00
24"	LF	193.00	178.00	180.00	184.00	182.00	196.00	188.00	197.00
27"	LF	227.00	209.00	212.00	216.00	214.00	230.00	220.00	231.00
30"	LF	273.00	251.00	255.00	260.00	257.00	277.00	265.00	278.00
36"	LF	352.00	324.00	329.00	336.00	332.00	357.00	342.00	359.00
42"	LF	433.00	398.00	404.00	413.00	408.00	439.00	421.00	441.00

Item	UNITS	St. John's	Halifax	Montreal	Ottawa	Toronto	Winnipeg	Calgary	Vancouver
33 36 00 Utility Septic Tanks									
SEPTIC TANKS									
Including excavation, stone bedding and backfilling									
Septic tank									
Steel horizontal:									
791 imp. gals.	EA	4,630	4,260	4,330	4,410	4,370	4,700	4,500	4,720
2,375 imp. gals.	EA	14,600	13,500	13,700	13,900	13,800	14,800	14,200	14,900
5,000 imp. gals.	EA	28,700	26,400	26,800	27,400	27,100	29,100	27,900	29,300
Disposal bed header pipes									
Cast iron, mechanical joint:									
4"	LF	70.80	65.10	66.10	67.40	66.80	71.80	68.80	72.10
Plastic:									
4"	LF	57.50	52.90	53.70	54.80	54.30	58.30	55.90	58.60
Plastic perforated:									
4"	LF	37.20	34.20	34.70	35.40	35.10	37.70	36.10	37.90
33 49 00 Storm Drainage Structures									
CATCH BASINS OR MANHOLES									
Catch basins, excavation and backfill included with pipe									
Poured concrete:									
2'0" x 2'0" x 4'0" deep	EA	2,600	2,390	2,430	2,470	2,450	2,630	2,520	2,650
Add for each additional 1' in depth	EA	314.00	289.00	293.00	299.00	296.00	318.00	305.00	320.00
Precast concrete:									
2'0" dia. x 4'0" deep	EA	2,190	2,020	2,050	2,090	2,070	2,230	2,130	2,240
Add for each additional 1' depth	EA	320.00	294.00	299.00	305.00	302.00	325.00	311.00	326.00
Manholes, excavation and backfill included with pipe									
Poured concrete:									
2'6" x 2'6" x 7'0" deep	EA	4,020	3,700	3,750	3,830	3,790	4,070	3,900	4,090
Add for each additional 1' depth	EA	373.00	343.00	348.00	356.00	352.00	378.00	363.00	380.00
Precast concrete:									
2'6" dia. x 7'0" deep	EA	3,400	3,130	3,180	3,240	3,210	3,450	3,310	3,470
Add for each additional 1' depth	EA	403.00	371.00	376.00	384.00	380.00	409.00	391.00	410.00
33 61 00 Hydronic Energy Distribution									
CHILLED WATER, DISTRIBUTION									
Including fittings, supports, guides and anchors,									
expansion joints and loops.									
Schedule 40 A-53 pipe									
In tunnel with 2" glass fibre insulation:									
3" dia.	LF	258.00	237.00	241.00	246.00	243.00	261.00	251.00	263.00
4" dia.	LF	286.00	263.00	267.00	272.00	270.00	290.00	278.00	291.00
5" dia.	LF	339.00	312.00	317.00	323.00	320.00	344.00	330.00	346.00
6" dia.	LF	378.00	348.00	353.00	360.00	357.00	383.00	367.00	385.00
8" dia.	LF	462.00	425.00	432.00	440.00	436.00	469.00	449.00	471.00
10" dia.	LF	594.00	547.00	555.00	566.00	561.00	603.00	578.00	606.00
12" dia.	LF	756.00	695.00	706.00	720.00	713.00	767.00	735.00	770.00
14" dia.	LF	821.00	755.00	766.00	782.00	774.00	832.00	797.00	836.00
In steel conduit including excavation & backfilling, av. 6' deep:									
3" dia.	LF	384.00	354.00	359.00	366.00	363.00	390.00	374.00	392.00
4" dia.	LF	439.00	404.00	410.00	419.00	415.00	446.00	427.00	448.00
5" dia.	LF	578.00	532.00	540.00	551.00	546.00	587.00	562.00	589.00
6" dia.	LF	659.00	606.00	616.00	628.00	622.00	668.00	640.00	672.00
8" dia.	LF	801.00	737.00	748.00	763.00	756.00	813.00	779.00	816.00
10" dia.	LF	960.00	883.00	896.00	914.00	905.00	973.00	932.00	978.00
12" dia.	LF	1,410	1,290	1,310	1,340	1,330	1,430	1,370	1,430
14" dia.	LF	1,690	1,550	1,580	1,610	1,590	1,710	1,640	1,720
33 63 00 Steam Energy Distribution									
STEAM DISTRIBUTION									
Including fittings, supports, guides and anchors, expansion joints and loops.									
Schedule 40 A-53 steam, schedule 80 seamless condensate.									
In tunnel with 2" calcium silicate insulation on steam and 1"									
glass fibre on condensate:									
3", 1 1/2"	LF	256.00	235.00	239.00	244.00	241.00	260.00	249.00	261.00
4", 2"	LF	271.00	249.00	253.00	258.00	255.00	275.00	263.00	276.00
5", 3"	LF	323.00	297.00	302.00	308.00	305.00	328.00	314.00	329.00
6", 3"	LF	368.00	339.00	344.00	351.00	347.00	374.00	358.00	375.00
8", 4"	LF	414.00	380.00	386.00	394.00	390.00	419.00	402.00	421.00
10", 5"	LF	582.00	535.00	543.00	554.00	549.00	590.00	565.00	593.00
12", 6"	LF	627.00	577.00	585.00	597.00	591.00	636.00	609.00	639.00
14", 6"	LF	795.00	731.00	742.00	757.00	750.00	806.00	772.00	810.00
In steel conduit including manhole, excavation and backfilling,									
average 6' deep:									
3", 1 1/2"	LF	452.00	416.00	422.00	431.00	427.00	459.00	440.00	461.00
4", 2"	LF	530.00	487.00	495.00	505.00	500.00	537.00	515.00	540.00
5", 3"	LF	607.00	559.00	567.00	579.00	573.00	616.00	590.00	619.00
6", 3"	LF	678.00	624.00	634.00	646.00	640.00	688.00	659.00	691.00
8", 4"	LF	817.00	752.00	763.00	779.00	771.00	829.00	794.00	833.00
10", 5"	LF	1,030	945.00	960.00	979.00	969.00	1,040	998.00	1,050
12", 6"	LF	1,380	1,270	1,290	1,320	1,300	1,400	1,340	1,410
14", 6"	LF	1,490	1,370	1,390	1,420	1,400	1,510	1,440	1,510

Item	UNITS	St. John's	Halifax	Montreal	Ottawa	Toronto	Winnipeg	Calgary	Vancouver
33 71 19 Electrical Underground Ducts & Manholes									
MANHOLES									
Concrete manholes									
5' x 5' single	EA	6,460	5,940	6,030	6,150	6,090	6,550	6,270	6,580
5' x 10' double	EA	11,300	10,400	10,600	10,800	10,700	11,500	11,000	11,600
UNDERGROUND DUCT BANKS									
Underground duct banks, 4" PVC pipe ducts & fittings including all excavation, concrete and backfilling									
In soft earth with backfill:									
1 duct	LF	55.60	51.10	51.90	52.90	52.40	56.40	54.00	56.60
2 ducts	LF	64.60	59.40	60.40	61.60	61.00	65.50	62.80	65.80
3 ducts	LF	83.70	77.00	78.20	79.70	78.90	84.90	81.30	85.30
4 ducts	LF	102.00	93.60	95.10	97.00	96.00	103.00	98.90	104.00
5 ducts	LF	122.00	113.00	114.00	117.00	116.00	124.00	119.00	125.00
6 ducts	LF	143.00	131.00	133.00	136.00	135.00	145.00	139.00	145.00
7 ducts	LF	162.00	149.00	151.00	154.00	153.00	164.00	157.00	165.00
8 ducts	LF	187.00	172.00	174.00	178.00	176.00	189.00	181.00	190.00
9 ducts	LF	199.00	183.00	186.00	190.00	188.00	202.00	193.00	203.00
10 ducts	LF	213.00	196.00	199.00	203.00	201.00	216.00	207.00	217.00
11 ducts	LF	237.00	218.00	222.00	226.00	224.00	241.00	231.00	242.00
12 ducts	LF	255.00	234.00	238.00	243.00	240.00	258.00	247.00	259.00
13 ducts	LF	269.00	247.00	251.00	256.00	254.00	273.00	261.00	274.00
14 ducts	LF	302.00	278.00	282.00	288.00	285.00	306.00	293.00	307.00
15 ducts	LF	321.00	295.00	299.00	305.00	302.00	325.00	311.00	327.00
In soft earth with granular backfill:									
1 duct	LF	62.40	57.40	58.20	59.40	58.80	63.20	60.60	63.50
2 ducts	LF	83.40	76.70	77.90	79.40	78.60	84.50	81.00	84.90
3 ducts	LF	92.40	85.00	86.30	88.00	87.20	93.70	89.80	94.10
4 ducts	LF	139.00	127.00	129.00	132.00	131.00	141.00	135.00	141.00
5 ducts	LF	157.00	144.00	146.00	149.00	148.00	159.00	152.00	160.00
6 ducts	LF	165.00	152.00	154.00	157.00	155.00	167.00	160.00	168.00
7 ducts	LF	200.00	184.00	187.00	191.00	189.00	203.00	194.00	204.00
8 ducts	LF	214.00	197.00	200.00	204.00	202.00	217.00	208.00	218.00
9 ducts	LF	230.00	212.00	215.00	219.00	217.00	233.00	224.00	234.00
10 ducts	LF	265.00	244.00	248.00	253.00	250.00	269.00	258.00	270.00
11 ducts	LF	276.00	254.00	258.00	263.00	260.00	280.00	268.00	281.00
12 ducts	LF	293.00	270.00	274.00	280.00	277.00	298.00	285.00	299.00
13 ducts	LF	330.00	303.00	308.00	314.00	311.00	334.00	320.00	336.00
14 ducts	LF	342.00	315.00	320.00	326.00	323.00	347.00	333.00	349.00
15 ducts	LF	372.00	342.00	347.00	354.00	351.00	377.00	361.00	379.00
In soft rock with granular backfill:									
1 duct	LF	77.90	71.60	72.70	74.20	73.50	79.00	75.70	79.30
2 ducts	LF	98.20	90.30	91.70	93.60	92.70	99.60	95.40	100.00
3 ducts	LF	106.00	97.80	99.30	101.00	100.00	108.00	103.00	108.00
4 ducts	LF	171.00	157.00	159.00	163.00	161.00	173.00	166.00	174.00
5 ducts	LF	193.00	177.00	180.00	184.00	182.00	196.00	187.00	197.00
6 ducts	LF	201.00	185.00	187.00	191.00	189.00	203.00	195.00	204.00
7 ducts	LF	231.00	212.00	215.00	220.00	218.00	234.00	224.00	235.00
8 ducts	LF	251.00	231.00	235.00	240.00	237.00	255.00	244.00	256.00
9 ducts	LF	276.00	254.00	258.00	263.00	261.00	280.00	268.00	281.00
10 ducts	LF	315.00	289.00	294.00	300.00	297.00	319.00	306.00	321.00
11 ducts	LF	323.00	297.00	302.00	308.00	305.00	328.00	314.00	329.00
12 ducts	LF	339.00	312.00	317.00	323.00	320.00	344.00	330.00	346.00
13 ducts	LF	372.00	342.00	347.00	354.00	351.00	377.00	361.00	379.00
14 ducts	LF	381.00	351.00	356.00	363.00	360.00	387.00	370.00	388.00
15 ducts	LF	401.00	369.00	374.00	382.00	378.00	406.00	389.00	408.00

SECTION D
CIQS LIST OF ELEMENTS

A. SHELL
A1 Substructure
  A11 Foundations
  A12 Basement Excavation

A2 Structure
  A21 Lowest Floor Construction
  A22 Upper Floor Construction
  A23 Roof Construction

A3 Exterior Enclosure
  A31 Walls Below Grade
  A32 Walls Above Grade
  A33 Windows & Entrances
  A34 Roof Covering

B. INTERIORS
B1 Partitions & Doors
  B11 Partitions
  B12 Doors

C. SERVICES
C1 Mechanical
  C11 Plumbing & Drainage
  C13 HVAC

C2 Electrical

D. SITE & ANCILLARY WORK
D1 Site Work
  D11 Site Development

Z. GEN. REQS. & ALLOWS.
Z1 Gen Reqs. & Fees
Z2 Allowances
  Z21 Design Allowance
  Z22 Escalation Allowance
  Z23 Construction Allowance

HOW TO READ "COMPOSITE UNIT RATES" METRIC AND IMPERIAL

Main heading shows metric or imperial listings for composite rates by material/system classification. Note that the number refers to the Canadian Institute of Quantity Surveyors (CIQS) breakdown.

Listings of composite units and rates are for use in preparing preliminary estimates or for comparative purposes. Rates in this section are basically built up from the prices appearing in Section C, Current Market Prices.

CIQS A2 Structure — METRIC COMPOSITE UNIT RATES

Item	UNITS	St. John's	Halifax	Montreal	Ottawa	Toronto	Winnipeg	Calgary	Vancouver
A2: STRUCTURE									
A21 Lowest Floor Construction									
FLOOR SLABS									
Concrete 21 MPa (3000 psi) 100 mm (4") thick with mesh reinforcement,									
150mm (6") layer of crushed stone and including screed and steel trowel finish									
Plain slab	m²	49.50	49.90	54.50	55.40	58.20	70.60	63.20	75.10
Slab with concrete skim slab 14 MPa (2000 psi) 75 mm (3")									
thick and waterproof fabric membrane 2 ply	m²	111.00	114.00	119.00	141.00	121.00	146.00	123.00	141.00
Add for each additional 25 mm (1") in thickness of concrete	m²	5.79	5.46	5.85	5.97	5.81	6.91	7.13	8.98
Extra for floor trench internal size 450 mm (18") wide x 300 mm									
(12") deep, constructed monolithically with slab, including all									
additional concrete, reinforcement, formwork and steel									
angle frame and 6 mm (1/4") plate cover	m	548.00	519.00	531.00	520.00	552.00	660.00	538.00	714.00
A22 Upper Floor Construction									
STEEL FRAME									
(Including steel floor deck, concrete slab, reinforcement and joint formwork.)									
3 storey live load 2.4 kPa (50 psf) plus partitions 1.2 kPa (25 psf)									
Not fireproofed:									
Bay size 8 m x 8 m (25' x 25')	m²	267.00	253.00	266.00	280.00	294.00	309.00	271.00	373.00
Bay size 9 m x 9 m (30' x 30')	m²	281.00	266.00	280.00	294.00	308.00	325.00	284.00	391.00
Bay size 11 m x 11 m (35' x 35')	m²	295.00	278.00	294.00	308.00	323.00	340.00	297.00	409.00
Bay size 12 m x 12 m (40' x 40')	m²	315.00	297.00	314.00	329.00	345.00	364.00	316.00	437.00
3 storey live load 3.6 kPa (75 psf) plus partitions 1.2 kPa (25 psf)									
Not fireproofed:									
Bay size 8 m x 8 m (25' x 25')	m²	278.00	263.00	277.00	291.00	305.00	322.00	281.00	387.00
Bay size 9 m x 9 m (30' x 30')	m²	292.00	276.00	291.00	305.00	320.00	337.00	294.00	405.00
Bay size 11 m x 11 m (35' x 35')	m²	309.00	291.00	307.00	322.00	337.00	356.00	310.00	428.00
Bay size 12 m x 12 m (40' x 40')	m²	336.00	316.00	334.00	349.00	366.00	387.00	335.00	464.00
10 storey live load 2.4 kPa (75 psf) plus partitions 1.2 kPa (25 psf)									
With fireproofing to steel and deck:									
Bay size 8 m x 8 m (25' x 25')	m²	325.00	385.00	321.00	334.00	349.00	366.00	330.00	428.00
Bay size 9 m x 9 m (30' x 30')	m²	335.00	390.00	331.00	344.00	360.00	378.00	339.00	443.00
Bay size 11 m x 11 m (35' x 35')	m²	348.00	402.00	344.00	358.00	374.00	393.00	351.00	461.00
Bay size 12 m x 12 m (40' x 40')	m²	368.00	420.00	364.00	378.00	395.00	415.00	369.00	487.00
10 storey live load 3.6 kPa (75 psf) plus partitions 1.2 kPa (25 psf)									
With fireproofing to steel and deck:									
Bay size 8 m x 8 m (25' x 25')	m²	334.00	393.00	330.00	343.00	359.00	376.00	338.00	441.00
Bay size 9 m x 9 m (30' x 30')	m²	344.00	399.00	340.00	353.00	369.00	388.00	347.00	455.00
Bay size 11 m x 11 m (35' x 35')	m²	360.00	413.00	356.00	370.00	386.00	406.00	362.00	477.00
Bay size 12 m x 12 m (40' x 40')	m²	380.00	431.00	375.00	390.00	407.00	429.00	380.00	503.00
CONCRETE FRAME									
(including concrete, reinforcement and formwork to slab columns and beams.)									
4 storey live load 3.0-4.0 kPa (60-80 psf)									
Bay size 6 m x 6 m (20' x 20') slab and flat drops	m²	252.00	255.00	271.00	280.00	296.00	322.00	274.00	324.00
Bay size 9 m x 9 m (30' x 30') slab and flat drops	m²	271.00	273.00	279.00	296.00	309.00	332.00	289.00	348.00
Bay size 12 m x 6 m (40' x 20') flat slab and beams	m²	318.00	344.00	369.00	376.00	388.00	457.00	362.00	428.00
Bay size 6 m x 12 m (20' x 40') joists slabs	m²	264.00	288.00	304.00	311.00	325.00	383.00	297.00	348.00
Bay size 12 m x 9 m (40' x 30') joists slabs	m²	275.00	300.00	314.00	322.00	335.00	393.00	306.00	360.00
4 storey live load 5.0 kPa (105 psf)									
Bay size 6 m x 6 m (20' x 20') slab and flat drops	m²	257.00	260.00	275.00	285.00	301.00	326.00	278.00	329.00
Bay size 9 m x 9 m (30' x 30') slab and flat drops	m²	282.00	284.00	289.00	308.00	320.00	342.00	298.00	360.00
Bay size 12 m x 6 m (40' x 20') flat slab and beams	m²	343.00	369.00	398.00	405.00	415.00	489.00	388.00	458.00
Bay size 6 m x 12 m (20' x 40') joists slabs	m²	281.00	305.00	319.00	328.00	341.00	398.00	312.00	367.00
Bay size 12 m x 9 m (40' x 30') joists slabs	m²	286.00	311.00	325.00	334.00	346.00	404.00	317.00	373.00
4 storey live load 7.0 kPa (140 psf)									
Bay size 6 m x 6 m (20' x 20') slab and flat drops	m²	264.00	269.00	282.00	293.00	308.00	333.00	284.00	337.00
Bay size 9 m x 9 m (30' x 30') slab and flat drops	m²	301.00	304.00	310.00	331.00	345.00	367.00	320.00	381.00
Bay size 12 m x 6 m (40' x 20') flat slab and beams	m²	344.00	370.00	393.00	403.00	413.00	483.00	387.00	459.00
Bay size 6 m x 12 m (20' x 40') joists slabs	m²	300.00	324.00	339.00	349.00	361.00	421.00	334.00	394.00
Bay size 12 m x 9 m (40' x 30') joists slabs	m²	325.00	352.00	361.00	372.00	384.00	442.00	353.00	419.00
15 storey live load 3.0-4.0 kPa (60-80 psf)									
Bay size 6 m x 6 m (20' x 20') slab and flat drops	m²	259.00	265.00	285.00	294.00	305.00	354.00	286.00	341.00
Bay size 9 m x 9 m (30' x 30') slab and flat drops	m²	278.00	282.00	292.00	309.00	317.00	361.00	298.00	356.00
Bay size 12 m x 6 m (40' x 20') flat slab and beams	m²	280.00	304.00	312.00	323.00	336.00	390.00	310.00	367.00
Bay size 6 m x 12 m (20' x 40') joists slabs	m²	280.00	283.00	305.00	313.00	329.00	362.00	303.00	356.00
Bay size 12 m x 9 m (40' x 30') joists slabs	m²	253.00	276.00	282.00	296.00	308.00	360.00	280.00	330.00
15 storey live load 8.0 kPa (160 psf)									
Bay size 6 m x 6 m (20' x 20') slab and flat drops	m²	274.00	282.00	298.00	310.00	319.00	367.00	299.00	357.00
Bay size 9 m x 9 m (30' x 30') slab and flat drops	m²	310.00	316.00	333.00	345.00	354.00	404.00	337.00	403.00
Bay size 12 m x 6 m (40' x 20') flat slab and beams	m²	315.00	340.00	346.00	359.00	370.00	425.00	342.00	408.00
Bay size 6 m x 12 m (20' x 40') joists slabs	m²	301.00	325.00	340.00	349.00	362.00	422.00	335.00	395.00
Bay size 12 m x 9 m (40' x 30') joists slabs	m²	311.00	337.00	348.00	359.00	371.00	429.00	341.00	404.00
WOOD JOISTED FLOORS									
Joists at 400 mm (16") o.c. with bridging									
39 mm x 184 mm (2" x 8") joists and 12 mm (1/2") plywood subfloor	m²	49.10	53.80	50.00	45.60	68.60	60.90	44.60	50.00
39 mm x 300 mm (2" x 12") joists and 19 mm (3/4") plywood subfloor	m²	55.30	61.60	56.80	52.70	75.90	65.40	49.20	54.20

Item	UNITS	St. John's	Halifax	Montreal	Ottawa	Toronto	Winnipeg	Calgary	Vancouver

A1: SUBSTRUCTURE

A11 Foundations

EXCAVATION BY MACHINE

(INCLUDING DISPOSAL OF SURPLUS MATERIAL)

Trench excavation for foundation walls 1.2 m (4') wide x 1.2 m (4') deep

In medium soil:

Item	UNITS	St. John's	Halifax	Montreal	Ottawa	Toronto	Winnipeg	Calgary	Vancouver
Backfill one side with excavated material,									
other side with imported granular material	m	80.40	87.90	88.80	83.10	93.70	122.00	108.00	153.00
Add for each additional 300 mm (12") depth (max 3600 mm (12') overall)	m	21.00	23.00	23.10	21.70	24.40	31.90	28.20	39.70
In rock:									
Backfill both sides with imported granular material	m	383.00	380.00	406.00	431.00	434.00	559.00	424.00	502.00
Add for each additional 300 mm (12") depth (max 3600 mm (12') overall)	m	97.20	96.50	103.00	109.00	110.00	142.00	108.00	128.00

Footing excavation for columns

In medium soil (top of footing at grade level):

Item	UNITS	St. John's	Halifax	Montreal	Ottawa	Toronto	Winnipeg	Calgary	Vancouver
900 mm x 900 mm x 200 mm (36" x 36" x 8")	EA	7.53	7.35	8.73	7.27	8.10	10.50	8.55	14.60
1200 mm x 1200 mm x 300 mm (48" x 48" x 12")	EA	17.60	17.20	20.40	17.00	19.00	24.60	20.00	34.20
1500 mm x 1500 mm x 400 mm (60" x 60" x 16")	EA	34.20	33.40	39.70	33.00	36.80	47.80	38.90	66.50
1800 mm x 1800 mm x 500 mm (72" x 72" x 20")	EA	61.30	59.80	71.00	59.10	65.90	85.60	69.50	119.00
2100 mm x 2100 mm x 600 mm (84" x 84" x 24")	EA	105.00	102.00	121.00	101.00	113.00	146.00	119.00	203.00
2400 mm x 2400 mm x 600 mm (96" x 96" x 24")	EA	137.00	133.00	158.00	132.00	147.00	191.00	155.00	265.00

Add for each additional 300 mm (12") depth (max 3600 mm (12') overall)

Item	UNITS	St. John's	Halifax	Montreal	Ottawa	Toronto	Winnipeg	Calgary	Vancouver
900 mm x 900 mm x 200 mm (36" x 36" x 8")	EA	15.30	14.90	17.00	14.50	16.10	21.50	17.00	28.10
1200 mm x 1200 mm x 300 mm (48" x 48" x 12")	EA	27.20	26.30	30.20	25.60	28.50	38.10	30.20	49.80
1500 mm x 1500 mm x 400 mm (60" x 60" x 16")	EA	42.50	41.20	47.30	40.10	44.60	59.70	47.20	78.10
1800 mm x 1800 mm x 500 mm (72" x 72" x 20")	EA	61.20	59.40	68.10	57.80	64.30	85.90	68.00	112.00
2100 mm x 2100 mm x 600 mm (84" x 84" x 24")	EA	83.40	80.80	92.70	78.60	87.50	117.00	92.60	153.00
2400 mm x 2400 mm x 600 mm (96" x 96" x 24")	EA	110.00	106.00	122.00	104.00	115.00	154.00	122.00	202.00

FOOTINGS

Assumed normal subsoil, bearing capacity 40 000 kg/m²
(8000 psf) (approximately), rates include bottom levelling,
formwork, reinforcing steel and 21 MPa (3000 psi) concrete

Wall footings

Item	UNITS	St. John's	Halifax	Montreal	Ottawa	Toronto	Winnipeg	Calgary	Vancouver
400 mm (16") wide x 200 mm (8") thick reinforced with 2 15 m (#4) bars....................	m	65.00	73.80	66.30	72.90	68.40	100.00	73.70	88.70
500 mm (20") wide x 200 mm (8") thick reinforced with 3 15 m (#4) bars....................	m	72.20	80.90	73.40	80.10	75.70	108.00	81.50	98.80
600 mm (24") wide x 300 mm (12") thick reinforced with 4 15 m (#4) bars....................	m	113.00	126.00	115.00	125.00	119.00	168.00	129.00	156.00
Column footings									
0.9 x 0.9 m x 0.25 m (36" x 36" x 10") thick reinforced with 5 15 m (#4) bars ea. way..	EA	160.00	186.00	167.00	179.00	167.00	238.00	179.00	218.00
1.2 m x 1.2 m x 0.3 m (48" x 48" x 12") thick reinforced with 6 20 m (#5) bars ea. way....	EA	319.00	362.00	330.00	350.00	331.00	458.00	355.00	437.00
1.5 m x 1.5 m x 0.4 m (60" x 60" x 16") thick reinforced with 7 25 m (#7) bars ea. way....	EA	566.00	635.00	582.00	615.00	587.00	789.00	629.00	779.00
1.8 m x 1.8 m x 0.5 m (72" x 72" x 20") thick reinforced with 7 30 m (#9) bars ea. way....	EA	926.00	1,030	949.00	999.00	959.00	1,270	1,030	1,280
2.1 m x 2.1 m x 0.6 m (84" x 84" x 24") thick reinforced with 10 30 m (#9) bars ea. way..	EA	1,380	1,510	1,400	1,470	1,420	1,840	1,530	1,910
2.4 m x 2.4 m x 0.7 m (96" x 96" x 28") thick reinforced with 11 35 m (#10) bars ea. way	EA	1,910	2,080	1,940	2,030	1,970	2,510	2,110	2,650

FOUNDATION WALLS

Concrete 21 MPa (3000 psi) reinforced with 15 kg steel per m² (3 lbs steel per sf)

Item	UNITS	St. John's	Halifax	Montreal	Ottawa	Toronto	Winnipeg	Calgary	Vancouver
300 mm (12") thick 1000 mm (40") high	m	327.00	342.00	339.00	341.00	341.00	455.00	367.00	440.00
Add for each additional 300 mm (12") in height....................................	m	98.10	102.00	102.00	102.00	102.00	137.00	110.00	132.00
Standard blockwork filled with concrete									
300 mm (12") thick 1000 mm (40") high	m	192.00	154.00	214.00	208.00	213.00	319.00	288.00	253.00
Add for each additional 300 mm (12") in height....................................	m	57.70	46.20	64.30	62.50	63.80	95.80	86.40	75.80

A12 Basement Excavation

(The following figures are guides only and should be supplemented
by information contained in section C. Special conditions dictating
wellpoint dewatering systems, shoring, soldier piling, timber lagging etc.,
must be assessed separately and added to project estimates as required.)

EXCAVATION BY MACHINE

(Including disposal of surplus material, backfilling with imported granular
material, weeping tiles to perimeter and trimming base ready to receive
concrete. Measure cube of basement to outside face of perimeter walls and from
underside of slab on grade.)

Simple building shape

Item	UNITS	St. John's	Halifax	Montreal	Ottawa	Toronto	Winnipeg	Calgary	Vancouver
In medium soil...	m³	31.00	30.80	36.40	31.20	34.70	39.30	35.70	57.70
In rock ripping...	m³	59.30	57.60	59.80	53.10	59.80	71.60	60.80	82.20
Complex building type									
In medium soil...	m³	50.70	51.50	57.90	51.20	56.90	66.70	60.40	92.70
In rock ripping...	m³	83.40	82.40	84.50	75.90	85.60	104.00	89.20	121.00

SPECIAL CONDITIONS

(Comparative rates are not shown as pricing for this is seldom done on any
elemental basis, but rather by particular study and specific solution (e.g., piling).
The outcome of each study normally defines a method. For information
on these methods consult unit price Section 31, Earthwork.)

Item	UNITS	St. John's	Halifax	Montreal	Ottawa	Toronto	Winnipeg	Calgary	Vancouver
A2: STRUCTURE									
A21 Lowest Floor Construction									
FLOOR SLABS									
Concrete 21 MPa (3000 psi) 100 mm (4") thick with mesh reinforcement, 150 mm (6") layer of crushed stone and including screed and steel trowel finish									
Plain slab	m²	49.50	49.90	54.50	55.40	58.20	70.60	63.20	75.10
Slab with concrete skim slab 14 MPa (2000 psi) 75 mm (3") thick and waterproof fabric membrane 2 ply	m²	111.00	114.00	119.00	141.00	121.00	146.00	123.00	141.00
Add for each additional 25 mm (1") in thickness of concrete	m²	5.79	5.46	5.85	5.97	5.81	6.91	7.13	8.98
Extra for floor trench internal size 450 mm (18") wide x 300 mm (12") deep, constructed monolithically with slab, including all additional concrete, reinforcement, formwork and steel angle frame and 6 mm (1/4") plate cover	m	548.00	519.00	531.00	520.00	552.00	660.00	538.00	714.00
A22 Upper Floor Construction									
STEEL FRAME									
(Including steel floor deck, concrete slab, reinforcement and joint formwork.)									
3 storey live load 2.4 kPa (50 psf) plus partitions 1.2 kPa (25 psf)									
Not fireproofed:									
Bay size 8 m x 8 m (25' x 25')	m²	267.00	253.00	266.00	280.00	294.00	309.00	271.00	373.00
Bay size 9 m x 9 m (30' x 30')	m²	281.00	266.00	280.00	294.00	308.00	325.00	284.00	391.00
Bay size 11 m x 11 m (35' x 35')	m²	295.00	278.00	294.00	308.00	323.00	340.00	297.00	409.00
Bay size 12 m x 12 m (40' x 40')	m²	315.00	297.00	314.00	329.00	345.00	364.00	316.00	437.00
3 storey live load 3.6 kPa (75 psf) plus partitions 1.2 kPa (25 psf)									
Not fireproofed:									
Bay size 8 m x 8 m (25' x 25')	m²	278.00	263.00	277.00	291.00	305.00	322.00	281.00	387.00
Bay size 9 m x 9 m (30' x 30')	m²	292.00	276.00	291.00	305.00	320.00	337.00	294.00	405.00
Bay size 11 m x 11 m (35' x 35')	m²	309.00	291.00	307.00	322.00	337.00	356.00	310.00	428.00
Bay size 12 m x 12 m (40' x 40')	m²	336.00	316.00	334.00	349.00	366.00	387.00	335.00	464.00
10 storey live load 2.4 kPa (75 psf) plus partitions 1.2 kPa (25 psf)									
With fireproofing to steel and deck:									
Bay size 8 m x 8 m (25' x 25')	m²	325.00	385.00	321.00	334.00	349.00	366.00	330.00	428.00
Bay size 9 m x 9 m (30' x 30')	m²	335.00	390.00	331.00	344.00	360.00	378.00	339.00	443.00
Bay size 11 m x 11 m (35' x 35')	m²	348.00	402.00	344.00	358.00	374.00	393.00	351.00	461.00
Bay size 12 m x 12 m (40' x 40')	m²	368.00	420.00	364.00	378.00	395.00	415.00	369.00	487.00
10 storey live load 3.6 kPa (75 psf) plus partitions 1.2 kPa (25 psf)									
With fireproofing to steel and deck:									
Bay size 8 m x 8 m (25' x 25')	m²	334.00	393.00	330.00	343.00	359.00	376.00	338.00	441.00
Bay size 9 m x 9 m (30' x 30')	m²	344.00	399.00	340.00	353.00	369.00	388.00	347.00	455.00
Bay size 11 m x 11 m (35' x 35')	m²	360.00	413.00	356.00	370.00	386.00	406.00	362.00	477.00
Bay size 12 m x 12 m (40' x 40')	m²	380.00	431.00	375.00	390.00	407.00	429.00	380.00	503.00
CONCRETE FRAME									
(Including concrete, reinforcement and formwork to slab columns and beams.)									
4 storey live load 3.0-4.0 kPa (60-80 psf)									
Bay size 6 m x 6 m (20' x 20') slab and flat drops	m²	252.00	255.00	271.00	280.00	296.00	322.00	274.00	324.00
Bay size 9 m x 9 m (30' x 30') slab and flat drops	m²	271.00	273.00	279.00	296.00	309.00	332.00	289.00	348.00
Bay size 12 m x 6 m (40' x 20') flat slab and beams	m²	318.00	344.00	369.00	376.00	388.00	457.00	362.00	428.00
Bay size 6 m x 12 m (20' x 40') joists slabs	m²	264.00	288.00	304.00	311.00	325.00	383.00	297.00	348.00
Bay size 12 m x 9 m (40' x 30') joists slabs	m²	275.00	300.00	314.00	322.00	335.00	393.00	306.00	360.00
4 storey live load 5.0 kPa (105 psf)									
Bay size 6 m x 6 m (20' x 20') slab and flat drops	m²	257.00	260.00	275.00	285.00	301.00	326.00	278.00	329.00
Bay size 9 m x 9 m (30' x 30') slab and flat drops	m²	282.00	284.00	289.00	308.00	320.00	342.00	298.00	360.00
Bay size 12 m x 6 m (40' x 20') flat slab and beams	m²	343.00	369.00	398.00	405.00	415.00	489.00	388.00	458.00
Bay size 6 m x 12 m (20' x 40') joists slabs	m²	281.00	305.00	319.00	328.00	341.00	398.00	312.00	367.00
Bay size 12 m x 9 m (40' x 30') joists slabs	m²	286.00	311.00	325.00	334.00	346.00	404.00	317.00	373.00
4 storey live load 7.0 kPa (140 psf)									
Bay size 6 m x 6 m (20' x 20') slab and flat drops	m²	264.00	269.00	282.00	293.00	308.00	333.00	284.00	337.00
Bay size 9 m x 9 m (30' x 30') slab and flat drops	m²	301.00	304.00	310.00	331.00	345.00	367.00	320.00	381.00
Bay size 12 m x 6 m (40' x 20') flat slab and beams	m²	344.00	370.00	393.00	403.00	413.00	483.00	387.00	459.00
Bay size 6 m x 12 m (20' x 40') joists slabs	m²	300.00	324.00	339.00	349.00	361.00	421.00	334.00	394.00
Bay size 12 m x 9 m (40' x 30') joists slabs	m²	325.00	352.00	361.00	374.00	384.00	442.00	353.00	419.00
15 storey live load 3.0-4.0 kPa (60-80 psf)									
Bay size 6 m x 6 m (20' x 20') slab and flat drops	m²	259.00	265.00	285.00	294.00	305.00	354.00	286.00	341.00
Bay size 9 m x 9 m (30' x 30') slab and flat drops	m²	278.00	282.00	292.00	309.00	317.00	361.00	298.00	356.00
Bay size 12 m x 6 m (40' x 20') flat slab and beams	m²	280.00	304.00	312.00	323.00	336.00	390.00	310.00	367.00
Bay size 6 m x 12 m (20' x 40') joists slabs	m²	280.00	283.00	305.00	313.00	329.00	362.00	303.00	356.00
Bay size 12 m x 9 m (40' x 30') joists slabs	m²	253.00	276.00	282.00	296.00	308.00	360.00	280.00	330.00
15 storey live load 8.0 kPa (160 psf)									
Bay size 6 m x 6 m (20' x 20') slab and flat drops	m²	274.00	282.00	298.00	310.00	319.00	367.00	299.00	357.00
Bay size 9 m x 9 m (30' x 30') slab and flat drops	m²	310.00	316.00	333.00	345.00	354.00	404.00	337.00	403.00
Bay size 12 m x 6 m (40' x 20') flat slab and beams	m²	315.00	340.00	346.00	359.00	370.00	425.00	342.00	408.00
Bay size 6 m x 12 m (20' x 40') joists slabs	m²	301.00	325.00	340.00	349.00	362.00	422.00	335.00	395.00
Bay size 12 m x 9 m (40' x 30') joists slabs	m²	311.00	337.00	348.00	359.00	371.00	429.00	341.00	404.00
WOOD JOISTED FLOORS									
Joists at 400 mm (16") o.c. with bridging									
39 mm x 184 mm (2" x 8") joists and 12 mm (1/2") plywood subfloor	m²	49.10	53.80	50.00	45.60	68.60	60.90	44.60	50.00
39 mm x 300 mm (2" x 12") joists and 19 mm (3/4") plywood subfloor	m²	55.30	61.60	56.80	52.70	75.90	65.40	49.20	54.20

Item	UNITS	St. John's	Halifax	Montreal	Ottawa	Toronto	Winnipeg	Calgary	Vancouver
CONCRETE SHEAR WALLS									
Unfinished reinforced concrete									
200 mm (8") thick, 14 kg steel per m² (3 lbs steel per sf)	m²	316.00	341.00	364.00	378.00	375.00	618.00	358.00	435.00
300 mm (12") thick, 17 kg steel per m² (3.5 lbs steel per sf)	m²	344.00	368.00	392.00	406.00	404.00	650.00	391.00	476.00
STAIRS									
ASSUMED SUPPORTED BY THE STRUCTURE									
Steel									
Pan stair 1200 mm (4') wide x 3600 mm (12') rise, half landing, including concrete infill and pipe railings	FLIGHT	12,400	11,000	13,200	14,400	15,300	16,900	15,500	20,200
Pan stair 1200 mm (4') wide x 3600 mm (12') rise, half landing, including precast terrazzo and landing and picket railings	FLIGHT	19,600	18,500	20,800	21,300	22,000	25,500	23,700	26,000
Concrete									
Cast-in-place concrete stair 1200 mm (4') wide x 3600 mm (12') rise, half landing, including fair concrete finish and pipe railings	FLIGHT	7,180	7,600	7,690	8,090	7,910	9,960	8,320	8,800
Cast-in-place concrete stair 1200 mm (4') wide x 3600 mm (12') rise, half landing, including quarry tile finish and picket railings	FLIGHT	11,400	11,600	11,800	12,700	12,300	15,000	12,800	13,700

A23 Roof Construction

STEEL FRAME
(Including 38 mm (1 1/2") deep roof deck.)
3 storey live load 3.0 kPa (60 psf), including 2 kPa (40 psf) snow load

Item	UNITS	St. John's	Halifax	Montreal	Ottawa	Toronto	Winnipeg	Calgary	Vancouver
Not fireproofed:									
Bay size 8 m x 8 m (25' x 25')	m²	163.00	150.00	152.00	161.00	166.00	172.00	144.00	235.00
Bay size 9 m x 9 m (30' x 30')	m²	171.00	158.00	159.00	169.00	173.00	181.00	151.00	246.00
Bay size 11 m x 11 m (35' x 35')	m²	201.00	185.00	187.00	198.00	204.00	213.00	177.00	286.00
Bay size 12 m x 12 m (40' x 40')	m²	218.00	200.00	203.00	214.00	221.00	231.00	193.00	309.00

10 storey live load 3.0 kPa (60 psf), including 2 kPa (40 psf) snow load

Item	UNITS	St. John's	Halifax	Montreal	Ottawa	Toronto	Winnipeg	Calgary	Vancouver
With fireproofing to steel and deck:									
Bay size 8 m x 8 m (25' x 25')	m²	267.00	321.00	251.00	262.00	269.00	280.00	245.00	360.00
Bay size 9 m x 9 m (30' x 30')	m²	279.00	332.00	262.00	274.00	282.00	293.00	255.00	376.00
Bay size 11 m x 11 m (35' x 35')	m²	294.00	344.00	277.00	289.00	297.00	309.00	268.00	396.00
Bay size 12 m x 12 m (40' x 40')	m²	310.00	356.00	291.00	303.00	313.00	326.00	282.00	417.00

CONCRETE FRAME
(Including concrete, reinforcement and formwork to slab columns and beams.)
4 storey live load 3.0-4.0 kPa (60-80 psf) including 2 kPa (40 psf) snow load

Item	UNITS	St. John's	Halifax	Montreal	Ottawa	Toronto	Winnipeg	Calgary	Vancouver
Bay size 6 m x 6 m (20' x 20') slab and flat drops	m²	252.00	255.00	271.00	280.00	296.00	322.00	274.00	324.00
Bay size 9 m x 9 m (30' x 30') slab and flat drops	m²	271.00	273.00	279.00	296.00	309.00	332.00	289.00	348.00
Bay size 12 m x 6 m (40' x 20') flat slab and beams	m²	318.00	344.00	369.00	376.00	388.00	457.00	362.00	428.00
Bay size 6 m x 12 m (20' x 40') joists slabs	m²	264.00	288.00	304.00	311.00	325.00	383.00	297.00	348.00
Bay size 12 m x 9 m (40' x 30') joists slabs	m²	283.00	307.00	323.00	333.00	345.00	404.00	315.00	369.00

15 storey live load 3.0-4.0 kPa (60-80 psf) including 2 kPa (40 psf) snow load

Item	UNITS	St. John's	Halifax	Montreal	Ottawa	Toronto	Winnipeg	Calgary	Vancouver
Bay size 6 m x 6 m (20' x 20') slab and flat drops	m²	259.00	265.00	284.00	294.00	305.00	353.00	286.00	340.00
Bay size 9 m x 9 m (30' x 30') slab and flat drops	m²	276.00	281.00	295.00	309.00	318.00	365.00	300.00	358.00
Bay size 12 m x 6 m (40' x 20') flat slab and beams	m²	280.00	304.00	312.00	323.00	336.00	390.00	310.00	367.00
Bay size 6 m x 12 m (20' x 40') joists slabs	m²	271.00	296.00	311.00	318.00	332.00	390.00	303.00	356.00
Bay size 12 m x 9 m (40' x 30') joists slabs	m²	275.00	300.00	314.00	322.00	335.00	393.00	306.00	360.00

A3: EXTERIOR ENCLOSURE

A31 Walls Below Ground Floor

CONCRETE
Cast in place
21 MPa (3000 psi)

Item	UNITS	St. John's	Halifax	Montreal	Ottawa	Toronto	Winnipeg	Calgary	Vancouver
300 mm (12") thick, 3000 mm (10') max. high, 17 kg (3.5 lb) reinforcement per m² (sf) and with 2 coats asphalt emulsion waterproofing	m²	408.00	418.00	438.00	487.00	464.00	709.00	436.00	522.00
300 mm (12") thick, 3600 mm (12') max. high, 22 kg (4.5 lbs) reinforcement per m² (sf) and with 2 coats asphalt emulsion waterproofing	m²	418.00	429.00	446.00	489.00	468.00	715.00	440.00	530.00
350 mm (14") thick, 4800 mm (16') max. high, 32 kg (6.5 lbs) reinforcement per m² (sf) and with 2 coats asphalt emulsion waterproofing	m²	452.00	466.00	479.00	526.00	503.00	747.00	469.00	566.00

MASONRY
Blockwork
Reinforced:

Item	UNITS	St. John's	Halifax	Montreal	Ottawa	Toronto	Winnipeg	Calgary	Vancouver
250 mm (10") thick with 12 mm (1/2") cement parging and 2 coats sprayed asphalt.	m²	269.00	218.00	270.00	285.00	302.00	417.00	351.00	348.00
300 mm (12") thick with concrete filling to voids 12 mm (1/2") cement parging and 2 coats sprayed asphalt	m²	320.00	266.00	322.00	341.00	356.00	481.00	419.00	429.00

A32 Walls Above Ground Floor

CONCRETE
Cast in place
21 MPa (3000 psi):

Item	UNITS	St. John's	Halifax	Montreal	Ottawa	Toronto	Winnipeg	Calgary	Vancouver
200 mm (8") thick, 3000 mm (10') high, with 20 kg (4 lbs) reinforcement per m² (sf), sandblasted finish and 25 mm (1") polystyrene insulation	m²	384.00	408.00	430.00	460.00	449.00	692.00	430.00	496.00
200 mm (8") thick, 3000 mm (10') high, with 20 kg (4 lbs) reinforcement per m² (sf), board-formed finish, 25 mm (1") polystyrene insulation and 100 mm (4") concrete block backup	m²	478.00	474.00	531.00	556.00	549.00	860.00	567.00	619.00

Item	UNITS	St. John's	Halifax	Montreal	Ottawa	Toronto	Winnipeg	Calgary	Vancouver
Precast concrete									
Solid load-bearing, white textured finish, 25 mm (1") moulded polystyrene insulation and 150 mm (6") concrete block backup	m²	691.00	619.00	572.00	556.00	584.00	909.00	719.00	799.00
Sandwich load-bearing panels with textured finish, 25 mm (1") moulded polystyrene insulation and 100 mm (4") concrete block backup	m²	715.00	648.00	585.00	569.00	600.00	942.00	738.00	873.00
Solid non-load-bearing, white exposed aggregate finish, 50 mm (2") moulded polystyrene insulation 100 mm (4") concrete block backup	m²	659.00	596.00	543.00	532.00	557.00	871.00	683.00	760.00
MASONRY									
Blockwork									
250 mm (10") with 2 coats silicone	m²	175.00	148.00	206.00	202.00	207.00	310.00	283.00	238.00
300 mm (12") with 2 coats silicone	m²	193.00	164.00	226.00	223.00	226.00	340.00	309.00	262.00
319 mm (12 1/2") hollow wall comprising 100 mm (4") architectural blockwork, 25 mm (1") moulded polystyrene insulation, 50 mm (2") cavity, 100 mm (4") block inner skin and 2 coats silicone	m²	319.00	335.00	363.00	365.00	377.00	526.00	479.00	418.00
Brickwork									
Solid walls:									
200 mm (8") wall with 100 mm (4") modular facing 100 mm (4") brick backup	m²	610.00	544.00	502.00	498.00	504.00	736.00	714.00	702.00
300 mm (12") wall with 100 mm (4") modular facing bonded with headers every 6th course to 200 mm (8") concrete block backing	m²	465.00	407.00	432.00	426.00	432.00	644.00	608.00	568.00
Hollow walls:									
300 mm (12") wall with 100 mm (4") modular facing, 50 mm (2") cavity, 50 mm (2") rigid insulation and 100 mm (4") concrete block backing	m²	406.00	353.00	382.00	368.00	380.00	563.00	530.00	493.00
350 mm (14") wall with 100 mm (4") modular facing, 12 mm (1/2") parging, 38 mm (1 1/2") cavity, 50 mm (2") rigid insulation and 150 mm (6") concrete block backing	m²	453.00	399.00	426.00	417.00	433.00	614.00	572.00	545.00
300 mm (12") wall with two 100 mm (4") modular facing skins, 50 mm (2") rigid insulation, 12 mm (1/2") parging and 38 mm (1 1/2") cavity	m²	624.00	555.00	514.00	512.00	528.00	739.00	713.00	707.00
Composite walls									
262 mm (10 1/2") wall with 100 mm (4") modular brick facing, polystyrene vapour barrier, 150 mm (6") metal studding, 100 mm (4") batt insulation, metal furring and drywall	m²	469.00	432.00	419.00	472.00	454.00	548.00	505.00	524.00
Stonework									
387 mm (15 1/2") wall with 100 mm (4") limestone ashlar sawn face, 12 mm (1/2") parging and 250 mm (10") concrete block backing	m²	813.00	1240.00	863.00	915.00	938.00	1060.00	998.00	1050.00
SIDING									
Metal siding with masonry backing									
Steel:									
0.711 mm (22 gauge) with baked enamel finish on z-bar sub girts and 300 mm (12") concrete block backing	m²	345.00	307.00	368.00	383.00	392.00	505.00	444.00	445.00
Aluminum:									
0.813 mm (21 gauge) with baked enamel finish, concealed fastenings on z-bar sub grits and 300 mm (12") concrete block backing	m²	371.00	332.00	396.00	411.00	422.00	537.00	469.00	474.00
Wood and board siding									
Cedar:									
19 mm x 250 mm (1" x 10") bevelled siding on wood furring with 250 mm (10") concrete block backup	m²	264.00	237.00	285.00	293.00	289.00	404.00	357.00	341.00
A33 Windows & Entrances									
ALUMINUM									
Based on 1200 mm x 1800 mm (4' x 6') opening, with baked enamel finish									
Non-thermally broken:									
Window with no vents and sealed tinted single glazing	m²	517.00	547.00	509.00	574.00	563.00	647.00	520.00	546.00
Window with one opening and sealed tinted double glazing	m²	763.00	773.00	758.00	893.00	833.00	926.00	734.00	768.00
Thermally broken:									
Window with no vents and sealed tinted single glazing	m²	591.00	637.00	584.00	648.00	611.00	694.00	532.00	642.00
Window with one opening and sealed tinted double glazing	m²	894.00	915.00	889.00	1040.00	943.00	1040.00	794.00	916.00
STEEL									
With baked enamel finish									
Industrial sash:									
With 20% ventilating sash and clear single glazing	m²	540.00	611.00	533.00	643.00	605.00	718.00	544.00	562.00
WOOD									
Redwood									
Based on 1200 mm x 1800 mm (4' x 6') opening:									
With lower ventilating unit and clear double glazing	m²	851.00	887.00	839.00	841.00	842.00	979.00	799.00	1070.00
ALUMINUM FRAMING SYSTEM									
With baked enamel finish									
Non-thermally broken:									
3000 mm - 3600 mm (10' - 12') flr/flr with 1200 mm (4') mullion spacing and tinted single glazing	m²	791.00	851.00	809.00	819.00	929.00	999.00	795.00	942.00
Thermally broken:									
3000 mm - 3600 mm (10' - 12') flr/flr with 1200 mm (4') mullion spacing and tinted double glazing	m²	928.00	1010.00	950.00	956.00	1060.00	1130.00	871.00	1130.00

Item	UNITS	St. John's	Halifax	Montreal	Ottawa	Toronto	Winnipeg	Calgary	Vancouver
A34 Roof Covering									
BUILT UP FELT ROOFING									
(Including wood cants and nailers, aluminum flashing									
450 mm (18") girth, insulation 75 mm (3") thick, and gravel.)									
High rise office building....................	m²	75.70	76.80	78.80	89.80	88.30	88.30	74.20	74.60
Low rise articulated office building	m²	86.50	89.40	89.30	99.90	104.00	103.00	84.30	85.80
FLUID APPLIED ROOFING									
Hot applied rubberized asphalt on base sheet									
including 75 mm (3") rigid insulation									
Low rise institutional building........................	m²	100.00	105.00	113.00	129.00	123.00	114.00	102.00	113.00
B1: PARTITIONS AND DOORS									
B11 Partitions									
Brickwork									
Modular red clay, single wythe, plastered one side............	m²	412.00	386.00	356.00	400.00	375.00	483.00	497.00	466.00
Modular backup, single wythe plaster both sides............	m²	404.00	400.00	368.00	460.00	402.00	459.00	504.00	452.00
Modular backup, double wythe plaster both sides	m²	590.00	566.00	521.00	611.00	556.00	684.00	722.00	666.00
Blockwork partitions									
Plain:									
Painted one side									
100 mm (4") thick...........	m²	119.00	97.60	146.00	143.00	142.00	215.00	194.00	165.00
150 mm (6") thick...........	m²	127.00	103.00	154.00	151.00	153.00	231.00	205.00	177.00
200 mm (8") thick...........	m²	139.00	114.00	167.00	165.00	166.00	252.00	225.00	193.00
Plastered and painted one side									
100 mm (4") thick...........	m²	239.00	226.00	263.00	307.00	275.00	346.00	351.00	298.00
150 mm (6") thick...........	m²	247.00	231.00	271.00	315.00	286.00	362.00	362.00	310.00
200 mm (8") thick...........	m²	259.00	242.00	284.00	329.00	299.00	383.00	382.00	326.00
Plastered and painted both sides									
100 mm (4") thick...........	m²	370.00	360.00	390.00	484.00	419.00	490.00	518.00	442.00
150 mm (6") thick...........	m²	378.00	365.00	398.00	492.00	430.00	506.00	529.00	454.00
200 mm (8") thick...........	m²	390.00	376.00	411.00	506.00	443.00	527.00	549.00	470.00
Architectural:									
Painted one side									
100 mm (4") thick...........	m²	151.00	178.00	162.00	173.00	180.00	252.00	223.00	208.00
150 mm (6") thick...........	m²	167.00	197.00	183.00	189.00	198.00	274.00	248.00	227.00
200 mm (8") thick...........	m²	186.00	221.00	200.00	211.00	223.00	310.00	276.00	255.00
Plastered and painted one side									
100 mm (4") thick...........	m²	271.00	306.00	279.00	337.00	313.00	383.00	380.00	341.00
150 mm (6") thick...........	m²	287.00	325.00	300.00	353.00	331.00	405.00	405.00	360.00
200 mm (8") thick...........	m²	306.00	349.00	317.00	375.00	356.00	441.00	433.00	388.00
Integrally coloured architectural:									
Painted one side									
100 mm (4") thick...........	m²	168.00	201.00	184.00	190.00	199.00	277.00	249.00	229.00
150 mm (6") thick...........	m²	179.00	213.00	194.00	205.00	217.00	300.00	267.00	246.00
200 mm (8") thick...........	m²	206.00	246.00	218.00	233.00	248.00	345.00	304.00	281.00
Painted both sides									
100 mm (4") thick...........	m²	288.00	329.00	301.00	354.00	332.00	408.00	406.00	362.00
150 mm (6") thick...........	m²	299.00	341.00	311.00	369.00	350.00	431.00	424.00	379.00
200 mm (8") thick...........	m²	326.00	374.00	335.00	397.00	381.00	476.00	461.00	414.00
Metal stud									
90 mm (3 5/8") thick:									
10 mm (3/8") drywall single board both sides	m²	87.00	86.30	84.90	95.40	99.50	109.00	78.20	120.00
12 mm (1/2") drywall single board both sides	m²	87.00	86.30	84.90	95.40	99.50	109.00	78.20	120.00
10 mm (3/8") drywall double board both sides	m²	128.00	127.00	126.00	139.00	145.00	169.00	116.00	182.00
12 mm (1/2") drywall double board both sides	m²	128.00	127.00	126.00	139.00	145.00	169.00	116.00	182.00
Wood stud									
38 mm x 89 mm (2" x 4") studs with 12 mm (1/2") drywall both sides...............	m²	61.50	61.90	62.00	67.40	69.80	88.00	57.40	88.70
B12 Doors									
Based on 900 mm x 2100 mm (3'0" x 7'0") single doors									
excluding hardware, including painting where applicable.									
Wood									
Hollow core:									
Paint grade birch in 0.914 mm (20 ga) hollow metal frame	Leaf	609.00	515.00	578.00	592.00	607.00	694.00	600.00	1140.00
Solid core:									
Paint grade birch in 1.219 mm (18 ga) hollow metal frame	Leaf	705.00	624.00	701.00	727.00	752.00	864.00	788.00	1250.00
Stain grade birch in 1.219 mm (18 ga) hollow metal frame	Leaf	700.00	648.00	690.00	698.00	745.00	848.00	787.00	747.00
Stain grade red oak in 1.219 mm (18 ga) hollow metal frame	Leaf	763.00	705.00	751.00	756.00	814.00	924.00	856.00	808.00
Plastic laminate faced, solid									
colours in 1.219 mm (18 gauge) hollow metal frame........................	Leaf	786.00	726.00	778.00	780.00	843.00	956.00	886.00	830.00
Metal									
Hollow steel honeycombed:									
In 1.219 mm (18 gauge) hollow metal frame........................	Leaf	698.00	648.00	698.00	812.00	778.00	951.00	824.00	810.00
Hollow steel stiffened:									
In 1.219 mm (18 gauge) hollow metal frame........................	Leaf	974.00	904.00	983.00	1,140	1,100	1,340	1,150	1,110
In 1.219 mm (18 gauge) hollow metal frame, door with									
600 mm x 600 mm (2' x 2') aperture glazed Georgian glazed									
wired glass	Leaf	1,200	1,140	1,210	1,390	1,350	1,630	1,370	1,370

Item	UNITS	St. John's	Halifax	Montreal	Ottawa	Toronto	Winnipeg	Calgary	Vancouver
FINISHING HARDWARE									
Per door, including locksets, butts, pulls, pushes and closers where applicable.									
Hotels	EA	698.00	629.00	677.00	704.00	816.00	853.00	718.00	732.00
Retail stores	EA	455.00	410.00	438.00	456.00	532.00	542.00	469.00	465.00
Apartment buildings	EA	308.00	278.00	302.00	311.00	365.00	379.00	322.00	317.00
Office buildings	EA	907.00	822.00	918.00	933.00	1040.00	1030.00	879.00	840.00
Hospitals	EA	982.00	883.00	985.00	1000.00	1120.00	1120.00	942.00	967.00
Schools	EA	808.00	731.00	821.00	835.00	922.00	914.00	774.00	748.00

C1: MECHANICAL

C11 Plumbing and Drainage

Plumbing cost including drainage, domestic water, etc.

Item	UNITS	St. John's	Halifax	Montreal	Ottawa	Toronto	Winnipeg	Calgary	Vancouver
Commercial building	/FIXT	4,370	4,020	4,080	4,160	4,120	4,430	3,870	4,450
Educational building	/FIXT	4,710	4,330	4,400	4,480	4,440	4,770	4,170	4,800
Residential building	/FIXT	1,170	1,070	1,090	1,110	1,100	1,180	1,030	1,190
SWIMMING POOL OLYMPIC SIZE									
with mechanical work including filtration, pool and deck drainage, water heating etc.	EA	506,000	465,000	472,000	482,000	477,000	513,000	448,000	515,000
GREASE INTERCEPTOR									
Cast iron type, 15 kg (33 lbs) fat capacity	EA	1,830	1,690	1,710	1,750	1,730	1,860	1,630	1,870
WATER PUMP STATION									
22,000 l (4850 gallon) tank, 11 kW 15 l/s 60 m (15 hp, 200 gpm, 200 ft.) head, centrifugal duplex pumps	EA	125,000	115,000	117,000	119,000	118,000	127,000	111,000	127,000

C13 Heating, Ventilation and Air Conditioning

HEATING

Hot water heating system (measure area serviced)

Item	UNITS	St. John's	Halifax	Montreal	Ottawa	Toronto	Winnipeg	Calgary	Vancouver
Including equipment and perimeter radiation	m²	94.80	87.20	88.50	90.30	89.40	96.10	84.00	96.60
Radiant in-floor hot water heating, PEX tubing	m²	71.70	65.90	66.90	68.30	67.60	72.70	63.50	73.00
Snow melting system including steel pipe, glycol charge, heat exchanger, pump and control (measure area serviced)	m²	102.00	94.20	95.60	97.60	96.60	104.00	90.80	104.00

VENTILATION

Sanitary exhaust system,

Item	UNITS	St. John's	Halifax	Montreal	Ottawa	Toronto	Winnipeg	Calgary	Vancouver
including fans ductwork and grilles	l/s	16.70	15.40	15.60	16.00	15.80	17.00	14.90	17.10
Propeller thru wall fan	l/s	2.19	2.02	2.05	2.09	2.07	2.23	1.95	2.24
Make-up air systems, including fan, heating coil, duct, diffusers, thermal insulation, and controls	l/s	37.10	34.10	34.70	35.40	35.00	37.60	32.90	37.80

AIR CONDITIONING

Central station systems

Item	UNITS	St. John's	Halifax	Montreal	Ottawa	Toronto	Winnipeg	Calgary	Vancouver
Chiller, cooling tower, distribution, AHU, ductwork & diffusers	kW	1,790	1,650	1,670	1,710	1,690	1,820	1,590	1,830
Air cooled chiller, distribution water, AHU, ductwork & diffusers	kW	1,530	1,400	1,430	1,450	1,440	1,550	1,350	1,560
Air cooled condenser, direct expansion, AHU, ductwork & diffusers	kW	1,260	1,160	1,180	1,200	1,190	1,280	1,120	1,290
Fan-coil system									
Chiller, cooling tower, individual room units with central primary air system	kW	2,120	1,950	1,980	2,020	2,000	2,150	1,880	2,160
Roof-top system									
Packaged unit, air cooled, gas-fired including ductwork and diffusers:									
18 kW (5TR) cooling, 50 kW (170 mbh) heating	EA	18,900	17,400	17,600	18,000	17,800	19,100	16,700	19,200
35 kW tonne (10 TR) cooling, 80 kW (270 mbh) heating	EA	39,600	36,500	37,000	37,800	37,400	40,200	35,200	40,400
53 kW (15 TR) cooling, 110 kW (375 mbh) heating	EA	54,700	50,300	51,100	52,100	51,600	55,500	48,500	55,700
70 kW (20 TR) cooling, 120 kW (410 mbh) heating	EA	63,500	58,400	59,300	60,500	59,900	64,400	56,300	64,700
Air distribution									
Air handling unit, ductwork, diffusers and grilles, automatic controls, thermal and acoustical insulation	l/s	45.30	41.60	42.30	43.10	42.70	45.90	40.10	46.10
Air conditioning equipment									
Absorption chiller	kW	629.00	578.00	587.00	599.00	593.00	637.00	557.00	640.00
Centrifugal chiller	kW	235.00	216.00	220.00	224.00	222.00	239.00	209.00	240.00
Cooling tower	kW	99.50	91.60	93.00	94.80	93.90	101.00	88.30	101.00

C2: ELECTRICAL

ELECTRICAL INSTALLATIONS

Office buildings (speculative), national code 70 regulation, substation, lighting fixture cost at average $165.00 (T-8 lamps), fire alarm, telephones, floor outlets. 1 per 30 m² (325 sf), parking in basement.

Ceiling grid empty conduit:

Item	UNITS	St. John's	Halifax	Montreal	Ottawa	Toronto	Winnipeg	Calgary	Vancouver
High-rise lighting intensity 700 lx (70 ft-c)	m²	137.00	126.00	128.00	130.00	129.00	139.00	121.00	139.00
Low-rise lighting intensity 700 lx (70 ft-c)	m²	145.00	134.00	136.00	138.00	137.00	147.00	129.00	148.00
High-rise lighting intensity 1000 lx (100 ft-c)	m²	142.00	131.00	133.00	135.00	134.00	144.00	126.00	145.00
Wireway and plug in lighting fixtures:									
High-rise lighting intensity 700 lx (70 ft-c)	m²	162.00	149.00	151.00	155.00	153.00	164.00	144.00	165.00
Low-rise lighting intensity 700 lx (70 ft-c)	m²	172.00	158.00	160.00	164.00	162.00	174.00	152.00	175.00
High-rise lighting intensity 1000 lx (100 ft-c)	m²	166.00	153.00	155.00	159.00	157.00	169.00	148.00	170.00

Item	UNITS	St. John's	Halifax	Montreal	Ottawa	Toronto	Winnipeg	Calgary	Vancouver
Heavy laboratories, national code 70 regulation, no parking facilities substation, 1000 lx (100 ft-c) at 347 V 1 V control, fixture, cost $275.00 (T-8 lamps), fire alarm, tel., emerg. gen., excl. security & special systems									
High rise:									
Load demand 160 W/m² (15 W/sf) lab area 40% of gfa	m²	413.00	380.00	386.00	394.00	390.00	419.00	367.00	421.00
Load demand 195 W/m² (18 W/sf) lab area 50% of gfa	m²	449.00	413.00	420.00	428.00	424.00	456.00	399.00	458.00
Load demand 215 W/m² (20 W/sf) lab area 60% of gfa	m²	492.00	452.00	459.00	469.00	464.00	499.00	436.00	501.00
Low rise:									
Load demand 160 W/m² (15 W/sf) lab area 40% of gfa	m²	405.00	372.00	378.00	386.00	382.00	411.00	359.00	413.00
Load demand 195 W/m² (18 W/sf) lab area 50% of gfa	m²	442.00	407.00	413.00	421.00	417.00	448.00	392.00	450.00
Load demand 215 W/m² (20 W/sf) lab area 60% of gfa	m²	484.00	446.00	452.00	462.00	457.00	491.00	430.00	494.00
LIGHTING SYSTEMS (net area lighted)									
Parking lots									
Davit steel poles, 2 heads, 250 W HPS integrated ballast, operating system wired to panel, complete:									
11 W/m² (1 W/sf)	m²	5.12	4.71	4.78	4.88	4.83	5.19	4.54	5.22
22 W/m² (2 W/sf)	m²	7.66	7.05	7.16	7.30	7.23	7.77	6.80	7.81
Supermarkets (against net area)									
Strip fluorescent	m²	54.40	50.00	50.80	51.80	51.30	55.10	48.20	55.40
Recessed HID	m²	60.30	55.50	56.30	57.50	56.90	61.20	53.50	61.50
Office building (against net area), lighting system operating and wired to panel, 347 V with standard LV switching, grid box system.									
700 lx (70 ft-c) average cost/fixture (T-8 lamps)									
$169.00	m²	71.00	65.30	66.30	67.70	67.00	72.00	63.00	72.40
$192.00	m²	79.60	73.20	74.30	75.90	75.10	80.70	70.60	81.10
$218.00	m²	84.80	78.00	79.20	80.80	80.00	86.00	75.20	86.40
ELECTRICAL HEATING									
Apartments, 2 to 3 storeys, heating load approx. 90 W/m² (8 W/sf), with baseboard convector units with integrated thermostats:									
Baked white enamel finish	kW	438.00	403.00	409.00	417.00	413.00	444.00	388.00	446.00
Offices, standard partitioning, heating load approximately 110 W/m² (10 W/sf), with baseboard convectors and room thermostats:									
Baked white enamel finish	kW	465.00	428.00	435.00	443.00	439.00	472.00	413.00	474.00
Stainless steel finish	kW	670.00	616.00	626.00	638.00	632.00	679.00	594.00	683.00
Banks and similar large window exposure, heating load 130 W/m² (12 W/sf), with central thermostat control:									
Baked white enamel finish	kW	475.00	437.00	444.00	452.00	448.00	482.00	421.00	484.00
Stainless steel finish	kW	686.00	631.00	641.00	653.00	647.00	696.00	608.00	699.00
SUBSTATIONS									
Indoor (vault type), 2 incoming h.t. lines, primary protection, load breaker and air circuit breaker, all busing, insulators, cutouts, transformer, grounding, etc., no secondary protection or distribution.									
12,000/347-600 V									
1,000 kVa	EA	97,200	89,400	90,800	92,600	91,700	98,600	86,200	99,000
1,500 kVa	EA	122,000	112,000	114,000	116,000	115,000	124,000	108,000	124,000
2,000 kVa	EA	164,000	151,000	153,000	157,000	155,000	167,000	146,000	167,000
Indoor (metal clad unit type), 2 incoming h.t. lines, primary protection, load breakers and air circuit breaker, all metering, transformer, including tentative allowance for secondary breaker type switchboard without main breaker.									
12,000/347-600 V									
1,000 kVa	EA	89,600	82,400	83,700	85,300	84,500	90,800	79,400	91,300
1,500 kVa	EA	111,000	102,000	104,000	106,000	105,000	113,000	98,700	113,000
2,000 kVa	EA	147,000	136,000	138,000	140,000	139,000	149,000	131,000	150,000
Outdoor, 2 incoming h.t. lines, steel switching structure, transformer fencing, lightning protection, grounding etc., does not include secondary protection.									
12,000/347-600 V									
1,000 kVa	EA	79,900	73,500	74,600	76,200	75,400	81,100	70,900	81,400
1,500 kVa	EA	100,000	92,100	93,600	95,400	94,500	102,000	88,800	102,000
2,000 kVa	EA	138,000	127,000	129,000	131,000	130,000	140,000	122,000	140,000
EMERGENCY SYSTEMS									
Diesel generator units including complete operating system, exhaust, cooling, oil system, control system.									
120/208 V 20 kW	EA	39,100	36,000	36,500	37,300	36,900	39,700	34,700	39,900
120/208 V 50 kW	EA	52,200	48,000	48,700	49,700	49,200	52,900	46,200	53,100
120/208 V 100 kW	EA	79,900	73,500	74,600	76,200	75,400	81,100	70,900	81,400
120/208 V 200 kW	EA	126,000	116,000	118,000	120,000	119,000	128,000	112,000	129,000
347/600 V 50 kW	EA	54,700	50,300	51,100	52,100	51,600	55,500	48,500	55,700
347/600 V 100 kW	EA	85,000	78,200	79,400	81,000	80,200	86,200	75,400	86,600
347/600 V 200 kW	EA	130,000	120,000	122,000	124,000	123,000	132,000	116,000	133,000
347/600 V 500 kW	EA	425,000	391,000	397,000	405,000	401,000	431,000	377,000	433,000

Item	UNITS	St. John's	Halifax	Montreal	Ottawa	Toronto	Winnipeg	Calgary	Vancouver
MOTOR CONTROL CENTERS									
To obtain probable cost of motor center, installed and operating, compute costs from motors connected to the center. Rates include all fuses, control transformers, pilot lights, push-button stations, etc.									
575 V breaker combination starters.									
Class 11, type b:									
Motors to 7.5 kW (10 hp)	/mtr	1,390	1,280	1,300	1,320	1,310	1,410	1,230	1,410
Motors 20 to 40 kW (30 to 50 hp)	/mtr	1,890	1,740	1,760	1,800	1,780	1,910	1,670	1,920
Motors 90 to 150 kW (125 to 200 hp)	/mtr	4,380	4,030	4,090	4,170	4,130	4,440	3,880	4,460
575 V fuse combination starter									
Class 11, type b:									
Motors to 7.5 kW (10 hp)	/mtr	1,270	1,170	1,190	1,210	1,200	1,290	1,130	1,300
Motors 75 to 110 kW (100 to 150 hp)	/mtr	1,890	1,740	1,760	1,800	1,780	1,910	1,670	1,920
Motors 130 to 220 kW (175 to 300 hp)	/mtr	4,300	3,960	4,020	4,100	4,060	4,360	3,820	4,380
Motors 190 to 300 kW (250 to 400 hp)	/mtr	12,700	11,700	11,900	12,100	12,000	12,900	11,300	13,000
575 V star delta breaker									
Class 11, type b:									
Motors to 55 kW (75 hp)	/mtr	3,760	3,460	3,510	3,590	3,550	3,820	3,340	3,830
Motors 75 to 110 kW (100 to 150 hp)	/mtr	5,060	4,650	4,720	4,820	4,770	5,130	4,480	5,150
Motors 130 to 220 kW (175 to 300 hp)	/mtr	11,300	10,400	10,600	10,800	10,700	11,500	10,100	11,600
COMMUNICATION SYSTEM									
Intercom system									
Complete with switchboard. Cost per system:									
Up to 50 lines	EA	41,200	37,900	38,500	39,300	38,900	41,800	36,600	42,000
Up to 100 lines	EA	82,200	75,600	76,700	78,300	77,500	83,300	72,900	83,700
Up to 200 lines	EA	118,000	108,000	110,000	112,000	111,000	119,000	104,000	120,000
Public address system									
Complete with wiring in hung ceiling. Cost per system:									
Up to 10 loudspeakers	EA	3,660	3,360	3,420	3,480	3,450	3,710	3,240	3,730
Up to 20 loudspeakers	EA	6,110	5,620	5,700	5,820	5,760	6,190	5,410	6,220
Up to 40 loudspeakers	EA	9,760	8,980	9,120	9,300	9,210	9,900	8,660	9,950
Add to above for the following:									
Microphone	EA	527.00	485.00	492.00	502.00	497.00	534.00	467.00	537.00
C.D., VCD, MP3, AM/FM stereo tuner	EA	2,270	2,090	2,120	2,160	2,140	2,300	2,010	2,310
LIGHTNING PROTECTION									
Complete installation of rods to include bonding of steel structure.									
High-rise structure:									
Up to 20 rods	/ROD	1,650	1,520	1,540	1,580	1,560	1,680	1,470	1,680
Up to 60 rods	/ROD	1,710	1,570	1,590	1,630	1,610	1,730	1,510	1,740
Medium-rise structure:									
Up to 20 rods	/ROD	1,300	1,200	1,220	1,240	1,230	1,320	1,160	1,330
Up to 60 rods	/ROD	1,380	1,270	1,290	1,310	1,300	1,400	1,220	1,400
Low-rise structure:									
Up to 20 rods	/ROD	975.00	897.00	911.00	929.00	920.00	989.00	865.00	994.00
Up to 60 rods	/ROD	1,030	946.00	960.00	980.00	970.00	1,040	912.00	1,050
SNOW MELTING COMPLETE									
System connected to panels, including controls, mineral insulation heating cable with nylon jacket.									
330 W/m² (30 W/sf)	m²	276.00	254.00	257.00	263.00	260.00	280.00	244.00	281.00
440 W/m² (40 W/sf)	m²	307.00	283.00	287.00	293.00	290.00	312.00	273.00	313.00

D1: SITE WORK

D11 Site Development

Item	UNITS	St. John's	Halifax	Montreal	Ottawa	Toronto	Winnipeg	Calgary	Vancouver
Seeding & sodding									
Rough grade, spread stock piled topsoil, fine grade & place sod	m²	16.40	16.20	13.90	14.40	14.80	18.60	15.70	16.30
Rough grade, spread stock piled topsoil, fine grade & seed	m²	11.30	10.80	10.10	10.60	10.50	12.30	9.91	11.60
Rough grade, spread imported topsoil, fine grade & place sod	m²	22.50	21.90	17.80	20.00	20.40	24.10	20.30	21.90
Rough grade, spread imported topsoil, fine grade & seed	m²	17.40	16.60	14.00	16.20	16.00	17.80	14.50	17.20
Road & parking									
Roadways, 8 m (25') wide, with 225 mm (9") crushed stone base, 75 mm (3") double layer asphalt and precast concrete curbs each side	m	634.00	635.00	580.00	611.00	624.00	881.00	705.00	872.00
Roadways, 3.6 m (12') wide, including crushed stone paving and 38 mm x 250 mm (2" x 10") cedar curbs to edges	m	45.10	44.20	38.40	40.00	39.40	52.30	39.90	50.10
Parking lots, including 150 mm (6") crushed stone base, 50 mm (2") single layer asphalt precast concrete bumpers at each car and painted parking lines	m²	46.10	48.20	42.90	44.60	40.50	58.00	51.10	76.50

Item	UNITS	St. John's	Halifax	Montreal	Ottawa	Toronto	Winnipeg	Calgary	Vancouver
Walkway & steps									
Walks, 1.2 m (4') wide, including 100 mm (4") crushed stone base and 50 mm (2") single layer asphalt	m	114.00	116.00	108.00	109.00	101.00	143.00	128.00	173.00
Walks, 1.2 m (4') wide, including 100 mm (4") crushed stone base and 125 mm (5") concrete, mesh and broom finish	m	93.40	96.90	98.40	104.00	116.00	158.00	119.00	117.00
Concrete steps to walks, 1.2 m (4') wide, including crushed stone base and broom finish (300 mm (12") tread and 150 mm (6") rise)	TREAD	105.00	111.00	112.00	121.00	135.00	182.00	133.00	131.00
Pedestrian and service tunnels for typical university installation, including reinforced concrete, waterproofing, excavation and backfill but not including mechanical and electrical services									
1800 mm (6') wide x 3000 mm (10') high	m	3,540	3,570	3,990	4,000	4,570	7,370	4,430	4,210
3000 mm (10') wide x 3000 mm (10') high	m	3,970	4,000	4,460	4,460	5,060	8,010	4,970	4,790
Fences & screens									
1800 mm (6') high cedar privacy fence 19 mm x 140 mm (1" x 6") alternate sides of 38 mm x 89 mm (2" x 4") rails including 89mm x 89mm (4" x 4") posts at 3000 mm (10') o.c. set in concrete	m	267.00	250.00	272.00	259.00	282.00	354.00	382.00	395.00
1800 mm (6') high decorative concrete block screen, including 1200 mm (4') deep block foundation wall below	m	550.00	526.00	618.00	615.00	643.00	947.00	842.00	716.00

Z1: GENERAL REQUIREMENTS & FEE

For preliminary estimating purposes the general contractor's site expenses, head office overhead and profit may be calculated on a percentage basis of the total net estimated cost

Complex Institutional Projects	%					8 - 12			
School Project	%					7 - 11			
Simple Commercial Projects	%					6 -1 0			

Z2: CONTINGENCIES/ALLOWANCES

Z21 Design

Initial estimates require the inclusion of a contingency sum for remeasured items, design development change, etc. This contingency may be reduced as more information becomes available enabling more detailed estimates to be prepared

	%					5 - 10			

Z22 Escalation

Provision should be made for likely cost increases between the date of estimate and the anticipated date of tender

	%					varies according to circumstance			

Z23 Construction

Allowance should be made for possible increases in contract cost resulting from unforeseen site conditions, design change during construction, etc.

New work	%					2 - 5			
Renovations and alterations	%					3 - 8			

Instructions for use, page 140. Main index, page 5.

Item	UNITS	St. John's	Halifax	Montreal	Ottawa	Toronto	Winnipeg	Calgary	Vancouver
A1: SUBSTRUCTURE									
A11 Foundations									
EXCAVATION BY MACHINE									
(INCLUDING DISPOSAL OF SURPLUS MATERIAL)									
Trench excavation for foundation walls 4' wide x 4' deep									
In medium soil:									
Backfill one side with excavated material,									
other side with imported granular material	LF	24.50	26.80	27.10	25.30	28.60	37.10	32.90	46.50
Add for each additional 12" depth (max 12' overall)	LF	6.40	7.01	7.03	6.61	7.45	9.72	8.59	12.10
In rock:									
Backfill both sides with imported granular material	LF	117.00	116.00	124.00	131.00	132.00	170.00	129.00	153.00
Add for each additional 12" depth (max 12' overall)	LF	29.60	29.40	31.40	33.30	33.60	43.30	32.90	39.10
Footing excavation for columns									
In medium soil (top of footing at grade level):									
36" x 36" x 8"	EA	7.53	7.35	8.73	7.27	8.10	10.50	8.55	14.60
48" x 48" x 12"	EA	17.60	17.20	20.40	17.00	19.00	24.60	20.00	34.20
60" x 60" x 16"	EA	34.20	33.40	39.70	33.00	36.80	47.80	38.90	66.50
72" x 72" x 20"	EA	61.30	59.80	71.00	59.10	65.90	85.60	69.50	119.00
84" x 84" x 24"	EA	105.00	102.00	121.00	101.00	113.00	146.00	119.00	203.00
96" x 96" x 24"	EA	137.00	133.00	158.00	132.00	147.00	191.00	155.00	265.00
Add for each additional 12" depth (max 12' overall)									
36" x 36" x 8"	EA	15.30	14.90	17.00	14.50	16.10	21.50	17.00	28.10
48" x 48" x 12"	EA	27.20	26.30	30.20	25.60	28.50	38.10	30.20	49.80
60" x 60" x 16"	EA	42.50	41.20	47.30	40.10	44.60	59.70	47.20	78.10
72" x 72" x 20"	EA	61.20	59.40	68.10	57.80	64.30	85.90	68.00	112.00
84" x 84" x 24"	EA	83.40	80.80	92.70	78.60	87.50	117.00	92.60	153.00
96" x 96" x 24"	EA	110.00	106.00	122.00	104.00	115.00	154.00	122.00	202.00
FOOTINGS									
Assumed normal subsoil, bearing capacity 8000 psf.									
(approximately), rates include bottom levelling,									
formwork, reinforcing steel and 3000 psi concrete									
Wall footings									
16" wide x 8" thick reinforced with 2 #4 bars	LF	19.80	22.50	20.20	22.20	20.90	30.50	22.50	27.00
20" wide x 8" thick reinforced with 3 #4 bars	LF	22.00	24.70	22.40	24.40	23.10	32.90	24.80	30.10
24" wide x 12" thick reinforced with 4 #4 bars	LF	34.50	38.30	35.00	38.10	36.10	51.10	39.30	47.70
Column footings									
36" x 36" x 10" thick reinforced with 5 #4 bars each way	EA	160.00	186.00	167.00	179.00	167.00	238.00	179.00	218.00
48" x 48" x 12" thick reinforced with 6 #5 bars each way	EA	319.00	362.00	330.00	350.00	331.00	458.00	355.00	437.00
60" x 60" x 16" thick reinforced with 7 #7 bars each way	EA	566.00	635.00	582.00	615.00	587.00	789.00	629.00	779.00
72" x 72" x 20" thick reinforced with 7 #9 bars each way	EA	926.00	1,030	949.00	999.00	959.00	1,270	1,030	1,280
84" x 84" x 24" thick reinforced with 10 #9 bars each way	EA	1,380	1,510	1,400	1,470	1,420	1,840	1,530	1,910
96" x 96" x 28" thick reinforced with 11 #10 bars each way	EA	1,910	2,080	1,940	2,030	1,970	2,510	2,110	2,650
FOUNDATION WALLS									
Concrete 3000 psi. reinforced with 3 lbs per sf									
12" thick 40" high	LF	99.70	104.00	103.00	104.00	104.00	139.00	112.00	134.00
Add for each additional 12" in height	LF	29.90	31.20	31.00	31.20	31.20	41.60	33.60	40.30
Standard blockwork filled with concrete									
12" thick 40" high	LF	58.60	46.90	65.30	63.50	64.90	97.30	87.80	77.00
Add for each additional 12" in height	LF	17.60	14.10	19.60	19.10	19.50	29.20	26.30	23.10
A12 Basement Excavation									
(The following figures are guides only and should be supplemented									
by information contained in section C. Special conditions dictating									
wellpoint dewatering systems, shoring, soldier piling, timber lagging etc., must be assessed									
separately and added to project estimates as required.)									
EXCAVATION BY MACHINE									
(Including disposal of surplus material, backfilling with									
imported granular material, weeping tiles to perimeter and									
trimming base ready to receive concrete. Measure cube of									
basement to outside face of perimeter walls and from									
underside of slab on grade.)									
Simple building shape									
In medium soil	CF	0.88	0.87	1.03	0.88	0.98	1.11	1.01	1.63
In rock ripping	CF	1.68	1.63	1.69	1.50	1.69	2.03	1.72	2.33
Complex building shape									
In medium soil	CF	1.43	1.46	1.64	1.45	1.61	1.89	1.71	2.63
In rock ripping	CF	2.36	2.33	2.39	2.15	2.42	2.94	2.52	3.42

Item	UNITS	St. John's	Halifax	Montreal	Ottawa	Toronto	Winnipeg	Calgary	Vancouver
SPECIAL CONDITIONS (Comparative rates are not shown as pricing for this is seldom done on any elemental basis, but rather by particular study and specific solution (e.g., piling). The outcome of each study normally defines a method. For information on these methods consult unit price Section 31, Earthwork.)									
A2: STRUCTURE									
A21 Lowest Floor Construction									
FLOOR SLABS									
Concrete 3000 psi 4" thick with mesh reinforcement, 6" layer of crushed stone and including screed and steel trowel finish									
Plain slab	SF	4.60	4.64	5.06	5.14	5.41	6.56	5.87	6.97
Slab with concrete skim slab 2000 psi 3" thick and 2 ply waterproof fabric membrane	SF	10.40	10.60	11.00	13.10	11.30	13.50	11.40	13.10
Add for each additional 1" in thickness of concrete	SF	0.54	0.51	0.54	0.55	0.54	0.64	0.66	0.83
Extra for floor trench internal size 18" wide x 12" deep constructed monolithically with slab, including all additional concrete, reinforcement, formwork and steel angle frame and 1/4" plate cover	LF	167.00	158.00	162.00	159.00	168.00	201.00	164.00	218.00
A22 Upper Floor Construction									
STEEL FRAME									
(Including steel floor deck, concrete slab, reinforcement and joint formwork.)									
3 storey live load 50 psf plus partitions 25 psf									
Not fireproofed:									
Bay size 25' x 25'	SF	24.80	23.50	24.70	26.00	27.30	28.70	25.20	34.60
Bay size 30' x 30'	SF	26.10	24.70	26.00	27.30	28.60	30.20	26.40	36.30
Bay size 35' x 35'	SF	27.40	25.90	27.30	28.60	30.00	31.60	27.60	38.00
Bay size 40' x 40'	SF	29.30	27.60	29.20	30.50	32.00	33.80	29.30	40.60
3 storey live load 75 psf plus partitions 25 psf									
Not fireproofed:									
Bay size 25' x 25'	SF	25.80	24.40	25.70	27.00	28.30	29.90	26.10	36.00
Bay size 30' x 30'	SF	27.10	25.60	27.00	28.30	29.70	31.30	27.30	37.70
Bay size 35' x 35'	SF	28.70	27.00	28.50	29.90	31.40	33.10	28.80	39.80
Bay size 40' x 40'	SF	31.20	29.30	31.00	32.50	34.00	35.90	31.10	43.10
10 storey live load 50 psf plus partitions 25 psf									
With fireproofing to steel and deck:									
Bay size 25' x 25'	SF	30.20	35.80	29.80	31.00	32.40	34.00	30.70	39.80
Bay size 30' x 30'	SF	31.10	36.30	30.80	32.00	33.40	35.10	31.50	41.20
Bay size 35' x 35'	SF	32.40	37.30	32.00	33.20	34.70	36.50	32.60	42.80
Bay size 40' x 40'	SF	34.20	39.00	33.80	35.10	36.70	38.60	34.30	45.30
10 storey live load 75 psf plus partitions 25 psf									
With fireproofing to steel and deck:									
Bay size 25' x 25'	SF	31.00	36.50	30.70	31.90	33.30	34.90	31.40	40.90
Bay size 30' x 30'	SF	32.00	37.00	31.60	32.80	34.30	36.00	32.30	42.30
Bay size 35' x 35'	SF	33.50	38.40	33.10	34.40	35.90	37.70	33.60	44.30
Bay size 40' x 40'	SF	35.30	40.00	34.90	36.20	37.80	39.80	35.30	46.80
CONCRETE FRAME									
(Including concrete, reinforcement and formwork to slab columns and beams.)									
4 storey live load 60-80 psf									
Bay size 20' x 20' slab and flat drops	SF	23.40	23.70	25.20	26.00	27.50	29.90	25.40	30.10
Bay size 30' x 30' slab and flat drops	SF	25.20	25.30	25.90	27.50	28.70	30.80	26.90	32.30
Bay size 40' x 20' flat slab and beams	SF	29.60	32.00	34.30	35.00	36.00	42.50	33.60	39.70
Bay size 20' x 40' joists slabs	SF	24.50	26.70	28.30	28.90	30.20	35.60	27.60	32.40
Bay size 40' x 30' joists slabs	SF	25.50	27.80	29.20	29.90	31.20	36.50	28.50	33.50
4 storey live load 105 psf									
Bay size 20' x 20' slab and flat drops	SF	23.80	24.20	25.60	26.50	28.00	30.30	25.80	30.60
Bay size 30' x 30' slab and flat drops	SF	26.20	26.40	26.80	28.60	29.70	31.70	27.70	33.40
Bay size 40' x 20' flat slab and beams	SF	31.80	34.30	37.00	37.60	38.60	45.50	36.10	42.60
Bay size 20' x 40' joists slabs	SF	26.10	28.40	29.60	30.40	31.60	37.00	29.00	34.10
Bay size 40' x 30' joists slabs	SF	26.60	28.90	30.20	31.00	32.20	37.60	29.50	34.70
4 storey live load 140 psf									
Bay size 20' x 20' slab and flat drops	SF	24.50	24.90	26.20	27.20	28.60	30.90	26.40	31.30
Bay size 30' x 30' slab and flat drops	SF	28.00	28.20	28.80	30.80	32.00	34.10	29.70	35.40
Bay size 40' x 20' flat slab and beams	SF	32.00	34.40	36.50	37.40	38.30	44.80	35.90	42.60
Bay size 20' x 40' joists slabs	SF	27.90	30.10	31.50	32.40	33.60	39.10	31.10	36.60
Bay size 40' x 30' joists slabs	SF	30.20	32.70	33.50	34.80	35.70	41.10	32.80	38.90
15 storey live load 60-80 psf									
Bay size 20' x 20' slab and flat drops	SF	24.00	24.60	26.40	27.30	28.30	32.80	26.60	31.60
Bay size 30' x 30' slab and flat drops	SF	25.80	26.20	27.10	28.70	29.40	33.50	27.70	33.10
Bay size 40' x 20' flat slab and beams	SF	26.00	28.20	29.00	30.00	31.20	36.20	28.80	34.10
Bay size 20' x 40' joists slabs	SF	26.00	26.30	28.30	29.10	30.60	33.60	28.20	33.10
Bay size 40' x 30' joists slabs	SF	23.50	25.70	26.20	27.50	28.60	33.50	26.00	30.70
15 storey live load 160 psf									
Bay size 20' x 20' slab and flat drops	SF	25.50	26.20	27.70	28.80	29.70	34.10	27.80	33.10
Bay size 30' x 30' slab and flat drops	SF	28.80	29.30	30.90	32.10	32.90	37.60	31.30	37.40

Item	UNITS	St. John's	Halifax	Montreal	Ottawa	Toronto	Winnipeg	Calgary	Vancouver
Bay size 40' x 20' flat slab and beams	SF	29.20	31.60	32.10	33.40	34.40	39.40	31.80	37.90
Bay size 20' x 40' joists slabs	SF	28.00	30.20	31.60	32.50	33.60	39.20	31.10	36.70
Bay size 40' x 30' joists slabs	SF	28.90	31.30	32.40	33.40	34.40	39.90	31.70	37.50

WOOD JOISTED FLOORS
Joists at 16" o.c. with bridging

Item	UNITS	St. John's	Halifax	Montreal	Ottawa	Toronto	Winnipeg	Calgary	Vancouver
2" x 8" joists and 1/2" plywood subfloor	SF	4.56	4.99	4.64	4.23	6.38	5.65	4.15	4.65
2" x 12" joists and 3/4" plywood subfloor	SF	5.14	5.73	5.27	4.90	7.05	6.08	4.57	5.03

CONCRETE SHEAR WALLS
Unfinished reinforced concrete

Item	UNITS	St. John's	Halifax	Montreal	Ottawa	Toronto	Winnipeg	Calgary	Vancouver
8" thick, 3 lbs steel per sf	SF	29.40	31.70	33.90	35.10	34.90	57.50	33.30	40.50
12" thick, 3.5 lbs steel per sf	SF	32.00	34.20	36.40	37.80	37.50	60.40	36.30	44.30

STAIRS
ASSUMED SUPPORTED BY THE STRUCTURE
Steel

Item	UNITS	St. John's	Halifax	Montreal	Ottawa	Toronto	Winnipeg	Calgary	Vancouver
Pan stair 4' wide x 12' rise, half landing, including concrete infill and pipe railings	FLIGHT	12,400	11,000	13,200	14,400	15,300	16,900	15,500	20,200
Pan stair 4' wide x 12' rise, half landing, including precast terrazzo and landing and picket railings	FLIGHT	19,600	18,500	20,800	21,300	22,000	25,500	23,700	26,000

Concrete

Item	UNITS	St. John's	Halifax	Montreal	Ottawa	Toronto	Winnipeg	Calgary	Vancouver
Cast-in-place concrete stair 4' wide x 12' rise, half landing, including fair concrete finish and pipe railings	FLIGHT	7,180	7,600	7,690	8,090	7,910	9,960	8,320	8,800
Cast-in-place concrete stair 4' wide x 12' rise, half landing, including quarry tile finish and picket railings	FLIGHT	11,400	11,600	11,800	12,700	12,300	15,000	12,800	13,700

A23 Roof Construction
STEEL FRAME
(Including 1 1/2" deep roof deck.)
3 storey live load 60 psf, including 40 psf snow load
Not fireproofed:

Item	UNITS	St. John's	Halifax	Montreal	Ottawa	Toronto	Winnipeg	Calgary	Vancouver
Bay size 25' x 25'	SF	15.10	14.00	14.10	15.00	15.40	16.00	13.40	21.80
Bay size 30' x 30'	SF	15.90	14.70	14.80	15.70	16.10	16.80	14.00	22.80
Bay size 35' x 35'	SF	18.70	17.20	17.40	18.40	18.90	19.80	16.50	26.60
Bay size 40' x 40'	SF	20.30	18.60	18.90	19.90	20.60	21.50	17.90	28.70

10 storey live load 60 psf, including 40 psf snow load
With fireproofing to steel and deck:

Item	UNITS	St. John's	Halifax	Montreal	Ottawa	Toronto	Winnipeg	Calgary	Vancouver
Bay size 25' x 25'	SF	24.80	29.90	23.30	24.40	25.00	26.00	22.70	33.40
Bay size 30' x 30'	SF	25.90	30.80	24.40	25.50	26.20	27.20	23.70	34.90
Bay size 35' x 35'	SF	27.30	32.00	25.70	26.80	27.60	28.70	24.90	36.80
Bay size 40' x 40'	SF	28.80	33.10	27.00	28.20	29.10	30.30	26.20	38.70

CONCRETE FRAME
(Including concrete, reinforcement and formwork to slab columns and beams.)
4 storey live load 60-80 psf including 40 psf snow load

Item	UNITS	St. John's	Halifax	Montreal	Ottawa	Toronto	Winnipeg	Calgary	Vancouver
Bay size 20' x 20' slab and flat drops	SF	23.40	23.70	25.20	26.10	27.50	29.90	25.40	30.10
Bay size 30' x 30' slab and flat drops	SF	25.20	25.30	25.90	27.50	28.70	30.80	26.90	32.30
Bay size 40' x 20' flat slab and beams	SF	29.60	32.00	34.30	35.00	36.00	42.50	33.60	39.70
Bay size 20' x 40' joists slabs	SF	24.50	26.70	28.30	28.90	30.20	35.60	27.60	32.40
Bay size 40' x 30' joists slabs	SF	26.30	28.60	30.00	30.90	32.10	37.60	29.30	34.30

15 storey live load 60-80 psf including 40 psf snow load

Item	UNITS	St. John's	Halifax	Montreal	Ottawa	Toronto	Winnipeg	Calgary	Vancouver
Bay size 20' x 20' slab and flat drops	SF	24.00	24.60	26.40	27.30	28.30	32.80	26.60	31.60
Bay size 30' x 30' slab and flat drops	SF	25.70	26.10	27.40	28.70	29.60	33.90	27.90	33.20
Bay size 40' x 20' flat slab and beams	SF	26.00	28.20	29.00	30.00	31.20	36.20	28.80	34.10
Bay size 20' x 40' joists slabs	SF	25.20	27.50	28.90	29.60	30.80	36.20	28.20	33.10
Bay size 40' x 30' joists slabs	SF	25.50	27.80	29.20	29.90	31.20	36.50	28.50	33.50

A3: EXTERIOR ENCLOSURE
A31 Walls Below Ground Floor
CONCRETE
Cast in place
3000 psi

Item	UNITS	St. John's	Halifax	Montreal	Ottawa	Toronto	Winnipeg	Calgary	Vancouver
12" thick, 10' max. high, 3.5 lbs. reinforcement per sf and with 2 coats asphalt emulsion waterproofing	SF	37.90	38.80	40.70	45.30	43.10	65.80	40.50	48.50
12" thick, 12' max. high, 4.5 lbs. reinforcement per sf and with 2 coats asphalt emulsion waterproofing	SF	38.90	39.80	41.40	45.50	43.40	66.40	40.90	49.20
14" thick, 16' max. high, 6.5 lbs. reinforcement per sf and with 2 coats asphalt emulsion waterproofing	SF	42.00	43.30	44.50	48.90	46.80	69.40	43.50	52.60

MASONRY
Blockwork
Reinforced:

Item	UNITS	St. John's	Halifax	Montreal	Ottawa	Toronto	Winnipeg	Calgary	Vancouver
10" thick with 1/2" cement parging and 2 coats sprayed asphalt	SF	24.90	20.30	25.10	26.50	28.00	38.70	32.60	32.30
12" thick with concrete filling to voids 1/2" cement parging and 2 coats sprayed asphalt	SF	29.70	24.70	29.90	31.70	33.10	44.70	38.90	39.80

Item	UNITS	St. John's	Halifax	Montreal	Ottawa	Toronto	Winnipeg	Calgary	Vancouver
A32 Walls Above Ground Floor									
CONCRETE									
Cast in place									
3000 psi:									
8" thick, 10' high, with 4 lbs. reinforcement per sf, sandblasted finish and 1" polystyrene insulation	SF	35.70	38.00	39.90	42.80	41.70	64.30	40.00	46.10
8" thick, 10' high, with 4 lbs. reinforcement per sf, board-formed finish, 1" polystyrene insulation and 4" concrete block backup	SF	44.40	44.10	49.40	51.70	51.00	79.90	52.70	57.50
Precast concrete									
Solid load-bearing, white textured finish, 1" moulded polystyrene insulation and 6" concrete block backup	SF	64.20	57.50	53.20	51.70	54.20	84.50	66.80	74.20
Sandwich load-bearing panels with textured finish, 1" moulded polystyrene insulation and 4" concrete block backup	SF	66.50	60.20	54.40	52.90	55.70	87.50	68.50	81.10
Solid non-load-bearing, white exposed aggregate finish, 2" moulded polystyrene insulation and 4" concrete block backup	SF	61.20	55.40	50.40	49.40	51.70	80.90	63.50	70.60
MASONRY									
Blockwork									
10" with 2 coats silicone	SF	16.30	13.70	19.10	18.70	19.20	28.80	26.30	22.10
12" with 2 coats silicone	SF	17.90	15.20	21.00	20.70	21.00	31.60	28.70	24.30
12 1/2" hollow wall comprising 4" architectural blockwork, 1" moulded polystyrene insulation, 2" cavity, 4" block inner skin and 2 coats silicone	SF	29.70	31.10	33.80	33.90	35.00	48.90	44.50	38.80
Brickwork									
Solid walls:									
8" wall with 4" modular facing 4" brick backup	SF	56.70	50.50	46.60	46.30	46.80	68.40	66.30	65.20
12" wall with 4" modular facing bonded with headers every 6th course to 8" concrete block backing	SF	43.20	37.80	40.10	39.60	40.20	59.80	56.50	52.80
Hollow walls:									
12" wall with 4" modular facing, 2" cavity, 2" rigid insulation, and 4" concrete block backing	SF	37.70	32.80	35.50	34.20	35.30	52.30	49.20	45.80
14" wall with 4" modular facing, 1/2" parging, 1 1/2" cavity, 2" rigid insulation, and 6" concrete block backing	SF	42.10	37.00	39.60	38.80	40.20	57.10	53.10	50.70
12" wall with two 4" modular facing skins, 2" rigid insulation, 1/2" parging and 1 1/2" cavity	SF	58.00	51.50	47.80	47.60	49.00	68.70	66.20	65.70
Composite walls									
10 1/2" wall with 4" modular brick facing, polystyrene vapour barrier, 6" metal studding, 4" batt insulation, metal furring and drywall	SF	43.60	40.20	39.00	43.90	42.10	50.90	46.90	48.70
Stonework									
15 1/2" wall with 4" limestone ashlar sawn face, 1/2" parging and 10" concrete block backing	SF	75.60	116.00	80.20	85.00	87.10	98.90	92.70	97.10
SIDING									
Metal siding with masonry backing									
Steel:									
22 gauge with baked enamel finish on z-bar sub girts and 12" concrete block backing	SF	32.00	28.50	34.20	35.60	36.40	47.00	41.20	41.40
Aluminum:									
21 gauge with baked enamel finish, concealed fastenings on z-bar sub grits and 12" concrete block backing	SF	34.50	30.80	36.80	38.20	39.20	49.90	43.50	44.00
Wood and board siding									
Cedar:									
1" x 10" bevelled siding on wood furring with 10" concrete block backup	SF	24.50	22.00	26.50	27.20	26.90	37.50	33.10	31.70
A33 Windows & Entrances									
ALUMINUM									
Based on 4' x 6' opening, with baked enamel finish									
Non thermally broken:									
Window with no vents and sealed tinted single glazing	SF	48.10	50.80	47.30	53.30	52.30	60.10	48.30	50.70
Window with one opening and sealed tinted double glazing	SF	70.90	71.80	70.40	82.90	77.40	86.00	68.20	71.40
Thermally broken:									
Window with no vents and sealed tinted single glazing	SF	54.90	59.20	54.20	60.20	56.80	64.50	49.40	59.60
Window with one opening and sealed tinted double glazing	SF	83.00	85.00	82.60	96.80	87.60	96.30	73.80	85.10
STEEL									
With baked enamel finish									
Industrial sash:									
With 20% ventilating sash and clear single glazing	SF	50.20	56.70	49.50	59.80	56.20	66.70	50.50	52.20
WOOD									
Redwood									
Based on 4' x 6' opening:									
With lower ventilating unit and clear double glazing	SF	79.10	82.40	78.00	78.10	78.20	91.00	74.20	99.20

Item	UNITS	St. John's	Halifax	Montreal	Ottawa	Toronto	Winnipeg	Calgary	Vancouver
ALUMINUM FRAMING SYSTEM									
With baked enamel finish									
Non-thermally broken:									
10' - 12' flr/flr with 4' mullion spacing and									
tinted single glazing....................	SF	73.50	79.10	75.20	76.10	86.30	92.80	73.90	87.50
Thermally broken:									
10' - 12' flr/flr with 4' mullion spacing and									
tinted double glazing....................	SF	86.20	94.10	88.30	88.80	98.80	105.00	80.90	105.00
A34 Roof Covering									
BUILT UP FELT ROOFING									
(Including wood cants and nailers, aluminum flashing									
18" girth, insulation 3" thick, and gravel.)									
High rise office building........................	SF	7.03	7.14	7.32	8.34	8.20	8.21	6.89	6.93
Low rise articulated office building............	SF	8.03	8.31	8.30	9.28	9.64	9.53	7.83	7.97
FLUID APPLIED ROOFING									
Hot applied rubberized asphalt on base sheet									
including 3" rigid insulation									
Low rise institutional building................	SF	9.29	9.78	10.50	12.00	11.40	10.60	9.46	10.50
B1: PARTITIONS AND DOORS									
B11 Partitions									
Brickwork									
Modular red clay, single wythe, plastered one side...........	SF	38.30	35.90	33.10	37.20	34.80	44.90	46.20	43.30
Modular backup, single wythe plaster both sides.............	SF	37.50	37.20	34.20	42.80	37.30	42.70	46.90	42.00
Modular backup, double wythe plaster both sides............	SF	54.80	52.50	48.40	56.80	51.70	63.60	67.10	61.80
Blockwork partitions									
Plain:									
Painted one side									
4" thick	SF	11.10	9.07	13.50	13.30	13.20	20.00	18.00	15.30
6" thick	SF	11.80	9.55	14.30	14.00	14.20	21.50	19.00	16.40
8" thick	SF	13.00	10.60	15.50	15.30	15.40	23.40	20.90	17.90
Plastered and painted one side									
4" thick	SF	22.20	21.00	24.40	28.50	25.60	32.20	32.60	27.70
6" thick	SF	23.00	21.40	25.10	29.30	26.60	33.60	33.60	28.80
8" thick	SF	24.10	22.50	26.30	30.60	27.80	35.60	35.50	30.30
Plastered and painted both sides									
4" thick	SF	34.40	33.40	36.20	45.00	38.90	45.50	48.10	41.00
6" thick	SF	35.10	33.90	37.00	45.70	40.00	47.00	49.10	42.10
8" thick	SF	36.20	34.90	38.20	47.00	41.20	49.00	51.00	43.60
Architectural:									
Painted one side									
4" thick	SF	14.10	16.50	15.00	16.10	16.70	23.40	20.70	19.30
6" thick	SF	15.60	18.30	17.00	17.60	18.40	25.50	23.00	21.10
8" thick	SF	17.30	20.50	18.50	19.60	20.70	28.80	25.60	23.70
Plastered and painted one side									
4" thick	SF	25.20	28.40	25.90	31.30	29.10	35.60	35.30	31.70
6" thick	SF	26.70	30.20	27.80	32.80	30.80	37.60	37.60	33.40
8" thick	SF	28.50	32.40	29.40	34.80	33.10	41.00	40.20	36.00
Integrally coloured architectural:									
Painted one side									
4" thick	SF	15.60	18.70	17.00	17.70	18.50	25.70	23.10	21.30
6" thick	SF	16.70	19.80	18.00	19.00	20.20	27.90	24.80	22.80
8" thick	SF	19.20	22.80	20.20	21.60	23.00	32.10	28.20	26.10
Plastered and painted both sides									
4" thick	SF	26.80	30.60	27.90	32.90	30.90	37.90	37.70	33.60
6" thick	SF	27.80	31.70	28.80	34.30	32.50	40.10	39.40	35.20
8" thick	SF	30.30	34.70	31.10	36.90	35.40	44.20	42.80	38.40
Metal stud									
3 5/8" thick:									
3/8" drywall single board both sides...........	SF	8.08	8.01	7.89	8.87	9.24	10.20	7.27	11.20
1/2" drywall single board both sides...........	SF	8.08	8.01	7.89	8.87	9.24	10.20	7.27	11.20
3/8" drywall double board both sides..........	SF	11.90	11.80	11.70	12.90	13.50	15.70	10.80	16.90
1/2" drywall double board both sides..........	SF	11.90	11.80	11.70	12.90	13.50	15.70	10.80	16.90
Wood stud									
2" x 4" studs with 1/2" drywall both sides	SF	5.71	5.75	5.76	6.26	6.48	8.17	5.34	8.24
B12 DOORS									
Based on 3'0" x 7'0" single doors excluding									
hardware, including painting where applicable.									
Wood									
Hollow core:									
Paint grade birch in 20 gauge hollow metal frame...........	Leaf	609.00	515.00	578.00	592.00	607.00	694.00	600.00	1140.00
Solid core:									
Paint grade birch in 18 gauge hollow metal frame...........	Leaf	705.00	624.00	701.00	727.00	752.00	864.00	788.00	1250.00
Stain grade birch in 18 gauge hollow metal frame...........	Leaf	700.00	648.00	690.00	698.00	745.00	848.00	787.00	747.00
Stain grade red oak in 18 gauge hollow metal frame...........	Leaf	763.00	705.00	751.00	756.00	814.00	924.00	856.00	808.00
Plastic laminate faced, solid									
colours in 18 gauge hollow metal frame...........	Leaf	786.00	726.00	778.00	780.00	843.00	956.00	886.00	830.00

Item	UNITS	St. John's	Halifax	Montreal	Ottawa	Toronto	Winnipeg	Calgary	Vancouver
Metal									
Hollow steel honeycombed:									
In 18 gauge hollow metal frame	Leaf	698.00	648.00	698.00	812.00	778.00	951.00	824.00	810.00
Hollow steel stiffened:									
In 18 gauge hollow metal frame	Leaf	974.00	904.00	983.00	1,140	1,100	1,340	1,150	1,110
In 18 gauge hollow metal frame, door with 2' x 2' aperture glazed with georgian glazed wired glass	Leaf	1,200	1,140	1,210	1,390	1,350	1,630	1,370	1,370

FINISHING HARDWARE

Per door, including locksets, butts, pulls, pushes and closers where applicable.

Item	UNITS	St. John's	Halifax	Montreal	Ottawa	Toronto	Winnipeg	Calgary	Vancouver
Hotels	EA	698.00	629.00	677.00	704.00	816.00	853.00	718.00	732.00
Retail stores	EA	455.00	410.00	438.00	456.00	532.00	542.00	469.00	465.00
Apartment buildings	EA	308.00	278.00	302.00	311.00	365.00	379.00	322.00	317.00
Office buildings	EA	907.00	822.00	918.00	933.00	1,040	1,030	879.00	840.00
Hospitals	EA	982.00	883.00	985.00	1,000	1,120	1,120	942.00	967.00
Schools	EA	808.00	731.00	821.00	835.00	922.00	914.00	774.00	748.00

C1: MECHANICAL

C11 Plumbing and Drainage

Plumbing cost including drainage, domestic water, etc.

Item	UNITS	St. John's	Halifax	Montreal	Ottawa	Toronto	Winnipeg	Calgary	Vancouver
Commercial building	/FIXT	4,370	4,020	4,080	4,160	4,120	4,430	3,870	4,450
Educational building	/FIXT	4,710	4,330	4,400	4,480	4,440	4,770	4,170	4,800
Residential building	/FIXT	1,170	1,070	1,090	1,110	1,100	1,180	1,030	1,190

SWIMMING POOL OLYMPIC SIZE

with mechanical work including filtration, pool and deck drainage, water heating etc.

Item	UNITS	St. John's	Halifax	Montreal	Ottawa	Toronto	Winnipeg	Calgary	Vancouver
	EA	506,000	465,000	472,000	482,000	477,000	513,000	448,000	515,000

GREASE INTERCEPTOR

Item	UNITS	St. John's	Halifax	Montreal	Ottawa	Toronto	Winnipeg	Calgary	Vancouver
Cast iron type, 33 lbs. fat capacity	EA	1,830	1,690	1,710	1,750	1,730	1,860	1,630	1,870

WATER PUMP STATION

4850 gallon tank, 15 hp. 200 gpm. 200 ft. head, centrifugal duplex pumps.

Item	UNITS	St. John's	Halifax	Montreal	Ottawa	Toronto	Winnipeg	Calgary	Vancouver
	EA	125,000	115,000	117,000	119,000	118,000	127,000	111,000	127,000

C13 Heating, Ventilation and Air Conditioning

HEATING

Hot water heating system (measure area serviced)

Item	UNITS	St. John's	Halifax	Montreal	Ottawa	Toronto	Winnipeg	Calgary	Vancouver
Including equipment and perimeter radiation	SF	8.80	8.10	8.22	8.39	8.31	8.93	7.81	8.97
Radiant in-floor hot water heating, PEX tubing	SF	6.66	6.12	6.22	6.34	6.28	6.75	5.90	6.78
Snow melting system including									
steel pipe, glycol charge, heat exchanger, pump and controls (measure area serviced)	SF	9.51	8.75	8.88	9.06	8.97	9.65	8.44	9.69

VENTILATION

Sanitary exhaust system,

Item	UNITS	St. John's	Halifax	Montreal	Ottawa	Toronto	Winnipeg	Calgary	Vancouver
including fans ductwork and grilles	CFM	7.90	7.27	7.38	7.53	7.46	8.02	7.01	8.05
Propeller thru wall fan	CFM	1.04	0.95	0.97	0.99	0.98	1.05	0.92	1.06
Make-up air systems, including fan, heating coil, duct,									
diffusers, thermal insulation and controls	CFM	17.50	16.10	16.40	16.70	16.50	17.80	15.50	17.80

AIR CONDITIONING

Central station systems

Item	UNITS	St. John's	Halifax	Montreal	Ottawa	Toronto	Winnipeg	Calgary	Vancouver
Chiller, cooling tower, distribution, AHU, ductwork & diffusers	TR	6,300	5,790	5,880	6,000	5,940	6,390	5,590	6,420
Air cooled chiller, distribution water, AHU, ductwork & diffusers	TR	5,370	4,940	5,010	5,110	5,060	5,440	4,760	5,470
Air cooled condenser, direct expansion, AHU, ductwork & diffusers	TR	4,440	4,080	4,140	4,230	4,180	4,500	3,930	4,520
Fan-coil system									
Chiller, cooling tower, individual room units with central primary air system	TR	7,450	6,860	6,960	7,100	7,030	7,560	6,610	7,590
Roof-top system									
Packaged unit, air cooled, gas-fired ductwork and diffusers:									
5 TR cooling, 170 mbh heating	EA	18,900	17,400	17,600	18,000	17,800	19,100	16,700	19,200
10 TR cooling, 270 mbh heating	EA	39,600	36,500	37,000	37,800	37,400	40,200	35,200	40,400
15 TR cooling, 375 mbh heating	EA	54,700	50,300	51,100	52,100	51,600	55,500	48,500	55,700
20 TR cooling, 410 mbh heating	EA	63,500	58,400	59,300	60,500	59,900	64,400	56,300	64,700
Air distribution									
Air handling unit, ductwork, diffusers and grilles, automatic controls, thermal and acoustical insulation	CFM	21.40	19.60	20.00	20.40	20.20	21.70	18.90	21.80
Air conditioning equipment									
Absorption chiller	TR	2,210	2,030	2,060	2,110	2,080	2,240	1,960	2,250
Centrifugal chiller	TR	827.00	761.00	773.00	788.00	781.00	839.00	734.00	843.00
Cooling tower	TR	350.00	322.00	327.00	333.00	330.00	355.00	310.00	357.00

C2: ELECTRICAL

ELECTRICAL INSTALLATIONS

Office buildings (speculative), national code 70 regulation, substation lighting fixture cost at average $165.00 (T-8 lamps), fire alarm, telephone, floor outlets, 1 per 325 SF, parking in basement.

Ceiling grid empty conduit:

Item	UNITS	St. John's	Halifax	Montreal	Ottawa	Toronto	Winnipeg	Calgary	Vancouver
High-rise lighting intensity 70 ft-c.	SF	12.70	11.70	11.90	12.10	12.00	12.90	11.30	12.90
Low-rise lighting intensity 70 ft-c.	SF	13.50	12.40	12.60	12.90	12.70	13.70	12.00	13.70
High-rise lighting intensity 100 ft-c.	SF	13.20	12.10	12.30	12.60	12.40	13.40	11.70	13.40

CIQS C2 Electrical — IMPERIAL COMPOSITE UNIT RATES

Item	UNITS	St. John's	Halifax	Montreal	Ottawa	Toronto	Winnipeg	Calgary	Vancouver
Wireway and plug in lighting fixtures:									
High-rise lighting intensity 70 ft-c	SF	15.10	13.90	14.10	14.40	14.20	15.30	13.40	15.40
Low-rise lighting intensity 70 ft-c	SF	16.00	14.70	14.90	15.20	15.10	16.20	14.10	16.30
High-rise lighting intensity 100 ft-c	SF	15.50	14.20	14.40	14.70	14.60	15.70	13.70	15.80
Heavy laboratories, national code 70 regulation, no parking facilities									
substation, 100 ft-c at 347 V 1 V control, fixture, cost $275.00									
fire alarm, tel., emergency generator, excl. security and special systems									
High rise:									
Load demand 15 W/sf lab area 40% of gfa	SF	38.40	35.30	35.90	36.60	36.20	38.90	34.10	39.10
Load demand 18 W/sf lab area 50% of gfa	SF	41.80	38.40	39.00	39.80	39.40	42.30	37.00	42.50
Load demand 20 W/sf lab area 60% of gfa	SF	45.70	42.00	42.70	43.50	43.10	46.30	40.50	46.60
Low rise:									
Load demand 15 W/sf lab area 40% of gfa	SF	37.60	34.60	35.10	35.80	35.50	38.20	33.40	38.30
Load demand 18 W/sf lab area 50% of gfa	SF	41.10	37.80	38.40	39.10	38.70	41.60	36.40	41.80
Load demand 20 W/sf lab area 60% of gfa	SF	45.00	41.40	42.00	42.90	42.50	45.60	39.90	45.90
LIGHTING SYSTEMS (net area lighted)									
Parking lots									
Davit steel poles, 2 heads, 250 W HPS ballast, operating									
system wired to panel, complete:									
1 W/sf	SF	0.48	0.44	0.44	0.45	0.45	0.48	0.42	0.48
2 W/sf	SF	0.71	0.65	0.66	0.68	0.67	0.72	0.63	0.73
Supermarkets (against net area)									
Strip fluorescent	SF	5.05	4.65	4.72	4.81	4.77	5.12	4.48	5.15
Recessed HID	SF	5.60	5.15	5.23	5.34	5.29	5.68	4.97	5.71
Office building (against net area), lighting system operating and									
wired to panel, 347 V with standard LV switching, grid box system.									
70 ft-c average cost/fixture (T-8 lamps)									
$169.00	SF	6.60	6.07	6.16	6.29	6.22	6.69	5.85	6.72
$192.00	SF	7.40	6.80	6.91	7.05	6.98	7.50	6.56	7.54
$218.00	SF	7.88	7.25	7.36	7.51	7.43	7.99	6.99	8.03
ELECTRICAL HEATING									
Apartments, 2 to 3 storeys, heating load approx. 8 W/sf,									
with baseboard convector and room thermostats:									
Baked white enamel finish	KW	438.00	403.00	409.00	417.00	413.00	444.00	388.00	446.00
Offices, standard partitioning, heating load approximately									
10 W/sf, with baseboard convectors and room thermostats:									
Baked white enamel finish	KW	465.00	428.00	435.00	443.00	439.00	472.00	413.00	474.00
Stainless steel finish	KW	670.00	616.00	626.00	638.00	632.00	679.00	594.00	683.00
Banks and similar large window exposure, heating load									
12 W/sf, with central thermostat control:									
Baked white enamel finish	KW	475.00	437.00	444.00	452.00	448.00	482.00	421.00	484.00
Stainless steel finish	KW	686.00	631.00	641.00	653.00	647.00	696.00	608.00	699.00
SUBSTATIONS									
Indoor (vault type), 2 incoming h.t. lines, primary									
protection, load breaker and air circuit breaker, all									
busing, insulators, cutouts, transformer, grounding,									
etc. no secondary protection or distribution.									
12,000/347-600 V									
1,000 kVa	EA	97,200	89,400	90,800	92,600	91,700	98,600	86,200	99,000
1,500 kVa	EA	122,000	112,000	114,000	116,000	115,000	124,000	108,000	124,000
2,000 kVa	EA	164,000	151,000	153,000	157,000	155,000	167,000	146,000	167,000
Indoor (metal clad unit type), 2 incoming h.t. lines, primary									
protection, load breakers and air circuit breaker, all									
metering, transformer, including tentative allowance for									
secondary breaker type switchboard without main breaker.									
12,000/347-600 V									
1,000 kVa	EA	89,600	82,400	83,700	85,300	84,500	90,800	79,400	91,300
1,500 kVa	EA	111,000	102,000	104,000	106,000	105,000	113,000	98,700	113,000
2,000 kVa	EA	147,000	136,000	138,000	140,000	139,000	149,000	131,000	150,000
Outdoor, 2 incoming h.t. lines, steel switching structure,									
transformer fencing, lightning protection, grounding,									
etc., does not include secondary protection.									
12,000/347-600 V									
1,000 kVa	EA	79,900	73,500	74,600	76,200	75,400	81,100	70,900	81,400
1,500 kVa	EA	100,000	92,100	93,600	95,400	94,500	102,000	88,800	102,000
2,000 kVa	EA	138,000	127,000	129,000	131,000	130,000	140,000	122,000	140,000
EMERGENCY SYSTEMS									
Diesel generator units including complete operating system,									
exhaust, cooling, oil system, control system.									
120/208 V 20 kW	EA	39,100	36,000	36,500	37,300	36,900	39,700	34,700	39,900
120/208 V 50 kW	EA	52,200	48,000	48,700	49,700	49,200	52,900	46,200	53,100
120/208 V 100 kW	EA	79,900	73,500	74,600	76,200	75,400	81,100	70,900	81,400
120/208 V 200 kW	EA	126,000	116,000	118,000	120,000	119,000	128,000	112,000	129,000
347/600 V 50 kW	EA	54,700	50,300	51,100	52,100	51,600	55,500	48,500	55,700
347/600 V 100 kW	EA	85,000	78,200	79,400	81,000	80,200	86,200	75,400	86,600
347/600 V 200 kW	EA	130,000	120,000	122,000	124,000	123,000	132,000	116,000	133,000
347/600 V 500 kW	EA	425,000	391,000	397,000	405,000	401,000	431,000	377,000	433,000

Item	UNITS	St. John's	Halifax	Montreal	Ottawa	Toronto	Winnipeg	Calgary	Vancouver

MOTOR CONTROL CENTERS

To obtain probable cost of motor center, installed and operating, compute costs from motors connected to the center. Rates include all fuses, control transformers, pilot lights, push-button stations, etc.

575 V breaker combination starters.

Class 11, type b:

Item	UNITS	St. John's	Halifax	Montreal	Ottawa	Toronto	Winnipeg	Calgary	Vancouver
Motors to 10 hp	/mtr	1,390	1,280	1,300	1,320	1,310	1,410	1,230	1,410
Motors 30 to 50 hp	/mtr	1,890	1,740	1,760	1,800	1,780	1,910	1,670	1,920
Motors 125 to 200 hp	/mtr	4,380	4,030	4,090	4,170	4,130	4,440	3,880	4,460

575 V fuse combination starter

Class 11, type b:

Item	UNITS	St. John's	Halifax	Montreal	Ottawa	Toronto	Winnipeg	Calgary	Vancouver
Motors to 10 hp	/mtr	1,270	1,170	1,190	1,210	1,200	1,290	1,130	1,300
Motors 100 to 150 hp	/mtr	1,890	1,740	1,760	1,800	1,780	1,910	1,670	1,920
Motors 175 to 300 hp	/mtr	4,300	3,960	4,020	4,100	4,060	4,360	3,820	4,380
Motors 250 to 400 hp	/mtr	12,700	11,700	11,900	12,100	12,000	12,900	11,300	13,000

575 V star delta breaker

Class 11, type b:

Item	UNITS	St. John's	Halifax	Montreal	Ottawa	Toronto	Winnipeg	Calgary	Vancouver
Motors to 75 hp	/mtr	3,760	3,460	3,510	3,590	3,550	3,820	3,340	3,830
Motors 100 to 150 hp	/mtr	5,060	4,650	4,720	4,820	4,770	5,130	4,480	5,150
Motors 175 to 300 hp	/mtr	11,300	10,400	10,600	10,800	10,700	11,500	10,100	11,600

COMMUNICATION SYSTEM

Intercom system

Complete with switchboard. Cost per system:

Item	UNITS	St. John's	Halifax	Montreal	Ottawa	Toronto	Winnipeg	Calgary	Vancouver
Up to 50 lines	EA	41,200	37,900	38,500	39,300	38,900	41,800	36,600	42,000
Up to 100 lines	EA	82,200	75,600	76,700	78,300	77,500	83,300	72,900	83,700
Up to 200 lines	EA	118,000	108,000	110,000	112,000	111,000	119,000	104,000	120,000

Public address system

Complete with wiring in hung ceiling. Cost per system:

Item	UNITS	St. John's	Halifax	Montreal	Ottawa	Toronto	Winnipeg	Calgary	Vancouver
Up to 10 loudspeakers	EA	3,660	3,360	3,420	3,480	3,450	3,710	3,240	3,730
Up to 20 loudspeakers	EA	6,110	5,620	5,700	5,820	5,760	6,190	5,410	6,220
Up to 40 loudspeakers	EA	9,760	8,980	9,120	9,300	9,210	9,900	8,660	9,950

Add to above for the following:

Item	UNITS	St. John's	Halifax	Montreal	Ottawa	Toronto	Winnipeg	Calgary	Vancouver
Microphone	EA	527.00	485.00	492.00	502.00	497.00	534.00	467.00	537.00
C.D., VCD, MP3, AM/FM stereo tuner	EA	2,270	2,090	2,120	2,160	2,140	2,300	2,010	2,310

LIGHTNING PROTECTION

Complete installation of rods to include bonding of steel structure.

High-rise structure:

Item	UNITS	St. John's	Halifax	Montreal	Ottawa	Toronto	Winnipeg	Calgary	Vancouver
Up to 20 rods	/ROD	1,650	1,520	1,540	1,580	1,560	1,680	1,470	1,680
Up to 60 rods	/ROD	1,710	1,570	1,590	1,630	1,610	1,730	1,510	1,740
Medium-rise structure:									
Up to 20 rods	/ROD	1,300	1,200	1,220	1,240	1,230	1,320	1,160	1,330
Up to 60 rods	/ROD	1,380	1,270	1,290	1,310	1,300	1,400	1,220	1,400
Low-rise structure:									
Up to 20 rods	/ROD	975.00	897.00	911.00	929.00	920.00	989.00	865.00	994.00
Up to 60 rods	/ROD	1,030	946	960	980	970	1,040	912	1,050

SNOW MELTING COMPLETE

System connected to panels, including controls, mineral insulation heating cable with nylon jacket.

Item	UNITS	St. John's	Halifax	Montreal	Ottawa	Toronto	Winnipeg	Calgary	Vancouver
30 W/sf	SF	25.60	23.60	23.90	24.40	24.20	26.00	22.70	26.10
40 W/sf	SF	28.60	26.30	26.70	27.20	26.90	29.00	25.30	29.10

D1: SITE WORK

D11 Site Development

Seeding & sodding

Item	UNITS	St. John's	Halifax	Montreal	Ottawa	Toronto	Winnipeg	Calgary	Vancouver
Rough grade, spread stock piled topsoil, fine grade & place sod	SY	13.70	13.50	11.60	12.00	12.40	15.60	13.10	13.60
Rough grade, spread stock piled topsoil, fine grade & seed	SY	9.45	9.03	8.44	8.86	8.78	10.30	8.29	9.70
Rough grade, spread imported topsoil, fine grade & place sod	SY	18.80	18.30	14.90	16.70	17.10	20.20	17.00	18.30
Rough grade, spread imported topsoil, fine grade & seed	SY	14.50	13.90	11.70	13.50	13.40	14.90	12.10	14.40

Road & parking

Item	UNITS	St. John's	Halifax	Montreal	Ottawa	Toronto	Winnipeg	Calgary	Vancouver
Roadways, 25' wide, with 9" crushed stone base, 3" double layer asphalt and precast concrete curbs each side	LF	193.00	194.00	177.00	186.00	190.00	269.00	215.00	266.00
Roadways, 12' wide, including crushed stone paving and 2" x 10" cedar curbs to edges	LF	13.70	13.50	11.70	12.20	12.00	15.90	12.20	15.30
Parking lots, including 6" crushed stone base, 2" single layer asphalt precast concrete bumpers at each car and painted parking lines	SF	4.28	4.48	3.99	4.14	3.76	5.39	4.75	7.11

Walkway & steps

Item	UNITS	St. John's	Halifax	Montreal	Ottawa	Toronto	Winnipeg	Calgary	Vancouver
Walks, 4' wide, including 4" crushed stone base and 2" single layer asphalt	LF	34.70	35.40	32.90	33.20	30.80	43.60	39.00	52.70
Walks, 4' wide, including 4" crushed stone base and 5" concrete, mesh and broom finish	LF	28.50	29.50	30.00	31.70	35.40	48.20	36.30	35.70
Concrete steps to walks, 4' wide, including crushed stone base and broom (12" tread and 6" rise)	TREAD	105.00	111.00	112.00	121.00	135.00	182.00	133.00	131.00

Pedestrian and service tunnels for typical university installation, including reinforced concrete, waterproofing, excavation and backfill but not including mechanical and electrical services.

Item	UNITS	St. John's	Halifax	Montreal	Ottawa	Toronto	Winnipeg	Calgary	Vancouver
6' wide x 10' high	LF	1,080	1,090	1,220	1,220	1,390	2,250	1,350	1,280
10' wide x 10' high	LF	1,210	1,220	1,360	1,360	1,540	2,440	1,510	1,460

Item	UNITS	St. John's	Halifax	Montreal	Ottawa	Toronto	Winnipeg	Calgary	Vancouver
Fences & screens									
6' high cedar privacy fence 1" x 6" alternate sides of 2" x 4" rails including 4" x 4" posts at 10' o.c. set in concrete	LF	81.40	76.20	82.90	78.90	86.00	108.00	116.00	120.00
6' high decorative concrete block screen, including 4' deep block foundation wall below	LF	168.00	160.00	188.00	187.00	196.00	289.00	257.00	218.00

Z1: GENERAL REQUIREMENTS & FEE

For preliminary estimating purposes the general contractor's site expenses, head office overhead and profit may be calculated on a percentage basis of the total net estimated cost

Item	UNITS								
Complex Institutional Projects	%					8 - 12			
School Project	%					7 - 11			
Simple Commercial Projects	%					6 - 1 0			

Z2: CONTINGENCIES/ALLOWANCES

Z21 Design

Initial estimates require the inclusion of a contingency sum for remeasured items, design development change, etc. This contingency may be reduced as more information becomes available enabling more detailed estimates to be prepared .... %   5 - 10

Z22 Escalation

Provision should be made for likely cost increases between the date of estimate and the anticipated date of tender .... %   varies according to circumstance

Z23 Construction

Allowance should be made for possible increases in contract cost resulting from unforeseen site conditions, design change during construction, etc.

Item	UNITS								
New work	%					2 - 5			
Renovations and alterations	%					3 - 8			

HOW TO READ "GROSS BLDG. COSTS—REPRESENTATIVE EXAMPLES"

Description of building type.

Breakdown of building elements.

First 3 columns show low and high costs per square metre, plus **average** costs for building elements.

These 3 columns show low and high costs per square foot, plus average costs for building elements.

Final column shows building element cost as a percentage of total cost.

This section offers a general guide to **overall** costs of 45 building types.

Costs are shown in both metric and imperial and based on gross floor area. Costs are shown for each building element with its proportion to the total cost. Prices are based on representative projects estimated in the Toronto market and must be adjusted to local conditions.

High and low prices are shown per square foot or square metre, and these indicate the +/- 10% from the averages, respectively. In the majority of cases, prices will fall between the high and low figures.

Note that costs for site work are not included because of a wide variation regardless of gross floor area.

SECTION E — GROSS BUILDING COSTS – REPRESENTATIVE EXAMPLES

MULTI LEVEL PARKING GARAGE: 1 level below grade plus 6 levels above ground, 700 cars, reinforced concrete frame. Excluding site. 264,700 SF (24,590 m2)

		SQUARE METERS			SQUARE FEET			%
		LOW	AVERAGE	HIGH	LOW	AVERAGE	HIGH	OF TOTAL
A1 substructure			41.58			3.86		5.4%
A2 structure			346.01			32.15		44.7%
A3 exterior enclosure			73.64			6.84		9.5%
B1 partitions & doors			3.60			0.33		0.5%
B2 finishes			76.21			7.08		9.9%
B3 fittings & equipment			48.87			4.54		6.3%
C1 mechanical			34.98			3.25		4.5%
C2 electrical			71.31			6.62		9.2%
Z1 general requirements & fee			77.36			7.19		10.0%
COMPLETE BUILDING		696.20	773.56	850.91	64.67	71.86	79.04	100.0%

PARKING GARAGE: 1 level below grade, 350 cars, reinforced concrete frame, heated. Excluding site 131,450 SF (12,210 m2)

		SQUARE METERS			SQUARE FEET			%
		LOW	AVERAGE	HIGH	LOW	AVERAGE	HIGH	OF TOTAL
A1 substructure			285.67			26.54		23.3%
A2 structure			390.17			36.25		31.8%
A3 exterior enclosure			112.26			10.43		9.1%
B1 partitions & doors			18.58			1.73		1.5%
B2 finishes			87.92			8.17		7.2%
B3 fittings & equipment			16.70			1.55		1.4%
C1 mechanical			124.59			11.57		10.2%
C2 electrical			68.60			6.37		5.6%
Z1 general requirements & fee			122.72			11.40		10.0%
COMPLETE BUILDING		1,104.49	1,227.21	1,349.93	102.61	114.01	125.41	100.0%

INDUSTRIAL (VEHICLE MAINTENANCE): Steel frame structure. Including administration, maintenance bays, storage and wash area. Excluding site. 150,700 SF (14,000 m2)

		SQUARE METERS			SQUARE FEET			%
		LOW	AVERAGE	HIGH	LOW	AVERAGE	HIGH	OF TOTAL
A1 substructure			153.84			14.29		10.3%
A2 structure			682.94			63.44		21.2%
A3 exterior enclosure			761.70			70.76		23.8%
B1 partitions & doors			119.79			11.13		2.5%
B2 finishes			105.42			9.79		3.2%
B3 fittings & equipment			67.19			6.24		4.3%
C1 mechanical			461.31			42.86		18.8%
C2 electrical			221.39			20.57		5.8%
Z1 general requirements & fee			231.62			21.52		10.0%
COMPLETE BUILDING		2,524.65	2,805.17	3,085.69	234.54	260.60	286.66	100.0%

WAREHOUSE: Bare, lightly serviced, single storey 30 ft. (9.5 m) eaves. Excluding site. 400,000 SF (37,160 m2)

		SQUARE METERS			SQUARE FEET			%
		LOW	AVERAGE	HIGH	LOW	AVERAGE	HIGH	OF TOTAL
A1 substructure			54.97			5.11		6.1%
A2 structure			259.27			24.09		28.9%
A3 exterior enclosure			233.52			21.69		26.0%
B1 partitions & doors			26.96			2.50		3.0%
B2 finishes			18.41			1.71		2.1%
B3 fittings & equipment			19.64			1.82		2.2%
C1 mechanical			125.38			11.65		14.0%
C2 electrical			69.12			6.42		7.7%
Z1 general requirements & fee			89.70			8.33		10.0%
COMPLETE BUILDING		807.27	896.97	986.66	74.99	83.32	91.65	100.0%

PUBLIC ADMINISTRATION BUILDING: 6 storeys above grade @ 390,065 SF, 1 level below grade parking. Including tenant fit-up. Excluding site. SF cost based on total area. 521,510 SF (48,450 m2)

		SQUARE METERS			SQUARE FEET			%
		LOW	AVERAGE	HIGH	LOW	AVERAGE	HIGH	OF TOTAL
A1 substructure			71.10			6.61		2.9%
A2 structure			403.62			37.50		16.6%
A3 exterior enclosure			428.07			39.77		17.6%
B1 partitions & doors			85.62			7.95		3.5%
B2 finishes			256.84			23.86		10.5%
B3 fittings & equipment			146.76			13.63		6.0%
C1 mechanical			478.09			44.42		19.6%
C2 electrical			322.27			29.94		13.2%
Z1 general requirements & fee			243.60			22.63		10.0%
COMPLETE BUILDING		2,192.37	2,435.97	2,679.56	203.68	226.31	248.94	100.0%

MULTI LEVEL PARKING GARAGE: Below grade only, 1 level below grade plus 3 levels above ground, 300 cars, reinforced concrete frame. Excluding site. 101,700 SF (9,450 m2)

		SQUARE METERS			SQUARE FEET			%
		LOW	AVERAGE	HIGH	LOW	AVERAGE	HIGH	OF TOTAL
A1 substructure			237.69			22.08		5.4%
A2 structure			576.57			53.56		44.6%
A3 exterior enclosure			190.27			17.68		9.5%
B1 partitions & doors			13.97			1.30		0.5%
B2 finishes			70.43			6.54		9.8%
B3 fittings & equipment			78.40			7.28		6.3%
C1 mechanical			130.71			12.14		4.6%
C2 electrical			81.62			7.58		9.3%
Z1 general requirements & fee			124.17			11.54		10.0%
COMPLETE BUILDING		1,353.45	1,503.83	1,654.21	125.74	139.71	153.68	100.0%

MULTI LEVEL PARKING GARAGE: 3 level above grade, 300 cars, reinforced concrete frame, heated. Excluding site 101,700 SF (9,450 m2)

		SQUARE METERS			SQUARE FEET			%
		LOW	AVERAGE	HIGH	LOW	AVERAGE	HIGH	OF TOTAL
A1 substructure			76.42			7.10		23.2%
A2 structure			404.78			37.60		31.7%
A3 exterior enclosure			168.48			15.65		9.1%
B1 partitions & doors			27.02			2.51		1.5%
B2 finishes			50.59			4.70		7.2%
B3 fittings & equipment			64.51			5.99		1.4%
C1 mechanical			102.92			9.56		10.3%
C2 electrical			72.60			6.74		5.7%
Z1 general requirements & fee			87.06			8.09		10.0%
COMPLETE BUILDING		948.94	1,054.38	1,159.82	88.16	97.95	107.75	100.0%

GROSS BUILDING COSTS — REPRESENTATIVE EXAMPLES

MULTI LEVEL PARKING GARAGE:
1 level below grade plus 6 levels above ground, 700 cars, reinforced concrete frame. Excluding site.
264,700 SF (24,590 m2)

	SQUARE METERS			SQUARE FEET			%
	LOW	AVERAGE	HIGH	LOW	AVERAGE	HIGH	OF TOTAL
A1 substructure		41.58			3.86		5.4%
A2 structure		346.01			32.15		44.7%
A3 exterior enclosure		73.64			6.84		9.5%
B1 partitions & doors		3.60			0.33		0.5%
B2 finishes		76.21			7.08		9.9%
B3 fittings & equipment		48.87			4.54		6.3%
C1 mechanical		34.98			3.25		4.5%
C2 electrical		71.31			6.62		9.2%
Z1 general requirements & fee		77.36			7.19		10.0%
COMPLETE BUILDING	696.20	773.56	850.91	64.67	71.86	79.04	100.0%

PARKING GARAGE:
1 level below grade, 350 cars, reinforced concrete frame, heated. Excluding site
131,450 SF (12,210 m2)

	SQUARE METERS			SQUARE FEET			%
	LOW	AVERAGE	HIGH	LOW	AVERAGE	HIGH	OF TOTAL
A1 substructure		285.67			26.54		23.3%
A2 structure		390.17			36.25		31.8%
A3 exterior enclosure		112.26			10.43		9.1%
B1 partitions & doors		18.58			1.73		1.5%
B2 finishes		87.92			8.17		7.2%
B3 fittings & equipment		16.70			1.55		1.4%
C1 mechanical		124.59			11.57		10.2%
C2 electrical		68.60			6.37		5.6%
Z1 general requirements & fee		122.72			11.40		10.0%
COMPLETE BUILDING	1,104.49	1,227.21	1,349.93	102.61	114.01	125.41	100.0%

INDUSTRIAL (VEHICLE MAINTENANCE):
Steel frame structure. Including administration, maintenance bays, storage and wash area. Excluding site.
150,700 SF (14,000 m2)

	SQUARE METERS			SQUARE FEET			%
	LOW	AVERAGE	HIGH	LOW	AVERAGE	HIGH	OF TOTAL
A1 substructure		153.84			14.29		10.3%
A2 structure		682.91			63.44		21.2%
A3 exterior enclosure		761.70			70.76		23.8%
B1 partitions & doors		119.79			11.13		2.5%
B2 finishes		105.42			9.79		3.2%
B3 fittings & equipment		67.19			6.24		4.3%
C1 mechanical		461.31			42.86		18.8%
C2 electrical		221.39			20.57		5.8%
Z1 general requirements & fee		231.62			21.52		10.0%
COMPLETE BUILDING	2,524.65	2,805.17	3,085.69	234.54	260.60	286.66	100.0%

WAREHOUSE:
Bare, lightly serviced, single storey 30 ft. (9.5 m) eaves. Excluding site.
400,000 SF (37,160 m2)

	SQUARE METERS			SQUARE FEET			%
	LOW	AVERAGE	HIGH	LOW	AVERAGE	HIGH	OF TOTAL
A1 substructure		54.97			5.11		6.1%
A2 structure		259.27			24.09		28.9%
A3 exterior enclosure		233.52			21.69		26.0%
B1 partitions & doors		26.96			2.50		3.0%
B2 finishes		18.41			1.71		2.1%
B3 fittings & equipment		19.64			1.82		2.2%
C1 mechanical		125.38			11.65		14.0%
C2 electrical		69.12			6.42		7.7%
Z1 general requirements & fee		89.70			8.33		10.0%
COMPLETE BUILDING	807.27	896.97	986.66	74.99	83.32	91.65	100.0%

PUBLIC ADMINISTRATION BUILDING:
6 storeys above grade @ 390,065 SF, 1 level below grade parking. Including tenant fit-up. Exluding site. SF cost based on total area.
521,510 SF (48,450 m2)

	SQUARE METERS			SQUARE FEET			%
	LOW	AVERAGE	HIGH	LOW	AVERAGE	HIGH	OF TOTAL
A1 substructure		71.10			6.61		2.9%
A2 structure		403.62			37.50		16.6%
A3 exterior enclosure		428.07			39.77		17.6%
B1 partitions & doors		85.62			7.95		3.5%
B2 finishes		256.84			23.86		10.5%
B3 fittings & equipment		146.76			13.63		6.0%
C1 mechanical		478.09			44.42		19.6%
C2 electrical		322.27			29.94		13.2%
Z1 general requirements & fee		243.60			22.63		10.0%
COMPLETE BUILDING	2,192.37	2,435.97	2,679.56	203.68	226.31	248.94	100.0%

PERFORMING ARTS CENTRE: 1000 seats. Including 2 performance halls, 1 multi-use hall and performance equipment. Excluding site. 66,860 SF (6,211 m2)		SQUARE METERS			SQUARE FEET			%
		LOW	AVERAGE	HIGH	LOW	AVERAGE	HIGH	OF TOTAL
	A1 substructure		150.58			13.99		3.2%
	A2 structure		835.41			77.61		17.7%
	A3 exterior enclosure		664.62			61.75		14.1%
	B1 partitions & doors		321.85			29.90		6.8%
	B2 finishes		310.16			28.81		6.6%
	B3 fittings & equipment		609.24			56.60		12.9%
	C1 mechanical		780.65			72.52		16.5%
	C2 electrical		574.89			53.41		12.2%
	Z1 general requirements & fee		471.93			43.84		10.0%
	COMPLETE BUILDING	4,247.40	4,719.33	5,191.27	394.59	438.43	482.28	100.0%

PRIVATE MUSEUM: 3 storeys plus 2 level basement. Excluding site. 39,500 SF (3,665 m2)		SQUARE METERS			SQUARE FEET			%
		LOW	AVERAGE	HIGH	LOW	AVERAGE	HIGH	OF TOTAL
	A1 substructure		263.62			24.49		5.5%
	A2 structure		835.41			77.61		17.4%
	A3 exterior enclosure		822.03			76.37		17.1%
	B1 partitions & doors		321.23			29.84		6.7%
	B2 finishes		310.16			28.81		6.5%
	B3 fittings & equipment		332.31			30.87		6.9%
	C1 mechanical		776.79			72.17		16.2%
	C2 electrical		658.00			61.13		13.7%
	Z1 general requirements & fee		479.95			44.59		10.0%
	COMPLETE BUILDING	4,319.55	4,799.50	5,279.45	401.29	445.88	490.47	100.0%

DISTRICT LIBRARY: Including meeting spaces and technical services. No basement area. Flat roof. Steel structure, brick & metal siding cladding. 30,140 SF (2,800 m2)		SQUARE METERS			SQUARE FEET			%
		LOW	AVERAGE	HIGH	LOW	AVERAGE	HIGH	OF TOTAL
	A1 substructure		135.35			12.57		7.2%
	A2 structure		492.79			45.78		18.0%
	A3 exterior enclosure		506.95			47.10		15.9%
	B1 partitions & doors		129.47			12.03		5.7%
	B2 finishes		165.82			15.40		7.6%
	B3 fittings & equipment		251.16			23.33		5.7%
	C1 mechanical		592.65			55.06		22.5%
	C2 electrical		364.26			33.84		7.3%
	Z1 general requirements & fee		237.46			22.06		10.0%
	COMPLETE BUILDING	2,588.32	2,875.91	3,163.50	240.45	267.17	293.89	100.0%

DAY CARE CENTRE: Wood framed construction, sloped roof, no basement area. Split face block and brick cladding. Residential type kitchen. No site work included. 3,010 SF (280 m2)		SQUARE METERS			SQUARE FEET			%
		LOW	AVERAGE	HIGH	LOW	AVERAGE	HIGH	OF TOTAL
	A1 substructure		233.12			21.66		7.2%
	A2 structure		302.72			28.12		18.0%
	A3 exterior enclosure		844.78			78.48		15.9%
	B1 partitions & doors		232.48			21.60		5.7%
	B2 finishes		233.04			21.65		7.6%
	B3 fittings & equipment		221.60			20.59		5.7%
	C1 mechanical		672.54			62.48		22.5%
	C2 electrical		564.31			52.42		7.3%
	Z1 general requirements & fee		297.41			27.63		10.0%
	COMPLETE BUILDING	3,241.80	3,602.00	3,962.20	301.16	334.63	368.09	100.0%

RECREATIONAL CENTRE: Including 1 arena, 1 pool, change rooms, library, gym and fitness centre and multi-use rooms. Excluding site. 125,950 SF (11,700m2)		SQUARE METERS			SQUARE FEET			%
		LOW	AVERAGE	HIGH	LOW	AVERAGE	HIGH	OF TOTAL
	A1 substructure		212.03			19.70		7.2%
	A2 structure		525.93			48.86		17.8%
	A3 exterior enclosure		465.23			43.22		15.8%
	B1 partitions & doors		166.16			15.44		5.6%
	B2 finishes		221.53			20.58		7.5%
	B3 fittings & equipment		166.16			15.44		5.6%
	C1 mechanical		648.12			60.21		22.0%
	C2 electrical		251.06			23.32		8.5%
	Z1 general requirements & fee		295.14			27.42		10.0%
	COMPLETE BUILDING	2,656.22	2,951.36	3,246.49	246.77	274.19	301.61	100.0%

COMMUNITY CENTRE:
Including gym, fitness centre multi-purpose room, no basement area. Flat roof. Steel structure, brick & metal siding cladding.
18,030 SF (1,675 m2)

		SQUARE METERS				SQUARE FEET		%
		LOW	AVERAGE	HIGH	LOW	AVERAGE	HIGH	OF TOTAL
	A1 substructure		137.29			12.75		7.2%
	A2 structure		345.24			32.07		18.0%
	A3 exterior enclosure		806.69			74.94		15.9%
	B1 partitions & doors		206.70			19.20		5.7%
	B2 finishes		167.25			15.54		7.6%
	B3 fittings & equipment		275.64			25.61		5.7%
	C1 mechanical		742.84			69.01		22.5%
	C2 electrical		380.05			35.31		7.3%
	Z1 general requirements & fee		275.55			25.60		10.0%
	COMPLETE BUILDING	3,003.53	3,337.25	3,670.98	279.03	310.03	341.03	100.0%

COMMUNITY POOL:
Including 6 lane pool, fitness centre and change rooms, public washrooms, concession area, admin office. Excludes site.
25,830 SF (2,400m2)

		SQUARE METERS				SQUARE FEET		%
		LOW	AVERAGE	HIGH	LOW	AVERAGE	HIGH	OF TOTAL
	A1 substructure		130.24			12.10		7.2%
	A2 structure		445.31			41.37		18.0%
	A3 exterior enclosure		705.50			65.54		15.9%
	B1 partitions & doors		176.09			16.36		5.7%
	B2 finishes		222.72			20.69		7.6%
	B3 fittings & equipment		422.24			39.23		5.7%
	C1 mechanical		707.41			65.72		22.5%
	C2 electrical		306.62			28.48		7.3%
	Z1 general requirements & fee		280.45			26.05		10.0%
	COMPLETE BUILDING	3,056.92	3,396.58	3,736.24	283.99	315.54	347.10	100.0%

COMMUNITY ARENA:
Including 1 ice surface 85' x 200', 500 seats, change rooms, public washrooms, concession area, admin office. Excludes site.
125,950 SF (11,700m2)

		SQUARE METERS				SQUARE FEET		%
		LOW	AVERAGE	HIGH	LOW	AVERAGE	HIGH	OF TOTAL
	A1 substructure		136.03			12.64		7.2%
	A2 structure		517.65			48.09		18.0%
	A3 exterior enclosure		501.20			46.56		15.9%
	B1 partitions & doors		122.86			11.41		5.7%
	B2 finishes		126.26			11.73		7.6%
	B3 fittings & equipment		291.41			27.07		5.7%
	C1 mechanical		610.40			56.71		22.5%
	C2 electrical		266.62			24.77		7.3%
	Z1 general requirements & fee		231.52			21.51		10.0%
	COMPLETE BUILDING	2,523.56	2,803.95	3,084.35	234.44	260.49	286.54	100.0%

FIRE STATION:
2 storey. Excluding site. Three bays, hose tower, administration area, sleeping area.
10,760 SF (1,000 m2)

		SQUARE METERS				SQUARE FEET		%
		LOW	AVERAGE	HIGH	LOW	AVERAGE	HIGH	OF TOTAL
	A1 substructure		177.58			16.50		9.3%
	A2 structure		428.98			39.85		12.3%
	A3 exterior enclosure		723.03			67.17		18.2%
	B1 partitions & doors		186.73			17.35		7.3%
	B2 finishes		151.49			14.07		6.4%
	B3 fittings & equipment		332.16			30.86		5.1%
	C1 mechanical		679.80			63.15		19.3%
	C2 electrical		335.08			31.13		12.1%
	Z1 general requirements & fee		271.34			25.21		10.0%
	COMPLETE BUILDING	2,957.57	3,286.19	3,614.81	274.76	305.29	335.82	100.0%

SMALL FIRE STATION:
1 storey. Excluding site. Two bays, wood framed
5,920 SF (550 m2)

		SQUARE METERS				SQUARE FEET		%
		LOW	AVERAGE	HIGH	LOW	AVERAGE	HIGH	OF TOTAL
	A1 substructure		233.72			21.71		9.3%
	A2 structure		589.56			54.77		12.3%
	A3 exterior enclosure		777.27			72.21		18.2%
	B1 partitions & doors		265.69			24.68		7.3%
	B2 finishes		99.70			9.26		6.4%
	B3 fittings & equipment		62.01			5.76		5.1%
	C1 mechanical		297.78			27.66		19.3%
	C2 electrical		277.21			25.75		12.1%
	Z1 general requirements & fee		234.26			21.76		10.0%
	COMPLETE BUILDING	2,553.48	2,837.20	3,120.92	237.22	263.58	289.93	100.0%

		SQUARE METERS			SQUARE FEET			%
		LOW	AVERAGE	HIGH	LOW	AVERAGE	HIGH	OF TOTAL
PSYCHIATRIC HOSPITAL: 2 storey, 325 beds. Excluding site and in-contract equipment. 503,370 SF (46,763 m2)	A1 substructure		134.39			12.49		2.8%
	A2 structure		570.48			53.00		12.0%
	A3 exterior enclosure		609.24			56.60		12.8%
	B1 partitions & doors		312.01			28.99		6.5%
	B2 finishes		276.93			25.73		5.8%
	B3 fittings & equipment		400.28			37.19		8.4%
	C1 mechanical		1,232.83			114.53		25.9%
	C2 electrical		754.55			70.10		15.8%
	Z1 general requirements & fee		476.75			44.29		10.0%
	COMPLETE BUILDING	4,290.71	4,767.46	5,244.20	398.63	442.92	487.21	100.0%

		SQUARE METERS			SQUARE FEET			%
		LOW	AVERAGE	HIGH	LOW	AVERAGE	HIGH	OF TOTAL
HIGH RISE HOSPITAL: 16 storeys above grade @ 430,400 SF, 1 level below grade parking. Concrete frame, masonry and curtain wall cladding. Excluding site and in-contract equipment. SF cost based on total area. 451,000 SF (41,898 m2)	A1 substructure		139.00			12.91		2.5%
	A2 structure		619.34			57.54		11.2%
	A3 exterior enclosure		609.24			56.60		11.0%
	B1 partitions & doors		314.25			29.19		5.7%
	B2 finishes		332.31			30.87		6.0%
	B3 fittings & equipment		587.46			54.58		10.6%
	C1 mechanical		1,340.93			124.58		24.2%
	C2 electrical		1,044.77			97.06		18.9%
	Z1 general requirements & fee		554.14			51.48		10.0%
	COMPLETE BUILDING	4,987.30	5,541.44	6,095.59	463.33	514.81	566.29	100.0%

		SQUARE METERS			SQUARE FEET			%
		LOW	AVERAGE	HIGH	LOW	AVERAGE	HIGH	OF TOTAL
HEALTH CENTRE (CLINIC): Single storey, no basement. Excluding site. 15,340 SF (1,425 m2)	A1 substructure		95.68			8.89		2.9%
	A2 structure		309.42			28.75		9.3%
	A3 exterior enclosure		523.39			48.62		15.7%
	B1 partitions & doors		283.68			26.35		8.5%
	B2 finishes		221.53			20.58		6.7%
	B3 fittings & equipment		166.16			15.44		5.0%
	C1 mechanical		889.96			82.68		26.8%
	C2 electrical		504.33			46.85		15.2%
	Z1 general requirements & fee		332.68			30.91		10.0%
	COMPLETE BUILDING	2,994.15	3,326.83	3,659.52	278.16	309.07	339.97	100.0%

		SQUARE METERS			SQUARE FEET			%
		LOW	AVERAGE	HIGH	LOW	AVERAGE	HIGH	OF TOTAL
REGIONAL HOSPITAL/ ACUTE CARE FACILITY: 1 and 2 storey combination. Masonry, curtain wall and metal cladding. Excluding site and in-contract equipment. 158,430 SF (14,718 m2)	A1 substructure		108.58			10.09		2.0%
	A2 structure		512.47			47.61		9.6%
	A3 exterior enclosure		609.24			56.60		11.4%
	B1 partitions & doors		315.37			29.30		5.9%
	B2 finishes		288.00			26.76		5.4%
	B3 fittings & equipment		588.64			54.69		11.0%
	C1 mechanical		1,340.93			124.58		25.1%
	C2 electrical		1,044.77			97.06		19.6%
	Z1 general requirements & fee		534.22			49.63		10.0%
	COMPLETE BUILDING	4,808.00	5,342.22	5,876.44	446.69	496.32	545.95	100.0%

		SQUARE METERS			SQUARE FEET			%
		LOW	AVERAGE	HIGH	LOW	AVERAGE	HIGH	OF TOTAL
LONG TERM CARE FACILITY: 280 beds, 2 storeys plus 1 level partial basement. Brick veneer cladding. Including lounge, dining room, kitchen, laundry, meeting hall and administration. Excluding site. 180,830 SF (16,800 m2)	A1 substructure		83.52			7.76		1.7%
	A2 structure		290.17			26.96		8.4%
	A3 exterior enclosure		277.93			25.82		7.2%
	B1 partitions & doors		237.12			22.03		4.5%
	B2 finishes		195.26			18.14		6.5%
	B3 fittings & equipment		243.43			22.61		4.1%
	C1 mechanical		544.42			50.58		37.5%
	C2 electrical		281.58			26.16		19.9%
	Z1 general requirements & fee		193.81			18.00		10.0%
	COMPLETE BUILDING	2,112.52	2,347.24	2,581.96	196.25	218.06	239.86	100.0%

INTERNATIONAL AIRPORT		SQUARE METERS			SQUARE FEET			%
		LOW	AVERAGE	HIGH	LOW	AVERAGE	HIGH	OF TOTAL
TERMINAL BUILDING:	A1 substructure		133.67			12.42		1.9%
50 gates. 3 levels above	A2 structure		946.80			87.96		13.6%
grade plus 1 service level	A3 exterior enclosure		720.01			66.89		10.3%
below grade. Excluding site,	B1 partitions & doors		199.39			18.52		2.9%
apron, fuel and navigational	B2 finishes		720.01			66.89		10.3%
systems, air traffic control	B3 fittings & equipment		1,661.56			154.36		23.8%
tower and tenant fit-up.	C1 mechanical		949.83			88.24		13.6%
3,710,600 SF (344,714 m2)	C2 electrical		949.78			88.24		13.6%
	Z1 general requirements & fee		697.89			64.84		10.0%
	COMPLETE BUILDING	**6,281.05**	**6,978.94**	**7,676.84**	**583.52**	**648.36**	**713.19**	**100.0%**

SMALL AIRPORT		SQUARE METERS			SQUARE FEET			%
		LOW	AVERAGE	HIGH	LOW	AVERAGE	HIGH	OF TOTAL
TERMINAL BUILDING:	A1 substructure		104.08			9.67		3.2%
Single storey, no basement.	A2 structure		458.11			42.56		14.1%
Steel framed. Metal cladding.	A3 exterior enclosure		664.62			61.75		20.4%
Excluding site, apron, fuel	B1 partitions & doors		166.16			15.44		5.1%
and navigational systems,	B2 finishes		232.61			21.61		7.1%
air traffic control tower and	B3 fittings & equipment		166.16			15.44		5.1%
tenant fit-up.	C1 mechanical		670.47			62.29		20.6%
24,000 SF (2,230 m2)	C2 electrical		472.13			43.86		14.5%
	Z1 general requirements & fee		326.04			30.29		10.0%
	COMPLETE BUILDING	**2,934.34**	**3,260.38**	**3,586.42**	**272.62**	**302.91**	**333.20**	**100.0%**

SHOPPING CENTRE:		SQUARE METERS			SQUARE FEET			%
		LOW	AVERAGE	HIGH	LOW	AVERAGE	HIGH	OF TOTAL
13 levels above grade @	A1 substructure		102.69			9.54		3.8%
346,780 SF, 6 levels below	A2 structure		554.57			51.52		20.7%
grade parking. Including	A3 exterior enclosure		713.40			66.28		26.6%
retail, theatres, restaurants,	B1 partitions & doors		226.54			21.05		8.5%
ice arena, bowling alley and	B2 finishes		126.26			11.73		4.7%
video arcade. Excluding site.	B3 fittings & equipment		233.68			21.71		8.7%
SF cost based on total area.	C1 mechanical		293.23			27.24		10.9%
694,120 SF (64,484 m2)	C2 electrical		162.14			15.06		6.0%
	Z1 general requirements & fee		268.06			24.90		10.0%
	COMPLETE BUILDING	**2,412.51**	**2,680.57**	**2,948.62**	**224.13**	**249.03**	**273.94**	**100.0%**

ELEMENTARY SCHOOL:		SQUARE METERS			SQUARE FEET			%
		LOW	AVERAGE	HIGH	LOW	AVERAGE	HIGH	OF TOTAL
45 classrooms. 4 storey.	A1 substructure		29.98			2.79		1.5%
Steel framed, brick cladding.	A2 structure		421.68			39.18		20.6%
Excluding site.	A3 exterior enclosure		279.43			25.96		13.6%
113,580 SF (10,551 m2)	B1 partitions & doors		188.36			17.50		9.2%
	B2 finishes		124.70			11.59		6.1%
	B3 fittings & equipment		152.10			14.13		7.4%
	C1 mechanical		436.39			40.54		21.3%
	C2 electrical		213.80			19.86		10.4%
	Z1 general requirements & fee		205.16			19.06		10.0%
	COMPLETE BUILDING	**1,846.44**	**2,051.60**	**2,256.76**	**171.55**	**190.61**	**209.67**	**100.0%**

ELEMENTARY SCHOOL:		SQUARE METERS			SQUARE FEET			%
		LOW	AVERAGE	HIGH	LOW	AVERAGE	HIGH	OF TOTAL
17 classrooms, with daycare	A1 substructure		194.31			18.05		1.4%
centre. 1 storey. Steel framed	A2 structure		243.66			22.64		20.3%
roof, block structure, brick	A3 exterior enclosure		462.36			42.95		13.6%
cladding. Excluding site.	B1 partitions & doors		231.60			21.52		9.2%
52,440 SF (4,870 m2)	B2 finishes		136.53			12.68		6.1%
	B3 fittings & equipment		71.52			6.64		7.4%
	C1 mechanical		431.64			40.10		21.6%
	C2 electrical		192.60			17.89		10.3%
	Z1 general requirements & fee		137.50			12.77		10.0%
	COMPLETE BUILDING	**1,891.55**	**2,101.72**	**2,311.89**	**175.72**	**195.25**	**214.77**	**100.0%**

		SQUARE METERS			SQUARE FEET			%
		LOW	AVERAGE	HIGH	LOW	AVERAGE	HIGH	OF TOTAL
ELEMENTARY SCHOOL:	A1 substructure		122.59			11.39		1.4%
21 classrooms	A2 structure		198.08			18.40		20.3%
2 storey. Steel framed	A3 exterior enclosure		392.08			36.42		13.6%
roof, block structure, brick	B1 partitions & doors		210.35			19.54		9.2%
cladding. Excluding site.	B2 finishes		129.91			12.07		6.1%
77,285 SF (7,180 m2)	B3 fittings & equipment		134.51			12.50		7.4%
	C1 mechanical		384.83			35.75		21.6%
	C2 electrical		188.69			17.53		10.3%
	Z1 general requirements & fee		125.49			11.66		10.0%
	COMPLETE BUILDING	1,697.88	1,886.53	2,075.18	157.73	175.26	192.78	100.0%

		SQUARE METERS			SQUARE FEET			%
		LOW	AVERAGE	HIGH	LOW	AVERAGE	HIGH	OF TOTAL
SECONDARY/HIGH	A1 substructure		71.67			6.66		3.0%
SCHOOL:	A2 structure		363.76			33.79		15.5%
3 storeys. Excluding site.	A3 exterior enclosure		364.15			33.83		15.5%
141,220 SF (13,119 m2)	B1 partitions & doors		184.04			17.10		7.8%
	B2 finishes		170.04			15.80		7.2%
	B3 fittings & equipment		200.27			18.61		8.5%
	C1 mechanical		499.45			46.40		21.2%
	C2 electrical		263.97			24.52		11.2%
	Z1 general requirements & fee		235.26			21.86		10.0%
	COMPLETE BUILDING	2,117.35	2,352.61	2,587.87	196.71	218.57	240.42	100.0%

		SQUARE METERS			SQUARE FEET			%
		LOW	AVERAGE	HIGH	LOW	AVERAGE	HIGH	OF TOTAL
UNIVERSITY LECTURE	A1 substructure		134.49			12.49		4.2%
HALL BUILDING:	A2 structure		551.39			51.23		17.1%
3 stories plus 1 level	A3 exterior enclosure		487.40			45.28		15.1%
basement. Curtain wall,	B1 partitions & doors		319.68			29.70		9.9%
copper metal siding and	B2 finishes		279.57			25.97		8.7%
precast concrete cladding.	B3 fittings & equipment		270.86			25.16		8.4%
Excluding site.	C1 mechanical		521.16			48.42		16.1%
102,080 SF (9,483 m2)	C2 electrical		341.82			31.76		10.6%
	Z1 general requirements & fee		322.93			30.00		10.0%
	COMPLETE BUILDING	2,906.37	3,229.30	3,552.23	270.01	300.01	330.01	100.0%

		SQUARE METERS			SQUARE FEET			%
		LOW	AVERAGE	HIGH	LOW	AVERAGE	HIGH	OF TOTAL
UNIVERSITY SPORTS	A1 substructure		62.70			5.82		3.4%
FACILITY:	A2 structure		710.09			65.97		13.2%
No ice surface, superior floor	A3 exterior enclosure		671.48			62.38		10.7%
finishes. Elevated indoor	B1 partitions & doors		134.05			12.45		5.5%
running track.	B2 finishes		223.37			20.75		4.3%
Concrete cladding.	B3 fittings & equipment		178.94			16.62		12.8%
Excluding site.	C1 mechanical		536.51			49.84		30.9%
115,280 SF (10,710 m2)	C2 electrical		235.16			21.85		9.3%
	Z1 general requirements & fee		247.71			23.01		10.0%
	COMPLETE BUILDING	2,700.01	3,000.01	3,300.01	250.83	278.70	306.57	100.0%

		SQUARE METERS			SQUARE FEET			%
		LOW	AVERAGE	HIGH	LOW	AVERAGE	HIGH	OF TOTAL
LABORATORY:	A1 substructure		175.70			16.32		3.3%
3 storey. Reinforced	A2 structure		689.45			64.05		13.1%
concrete. Curtain wall,	A3 exterior enclosure		553.85			51.45		10.5%
masonry and precast	B1 partitions & doors		286.37			26.60		5.4%
concrete cladding.	B2 finishes		221.53			20.58		4.2%
Excluding site.	B3 fittings & equipment		664.62			61.75		12.6%
54,620 SF (5,074 m2)	C1 mechanical		1,583.56			147.12		30.0%
	C2 electrical		574.89			53.41		10.9%
	Z1 general requirements & fee		527.77			49.03		10.0%
	COMPLETE BUILDING	4,749.97	5,277.74	5,805.52	441.28	490.31	539.34	100.0%

COLLEGE LIBRARY:
2 storeys plus 1 level basement. Curtain wall and stone cladding. Including shelving. Excluding site. 37,540 SF (3,487 m2)

		SQUARE METERS			SQUARE FEET			%
		LOW	AVERAGE	HIGH	LOW	AVERAGE	HIGH	OF TOTAL
	A1 substructure		92.09			8.56		3.0%
	A2 structure		422.00			39.21		13.8%
	A3 exterior enclosure		537.31			49.92		17.6%
	B1 partitions & doors		157.89			14.67		5.2%
	B2 finishes		267.21			24.82		8.8%
	B3 fittings & equipment		170.04			15.80		5.6%
	C1 mechanical		673.17			62.54		22.1%
	C2 electrical		423.18			39.31		13.9%
	Z1 general requirements & fee		304.77			28.31		10.0%
	COMPLETE BUILDING	2,742.89	3,047.66	3,352.42	254.83	283.14	311.46	100.0%

PROVINCIAL COURTHOUSE:
13 courtrooms. 3 storeys plus 2 level basement. Excluding parking and site. 131,250 SF (12,193 m2)

		SQUARE METERS			SQUARE FEET			%
		LOW	AVERAGE	HIGH	LOW	AVERAGE	HIGH	OF TOTAL
	A1 substructure		126.71			11.77		2.9%
	A2 structure		545.78			50.70		12.4%
	A3 exterior enclosure		490.12			45.53		11.2%
	B1 partitions & doors		188.30			17.49		4.3%
	B2 finishes		387.69			36.02		8.8%
	B3 fittings & equipment		830.77			77.18		18.9%
	C1 mechanical		715.16			66.44		16.3%
	C2 electrical		662.68			61.57		15.1%
	Z1 general requirements & fee		438.58			40.74		10.0%
	COMPLETE BUILDING	3,947.21	4,385.79	4,824.37	366.70	407.44	448.19	100.0%

CHURCH:
1 storey plus 1 level basement. Cedar cladding. Excluding site. 11,290 SF (1,049 m2)

		SQUARE METERS			SQUARE FEET			%
		LOW	AVERAGE	HIGH	LOW	AVERAGE	HIGH	OF TOTAL
	A1 substructure		293.39			27.26		10.2%
	A2 structure		452.65			42.05		15.7%
	A3 exterior enclosure		745.35			69.25		25.9%
	B1 partitions & doors		122.40			11.37		4.3%
	B2 finishes		177.85			16.52		6.2%
	B3 fittings & equipment		233.37			21.68		8.1%
	C1 mechanical		324.68			30.16		11.3%
	C2 electrical		237.41			22.06		8.3%
	Z1 general requirements & fee		287.46			26.71		10.0%
	COMPLETE BUILDING	2,587.10	2,874.56	3,162.01	240.35	267.06	293.76	100.0%

LOW RISE CONDOMINIUM:
63 units. 5 storeys above grade @ 60,149 SF. 2 levels below grade parking. Medium quality. Excluding site. SF cost based on total area. 101,547 SF (9,434 m2)

		SQUARE METERS			SQUARE FEET			%
		LOW	AVERAGE	HIGH	LOW	AVERAGE	HIGH	OF TOTAL
	A1 substructure		159.38			14.81		7.3%
	A2 structure		566.94			52.67		25.9%
	A3 exterior enclosure		389.53			36.19		17.8%
	B1 partitions & doors		145.68			13.53		6.6%
	B2 finishes		146.07			13.57		6.7%
	B3 fittings & equipment		170.43			15.83		7.8%
	C1 mechanical		261.69			24.31		11.9%
	C2 electrical		142.89			12.35		6.1%
	Z1 general requirements & fee		219.18			20.36		10.0%
	COMPLETE BUILDING	1,972.61	2,191.79	2,410.97	183.26	203.62	223.98	100.0%

CORPORATE OFFICE COMPLEX:
5 storeys. Curtain wall, metal panel and stone cladding. Excluding site. 427,000 SF (39,670 m2)

		SQUARE METERS			SQUARE FEET			%
		LOW	AVERAGE	HIGH	LOW	AVERAGE	HIGH	OF TOTAL
	A1 substructure		57.30			5.32		1.9%
	A2 structure		464.64			43.17		15.6%
	A3 exterior enclosure		478.14			44.42		16.1%
	B1 partitions & doors		125.82			11.69		4.2%
	B2 finishes		314.55			29.22		10.6%
	B3 fittings & equipment		199.72			18.55		6.7%
	C1 mechanical		510.06			47.39		17.1%
	C2 electrical		530.33			49.27		17.8%
	Z1 general requirements & fee		297.84			27.67		10.0%
	COMPLETE BUILDING	2,680.56	2,978.40	3,276.24	249.03	276.70	304.37	100.0%

CORPORATE OFFICE		SQUARE METERS			SQUARE FEET			%
		LOW	AVERAGE	HIGH	LOW	AVERAGE	HIGH	OF TOTAL
7 storeys. Curtain wall, metal panel and stone cladding. No fit-up included. No parking levels. Excluding site. 100,050 SF (9,295 m2)	A1 substructure		52.06			4.84		1.9%
	A2 structure		574.52			53.37		15.5%
	A3 exterior enclosure		452.39			42.03		16.0%
	B1 partitions & doors		75.90			7.05		4.2%
	B2 finishes		172.40			16.02		10.5%
	B3 fittings & equipment		92.45			8.59		6.7%
	C1 mechanical		482.90			44.86		17.4%
	C2 electrical		291.97			27.12		17.8%
	Z1 general requirements & fee		197.51			18.35		10.0%
	COMPLETE BUILDING	2,152.89	2,392.10	2,631.31	200.00	222.23	244.45	100.0%

COMMERCIAL RETAIL UNIT:		SQUARE METERS			SQUARE FEET			%
		LOW	AVERAGE	HIGH	LOW	AVERAGE	HIGH	OF TOTAL
Mainly stucco exterior wall finish. Interior finishing at tenant's expense. Medium quality. Excluding surface parking. 20,300 SF (1,885 m2)	A1 substructure		105.57			9.81		7.6%
	A2 structure		285.95			26.57		20.7%
	A3 exterior enclosure		613.06			56.96		44.4%
	B1 partitions & doors		36.43			3.38		2.6%
	B2 finishes		7.81			0.73		0.6%
	B3 fittings & equipment		0.49			0.05		0.0%
	C1 mechanical		148.42			13.79		10.7%
	C2 electrical		45.54			4.23		3.3%
	Z1 general requirements & fee		138.14			12.84		10.0%
	COMPLETE BUILDING	1,243.27	1,381.41	1,519.55	115.52	128.36	141.19	100.0%

POST OFFICE:		SQUARE METERS			SQUARE FEET			%
		LOW	AVERAGE	HIGH	LOW	AVERAGE	HIGH	OF TOTAL
Single storey with no basement. Brick veneer cladding. Excluding site. 12,520 SF (1,162 m2)	A1 substructure		142.09			13.20		7.7%
	A2 structure		160.11			14.87		8.7%
	A3 exterior enclosure		468.92			43.56		25.5%
	B1 partitions & doors		129.01			11.99		7.0%
	B2 finishes		120.79			11.22		6.6%
	B3 fittings & equipment		117.51			10.92		6.4%
	C1 mechanical		362.09			33.64		19.7%
	C2 electrical		151.93			14.11		8.3%
	Z1 general requirements & fee		183.61			17.06		10.0%
	COMPLETE BUILDING	1,652.45	1,836.06	2,019.66	153.51	170.57	187.62	100.0%

MOVIE THEATRE COMPLEX:		SQUARE METERS			SQUARE FEET			%
		LOW	AVERAGE	HIGH	LOW	AVERAGE	HIGH	OF TOTAL
12-plex, 3,475 seats. Steel framed, stucco and curtain wall cladding. Including concession, food retail, party rooms and video arcade. Excluding site. 83,460 SF (7,750 m2)	A1 substructure		88.68			8.24		2.8%
	A2 structure		588.58			54.68		18.8%
	A3 exterior enclosure		610.86			56.75		19.6%
	B1 partitions & doors		299.08			27.79		9.6%
	B2 finishes		354.46			32.93		11.4%
	B3 fittings & equipment		188.30			17.49		6.0%
	C1 mechanical		469.33			43.60		15.0%
	C2 electrical		211.06			19.61		6.8%
	Z1 general requirements & fee		312.26			29.01		10.0%
	COMPLETE BUILDING	2,810.35	3,122.61	3,434.87	261.09	290.10	319.11	100.0%

PENITENTIARY:		SQUARE METERS			SQUARE FEET			%
		LOW	AVERAGE	HIGH	LOW	AVERAGE	HIGH	OF TOTAL
Housing 1200 inmates. 2 storey. Including male and female housing, medical and segregation units, support services, administration, gymnasium and workshops. Excluding site. 269,370 SF (25,025 m2)	A1 substructure		117.63			10.93		3.3%
	A2 structure		357.67			33.23		10.2%
	A3 exterior enclosure		465.23			43.22		13.2%
	B1 partitions & doors		487.40			45.28		13.9%
	B2 finishes		177.24			16.47		5.0%
	B3 fittings & equipment		243.70			22.64		6.9%
	C1 mechanical		893.95			83.05		25.4%
	C2 electrical		422.13			39.22		12.0%
	Z1 general requirements & fee		351.66			32.67		10.0%
	COMPLETE BUILDING	3,164.95	3,516.61	3,868.27	294.04	326.71	359.38	100.0%

		SQUARE METERS			SQUARE FEET			%
		LOW	AVERAGE	HIGH	LOW	AVERAGE	HIGH	OF TOTAL
PENITENTIARY SEGREGATION UNIT: 9 cells, maximum security. Single storey. Excluding site. 5,660 SF (530 m2)	A1 substructure		167.77			15.59		3.7%
	A2 structure		445.55			41.39		9.8%
	A3 exterior enclosure		875.08			81.30		19.3%
	B1 partitions & doors		664.62			61.75		14.6%
	B2 finishes		199.39			18.52		4.4%
	B3 fittings & equipment		77.54			7.20		1.7%
	C1 mechanical		1,118.01			103.87		24.6%
	C2 electrical		537.61			49.95		11.8%
	Z1 general requirements & fee		453.95			42.17		10.0%
	COMPLETE BUILDING	**4,085.57**	**4,539.52**	**4,993.47**	**379.57**	**421.74**	**463.92**	**100.0%**

		SQUARE METERS			SQUARE FEET			%
		LOW	AVERAGE	HIGH	LOW	AVERAGE	HIGH	OF TOTAL
POLICE STATION: 6 cells. 2 storey with no basement. Including administration, conference room, exercise room and showers. Excluding site. 16,700 SF (1550 m2)	A1 substructure		55.70			5.17		1.8%
	A2 structure		614.71			57.11		20.0%
	A3 exterior enclosure		530.39			49.27		17.2%
	B1 partitions & doors		299.35			27.81		9.7%
	B2 finishes		144.00			13.38		4.7%
	B3 fittings & equipment		177.24			16.47		5.8%
	C1 mechanical		581.06			53.98		18.9%
	C2 electrical		369.36			34.31		12.0%
	Z1 general requirements & fee		307.98			28.61		10.0%
	COMPLETE BUILDING	**2,771.81**	**3,079.79**	**3,387.77**	**257.50**	**286.11**	**314.72**	**100.0%**

		SQUARE METERS			SQUARE FEET			%
		LOW	AVERAGE	HIGH	LOW	AVERAGE	HIGH	OF TOTAL
POLICE TRAINING FACILITY: Singe story facility, no basement. Including 18 position firing range, including equipment and acoustic package. LEED Silver. 84,600 SF (7,860 m2)	A1 substructure		117.58			10.92		1.8%
	A2 structure		422.78			39.28		19.8%
	A3 exterior enclosure		464.13			43.12		17.1%
	B1 partitions & doors		145.09			13.48		9.7%
	B2 finishes		65.11			6.05		4.7%
	B3 fittings & equipment		1,044.80			97.06		5.7%
	C1 mechanical		773.43			71.85		19.1%
	C2 electrical		309.91			28.79		12.1%
	Z1 general requirements & fee		334.28			31.05		10.0%
	COMPLETE BUILDING	**3,309.40**	**3,677.11**	**4,044.82**	**307.44**	**341.60**	**375.76**	**100.0%**

Conversion Factors and Abbreviations

Metric Conversion Factors for Use in the Construction Industry

LENGTH	Imperial to Metric	Metric to Imperial	Metric Unit	Symbol		Imperial to Metric	Metric to Imperial	Metric Unit	Symbol
Inches	25.4	.039 370 1	millimetres	mm	Millions				
Feet	.3048	3.280 84	metres	m	gals/day	.005 261 88	19.0053	cu. metres/sec	m^3/s
Yards	.9144	1.093 61	metres	m	**FORCE**				
Miles	1.609 344	.621 371	kilometres	km	Pounds force	4.448 22	.224 809	newtons	N
Fathoms	1.8288	.546 806 6	metres	m	Tons force (short)	8.896 44	.112 404	kilonewtons	kN
AREA					**PRESSURE**				
Sq. inches	645.16	.001 550	sq. millimetres	mm^2	Tons/sq. inch (short)	13.789 514	.072 519	megapascals	MPa
Sq. feet	.092 903	10.7639	sq. metres	m^2	Pounds/sq. inch	6.894 76	.1450376	kilopascals	kPa
Sq. yards	.836 127	1.195 99	sq. metres	m^2	Pounds/sq. foot	47.8803	.020 8854	pascals	Pa
Acres	.404 686	2.471 05	hectares	ha					
Sq. miles	2.589 99	.386 102	sq. kilometres	km^2	**ENERGY**				
VOLUME					Kilowatt hours	3.6	.277 778	megajoules	MJ
Cu. inches	16 387.1	61.0237×10^{-6}	cu. millimetres	mm^3	BTUs	1.055 06	.947 817	kilojoules	kJ
Cu. feet	.028 316 8	35.3147	cu. metres	m^3	Foot pounds (force)	1.355 82	.737 562	joules	J
Cu. yards	.764 555	1.307 95	cu. metres	m^3	**POWER**				
Fluid oz.	28.413	.035 195 1	millilitres	ml	Horsepower	.745 700	1.341 02	kilowatts	kW
Pints	568.261	.001 759 76	millilitres	ml	BTU/hour	.293 071	3.412 14	watts	W
Gallons	4.546 09	.219 969	litres	l	Footpounds/sec	1.355 82	.737 562	watts	W
MASS					**ILLUMINATION**				
Grains	.064 798 91	15.432 36	grams	g	Lumens/sq. foot	10.7639	.092 903	lux	lx
Ounces	28.3495	.035 274	grams	g					
Pounds	.453 592	2.204 62	kilograms	kg					
Tons (short)	.907 184	1.102 312	tonnes	t					
VOLUME RATE OF FLOW									
Cu. ft/sec	.028 316 8	35.3147	cu. metres/sec	m^3/s					
Cu. ft/min	.471 947	2.118 88	litres/sec	l/s					
Gals/min	.075 768 2	13.198 2	litres/sec	l/s					
Gals/hour	.001 262 8	791.891	litres/sec	l/s					

Abbreviations: Imperial Sections

Amp, A .... ampere
BTU .... British Thermal Unit
cct .... circuit
CF, cf .... cubic foot (feet)
CFM, cfm .... cubic foot (feet) per minute
ci .... cast iron
CIQS .... Canadian Institute of Quantity Surveyors
CLF .... One hundred linear feet
cond .... conduit
conn .... connector
CY, dia .... cubic yard, diameter
D4S .... dressed four sides
EA, ea .... each
EDR .... equivalent direct radiation
EMT .... electrical metallic tubing
eqpt .... equipment
FBM, fbm .... foot board measure
Fdn .... foundation
Fixt .... fixture
fpm .... feet per minute
F.C. .... foot candles
ftg .... footing
ga .... gauge
gfa .... gross floor area
gal .... gallon
galv. .... galvanized
gpm .... gallons per minute
G1S .... good one side

hp .... horsepower
hr(s) .... hour(s)
h.t. .... high tension
ibr .... Institute of Biler and
.... Radiator Manufacturers specification
ici .... iron body, cast iron flanged
incl .... included
induct .... induction
ksi .... thousand pounds per square inch
kV .... kilovolt
kVA .... kilovolt ampere
kVAc .... kilovolt ampere capacitance
kW .... kilowatt
ibs/lf, LBS .... pounds per linear foot, pounds
Lf, lf .... linear foot
LF Dist .... linear foot distribution
lin. yd. .... linear yard
max .... maximum
mbh .... thousand BTUs per hour
MCF .... thousand cubic feet
mcm .... one thousandths of a square inch
meterg .... metering
MFBM .... thousand foot board measure
MGH .... thousand gallons per hour
m.i. .... malleable iron
min .... minimum
MLF .... thousand linear feet
mm .... millimetre

MSY .... thousand square yards
mtg .... mounting
mtr .... motor
nb .... nickel bronze
No .... number
oc .... on centre
os & y .... outside screw & yoke
OWSJ .... open web steel joist
oz .... ounce
prot .... protection
psf .... pounds per square foot
psi .... pounds per square inch
PVC .... polyvinyl chloride
rpm .... revolutions per minute
sch .... schedule
self pro .... self propelled
SF .... square foot
$/MCF .... dollars per thousand cubic feet
S4S .... sanded four sides
SY .... square yard
T&G .... tongue & groove
ttw .... through the wall
U ground .... underground
uncompl .... uncompleted
V .... volt
W .... watt
wf .... wash fountain
W/sq ft. .... watts per square foot

Go beyond the pages

Access
Quarterly
Data
Updates

Explore
Video
Resources

Attend
Product
Training
Webinars

For more information visit our website at www.RSMeans.com

Our Online Estimating Solution

Competitive Cost Estimates Made Easy

Our online estimating solution is a web-based service that provides accurate and up-to-date cost information to help you build competitive estimates or budgets in less time.

Quick, intuitive, easy to use and automatically updated, you'll gain instant access to hundreds of thousands of material, labor, and equipment costs from RSMeans' comprehensive database, delivering the information you need to build budgets and competitive estimates every time.

With our online estimating solutions, you can perform quick searches to locate specific costs and adjust costs to reflect prices in your geographic area. Tag and store your favorites for fast access to your frequently used line items and assemblies and clone estimates to save time. System notifications will alert you as updated data becomes available. This data is automatically updated throughout the year.

Our visual, interactive estimating features help you create, manage, save and share estimates with ease! You'll enjoy increased flexibility with customizable advanced reports. Easily edit custom report templates and import your company logo onto your estimates.

	Core	Advanced	Complete
Unit Prices	✓	✓	✓
Assemblies	⊘	✓	✓
Sq Foot Models	⊘	⊘	✓
Editable Sq Foot Models	⊘	⊘	✓
Editable Assembly Components	⊘	✓	✓
Custom Cost Data	⊘	✓	✓
User Defined Components	⊘	✓	✓
Advanced Reporting & Customization	⊘	✓	✓
Union Labor Type	✓	✓	✓

Continue to check our website at www.RSMeans.com for more product offerings.

Estimate with Precision

Find everything you need to develop complete, accurate estimates.

- Verified costs for construction materials
- Equipment rental costs
- Crew sizing, labor hours and labor rates
- Localized costs for U.S. and Canada

Save Time & Increase Efficiency

Make cost estimating and calculating faster and easier than ever with secure, online estimating tools.

- Quickly locate costs in the searchable database
- Create estimates in minutes with RSMeans cost lines
- Tag and store favorites for fast access to frequently used items

Improve Planning & Decision-Making

Back your estimates with complete, accurate and up-to-date cost data for informed business decisions.

- Verify construction costs from third parties
- Check validity of subcontractor proposals
- Evaluate material and assembly alternatives

Increase Profits

Use our online estimating solution to estimate projects quickly and accurately, so you can gain an edge over your competition.

- Create accurate and competitive bids
- Minimize the risk of cost overruns
- Reduce variability

Unit prices according to the latest MasterFormat®

Online Estimating Solution

For more information visit our website at www.RSMeans.com

Seminar Schedule and Professional Development

2018 Seminar Schedule   ☎ 877-620-6245

Note: call for exact dates, locations, and details as some cities are subject to change.

Location	Dates	Location	Dates
Seattle, WA	January and August	San Francisco, CA	June
Dallas/Ft. Worth, TX	January	Bethesda, MD	June
Austin, TX	February	El Segundo, CA	August
Anchorage, AK	March and September	Dallas, TX	September
Las Vegas, NV	March	Raleigh, NC	October
New Orleans, LA	March	Salt Lake City, UT	October
Washington, DC	April and September	Baltimore, MD	November
Phoenix, AZ	April	Orlando, FL	November
Toronto	May	San Diego, CA	December
Denver, CO	May	San Antonio, TX	December

Gordian also offers a suite of online RSMeans data self-paced offerings. Check our website www.RSMeans.com for more information.

Self-Paced Professional Development Courses

Training on how to use RSMeans data and estimating tools, as well as Professional Development courses on industry topics are now offered in a convenient self-paced format. These courses are on-demand and allow more flexibility to learn around your busy schedule, while saving the cost of travel and time.

Current course offerings include:
Facilities Construction Estimating—our best-selling live class now available as an on-demand training course! Let the subject matter experts of construction estimating—the RSMeans Engineering Staff—walk you through the basics and much more of estimating for renovation and facilities construction.

RSMeansOnline.com Training—learn the ins and outs of the flagship delivery method of RSMeans data!

The Construction Process—how much do you and your team really know about the ins and outs of the "contract-side" of a construction project? This self-paced course will clarify best practices for items such as schedules, change orders, and project closeout.

These self-paced training courses can be completed over the course of 45 days and are comprised of multiple lessons with documentation, video presentation, software simulation, assessment quizzes and certificate of completion.

Site Work Estimating with RSMeans data

This new one-day program focuses directly on site work costs, a unique portion of most construction projects that often is the wild card in determining whether you have developed a good estimate or not. Accurately scoping, quantifying, and pricing site preparation, underground utility work, and improvements to exterior site elements are often the most difficult estimating tasks on any project. The program takes the participant from preparing a never-developed site through underground utility installation, pad preparation, paving and sidewalks, and landscaping. Attendees will use the full array of site work cost data through the RSMeans online program and participate in exercises to strengthen their estimating skills.

Some of what you'll learn:
- Evaluation of site work and understanding site scope of work.
- Site work estimating topics including: site clearing, grading, excavation, disposal and trucking of materials, erosion control devices, backfill and compaction, underground utilities, paving, sidewalks, fences & gates, and seeding & planting.
- Unit price site work estimates—Correct use of RSMeans site work cost data to develop a cost estimate.
- Using and modifying assemblies—Save valuable time when estimating site work activities using custom assemblies.

Who should attend: Engineers, contractors, estimators, project managers, owner's representatives, and others who are concerned with the proper preparation and/or evaluation of site work estimates.

Please bring a laptop with ability to access the internet.

Registration Information

Register early and save up to $100!

Register 30 days before the start date of a seminar and save $100 off your total fee. Note: This discount can be applied only once per order. It cannot be applied to team discount registrations or any other special offer.

How to register

By Phone
Register by phone at 877-620-6245

Online
Register online at
www.RSMeans.com/products/seminars.aspx

Note: Purchase Orders or Credits Cards are required to register.

Two-day seminar registration fee - $1,045.

One-Day Construction Cost Estimating or Building Systems and the Construction Process - $630.

Government pricing

All federal government employees save off the regular seminar price. Other promotional discounts cannot be combined with the government discount.

Team discount program

For over five attendee registrations. Call for pricing: 781-422-5115

Refund policy

Cancellations will be accepted up to ten business days prior to the seminar start. There are no refunds for cancellations received later than ten working days prior to the first day of the seminar. A $150 processing fee will be applied for all cancellations. Written notice of the cancellation is required. Substitutions can be made at any time before the session starts. No-shows are subject to the full seminar fee.

Note: Pricing subject to change.

AACE approved courses

Many seminars described and offered here have been approved for 14 hours (1.4 recertification credits) of credit by the AACE International Certification Board toward meeting the continuing education requirements for recertification as a Certified Cost Engineer/Certified Cost Consultant.

AIA Continuing Education

We are registered with the AIA Continuing Education System (AIA/CES) and are committed to developing quality learning activities in accordance with the CES criteria. Many seminars meet the AIA/CES criteria for Quality Level 2. AIA members may receive 14 learning units (LUs) for each two-day RSMeans course.

Daily course schedule

The first day of each seminar session begins at 8:30 a.m. and ends at 4:30 p.m. The second day begins at 8:00 a.m. and ends at 4:00 p.m. Participants are urged to bring a hand-held calculator since many actual problems will be worked out in each session.

Continental breakfast

Your registration includes the cost of a continental breakfast and a morning and afternoon refreshment break. These informal segments allow you to discuss topics of mutual interest with other seminar attendees. (You are free to make your own lunch and dinner arrangements.)

Hotel/transportation arrangements

We arrange to hold a block of rooms at most host hotels. To take advantage of special group rates when making your reservation, be sure to mention that you are attending the RSMeans Institute data seminar. You are, of course, free to stay at the lodging place of your choice. (Hotel reservations and transportation arrangements should be made directly by seminar attendees.)

Important

Class sizes are limited, so please register as soon as possible.

Professional Development

NOTES

NOTES